Communications
in Computer and Information Science   75

Song Lin   Xiong Huang (Eds.)

Advanced Research on Computer Education, Simulation and Modeling

International Conference, CESM 2011
Wuhan, China, June 18-19, 2011
Proceedings, Part I

 Springer

Volume Editors

Song Lin
International Science & Education Researcher Association
Wuhan Branch, No.1, Jiangxia Road
Wuhan, China
E-mail: 30978376@qq.com

Xiong Huang
International Science & Education Researcher Association
Wuhan Branch, No.1, Jiangxia Road
Wuhan, China
E-mail: 499780828@qq.com

ISSN 1865-0929   e-ISSN 1865-0937
ISBN 978-3-642-21782-1   e-ISBN 978-3-642-21783-8
DOI 10.1007/978-3-642-21783-8
Springer Heidelberg Dordrecht London New York

Library of Congress Control Number: 2011929161

CR Subject Classification (1998): J.1, I.6, H.2, I.4, I.2, F.1-2, H.3-4

Typesetting: Camera-ready by author, data conversion by Scientific Publishing Services, Chennai, India

Printed on acid-free paper

Springer is part of Springer Science+Business Media (www.springer.com)

Preface

The International Science & Education Researcher Association(ISER) puts its focus on the study and exchange of academic achievements of international researchers, and it also promotes educational reform in the world. In addition, it serves as an academic discussion and communication platform, which is beneficial for education and for scientific research, thus aiming to stimulate researchers in their work.

The CESM conference is an integrated event concentrating on computer education, simulation, and modeling. The goal of the conference is to provide researchers working in the field of computer education, simulation, and modeling based on modern information technology with a forum to share new ideas, innovations, and solutions. CESM 2011 was held during June 18-19, in Wuhan, China, and was co-sponsored by the International Science & Education Researcher Association, Beijing, Gireida Education Co. Ltd, and Wuhan University of Science and Technology, China. Renowned keynote speakers were invited to deliver talks, giving participants the chance to discuss their work with the speakers face to face.

In these proceeding, you can learn more about the field of computer education, simulation, and modeling from the contributions of several international researchers. The main role of the proceedings is to be used as a means of exchange of information for those working in this area. The Organizing Committee made great efforts to meet the high standards of Springer's *Communications in Computer and Information Science (CCIS)* series Firstly, poor-quality papers were rejected after being reviewed by anonymous referees. Secondly, meetings were held periodically for reviewers to exchange opinions and suggestions. Finally, the organizing team held several preliminary sessions before the conference. Through the efforts of numerous individuals and departments, the conference was successful and fruitful.

During the organization, we received help from different people, departments, and institutions. Here, we would like to extend our sincere thanks to the publishers of CCIS, Springer, for their kind and enthusiastic assistance and support of our conference. Secondly, the authors should also be thanked for their submissions. Thirdly, the hard work of the Program Committee, the Program Chairs, and the reviewers is greatly appreciated.

In conclusion, it was the team effort of all these people that made our conference such a success. We welcome any suggestions that may help improve the conference in the future and we look forward to seeing all of you at CESM 2012.

April 2011   Song Lin

Committee

Honorary Chairs

Chen Bin   Beijing Normal University, China
Hu Chen   Peking University, China
Chunhua Tan   Beijing Normal University, China
Helen Zhang   University of Munich, Germany

Program Committee Chairs

Xiong Huang   International Science & Education Researcher Association, China
Li Ding   International Science & Education Researcher Association, China
Zhihua Xu   International Science & Education Researcher Association, China

Organizing Chair

ZongMing Tu   Beijing Gireida Education Co. Ltd., China
Jijun Wang   Beijing Spon Technology Research Institution, China
Quan Xiang   Beijing Prophet Science and Education Research Center, China

Publication Chairs

Song Lin   International Science & Education Researcher Association, China
Xiong Huang   International Science & Education Researcher Association, China

Program Committee

Sally Wang   Beijing Normal University, China
Li Li   Dongguan University of Technology, China
Bing Xiao   Anhui University, China
Z.L. Wang   Wuhan University, China
Moon Seho   Hoseo University, Korea
Kongel Arearak   Suranaree University of Technology, Thailand
Zhihua Xu   International Science & Education Researcher Association, China

Co-sponsored by:

International Science & Education Researcher Association, China
VIP Information Conference Center, China

Reviewers of CESM 2011

Chunlin Xie	Wuhan University of Science and Technology, China
Lin Qi	Hubei University of Technology, China
Xiong Huang	International Science & Education Researcher Association, China
Gang Shen	International Science & Education Researcher Association, China
Xiangrong Jiang	Wuhan University of Technology, China
Li Hu	Linguistic and Linguistic Education Association, China
Moon Hyan	Sungkyunkwan University, Korea
Guang Wen	South China University of Technology, China
Jack H. Li	George Mason University, USA
Marry Y. Feng	University of Technology Sydney, Australia
Feng Quan	Zhongnan University of Finance and Economics, China
Peng Ding	Hubei University, China
Song Lin	International Science & Education Researcher Association, China
XiaoLie Nan	International Science & Education Researcher Association, China
Zhi Yu	International Science & Education Researcher Association, China
Xue Jin	International Science & Education Researcher Association, China
Zhihua Xu	International Science & Education Researcher Association, China
Wu Yang	International Science & Education Researcher Association, China
Qin Xiao	International Science & Education Researcher Association, China
Weifeng Guo	International Science & Education Researcher Association, China
Li Hu	Wuhan University of Science and Technology, China
Zhong Yan	Wuhan University of Science and Technology, China
Haiquan Huang	Hubei University of Technology, China
Xiao Bing	Wuhan University, China
Brown Wu	Sun Yat-Sen University, China

Table of Contents – Part I

Model and Algorithm for Time-Dependent Team Orienteering
Problem 1
   Jin Li

Computer Aided Match Method for Matching the Electrical Motor and
the Gearbox of the Pure Electrical Vehicle 8
   HongBin Li, Jian Wang, and JingNuo Yu

Research and Implementation of Dots-and-Boxes Chessboard Based on
the Game Strings-and-Coins 14
   Dongming Li, Shuqin Li, and Hua Bao

Research on Teaching of "Object-Oriented Programming" Course for
Bachelor Students 21
   Zhaoxue Chen and Bei Dai

Modeling of Flight Delay State-Space Model 26
   HaiYan Chen, JianDong Wang, and Hao Yan

An Image Fusion Algorithm Based on Discrete Wavelet Transform and
Canny Operator 32
   Ai Deng, Jin Wu, and Shen Yang

A Novel Method of Stabilizing the Vibration Velocity at the End of
Piezoelectric Transducers 39
   HuiJuan Dong, Jian Wu, WeiGang Bao, and GuangYu Zhang

The Optimization Model of Campus Network Port Resources Based on
Queuing Theory 47
   Banteng Liu, Xuejun Wu, Juhua Chen, Guoyong Dai, and yue Ruan

The Intelligent Algorithm of the Biorthogonal Quarternary Wavelet
Packs and Applications in Physics 53
   Hailin Gao and Ruohui Liu

The Traits of Orthogonal Nonseparable Binary-Variable Wavelet Packs
in Two-Dimensional Function Space 59
   Guoqiang Wang and Rui Wei

The Biorthogonal Features of the Ternary Vector-Valued Wavelet
Wraps with Filter Functions and Pseudoframes 66
   Honglin Guo and Zhihao Tang

The Nice Characters of Orthogonal Bidimensional Vector Wavelet
Packs and Orthogonal Binary Framelets 73
    Jinfan Yang and Sanhua Song

Research on New Tabu Search Algorithm for Min-Max Vehicle Routing
Problem 79
    Chunyu Ren

Application of Measurement and Control Technology of Digital for the
Power Inverter 85
    Huanqi Tao and Yuchuan Wu

The Design of Image Process Software of Dispensing Systems 92
    Lianjun Hu, Guixu Chen, Xiaohui Zeng, and Hong Song

Research of SOAP Message Security Model on Web Services 98
    Shujun Pei and Deyun Chen

Application of Real Options Analysis for R&D Project Valuation in
High-Tech Public Corporation 105
    Kai Zhang

A Fixed Point Theory for Quasi-Contractive Mappings in Ordered
Sets 112
    Jiawei Chen, Zhongping Wan, Zhanyi Ao, and Liuyang Yuan

A New Optimization Approach for Grey Model GM(1,1) 117
    Zhanyi Ao, Xiao-qing Ou, and Shaohua Zhu

Approach of Web2.0 Application Pattern Applied to the Information
Teaching 123
    *GuangMin Li, Min Liu, GuoPing Li, ZiYun Wang, and
WenJing Chen*

Research and Analysis of TD-SCDMA Uplink Capacity 128
    Hao Chen, Tong Yang, Jian-fu Teng, and Hong He

Simulation of Micro Stage System Based on BP Neural Network
Control 134
    Jianying Shen

Study on the Monolithic Muffler Acoustic Field Performance of the
Train Air-Conditioning 139
    Xuquan Li, Yaohua Wei, Minjie Gu, Gang Wang, and Songtao Hu

Cell Status Diagnosis for the Aluminum Production on BP Neural
Network with Genetic Algorithm 146
    Shuiping Zeng, Jinhong Li, and Lin Cui

The Application of Project Isomerization Teaching Method in Database
Course Design   153
    Qin Liu

Use of Anaerobic Sludge for Manufacturing Light Ceramsite   159
    Hui Li

The Application Research on Anti-counterfeiting of Fractal Graphics in
Color Printing Based on Newton Iteration and Escape Time
Algorithm.   163
    Fucheng You and Yujie Chen

Rainfall Infiltration Influence to Asphalt Concrete Pavement   170
    Jilei Hu, Xiaochu Wang, and Rendong Guo

The Research on Anti-counterfeiting of Fractal Graphics in Color
Printing Based on Escape Time Algorithm of Julia-set   174
    Fucheng You and Yingjie Liu

On Virtual Expert of Knowledge Management an Extenics Oriented
Ontology   180
    Feng Liu

The Study on College Sports Education Reform Based on the Learning
Organization Theory   186
    Li Gang

The Implementing and Researching of BIT in Airborne Computer   192
    Xinyu Tian, Xiaolin Zhang, Haitao Wu, and Ying Yao

Existence of Periodic Solution for Fuzzy Cellular Neural Networks with
Time-Varying Delays   199
    Qianhong Zhang, Lihui Yang, and Daixi Liao

A Simulation and Experiments of Rapeseed Logistics Supply System
Based on Flexsim Software   207
    Dejun liu, Guangsheng Zhang, Xiurong Zhao, and Claus Age Søresen

Roll Stability Performance Simulation of Tractor-Semitrailer Based on
ARCSIM   213
    Xiaomei Liu, Jun Li, and Jianrong Zhou

A Class of Hybrid Projection Methods with Perturbations   219
    Meixia Li

A Research into "PRAMs" Mode of Orders Education   226
    Hanyu Guo, Xiujuan Yan, and Jianfeng Hu

A New Method of Sound Travel-Time Measurement in Stored Grain. . . .   232
    Guannan Chen, Hua Yan, Yinggang Zhou, and Lijun Liu

ILOG and MAS Based Framework of Job-Shop Scheduling System   238
    LiZhi Qin and QingSong Li

The Infiltration Numerical Simulation for Several Kinds of Unsaturated
Soil under Rainfall Condition   243
    Dongfang Tian

The Research and Exploration of Project Course Developmental
Evaluation in Higher Vocational Colleges Software Major   248
    Gang Teng and Qian Wu

Bidirectional Matching Algorithm for Target Tracking Based on
SIFT   253
    Zhenxing Wu, Jingling Wang, Chuanzhen Li, Yue Yan, and
    Chen Chu

The Design and Implementation of a Kind of Simple and Easy Access
to Database Framework   259
    Pin Yuan, Jia Chen, and Xi'an Lou

A Brief Study on the Theory and Application of Interactive
Simulation   266
    F.Y. Ma, Jinguo Li, Weiwei Wu, Lijun Cai, and Wei Li

Evaluation on Chinese Defense Expenditures from 1978-2009—From
View of International Comparison   273
    Ling Li, Yu Wang, and Sheng Zhou

Construction of Exact Traveling Wave for KP-Type Equation Based on
Symbolic Computation   280
    Qingfu Li and Ruihua Cheng

Comparison and Application of Time-Frequency Analysis Methods for
Nonstationary Signal Processing   286
    Qiang Zhu, Yansong Wang, and Gongqi Shen

Design of Adaptive Filter Based on Matlab and Simulink   292
    YanPing He and HaiDong Zhang

Research on an Improved Method for Maximum Power Point Tracking
of Photovoltaic   298
    Bin Wang, Chunfu Gao, Xinsheng He, and Zhiyong Luo

Application of RBF Neural Network Model on Forecasting Tourists
Quantity in Hainan Province   305
    HuaiQiang Zhang and JingBing Li

A Set of Algorithm to Simulate the Dynamics of Land System   312
    Xiangzheng Deng and Xin Wen

Computer-Based Estimation System for Land Productivity   317
  Xiangzheng Deng, Qunou Jiang, and Xin Wen

An Algorithm to Simulate the Equilibrium of Land Use Structures   322
  Xin Wen and Xiangzheng Deng

An Evacuation Simulation Based on Boltzmann Distribution   327
  Hao Lian, Ang Li, Yang Tian, and Ying Chen

On Self-adaptability of the Higher Vocational Education   335
  Guanlong Luo, Jianjun Yun, and Jie Tang

Design and Implementation of Middle Layer for Off-line Query Based
on JSF and Hibernate Framework   341
  Zheqiong Yan, Jia Chen, and Minggang Wang

Reliability Analysis of Real-Time Multitasking Software Based on
Neural Network   347
  Xiang Chen, Wei Hou, and Yong Zhang

Construction of Distance Education System Based on Online Game
Operation Mode   353
  Xiang Chen, Xue-feng Zhou, and Yong Zhang

Modeling and Optimization Algorithm of FMS Logistics System Based
on Petri Nets and PSO   359
  Wei Yang, ZhiGang Bing, GuiPing Yi, and QuanLi Li

Variable Fuzzy Sets and Its Application in Flood Disaster Loss
Evaluation   366
  Qiong Li

An Improved Algorithm for PAPR Reduction of OFDM Systems   372
  Yazhen Li, Xinhui Zhou, and Jing Guan

The Design and Realization of Experiment Platform in Airborne
Equipments   379
  Ying Gao, Tao Jiang, Lei Lei, and Shuxia Guo

Considerations of the Subject Teaching Method Applying in the
Information Technology Course   385
  Yaqing Shi, Meijuan Wang, and Tingting Zhang

Research on Localization Technology in Wireless Sensor Networks   392
  XingHua Ma, ZhiGang Bing, and YuQiu Tang

Development of a Catastrophe Model to Assess the Allocation
Efficiency of Competitive Sports Resources in China   399
  Qian Wang

MPCS: A Wireless Communication Protocol for Ubiquitous Industrial
Environment 405
     Yuhuang Zheng

Study on Throughput of Network with Selfish Nodes Based on IEEE
802.15.4 411
     Haiping Li, Jianlin Mao, Ning Guo, and Bin Zhang

Attraction for Stochastic Cellular Neural Networks 418
     Li Wan and Qinghua Zhou

Designing on a Special Algorithm of Triple Tree Based on the Analysis
of Data Structure 423
     Min Wang and Yunfei Li

Application of Wireless Communication in Temperature
Measurement 428
     Dejie Song, Boxue Tan, and Wenfeng Liu

Study of the Supply Chain Finance Operational Risk 434
     Di Wang and Baosen Wang

Stability Faults Detecting and Quality Attributes Assessing of Network
information 441
     Sheng Qi Li

Using Concepts in Grid Data Organization 447
     Yan Mao and Li Kai Han

Security Scheme in Wireless Grid 453
     Yue Hong Zhang, Li Hao, and Zhong Shan Yang

Author Index 459

Table of Contents – Part II

The Reform and Practice of Open Teaching for Micro-Computer
Principle and Interface Technology 1
   Zheng Nong

Numerical Simulations on Fire and Analysis of the Spread
Characteristics of Smoke in Supermarket 7
   Daijian Ling and Kaihui Kan

Numerical Simulation of Nonlinear Filtering Problem 14
   Zhen Liu, Fangfang Dong, and Luwei Ding

An Wavelet Multi-scale Edge Detection Algorithm Based on Adaptive
Dual Threshold 20
   Ni Zhao and HuaPeng Zhang

Credibility Evaluation of Information Service Platform Based on
SOA-Extended 26
   JingJing Yan, TingJie Lv, LongFei Guo, and ZiMu Zhang

Saving Energy Control of Auxiliary Fan 33
   Xian-wei Xu, Jin-bao Xu, Yang Liu, Nan Hu, and JIan-xin Gao

The Denotational Semantics Definition of PLC Programs Based on
Extended λ-Calculus 40
   Litian Xiao, Ming Gu, and Jiaguang Sun

ADRC with Synthesis Tuning Algorithm for Main Steam Pressure of
CFBB 47
   Qiang Ma, Qi Xv, and Weishu Wang

Comparing and Analyzing on Value-Passing between Pages in
ASP.NET 53
   Jin Wang

A Retrieval System of Internet Audio Public Opinion Based on
Dynamic Keyword Spotting 59
   Bo Xie, Dongliang Dai, and Xiaojun Li

An Image De-noising Algorithm Based on Improved Wavelet Threshold
Scheme 67
   Li Zhang and Bing Tang

Experiences on Teaching "Computer Program Design" in Military
Academy by Applying Constructivism   73
    MeiJuan Wang, YaQing Shi, ZhengHong Qiao, and XiaoYu Lei

IT Infrastructure, E-commerce Capabilities and Firm Performance:
A Empirical Test Based on China Firm Data   79
    Kuang Zhijun

Remote Sensing Image Segmentation Using Mean Shift Method   86
    Fang Wan and Fei Deng

An Image Registration Method Based on Feature Matching   91
    Fang Wan and Fei Deng

An Exploration of Research and Innovation in Basic Teaching   96
    TingTing Zhang, YongChun Yu, XiaoLi Wu, and YaQin Si

An Improvement Method of Fractional-Order Filter Approximation   101
    Yanzhu Zhang and Jingjiao Li

Phased Experimental Teaching in the College Course of *Computer and
Information Technology*   107
    *Nanli Zhu, Yu Yao, Jianbo Fan, Yongping Zhang, Meng Zou, and
    Peng An*

Modeling and Simulation of the Underground Mining Transportation
System   116
    Lei Xu, Sheng Ye, Guilin Lu, and Zhen Zhang

Database System Development for Cement Factory   122
    Wu Xie, Huimin Zhang, Zili Qin, and Huacheng Zhang

A Feedback Comprehensive Evaluation Method with Data Mining   128
    Wu Xie, Huimin Zhang, and Zengshan Meng

eTOM Business Processes Conception in NGN Monitoring   133
    *B. Raouyane, M. Bellafkih, M. Errais, D. Leghroudi, D. Ranc, and
    M. Ramdani*

Identifying Oligomeric Proteins Based on a Self-constructed Dataset   144
    Tong Wang, Wenan Tan, and Lihua Hu

The Effect of IT Capability on Firm Performance   149
    Ping Fan

The Development and Deployment of a Computer Network Laboratory
Education Service Platform   155
    Chenyang Yan

Obscene Picture Identification Based on Wavelet Transform and
Support Vector Machine 161
    Chun Liu, Changsheng Xie, Guangxi Zhu, and Qingdong Wang

The Design and Implementation of a Course Scheduling System........ 167
    Ping Guo, Lin Zhu, and Shuai-Shuai Chen

An Simulate Micro Hard Disk Read-Write Channel Servo Signal System
Design on FPGA 174
    Qingdong Wang, Changsheng Xie, Dexiu Huang, and Chun Liu

A New Method for Constructing Concept Maps in Adaptive E-Learning
Systems 180
    Mohammed AL-Sarem, Mostafa Bellafkih, and Mohammed Ramdani

Abnormal Event Detection Method for ATM Video and Its
Application 186
    Min Yi

Web Service-Based Enterprise Data Service Center for Exchanging
Common Data of Enterprise...................................... 193
    WenLin Pan, TieHu Tang, and ChangHua Qiu

Research on Addition of Aluminum Fluoride for Aluminum Reduction
Cell Based on the Neural Network 200
    Shuiping Zeng, Rongjuan Wang, and Yuqi Guo

Hot Topic Detection on Chinese Short Text 207
    Cheng Zhang, Xinghua Fan, and Xianlin Chen

Research on Digital Campus Based on Cloud Computing.............. 213
    Nian Liu and Geng Li

The Computer Modeling of the Ball Gear of Concave Cone Teeth 219
    Huran Liu

The Computer Simulation of the "SFT" and "HFT" Method on the
CNC Hypoid Cutting Machine.................................... 225
    Huran Liu

The Computer-Aided Assembly of Pneumatic Motor with Offset
Swinging Planetary Drives of Bevel Gear.......................... 231
    Huran Liu

Programming Calculation of Slope Stability Safety
Coefficient 235
    Wei Lei

Qualitative Assessment of the Influence of 2010 Shanghai World Expo
on the Tourist Industry in World Expo Circle 241
    Xiujuan Gao

An Optimized Color Image Steganography Using LFSR and DFT
Techniques   247
    Asghar Shahrzad Khashandarag, Ahmad Habibizad Navin,
    Mir Kamal Mirnia, and Hamid Haji Agha Mohammadi

Evaluation for the Flawlessness of New Energy Industry Chain Based
on Rough Sets and BP Neural Networks   254
    Wei Li, Dan Wang, and Yunqiao Ti

Optimizing Industry Structure of HeBei Province Based on Low
Carbon Economy   261
    Wei Li, Zuxin Zhang, and Man Wei

The Competitiveness of Photovoltaic Industry in Hebei Province Fuzzy
Comprehensive Evaluation of the AHP   267
    Wei Li, Man Wei, and Zuxin Zhang

Design of Distributed Communications Data Query Algorithm Based
on the Cloud Computing of Hadoop   273
    Luo Jun

Information Technology and "Meaningful Transfer - Led Explore "
Teaching Concepts   281
    PingHua Huang and SuMin Han

The Research and Application of Generating 3D Urban Simulation
Quickly in a Single-View Way   287
    Long-Bao Mei and Chuan Gao

Numerical Analysis of Twist for a Horizontal Axis Turbine Blade   293
    Youfeng Zhu and Yongsheng Ren

The Computer Simulation of the Half-Forming Principle of Carbide
Bur   299
    Huran Liu

The CNC Simulation of the End Milling of the Sculptured Surfaces   305
    Huran liu

The Computer Simulation for the Pneumatic Motor with Planetary
Drive of Bevel Gear   312
    Huran liu

Prediction of Homo-oligomeric Protein Types by a Dimension
Reduction Method   318
    Tong Wang, Xiaoxia Cao, and Xiaoming Hu

Research of Optimal Design for Gravity Dam Based on Niche Genetic
Algorithm   323
    Liangming Hu, Feng Chen, and Yizhi Li

A Pilot Study on Comprehensive Evaluating Indicators System for
Acceptability of Real Time Communication Software Based on AHP ...   329
    Jifeng Guo

The Research on a New Image Enhancement Algorithm Based on
Retinex Theory   336
    Qin Guang

Application of Combined Grey Neural Network for the BTP Forecasting
in Sintering Process   343
    Rui Wang and Qiang Song

FMH and Its Application in Chinese Stock Market   349
    Yuling Wang, Juan Wang, Yanjun Guo, Xinjue Wu, and Jing Wang

Sentiment Classification of Documents Based on Latent Semantic
Analysis   356
    Lan Wang and Yuan Wan

Product Innovative Development for the Laser Orientation Projection
Device   362
    Ruilin Lin

An Improved Quantum Genetic Algorithm for Knapsack Problem   368
    Ning Guo, Fenghong Xiang, Jianlin Mao, and Rui Wang

Innovations in the Teaching of Building Physics with Ecotect   374
    Jian Yao and Chengwen Yan

Study of Microwave Attenuation from Dust Particle   379
    Qianzhao Lei

A Linear Localization Algorithm for Wireless Sensor Network Based on
RSSI   384
    Feng Liu, Hao Zhu, Zonghai Gu, and Yan Liu

Database System of University Sports Meet   390
    Wu Xie, Huimin Zhang, and Tong Li

Shoe Last Free-Form Surface Reconstruction Technique Based on
Reverse Engineering   396
    Xiang Chen and Xin Zhang

Product Innovative Development for the Datum Orientation Triangle . . .   403
    Ruilin Lin

A Distributed Certification Method for Peer-to-Peer System Based on
Biological Information   409
    Zhenhua Tan, Guangming Yang, Zhiliang Zhu, Wei Cheng, and
    Guiran Chang

Characters of a sort of Finitely Supported Wavelet Bases for Sobolev
Space 415
    Yongcai Hu and Qingjiang Chen

The Novel Characteristics of Two-Directional Multi-scale Binary
Small-Wave Wraps with Short Support 421
    Dong Liao and Guodong Xu

Algorithms and Methods for Emotional Mandarin Speech Synthesis 428
    HuaPeng Zhang

Energy Savings Potential for Buildings in Hot Summer and Cold
Winter Zone 434
    Tianhong Wang and Jian Yao

Research on Initial Trust in a B2C E-Vendor 438
    Hanyang Luo

Prediction of Protein O-Glycosylation Sites by Kernel Principal
Component Analysis and Artificial Neural Network.................. 445
    Xue-mei Yang

Analyzing the Effect and Selecting the Parameter of Bioradar Antenna
for Measurement 451
    Hui Xu, Bangyu Li, Xinsheng Che, and Jian Ren

Design of a CAI System for Translation Teaching 457
    Zheng Wang

Author Index.. 463

Model and Algorithm for Time-Dependent Team Orienteering Problem

Jin Li

College of Computer Science & Information Engineering,
Zhejiang Gongshang University, Hangzhou, P.R. China
Jinli @mail.zjgsu.edu.cn

Abstract. In the team orienteering problem (TOP) a set of locations is given, each with a score. The goal is to determine a fixed number of routes, limited in length, that visit some locations and maximize the sum of the collected scores. The team orienteering problem is often used as a starting point for modeling many combinatorial optimization problems. This paper studies the time-dependent team orienteering problem considering the travel cost varying with time and visiting time constraints. After a mixed integer programming model is proposed, a novel optimal dynamic labeling algorithm is designed based on the idea of network planning and dynamic programming. Finally, a numerical example is presented to show the validity and feasibility of this algorithm.

Keywords: Team orienteering problem; time-dependent network; travel time; optimal algorithm.

1 Introduction

In the orienteering problem (OP) a set of n locations i is given, each with a score s_i. The starting point (location1) and the end point (location n) are fixed. The time t_{ij} needed to travel from location i to j be known for all location pairs. A given T limits the time to visit locations. The goal of the OP is to determine a single route, limited by T, in order to maximize the total collected score. Each location can be visited at most once. The Team Orienteering Problem (TOP) is an OP that maximizes that total collected score of m routes, each limited to T. The team orienteering problem (TOP) first appeared in Butt and Cavalier [1] under the name of the Multiple Tour Maximum Collection Problem. The term TOP, first introduced in Chao et al. [2], comes from a sporting activity: team orienteering. A team consists of several members who all begin at the same starting point. Each member tries to collect as many reward points as possible within a certain time before reaching the finishing point. Available points can be awarded only once. Chao et al. [2] also created a set of instances, used nowadays as standard benchmark instances for the TOP.

The TOP is an extension to multiple-vehicle of the orienteering problem (OP), also known as the selective traveling salesman problem (STSP). The TOP is also a generalization of vehicle routing problems (VRPs) where only a subset of customers can be

S. Lin and X. Huang (Eds.): CESM 2011, Part I, CCIS 175, pp. 1–7, 2011.

serviced. As an extension of these problems, the TOP clearly appears to be NP-hard. Many TOP real applications are described in the literature: athlete recruiting from high schools [3], technician routing and scheduling problem [4], TSPs with profits [5], etc. Butt et al. [6] present an exact algorithm based on column generation to solve the TOP. They deal with problems up to 100 locations, provided that the number of selected locations in each tour remains small. Boussier et al. [7] propose a branch-and-price approach to solve problems with up to 100 locations. Only problems in which the number of possible locations in a route is low, namely, up to about 15 per route, can be solved in less than 2h of calculation. The first published TOP heuristic was developed by Chao et al [8]. Tang and Miller-Hooks [4] developed a tabu search heuristic embedded in an adaptive memory procedure. Archetti et al. [9] came up with two variants of a tabu search heuristic and a slow and fast Variable Neighbourhood Search (VNS) algorithm. Ke et al. [10] developed four variants of an ant colony optimization approach for the TOP. Vansteenwegen et al. [11, 12] implemented a Guided Local Search (GLS) and a skewed Variable Neighbourhood Search (SVNS) algorithm. Souffriau et al. [13] designed a path relinking metaheuristic approach. Bouly et al. [14] proposed a simple hybrid genetic algorithm.

However, most of the previous research for TOP in the literature seldom takes into account changes to the network over time. Clearly, the route between two locations does not depend only on the distance traveled, but on many other time dependent properties of the network such as congestion levels, incident location, and construction zone on certain road segments, which would change the travel cost on that segment. Therefore, based on above literature, this paper will consider the time-dependent team orienteering problem (TDTOP for short) which meets the needs to real-world problems. Here, the transportation cost of traveling (time cost in our terminology) varies with time and the travel cost from one location to another depends on the start time. So decision-makers could choose the right route, locations and departure time according to their own situation.

The remaining of this paper is structured as follows: the time-dependent team orienteering problem is described in Section 2. A mixed integer programming model for TDTOP is proposed, and an optimal dynamic labeling algorithm is designed in Section 3. Moreover, in Section 4, a numerical example is introduced to show the validity and feasibility of the algorithm. Finally, the concluding remarks and further research are included in Section 5.

2   Problem Description

Given a transportation network $G = (V, E)$, where $V = \{v_i \mid i = 1,2,\cdots,n\}$ is the node set, $E = \{e_{ij} \mid v_i, v_j \in V\}$ is the edge set, if v_i is adjacent with v_j, then there is one edge e_{ij} between them. $P(i)$: Set of predecessor nodes of node v_i; $S(i)$: Set of successor nodes of node v_i; R: Set of multiple routes, $R = \{r_d \mid d = 1,2,\cdots,m\}$; $\overline{V}$: Set of unvisited nodes; T: The total time budget of the route; s_i: Score of node v_i; vt_i: Visiting time on node v_i; a_i: Arrival time at node v_i; b_i: Departure time from node v_i; $t_{ij}(t)$:

Travel time on edge e_{ij} when the entry time is t; $x_{ijd}(t)$: if edge e_{ij} on route r_d is entered at time t, then $x_{ijd}(t) = 1$, else $x_{ijd}(t) = 0$.

This paper will study the team orienteering problem on transportation network with a given source and destination node, in which the travel cost is dependent on time and primarily on the start time on the edge. It is assumed that time is discredited into small units (such as 1 hour or less 10 minutes). In the TDTOP, each location has a score. It consists in visiting some of the locations in order to maximize the total collected score of multiple tours within a given time budget. And each location can be visited at most once. We don't consider the phenomenon of return and round in traveling road. The road segments may not satisfy the "first-in-first out" property. On this basis, taking into account the application in real world, this paper will consider time-dependent travel cost, location stay time and total transportation time constraint to study the team orienteering problem. Therefore, the time-dependent team orienteering problem is actually a multi-routes-selection one in the time-dependent network with the determination of the departure time from each node on the selected route.

Time and spatial dimensions are used to represent the selected routes, where time is discrete time unit and space is expressed as $V = \{v_i \mid i \in [1,|V|]\}$. So, every selected route is a list constitute in elements (v_i, a_i, b_i), the selected route r_d is presented: $P_d(v_1, v_n) = \{(v_1, a_1, b_1), (v_{d_1}, a_{d_1}, b_{d_1}), \cdots, (v_{d_w}, a_{d_w}, b_{d_w}), (v_n, a_n, b_n)\}$, where v_1 is the source node, v_n is the destination node, and d_i ($i = 1, 2, \cdots, w$) is the node subscript on route r_d. The route r_d is expressed as $r_d = \{v_1, v_{d_1}, \cdots, v_{d_w}, v_n\}$.

3 Model and Algorithm

3.1 Mathematical Model

Choose node v_1 as the source point and node v_n as the destination point. So we establish the following mixed integer programming model.

$$\max \sum_{t=1}^{T} \sum_{d=1}^{m} \sum_{i=2}^{n-1} \sum_{j \in S(i)} s_i x_{ijd}(t) \tag{1}$$

$$s.t. \sum_{t=1}^{T} \sum_{d=1}^{m} \sum_{j \in S(1)} x_{1jd}(t) = \sum_{t=1}^{T} \sum_{d=1}^{m} \sum_{i \in P(n)} x_{ind}(t) = m \tag{2}$$

$$\sum_{t=1}^{T} \sum_{i \in P(k)} x_{ikd}(t) = \sum_{t=1}^{T} \sum_{j \in S(k)} x_{kjd}(t), \ \forall k = 2, \cdots, n-1, \ \forall d = 1, \cdots, m \tag{3}$$

$$\sum_{t=1}^{T} \sum_{d=1}^{m} \sum_{j \in S(i)} x_{ijd}(t) \le 1, \forall i = 2, \cdots, n-1 \tag{4}$$

$$\sum_{t=1}^{T}\sum_{d=1}^{m}\sum_{i\in P(j)}(t+t_{ij}(t))x_{ijd}(t)=a_j, \ \forall\, j=2,\cdots,n \tag{5}$$

$$\sum_{t=1}^{T}\sum_{d=1}^{m}\sum_{j\in S(i)}tx_{ijd}(t)=a_i+vt_i, \ \forall\, i=1,\cdots,n-1 \tag{6}$$

$$a_1=1, a_n\le T \tag{7}$$

$$a_i>0, \forall\, i=1,\cdots,n \tag{8}$$

$$x_{ijd}(t)=0,1, \ \ \forall\, e_{ij}\in E, \ \ \forall\, d=1,\cdots,m, \ \ \forall\, t=1,\cdots,T \tag{9}$$

The objective of the TDTOP is to maximize the total collected score, as shown in (1). In this formulation, constraint (2) and (3) are flow-conservation constraints. Constraint (4) ensures that every location is visited at most once. Constraint (5) and (6) guarantees that if one edge is visited in a given tour, the arrival time of the edge following node is the sum of the preceding arrival time, visiting time and the edge travel time. Constraint (7) is the start time and latest finish time constraint. Constraint (8) and (9) are the variables constraint.

3.2 Optimal Algorithm

Definition 1. (i,a_j,k) is the label of node v_j, where i is the subscript of node v_i followed by node v_j, and k shows what stage it is.

Definition 2. L_k is the set of nodes belong to the k stage, for $\forall v_j\in L_k$, $P_{k-1}(j)$ is the set of predecessor nodes belong to the $k-1$ stage, $P_{k-1}(j)=L_{k-1}\cap P(j)$.

Definition 3. $U_k(j,t)$ represents the optimal collected score from sourcing node to the node v_j at time t on stage k, $v_j\in L_k$.

Definition 4. $U(i)$ represents the optimal collected score from sourcing nodes v_1 to node v_i. So, $U(i)=\max\{U_k(i,a_i)\,|\,k=1,2,\cdots,K\}$, where K is the maximum of stages division.

According to the idea of network planning and dynamic programming, a novel dynamic node labeling algorithm is presented in the following.

Step 1 (Initialization). Given the score s_i and visiting time vt_i on node v_i, $i=2,\cdots,n-1$. Let $s_1=s_n=0$, $vt_1=vt_n=0$, $d=1$, $\overline{V}=V$;

Step 2 (Stages division). According to the arcs on the route, the time dependent network $G=(\overline{V},E)$ is divided into K stages; v_1 is the sourcing node, let $a_1=1$, $k=0$, $U_0(1,1)=0$;

Step 3 (Calculation of arrival time on stage k). For each node v_j in L_k, we find the $P_{k-1}(j)$ which is the predecessor nodes set of v_j ; for $v_i \in P_{k-1}(j)$, calculating $a_j = a_i + vt_i + t_{ij}(b_i)$, if $a_j > T$, then $U_k(j,a_j) = 0$, else go to step 4.

Step 4 (Calculation of the collected score and labeling on stage k). Calculating the total collected score to node v_j at time a_j , $U_k(j,t) = \max\limits_{i \in T(i,t)} (U_{k-1}(i,a_i) + s_i)$, labeling (i, a_j, k) ;

Step 5 (Judgment of the iteration on stage k). Let $L_k = L_k \setminus \{v_j\}$, if $L_k = \phi$, then the iteration is finished on stage k ; if $k = K$, then go to step 6, else $k = k+1$, go to step 3;

Step 6 (Calculation of the total collected score). Calculating $U(n) = \max\limits_k U_k(n,a_n)$;

Step7 (Backward the maximum collected score route). According to the label, re-verse deduction and find out the maximum collected score route: $P_d(v_1,v_n) = \{(v_1,a_1,b_1),(v_{d_1},a_{d_1},b_{d_1}),\cdots,(v_{d_w},a_{d_w},b_{d_w}),(v_n,a_n,b_n)\}$, the visiting route is $r_d = \{v_1,v_{d_1},\cdots,v_{d_w},v_n\}$;

Step 8 (Judgment of the iteration in route set R). Update $\overline{V} = \overline{V} \setminus \{v_{d_1},\cdots,v_{d_w}\}$, if $\overline{V} = \{v_1,v_n\}$, then the iteration is finished, else if $d = m$, then the iteration is finished, else $d = d+1$,go to step 2.

4 Numerical Example

The efficiency and feasibility of algorithm would be demonstrated by the following numerical example in this section. Given a TDTOP directed graph, where there are 20 nodes and 189 edges, node 1 is the sourcing point, node 20 is the destination point. To simplify the problem, we only consider the one-way travel. The time budget is $T=80$. The graph parameters are set as follows: The average travel time on edges is random integer in [3, 20]; The travel time on edges at each time is random integer of the fluctuation range $\alpha =30\%$ to edge average travel time; The average visiting time is random integer in [5,15] as shown in table 1 where the average visiting time for node 1 and node 20 is 0; The score for every node is random integer in [1,10] as shown in table 2.

Table 1. The average visiting time for every node

nodes	1	2	3	4	5	6	7	8	9	10
vt_i	0	8	10	8	12	15	8	6	7	14
nodes	11	12	13	14	15	16	17	18	19	20
vt_i	13	5	8	6	9	5	5	8	9	0

Table 2. The score for every node

nodes	1	2	3	4	5	6	7	8	9	10
s_i	0	6	5	3	4	1	3	4	10	7
nodes	11	12	13	14	15	16	17	18	19	20
s_i	5	5	10	6	5	9	6	7	10	0

According to the dynamic node labeling algorithm, a simulation program is developed with MATLAB 7.0 and the optimal routes for TDTOP are designed as shown in the following.

Given $m = 2$, $R = \{r_d \mid d = 1,2\}$, $\overline{V} = V = \{i \mid i = 2, \cdots, 19\}$, $a_1 = 1$; When $d = 1$, the stages are divided as shown in table 3. According to the algorithm iteration steps, the route is: $P_1(1,20) = \{(1,1,1),(7,3,11),(8,15,21),(9,25,32),(14,35,41),(16,54,59),(19,62,71),(20,74,74)\}$. The route travel time is 74 and the total collected score is 42. When $d = 2$, the unvisited node set is $\overline{V} = \{i \mid i = 2, \cdots, 19\} \setminus \{7,8,9,14,16,19\}$ and the stages are divided as shown in table 4. So, the route is $P_2(1,20) = \{(1,1,1),(2,6,14),(11,17,30),(12,33,38),(13,48,56),(18,66,74),(20,79,79)\}$.The route travel time is 79 and the total collected score is 33.

Table 3. Stages division when $d=1$

Stage	0	1	2	3	4	5	6	7	8	9
Node Set	{1}	{2-19}	{3-20}	{4-20}	{5-20}	{6-20}	{7-20}	{8-20}	{9-20}	{10-20}
Stage	10	11	12	13	14	15	16	17	18	19
Node Set	{11-20}	{12-20}	{13-20}	{14-20}	{15-20}	{16-20}	{17-20}	{18-20}	{19,20}	{20}

Table 4. Stages division when $d=2$

Stage	0	1	2	3	4	5	6
Node Set	{1}	{2-6,10-13, 15,17,18}	{3-6,10-13, 15,17,18,20}	{4-6,10-13, 15,17,18,20}	{5,6,10-13, 15,17,18,20}	{6,10-13,15, 17,18,20}	{10-13,15, 17,18,20}
Stage	7	8	9	10	11	12	13
Node Set	{11-13,15, 1718,20}	{12,13,15, 17,18,20}	{13,15,17, 18,20}	{15,17,18,20}	{17,18,20}	{18,20}	{20}

5 Conclusion

The team orienteering problem is often used as a starting point for modeling many combinatorial optimization problems. The study on time-dependent team orienteering problem is rarely performed at present, especially the travel cost varying with time, which makes it rather difficult to solve the problem. Based on previous literatures, a time-dependent team orienteering problem considering the time-varying travel cost and location visiting time is studied. A corresponding mixed integer programming model is presented and an optimal dynamic labeling algorithm is also designed based on the idea of network planning and dynamic programming. Then the validity and feasibility of the algorithm is demonstrated by a numerical example. The study of this problem is beneficial for decision-makers to choose the right route, locations and departure time according to their own situation in limited time budget. Further study will consider more realistic factors such as the time windows and capacity constraints of locations.

Acknowledgments. This work was supported by Natural Foundation of China (NSFC 70432001) and Shanghai Leading Academic Discipline Project (B210).

References

1 Butt, S., Cavalier, T.: A heuristic for the multiple tour maximum collection problem. Comput. Oper. Res. 21, 101–111 (1994)
2 Chao, I.M., Golden, B., Wasil, E.: The team orienteering problem. Eur. J. Oper. Res. 88, 464–474 (1996)
3 Butt, S., Cavalier, T.: A heuristic for the multiple tour maximum collection problems. Computers and Operations Research 21, 101–111 (1994)
4 Tang, H., Miller-Hooks, E.: A tabu search heuristic for the team orienteering problem. Comput. Oper. Res. 32, 1379–1407 (2005)
5 Feillet, D., Dejax, P., Gendreau, M.: Traveling salesman problems with profits. Transp. Sci. 39(2), 188–205 (2005)
6 Butt, S., Ryan, D.: An optimal solution procedure for the multiple tour maximum collection problem using column generation. Computer and Operations Research 26, 427–441 (1999)
7 Boussier, S., Feillet, D., Gendreau, M.: An exact algorithm for the team orienteering problem. 4OR 5, 211–230 (2007)
8 Chao, I., Golden, B., Wasil, E.: Theory and methodology—the team orienteering problem. European Journal of Operational Research 88, 464–474 (1996)
9 Archetti, C., Hertz, A., Speranza, M.: Metaheuristics for the team orienteering problem. Journal of Heuristics 13, 49–76 (2007)
10 Ke, L., Archetti, C., Feng, Z.: Ants can solve the team orienteering problem. Computers & Industrial Engineering 54, 648–665 (2008)
11 Vansteenwegen, P., Souffriau, W., et al.: Metaheuristics for tourist trip planning. Metaheuristics in the Service Industry. LNEMS, vol. 624. Springer, Berlin (2009) (to appear) ISBN: 978-3-642-00938-9
12 Vansteenwegen, P., Souffriau, W., Vanden Berghe, G., Van Oudheusden, D.: A guided local search metaheuristic for the team orienteering problem. European Journal of Operational Research 196(1), 118–127 (2009)
13 Souffriau, W., Vansteenwegen, P., et al.: A path relinking approach for the team orienteering problem. Computers & Operations Research 37(11), 1853–1859 (2010)
14 Bouly, H., Dang, D.C., Moukrim, A.: A memetic algorithm for the team orienteering problem. 4OR-QJ Oper. Res 8, 49–70 (2010)

Computer Aided Match Method for Matching the Electrical Motor and the Gearbox of the Pure Electrical Vehicle

HongBin Li, Jian Wang, and JingNuo Yu

Communications School of Ludong University,
264025 Yantai, China
{lhbmv,yujingnuo}@126.com, wangjdl@163.com

Abstract. To improve the power performance and economy synchronously, a computer aided matching method for match gearbox and the electrical motor of the pure electrical vehicle is proposed. The method is based on the testing data of the electrical motor. The maximum ratio, the minimum ratio, the gears number and other ratios are chosen according the analysis result of these testing data. The MATLAB is used as the calculating tool. The matching results of the designing case shows that this method is effectively.

Keywords: Computer aided, Matching, Gearbox, Pure electrical vehicle, MATLAB.

1 Introduction

In order to cope with the challenge of the energy contraction, pollution, the pure electrical vehicle which adopts the electrical motor as the driving part has become the researching hotspot. Contrasting with the engine, the power of the electrical motor is constant in wide speed scale. Hence, the gearbox in the pure electrical can be replaced by a fixed reducer whose ratio is optimized. [1-2] But if the speed of the vehicle leave the optimization point, the optimization are all declined. Then the two ratios gearbox is used presently. [3-4] But these two ratios of the gearbox are designed only according the power performance.

To improve the power and economy performance synchronously, the gearbox must be designed correspond the character of the electrical motor. So a computer aided matching method for match gearbox and the electrical motor of the pure electrical vehicle is proposed based on the MATLAB.

2 Choosing the Power of the Electrical Motor

The pure electrical vehicle designed in this paper is a low speed vehicle. Whose full-load weight is 2000kg, the maximum speed is 100km/h, the maximum grade ability is 30%, the acceleration time from 0 to 50km/h is 10 seconds.

Refer to reference [5], the power of the electrical motor should not less than the loading power according the maximum speed. Viz.

S. Lin and X. Huang (Eds.): CESM 2011, Part I, CCIS 175, pp. 8–13, 2011.
© Springer-Verlag Berlin Heidelberg 2011

$$P_e \geqslant (Gfu_{amax}/3600 + C_D Au^3_{amax}/76410)/\eta_T . \tag{1}$$

Where, the P_e is the power of the motor, the η_T which equals to 0.912 is the transmission efficiency, the G equals to 2000kg multiplies 9.8 is the weight, the f equals to 0.014 is the roll resistance coefficient, the u_{amax} equals to 100km/h is the maximum speed, the C_D equals to 0.35 is the wind resistance coefficient, the A equals to 1.9 is the aweather.

The driving resistance power curve which is shown is Fig. 1 can be plotted using MATLAB according equation (1), the required power of the motor is 17.8kw. So a permanent magnetic motor whose power is 20kw is chosen.

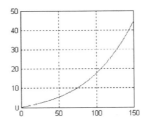

Fig. 1. Driving resistance power curve

3   Computer Aided Analysis Method for the Character of the Motor

The output torque and the efficiency of the system which composed by the motor and the motor controller are measured using dynamometer. The voltage of the accelerating pedal is varied from 0.9V to 4.28V. The character of the motor is measures from the 1.0V to 4.2V taken the 0.2V as the interval. Then, seventeen groups of data are obtained.

Here, the analysis process of the data measured while the pedal voltage is 2.8V using MATLAB is described.

After importing the mdf file which generated by the experimental device, the curve of the output torque and efficiency can be plotted as Fig. 2 and Fig. 3 using "plot" command. For the convenience of following analysis, the curve should be fitted using the fitting tool provide by the MATLAB. It is shown in Fig. 2 that there is an inflexion between the torque of low speed and the torque of the high speed, so the output torque curve is fitted piecewise. But the efficiency curve is smoothly, so the efficiency curve is fitted in total. The fitted curves are shown in Fig. 4 and Fig. 5.

The fitted output torque curves and the efficiency curves of the seventeen groups data are plotted in Fig. 6 and Fig. 7. Then, the fitted power and the efficiency curve while the pedal voltage is 4.2V is plotted in Fig. 8 and Fig. 9.

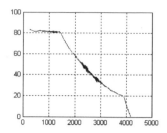
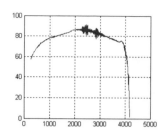

Fig. 2. Torque curve based on original data   **Fig. 3.** Efficiency curve based on original data

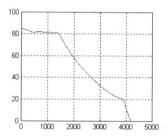

Fig. 4. Torque curve based on fitted function **Fig. 5.** Efficiency curve based on fitted function

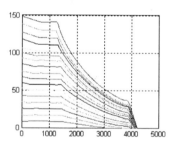
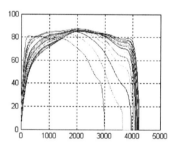

Fig. 6. Torque curve total   **Fig. 7.** Efficiency curve total

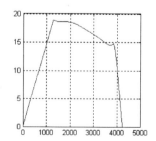
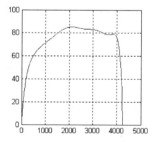

Fig. 8. Power curve of 4.2V pedal voltage   **Fig. 9.** Efficiency curve of 4.2V pedal voltage

It is shown in Fig. 8 that the maximum actual power is 18.9kw, so it can suit the required power.

Then the mapping characteristics of the motor should be plotted. There are two kinds of mapping characteristics. The first kind of mapping characteristics whose vertical axis is torque is shown in Fig. 10. To draw this kind of mapping characteristics, a matrix which includes the output torque and the efficiency in different pedal voltage and different speed is calculated using the fitted output torque function and the fitted efficiency function firstly, then the mesh grid is established using the "meshgrid" command and the grid is assigned using the "griddata" command, then the mapping characteristics could be drawn using the "contour" command. The second kind of mapping characteristics whose vertical axis is pedal voltage is shown in Fig. 11. To draw these kind of mapping characteristics, a matrix which includes the efficiency in different pedal voltage and different speed is calculated using the fitted efficiency function firstly, then he mapping characteristics could be drawn using the "contour" command.

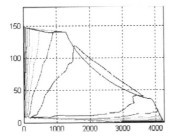

Fig. 10. Mapping characteristics 1   **Fig. 11.** Mapping characteristics 2

The efficiency of the motor is 80% within the innermost scope of Fig. 10 and Fig. 11. It can been seen that the high efficiency area of the motor is wider than it of the engine.

4   Computer Aided Matching Method for the Motor and the Gearbox

Once the motor performance had been analyzed, the maximum ratio, the minimum ratio and the gears number could be designed under the help of MATLAB.

To improve the power performance and economy synthetically, the motor should work in the high efficiency area and fulfill the required power. So the motor speed while the maximum speed is chosen in the speed scale in which the motor power is greater than17.8kw and the speed scale in which the efficiency is higher than 80%. Then the 2350rpm is chosen. The proportionality between 2350rpm and 100km/h which equals 2.631 is chosen as the minimum ratio of the gearbox.

The climbing capacity and the accelerating capacity should be considered while choosing the maximum ratio. The climbing force that required during the climbing process is:

$$F_{rmax} = F_f + F_{imax} .$$ (2)

Where, the F_f is the roll resistance, the F_{imax} is the gradient resistance.

According equation (2), the required climbing force whose value is 5895.6N is calculated using MATLAB.

The accelerating resistance during the accelerating process is:

$$F_j = \delta \, mdu/dt .$$ (3)

Where, the δ which equals to 1.35 is the rotating mass conversion coefficient.

According equation (3), the accelerating resistance whose value is 3750N is calculated using MATLAB.

Then the required maximum driving force is 6600N. So the maximum ratio of the gearbox is 14 in accordance with the maximum output torque of the motor while the pedal voltage is the largest which shown in Fig. 6.

Based on the method to drawing the mapping characteristics whose vertical axis is pedal voltage, the maximum and the minimum ratio designed in the foregoing paragraphs, the contour which depicts the 80% efficiency area is shown in Fig. 12.

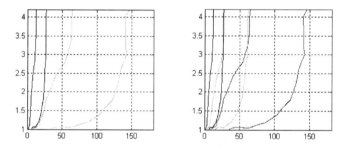

Fig. 12. 80% Efficiency area of two gears **Fig. 13.** 80% Efficiency area of three gears

It can be seen from Fig. 12, the 80% efficiency area of the minimum ratio and the 80% efficiency area of the maximum ratio does not coincide. So the difference between the efficiency before shift and the efficiency after shift is large, the economy of the vehicle is not high using two gears gearbox, the gears should be more.

Then, a three gears gearbox is adopted. The ratio of the middle gears is 6.07 while the geometric progression is adopted to distribute the ratio of all gears. The contour which depicts the 80% efficiency area drawn by MATLAB is shown in Fig. 13.

It can be seen, that the 80% efficiency area of the minimum ratio and the 80% efficiency area of the middle ratio has a large concurrent area, so does the 80% efficiency area of the middle ratio and the 80% efficiency area of the maximum ratio. The economy of the vehicle could be increase if the gearbox is shifted in the concurrent area.

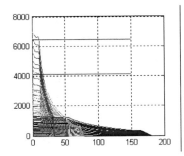

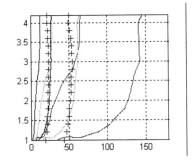

Fig. 14. Driving force of different ratios   **Fig. 15.** 80% efficiency area and force intersection

The driving force curve of different ratios and the resistance force curve which is shown in Fig. 14 can be plotted using MATLAB. It can be seen from Fig.14 that the power performance is satisfied. Then plot the intersection point of the driving force of the same pedal voltage and different ratios using "+" in Fig. 13, which is shown in Fig. 15. the intersection point is gained using "ginput" command in Fig. 14.

It can be seen that the intersection point curve of the driving force pass through the high efficiency concurrent area when the pedal voltage is low. Therefore, the power performance and the economy could be satisfied simultaneously.

5 Conclusion

A computer aided matching method for match gearbox and the electrical motor of the pure electrical vehicle based on the MATLAB is described in the forgoing paragraph by a particular designing case.

The method is based on the character of the motor, so the power performance and the economy could be satisfied simultaneously.

The whole matching process is visible by the assistance of MATLAB, so the designing productivity is increased.

If an automated transmission system is adopted in the pure electrical vehicle, the shifting schedule could be obtained expediently using this computer aided matching method.

References

1. Liu, H., Yin, H., Wang, Q., Liu, P.: Design and Simulation of Power-train Matching for Micro-electric Cars. Micro Electrical Motor 43, 56–58 (2010)
2. Ji, F., Gao, F., Wu, Z.: Interval Optimization Method of Power Train Parameters in Pure Electric Car. Transactions of the Chinese Society for Agricultural Machinery 37, 5–7 (2006)
3. Zeng, H., Huang, J.: The Matching of EV between the Motor and Transmission. Equipment Manufacturing Technology 2, 40–42 (2010)
4. Zha, H., Zong, Z., Liu, Z., Wu, Q.: Matching Design and Simulation of Power Train Parameters for Electrical Vehicle. ACTA Scientiarum Natrualium Universitatis Sunyatseni 49, 4–51 (2010)
5. Yu, Z.: Automotive Theory, 2nd edn. Mechanical Industry Press, Beijing (1999)

Research and Implementation of Dots-and-Boxes Chessboard Based on the Game Strings-and-Coins

Dongming Li, Shuqin Li, and Hua Bao

Department of Computer Science Beijing Information & Science Technology University,
Beijing China 100192
lishuqin_de@126.com

Abstract. The model of computer game system is important for us to make careful analyses of games; generally this model includes description of the board, rules of the game, searching method and estimation value. Dots-and-Boxes is a familiar paper and pencil game for two players, while Strings-and-Coins is a game invented by Elwin Berlekamp to generalize Dots-and-Coins to general graphs. In this paper we made a detailed analysis trying to talk about if the two games are equivalent and to discuss how to describe the Dots-and-Coins chessboard by generalizing Strings-and-Coins graphs. Because of the advantage of Stings-and-Coins that it can be played on any graph, it can simplify certain Dots-and-Boxes observations and is convenient to recognize the chain or cycle formed in the process of playing game, compared with other descriptions of board, this way is effective in improving the efficiency of programs.

Keywords: computer game; dots and boxes; description of chessboard; Strings and Coins.

1 Introduction

Computer gambling, which is also called Machine Gambling, has a simple definition that it tries to make machines think like human while playing chess. Computer gambling is one of the important research fields of artificial intelligence (AI) and an important aspect of proving the level of AI [1]. In 1997, an artificial intelligence milestone, IBM's Deep Blue conquered Kasparov, the international champion of chess, this match is a classic competition between human and computer, it indicates that computer gambling can achieve the level of world champion.

There are many Computer gambling like Dots-and-Boxes, Gobang, Chinese Chess and Go. In this paper we took a deep research on the description of Dots and Boxes chessboard.

2 Stings-and-Coins and Dots-and-Boxes

The Fig.1 indicates the description of Dots and Boxes board, and we can see that it is a 6*6 dots matrix or 5*5 boxes matrix, also it can have another size, the rules of the game

S. Lin and X. Huang (Eds.): CESM 2011, Part I, CCIS 175, pp. 14–20, 2011.

are that each player connect adjacent dots on alternate turns, it is required that you should only connect adjacent dots and should not make cater corners; the lines, which are also called edges, are not belong to any side, and we only take boxes into account. You can get a box by connecting the four adjacent dots with lines, and when you make a box, you can put your name in it, and move again, when all boxes are formed, the game is over, and the winner is the one who get the most boxes.

Strings-and-Coins is another game invented by Elwin Berlekamp and we can use it to generalize Dots-and-Coins to general graphs. The rules of game Strings-and-Games are simply, the players alternate cutting strings. When a player cuts all the edges surrounding a coin, he takes the coin and moves again. The player with the most coins wins the game.

Strings-and-Coins is played on the dual graph of Dots-and-Boxes, which means the following: For any Dots-and-Boxes position, the corresponding Strings-and-Coins game is constructed by considering the boxes as coins, and the edges of the Dots-and-Boxes game as strings. It is seen that placing an edge in the Dots-and-Boxes position separates two boxes, so this has exactly the effect of cutting a string in the corresponding Strings-and-Coins position. From this point of view, the two games are equivalent.

3   The New Description of Dots Chessboard Based on Strings-and-Coins

The traditional description of the Dots chessboard is a 6*6 dots grid, and a 2*2 sub grid is called a box, the nodes(i,j)and(k,l)are adjacent only when the expression |i-k|+|j-l|=1 exists, when the four edges of one box are all connected then the box will be got by the player. Inspired by the equivalent game Strings-and-Coins, we can deprive the ideas that providing another easier description of the board. Fig.1 shows the initial board in traditional way, while Fig.2 shows the Strings-and-Coins chessboard.

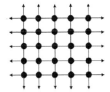

Fig. 1. The traditional description   **Fig. 2.** The Strings-and-Coins chessboard

The corresponding relationship of the two types of boards:

● Boxes correspond with coins

Fig.1 shows the initial Dots chess board of 6*6 type and we can get 5*5 boxes in this Dots-and-Boxes board, while Fig.2 shows the description of Stings-and-Coins chess board of 5*5 type. We can consider the boxes in Dots-and-Boxes as the coins in the Strings-and-Coins, so we get the corresponding relationship of boxes and coins.

● Edges correspond with strings

The initial chess board of Dots-and-Boxes has no connected edges at all, but in Stings-and-Coins chess board, each coin is connected with four strings, we can consider the edges of the Dots-and-Boxes game as strings, but it is seen that placing an edge in the Dots game position separates two boxes, so this has exactly the effect of cutting a string in the corresponding Strings-and-Coins position. Similarly each coin has a degree property which represents the count of strings connected to it.

Each edge in Dots will has the corresponding position in Strings, and the followed illustration Fig.3 shows how the edges correspond with strings.

Fig. 3. The corresponding relationship of edges and strings

In Fig.3, the left one is a box in Dots and it can have four edges a, b, c and d while the right one is a coin with four strings a, b, c and d connected to it in Strings game. When placing the edge a in the left Dots box, it will has the same effect in the right coin by cutting the corresponding string, when all of the four edges of one box are connected, it represents that all of the four strings will be cut from the coin, and Fig.4 illustrates the coin's corresponding state while setting an edge a in the left box, we will see that in Strings the string of this coin has been removed.

Fig. 4. The corresponding relationship when placing one edge in Dots

● The corresponding relationship of chains and cycles

Fig.5 shows that a chain has been made, and from what we talked above we can easily know how to get the corresponding graph in Strings-and-Coins game. The way is just to cut the corresponding strings and we will get the right chessboard description like what Fig.6 shows. We can see that the representation of chain in Strings-and-Coins is clearer and it is vivid for us to judge if there's a chain exists or distinguish the different coins. Similarly, Fig.7 shows the corresponding relationship of cycles in two games.

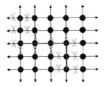

Fig. 5. The chain in Dots-and-Boxes   **Fig. 6.** The corresponding chain in Strings-and-Coins

Fig. 7. The cycle in Dots-and-Boxes   **Fig. 8.** The cycle in Strings-and-Coins

4   The Design and Implementation of Dots Chessboard Based on the Game Strings-and-Coins

Based on the analysis of Strings-and-Coins, we can play Dots-and-Boxes in a general graph, and in section III we have provided the simply design of the description of chessboard, and in this section we will provide an simply implementation of the program of playing the game Dots-and-Boxes.

In the previous section we have seen how the game of Dots-and-Boxes must be played. Now we will outline how to implement the suggested theory in a game playing system.

● Game rule implementation

We should make sure that both player obey the rules and make their moves when they are supposed to, like that you can choose if you make move first or make the computer move first, and when the player get boxes(coins) he/she should make another move unit no boxes can be obtain in this turn.

So we should keep track of the moves in program made on the board to check for illegal moves and to keep track of the score of both players. This is enough to play a complete game of Dots-and-Boxes or Strings-and-Coins, obeying the rules as described in sections above, also we need to keep track of a few other features of the game in order to implement a game playing device. The structures that arise during the game must be represented after each move. during the game, just like an human player this is not something that needs to be updated just before the computer's next turn, but every time a move is made since everybody thinks all the time, not only when it's one's turn.

● Game representation

By the function DoMove We will keep track whose turn it is in the game and keeps the score. We can set who moves first at the beginning of the game, like the human player first or the computer first. At the beginning of the game it prints the empty board. After the first move, it assigns the turn to another player and wait for the move after which it switches turns again. Every move will be recorded in a log file. After each move it checks whether the turns must be switched and assigns the move to the player to move next. For both players the same protocol is used every turn. First the current playing field is printed then the move is made. After the move is made it is added to the move list and updated in the playing field after which the structure list is updated by adjusting all structures to the new situation.

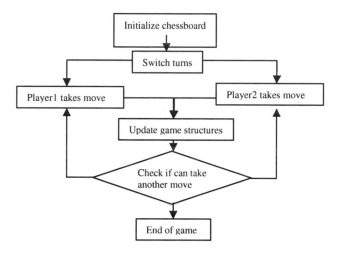

Fig. 9. The simplest flow of Dots-and-Boxes playing system

● Chessboard representation

This playing board consists of n*m boxes. The playing field is stored in three arrays: Square array, Horizontal edge array and Vertical edge array. In the square array, we will store the each coin in the chessboard, including its location, the count of edges connected to it. The Square array is a two-dimension array, it also stores the ground node existed in the Strings-and-Coins. The ground nodes are not like the nodes in the center area, the degree of each ground node is 1, that means only one edge connected to it at most. But the other coins will each has four edges connected to it, and it will have the degree of four. When the node is formed which is also means the four edges are all removed from it, its property of degree will be zero, and this coin will be got by one player, and its value of property owner will indicate this player.

The type of the elements of Square array is Node, the detailed definition of class node is represented by Fig.10.In this class the pointer array edge[4] is used for storing the four strings connected to each coin, and the property degree represents the count of strings connected to one coin.

We will store all the horizontal edges in the Horizontal edge array, each edge has the information of the two nodes to which it is connected, and this is similarly to vertical edges. Each edge will have the property of removed, when it is removed from one connected coin, the value of this property will be one. Each array element in the horizontal array imply indicates the location of one horizontal string and the information

```
Class Node
{
    Public:
        Edge* NextEdge(Edge* Next);
        Node* NextNode(Edge* Next);

        Int x,y;//the location of this coin
        Edge* edge[4];//the four edges connected to this coin

        Int degree;//the count of edges connected to it
        Int owner;//the player got this coin
        Int ground;//is it a ground node
}
```

Fig. 10. The definition of Node

about the start node and end node of this edge. For example, horizontal[1][0] represents that this string is an horizontal string and it is connected by the nodes square[0][1] and square[1][1].Similarly each array element in the array vertical[6][6] indicates that this string is a vertical string and it is connected by the nodes square[1][0] and square[1][1].Fig.11 shows the detailed definition of the string class.

```
Class Edge
{
    Public:
        Int length;
        Node* node[2];
        Edge* next;
        Edge* prev;
        Int removed;
}
```

Fig. 11. The definition of Edge

● Game structure representation

In Dots-and-Boxes game, the count of chains is the key for the player to win a Dots game, and the Chain Rule tells you how many chains you should make to force your opponent to open the first long chain or cycle:

If there is an odd numbers of dot, then the first player should make an odd number of chains and the second player an even number of chains.

If there is an even number of total dots, then the first player should make an even number of chains and the second player an odd number of chains.

For the board sizes of 6*6 dots (5*5 boxes), we can get it that first player should make an even number of chains, and second player should make an odd number of chains.

So the chain is an important aspect of wining the Dots game, and in our board description, how to inspect that if the chain is formed after one move and get the count of chains is important for the player or program.

All structures that are discovered during the game will be stored in corresponding lists. Each structure will have its own list, like that the chain will be stored in the chain list, and cycle will be stored in the cycle list. Chains or cycles will be stored in the array Chains [] or Cycles [], so we can easily get the chain and the count of chains or cycles that will be used in other methods. Each new structure that discovered in during the game will be stored and the full structure of the game will be changed also.

The keys of these lists are the different kinds of structures we distinguish. We keep track of the total number of current and past structures. We keep a list of the following different structures: chains of all lengths, loops of all lengths, joints, handouts. The values that these keys correspond with are arrays containing the boxes that form that particular structure. In the case of a joint the array contains the joint box and the names of the structures that are connected to that joint.

5 Conclusion

In this paper we introduced a corresponding chessboard description of the game Dots-and-Boxes based on the equivalent game Strings-and-Coins, it is clearly that by this way we can simply the traditional description of board and to reduce the complexity of computing the count of chains or cycles. it is much more convenient for programs to judge if there's a chain formed after one move. Also we made a simply implementation of the new chessboard and shows how to form chains or cycles in the process of game.

Acknowledgments

This research is sponsored by the Funding Project for Academic Human Resources Development in Institutions of Higher Learning Under the Jurisdiction of Beijing Municipality (PHR201007131), by the Funding Project for Graduate Science and Technology Innovation Projects of Beijing Information & Science Technology University, by the Funding Project for Science and Technology Research of Beijing Information & Science Technology University (1025013).

References

1. Xu, X., Deng, Z., Wang, J.: Challenging issues facing computer game research. Caai Transactions on Intelligent Systems 3(4), 288–293 (2008)
2. Lian, L., Xu, X.-h., Zhang, X., Yan, N.: Key Technologies Analysis of Dots and Boxes Game System. Progress of Artificial Intelligence in China 2009, 719–724 (2009)
3. Calabro, C.: Analysis of dead boxes in dots-n-boxes, http://www.cseweb.ucsd.edu/ccalabro/
4. Vardi, I.: The mathematical theory of dots, http://www.cf.geocities.com
5. Chrisc Berlekamp, E.R.: The dots-and-boxes game. A K Peters Ltd, Stanford (2000)
6. Blom, G.M.: An Artificial Intelligence approach to Dots-and-Boxes. Multi-Agent systems (2007)

Research on Teaching of "Object-Oriented Programming" Course for Bachelor Students

Zhaoxue Chen and Bei Dai

School of medical instrument & food engineering,
University of Shanghai for Science and Technology, Shanghai, 200093
chenzhaoxue@163.com

Abstract. This paper is dedicated to teaching issues of the Object-Oriented Programming course for bachelor students. It emphasizes specially on problems such as choosing C++ as programming language at the first stage of teaching, percentage-optimized hybrid bi-lingual teaching, careful choice of textbook and teaching materials, etc. It insists that the teachers ought to be careful and considerate in designing various phases of the delivery of the course and provide the right teaching or referencing materials according to the knowledge foundation of different students. Moreover, necessary regular teaching methods would turn out effective during the process of teaching, which has been proved by the author's five-year teaching practice.

Keywords: C++, Object-Oriented programming, hybrid bilingual teaching.

1 Introduction

At present, the object-oriented idea is popular almost in every computer application field, and many universities have opened relevant courses. When it comes to the object-oriented thought, people seldom introduce abstract concepts directly. They usually integrate specific object-oriented programming language with the object-oriented idea in their introductory teaching, and further strengthen these ideas in various related courses or computer knowledge teaching. It is an important task in modern computer related teaching how to take appropriate measures to implement successful object-oriented introductory teaching. This will directly influence the students in their deep understanding of the modern computer system development and implementation principle dominated by advanced OOP idea. So it is necessary to perform in-depth study, discuss and practice on teaching issues of the 《Object-Oriented Programming》 course.

Combining the Chinese current students' characteristics, to satisfy most students' teaching needs, this paper argues that it carries out in the form of C++ language mainly and chooses appropriate classical textbook at home and abroad in introductory teaching of object-oriented programming courses. In teaching methods, bilingual teaching proportion should be increased, practicing should be emphasized and appropriate, ancillary practice material according to different knowledge foundation of each student should be provided. Then a better teaching effect will be achieved with the help of necessary teaching skills.

S. Lin and X. Huang (Eds.): CESM 2011, Part I, CCIS 175, pp. 21–25, 2011.

2 To Choose C++ Language as the Initial Introductory Language Paper Preparation

There are two choices of Java and C++ in terms of selection of the initial introduction for teaching of the 《 Object-Oriented Programming》 course. As to choosing what kind of language to teach, each has advantages and disadvantages. Java belongs to languages of network era with its many merits. But C++ has its many excellent characteristics as well with a long history and plenty of code resources. The language of C++ has some irreplaceable advantages over Java in special attention to code execution efficiency of image and graphics processing together with operating system developing and the underlying driver programming. In addition, considering expansion of enrollment of Chinese high education in recent years, base knowledge of students becomes relatively worse. The ability gap among students becomes bigger and introductory teaching of computer languages is usually performed based on C language. Owing to C++ language is a superset and object-oriented expanding version of the C language, it is a better choice to choose C++ language in the initial teaching of object oriented programming course. During the course of C++ teaching based on C language, the C language can also be reviewed for necessity, which can make the teaching suit for various learning abilities of students and also follows the rules of study from easy to difficult, from simplest to more complex in the process of knowledge learning.

Previous C language learning process can be integrated into an organic iteration while C++ learning in accordance with spiral progressive learning laws. The C++ language is naturally introduced while reviewing content of C language. Most students have C language foundation, which can help students grasping and deepening the understanding of relationship between two languages by highlighting superiority of the object-oriented idea and contrasting C++ and C language during the teaching.

The C++ language in application development has the most extensive adaptability in different technological fields. It is suitable for teaching for students with various majors, whether under the subject of computer or not. For undergraduates, their research direction remains uncertain, so they have great plasticity with further developing potential and space. Mastering C++ language contributes to their future employment and career development. It is more cost-effective than to master Java.

3 Adopting the Hybrid Bilingual Teaching Method

Many Chinese universities are carrying out the bilingual teaching to assure that their students have international quality. But according to the author's teaching practice of several years, it is not so good to perform one-sided emphasis on traditional bilingual teaching, so it is necessary to make concrete analysis of concrete conditions and select appropriate bilingual teaching proportion based on students' basis while teaching. The author has found that the effect of utilizing fully bilingual teaching among Chinese undergraduates is not satisfactory enough in C++ teaching. In addition to the reason of whole declining of the students' quality, students' and teachers' English quality is also an important reason. Besides, C++ is relatively difficult to be understood. Based on the characteristics of the students, the author has found that hybrid bilingual teaching method can not only achieve the goal of the general fully bilingual teaching, but also can be helpful for the delivery and teaching of course contents. Here, the so-called hybrid bilingual teaching is that teachers use PPT or board writing in English and teach in Chinese in key areas as teaching. If necessary, teachers can use English in the key reading materials and exercises. This teaching method is obviously not only reduced degree of difficulty of teaching compared with the pure bilingual teaching, but also has advantages over pure Chinese teaching because a number of related documents and compiler debugging message are expressed in English especially for C++ course. Using pure Chinese teaching it will obviously have an adverse effect on learning and mastering such kind of knowledge. Undergraduates are able to avoid the irrelevant obstacle caused by the limitation of teachers' oral expression and the students' listening comprehension adopting hybrid bilingual teaching instead. They can directly take account of the key knowledge understanding in spite of different abilities of reading English for students. Certainly, those undergraduates with excellent ability of English expressing or enough extra energy are suggested to read some original English materials closely relation to the teaching issue for further improvements on abilities of language expression, knowledge applying and comprehension to this course.

《Object-Oriented Programming》 in the use of hybrid bilingual teaching must also try to increase English teaching proportion as much as possible. First it is determined by objective requirement of the course, for it is almost impossible to build sound program with no errors for programming, debugging is generally required wherein most of help documentation or messages are provided in English. Although most of these tips are written by special document writing workers in most understandable form, the students not majored in computer science are difficult to deduce its specific technological meaning by regular English context. The university is also unlikely to set up English computer courses to help students improving their understanding. So it is necessary to combine introducing related English terms in corresponding courses. It is better to combine computer experiment and other teaching links while doing this to increase repetition rate of the terms and then deepen the understanding of related terminology and knowledge from various perspectives.

4   To Use Both the English and Chinese Version of Classical Textbooks Abroad

To use both the English and Chinese version of the classical textbooks abroad provides enough teaching resources corresponding to different abilities and knowledge foundation of different students. With the overflowing C++ textbooks home and abroad in text book markets, it is especially important to select the right textbook of C++ language among the intimidating thick ones as well as most thin handbooks. According to the author's teaching experience, the classical textbooks abroad is highly recommended but meanwhile the corresponding translated Chinese version should also be considered to judge whether the translated version meets the criteria of elegance, honesty and fluency or not. It would be best if we could have both the Chinese version and English version of the textbook, so that, on one hand, the high-level students are able to have direct access to the original information; on the other hand, students who are not so competent in English language skills could consult both versions as reference. In this way, the demand raised by students' wide ability gap could be met with sufficient bilingual resources. At the same time, it should also be emphasized to adopt which edition of a certain textbook while teaching. Generally speaking, the revised edition is better than earlier editions by taking into consideration the feedback of the readers. What's more, some highly recommended Chinese reference books can be used as a supplementary for such indigenous publications are more suitable in domestic environment as to content and logic. Teachers should decide on at least one Chinese reference book in case students may be tired of reading the same textbook over and over again. Two books with different style for the same course would help to deepen their understanding of related knowledge points and reduce difficulties while learning.

5   Advice on Regular Items While Teaching

As to the design of C++ Object-Oriented Programming course, teachers should not only transmit the idea of object-orientation but also demonstrate common knowledge of programming. What is more, they need to smoothly and gradually transform their thinking pattern from structural programming to object-oriented programming pattern. To achieve these three goals, it is necessary to appeal to the meticulous design of various stages in the whole teaching process. In inculcating the object-orientation thoughts, obstacles caused by complex grammar should be cleared away as clean as possible; on the other hand, in teaching the C++ grammar, the object-orientation thinking pattern should be considered and integrated.

Firstly, the learning of C++ programming asks for a great quantity of conception exercises and hand-on experience. Consequently, the teachers must provide the students with enough quizzes for self-assessment as to their cognition process in order to master the fragile pieces of knowledge points in learning; at the same time, regarding the computer programming language learning as a gradual and accumulating procedure, quizzes and final examinations should be used by teachers as a means of urging the students to learn. The quizzes mainly stress on the key concepts while the finals dwell on comprehensive problems solving in this subject. In this way, the students' mastery of the studied knowledge could be assessed in an all-around way.

Secondly, in the teaching of hand-on practice on the computer, the choosing of exercise should be both interesting and comprehensive so as to build up the students' ability of putting what they have learned in class to practice. Meanwhile, teachers could help students in improving their use of grammars so they can have better understanding of grammars and more excellent ability in correcting their programs with the help of English help documentation and tips.

Besides, the curriculum design exercises the teacher assigned for their students need to be raised to a higher level of comprehension and at best to be accomplished through cooperative teamwork. This would nurture team-work awareness within the students and stick to the essence of modern software projects.

Being extensively applicable in different area of computer technology, the advanced ideas of object-orientation requires that teachers should provide more interdisciplinary reading materials so that students would develop a deeper and more overall understanding of object-orientation, thus establishing the foundation of further mastering other object-oriented tools.

What should be paid special attention to is that discussion and seminars need to be held regularly among C++ teaching team so that different parts in teaching integrate better within the same theme of teaching.

6 Conclusions

By taking into integrating the specific characteristics of both the course itself and potentials of Chinese students, the paper insists that C++ language should be adopted at the initial stage and excellent classical textbook home and abroad should be attached as well; while as to hybrid bi-lingual teaching methods, the percentage of English teaching should be multiplied to the maximum. The teachers ought to be careful and considerate in designing various phases of the delivery of the course and choose the right textbook according to the knowledge foundation of different students. On these bases, necessary regular teaching methods would turn out effective during the process of teaching, which has been proved by the author's five-year teaching practice.

Acknowledgments. This work is under the auspice of Shanghai Municipal Education Commission to Scientific Innovation Research Funds (No. 11YZ116).

Modeling of Flight Delay State-Space Model

HaiYan Chen, JianDong Wang, and Hao Yan

College of Computer Science and Technology, Nanjing University of Aeronautics and
Astronautics, 210016, Nanjing, P.R. China
LNCS@Springer.com

Abstract. Flight delay prediction remains an important research topic due to its
dynamic nature. Dynamic data-driven approach might provide a solution to this
problem. To apply the approach, a flight delay state-space model is required to
represent relationship among system states, as well as relationship between system states and input/output variables. Based on the analysis of delay event sequence, a state-space model was established and the input variable was studied.
A genetic EM algorithm was applied to obtain global optimal estimates of parameters used in the mode. Validation based on probability interval tests shows
that: the model has reasonable goodness of fit to the historical flight data, and
the search performance of traditional EM algorithm can be improved by ideals
of Genetic Algorithm.

Keywords: Flight Delay Prediction, Dynamic Data-driven Approach,
State-space Model, Genetic Algorithm.

1 Introduction

As a result of excessive demand for air transportation, flight delay becomes an urgent
problem that exacerbates national transportation bandwidth limitations. Over the past
decade, researches were focused on analyzing flight delay factors, predicting delay
and propagation, and decreasing delays and other issues [1-3]. Real-time prediction of
flight delay is essentially state estimation of dynamic system. Flight operation process
is monitored in real time, which provides an opportunity to apply dynamic data-driven
approach [4] to achieve more accurate and more reliable prediction. The challenge
remains in establishment of the delay state-space model, which is the foundation in
applying the dynamic data-driven approach.

In this paper, a flight delay state-space model was proposed with a statistic way to
calculate delay caused by random factors. In order to search for maximum likelihood
estimates of parameters in the model, Genetic Algorithm (GA) was combined with the
traditional EM Algorithm to avoid the local maximum problem. Model validation and
performance comparison of the two EM algorithms were given as well.

2 State-Space Model of Flight Delay

2.1 State-Space Model of Flight Delay

From departure at an airport to arrival at the destination, an aircraft accomplishes a
flight task. For efficiency and cost considerations, an aircraft should perform multiple

S. Lin and X. Huang (Eds.): CESM 2011, Part I, CCIS 175, pp. 26–31, 2011.

tasks consecutively each day. Assume d denotes a departure event and a denotes an arrival event. Then the discrete event sequence of an aircraft performs in a day can be written as $d_1a_1d_2a_2...d_na_n$, where the state of the next event only depends on the state of the current event, not on the state of the past event. The discrete events sequence is a Markov chain. Therefore, the relationship among states can be represented in a state-space model, which can be expressed as:

$$x_{i+1}=x_i+u_i+w_i \tag{1}$$

$$y_i=x_i+v_i \tag{2}$$

Where x_i denotes the state variable, u_i denotes the system input, y_i denotes the measurements, w_i and v_i denote the process and measurement noise, respectively. The system model (1) describes the evolution of the state variables over the sequence, whereas the measurement model (2) represents how measurements relate to the state variables. If an aircraft accomplish n flight tasks, then we have $i=1,...,2n$. When i is an odd number, x_i denotes a departure delay state or an arrival delay state, vise versa.

Flight delay in this paper represents the difference between the actual flight time and the scheduled flight time. Random factors such as weather, baggage check-ins, and mechanical failures may result in a delayed flight. On the other hand, an early flight task completion is achievable through planning methods and strategies. Flight delays caused by these uncertainties can be added to the model as u_i. Additionally, air turnaround time and ground turnaround time correspond to two uncorrelated processes. Values of u_i for different models should be estimated in two delay states. However, the relationship between the uncertainties and flight delays are not to be represented by any mathematical models, which leaves the calculation of u_i a key problem in establishment of the state-space model.

2.2 Modeling of the System Input

In general, x_i is the departure delay from an upstream airport, u_i is represented as the delay in air. When $u_i < 0$, it is actually denoted as flight time compensation. Earlier statistics show that the longer itinerary duration a flight is to take, the more compensation the flight can obtain. Therefore, a more effective way to represent u_i is given as following:

$$u_i = sf_i * r_i \tag{3}$$

Where sf_i denotes the scheduled flight time between airports, r_i denotes the delay of per scheduled flight time, or delay rate. The density distribution of the delay rate is shown in Fig.1.

The delay rates vary significantly in distribution, decreasing sharply as a function of the distance from the center, which suggests us to use a finite mixture model [5] to describe the delay rate distribution. The density distribution g of delay rate is modeled as a function with m mixed components. The mixture density of the ith point is written as:

$$g(r_i|\Theta)=\sum_{j=1}^{m} \alpha_j \psi_j(r_i|\theta_j) \tag{4}$$

Where $\Theta=(\alpha_i,...,\alpha_m,\theta_1,...,\theta_m)$ is the parameter vector, $\alpha_j(\alpha_j \in [0,1], \sum_{j=1}^{m}\alpha_j=1$) is the mixing weight of jth component, and $\psi_j(r_i|\theta_j)$ is the density function of jth component depending on parameter θ_j. In this paper, we assume that g is a normal mixture model. And θ_j is denoted as $\theta_j =(\mu_j,\Sigma_j)$, where μ denotes the mean and Σ denotes the covariance matrix.

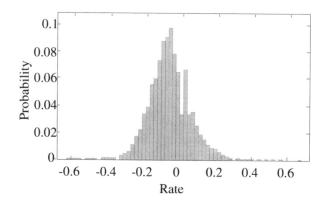

Fig. 1. Density Distribution of Original Delay Rate

2.3 Parameter Estimation Based on Genetic EM Algorithm

EM algorithm is the most popular and effective method for parameter estimation.It is an iterative two-step procedure: E-step and M-step. The E-step calculates the expectation of the log likelihood on the observed data R and the current value of Θ. The M-step updates the corresponding estimate of Θ. After a certain number of iterations, the algorithm obtains the local optimal value of Θ. In order to avoid the local maximum problem associated with the traditional EM algorithm, ideals of GA can be applied to EM to find the global optimum. The combination of GA and EM is known as genetic EM algorithm [6]. The procedure of the genetic EM algorithm is shown as following.

```
Initial: oldChrom, Emrate,bestFit,oldFit;
while (bestFit-oldFit) > EMRate
            fitV = Evaluation (oldChrom,R);
            newChrom = Selection(oldChrom, fitV,ps);
            newChrom = Crossover(newChrom, k, pc);
            newChrom = Mutation(newChrom, pm);
            newChrom = EM(newChrom,R);
            oldFit = bestFit;
            bestFit = max(fitV);
            newChrom = sortByMiu(newChrom);
            oldChrom = newChrom;
end
```

The fitness function used in the genetic EM algorithm is the log likelihood function of Θ defined in equation (5) and calculation stops when improvement of the fitness function value decreases below a given threshold.

$$\log L(\Theta|r)=\sum_{i=1}^{n}\sum_{j=1}^{m}\{\log\alpha_{j}+\log\psi_{j}(r_{i}|\theta_{j})\} \tag{5}$$

3 Case Study and Test

The flight operation data used in this case study was provided by a domestic airline. Information like arrival delay, upstream delay propagation and delay rate was extracted from the experimental data which was also divided into several groups categorized by operating date, test set (only one set), and training set (excepting the test set). Parameters were estimated in the genetic EM algorithm on the training set. The fitness of the model was validated on the test set.

3.1 Density Estimation of Delay Rate

Density estimation of delay rate was implemented in Matlab7.1. In Fig. 1, the distribution represents a mixture of normal distributions rather than a single normal distribution. Assuming component number m=1,2,3,4, we obtained one single model and three mixture models after parameter estimation. As a result, Fig. 2 shows a fitted distribution with two components.

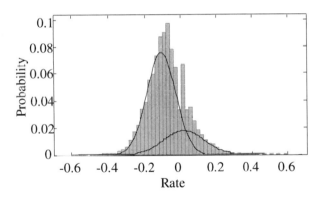

Fig. 2. Fitted Distribution with Two Components

3.2 Fitness Test of the Model

Since the normal mixture models from above are mixtures of normal distributions, general test methods cannot be directly applied to fitness test for the model. Therefore, a probability interval based test was used with steps shown as following:

Step1. Find a interval $[p_1,p_2]$ to contain P% of the values from a normal distribution;

Step2. Compute the inverse of the normal cumulative distribution function with parameters μ_i and Σ_i at the corresponding probabilities: $[a_i,b_i]=$norminv $([p_1,p_2],\mu_i,\Sigma_i)$;

Step3. Calculate the mixed delay time interval [a,b]: $a=\sum_{i=1}^{m}\alpha_i a_i,\quad b=\sum_{i=1}^{m}\alpha_i b_i$;

Step4. On the test set, calculate the proportion of the values fall interval [a,b];

In the tests, two intervals were set as P=90, $[p_1,p_2]=[0.05,0.95]$ and P=80, $[p_1,p_2]=[0.1,0.9]$. Results from all four tests on these models are listed in Table 1. For the case study, the normal mixture model with two components has the best fitness.

Table 1. Results of the model tests

m	P%	
	90%	80%
2	90.29%	85.32%
3	87.67%	79.48%
4	83.05%	75.33%

3.3 Performance Validation of the Genetic EM Algorithm

On the same stop criteria, log likelihood values produced in all iterations from the two EM algorithms with m=3 were collected and shown in Fig. 3. It can be concluded that, in each step, the genetic EM algorithm achieves better log likelihood value, which represents higher effectiveness.

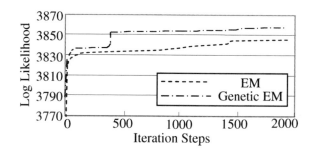

Fig. 3. The log likelihood values of genetic EM and EM

4   Conclusions and Further Work

In this paper, we demonstrated the modeling process of flight delay state-space model. The genetic EM algorithm was used to find the global optimal estimates of the parameters in the normal mixture model. Case study shows that the model has an excellent fit to the real data in both mixture density distribution calculation and the probability interval tests. In conclusion, the traditional EM algorithm can be opti-mized and become more efficient by introducing GA methods in finding the global optimum. Most importantly, the flight delay state-space model proposed in this paper would make it possible to apply the dynamic data-driven prediction into the air trans-portation industry in the near future.

References

1. Abdelghany, K.F., Shah, S.S., Raina, S., et al.: A model for projecting flight delays during irregular operation conditions. Journal of Air Transport Management 10(6), 385–394 (2004)
2. Hsu, C.L., Hsu, C.C., Li, H.C.: Flight delay propagation, allowing for behavioral response. International Journal of Critical Infrastructures 3(3/4), 301–326 (2007)
3. AhmadBeygi, S., Cohna, A., Lapp, M.: Decreasing airline delay propagation by re-allocating scheduled slack. IIE Transactions 42(7), 478–489 (2010)
4. Darema, F.: Introduction to the ICCS 2007 Workshop on Dynamic Data Driven Applications Systems. In: International Conference on Computational Science (1), pp. 955–962 (2007)
5. McLachlan, G., Peel, D.: Finite Mixture Models. John Wiley, New York (2000)
6. Pernkopf, F., Bouchaffra, D.: Genetic-Based EM Algorithm for Learning Gaussian Mixture Models. IEEE Transactions on Pattern Analysis and Machine Intelligence 27(8), 1344–1348 (2005)

An Image Fusion Algorithm Based on Discrete Wavelet Transform and Canny Operator

Ai Deng, Jin Wu, and Shen Yang

Dept. of Information Science and Engineering,
Wuhan University of Science and Technology, Wuhan, P.R. China
dengai131@126.com, wujin1988@163.com, 317987@qq.com

Abstract. Choosing one reliable and effective fusion method to determine fusion coefficients is the key of the image fusion. This text puts forwards a new algorithm based on discrete wavelet transform (DWT) and canny operator from the perspective of the edge detection. First make original images multi-scale decomposed using DWT, and then acquire the level, vertical as well as diagonal edge information by detecting low-frequency and high-frequency components' edges. Whereafter carry out a comparison of the energy of each pixel and consistency verification to more accurately determine the edge points and ensure the clarity of the fusion image. The comparison between the traditional method and this new method is made from the three aspects: independent factors, united factors and comprehensive evaluation. The experiment proved the usefulness of the method, which is able to keep the edges and obtain better visual effect.

Keywords: image fusion; wavelet transform; canny operator; edge detection.

1 Introduction

Image fusion, an important branch of data fusion, aims to make a multi-level multi-aspect processing and synthesis towards multiple source images from multi-sensor, as a result of maximizing the complete information of the objectives and background[1] Multi-source images include multi-sensor images, multi-source remote sensing images, multi-focus images and time series (dynamic) images. This paper mainly analyzes multi-focus images fusion. It's very difficult to get a completely clear image for the identical optical sensor resulting from the restriction of the depth of the field when sensors image the same scene[2]. Multi-focus images have different clear domain and fuzzy domain. The fusion goal lies to synthesize all clear domain of all original images in order to gain a fusion image with optimum clarity.

Recently, fusion algorithms based on multi-resolution decomposition have been extensively studied. Multi-resolution decomposition enables to decompose a image into several images with a progressive lower resolution, that is the decomposition can generate a set of low-pass or band-pass images. This hierarchical structure makes full use of the local information and the global information of images[3]. In 1983, Laplacian pyramid transform was proposed by Burt P.J. and Adelson E. H., which was the first multi-resolution fusion algorithm[4]. Subsequently, contrast pyramid transform, morphological pyramid transform and gradient pyramid transform were all used in

S. Lin and X. Huang (Eds.): CESM 2011, Part I, CCIS 175, pp. 32–38, 2011.
© Springer-Verlag Berlin Heidelberg 2011

image fusion. As the development of the wavelet theory, wavelet transform has been paid much attention due to its good time-frequency characteristic[5] . After the emergency of fast algorithm of orthogonal wavelet transform, wavelet transform becomes more efficient[6], the fusion method based on DWT has been a hot research topic. This paper select Daubechies, bi-orthogonal wavelet to make wavelet transform, multi-scale decomposing the images.

The traditional rules, such as averaging low frequency coefficients and selecting maximum or absolute maximum of high frequency coefficients and so on, have a common defect that the improvement of fuzzy domain quality is at the expense of the debasement of clear domain quality. This fusion effect and ideal effect exist certain deviation. This article introduces canny operator to detect low-frequency and high-frequency components' edges and makes comparison of the energy of each pixel and consistency verification to determine the edge points and ensure the clarity of the fusion image.

2   Image Multiscale Decomposition

Wavelet analysis provides an self-adaptive and localized analysis, which is applicable to time domain and frequency domain. This analysis can focus on any details of the time domain and frequency domain. Multi-scale decomposition of the image based on DWT extract low frequency information, as well as, horizontal, vertical and diagonal directions of the high frequency details.

When it comes to using DWT to Multi-scale decomposition, Mallat fast algorithm is most people's first choice. This algorithm requires a two-dimensional scaling function $\varphi(x, y)$ and three-dimensional wavelet functions $\psi^1(x, y)$, $\psi^2(x, y)$ and $\psi^3(x, y)$. The Fourier Transform of scaling function has low-pass filter characteristic, while the Fourier Transform of wavelet function has high-pass filter characteristic. Constructing low-pass filter and high-pass filter by the scaling function and wavelet function[7], and then you can decompose the image. In this way, a separable scaling function is constructed:

$$\varphi(x, y) = \varphi(x)\varphi(y) \tag{1}$$

And three direction-sensitive wavelet functions are constructed too:

$$\psi^1(x, y) = \varphi(x)\psi(y) \tag{2}$$

$$\psi^2(x, y) = \psi(x)\varphi(y) \tag{3}$$

$$\psi^3(x, y) = \psi(x)\psi(y) \tag{4}$$

$\psi^1(x, y)$ corresponds to the change of horizontal direction, $\psi^2(x, y)$ corresponds to the change of vertical direction, $\psi^3(x, y)$ corresponds to the change of diagonal direction. Decomposition of the image by two-dimensional Mallat algorithm[8] can be expressed as the following equations.

$$A_{j+1}(x, y) = \sum_{x \in Z} \sum_{y \in Z} f(x, y) \varphi_j(x) \varphi_j(y) \tag{5}$$

$$D_{j+1}^1(x, y) = \sum_{x \in Z} \sum_{y \in Z} A_j(x, y) \varphi_j(x) \psi_j(y) \tag{6}$$

$$D_{j+1}^2(x, y) = \sum_{x \in Z} \sum_{y \in Z} A_j(x, y) \psi_j(x) \varphi_j(y) \tag{7}$$

$$D_{j+1}^3(x, y) = \sum_{x \in Z} \sum_{y \in Z} A_j(x, y) \psi_j(x) \psi_j(y) \tag{8}$$

Reconstruction of the image can be expressed as the following equations:

$$F = \sum_{x \in Z} \sum_{y \in Z} (A_{j+1} \tilde{\varphi}_{j+1} \tilde{\varphi}_{j+1} + D_{j+1}^1 \tilde{\varphi}_{j+1} \tilde{\psi}_{j+1} + D_{j+1}^2 \tilde{\psi}_{j+1} \tilde{\varphi}_{j+1} + D_{j+1}^3 \tilde{\psi}_{j+1} \tilde{\psi}_{j+1}) \tag{9}$$

A_{j+1} is the approximate coefficient of the image, D_{j+1}^1 is the horizontal detail co-efficient of the image, D_{j+1}^2 is the vertical detail coefficient of the image, D_{j+1}^3 is the diagonal detail coefficient of the image.

Show as the Figure 1 below:

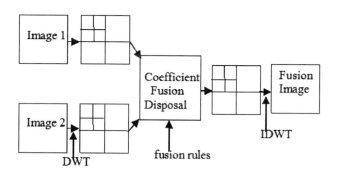

Fig. 1. Image decomposition and reconstruction

3   Image Fusion

Low-frequency component A_{j+1} and high-frequency components D_{j+1}^1, D_{j+1}^2, D_{j+1}^3 are carried out edge detection using canny operator. In this way, the horizontal and vertical detail information of them are extracted. Meanwhile, make a convolution be-tween a 3×3 template and the each frequency domain to acquire the diagonal edge information. Then the low- frequency coefficients' edge information EA_1, EA_2, EA_3

of the three directions and the high- frequency coefficients' ED_1, ED_2, ED_3 are all gained.

The energy of low-frequency coefficient's each pixel is defined as follows:

$$EA(x, y) = EA_1^2(x, y) + EA_2^2(x, y) + EA_3^2(x, y) \tag{10}$$

The energy of high-frequency coefficient's each pixel is defined as follows:

$$ED(x, y) = ED_1^2(x, y) + ED_2^2(x, y) + ED_3^2(x, y) \tag{11}$$

Calculate each point's energy $E1(x, y)$, $E2(x, y)$ of the frequency domain coefficients of original images and make a comparison to determine the fused low-frequency coefficient FA and fused high-frequency coefficient FD (three directions):

$$FA(x, y) = \begin{cases} A1(x, y), & EA1(x, y) \geq EA2(x, y) \\ \\ A2(x, y), & EA1(x, y) < EA2(x, y) \end{cases} \tag{12}$$

$$FD(x, y) = \begin{cases} D1(x, y), & ED1(x, y) \geq ED2(x, y) \\ \\ D2(x, y), & ED1(x, y) < ED2(x, y) \end{cases} \tag{13}$$

Then, implement a consistency verification towards the frequency domain coefficient by a 3 × 3 template, which is an essential part. If the fusion coefficient of certain region's center is selected from the transformed coefficient of the original image 1, however, the other 5 or more than 5 fusion coefficients in this region are selected from the transformed coefficient of the original image 2, the fusion coefficient of the region's center should be changed to the transformed coefficient of the original image 2. As for the boundary coefficient, the consistency verification rule is altered to first make up zeros and then compare them. Finally, the fused image can be generated adopting inverse discrete wavelet transform(IDWT).

4   Experiment Result and Data Analysis

The image fusion algorithm has been achieved using MATLAB 7. 0. 1 platform. The original image 1 used in the experiment is that the center is fuzzy and the vicinity is clear, and the original image 2 is just opposite. Show as the Figure 2 below.

Make a comparison of the following methods: a traditional rule that averages low frequency coefficients and selects absolute maximum of high frequency coefficients; this article's new fusion method is separately utilized at the low-frequency coefficient, the high-frequency coefficient and the low- high-frequency. The fusion results are shown in the Figure 3. Fig.3 (a) is the result of the traditional method of average. Fig.3 (b) is the method of this article acting on the high-frequency coefficient (method of this article 1). Fig.3 (c) is the method of this article acting on the low-frequency coefficient (method of this article 2). Fig.3 (d) is the method of this article acting on the low-high-frequency coefficient (method of this article 3).

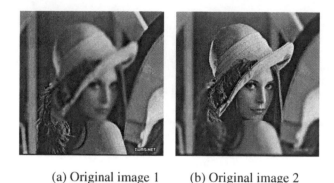

(a) Original image 1   (b) Original image 2

Fig. 2. Original images

(a) Method of average   (b) Method of this article 1

(c) Method of this article 2   (d) Method of this article 3

Fig. 3. Comparison of four fused images

Qualitative analysis displays that the visual effects of the latter two fused images are better than that of the first two images. Then make a quantitative analysis from three respects: independent factors (IF), united factors (UF) as well as comprehensive evaluation (CE)[9] . Mean value (MV) reflects average brightness as to human eyes. Mean gradient (MV) indicates the clarity, detail contrast and texture transformation features. Information entropy (IE) can show the quantity of image information. Deviation index (DI) reflects the deviation between fused images and reference image and the smaller its value is, the closer two images' similarity is[10].

$$DI = \frac{1}{r \times c} \left| \sum_{i=1}^{r} \sum_{j=1}^{c} \text{Re} f(i, j) - \sum_{i=1}^{r} \sum_{j=1}^{c} fR(i, j) \right| \tag{14}$$

Ref is the reference image, r and c represent the image's width and length. Edge preservation (EP) expresses a image's edge information. It and average energy of wavelet coefficients (WAE) both can indicate a image's resolution and clarity.

$$EP = \frac{\sum_{i=1}^{r} \sum_{j=1}^{c} [Q_1(i, j) \cdot w_1(i, j) + Q_2(i, j) \cdot w_2(i, j)]}{\sum_{i=1}^{r} \sum_{j=1}^{c} [w_1(i, j) + w_2(i, j)]} \tag{15}$$

$Q_1(i, j)$ and $Q_2(i, j)$ represently show the edge information retention of each pixel. $w_1(i, j)$ and $w_2(i, j)$ reflect the absolute value of the gradient of each pixel. Mean value, mean gradient, information entropy, deviation index and edge preservation all have corresponding improvements. The fused images' average energy of wavelet coefficients is more than that of two original images. The experiment data are shown in the Table 1. I1, and I2 represent two original images. TM represents the traditional method. HI, LI and LHI respectively represent high-frequency coefficient fusion improvement, low-frequency coefficient fusion improvement and low-high-frequency coefficient fusion improvement.

Table 1. Comparison of fusion methods

	IF			UF	CE	
	MV	*MG*	*IE*	*DI*	*EP*	*WAE*
I 1	98.3719	48.3449	7.4612	1.3037		0.0314
I 2	98.3657	49.7548	7.4352	1.3582		0.0291
TM	98.5281	53.2725	7.4462	1.2221	0.2140	0.0565
HI	98.5296	53.2876	7.4453	1.2216	0.2142	0.0565
LI	98.5517	65.3368	7.5029	0.0531	0.2300	0.0565
LHI	98.5520	65.3482	7.5019	0.0530	0.2301	0.0565

5 Conclusion

To sum up, the relevant experiments show that the image fusion algorithm based on discrete wavelet transform and canny operator can be used on multi-focus images fusion, which enables to achieve a well-effect fused image with higher clarity and improve the regarding performance index. It makes good use of local time-frequency characteristic and keeps image edge information better.

Acknowledgement

I hereby experss gratitude to my dear teacher Jin Wu and Shen Yang , without their effort, this thesis can not be accomplished. It is to acknowledge that this project has been sponsored by Hubei Natural Science Foundation (Grant No. 2010CDB03301).

References

1 Llinas, J., Edward, W.: Multisensor data fusion. Artech House, Boston (1990)
2 Yang, X., Yang, W.H., Pei, J.H.: Different focus points images fusion based on wavelet decomposition. Acta Electronica Sinica 29(6), 846–848 (2001)
3 Nunez, J., Otazu, X., Fors, O., et al.: Multiresolution-based image fusion with additive wavelet decomposition. IEEE Trans. on Geoscience and Remote Sensing 37(3), 1204–1211 (1999)
4 Burt, P.J., Adelson, E.H.: The Laplacian pyramid as a compact image code. IEEE Trans. on Communications 31(4), 532–540 (1983)
5 Yan, D.M., Zhao, Z.M.: Wavelet decomposition applied to image fusion. In: Proc. Int. Conf. on Info-tech and Info-net, pp. 291–295. IEEE Press, New Jersey (2001)
6 Mallat, S.G.: Multifrequency channel decompositions of images and wavelet models. IEEE Trans. on Acoustics Speech and Signal Processing 37(12), 2091–2110 (1989)
7 Li, J., Li, X.: Digital image processing, pp. 55–67. Tsinghua University Press, Beijing (2007)
8 Jing, Z., Xiao, G., Li, Z.: Image Fusion: Theory and Applications, pp. 70–86. Higher Education Press, Beijing (2007)
9 Krista, A., Yun, Z., Peter, D.: Wavelwt based image fusion techniques——An introduction, review and comparision. ISPRS Journal of Photogrammetry & Remote Sensing 62(4), 249–263 (2007)
10 Liu, G., Yang, W.: A wavelet-decomposition-based image fusion scheme and its performance evaluation. Aeta Automatica Sinica 28(11), 927–934 (2002)

A Novel Method of Stabilizing the Vibration Velocity at the End of Piezoelectric Transducers*

HuiJuan Dong[1], Jian Wu[2], WeiGang Bao[1], and GuangYu Zhang[1]

[1] School of Mechatronics Engineering of Harbin Institute of Technology, Harbin, 150001
[2] Pearl River Water Research Institute, Pearl River Water Resources Committee, Guangzhou, 510611

Abstract. The vibration velocity at the end of a piezoelectric transducer is difficult to be stabilized. This paper theoretically analyzes the relationship of its admittance and frequency, and the main reasons of over voltage and over current caused by the traditional current-based stabilizing vibration velocity method. In light of the above, the authors present a novel method, which takes advantages over the traditional one in terms of the time and the amplitude of the overshoot voltage or current. Accordingly, the transducer and its generator can be effectively protected.

Keywords: piezoelectric transducer, admittance, frequency, current-based stabilizing vibration velocity.

1 Introduction

The vibration velocity at the output end of a transducer is required constant during the ultrasonic machining process, but it fluctuates with the changes of load [1]. And thus an ultrasonic generator should have a function of keeping the vibration velocity constant automatically. As the vibration velocity is proportional to the current of the transducer [2][3], the traditional current-based stabilizing vibration velocity method [4] is available, in which the exciting voltage of the transducer is adjusted after the resonant frequency being successfully traced to keep its current constant. It is noted that the traditional method only offers an efficient solution under the condition of load being increasing. However, an unacceptable increasing of the current using the traditional method was seen in tests when the load decreased, which might cause the damage of the transducer.

In order to solve these problems, a novel method termed as asymmetric automatic regulation of the vibration velocity was described and implemented in this work. The point is that the increasing velocity of the exciting voltage is slower than that of the resonant frequency when the load increases. And the decreasing velocity of the exciting voltage is faster than that of the resonant frequency when the load decreases. The experiments carried out demonstrated that it takes advantage over the traditional method mentioned in terms of the accuracy of stabilizing the current and the transducer safety.

* Sponsored by National Natural Sciences Foundation of China (50674036).

S. Lin and X. Huang (Eds.): CESM 2011, Part I, CCIS 175, pp. 39–46, 2011.
© Springer-Verlag Berlin Heidelberg 2011

2   The Traditional Constant Current Method and Its Shortages

The equivalent circuit of a transducer near its mechanical resonant frequency is shown in Fig.1 [5][6].

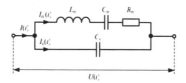

Fig. 1. Equivalent circuit of a piezoelectric transducer

$U(t)$ and $I(t)$ are the transducer's exciting voltage and its current at time t. L_m, C_m and R_m compose the mechanical arm. C_e is named as the electrical arm. $I(t)$ may be described below.

$$I(t) = I_m(t) + I_e(t) = \frac{U(t)}{Z_m(\omega)} + \frac{U(t)}{Z_e(\omega)}. \tag{1}$$

In which ω is the exciting frequency of the transducer, $Z_m(\omega)$ is the impedance of the mechanical arm, $Z_e(\omega)$ is the impedance of the electrical arm.

Assuming that the transducer is excited at the resonant frequency ω_s, which satisfies the equations below:

$$Z_m(\omega_s) \ll Z_e(\omega_s)$$
$$I(t) \approx I_m(t) \gg I_e(t) \tag{2}$$

Equation (2) shows that keeping $I(t)$ constant at ω_s is to stabilize the vibration velocity, which is the basis of the traditional current-based stabilizing vibration velocity method.

Assuming that ω is far away from ω_s, the equations below are satisfied:

$$Z_m(\omega) \gg Z_e(\omega)$$
$$I(t) \approx I_e(t)$$
$$I_m(t) \approx 0 \tag{3}$$

Equation(3) implies that the vibration speed is nearly zero at ω. Therefore, the vibration velocity could be stabilized using the traditional method only after the resonant frequency being successfully traced.

3   The Novel Method of Stabilizing the Vibration Velocity

The impedance $Z(\omega)$ and the conductance $G[\omega(t)]$ of the transducer [7][8] are given in equation (4)

$$Z(\omega) = \frac{1}{G[\omega(t)]} = \frac{(\omega^2 L_m C_m - 1) - j\omega C_m R_m}{\omega^2 C_e C_m R_m + j[\omega^3 L_m C_e C_m - \omega(C_e + C_m)]} \tag{4}$$

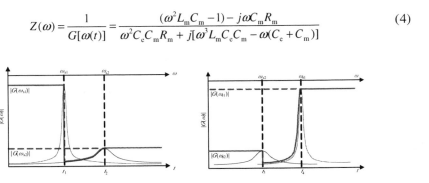

(a) ω_s shifts from ω_{s1} to ω_{s2} (b) ω_s shifts from ω_{s2} back to ω_{s1}

Fig. 2. $|G[\omega(t)]|$ varying with ω and t

$G[\omega(t)]$ of a transducer with and without load are respectively shown in black and blue in Fig.2, which is ω dependent. Their corresponding maximum values, $|G(\omega_{s1})|$ and $|G(\omega_{s2})|$, are obtained at ω_{s1} and ω_{s2}. When ω_s shifts from ω_{s1} to ω_{s2} at t_1, $|G[\omega(t)]|$ follows the red curve in graph (a). Subsequently ω_s shifts back from ω_{s2} to ω_{s1} at t_3, $|G[\omega(t)]|$ follows the red curve in graph (b).

In order to stabilize the output vibration velocity, it is required to regulate the voltage $U(t)$ when $|G[\omega(t)]|$ being changed. This can be described in equation (5).

$$I(t) = U(t)|G(\omega)| \tag{5}$$

In graph (b), $|G[\omega(t)]|$ will increase at t_4 when ω_s being locked. Due to the fact of the voltage still not being regulated using the traditional method, the current $U(t)|G(\omega)|$ might go beyond the limit. In light of the above, a novel method termed as asymmetric automatic regulation of the vibration velocity was described in this work. The voltage increase speed should be much slower than the frequency regulation speed ($dU(t)/dt \ll d\omega/dt$) when $|G[\omega(t)]|$ decreases immediately at the beginning of the load being changed. Subsequently, $|G[\omega(t)]|$ monotonically increases during the process of the frequency-tracing. The voltage decrease speed should be much faster than $d\omega/dt$ to ensure transducer's current not overshoot.

4   Structure of the Ultrasonic Power Based on Asymmetric Regulation of the Vibration Velocity

The ultrasonic power based on asymmetric regulation of the vibration velocity is constructed and evaluated in this paper, illustrated in Figure 3.

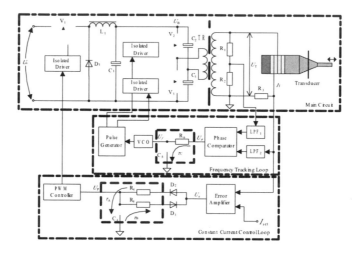

Fig. 3. Schematic of the asymmetric regulation-based ultrasonic power

The power system is composed by three parts, Main Circuit, Constant Current Loop and Frequency Tracking Loop, which are partitioned by a dot-dash line.

The principle of Main Circuit is detailed below. V_1, D_1, L_1 and C_1 constitute the voltage adjustment circuit. Its output voltage U_B provides variable working voltage for the half-bridge converter circuit, which is constituted by V2 and V3. Moreover, the output of the half-bridge converter circuit drives a transducer through a transformer TR.

The principle of Constant Current Loop is described. The transducer's current, which is the input of Constant Current Loop, is sampled through resistance R3 and sent to an Error Amplifier. $\tau_A = R_4C_4$ represents the increasing speed of U_B, and the smaller τ_A is, the faster the speed increases. $\tau_B = R_5C_4$ decides the decreasing speed of U_B, and the smaller τ_B is, the faster the speed decrease. The method proposed in this paper makes sure that the decreasing speed of U_B is much faster than the increasing one by setting $\tau_A \gg \tau_B$.

The principle of Frequency tracking is: the transducer's voltage is gained through R1 and R2, and its current value is sampled through R3. Their phase difference $\theta(\omega)$ in equation (4) is sent to Phase Comparator through two low-pass filters LPF1 and LPF2, and subsequently is used to regulate U_θ to realize frequency tracking. $\tau_C = R_6C_5$ stands for the speed of frequency tracking. $\tau_A \gg \tau_C \gg \tau_B$ is set in this work to realize the asymmetrical automatic steady speed control, which means that the decreasing speed of U_B is faster than the frequency tracking speed, and they both are faster than the increasing speed of U_B.

5 Simulation Experiments and Analysis

This section demonstrates the novel method by using the simulation-based analysis. Parameters of the transducer with and without load is listed in Table 1.

Table 1. Parameters of the transducer under with and without load

	L_m (mH)	C_m(pF)	$R_m(\Omega)$	C_e(nF)	f_s(kHz)
without load	140.5	459.0	35	12.17	19.814
with load	140.5	420.0	450	12.17	20.707

It is supposed that the working current of the transducer in test is 1A.

5.1   The Traditional Constant Current-Based Steady Speed Method

Parameters in Fig.3 are set as $\tau_A = \tau_B \gg \tau_C$, $\tau_A = \tau_B = 5 \times 10^{-4}$s, $\tau_C = 5 \times 10^{-5}$s. The results of the simulation are shown in Fig.4.

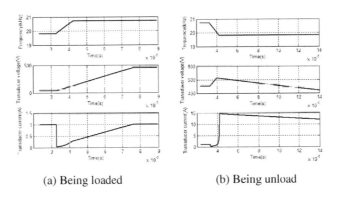

(a) Being loaded   (b) Being unload

Fig. 4. Voltage & current of the transducer varied with ω using the traditional method

As shown in Fig.4(a), when the transducer being loaded, the admittance of transducer follows the red curve in Figure 2(a) and the current value decreases to zero instantly. The frequency tracking costs 1×10^{-5} seconds, and the voltage adjustment costs about 4×10^{-4} seconds. It shows that both the voltage and current can increase steadily when using the traditional method. As shown in Figure 4(b), when the transducer being unload, the current also decreases to zero instantly, and subsequently increases to nearly 15A right after frequency tracking completes. Accordingly, the traditional method can't be well suited to the situation of the load being decreased.

5.2   The Asymmetric Automatic Steady Speed Method

Parameters are set, $\tau_A = 5 \times 10^{-4}$s, $\tau_B = 5 \times 10^{-6}$s, $\tau_C = 5 \times 10^{-5}$s, $\tau_A \gg \tau_C \gg \tau_B$. It implies that the speed of the voltage decrease is faster than that of frequency tracking, which is faster than that of voltage increase. The voltage and current of the transducer being varied with ω_s using the proposed method are simulated and shown in Fig.5 under the two conditions.

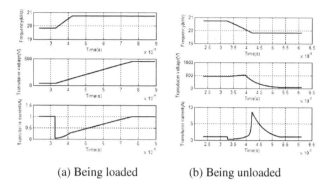

(a) Being loaded   (b) Being unloaded

Fig. 5. Voltage and current being varied with ω_s using the proposed method

When the transducer being loaded shown in Fig.5(a), the current decreases to zero instantly. The voltage and current both increase steadily, which is the same as using the traditional method. When transducer being unload shown in Fig.5(b), the current also decreases to zero instantly, and subsequently increases to 9A right after frequency tracking completes. Though the current overshoot appears, the proposed method takes advantages over the traditional method of its overshoot value and overshoot time.

5.3   Parameters Effect on Characteristic of the Novel Method

The set of $\tau_A \gg \tau_C \gg \tau_B$ is the base of the proposed method. The effect of three parameters on the overshoot are analyzed below. Supposing that $\tau_C = 5\times10^{-5}$s, overshoot of the voltage and currentare are simulated and shown in Figure 6 and Figure 7 under both conditions of the transducer being loaded and unloaded.

As shown in Figure 6, voltage and current both won't be overshooted when transducer being load. It is noted that the regulation process will be shorter when speed of

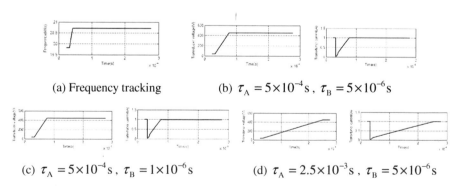

(a) Frequency tracking   (b) $\tau_A = 5\times10^{-4}$s, $\tau_B = 5\times10^{-6}$s

(c) $\tau_A = 5\times10^{-4}$s, $\tau_B = 1\times10^{-6}$s   (d) $\tau_A = 2.5\times10^{-3}$s, $\tau_B = 5\times10^{-6}$s

Fig. 6. Overshoot of the voltage and current when the transducer being load

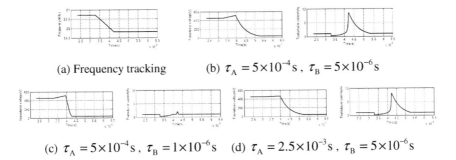

(a) Frequency tracking   (b) $\tau_A = 5 \times 10^{-4}$ s, $\tau_B = 5 \times 10^{-6}$ s

(c) $\tau_A = 5 \times 10^{-4}$ s, $\tau_B = 1 \times 10^{-6}$ s   (d) $\tau_A = 2.5 \times 10^{-3}$ s, $\tau_B = 5 \times 10^{-6}$ s

Fig. 7. Overshoot of the voltage and current when the transducer being unload

voltage increase is faster (or τ_A is smaller). However, speed of voltage decrease(τ_B) doesn't affect the regulation process at all.

As shown in Figure 7, when load decreases, the slower the voltage increases, the smaller the overshoot of incentive voltage will be. The overshoot v and the voltage current both depend on the speed of voltage decrease (or τ_B). The faster the voltage decreases (or τ_B is smaller), the smaller overshoot of the current will be.

6 Conclusions

The asymmetric automatic steady speed control method proposed in this paper offer a solution to protect devices by reasonably setting up/down speed of driven voltage and frequency tracking speed. The faster the speed of the voltage decreases, the smaller overshoot is. By comparison with the traditional method, the transducer controlled using the proposed method will be subjected to a smaller overshoot of voltage and current, no matter how the load changes in the process.

References

1. Mortimer, B., du Bruyn, T., Davies, J., Tapson, J.: High power resonant trancking amplifier using admittance locking. Ultrasonics 39, 257–261 (2001)
2. Chen, Z., Zhao, C., Huang, W.: An Effective Frequency Tracking Control and Balancing Compensation between CW & CCW Rotation Speed Techniques for Ultrasonic Motor. In: 2004 IEEE International Ultrasonics, Ferroelectrics and Frequency Control Joint 50th Anniversary Conference, pp. 2251–2254 (2004)
3. Shuyu, L., Fucheng, Z.: Measurement of ultrasonic power and electro-acoustic efficiency of high power transducers. Ultrasonics 37, 549–554 (2000)
4. Xu, L.: Amplitude controlling in ultrasonic machining. Electromachining & Mould (6), 24–26&III-VI (2004) (in Chinese)
5. Mizutani, Y., Suzuki, T., Ikeda, H., Yoshida, H.: Automatic Frequency Control for Maximizing RF Power Fed to Ultrasonic Transducer Operating at 1MHz. Thirty-First IAS Annual Meeting, IAS 1996, Conference Record of the 1996 IEEEIndustry Applications Conference, 1996, vol. 3, 1585–1588 (1996)

6. Parrini, L.: Member: Design of Advanced Ultrasonic Transducers for welding devices. IEEE Transactions on Ultrasonics, Ferroelectrics, and Frequency Control 48(6), 1632–1639 (2001)
7. Mizutani, Y., Suzuki, T., Ikeda, H., Yoshida, H.: Power Maximizing of Ultrasonic Transducer Driven by MOS-FET Inverter Operating at 1MHz. In: Proceedings of the 1996 IEEE IECON 22nd International Conference on Industrial Electronics, Control, and Instrumentation, 1996, vol. 2, pp. 983–986 (1996)
8. Dong, H.-j., Zhang, G.-y., Zhang, Q.-x.: CAI He-gao: Automatic stabilization of velocity for ultrasonic vibration system. Journal of Harbin Institute of Technology (New Series) 8(1), 4–7 (2001)

The Optimization Model of Campus Network Port Resources Based on Queuing Theory

Banteng Liu[1], Xuejun Wu[2,*], Juhua Chen[2], Guoyong Dai[2], and yue Ruan[2]

[1] Zhejiang Shuren University, College of Information, 310015, Hangzhou, China
[2] Zhejiang University of Technology, College of Science, 310023, Hangzhou, China
wuxj@zjut.edu.cn

Abstract. In this paper, give full consideration to the Internet utilization, waste rate, complaint rate and other indicators, building on the model about campus network issues. Through the study of campus information network this stochastic service system, analyzed the service quality and system resources this pair of contradictions, application of the principle of queuing theory, the mathematical model was established, determined the communication port number, and adjusted the charge system, on the basis of ensuring regular service quality indicators, making service facilities cost economic and reasonable.

Keywords: operations research,stochastic service system,queuing theory.

1 Introduction

Today's society has entered the information society, information has become a core element of social and economic development, information technology has become the trend in today's world, our campus network construction is gradually warming up, and digital campus continues to accelerate the pace of construction. Many areas and schools regarded construction of the campus network as a symbol of modernization. According to the construction of campus net needs to solve the following tasks: 1. Determine the port number and the ratio of number of Internet users.2. Discussion on an average day each user Internet 1h, 1.5 h, 2h, 3h, 4h, the possibility of 5h, appear because of the line is busy user wants to Internet instead produced the possibility and communication port complain the average usage, 3. In order to control the Internet time, gives a kind of reasonable piecewise timing charging circuits' scheme[1].

The key to solve mission in the following: 1. the task requires us to fully consider Internet indices (such as Internet utilization, waste rate, complaint rate, etc.), determined the port number and the ratio of number of Internet users. How to explain the correctness and rationality of results we obtained become a problem we need to consider[2]. We can use multi-objective programming unit above three index reunification together, establish evaluation function, and how to establish evaluation function becomes a key to solve this problem. 2. Any campus network construction, and must have the earlier investigation data. In the completion of tasks of process, we

---

* Corresponding author.

S. Lin and X. Huang (Eds.): CESM 2011, Part I, CCIS 175, pp. 47–52, 2011.
© Springer-Verlag Berlin Heidelberg 2011

need college students surf the Internet time distribution to support our model construction. Due to the title didn't give any data, gave us the process brings some difficulty. Through research online to find previous results, by normalized, the average time they can get all kinds of online distribution of Internet time, it is our other key to solve task[3]. 3. In order to prevent students from excessive online, the school adopted the segmented pricing strategy, how to formulate a reasonable sub-function to effectively reduce the price students time spent online is the problem.We only need to resolve the above three key can effectively completed the topic request of three tasks.

2 Queuing Models

The accounting management gateway is actually a fairly typical stochastic service system, from network management perspective, this service gateway is a dynamic real-time parallel queuing system more reception, and its characteristics are as follows:

   System service object is campus network users, they in turn, randomly arrival, independent, the process to reach is steady. Therefore, the user can be formed by the arrival of the sequence in turn as input stream, can verify the input stream satisfy poisson (poisson) input, also called the simplest flow conditions, namely the stability, without the aftereffects character, single character also called universality. The system is stable, and then we can get the statistics of the arrival rate of input stream. For poisson flow, in length as t time arrived within the probability of a customer k to random poisson distribution In a certain period, due to the campus network inside each user can be repeated several times online, so that users can be regarded as the general source is unlimited[4].

   When a user arrives within the campus network, if the system is full of members, the user's service request was rejected, when he tried to log in again, the request shall be considered as a new user;. If the system is not full, then accept the user's request, allow the user access to a system, Therefore queuing rule is loss system, the queue length $L_q = 0$ and waiting time $W_q = 0$. If the customers arrive queuing system, all service has been taken up by first customers, then they will automatically left the system never comes[5].

   Due to the system to serve the way at by turns every user, so each user into the system were to enjoy exactly the same service, from a logical point of view, that the system can have multiple virtual and independent service desk, its service capabilities is same, and every time services only one user, therefore the system virtual station number just equals the number of customers in the system, and with the number of user dynamically changes. Through the long period of statistics, we can get the user login time of the mean value $1 / \mu$ (μ for reception service efficiency), in theory, as long as the number of users in the system does not exceed the limit of capacity, for any user number k, users can't feel reception available resources reduce, we believe that the average service rate of each desk is the same μ, and the user's Internet time obeys the negative exponential distribution parameter.

In summary, the service system is real-time queuing system for more than a desk. According to the changes of input process, queuing rules and service mechanism, by analyzing the information we can know that the problem with queuing model with Ken Doyle (D.G.Kendall) proposed currently in queuing theory widely used in "Kendall mark" can be represented by $M / M / n / n / \infty$.

According to the meaning of problems, each user on an average day time online 1.5 hours, subscribers 150 person, can be given time unit of subscribers for 150/16 people/hour. $N(t)$ Process is a thickening and elimination process which has the following parameter:

$$\begin{cases} \mu_k = k\mu \\ \lambda_k = \lambda & k \le n \\ \lambda_k = 0 & k > n \end{cases} \qquad (1)$$

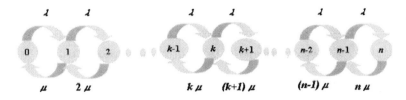

Fig. 1. $M / M / n / n / \infty$ system state probability distribution and state transfer speed diagram

Assuming the system state is k (ie k users on the Internet) the probability is P_k, from this figure we can easy to get: Transfer rate = transfer out rate, steady-state probability should satisfy the relationship:

$$\begin{cases} \lambda P_0 = \mu P_1 \\ \lambda P_{k-1} = \mu P_k \\ \sum_{k=0}^{n} P_k = 1 \end{cases} \qquad (2)$$

According to the recursive formula can be solved:

$$P_k = \frac{1}{k!}\left(\frac{\lambda}{\mu}\right)^k P_0 \qquad (3)$$

Among them $P_0 = \left[\sum_{k=0}^{n} \frac{1}{k!}\left(\frac{\lambda}{\mu}\right)^k\right]^{-1}$, $\rho = \frac{\lambda}{\mu}$ .Then steady-state solution is:

$$P_k = \frac{\dfrac{\rho^k}{k!}}{1+\rho+\dfrac{\rho^2}{2}+...+\dfrac{\rho^k}{k!}} \qquad (4)$$

The average number of port $L_s = n\left(\dfrac{\lambda}{\mu}\right)(1-P_n)$,The probability of system full

is P_n the probability that port has free users and can connect to the Internet

is $\overline{P}=1-P_n$ when $k=n$, and then P_n is the probability that a user is rejected.

Table 1. Queuing model tables

$1/\mu$	λ/μ	P_{16}	$\overline{P}$	L_s
1	9.375	0.0146671	0.985323	9.2375
1.5	14.0625	0.116352	0.883648	12.4263
2	18.75	0.257403	0.742597	13.9237
3	28.125	0.467174	0.532826	14.9857
4	37.5	0.590668	0.409332	15.35
5	46.875	0.668793	0.331207	15.5253

In theory, as long as the number of users in the system does not exceed capacity limit, for any user number k, users can't feel reception available resources reduce. We believe that the average service rate of each desk is the same μ , and the user's Internet time obeys the negative exponential distribution parameter. However, in real network systems, because information is transmitted by packets, different user data pack will constantly collide. In the case of the system's hardware resources is limited, when the number of user k increases to a degree, users can obviously felt the efficiency of system service decrease, it will affect the user's mental state, thus affecting their Internet time. Therefore, when the system is to have multiple users, each at the reception desk for an average service rate although same μ_n , but with less than μ , and its distribution is not negative exponential distribution, will become the general distribution. Showed by $M/G/n/n/\infty$, this service system's structure as shown in the diagram.

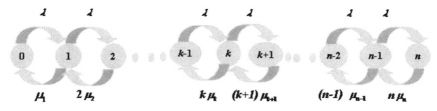

Fig. 2. $M/G/n/n/\infty$ system state probability distribution and state transfer speed diagram

The figure shows: the shift from state $k-1$ to state k rate is λP_{k-1}, from state k to state $k-1$ transfer rate is $k\mu_k P_k$, when the system is in stable state, each state of pass in and out of subscribers is equal, so we can get the differential equations are as follows:

$$\begin{cases} \lambda P_0 = \mu_1 P_1 \\ (\lambda + k\mu_k) P_k = (k+1)\mu_{k+1} P_{k+1} + \lambda P_{k-1} & k < n \\ \lambda P_{k-1} = n\mu_n P_n & k = n \end{cases} \tag{5}$$

It is available from the above recursive equation:

$$\begin{cases} P_k = \dfrac{\lambda P_{k-1}}{k\mu_k} = \dfrac{\lambda^2 P_{k-2}}{k(k-1)\mu_k\mu_{k-1}} = \cdots = \dfrac{\lambda^k P_0}{k!\mu_k\mu_{k-1}\cdots\mu_1} \\ \sum_{k=0}^{n} P_k = P_0\left(1+\sum_{k=1}^{n}\dfrac{\lambda^k}{k!\mu_k\mu_{k-1}\cdots\mu_1}\right) = 1 \Rightarrow P_0 = \left[1+\sum_{k=1}^{n}\dfrac{\lambda^k}{k!\mu_k\mu_{k-1}\cdots\mu_1}\right]^{-1} \end{cases} \tag{6}$$

So get probability formula when system states is k

$$P_k = \frac{\lambda^k P_0}{k!\mu_k\mu_{k-1}\cdots\mu_1} = \frac{\lambda^k}{k!\mu_k\mu_{k-1}\cdots\mu_1\left(1+\sum_{k=1}^{n}\dfrac{\lambda^k}{k!\mu_k\mu_{k-1}\cdots\mu_1}\right)} \tag{7}$$

In theory, if the number of users k is not more than system limit. It has a little influence on the Internet time, the average service rate of reception desk is unchanged, and $\mu_k = \mu_{k-1} = \cdots = \mu_1 = \mu$.

In practical application, along with the increase of the number of users, the entire system service efficiency will gradually decrease, the user average Internet time has been gradually made longer, make each reception average service rate μ_k less than theoretical value μ, When k increases to a certain extent, the system service efficiency will be dropped dramatically, this will produce greatly influences on user's psychological.

According to because the user is sensitive to the network speed, so they would have written off the net, leaving the service system. The number of user enters and leave the system began to tend to a new equilibrium, the number of system users will no longer be increased, thus constraints: $n\mu_n \geq \lambda$.

Calculation can be assumed $\mu_k = \dfrac{\mu}{\omega^k}$, in which ω is the user-sensitive factor, and $1 < \omega < 1.1$, then:

$$P_k = \frac{\rho^k \omega^{k(k+1)/2}}{k! \sum_{k=0}^{n} \frac{\rho^k \omega^{k(k+1)/2}}{k!}} \tag{8}$$

For parameters ω, it reflects the psychological sensitive degree of users to system service efficiency, in the time online billing service system, users' demands about network speed is higher in the psychological, this ω is bigger than that ω which according to flow billing system. We can use historical data, using the least-square method to estimate parameters ω's value and the random error distribution. Finally can according to ω, to determine the distribution of immediately error μ_k.

3 Concluion

This queuing theory model give a more accurate description of the campus information network service system, based on the system of various operation index calculation, determines the system scale and reasonably adjust charging scheme. In actual applications can greatly improve the system efficiency.

References

1. Sun, L.-m., Li, J.-z., Chen, Y., Zhu, H.-s.: Wireless sensor networks, vol. 5, pp. 1–15. Tsinghua University Press, Beijing (2005)
2. Zhang, L., et al.: The protocol of sensor networks clustering based on cluster head. Computer Applications and Software 8(24), 133–134 (2007)
3. Yang, Y., et al.: A new method of data transmission of passive wireless sensor networks. Computer Science 4(36), 27–30 (2009)
4. Huang, L.-s., et al.: The research of random configuration of coverage and connectivityof wireless sensor network node. 11(26), 2567–2569 (2006)
5. Hill, J.L.: System Architecture for Wireless Sensor Networks. UCA, Berkeley

The Intelligent Algorithm of the Biorthogonal Quarternary Wavelet Packs and Applications in Physics

Hailin Gao[1,*] and Ruohui Liu[2]

[1] Department of Fundamentals, Henan Polytechnic Institute, Nanyang, 473009
[2] Dept. of Computer Science, Huanghuai University, Zhumadian 463000, China
{zxc123wer,sxxa66xauat}@126.com

Abstract. The rise of wavelet analysis in applied mathematics is due to its applications and the flexibility. In this article, the notion of orthogonal nonseparable four-dimensional wavelet packets, which is the generalization of orthogonal univariate wavelet packets, is introduced. An approach for designing a sort of biorthogonal vector-valued wavelet wraps in three-dimensional space is presented and their biorthogonality traits are characterized by virtue of iteration method and time-frequency representation method. The biorthogonality formulas concerning the-se wavelet wraps are established. Moreover, it is shown how to draw new Riesz bases of space $L^2(R^4)$ from these wavelet wraps. The quarternary dual frames ia also discussed.

Keywords: B-spline function; quarternary; vector-valued wavelet wraps; Riesz bases; iteration method; time-frequency analysis representation.

1 Introduction

Although the Fourier transfer has been a major tool in analysis for overa century, it has a scrious lacking for signal analysis in that it hides in its phases information concerning the moment of emission and duration of a signal. What was needed was a localed time-frquency representation which has this information encoded in it. Transform and Gabor Transform were used for harmonic studies of nonstationary power system waveforms which are basically Fourier Transform-based methods. Wavelet analysis has become a developing branch of mathematics for over twenty years. The main feature of the wavelet transform is to hierarchically decompose general functions, as a signal or a process, into a set of approximation functions with different scales. The last two decades or so have witnessed the development of wavelet theory[1]. Wavelet packs, owing to their good properties, have attracted considerable attention. They can be widely applied in science and engineering [4,5]. Coifman R. R. and Meyer Y. firstly introduced the notion for orthogonal wavelet packs which were used to decompose wavelet components. Chui C K.and Li Chun L.[6] generalized the concept of orthogonal wavelet packs to the case of non-orthogonal wavelet packs so that wavelet packets can be employed in the case of the spline wavelets and so on. The introduction for biorthogonal

---

* Corresponding author.

S. Lin and X. Huang (Eds.): CESM 2011, Part I, CCIS 175, pp. 53–58, 2011.
© Springer-Verlag Berlin Heidelberg 2011

wavelet packs attributes to Cohen and Daubechies.Tensor product multivariate wavelet packs has been constructed by Coifman and Meyer. The introduction for the notion on nontensor product wavelet packs attributes to Shen [7]. Since the majority of information is multidimensional information, many researchers interest themselves in the investigation into multivariate wavelet theory. But, there exist a lot of obvious defects in this method, such as, scarcity of designing freedom. Therefore, it is signifi-cant to investigate nonseparable multivariate wavelet theory. Nowadays, since there is little literature on biorthogonal wavelet packs, it is necessary to investigate biorthogo-nal wavelet packs. The notion for nonseparable orthogonal quarternary wavelet packs is given and a procedure for constructing them is described. Next, the biorthogonality property of nonseparable quarternary wavelet packs is studied.Wavelet packs, owing to their nice characteristics, have been widely applied to signal Yang [8] constructed a-scale orthogonal multiwavelet wraps that were more flexible in applications. It is known that the majority of information is multi-dimensional information. Shen introduced multivariate orthogonal wavelets which may be used in a wider field. Thus, it is necessary to generalize the concept of multivariate wavelet wraps to the case of quarternary nonseparable vector-valued wavelets. The goal of this paper is to give the definition and the constructing procedure of orthogonal quarternary wavelet wraps and characterize their properties.

2   The Four-Dimensional General Multiresolution Analysis

We start from the following notations. Z and N stand for integers and nonnegative integers, respectively. Let R be the set of all real numbers. R^4 denotes the 4- dimensional *Euclidean* space. By $L^2(R^4)$, we denote the square integrable function space on R^4. Set $x = (x_1, x_2, x_3, x_4) \in R^4$, $u = (u_1, u_2, u_3, u_4)$, $\omega = (\omega_1, \omega_2, \omega_3, \omega_4)$, $z_t = e^{-i\omega_t/2}$, where $t = 1, 2, 3, 4$. The inner product for any $\varphi(\chi), \hbar(\chi) \in L^2(R^4)$ and the Fourier transform of $\varphi(\chi)$ are defined as, respectively

$$\langle \varphi, \hbar \rangle = \int_{R^4} \varphi(\chi)\overline{\hbar(\chi)}d\chi, \quad \hat{\hbar}(\omega) = \int_{R^4} \hbar(\chi)e^{-i\chi \cdot \omega}d\chi,$$

where $\omega \cdot x = \omega_1 x_1 + \omega_2 x_2 + \omega_3 x_3 + \omega_4 x_4 = $ and $\overline{\hbar(\chi)}$ denotes the conjugate. There exist 256 elements $\mu_0, \mu_1, \cdots, \mu_{255}$ in Z_+^4 by finite group theory such that $a = \det(A)$, $Z^4 = \bigcup_{\mu \in \Gamma_0}(\mu + AZ^4)$; $(v_1 + AZ^4) \bigcap (v_2 + AZ^4) = \varnothing$, where $\Gamma_0 = \{v_0, v_1, \cdots, v_{255}\}$ denotes the set of all different representative elements in the quotient group $Z^4/(AZ^4)$ and v_1, v_2 denote two arbitrary distinct elements in Γ_0, A is a 4×4 integer matrix. Set $v_0 = \underline{0}$, where $\underline{0}$ is the null of Z_+^4. Let $\Gamma = \Gamma_0 - \{\underline{0}\}$ and Γ, Γ_0 be two index sets. By $L^2(R^4, C^v)$, we denote the aggregate of all vector-valued functions $\Phi(x)$, that is, $L^2(R^4, C^v) := \{\Phi(x) = (\varnothing_1(x), \varnothing_2(x), \cdots, \varnothing_v(x))^T : \varnothing_l(x) \in L^2(R^4), l = 1, 2, \cdots, v\}$, where T means the transpose of a vector. Video images and digital films are examples of vector-valued functions where $\varnothing_l(x)$ in the above $\Phi(x)$ denotes the pixel on the l th column at the point x.

The multiresolution analysis method is an important approach to obtaining wave-lets and wavelet packs. We introduce the notion of multiresolution analysis of $L^2(R^4)$. Let $\phi(x) \in L^2(R^4)$ satisfy the following refinement equation:

$$\phi(x) = \sqrt{a} \cdot \sum_{u \in Z^4} d(u)\phi(Ax - u) \tag{1}$$

where $\{d(u)\}_{u \in Z^4}$ is a real number sequence and $\phi(x)$ is called a scaling function. Taking the Fourier transform for the both sides of refinement equation (1), we have

$$\hat{\phi}(A\omega) = D(\omega)\hat{\phi}(\omega) \tag{2}$$

Define a subspace $U_l \subset L^2(R^4)$ ($l \in Z$) by

$$U_l = clos_{L^2(R^4)} \left\langle |\det(A)|^l \phi(A^l x - n) : n \in Z^4 \right\rangle, \tag{3}$$

We say that $\Upsilon(x)$ in (1) generates a multiresolution analysis $\{U_j\}_{j \in Z}$ of $L^2(R^4)$, if the sequence $\{U_l\}_{l \in Z}$, defined in (3) satisfies the below: (a) $U_l \subset U_{l+1}, \forall l \in Z$; (b) $\bigcap_{l \in Z} U_l = \{0\}$; $\bigcup_{l \in Z} U_l$ is dense in $L^2(R^4)$; (c) $f(x) \in U_l \Leftrightarrow f(Ax) \in U_{l+1}$, $\forall l \in Z$; (d) the family $\{|\det(A)|^{2^l} \phi(A^l x - n) : n \in Z^4\}$ is a Riesz basis for U_l.

Let W_l ($l \in Z$) denote the orthogonal complementary subspace of U_l in U_{l+1} and order $A = 2I_1$, also assume that there exists a vector-valued function $F(x) = (f_1(x), f_2(x), \cdots, f_{15}(x))^T$ (see [7]) forms a Riesz basis for W_l, i.e,

$$W_l = clos_{L^2(R^4)} \left\langle f_v(2^l \cdot -u) : v = 1, 2, \cdots, 15; u \in Z^4 \right\rangle, l \in Z \tag{4}$$

From (4), it is clear that $f_1(x), f_2(x), \cdots, f_{15}(x) \in W_0 \subset U_1$. Therefore, there exist fifteen real sequences $\{b^{(l)}(u)\}$ ($l = 1, 2, \cdots 15, u \in Z^4$) such that

$$f_l(x) = 16 \cdot \sum_{u \in Z^4} b^{(l)}(u)\phi(2x - u), l \in \Gamma, u \in Z^4. \tag{5}$$

Definition 1. We say that a pair of vector-valued functions $\Phi(x), \tilde{\Phi}(x) \in L^2(R^4, C^v)$ are biorthogonal, if their translations satisfy

$$[\Phi(\cdot), \tilde{\Phi}(\cdot - n)] = \delta_{0,n} I_v, \quad n \in Z^4, \tag{6}$$

where I_v denotes the $v \times v$ indentity matrix and $\delta_{0,n}$ is the Kronecker symbol.

Definition 2. A sequence of vector-valued functions $\{T_n(x)\}_{n \in Z^4} \subset U \subset L^2(R^4, C^v)$ is called a Riesz basis of U if itsatisfies (i) for any $G(x) \in U$, there exists a unique $v \times v$ matrix sequence $\{P_n\}_{n \in Z^4} \in \ell^2(Z^4)^{v \times v}$ such that

$$G(x) = \sum_{n \in Z^4} P_n T_n(x), \quad x \in R^4, \tag{7}$$

where $\ell^2(Z^4)^{v \times v} = \{P : Z^4 \to C^{u \times u}, \|P\|_2 = \sum_{l,s=1}^{v} \sum_{n \in Z^4} |q_{l,s}(n)|^2)^{\frac{1}{2}} < +\infty\}$, (ii) there exist two constants $0 < C_1 \le C_2 < +\infty$ such that, for any matrix sequence $\{M_n\}_{n \in Z^3}$, the following equality follows.i.e.,

$$C_1 \|\{M_n\}\|_* \leq \| \sum_{n \in Z^3} M_n H_n(x) \| \leq C_2 \|\{M_n\}\|_*, \tag{8}$$

We say that $f_\mu(x), \tilde{f}_\mu(x) \in L^2(R^4), \mu \in \Gamma$ are pairs of biorthogonal vector-valued wavelets associated with a pairof biorthogonal vector-valued scaling functions $\phi(x)$ and $\tilde{F}(x)$, if the family $\{\Psi_\mu(x-n), n \in Z^3, \mu \in \Gamma\}$ is a Riesz basis of subspace X_0, and

$$[\phi(\cdot), \tilde{f}_\mu(\cdot - n)] = 0, \quad \mu \in \Gamma, \quad n \in Z^4. \tag{9}$$

$$[\tilde{\phi}(\cdot), f_\mu(\cdot - k)] = 0, \quad \mu \in \Gamma, \quad k \in Z^4. \tag{10}$$

$$X_j^{(\mu)} = \overline{Span\{\Psi_\mu(M^j \cdot - n) : n \in Z^3, \}}, \mu \in \Gamma, j \in Z. \tag{11}$$

Similar to (5) and (9), there exist 64 finitely supported sequences of $v \times v$ complex constant matrice $\{\tilde{d}_k\}_{k \in Z^4}$ and $\{\tilde{B}_k^{(\mu)}\}_{k \in Z^3}$, $\mu \in \Gamma$ such that $\tilde{\phi}(x)$ and $\tilde{f}_\mu(x)$ satisfy the refinement equations:

$$\tilde{\phi}(x) = \sum_{k \in Z^4} \tilde{d}_k \tilde{\phi}(Ax - k), \tag{12}$$

$$\tilde{f}_t(x) = 16 \cdot \sum_{k \in Z^4} \tilde{b}^{(t)}(k) \tilde{\phi}(2x - k), t \in \Gamma, k \in Z^4. \tag{13}$$

3   The Traits and Features of a Sort of Quarternary Wavelet Wraps

We begin with the following notations:

$$\Gamma_0(x) = \phi(x), \quad \Gamma_t(x) = f_t(x), \quad d^{(0)}(u) = d(u), \quad d^{(t)}(u) = b^{(t)}(u), \quad t \in \Gamma, \quad u \in Z^4$$

Definition 1. A set of functions $\{\Gamma_{16n+v}(x) : n = 0, 1, 2, \cdots, v = 0,1,2,\cdots,15\}$ is called a nonseparable four-dimensional wavelet wraps with respect to the orthogonal scaling function $\phi(x)$, where

$$\Gamma_{16n+v}(x) = \sum_{k \in Z^4} d^{(t)}(n) \Gamma_v(2x - k), \quad v \in \Lambda_0 = \{0,1,2,\cdots 15\}, \tag{14}$$

By implementing the Fourier transform for the both sides of (14), we have

$$\hat{\Gamma}_{16n+v}(\omega) = D^{(v)}(z_1, z_2, z_3, z_4) \cdot \hat{\Gamma}_n(\omega/2). v \in \Lambda_0. \tag{15}$$

$$D^{(v)}(z_1, z_2, z_3, z_4) = D^{(v)}(\omega/2) = \sum_{k \in Z^4} d^{(v)}(k) z_1^{k_1} z_2^{k_2} z_3^{k_3} z_4^{k_4} \tag{16}$$

Lemma 1 [7]. Let $h(x) \in L^2(R^4)$. Then $\phi(x)$ is an orthogonal function if and only if

$$\sum_{u \in Z^4} |\hat{h}(\omega + 2u\pi)|^2 = 1. \tag{17}$$

Lemma 2. Assuming that $\phi(x)$ is an orthogonal scaling function. $P(z_1, z_2, z_3, z_4)$ is the symbol of the sequence $\{d(u)\}$ defined in (3).Then we have

$$\Omega = \left| P(z_1, z_2, z_3, z_4) \right|^2 + \left| P(-z_1, -z_2, -z_3, -z_4) \right|^2 + \left| P(-z_1, z_2, z_3, z_4) \right|^2$$

$$+ \left| P(z_1, -z_2, z_3, z_4) \right|^2 + \left| P(z_1, z_2, -z_3, z_4) \right|^2 + \left| P(z_1, z_2, z_3, -z_4) \right|^2$$

$$+ \left| P(-z_1, -z_2, z_3, z_4) \right|^2 + \left| P(-z_1, z_2, -z_3, z_4) \right|^2 + \left| P(-z_1, z_2, z_3, -z_4) \right|^2$$

$$+ \left| P(z_1, -z_2, -z_3, z_4) \right|^2 + \left| P(z_1, -z_2, z_3, -z_4) \right|^2 + \left| P(z_1, z_2, -z_3, -z_4) \right|^2$$

$$+ \left| P(-z_1, -z_2, -z_3, z_4) \right|^2 + \left| P(-z_1, -z_2, z_3, -z_4) \right|^2 + \left| P(-z_1, z_2, -z_3, -z_4) \right|^2 + \left| P(z_1, -z_2, -z_3, -z_4) \right|^2 = 1$$

Lemma 3. If $f_\nu(x)$ ($\nu = 0, 1, \cdots, 15$) are orthogonal wavelet functions associated with $\phi(x)$. Then we have

$$\Xi_{\lambda, \mu} = \sum_{j=0}^{1} \{ D^{(\lambda)}((-1)^j z_1, (-1)^j z_2, (-1)^j z_3, (-1)^j z_4) . D^{(\nu)}((-1)^j z_1, (-1)^j z_2, (-1)^j z_3, (-1)^j z_4)$$

$$+ D^{(\lambda)}((-1)^{j+1} z_1, (-1)^j z_2, (\ 1)^j z_3, (\ 1)^j z_4) \cdot \overline{D^{(\nu)}((-1)^{j+1} z_1, (-1)^j z_2, (-1)^j z_3, (-1)^j z_4)}$$

$$+ D^{(\lambda)}((-1)^j z_1, (-1)^{j+1} z_2, (-1)^j z_3, (-1)^j z_4) . \overline{D^{(\nu)}((-1)^j z_1, (-1)^{j+1} z_2, (-1)^j z_3, (-1)^j z_4)}$$

$$+ D^{(\lambda)}((\ 1)^j z_1, (\ 1)^j z_2, (-1)^{j+1} z_3, (-1)^j z_4) \} \overline{D^{(\nu)}((-1)^j z_1, (-1)^j z_2, (-1)^{j+1} z_3, (-1)^j z_4)} \}$$

$$+ D^{(\lambda)}((-1)^j z_1, (-1)^j z_2, (-1)^j z_3, (-1)^{j+1} z_4) \cdot \overline{D^{(\nu)}((-1)^j z_1, (-1)^j z_2, (-1)^j z_3, (-1)^{j+1} z_4)}$$

$$+ D^{(\lambda)}((-1)^{j+1} z_1, (-1)^j z_2, (-1)^{j+1} z_3, (-1)^j z_4) . \overline{D^{(\nu)}((-1)^{j+1} z_1, (-1)^j z_2, (-1)^{j+1} z_3, (-1)^j z_4)}$$

$$+ D^{(\lambda)}((-1)^{j+1} z_1, (-1)^j z_2, (-1)^j z_3, (-1)^{j+1} z_4) . \overline{D^{(\nu)}((-1)^{j+1} z_1, (-1)^j z_2, (-1)^j z_3, (-1)^{j+1} z_4)}$$

$$= \delta_{\lambda, \nu}, \quad \lambda, \nu \in \{0, 1, 2, \cdots, 15\}. \tag{18}$$

Theorem 1 [6]. For $n \in Z_+$, $\nu \in Z^4$, we have

$$\left\langle \Gamma_n(\cdot), \Gamma_n(\cdot - v) \right\rangle = \delta_{0, v} \tag{19}$$

Theorem 2 [6]. For $u \in Z^4$ and $n \in Z_+$, $\iota \in \{0, 1, 2, \cdots, 14, 15\}$, we have

$$\left\langle \Gamma_{16n}(\cdot), \Gamma_{16n+\nu}(\cdot - u) \right\rangle = \delta_{0, \nu} \delta_{0, u}. \tag{20}$$

Proof. By Lemma 1 and 3, and formulas (14) and $\nu \in \{0, 1, \cdots, 15\}$, we get that

$$(2\pi)^4 \left\langle \Gamma_{16n}(\cdot), \Gamma_{16n+\nu}(\cdot - u) \right\rangle$$

$$= \int_{R^4} D^{(0)}(z_1, z_2, z_3, z_4) \overline{D^{(\nu)}(z_1, z_2, z_3, z_4)} \cdot \left| \hat{\Gamma}_n(\omega/2) \right|^2 \cdot \exp\{iu\omega\} d\omega$$

$$= \int_{[0, 4\pi]^4} D^{(0)}(z_1, z_2, z_3, z_4) \overline{D^{(\nu)}(z_1, z_2, z_3, z_4)}$$

Theorem 3. For every $u \in Z^4$ and $m, n \in Z_+$, we have

$$\langle \Gamma_m(\cdot), \Gamma_n(\cdot - k) \rangle = \delta_{m,n} \delta_{0,k} . \tag{21}$$

Proof. For the case of $m = n$, (20) follows from Theorem 1. As $m \neq n$ and $m, n \in \Omega_0$, equality (20) can be established from Theorem 2, where $\Lambda = \{0,1,2,\cdots,15\}$. In what follows, assuming that m is not equal to n and at least one of $\{m, n\}$ doesn't belong to Γ_0, rewrite m, n as $m = 16m_1 + \lambda_1$, $n = 16n_1 + \mu_1$, where $m_1, n_1 \in Z_+$, and $\lambda_1, \mu_1 \in \Gamma_0$.

Case 1. If $m_1 = n_1$, then $\lambda_1 \neq \mu_1$. By (14), (16) and (18), (20) holds, since

$$(2\pi)^4 \langle \Gamma_m(\cdot), \Gamma_n(\cdot - k) \rangle = \int_{R^4} \overline{\hat{\Gamma}_{16m_1+\lambda_1}(\omega)} \overline{\hat{\Gamma}_{16n_1+\mu_1}(\omega)} \cdot \exp\{ik\omega\} d\omega$$

$$= \int_{[0,4\pi]^4} D^{(\lambda_1)}(z_1,z_2,z_3,z_4) \sum_{v \in Z^4} \hat{\Gamma}_{m_1}(\omega/2 + 2v\pi) \cdot \overline{\hat{\Gamma}_{m_1}(\omega/2 + 2v\pi)} \overline{D^{(\mu_1)}(z_1,z_2,z_3,z_4)} \cdot e^{ik\omega} d\omega$$

$$= \int_{[0,2\pi]^4} \Xi_{\lambda_1,\mu_1} \cdot \exp\{ik\omega\} d\omega = 0.$$

Therefore, $\langle \Lambda_m(\cdot), \Lambda_n(\cdot - k) \rangle = 0$.

Theorem 4 [7]. Let $\phi(x), \tilde{\phi}(x), \hbar_l(x)$ and $\tilde{\hbar}_l(x), l \in J$ be functions in $L^2(R^3)$ defined by (28), (29), (33) and (34), respectively. Assume that conditions in Theorem 1 are satisfied. Then, for any function $f(x) \in L^2(R^3)$, and any integer n,

$$\sum_{u \in Z^3} \langle f, \tilde{\phi}_{n,u} \rangle \phi_{n,u}(x) = \sum_{t=1}^{7} \sum_{s=-\infty}^{n-1} \sum_{u \in Z^3} \langle f, \tilde{\hbar}_{t:s,u} \rangle \hbar_{t:s,u}(x). \tag{27}$$

References

1. Telesca, L., et al.: Multiresolution wavelet analysis of earthquakes. Chaos, Solitons & Fractals 22(3), 741–748 (2004)
2. Iovane, G., Giordano, P.: Wavelet and multiresolution analysis: Nature of ε^∞ Cantorian space-time. Chaos, Solitons & Fractals 32(4), 896–910 (2007)
3. Zhang, N., Wu, X.: Lossless Compression of Color Mosaic Images. IEEE Trans. Image Processing 15(16), 1379–1388 (2006)
4. Chen, Q., et al.: A study on compactly supported orthogo-nal vector-valued wavelets and wavelet packets. Chaos, Soli-tons & Fractals 31(4), 1024–1034 (2007)
5. Shen, Z.: Nontensor product wavelet packets in L₂(Rˢ). SIAM Math. Anal. 26(4), 1061–1074 (1995)
6. Li, S., et al.: A Theory of Geeneralized Multiresolution Structure and Pseudoframes of Translates. J. Fourier Anal. Appl. 6(1), 23–40 (2001)
7. Chen, Q., Huo, A.: The research of a class of biorthogonal compactly supported vector-valued wavelets. Chaos, Solitons & Fractals 41(2), 951–961 (2009)

The Traits of Orthogonal Nonseparable Binary-Variable Wavelet Packs in Two-Dimensional Function Space

Guoqiang Wang[*] and Rui Wei

Department of Computer Science, Huanghuai University, Zhumadian, 463000, China
nysslt88@126.com

Abstract. In this paper, the concept of orthogonal non-tensor bivariate wavelet packs, which is the generalization of orthogonal univariate wavelet packs, is pro -posed by virtue of analogy method and iteration method. Their orthogonality property is investigated by using time-frequency analysis method and variable se-paration approach. Three orthogonality formulas concerning these wavelet packs are obtained. Moreover, it is shown how to draw new orthonormal bases of space $L^2(R^2)$ from these wavelet wraps. A procedure for designing a class of orthogonal vector-valued finitely supported wavelet functions is proposed by virtue of filter bank theory and matrix theory.

Keywords: Nonseparable; binary wavelet packs; Sobelev space; Bessel sequence; orthonormal bases; time frequency analysis method.

1 Introduction and Notations

Although the Fourier transform has been a major tool in analysis for over a century, it has a serious laking for signal analysis in that it hides in its phases information concerning the moment of emission and duration of a signal. Wavelet analysis [1] has been developed a new branch for over twenty years. Its applications involve in many areas in natural science and engineering technology. The main advantage of wavelets is their time-frequency localization property. Many signals in areas like music, speech, images, and video images can be efficiently represented by wavelets that are translations and dilations of a single function called mother wavelet with bandpass property. Wavelet packets, owing to their good properties, have attracted considerable attention. They can be widely applied in science and engineering [2,3]. Coifman R. R. and Meyer Y. firstly introduced the notion for orthogonal wavelet packets which were used to decompose wavelet components. Chui C K.and Li Chun L.[4] generalized the concept of orthogonal wavelet packets to the case of non-orthogonal wavelet packets so that wavelet packets can be employed in the case of the spline wavelets and so on. Tensor product multivariate wavelet packs has been constructed by Coifman and Meyer. The introduction for the notion on nontensor product wavelet packs attributes

---

[*] Corresponding author.

S. Lin and X. Huang (Eds.): CESM 2011, Part I, CCIS 175, pp. 59–65, 2011.
© Springer-Verlag Berlin Heidelberg 2011

to Shen Z [5]. Since the majority of information is multidimensional information, many researchers interest themselves in the investigation into multivariate wavelet theory. The classical method for constructing multivariate wavelets is that separable multivariate wavelets may be obtained by means of the tensor product of some univariate wavelets. But, there exist a lot of obvious defects in this method, such as, scarcity of designing freedom. Therefore, it is significant to investigate nonseparable multivariate wavelet theory. Nowadays, since there is little literature on biorthogonal wavelet packets, it is necessary to investigate biorthogonal wavelet packs.

In the following, we introduce some notations. Z and Z_+ denote all integers and all nonnegative integers, respectively. R denotes all real numbers. R^2 denotes the 2-dimentional *Euclidean* space. $L^2(R^2)$ denotes the square integrable function space. Let $x = (x_1, x_2) \in R^2$, $\omega = (\omega_1, \omega_2) \in R^2$, $k = (k_1, k_2) \in Z^2$, $z_1 = e^{-i\omega_1/2}$, $z_2 = e^{-i\omega_2/2}$. The inner product for any functions $\phi(x)$ and $\lambda(x)$ ($\phi(x), \lambda(x) \in L^2(R^2)$) and the Fourier transform of $\lambda(x)$ are defined, respectively, by

$$\langle \phi, \lambda \rangle = \int_{R^2} \phi(x)\overline{\lambda(x)}\,dx, \quad \hat{\lambda}(\omega) = \int_{R^2} \lambda(x)e^{-i\omega \cdot x}\,dx,$$

where $\omega \cdot x = \omega_1 x_1 + \omega_2 x_2$ and $\overline{\lambda(x)}$ denotes the complex conjugate of $\lambda(x)$. Let R and C be all real and all complex numbers, respectively. Z and N denote, respectively, all integers and all positive integers. Set $Z_+ = \{0\} \cup N, a, s \in N$ as well as $a \geq 2$ By algebra theory, it is obviously follows that there are a^2 elements $d_0, d_1, \cdots, d_{a^2-1}$ in $Z_+^2 = \{(z_1, z_2): z_1, z_2 \in Z_+\}$ such that $Z^2 = \bigcup_{d \in \Omega_0}(d + aZ^2)$; $(d_1 + aZ^2) \cap (d_2 + aZ^2) = \phi$, where $\Omega_0 = \{d_0, d_1, \cdots, d_{a^2-1}\}$ denotes the aggregate of all the different representative elements in the quotient group $Z^2/(aZ^2)$ and order $d_0 = \{\underline{0}\}$ where $\{\underline{0}\}$ is the null element of z_+^2 and d_1, d_2 denote two arbitrary distinct elements in Ω_0. Let $\Omega = \Omega_0 - \{\underline{0}\}$ and Ω, Ω_0 to be two index sets. Define, By $L^2(R^2, C^s)$, we denote the set of all vector-valued functions $L^2(R^2, C^s) := \{\hbar(x), = (h_1(x)), h_2(x), \cdots, h_u(x))^T : h_l(x) \in L^2(R^2), l = 1, 2, \cdots, s\}$, where ^{T} means the transpo--se of a vector. For any $\hbar \in L^2(R^2, C^s)$ its integration is defined as follows $\int_{R^2} \hbar(x)dx = (\int_{R^2} h_1(x)dx, \int_{R^2} h_2(x)dx, \cdots, \int_{R^2} h_s(x)dx)^T$.

De nition 1. A sequence $\{\hbar_n(y)_{n \in Z^2} \subset L^2(R^2, C^s)\}$ is called an orthogonal set, if

$$\langle \hbar_n, \hbar_v \rangle = \delta_{n,v} I_s, \quad n, v \in Z^2, \tag{1}$$

where I_s stands for the $s \times s$ identity matrix and $\delta_{n,v}$, is generalized Kronecker symbol, i.e., $\delta_{n,v} = 1$ as $n = v$ and $\delta_{n,v} = 0$, otherwise.

2 The Two-Dimensional Multiresolution Analysis

Firstly, we introduce multiresolution analysis of space $L^2(R^2)$. Wavelets can be constructed by means of multiresolution analysis. In particular, the existence theorem[8] for higher-dimentional wavelets with arbitrary dilation matrice has been given. Let $h(x) \in L^2(R^2)$ satisfy the following refinement equation:

$$h(x) = a^2 \cdot \sum_{n \in Z^2} b_n \cdot h(ax - n) \tag{2}$$

where $\{b(n)\}_{n \in Z^2}$ is real number sequence which has only finite terms.and $h(x)$ is called scaling function. Formula (1) is said to be two-scale refinement equation. The frequency form of formula (1) can be written as

$$\hat{h}(\omega) = B(z_1, z_2)\hat{h}(\omega/a), \tag{3}$$

where

$$B(z_1, z_2) = \sum_{(n_1, n_2) \in Z^2} b(n_1, n_2) \cdot z_1^{n_1} \cdot z_2^{n_2}. \tag{4}$$

Define a subspace $X_j \subset L^2(R^2)$ $(j \in Z)$ by

$$X_j = clos_{L^2(R^2)} \langle a^j h(a^j \cdot - n) : n \in Z^2 \rangle. \tag{5}$$

Definition 2. We say that $h(x)$ in (2) generate a multiresolution analysis $\{X_j\}_{j \in Z}$ of $L^2(R^2)$, if the sequence $\{X_j\}_{j \in Z}$ defined in (4) satisfy the following properties: (i) $X_j \subset X_{j+1}$, $\forall j \in Z$; (ii) $\bigcap_{j \in Z} X_j = \{0\}$; $\bigcup_{j \in Z} X_j$ is dense in $L^2(R^2)$; (iii) $f(x) \in X_k \Leftrightarrow f(ax) \in X_{k+1}, \forall k \in Z$; (iv) the family $\{h(a^j x - n) : n \in Z^2\}$ forms a *Riesz* basis for the spaces X_j.

Let $Y_k (k \in Z)$ denote the complementary subspace of X_j in X_{j+1}, and assume that there exist a vector-valued function $\Psi(x) = \{\psi_1(x), \psi_2(x), \psi_3(x)\}$ constitutes a *Riesz* basis for Y_k, i.e.,

$$W_j = clos_{L^2(R^2)} \langle \psi_{\lambda:j,n} : \lambda = 1, 2, \cdots, a^2 - 1; \ n \in Z^2 \rangle, \tag{6}$$

where $j \in Z$, and $\psi_{\lambda:j,k}(x) = a^{j/2}\psi_\lambda(a^j x - n)$, $\lambda = 1, 2, \cdots, a^2 - 1; \ n \in Z^2$. Form condition (5), it is obvious that $\psi_1(x), \psi_2(x), \psi_3(x)$ are in $Y_0 \subset X_1$. Hence there exist three real number sequences $\{q_n^{(\lambda)}\}(\lambda \in \Delta = \{1, 2, \cdots, a^2 - 1\}, \ n \in Z^2)$ such that

$$\psi_\lambda(x) = a^2 \cdot \sum_{n \in Z^2} q_n^{(\lambda)} h(ax - n), \tag{7}$$

Formula (7) in frequency domain can be written as

$$\hat{\psi}_\lambda(\omega) = Q^{(\lambda)}(z_1, z_2)\hat{h}(\omega/a), \quad \lambda = 1, 2, \cdots, a^2 - 1. \tag{8}$$

where the signal of sequence $\{q_k^{(\lambda)}\}(\lambda = 1, 2, \cdots, a^2 - 1, \; k \in Z^2)$ is

$$Q^{(\lambda)}(z_1, z_2) = \sum_{(n_1, n_2) \in Z^2} q_{(n_1, n_2)}^{(\lambda)} \cdot z_1^{n_1} \cdot z_2^{n_2}. \tag{9}$$

A bivariate function $h(t) \in L^2(R^2)$ is called a semiorthogonal one, if

$$\langle h(\cdot), h(\cdot - n) \rangle = \delta_{0,n}, \; n \in Z^2. \tag{10}$$

We say $\Psi(x) = (\psi_1(x), \psi_2(x), \psi_3(x))^T$ is a semiorthogonal bivariate vector-valued wavelets associated with the scaling function $h(t)$, if they satisfy:

$$\langle h(\cdot), \psi_v(\cdot - n) \rangle = 0, \; v \in \Delta, \; n \in Z^2, \tag{11}$$

$$\langle \psi_\lambda(\cdot), \psi_v(\cdot - n) \rangle = \delta_{\lambda,v}\delta_{0,n}, \; \lambda, v \in \Delta, \; n \in Z^2 \tag{12}$$

3   The Traits of Nonseparable Bivariate Wavelet Packs

To construct wavelet packs, we introduce the following notation: $a = 2, \Lambda_0(x) = h(x)$, $\Lambda_v(x) = \psi_v(x), b^{(0)}(k) = b(k), \; b^{(v)}(k) = q^{(v)}(k)$, where $v \in \Delta$ We are now in a position of introdu- cing orthogonal trivariate nonseparable wavelet packets.

Definition 3. A family of functions $\{\Lambda_{4n+v}(x) : n = 0, 1, 2, 3, \cdots, \; v \in \Delta\}$ is called a nonseparable bivariate wavelet packs with respect to the semiorthogonal scaling function $\Lambda_0(x)$, where

$$\Lambda_{4n+v}(x) = \sum_{k \in Z^2} b^{(v)}(k) \Lambda_n(2x - k), \tag{13}$$

where $v = 0, 1, 2, 3$. By taaking the Fourier transform for the both sides of (12), we have

$$\hat{\Lambda}_{4n+v}(\omega) = B^{(v)}(z_1, z_2) \cdot \hat{\Lambda}_n(\omega/2). \tag{14}$$

where

$$B^{(v)}(z_1, z_2) = B^{(v)}(\omega/2) = \sum_{k \in Z^2} b^{(v)}(k) z_1^{k_1} z_2^{k_2} \tag{15}$$

Lemma 1 [6]. Let $\hbar(x) \in L^2(R^2)$. Then $\hbar(x)$ is an orthogonal one if and only if

$$\sum_{k \in Z^2} |\hat{\hbar}(\omega + 2k\pi)|^2 = 1. \tag{16}$$

Lemma 2. Assuming that $\hbar(x)$ is an semiorthogonal scaling function. $B\left(z_1, z_2\right)$ is the symbol of the sequence $\{b(k)\}$ defined in (3). Then we have

$$\Pi = \left|B(z_1, z_2)\right|^2 + \left|B(-z_1, z_2)\right|^2 + \left|B(z_1, -z_2)\right|^2 + \left|B(-z_1, -z_2)\right|^2 \tag{17}$$

Proof. If $\hbar(x)$ is an orthogonal bivariate function, then $\sum_{k\in Z^2}\left|\hat{h}\left(\omega + 2k\pi\right)\right|^2 = 1$.
Therefore, by Lemma 1 and formula (2), we obtain that

$$1 = \sum_{k\in Z^2} |\, B(e^{-i(\omega_1/2 + k_1\pi)}, e^{-i(\omega_2/2 + k_2\pi)})\cdot\hat{h}((\omega_1, \omega_2)/2 + (k_1, k_2)\pi)\,|^2$$

$$= |\,B(z_1, z_2)\sum_{k\in Z^2}\hat{h}(\omega + 2k\pi)\,|^2 + |\,B(-z_1, z_2)\cdot\sum_{k\in Z^2}\hat{h}(\omega + 2k\pi + (1,0)\pi)\,|^2$$

$$+ |\,B(z_1, -z_2)\cdot\sum_{k\in Z^2}\hat{h}(\omega + 2k\pi + (0,1)\pi)\,|^2 + |\,B(-z_1, -z_2)\cdot\sum_{k\in Z^2}\hat{h}(\omega + 2k\pi + (1,1)\pi)\,|^2$$

$$= \left|B(z_1, z_2)\right|^2 + \left|B(-z_1, z_2)\right|^2 + \left|B(z_1, -z_2)\right|^2 + \left|B(-z_1, -z_2)\right|^2$$

This complete the proof of Lemma 2. Similarly, we can obtain Lemma 3 from (3), (8), (13).

Lemma 3. If $\psi_v(x)$ ($v = 0,1,2,3$) are orthogonal wavelet functions associated with $h(x)$. Then we have

$$\sum_{j=0}^{1}\{B^{(\lambda)}((-1)^j z_1, (-1)^j z_2)\overline{B^{(v)}((-1)^j z_1, (-1)^j z_2)} + B^{(\lambda)}((-1)^{j+1} z_1, (-1)^j z_2)$$

$$\cdot \overline{B^{(v)}((-1)^{j+1} z_1, (-1)^j z_2)}\} := \Xi_{\lambda,\mu} = \delta_{\lambda,v}, \quad \lambda, v \in \{0,1,2,3\}. \tag{18}$$

For an arbitrary positive integer $n \in Z_+$, expand it by

$$n = \sum_{j=1}^{\infty} v_j 4^{j-1}, \quad v_j \in \Delta = \{0,1,2,3\}. \tag{19}$$

Lemma 4. Let $n \in Z_+$ and n be expanded as (17). Then we have

$$\hat{\Lambda}_n(\omega) = \prod_{j=1}^{\infty} B^{(v_j)}(e^{-i\omega_1/2^j}, e^{-i\omega_2/2^j})\hat{\Lambda}_0(0).$$

Lemma 4 can be inductively proved from formulas (14) and (18).

Theorem 1. For $n \in Z_+$, $k \in Z^3$, we have

$$\left\langle \Lambda_n(\cdot), \Lambda_n(\cdot - k)\right\rangle = \delta_{0,k}. \tag{20}$$

Proof. Formula (20) follows from (10) as n=0. Assume formula (20) holds for the case of $0 \leq n < 4^{r_0}$ (r_0 is a positive integer). Consider the case of $4^{r_0} \leq n < 4^{r_0+1}$. For $v \in \Delta$, by induction assumption and Lemma 1, Lemma 3 and Lemma 4, we have

$$(2\pi)^2 \left\langle \Lambda_n(\cdot), \Lambda_n(\cdot - k) \right\rangle = \int_{R^2} \left| \hat{\Lambda}_n(\omega) \right|^2 \cdot \exp\{ik\omega\} d\omega$$

$$= \sum_{j \in Z^2} \int_{4\pi j_1}^{4\pi(j_1+1)} \int_{4\pi j_2}^{4\pi(j_2+1)} \left| B^{(\nu)}(z_1, z_2) \cdot \hat{\Lambda}_{[\frac{n}{8}]}(\frac{\omega}{2}) \right|^2 \cdot e^{ik\omega} d\omega$$

$$= \int_0^{4\pi} \int_0^{4\pi} \left| B^{(\nu)}(z_1, z_2, z_3) \right|^2 \sum_{j \in Z^2} |\hat{\Lambda}_{[\frac{n}{8}]}(\frac{\omega}{2} + 2\pi j)|^2 \cdot e^{ik\omega} d\omega$$

$$= \int_0^{4\pi} \int_0^{4\pi} \left| B^{(\nu)}(z_1, z_2, z_3) \right|^2 \cdot e^{ik\omega} d\omega = \int_0^{2\pi} \int_0^{2\pi} \Pi \cdot e^{ik\omega} d\omega = \delta_{o,k}$$

Thus, we complete the proof of theorem 1.

Theorem 2. For every $k \in Z^2$ and $m, n \in Z_+$, we have

$$\left\langle \Lambda_m(\cdot), \Lambda_n(\cdot - k) \right\rangle = \delta_{m,n} \delta_{0,k}. \tag{21}$$

Proof. For the case of $m = n$, (20) follows from Theorem 1. As $m \neq n$ and $m, n \in \Omega_0$, the result (20) can be established from Theorem 2, where $\Omega_0 = \{0, 1, 2, 3\}$. In what follows, assuming that m is not equal to n and at least one of $\{m, n\}$ doesn't belong to Ω_0, rewrite m, n as $m = 4m_1 + \lambda_1$, $n = 4n_1 + \mu_1$, where $m_1, n_1 \in Z_+$, and $\lambda_1, \mu_1 \in \Omega_0$.

Case 1. If $m_1 = n_1$, then $\lambda_1 \neq \mu_1$. By (17), formulas (21) follows, since

$$(2\pi)^2 \left\langle \Lambda_m(\cdot), \Lambda_n(\cdot - k) \right\rangle = \int_{R^2} \hat{\Lambda}_{4m_1 + \lambda_1}(\omega) \overline{\hat{\Lambda}_{4n_1 + \mu_1}(\omega)} \cdot \exp\{ik\omega\} d\omega$$

$$= \int_{R^2} B^{(\lambda_1)}(z_1, z_2) \hat{\Lambda}_{m_1}(\omega/2) \cdot \overline{\hat{\Lambda}_{n_1}(\omega/2)} \overline{B^{(\mu_1)}(z_1, z_2)} \cdot \exp\{ik\omega\} d\omega$$

$$= \int_{[0,4\pi]^2} B^{(\lambda_1)}(z_1, z_2) \sum_{s \in Z^2} \hat{\Lambda}_{m_1}(\omega/2 + 2s\pi) \cdot \overline{\hat{\Lambda}_{m_1}(\omega/2 + 2s\pi)} \overline{B^{(\mu_1)}(z_1, z_2, z_3)} \cdot e^{ik\omega} d\omega$$

$$= \frac{1}{(2\pi)^2} \int_{[0,2\pi]^2} \Xi_{\lambda_1, \mu_1} \cdot \exp\{ik\omega\} d\omega = O.$$

Case 2. If $m_1 \neq n_1$ we order $m_1 = 4m_2 + \lambda_2$, $n_1 = 4n_2 + \mu_2$, where $m_2, n_2 \in Z_+$, and $\lambda_2, \mu_2 \in \Omega_0$. If $m_2 = n_2$, then $\lambda_2 \neq \mu_2$. Similar to Case 1, we have (21) follows. That is to say, the proposition follows in such case. As $m_2 \neq n_2$, we order $m_2 = 2m_3 + \lambda_3$, $n_2 = 2n_3 + \mu_3$, once more, where $m_3, n_3 \in Z_+$, and $\lambda_3, \mu_3 \in \Omega_0$. Thus, after taking finite steps (denoted by r), we obtain $m_r, n_r \in \Omega_0$, and

$\lambda_r, \mu_r \in \Omega_0$. If $\alpha_r = \beta_r$, then $\lambda_r \neq \mu_r$. Similar to Case 1, (21) holds. If $\alpha_r \neq \beta_r$, Similar to Lemma 1, we conclude that

$$\langle \Lambda_m(\cdot), \Lambda_n(\cdot-k) \rangle = \frac{1}{(2\pi)^2} \int_{R^2} \hat{\Lambda}_{4m_1+\lambda_1}(\omega) \overline{\hat{\Lambda}_{4n_1+\mu_1}(\omega)} \cdot e^{ik\omega} d\omega$$

$$= \frac{1}{(2\pi)^2} \int_{[0,2^{r+1}\pi]^2} \{\prod_{t=1}^{r} B^{(\lambda_t)}(\frac{\omega}{2^t})\} \cdot O \cdot \{\prod_{t=1}^{r} B^{(\mu_t)}(\omega/2^t)\} \cdot e^{ik\omega} d\omega = O.$$

References

1. Telesca, L., et al.: Multiresolution wavelet analysis of earthquakes. Chaos, Solitons & Fractals 22(3), 741–748 (2004)
2. Iovane, G., Giordano, P.: Wavelet and multiresolution analysis: Nature of ε^{∞} Cantorian space-time. Chaos, Solitons & Fractals 32(4), 896–910 (2007)
3. Zhang, N., Wu, X.: Lossless Compression of Color Mosaic Images. IEEE Trans. Image Processing 15(16), 1379–1388 (2006)
4. Chen, Q., et al.: A study on compactly supported orthogonal vector-valued wavelets and wavelet packets. Chaos, Solitons & Fractals 31(4), 1024–1034 (2007)
5. Shen, Z.: Nontensor product wavelet packets in $L_2(R^s)$. SIAM Math. Anal. 26(4), 1061–1074 (1995)
6. Chen, Q., Qu, X.: Characteristics of a class of vector-valued nonseparable higher-dimensional wavelet packet bases. Chaos, Solitons & Fractals 41(4), 1676–1683 (2009)
7. Chen, Q., Qu, X.: Characteristics of a class of vector-valued nonseparable higher-dimensional wavelet packet bases. Chaos, Solitons & Fractals 41(4), 1676–1683 (2009)
8. Chen, Q., Huo, A.: The research of a class of biorthogonal compactly supported vector-valued wavelets. Chaos, Solitons & Fractals 41(2), 951–961 (2009)

The Biorthogonal Features of the Ternary Vector-Valued Wavelet Wraps with Filter Functions and Pseudoframes

Honglin Guo[1,*] and Zhihao Tang[2]

[1] Department of Fundamentals, Henan Polytechnic Institute, Nanyang, 473009
[2] Dept. of Fundamentals, Henan Polytechnic Institute,
Nanyang, 473009, P.R. China
{sxxallxauat,jhnsx123}@126.com

Abstract. The rise of wavelet analysis in applied mathematics is due to its applications and the flexibility. Vector-valued wavelet wraps with multi-scale dilation factor of space $L^2(R^3, C^\nu)$ is introduced, which is the generalization of multivariate wavelet packs. An approach for designing a sort of biorthogonal vector-valued wavelet wraps in three-dimensional space is presented and their biorthogonality traits are characterized by virtue of iteration method and time-frequency analysis method. The biorthogonality formulas concerning these wavelet wraps are established. Moreover, it is shown how to draw new Riesz bases of space $L^2(R^3, C^\nu)$ from these wavelet wraps. The pyramid decomposition scheme based on pseudoframes is established.

Keywords: B-spline function; trivariate; vector-valued wavelet wraps; Riesz bases; iteration method; time-frequency analysis representation.

1 Introduction

The frame theory has been one of powerful tools for researching into wavelets. Although the Fourier transform has been a major tool in analysis for over a century, it has a serious laking for signal analysis in that it hides in its phases information concerning the moment of emission and duration of a signal. Every frame(or Bessel sequence) determines an analysis operator, the range of which is important for a lumber of applications. Multiwavelets can simultaneously possess many desired properties such as short support, orthogonality, symmetry, and vanishing moments, which a single wavelet cannot possess simultaneously. This suggests that multiwavelet systems can provide perfect reconstruction, good performance at the boundaries (symmetry), and high approximation order (vanishing moments). Already they have led to exciting applications in signal analysis [1], fractals [2] and image processing [3], and so on. Vector-valued wavelets are a sort of special multiwavelets Chen [4] introduced the notion of orthogonal vector-valued wavelets.However, vector-valued wavelets and multiwavelets are different in the following sense. Pre-filtering is usually required for discrete multiwavelet transforms [5] but not necessary for discrete vector-valued

---

* Corresponding author.

S. Lin and X. Huang (Eds.): CESM 2011, Part I, CCIS 175, pp. 66–72, 2011.
© Springer-Verlag Berlin Heidelberg 2011

transforms. Wavelet wraps, owing to their nice characteristics, have been wid-ely applied to signal processing [6],code theory, image compression, solving integral equation and so on. Coifman and Meyer firstly introduced the notion of univariate or - thogonal wavelet wraps. Yang [7] constructed a-scale orthogonal multiwavelet wraps that were more flexible in applications. It is known that the majority of information is multi-dimensional information. Shen [8] introduced multivariate orthogonal wavelets which may be used in a wider field. Thus, it is necessary to generalize the concept of multivariate wavelet wraps to the case of multivariate vector-valued wavelets. The go -al of this paper is to give the definition and the construction of bioorthogonal vector-valued wavelet wraps and desingt new Riesz bases of $L^2(R^3, C^v)$.

2 The Preliminaries on Vector-Valued Function Space

We begin with some notations. Set $Z_+ = \{0\} \cup N$, s, $n, v \in N$ and $s, n, v \geq 2$, $Z^3 = \{(z_1, z_2, z_3): z_r \in Z, r = 1, 2, 3\}$, $Z_+^3 = \{\{(z_1, z_2, z_3): : z_r \in z_+, r = 1, 2, 3\}$. For any X, $X_1, X_2 \subset R^3$, denoting by $4X = \{4x : x \in X\}$, $X_1 + X_2 = \{x_1 + x_2 : x_1 \in X_1, x_2 \in X_2\}$, $X_1 - X_2 = \{x_1 = \{x_1 - x_2 : x_1 \in X_1, x_2 \in X_2\}$. There exist 64 elements μ_0, $\mu_1, \cdots, \mu_{63}$ in Z_+^4 by finite group theory such that $Z^3 = \cup_{\mu \in \Gamma_0} (\mu + MZ^3)$; $m = \det(M)$, $(\mu_1 + MZ^3) \cap (\mu_2 + MZ^3) = \varnothing$, where $\Gamma_0 = \{\mu_0, \mu_1, \cdots, \mu_{63}\}$ denotes the set of all different representative elements in the quotient group $Z^3 / (MZ^3)$ and μ_1, μ_2 denote two arbitrary distinct elements in Γ_0, M is a 3×3 matrix Set $\mu_0 = \underline{0}$, where $\underline{0}$ is the null of Z_+^3. Let $\Gamma = \Gamma_0 - \{\underline{0}\}$ and Γ, Γ_0 be two index sets.By $L^2(R^3, C^v)$, we denote the aggregate of all vector- valued functions $H(x)$, i.e., $L^2(R^3, C^v) := \{H(x) = (h_1(x), h_2(x), \cdots, h_v(x))^T : h_l(x) \in L^2(R^3), l = 1, 2, \cdots, v\}$, where T means the transpose of a vector. Video images and digital films are examples of vector-valued functions where $\varnothing_l(x)$ in the above $H(x)$ denotes the pixel on the l th column at the point x. For $H(x) \in L^2(R^3, C^v)$, $\|H\|$ denotes the norm of vector-valued function $H(x)$, i.e., $\|H\| := (\sum_{l=1}^v \int_{R^3} |h_l(x)|^2 \, dx)^{1/2}$ .In the below $*$ means the transpose and the complex conjugate, and its integration is defined to be

$$\int_{R^3} H(x) dx = (\int_{R^3} h_1(x) dx, \int_{R^3} h_2(x) \, dx, \cdots\cdots, \int_{R^3} h_v(x) dx)^T.$$

The Fourier transform of $H(x)$ is defined as $\hat{H}(\gamma) := \int_{R^3} H(x) \cdot e^{-ix \cdot \gamma} dx$, where $x \cdot \gamma$ denotes the inner product of real vectors x and γ. For $F, H \in L^2(R^3, C^v)$, their *symbol in ner product* is defined by

$$[F(\cdot), H(\cdot)] := \int_{R^s} F(x) H(x)^* dx, \tag{1}$$

Definition 1. We say that a pair of vector-valued functions $H(x), \widetilde{H}(x) \in L^2(R^3, C^v)$ are biorthogonal, if their translations satisfy

$$[H(\cdot), \widetilde{H}(\cdot - n)] = \delta_{0,n} I_v, \quad n \in Z^3, \tag{2}$$

where I_v denotes the $v \times v$ indentity matrix and $\delta_{0,n}$ is the Kronecker symbol.

Definition 2. A sequence of vector-valued functions $\{H_n(x)\}_{n \in Z^3} \subset U \subset L^2(R^3, C^v)$ is called a Riesz basis of U if itsatisfies *(i)* for any $G(x) \in U$, there exists a unique $v \times v$ matrix sequence $\{Q_n\}_{n \in Z^3} \in \ell^2(Z^3)^{v \times v}$ such that

$$G(x) = \sum_{n \in Z^3} Q_n H_n(x), \quad x \in R^3, \tag{3}$$

where $\ell^2(Z^3)^{v \times v} = \{Q : Z^3 \to C^{u \times u}, \|Q\|_2 = \sum_{l,s=1}^{v} \sum_{n \in Z^4} |q_{l,s}(n)|^2)^{\frac{1}{2}} < +\infty\}$, *(ii)* there exist two constants $0 < C_1 \le C_2 < +\infty$ such that, for any matrix sequence $\{M_n\}_{n \in Z^3}$, the following equality follows.i.e.,

$$C_1 \|\{M_n\}\|_* \le \| \sum_{n \in Z^3} M_n H_n(x) \| \le C_2 \|\{M_n\}\|_*, \tag{4}$$

In what follows, we introduce the notion of vector- valued multiresolution analysis and give the definition of biorthogonal vector-valued wavelets of space $L^2(R^3, C^v)$.

Definition 3. A vector-valued multiresolution analysis of the space $L^2(R^3, C^v)$ is a nested sequence of closed subspaces $\{Y_\ell\}_{\ell \in Z}$ such that (i) $Y_\ell \subset Y_{\ell+1}, \forall \ell \in Z$; (ii) $\bigcap_{\ell \in Z} Y_\ell = \{0\}$ and $\bigcup_{\ell \in Z} Y_\ell$ is dense in $L^2(R^3, C^v)$, where 0 denotes an zero vector of space R^v; (iii) $\Phi(x) \in Y_\ell \Leftrightarrow \Phi \ (Mx) \in Y_{\ell+1}, \forall \ell \in Z$; (iv) there exists $F(x) \in Y_0$,called a vector-valued scaling function, such that its translates $F_n(x) := F(x - n), \quad n \in Z^3$ forms a Riesz basis of subspace Y_0.

Since $F(x) \in Y_0 \subset Y_1$, by Definition 3 and (4) there exists a finitely supported sequence of constant $v \times v$ matrice $\{\Omega_n\}_{n \in Z^3} \in \ell^2(Z^3)^{v \times v}$ such that

$$F(x) = \sum_{n \in Z^3} \Omega_n F(Mx - n). \tag{5}$$

Equation (6) is called a refinement equation. Define

$$m \cdot \Omega(\gamma) = \sum_{n \in Z^3} \Omega_n \cdot \exp\{-in \cdot \gamma\}, \quad \gamma \in R^3. \tag{6}$$

where $\Omega(\gamma)$, which is $2\pi Z^s$ fun., is called a symbol of $F(x)$. Thus, (6) becomes

$$\hat{F}(M\gamma) = \Omega(\gamma)\hat{F}(\gamma), \quad \gamma \in R^3. \tag{7}$$

Let $X_{j,} j \in Z$ be the direct complementary subspace of Y_j in Y_{j+1}. Assume that there exist 63 vector-valued functions $\psi_\mu(x) \in L^2(R^3, C^v), \mu \in \Gamma$ such that their tran- slations and dilations form a Riesz basis of $X_{j,}$ i.e.,

$$X_j = \overline{(span\{\Psi_\mu(M^j \cdot -n) : n \in Z^3, \mu \in \Gamma\})}, \quad j \in Z. \tag{8}$$

Since $\Psi_\mu(x) \in X_0 \subset Y_1$, $\mu \in \Gamma$, there exist 63 finitely supported sequences of constant $v \times v$ matrice $\{B_n^{(\mu)}\}_{n \in Z^4}$ such that

$$\Psi_\mu(x) = \sum_{n \in Z^3} B_n^{(\mu)} F(Mx - n), \quad \mu \in \Gamma. \tag{9}$$

By implementing the Fourier transform for the both sides of (9) , we have

$$\hat{\Psi}_\mu(M\gamma) = \mathcal{B}^{(\mu)}(\gamma)\hat{\Phi}(\gamma), \quad \gamma \in R^3, \quad \mu \in \Gamma. \tag{10}$$

where

$$m \cdot \mathcal{B}^{(\mu)}(\gamma) = \sum_{n \in Z^3} B_n^{(\mu)} \cdot \exp\{-in \cdot \gamma\}, \quad \mu \in \Gamma. \tag{11}$$

If $F(x), \tilde{F}(x) \in L^2(R^3, C^v)$ are a pair of biorthogonal vector-valued scaling functions, then

$$[F(\cdot), \tilde{F}(\cdot - n)] = \delta_{0,n} I_v, \quad n \in Z^3. \tag{12}$$

We say that $\Psi_\mu(x), \tilde{\Psi}_\mu(x) \in L^2(R^3, C^v), \mu \in \Gamma$ are pairs of biorthogonal vector-valued wavelets associated with a pairof biorthogonal vector-valued scaling functions $F(x)$ and $\tilde{F}(x)$, if the family $\{\Psi_\mu(x - n), n \in Z^3, \mu \in \Gamma\}$ is a Riesz basis of subspace X_0, and

$$[F(\cdot), \tilde{\Psi}_\mu(\cdot - n)] = 0, \quad \mu \in \Gamma, \quad n \in Z^3. \tag{13}$$

$$[\tilde{F}(\cdot), \Psi_\mu(\cdot - n)] = 0, \quad \mu \in \Gamma, \quad n \in Z^3. \tag{14}$$

$$X_j^{(\mu)} = \overline{Span\{\Psi_\mu(M^j \cdot -n) : n \in Z^3, \}}, \mu \in \Gamma, j \in Z. \tag{15}$$

Similar to (5) and (9), there exist 64 finitely supported sequences of $v \times v$ complex constant matrice $\{\tilde{\Omega}_k\}_{k \in Z^3}$ and $\{\tilde{B}_k^{(\mu)}\}_{k \in Z^3}$, $\mu \in \Gamma$ such that $\tilde{F}(x)$ and $\tilde{\Psi}_\mu(x)$ satisfy the refinement equations:

$$\tilde{F}(x) = \sum_{k \in Z^3} \tilde{\Omega}_k \tilde{F}(Mx - k), \tag{16}$$

3   The Biorthogonality Features of a Sort of Wavelet Wraps

Denoting by $G_0(x) = F(x), G_\mu(x) = \tilde{\Psi}_\mu(x), \tilde{G}_0(x) = F(x), \tilde{G}_\mu(x) = \tilde{\Psi}_\mu(x), Q_k^{(0)} = \Omega_k$, $Q_k^{(\mu)} = B_k^{(\mu)}, \tilde{Q}_k^{(0)} = \tilde{\Omega}_k, \tilde{Q}_k^{(\mu)} = \tilde{B}_k^{(\mu)}, \mu \in \Gamma, k \in Z^3, M = 4I_v$. For any $\alpha \in Z_+^3$ and the given vector-valued biorthogonal scaling functions $G_0(x)$ and $\tilde{G}_0(x)$, iterititvely define, respectively,

$$G_\alpha(x) = G_{4\sigma+\mu}(x) = \sum_{k\in Z^3} Q_k^{(\mu)} G_\sigma(4x-k), \quad \mu \in \Gamma_0, \qquad (18)$$

$$\tilde{G}_\alpha(x) = \tilde{G}_{4\sigma+\mu}(x) = \sum_{k\in Z^3} \tilde{Q}_k^{(\mu)} \tilde{G}_\sigma(4x-k), \quad \mu \in \Gamma_0. \qquad (19)$$

where $\sigma \in Z_+^3$ is the unique element such that $\alpha = 4\sigma + \mu$, $\mu \in \Gamma_0$ follows.

Lemma 1[4]. Let $F(x), \tilde{F}(x) \in L^2(R^3, C^\nu)$. Then they are biorthogonal if and only if

$$\sum_{k\in Z^3} \hat{F}(\gamma + 2k\pi) \hat{\tilde{F}}(\gamma + 2k\pi)^* = I_\nu. \qquad (20)$$

Definition 4. We say that two families of vector-valued functions $\{G_{4\sigma+\mu}(x), \sigma \in Z_+^3, \mu \in \Gamma_0\}$ and $\{\tilde{G}_{4\sigma+\mu}(x), \sigma \in Z_+^3, \mu \in \Gamma_0\}$ are vector-valued wavelet packets with respect to a pair of biorthogonal vector-valued scaling functions $G_0(x)$ and $\tilde{G}_0(x)$, resp., where $G_{4\sigma+\mu}(x)$ and $\tilde{G}_{4\sigma+\mu}(x)$ are given by (18) and (19), respectively.

Applying the Fourier transform for the both sides of (18) and (19) yields, resp.,

$$\hat{G}_{4\sigma+\mu}(\gamma) = Q^{(\mu)}(\gamma/4)\hat{G}_\sigma(\gamma/4), \quad \mu \in \Gamma_0, \qquad (21)$$

$$\hat{\tilde{G}}_{4\sigma+\mu}(4\gamma) = Q^{(\mu)}(\gamma)\hat{\tilde{G}}_\sigma(\gamma), \quad \mu \in \Gamma_0, \qquad (22)$$

Lemma 2 [6]. Assume that $G_\mu(x)$, $\tilde{G}_\mu(x) \in L^2(R^3, C^\nu)$, $\mu \in \Gamma$ are pairs of biorthogonal vector-valued wavelets associated with a pair of biorthogonal scaling functions $G_0(x)$ and $\tilde{G}_0(x)$. Then, for $\mu, \nu \in \Gamma_0$, we have

$$\sum_{\rho\in\Gamma_0} Q^{(\mu)}((\gamma+2\rho\pi)/4)\tilde{Q}^{(\nu)}((\gamma+2\rho\pi)/4)^* = \delta_{\mu,\nu}I_\nu. \qquad (23)$$

Lemma 3 [6]. Suppose $\{G_\alpha(x), \alpha \in Z_+^3\}$ and $\{\tilde{G}_\alpha(x), \alpha \in Z_+^3\}$ are wavelet packets with respect to a pair of biorthogonal vector-valued functions $G_0(x)$ and $\tilde{G}_0(x)$. Then, for $\alpha \in Z_+^3$, we have

$$[G_\alpha(\cdot), \tilde{G}_\alpha(\cdot - k)] = \delta_{0,k}I_\nu, \quad k \in Z^3. \qquad (24)$$

Theorem 1 [8]. Assume that $\{G_\beta(x), \beta \in Z_+^3\}$ and $\{\tilde{G}_\beta(x), \beta \in Z_+^3\}$ are vector-valued wavelet packets with respect to a pair of biorthogonal vector-valued functions $G_0(x)$ and $\tilde{G}_0(x)$, respectively. Then, for $\beta \in Z_+^3, \mu, \nu \in \Gamma_0$, we have

$$[G_{4\beta+\mu}(\cdot), \tilde{G}_{4\beta+\nu}(\cdot - k)] = \delta_{0,k}\delta_{\mu,\nu}I_\nu, \quad k \in Z^3. \qquad (25)$$

Theorem 2. If $\{G_\beta(x), \beta \in Z_+^3\}$ and $\{\tilde{G}_\beta(x), \beta \in Z_+^3\}$ are vector-valued wavelet wraps with respect to a pair of biorthogonal vector scaling functions $G_0(x)$ and $\tilde{G}_0(x)$, then for any $\alpha, \sigma \in Z_+^3$, we have

$$[G_\alpha(\cdot), \tilde{G}_\sigma(\cdot - k)] = \delta_{\alpha,\sigma}\delta_{0,k}I_v, \quad k \in Z^3. \tag{26}$$

Proof. When $\alpha = \sigma$, (26) follows by Lemma 3. as $\alpha \neq \sigma$ and $\alpha, \sigma \in \Gamma_0$, it follows from Lemma 4 that (26) holds, too. Assuming that α is not equal to β, as well as at least one of $\{\alpha, \sigma\}$ doesn't belong to Γ_0, we rewrite α, σ as $\alpha = 4\alpha_1 + \rho_1$, $\sigma = 4\sigma_1 + \mu_1$, where $\rho_1, \mu_1 \in \Gamma_0$.

Case 1. If $\alpha_1 = \sigma_1$, then $\rho_1 \neq \mu_1$. (26) follows by virtue of (24), (25) as well as Lemma 1 and Lemma 2, i.e.,

$$[G_\alpha(\cdot), \tilde{G}_\sigma(\cdot - k)] = \frac{1}{(2\pi)^3}\int_{R^3} \hat{G}_{4\alpha_1+\rho_1}(\gamma)\hat{\tilde{G}}_{4\sigma_1+\mu_1}(\gamma)^* \cdot \exp\{ik \cdot \gamma\}d\gamma$$

$$= \frac{1}{(2\pi)^3}\int_{[0,2\pi]^3}\delta_{\rho_1,\mu_1}I_v \cdot \exp\{ik \cdot \gamma\}d\gamma = O.$$

Case 2. If $\alpha_1 \neq \sigma_1$, order $\alpha_1 = 4\alpha_2 + \rho_2$, $\sigma_1 = 4\sigma_2 + \mu_2$, where $\alpha_2, \sigma_2 \in Z_+^3$, and $\rho_2, \mu_2 \in \Gamma_0$. If $\alpha_2 = \sigma_2$, then $\rho_2 \neq \mu_2$. Similar to Case 1, (28) follows. As $\alpha_2 \neq \sigma_2$, order $\alpha_2 = 4\alpha_3 + \rho_3$, $\sigma_2 = 4\sigma_3 + \mu_3$, where $\alpha_3, \sigma_3 \in Z_+^3$, $\rho_3, \mu_3 \in \Gamma_0$. Thus, taking finite steps (denoted by κ), we obtain $\alpha_\kappa \in \Gamma_0$, and $\rho_\kappa, \mu_\kappa \in \Gamma_0$.

$$8\pi^3[G_\alpha(\cdot), \tilde{G}_\sigma(\cdot - k)] = \int_{R^3}\hat{G}_\alpha(\gamma)\hat{\tilde{G}}_{\sigma_1}(\gamma)^* \cdot e^{ik \cdot \gamma}d\gamma$$

$$= \int_{R^3}\hat{G}_{4\alpha_1+\lambda_1}(\gamma)\hat{\tilde{G}}_{4\beta_1+\mu_1}(\gamma)^* \cdot \exp\{ik \cdot \gamma\}d\gamma = \cdots\cdots\cdots\cdots$$

$$= \int_{[0,2\cdot4^\kappa\pi]^3}\{\prod_{l=1}^{\kappa}Q^{(\rho_l)}(\gamma/4^l)\}\cdot O \cdot \{\prod_{l=1}^{\kappa}\tilde{Q}^{(\mu_l)}(\gamma/4^l)\}^* \cdot \exp\{-ik \cdot \gamma\}d\gamma = O.$$

Therefore, for any $\alpha, \sigma \in Z_+^3$, result (26) is established.

For any $v = (v_1, v_2, v_3) \in Z^3$, the translation operator S is defined to be $(S_{va}\lambda)(x) = \lambda(x - va)$, where a is a positive constant real number.

Theorem 3 [7]. Let $\phi(x), \tilde{\phi}(x), \hbar_t(x)$ and $\tilde{\hbar}_t(x), t \in J$ be functions in $L^2(R^3)$ defined by (30), (31), (33) and (34), respectively. Assume that conditions in Theorem 1 are satisfied. Then, for any function $f(x) \in L^2(R^3)$, and any integer n,

$$\sum_{u \in Z^3}\langle f, \tilde{\phi}_{n,u}\rangle\phi_{n,u}(x) = \sum_{t=1}^{7}\sum_{s=-\infty}^{n-1}\sum_{u \in Z^3}\langle f, \tilde{\hbar}_{t:s,u}\rangle\hbar_{t:s,u}(x). \tag{27}$$

References

1. Telesca, L., et al.: Multiresolution wavelet analysis of earthquakes. Chaos, Solitons & Fractals 22(3), 741–748 (2004)
2. Iovane, G., Giordano, P.: Wavelet and multiresolution analysis:Nature of Cantorian space-time. Chaos, Solitons & Fractals 32(4), 896–910 (2007)
3. Zhang, N., Wu, X.: Lossless Compression of Color Mosaic Images. IEEE Trans. Image Processing 15(16), 1379–1388 (2006)
4. Chen, Q., et al.: A study on compactly supported orthogo-nal vector-valued wavelets and wavelet packets. Chaos, Solitons & Fractals 31(4), 1024–1034 (2007)
5. Shen, Z.: Nontensor product wavelet packets in $L_2(R^s)$. SIAM Math. Anal. 26(4), 1061–1074 (1995)
6. Chen, Q., Cheng, Z., Feng, X.: Multivariate Biorthogonal Multiwavelet packets. Mathematica Applicata 18(3), 358–364 (2005) (in Chinese)
7. Li, S., et al.: Theory of Geeneralized Multiresolution Structure and Pseudoframes of Translates. J. Fourier Anal. Appl. 6(1), 23–40 (2001)
8. Chen, Q., Huo, A.: The research of a class of biorthogonal compactly supported vector-valued wavelets. Chaos, Solitons & Fractals 41(2), 951–961 (2009)

The Nice Characters of Orthogonal Bidimensional Vector Wavelet Packs and Orthogonal Binary Framelets

Jinfan Yang[*] and Sanhua Song

Department of Computer Science, Huanghuai University, Zhumadian, 463000, China
jhnsx123@126.com

Abstract. Wavelet analysis has become a developing branch of mathematics for over twenty years. It has been a powerful tool for exploring and solving many complicated problems in natural science and engineering computation. In this work, the notion of orthogonal vector bivariate wavelet packs and wavelet frame packs, which are generalization of uni-wavelet packets, is introduced. A new procedure for designing these vector bivariate wavelet packs is presented. Their characteristics are studied by using time-frequency analysis method, Banach space theory and finite group theory. Orthogonal formulas concerning the wavelet packs are established. The biorthogonality formulas concerning these wavelet wraps are established. Moreover, it is shown how to draw new Riesz bases of space $L^2(R^2, C^\nu)$ from these wavelet wraps.

Keywords: Banach space theorem, Bivariate, vector wavelet wraps, Riesz bases, Bessel sequence, time-frequency analysis representation.

1 Introduction and Notations

The wavelet theory has been one of powerful tools for researching into wavelets. Although the Fourier transform has been a major tool in analysis for over a century, it has a serious laking for signal analysis in that it hides in its phases information concerning the moment of emission and duration of a signal. Since 1986, wavelet analysis has become a developing branch of mathematics. Wavelet packets have been applied to signal processing [1], image compression [2] so on. Coifman and Meyer are those who firstly introduced the notion of univariate orthogonal wavelet packets. Shen[3] constructed the multivariate orthogonal wavelet packets. Wavelet packets include multiple orthonormal basis , which means that a signal could be represented in many different ways by using wavelet packets. But the performances in presenting the specified signal are different using different bases. The one which could provide the best performance according to some criterion will be the best basis. Nowadays, most of the related studies use the algorithm proposed by Coisman and Wickerhanser to select the best basis. Vector-valued wavelets are a class of generalized multiwavelets. Xia [4] introduced the notion of orthogonal vector-valued wavelets. Moreover, he studied the existence

---

[*] Corresponding author.

S. Lin and X. Huang (Eds.): CESM 2011, Part I, CCIS 175, pp. 73–78, 2011.
© Springer-Verlag Berlin Heidelberg 2011

and construction of vector-valued wavelets. However, vector-valued wavelets [5] and multiwavelets are different. Hence, studying vector-valued wavelets is useful in multiwavelet theory and representations of signals. It is known that the majority of information is multi-dimensional information. Thus, it is significant and necessary to generalize the concept of multivariate wavelet packets to the case of multiple vector-valued multivariate wavelets. Based on some ideas from [3], the goal of this paper is to discuss the properties of multiple vector-valued multivariate wavelet packets. Let R and C be all real and all complex numbers, respectively. Z and N denote, respectively, all integers and all positive integers. Set $Z_+ = \{0\} \cup N, a, s \in N$ as well as $a \geq 2$ By algebra theory, it is obviously follows that there are a^2 elements $d_0, d_1, \cdots, d_{a^2-1}$ in $Z_+^2 = \{(z_1, z_2) : z_1, z_2 \in Z_+\}$ such that $Z^2 = \bigcup_{d \in \Omega_0} (d + aZ^2)$; $(d_1 + aZ^2) \cap (d_2 + aZ^2) = \phi$, where $\Omega_0 = \{d_0, d_1, \cdots, d_{a^2-1}\}$ denotes the aggregate of all the different representative elements in the quotient group $Z^2 / (aZ^2)$ and order $d_0 = \{\underline{0}\}$ where $\{\underline{0}\}$ is the null element of z_+^2 and d_1, d_2 denote two arbitrary distinct elements in Ω_0. Let $\Omega = \Omega_0 - \{\underline{0}\}$ and Ω, Ω_0 to be two index sets. Define, By $L^2(R^2, C^s)$, we denote the set of all vector-valued functions $L^2(R^2, C^s) := \{\hbar(y) = (h_1(y)), h_2(y), \cdots, h_u(y))^T : h_l(y) \in L^2(R^2), l = 1, 2, \cdots, s\}$, where T means the transpose of a vector. For any $\hbar \in L^2(R^2, C^s)$ its integration is defined as $\int_{R^2} \hbar(y) dy = (\int_{R^2} h_1(y) dy, \int_{R^2} h_2(y) dy, \cdots, \int_{R^2} h_s(y) dy)$, and the Fourier transform of $\hbar(y)$ is defined by

$$\hat{\hbar}(\omega) := \int_{R^2} \hbar(y) \cdot \exp\{-i\langle y, \omega \rangle\} dy, \tag{1}$$

where $\langle y, \omega \rangle$ denotes the inner product of y and ω. For multiple vector-valued functions $< \hbar, \Lambda >$ denotes their symbol inner product, i.e.,

$$\langle \hbar, \Lambda \rangle := \int_{R^2} \hbar(y) \Lambda(y)^* dy, \tag{2}$$

where $*$ means the transpose and the complex conjugate.

Definition 1. A sequenc $\{\hbar_n(y)_{n \in Z^2} \subset L^2(R^2, C^s)\}$ is called an orthogonal set, if

$$\langle \hbar_n, \hbar_v \rangle = \delta_{n,v} I_s, \quad n, v \in Z^2, \tag{3}$$

where I_s stands for the $s \times s$ identity matrix and $\delta_{n,v}$, is generalized Kronecker symbol, i.e., $\delta_{n,v} = 1$ as $n = v$ and $\delta_{n,v} = 0$, otherwise.

Definition 2. A sequence of vector-valued functions $\{\hbar_n(y)\}_{n \in Z^2} \subset W \subset L^2(R^2, C^s)$ is called a Riesz basis in W, if it satisfies

(i) For any $\Lambda(y) \in W$, there exists a unique $s \times s$ matrix sequence $\{P_n\}_{n \in Z^2}$ such that

$$\Lambda(y) = \sum_{n \in Z^2} P_n \hbar_n(y), \quad y \in R^2. \tag{4}$$

(ii) There exist constants $0 < C_1 \le C_2 < \infty$ such that, for any constant matrix sequence $\{P_n\}_{n \in Z^2}$, we have,

$$C_1 \|\{P_n\}\|_+ \le \left\| \sum_{n \in Z^2} P_n(y) \hbar_n(y) \right\|_2 \le C_2 \|\{P_n\}\|_+ \tag{5}$$

Where $\|\{P_n\}\|_+$ denotes the norm of sequence $\{P_n\}_{n \in Z^2}$

We consider any functions $\hbar(x)$, $\lambda(x)$ in space $L^2(R^2)$ with the inner product:

$$\langle \lambda, \hbar \rangle = \int_{R^2} \lambda(x) \overline{\hbar(x)}\, dx, \quad \hat{\hbar}(\omega) = \int_{R^2} \hbar(x) e^{-x \cdot \omega}\, dx.$$

As usual, $\hat{\hbar}(\omega)$ denotes the Fourier transform of any function $\hbar(x) \in L^2(R^2)$.

2   Vector-Valued Multiresolution Analysis

Definition 3. Let Ω be a separable Hilbert space and Λ be an index set. We recall that a sequence $\{\Gamma_\iota : \iota \in \Lambda\} \subseteq \Omega$ is a frame for Ω if there exist two positive constants A_1, A_2 such that

$$\forall \xi \in \Omega, \quad A_1 \|\xi\|^2 \le \sum_{\iota \in \Lambda} |\langle \xi, \Gamma_\iota \rangle|^2 \le A_2 \|\xi\|^2, \tag{6}$$

where $\|\xi\|^2 = \langle \xi, \xi \rangle$, and A_1, A_2 are called frame bounds. A sequence $\{\hbar_\iota : \iota \in \Lambda\} \subseteq \Omega$ is a tight one if we can choose $A_1 = A_2$. A frame $\{\hbar_\iota : \iota \subset \Lambda\}$ is an exact frame if it ceases to be a frame when any one of its elements is removed. If $A_1 = A_2 = 1$, then it follows from (1) that

$$\forall \xi \in \Omega, \quad \xi = \sum_{\iota \in \Lambda} \langle \xi, \Gamma_\iota \rangle \Gamma_\iota$$

A sequence $\{\Gamma_\iota : \iota \in \Lambda\} \subseteq \Omega$ is a Bessel sequence if (only) the upper inequality of (1) follows. If only for all $\hbar \in U \subset \Omega$, the upper inequality of (1) holds, the sequence $\{\Gamma_\iota : \iota \in \Lambda\} \subseteq \Omega$ is a Bessel sequence with respect to (w.r.t.) U. Moreover, we assume that $U \subset \Omega$ is a closed subspace, if for all $\lambda \in U$, there exist two real numbers A_1, $A_2 > 0$ such that $A_1 \|\lambda\|^2 \le \sum_{\iota \in \Lambda} |\langle \lambda, \Gamma_\iota \rangle|^2 \le A_2 \|\lambda\|^2$, the sequence $\{\Gamma_\iota : \iota \in \Lambda\} \subseteq \Omega$ is called an U – subspace frame. In this section, we introduce the notion of vector-valued multiresolution analysis.

Definition 4. A vector-valued multiresolution analysis of $L^2(R^2, C^s)$ is a nested sequence of closed subspaces $\{X_j\}_{j \in Z}$ such that (i) $X_j \subset X_{j+1}$, $j \in Z$; (ii) $\bigcap_{j \in Z} X_j = \{O\}$ and $\bigcup_{j \in Z} X_j$ is dense in $L^2(R^2, C^s)$, where O denotes $s \times s$ zero matrix; (iii) $\hbar(y) \in X_j \Leftrightarrow \hbar(ay) \in X_{j+1}, \forall j \in Z$; (iv) there is a vector-valued function $f(y) \in X_0$ such that $\{f_n(y) := f(y-n) : n \in Z^2\}$ form a Riesz basis for subspace $f(y) \in X_0$ .Since $f(y) \in X_0 \subset X_1$, by definition and (4) there exist a finite supported constant $s \times s$ matrix sequence $\{M_n\}_{n \in Z^2}$ such that

$$f(y) = \sum_{n \in Z^2} M_n f(ay - n), \tag{7}$$

$$\hat{f}(a\omega) = M(\omega)\hat{f}(\omega), \omega \in R^2, \tag{8}$$

where $M(\omega) = \frac{1}{a^2} \sum_{n \in Z^2} M_n \cdot e^{-i\langle n, \omega \rangle}$. Equation (7) is called a refinement equation and

$f(y)$ a vector-valued scaling function. Let $U_j, j \in Z$ be the direct complementary subspace of X_j in X_{j+1} and there exist $a^2 - 1$ vector-valued function $\Phi_\rho(y) \in L^2(R^2, C^s), \rho \in \Omega$, such that the translates and dilations of $\Phi_\rho(y)$ form a Riesz basis of U_j, i.e.

$$U_j = clos_{L^2(R^2, C^s)} \langle \Phi_\rho(a^j \cdot -n) : n \in Z^2, \rho \in \rangle. \tag{9}$$

Since $\Phi_\rho(y) \in U_0 \subset V_1, \rho \in \Omega$ there exist $a^2 - 1$ finite supported constant matrix sequences $\{B_n^\rho\}_{n \in Z^2}$ such that

$$\Phi_\rho(y) = \sum_{n \in Z^2} B_n^\rho f(ay - n), \rho \in \Omega, \tag{10}$$

The vector-valued functions $f(x) \in L^2(R^2, C^s)$ is said to be an orthogonal one, if

$$\langle f(\cdot), f(\cdot - n) \rangle = \delta_{0,n} I_s, n \in Z^2, \tag{11}$$

We say that $\Phi_\rho(y) \in L^2(R^2, C^s), \rho \in \Omega$ are orthogonal vector-valued wavelets associated with an orthogonal vector-valued scaling functions $\Phi_\rho(y)$ if $\{\Phi_\rho(y-n), n \in Z^2, \rho \in \Omega\}$ is a Riesz basis of U_0, and

$$\langle f(\cdot), \Phi_\rho(\cdot - n) \rangle = 0, \rho \in \Omega, n \in Z^2. \tag{12}$$

$$\langle \Phi_\rho(\cdot), \Phi_\rho(\cdot - n) \rangle = \delta_{\rho,\mu} \delta_{0,n} I_s, \rho, \mu \in \Omega. \tag{13}$$

3 The Orthogonality Traits of Vector-Valued Wavelet Wraps

To introduce the vector-valued wavelet packets, we set

$\Psi_0(y) = f(y), \Psi_\rho(y) = \Phi_\rho(y)$, $P_n^{(0)} = M_n, P_n^{(\rho)} = B_n^{(\rho)}, \rho \in \Omega, n \in Z^2$.

Then, the equations (7) and (10), which $f(y)$ and $\Phi_\rho(y)$ satisfy can be written as

$$\Psi_\rho(y) = \sum_{n \in Z^2} P_n^{(\rho)} \Psi_{\underline{0}}(ay - n), \rho \in \Omega_0. \tag{14}$$

For any α and the given vector-valued orthogonal scaling function $f(y)$, let

$$\Psi_\alpha(y) = \Psi_{a\beta+\lambda}(y) = \sum_{n \in Z^2} P_n^{(\lambda)} \Psi_\beta(ay - n), \quad \lambda \in \Omega_0. \quad \lambda \in \Omega_0 \tag{15}$$

Definition 5. The family of vector-valued functions $\{\Psi_{a\beta+\lambda}(y), \beta \in Z_+^2, \lambda \in \Omega_0\}$ is called vector-valued wavelet packs with respect to the vector-valued scaling function $f(y)$ where $\Psi_{a\beta+\lambda}(y)$ is given by (16).

$$\Psi_\alpha(x) = \Psi_{a\sigma+\mu}(x) = \sum_{k \in Z^2} Q_k^{(\mu)} \Psi_\sigma(ax - k), \quad \mu \in \Gamma_0, \tag{16}$$

where $\sigma \in Z_+^2$ is the unique element such that $\alpha = a\sigma + \mu$, $\mu \in \Gamma_0$ follows.

Lemma 1[4]. Let $F(x), \tilde{F}(x) \in L^2(R^2, C^v)$. Then they are biorthogonal if and only if

$$\sum_{k \in Z^2} \hat{F}(\gamma + 2k\pi)\hat{\tilde{F}}(\gamma + 2k\pi)^* = I_s. \tag{17}$$

Lemma 2[6]. Assume that $\Psi_\mu(x) \in L^2(R^2, C^s)$, $\mu \in \Gamma$ an orthogonal vector-valued wavelets associated with orthogonal scaling functions $\Psi_0(x)$. Then, for $\mu, \nu \in \Omega_0$, we have

$$\sum_{\rho \in \Omega_0} \mathcal{P}^{(\mu)}((\gamma + 2\rho\pi)/a)\mathcal{P}^{(\nu)}((\gamma + 2\rho\pi)/a)^* = \delta_{\mu,\nu} I_s. \tag{18}$$

Lemma 3[6]. Suppose $\{\Psi_\alpha(x), \alpha \in Z_+^2\}$ are wavelet packets with respect to orthogonal vector-valued functions $\Psi_0(x)$. Then, for $\alpha \in Z_+^3$, we have

$$[\Psi_\alpha(\cdot), \Psi_\alpha(\cdot - k)] = \delta_{0,k} I_s, \quad k \in Z^2. \tag{19}$$

Theorem 1[8]. Assume that $\{\Psi_\alpha(x), \alpha \in Z_+^2\}$ are wavelet packets with respect to orthogonal vector-valued functions $\Psi_0(x)$. Then, for $\beta \in Z_+^2, \mu, \nu \in \Omega_0$, we have

$$\langle \Psi_{a a\beta+\mu}(\cdot), \Psi_{a\beta+\nu}(\cdot - m) \rangle = \delta_{0,k} \delta_{\mu,\nu} I_s, \quad m \in Z^2. \tag{20}$$

Theorem 2. If $\{G_\beta(x), \beta \in Z_+^2\}$ is vector-valued wavelet wraps with respect to a pair of biorthogonal vector scaling functions $G_0(x)$, then for any $\alpha, \sigma \in Z_+^3$, we have

$$[G_\alpha(\cdot), \tilde{G}_\sigma(\cdot - k)] = \delta_{\alpha,\sigma} \delta_{0,k} I_v, \quad k \in Z^2. \tag{21}$$

Proof. When $\alpha = \sigma$, (21) follows by Lemma 3. as $\alpha \neq \sigma$ and $\alpha, \sigma \in \Gamma_0$, it follows from Lemma 4 that (21) holds, too. Assuming that α is not equal to β, as well as at least one of $\{\alpha, \sigma\}$ doesn't belong to Γ_0, we rewrite α, σ as $\alpha = a\alpha_1 + \rho_1$, $\sigma = a\sigma_1 + \mu_1$, where $\rho_1, \mu_1 \in \Gamma_0$.

Case 1. If $\alpha_1 = \sigma_1$, then $\rho_1 \neq \mu_1$. (21) follows by virtue of (19), (20) as well as Lemma 1 and Lemma 2, i.e.,

$$[G_\alpha(\cdot), \tilde{G}_\sigma(\cdot - k)] = \frac{1}{(2\pi)^2} \int_{R^2} \hat{G}_{a\alpha_1+\rho_1}(\gamma)\hat{\tilde{G}}_{a\sigma_1+\mu_1}(\gamma)^* \cdot \exp\{ik \cdot \gamma\} d\gamma$$

$$= \frac{1}{(2\pi)^2} \int_{[0,2\pi]^2} \delta_{\rho_1,\mu_1} I_s \cdot \exp\{ik \cdot \gamma\} d\gamma = 0.$$

Case 2. If $\alpha_1 \neq \sigma_1$, order $\alpha_1 = a\alpha_2 + \rho_2$, $\sigma_1 = a\sigma_2 + \mu_2$, where $\alpha_2, \sigma_2 \in Z_+^2$, and $\rho_2, \mu_2 \in \Gamma_0$. If $\alpha_2 = \sigma_2$, then $\rho_2 \neq \mu_2$. Similar to Case 1, (21) follows. As $\alpha_2 \neq \sigma_2$, order $\alpha_2 = a\alpha_3 + \rho_3$, $\sigma_2 = a\sigma_3 + \mu_3$, where $\alpha_3, \sigma_3 \in Z_+^2$, $\rho_3, \mu_3 \in \Omega_0$. Thus, taking finite steps (denoted by κ), we obtain $\alpha_\kappa \in \Gamma_0$, and $\rho_\kappa, \mu_\kappa \in \Gamma_0$.

$$8\pi^2[G_\alpha(\cdot), \tilde{G}_\sigma(\cdot - k)] = \int_{R^2} \hat{G}_\alpha(\gamma)\hat{\tilde{G}}_{\sigma_1}(\gamma)^* \cdot e^{ik\cdot\gamma} d\gamma$$

$$= \int_{R^2} \hat{G}_{a\alpha_1 + \lambda_1}(\gamma)\hat{\tilde{G}}_{a\beta_1 + \mu_1}(\gamma)^* \cdot \exp\{ik\cdot\gamma\} d\gamma = \cdots\cdots\cdots\cdots\cdots\cdots$$

$$= \int_{[0,2\cdot a^\kappa\pi]^2} \{\prod_{l=1}^{\kappa} \mathcal{Q}^{(\rho_l)}(\gamma/a^l)\} \cdot O \cdot \{\prod_{l=1}^{\kappa} \tilde{\mathcal{Q}}^{(\mu_l)}(\gamma/a^l)\}^* \cdot \exp\{-ik\cdot\gamma\} d\gamma = O.$$

Therefore, for any $\alpha, \sigma \in Z_+^2$, result (21) is established.

For any $v = (v_1, v_2) \in Z^2$, the translation operator S is defined to be $(S_{va}\lambda)(x) = \lambda(x - va)$, where a is a pasitive constant real number.

Theorem 3 [7]. Let $\phi(x), \tilde{\phi}(x), \hbar_l(x)$ and $\tilde{\hbar}_l(x), l \in J$ be functions in $L^2(R^2)$. Assume that conditions in Theorem 1 are satisfied. Then, for any function $f(x) \in L^2(R^2)$, and any integer n, we have

$$\sum_{u \in Z^2} \langle f, \tilde{\phi}_{n,u} \rangle \phi_{n,u}(x) = \sum_{l=1}^{7} \sum_{s=-\infty}^{n-1} \sum_{u \in Z^2} \langle f, \tilde{\hbar}_{l:s,u} \rangle \hbar_{l:s,u}(x). \tag{22}$$

References

1. Telesca, L., et al.: Multiresolution wavelet analysis of earthquakes. Chaos, Solitons & Fractals 22(3), 741–748 (2004)
2. Iovane, G., Giordano, P.: Wavelet and multiresolution analysis: Nature of ε^∞ Cantorian space-time. Chaos, Solitons & Fractals 32(4), 896–910 (2007)
3. Zhang, N., Wu, X.: Lossless Compression of Color Mosaic Images. IEEE Trans. Image Processing 15(16), 1379–1388 (2006)
4. Chen, Q., et al.: A study on compactly supported orthogo-nal vector-valued wavelets and wavelet packets. Chaos, Solitons & Fractals 31(4), 1024–1034 (2007)
5. Shen, Z.: Nontensor product wavelet packets in $L_2(R^2)$. SIAM Math. Anal. 26(4), 1061–1074 (1995)
6. Chen, Q., Qu, X.: Characteristics of a class of vector-valued nonseparable higher-dimensional wavelet packet bases. Chaos, Solitons & Fractals 41(4), 1676–1683 (2009)
7. Li, S., et al.: A Theory of Geeneralized Multiresolution Structure and Pseudoframes of Translates. J. Fourier Anal. Appl. 6(1), 23–40 (2001)
8. Chen, Q., Huo, A.: The research of a class of biorthogonal compactly supported vector-valued wavelets. Chaos, Solitons & Fractals 41(2), 951–961 (2009)

Research on New Tabu Search Algorithm for Min-Max Vehicle Routing Problem

Chunyu Ren

School of Information science and technology, Heilongjiang University,
15080 Harbin, China
rency2004@163.com

Abstract. In order to satisfy with the individual and various demand of customer, the present study is focused on the Min-Max Vehicle Routing Problem. According to the characteristics of model, new tabu search algorithm is used to get the optimization solution. It applies newly improved insertion method to construct initial solution, to improve the feasibility of the solution; centers the longest route to design dual layered random operation to construct its neighborhood, to realize the strategy of optimizing between and within the route, to boost the efficiency and quality of the searching. Applies auto adaptive tabu length to control the searching capability dynamically; At last, it uses simulated experiments to prove the effectiveness and feasibility of this algorithm, and provides clues for massively solving practical problems.

Keywords: MMVRP, new tabu search algorithm, improved insertion method, dual layered random operation, auto adaptive tabu length.

1 Introduction

In the recent years, with the development of the modern logistics, vehicle routing problem has received widespread attention. Optimizing the problem can increase economic efficiency of logistics distribution. When it comes to solve massive complicated problems, the intelligent algorithm has wider application. Yuvraj applied large-scale ant colony algorithm to solve VRPB [1]. Ai designed a particle swarm optimization algorithm based on multiple social structures to solve pickup-delivery problem [2].

In practice, there exists a type of problems, whose aim is not to demand the shortest distance of the whole route, but to demand the shortest distance of the longest sub route throughout the whole route, for which is called Min-Max Vehicle Routing Problem, MMVRP. Michael firstly solved the minimum boundary value of the objective function in MMVRP, and then used tabu search algorithm to get the solution [3]. Sema studied the school commuting bus MMVRP, and used the tabu search algorithm of the Cross and Or-opt Exchange Algorithm [4]. Arkin divided the n number of routes created by MMVRP into n number of sub regions of solving TSP problem and applied approximate algorithm to get the solution [5].

Considering the complexity of MMVRP, the essay proposed to apply new tabu search algorithm.

S. Lin and X. Huang (Eds.): CESM 2011, Part I, CCIS 175, pp. 79–84, 2011.

2 Mathematical Model

$$Z = Min\left\{ Max \sum_{i \in S} \sum_{j \in S} \sum_{k \in V} X_{ijk} d_{ij} \right\} \tag{1}$$

Constraints:

$$\sum_{i \in H} \sum_{j \in S} q_i X_{ijk} \leq W_k, \quad k \in V \tag{2}$$

$$\sum_{i \in S} X_{ijk} = Y_{ik}, \quad j \in S, \quad k \in V \tag{3}$$

$$\sum_{j \in S} X_{ijk} = Y_{ik}, \quad i \in S, \quad k \in V \tag{4}$$

$$\sum_{i \in S} \sum_{j \in S} x_{ijk} \leq |m| - 1, \quad \forall m \subseteq \{2,3...,n\}, \quad k \in V \tag{5}$$

In the formula: $G\{g_r|r=1,...R\}$ is a series of aggregations of distribution centre in the place R (this essay only has one); $H\{h_i|i=R+1,..R+N\}$ is a series of clients' aggregations in the place N ; $S\{G \} \cup \{H \}$ is the combination of all distribution centres and clients. $V\{v_k|k=1,..K\}$ is travel vehicle k 's aggregation; q_i is the demand amount of client $i(i \in H)$; W_k is travel vehicle k 's loading capacity; d_{ij} is the linear distance from client i to client j .

3 Parameter Design for Tabu Search Algorithm

3.1 The Formation of Initial Solution

Given h_k as the total number of client nodes served by vehicle k , aggregation $R_k = \{ y_{ik} | 0 \leq i \leq h_k \}$ to correspond the client nodes served by the number k vehicle, Y_{ik} signified that vehicle k served in node i , Y_{0k} signified that the number k vehicle's beginning point was distribution centre. The procedures as such:

Step1: Order vehicles' initial remaining load capacity: $w_k^1 = w_k$, $k = 0$, $h_k = 0$, $R_k = \Phi$;

Step2: The demand amount corresponding to the i client node in a route q_i , order $k = 1$;

Step3: if $q_i \leq w_k^1$, then order $w_k^1 = Min\{(w_k^1 - q_i), w_k\}$, if not turn to Step6;

Step4: if $w_k^1 - q_i \leq w_k$, and $D_{i-1} + D_i \leq D_k$; then $R_k = R_k \bigcup \{i\}$, $h_k = h_k + 1$ if not turn to Step6;

Step5: if $k > K$, then $k = K$, otherwise, $k = k$;

Step6: $k = k + 1$, turn to Step3;

Step7: $i = i + 1$, turn to Step2;

Step8: repeat Step2-7, K recorded the total used vehicles, R_k recorded a group of feasible routes.

3.2 Inner Neighborhood Operation

Specific procedures as such:

(1) 1-move

$1 - move$ is a heuristic algorithm the same as operators $(1, 0)$ and $(0, 1)$, which can effectively improve the quality of solutions and the feasibility of poor solutions.

(2) 2-opt

$k(i)$ signified the neighbor point of the client point i in the route l, and $a(i, j)$ signified to change the direction of the route from i to j. That was in the l route, the client points were: $(0,1,2,...,n,0)$, in it, 0 signified distribution centre. The procedures of the $2 - opt$ neighborhood operation were as such:

Step1: $i_1 := 1, i := 0$;

Step2: if $i > n - 2$, end; otherwise, turn to Step3;

Step3: revise $i_2 := k(i_1)$, $j_1 := k(i_2)$, $j := i + 2$;

Step4: if $j > n$, turn to Step8, if not, turn to Step5;

Step5: $j_2 := s(j_1)$, change route l as such (1) $a(i_2, j_1)$, (2) alternately used (i_1, j_1) and (i_2, j_2), substitute (i_1, i_2) and (j_1, j_2);

Step6: If the changed route l_1 is feasible, and better than l, revise l, if not, turn to Step7;

Step7: $j_1 := j_2$, $j := j + 1$, return to Step4;

Step8: $i_1 := i_2$, $i := i + 1$, return to Step2.

3.3 Outer Neighborhood Operation

(1) 2-opt*

That is in the route l, the client points are $(0,1,2,...,n,0)$, in the route k, the client points are $(0,1,2,...,m,0)$, in it, 0 signifies distribution centre.

Step1: Randomly choose n number of client points in the route l, for each client point i, choose client point j nearby the route k, if exist, exchange chains $(i, i+1), (j, j+1)$;

Step2: Conduct $2 - opt$ neighborhood operation in the exchanged routes l^1 and k^1, to obtain feasible solution;

Step3: Calculate the exchanged objective function f^1, if $f^1 > f$, turn to Step4; if not, turn to Step5;

Step4: If the current optimal solution does not exist in the tabu list, update tabu list, input the obtained optimal solution into the tabu list, simultaneously remove out the ban-lifted elements; otherwise, turn to Step5;

Step5: $i = i+1$, turn to Step1;

Step6: repeat Step1- 5, till the current optimal solution can not update.

3.4 Adaptive Tabu Length

In order to ensure effectiveness of the tabu list, during the whole process of searching, make L_{min}, L_{max} as its variable region $\left[a\sqrt{N}, b\sqrt{N}\right]$, in it $0 < a < b$. So the tabu length L's variable scope is the formula as the following:

$$L = \lambda L_{min} + (1-\lambda)L_{max} \qquad (6)$$

In the formula, L_{min} and L_{max} are the upper and lower bound of tabu length L's dynamic change respectively, N refers to the number of clients, the weighing coefficient is $0 \le \lambda \le 1$.

4   Experimental Calculation and Result Analysis

Example One: The data originates from Document [6]. There are one depot and 20 client nodes, the coordinates and demand amount of each node is created randomly, as indicated in table 1; give six vehicles of the same type, and the load capacity is 8.

Table 1. Known condition of examples

Item	coordinate	Distribution amount	Item	coordinate	Distribution amount
0	(52,4)	0			
1	(15,49)	1.64	11	(24,89)	2.35
2	(0,61)	1.31	12	(19,25)	2.60
3	(51,15)	0.43	13	(20,99)	1.00
4	(25,71)	3.38	14	(73,91)	0.65
5	(38,62)	1.13	15	(100,95)	0.85
6	(35,45)	3.77	16	(7,73)	2.56
7	(100,4)	3.84	17	(69,86)	1.27
8	(10,52)	0.39	18	(24,3)	2.69
9	(26,79)	0.24	19	(66,14)	3.26
10	(87,7)	1.03	20	(9,30)	2.97

4.1   Solution of New Tabu Search Algorithm

This algorithm adopts the following parameters as part. The maximum iterative times are max_ *iter* =500, tabu length is $\alpha = 2$, $\beta = 3$, $\lambda = 0.6$, and candidate solution

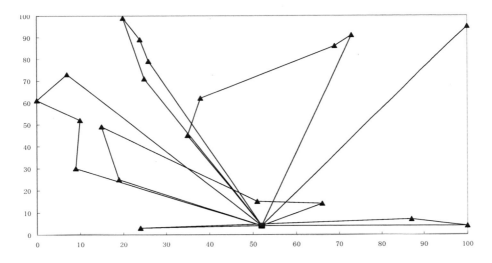

Fig. 1. Optimization route of MMVRP using new tabu search algorithm

Table 2. Optimal results by new tabu search algorithm

Line No.	Running Path	Mileage
1	0-16-2-8-20-0	181.416
2	0-9-11-13-4-0	201.293
3	0-18-10-7-0	152.486
4	0-6-5-17-14-0	196.754
5	0-15-0	205.767
6	0-12-1-3-19-0	145.202
The Total Mileage	1082.918 km	
Average Mileage	180.486	
The longest line	205.767	

amount is 50. Here, the longest line is 205.767 km, the corresponding optimal total length of 1082.918 km. The concrete route can be seen in table 2 and figure 1.

4.2 Analysis on Three Algorithms

Compared the optimal scheme of reference [6], the proposed new tabu search algorithm has a strong search capability, high computational efficiency.

Table 3. Comparison among GA, TS and Algorithm of this study

	GA	TS	NTS
The Total Mileage	1106.237	1095.136	1083.411
Average Mileage	184.373	182.523	180.5685
The longest line	205.767	205.767	205.767

5 Conclusions

Therefore, it is more practical significance and value so as to reduce operating cost and improve economic benefit.

Acknowledgment

This paper is supported by project of Heilongjiang Provincial Education Department of Science & Technology (No. 11551332).

References

1. Gajpal, Y., Abad, P.L.: Multi-ant colony system (MACS) for a vehicle routing problem with backhauls. European Journal of Operational Research 196, 102–117 (2009)
2. Ai, T.J., Kachitvichyanukul, V.: A particle swarm optimization for the vehicle routing problem with simultaneous pickup and delivery. Computers and Operations Research 36, 1693–1702 (2009)
3. Serna, C.R.D., Bonrostro, J.P.: Minmax vehicle routing problems: application to school transport in the province of Burgos (Spain). In: International Conference on Computer-aided Scheduling of Public Transport, vol. 505, pp. 297–317 (2000)
4. Molloy, M., Reed, B.: A Bound on the Strong Chromatic Index of a Graph. Journal of Combinatorial Theory, Series B 69, 103–109 (1997)
5. Arkin, E.M., Hassin, R., Levin, A.: Approximations for minimum and min-max vehicle routing problems. Algorithms Archive 59, 1–18 (2006)
6. Xia, L.: Research on Vehicle Routing Problem. PhD thesis of Huazhong University of Science and Technology, pp. 24–44 (2007)

Application of Measurement and Control Technology of Digital for the Power Inverter

Huanqi Tao and Yuchuan Wu

College of Electronics and Information Engineering,
Wuhan Textile University, Wuhan, China
taohq@163.com, wychuan007@qq.com

Abstract. The inverters control technology becomes a research hotspot, because the inverter is a important equipment, which connects the photovoltaic grid-connected system and the grid. In this paper, the structure and the principle of the photovoltaic grid-connected system were introduced in brief, then the control scheme and its digital implementation were analyzed in detail. then practical significance and developmental prospect to the technology based on digitalization about power converter are described in detail; and new direction of study is explored for the development about electrical engineering discipline and application of the technology about solar energy.

Keywords: grid-connected inverter, photovoltaic, measurement and control technology, digital signal processing, electrical engineering.

1 Introduction

With the continuous exploitation and consumption of fossil energy, and the ramatic changes in global climate, Human beings are even more conscious of the importance and the urgency of the development of clean energy. In a variety of the clean energy among, Solar energy is the most widely used of clean energy, Solar power station is the 21st century's most promising renewable energy one of the ways. However, the original form of solar cells are the DC power supply, to achieve with the existing communication network consistent with a common, unified power supply, must go through a transformation process, to achieve a wide range of applications. therefore, The major components of sunlight power plant, including solar cell matrix, batteries, inverter and control of detection devices, one of the inverter system and its control technology is an important research content and direction for the application of solar energy [1].

2 Power Conversion Technology and Inverter

Power conversion technologies, including two directions: First, AC to DC power supply technology for mobile devices to provide AC or DC power supply, such as the various battery charging control, a direct impact on battery life and efficiency; II is the DC power into AC power of technology: for example, photovoltaic solar energy is

S. Lin and X. Huang (Eds.): CESM 2011, Part I, CCIS 175, pp. 85–91, 2011.

converted to AC power control technology, often referred to as inverter technology that transform, the mapping device known as the inverter. Overall, both the AC-DC or DC-AC, are different according to the need to convert AC or DC power supply specifications into a unified form. Because all the advantages of AC power, making it the most electricity in the form of electrical equipment uniform. Therefore, the power conversion technology mainly refers to the DC power into AC power inverter technology, to adapt to different forms of energy require the use of uniform in a variety of power supply voltage electrical equipment, as well as flexibility for grid transmission and distribution power. With the increase in energy demand and solar energy, inverters and inverter technology becomes more and more important[2]. Can be said to a variety of power conversion technology is a solar photovoltaic energy in particular, an important link in energy utilization. Based on this, on the converter and inverter technology, the basic requirements are: the power supply at the same time, to improve and enhance the power of the power factor; to improve and enhance the ability of anti-electromagnetic interference, reducing harmonic pollution; lower conversion loss, improve efficiency (high efficiency); reduce manufacturing costs, reduce size and weight; improve stability and reliability. The 5 aspects of the basic requirements for the technology we provide a broad research topic.

3   Status of the Inverter

With the development of technology and the increasing energy demand in recent years, power conversion technology has also been rapid development. The following application status of the inverter for a brief introduction.

3.1   Solar Photovoltaic Power Stations with the Characteristics of the Inverter

Inverter solar photovoltaic power station, power supply and power electronics has become a hot research topic industry. As shown in Figure 1. Solar PV power plant has three inverter characteristics different from other inverters.

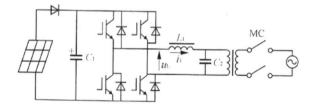

Fig. 1. Solar PV Inverter

First, high efficiency: It is now commonly used in photoelectric conversion efficiency of solar cell matrix <15%, very low, if the inverter efficiency is low, the solar cells convert to the power loss finally out, a great pity, therefore, required inverter high efficiency. Otherwise, the matrix must increase the number of solar modules, increasing the area occupied by matrix, thus greatly increasing the solar photovoltaic power plant investment in equipment and civil charges. Therefore, the following general requirements 10kVA inverter efficiency to> 90%, 10kVA inverter efficiency is more than "95%.

Second, small waveform distortion high power factor: and grid solar power plant output to be associated with the external power grid, the inverter output waveform must be consistent with the external power grid. Requirements of the waveform distortion <5%, high harmonic content of "3%, power factor close to 1. Independent inverter solar power stations can be larger waveform distortion (<10%), but, in order to reduce transmission line losses, and hope the waveform close to sinusoidal, power factor close to 1, to reduce reactive power consumption [3], [4].

Third, the use of high: the majority required for stand-alone solar power plants in remote mountainous areas and islands, requiring the inverter can withstand relatively harsh conditions of use, while ensuring maintenance of conditions in a small amount of long-term work. Because most solar power plants and grid for the family, requiring a small inverter electromagnetic interference, does not affect people's living environment, does not prevent the normal operation of other appliances.

3.2 Uninterruptible Power Supply UPS Inverter Characteristics

Off-line UPS in the inverter, a small power (5kVA below) mainly, as shown in Figure 2. Mainly mains filtering, voltage adjustment, in order to provide a more stable load voltage, through the charger into chemical energy into electrical energy stored in the battery, the event of a power interruption, the grid voltage or grid frequency is outside the inverter input range can be in a very short time (few ms) opened its reserve power, power to the load, the inverter is characterized by such a high conversion efficiency, easy maintenance and low prices, for the vast majority of small and medium-power users power protection choice.

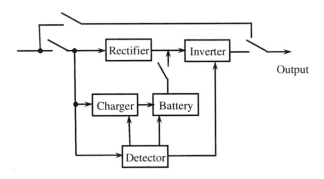

Fig. 2. UPS inverter

In-line UPS to the power inverter (5kVA and above) the main inverter is always in working condition, and electrical equipment to run, in the power supply's main function is to state regulation and to prevent voltage fluctuations and interference, to avoid low-quality long-term electricity load has been an infringement, once the electricity interruption, the inverter will use the machine provided by the battery power to maintain the normal operation of the load, power conversion time is zero, truly non-stop for electricity. Inverter type of high quality, but expensive.

Online interactive with the main inverter to the network, which combines off-line power supply with high efficiency and high quality features, and off-line inverter switching time is short compared to[5].

In short, the uninterruptible power supply UPS's inverter should be included in the traditional sense of the following links and features: power in a variety of complex operating environment; in the operation will not generate additional electricity interference; output performance indicators should be is a comprehensive, high quality, and that can meet the requirements of the load; inverter itself should have a high efficiency, close to the actual output of electricity capacity; is a high degree of intelligence equipment, a highly intelligent self-test function automatically display, alarm, status memory, and communications functions; inverter not only by its direct power supply to the various hardware devices to provide comprehensive protection, in the Internet age, they should also be run to the software and data transmission means to provide safe and reliable protection, configure the power monitoring software, with remote management capabilities to enable users to perform network management platform inverter and monitoring and data communication between the operations.

3.3 Emergency Power Supply System (EPS) Inverter Characteristics

Emergency Power Supply System (EPS) has been widely used in construction of electrical fields and special occasions, emergency power, known as the "urban lifeline systems," the important part.. As shown in Figure 3. One of the main design idea is the inverter power suddenly interrupted in the city to provide safe and reliable emergency power supply to avoid a disaster when the personal injury and property damage as a principle. Therefore, the inverter should focus on its safety, reliability, applicability and reasonableness.

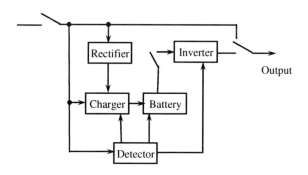

Fig. 3. EPS inverter

Main features are:

Power conversion time is usually in milliseconds (25ms), in order to ensure timeliness of supply; load adaptability, including capacitive, inductive, mixed load, overload and impact resistance and strong;

More output, the failure to prevent the output of a single formation; the fire linkage and remote control signals, can be manual and automatic conversion; environmental adaptability for a variety of harsh environments, to prevent high and low temperature, humidity, salt spray, dust , vibration and rat-bite and other measures;

Long life, fast charging the battery capacity and management capacity; energy saving, high efficiency, low operating costs; no smoke, no noise, pollution, etc.; maintenance is simple, low maintenance costs;

There unattended, automatic operation; alarm complete, timely provision of a variety of abnormal conditions of the police; a strong start, to avoid the protected link fails to start after the battery [6].

In summary, the inverter technology to solve the problem now is still the efficiency, cost, performance, quality, volume, and to adapt to harsh conditions.

4 Inverter Technology Trends and Requirements

As the energy consumption requirements, people will seek all possible energy sources, despite the inverter technology which is not wholly satisfactory, but there are broad prospects and needs.

Improve energy supply and demand, need the support of the power inverter technology.

With the increasing demands of social life, people need a stable, safe and reliable power supply, power inverter technology needed for security.

With the increasing environmental pressures, the need for different forms of clean energy, which also requires inverter technologies.

The face of sudden disasters and accidents, will have to minimize damage and emergency rescue facilities are available. Power inverter technology also need to support [7]. Such as the 2003 blackouts in North America a large area to need to be a large number of inverters.

5 Power of Digital Measurement and Control Technology Transform the Content and Prospects

5.1 Measurement and Control Technology of Digital Content

Measurement and control technology of digital power conversion, including the following aspects, each side is also can contain a number of topics:

Digital conversion and control of the maximum power output; Digital Inverter adjustment, automatic power factor improvement; digital inverter fault diagnosis and maintenance; digital power of information transmission and human-computer interaction network [8].

5.2 Digital Control Technology Prospects

Control of digital power conversion technology research for the discipline of electrical engineering and the development of opening up new research directions.

Traditional electrical engineering, are concentrated in the power system generation, distribution and electricity and so-called high power applications. Study of digital power conversion, digital control of power opens up new fields of technology, the traditional expertise and modern digital information technologies for power transmission of information, weak control the strong power to find a new starting point, and promote the continuous development of disciplines, with broad prospects.

Promote the study of new electronic components; for new control methods and technology research, such as fuzzy control and chaos control; promoting a new integrated circuit design and research; open up new directions for training professionals and broaden the application of electrical engineering basis and scope, thereby contributing to improving the overall quality of students; for electrical engineering curriculum updates and improvements: such as "Power Electronics", "switching power supply technology", "power electronics" and other courses to add new content will be directly .

5.3 Digital Control Technology Application Projects

Control of digital power conversion technology for solar photovoltaic projects and future applications of new energy sources play an important role.

Digital Control of the results of application projects for the photovoltaic project to provide technical support; to future talent needs of PV projects provide an effective guarantee and order services; life scenarios for the future needs of the power supply providing power inverter, such as roof type, construction and decoration embedded, portable, intelligent power converter.

6 Conclusion

The solar photovoltaic power generation in the 21st century's most promising clean energy sources, its control and conversion technology has become the science and technology, extensive research hotspot, the digital control will be the most promising development in the technology direction, in promoting the application of clean energy will play an important role.

Acknowledgment

This work was supported by Hubei Province Clean Development Mechanism (CDM) service center support; Got also the careful guidance of CESM expert group; Authors thank them for their help. Even more thank all the members of the project team.

References

1. Wang, L., He, X.: Comparison and Analysis Among Control Methods for UPS. Power Supply Technology Application 8(1), 46–50 (2005)
2. Huang, S.: Power Supply on the Arc Welder and Digital Control of Power. China machine press, Beijing (2007)

3. Wang, F., Wu, S., Xu, J., et al.: Modeling and Simulation of V2 Controlled Switching Converters. In: International Conference on Communications Circuijts and Systems, vol. (11), pp. 613–617 (2003)
4. Chen, Y., Zhang, W., Zhou, J., et al.: Summarize of Control Technology based on Power Converter. Electrotechnical Application (4), 4–9 (2008)
5. Feng, G., Meyer, E., Liu, Y.: High Performance Digital Control Algorithms for DC-DC Converters based on the Principle of Capacitor Charge Balance. In: 37th IEEE Power Electronics Conference of PESC 2006 (2006)
6. Jidin, A.b., Idris, N.R.N., Senior Member: Sliding Mode Variable Structure Control Design Principles and Application to DC Drives. In: Power and Energy Conference, pp. 78–82 (2004)
7. Yang, J., Chai, L.: Application and Development of Digital Technology in Switching Power Supply Control. Power World (2), 6–8 (2006)
8. He, M., Xu, J., Hu, X.: Digital Controller of DC-DC Switching Converters based on FPGA. Power Electronics 41(6), 71–73 (2007)

The Design of Image Process Software of Dispensing Systems

Lianjun Hu[1], Guixu Chen[2,3], Xiaohui Zeng[2], and Hong Song[2]

[1] School of Mechanical Engineering, Sichuan University of Science & Engineering, 643000,
Zigong, China
[2] School of Automation and Electronic Information Engineering, Sichuan University of Science
& Engineering, 643000, Zigong, China
[3] Shaxian Power supply corporation of Fujian province, 365500, Fujian, China
{hlj28288,cgx8287,sh8887878}@sina.com, xh-z@sohu.com

Abstract. Most kinetic control systems available domestically, such as dispensing systems, do not have image processing functions. In the paper, image process software based on VB language and MATLAB language is designed, and it is used successfully on a dispensing test system. Degree of automation can be improved through two functions of the software. One is whether coordinates are correct or not can be determined from images. The other is real coordinates from encoders can be read automatically through the image processing. Experiments show the validity of the image process software.

Keywords: Dispensing system, VB, Image process, MATLAB.

1 Introduction

Kinetic control systems as independent industrial automation control products have been accepted at more and more domains. Enormous amount of monies are put into by governments and large-scale enterprises for developing their own kinetic control systems [1]. After developments of many years, as for dispensing systems, techniques of produces has improved greatly at home, but there are still distances compared with produces abroad. Moreover, kinetic control systems of dispensing systems available at home and abroad have no image process functions. Therefore, a solution of image processing software based on VB and MATLAB language is proposed in the paper.

2 Hybrid Programming of VB Software and MATLAB

There are mainly four interface methods between VB programs and MATLAB programs: dynamic data exchange technologies, ActiveX technologies, Matrx VB technologies import and COM technologies import.

   (1) Dynamic data exchange technologies. Communications between Microsoft Window application programs are allowed by exchanging data. Dynamic data exchange technologies can not work out of MATLAB environments.

S. Lin and X. Huang (Eds.): CESM 2011, Part I, CCIS 175, pp. 92–97, 2011.
© Springer-Verlag Berlin Heidelberg 2011

(2) ActiveX technologies. MATLAB programs can be called as ActiveX parts of VB programs through ActiveX interfaces. ActiveX technologies can not work out of MATLAB environments either.

(3) Import Matrx VB technologies. Matrx VB is MABLAB library files for VB languages provided by Math Works. The advantage is that it can work out of MATLAB environments. But because it is a third-party control, it can be acquired only by purchase with limited functions.

(4) Import COM technologies. COM technologies are object models released based on modules. These kinds of object models make modules called by VB language to communicate under a uniform mode. By using own COM Builder tool of MATLAB software, M files can be transferred to COM modules, which are modules in processes of computers and are stored in DLL format that can be called directly in VB programs.

Because the system software is integrated in a PC, VB languages are used to develop application programs along with COM technologies.

3 Architecture of the Software Platform

MATLAB COM modules are called by VB programs to accomplish interfacing tasks of the system. Channels between VB program modules and MATLAB program modules are established through COM modules, and communications between modules are also carried on through COM modules. The architecture of the software platform includes VB visual interface, M files (algorithms), COM modules and image display four parts, as shown in figure 1. Images acquired from a CCD camera are sent into computers and captured by ezVidCap modules of the VB software. And images are displayed on a VB visual interface after image processing by M-file algorithms of COM modules [2].

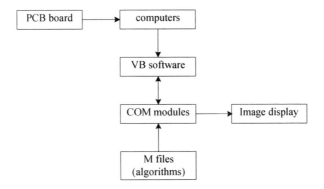

Fig. 1. Basic structure of the software

4   The Design and Call of COM Modules

4.1   M-File Algorithm Programming

The algorithm function file is programmed in the MATLAB M-file editor with one
input parameter and saved as jc.m file.

```
function [a,b,c,d]=myfind(r)
  I=imread(r);
  I1=im2double(I);
  I2=rgb2gray(I1);
  [thr,sorh,keepapp]=ddencmp('den','wv',I2);
  I3=wdencmp('gbl',I2,'sym4',2,thr,sorh,keepapp);
  I4=medfilt2(I3,[9 9]);
  I5=imresize(I4,0.2,'bicubic');
  ss=edge(I5,'sobel');
  figure;
  subplot(1,3,1);
  imshow(ss);
  title('SobelËã×Ó');
  [m,n]=find(ss==1);
  a=m(1)
  b=m(2)
  c=m(3)
```

4.2   The Creation of COM Modules

COM Builder is a COM builder provided by MATLAB software which can transfer
M-file algorithms into independent COM modules [3]. Objects built can be used under any developing environment which supports COM objects. A COM module could
involve many classes and each class can include many M files. Class files will be
after compiling of M files.

Fig. 2. Project naming dialog

Compiling steps of COM modules by MATLAB software are as followings.

① Create a project.

② Add M files into the project.

③ compile modules. Command mbuild – setup is inputted in MATLAB command window for selecting compiling tools. MATLAB COM Builder is started by inputting command Comtool. Select "File→New Project" in COM Builder and set option "Component Name" with PCB to create PCB class automatically, as shown in figure 2. If MATLAB graphics library is needed, select option "Create a singleton MCR". Properties sets of modules is as shown in figure 3. If files are needed to be added into a project, then select "Project→AddFile" of PCB at the left side of the workspace, and select compiled M file jc.m. An object file is built and PCB _1_0.DLL module is

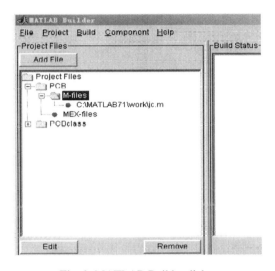

Fig. 3. MATLAB Builder dialog

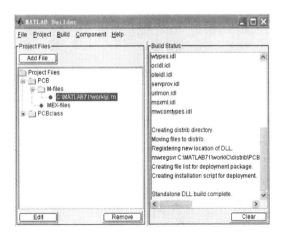

Fig. 4. MATLAB Builder dialog

outputted by selecting option "COMObject" of option "Build". Information of version, methods, properties, events and interfaces of the module built are as shown in figure 4.

4.3 The Call of COM Modules

Create a new project under VisualBasic environment. Select "project→references" at the menu bar. PCB 1.0 type library is added into the reference list. And then PCB-1-0.DLL module can be called in Visual Basic programs. Partial call program codes of COM modules in the VB program is as followings.

```
Private Sub Command1_Click()
  Dim gh As PCB.PCB
  Set gh = New PCB.PCB
  Call gh.jc(4, a, b, c, d, App.Path & "\jlsy.jpg")
  x = (a + b + c + d) \ 4
  Print a
  Print vbCrLf
  Print b
  Print vbCrLf
  Print c
  Print vbCrLf
  Print d
  Print vbCrLf
  Print x
  Print vbCrLf
End Sub
```

Simulated image jlsy.jpg of the PCB board is placed under the install catalogue of the VB software, which provides a way for dispensing position identification in a real environment afterwards. A button with Caption property "image processing" is placed on the VB interface. Sobels operator [4] is mainly used in the processing of images. Processing impressions can be obtained if the image processing button is pushed, as shown in figure 5.

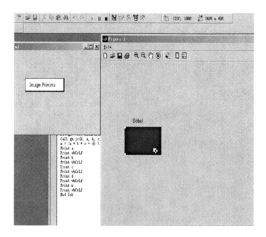

Fig. 5. Running result of the software

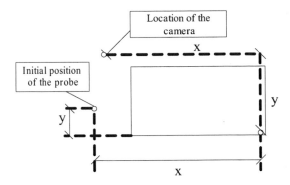

Fig. 6. Camera location

The result of calling COM modules can be seen clearly in the figure 5. The average vertical ordinate of simulated PCB images is 11. Therefore, real positions can be calculated by certain proportions. In my research, positions can be obtained through PCB board simulating method under an ideal environment. Because PCB boards are fixed on X-Y workbenches in real dispensing environments, PCB boards will move when X-Y workbenches move and CCD cameras are fixed in installations, as shown in figure 6. Hence, real positions can be obtained.

In position-settings, buttons of the upper computer is operated and X-Y workbench moves to the position set. At the same time, the camera is opened and the current position is captured. Finally, image processing button is pushed. Therefore, it can be told whether the position of the dispensing is at the center of the image. If the position is out of areas allowed, the position should be adjusted to its presets in order to ensure the accuracy of the dispensing.

5 Conclusion

The image process software designed has been used successfully in multi-axis kinetic control systems, through which the automatic level of dispensing systems has been improved greatly. The software can also be used in similar kinetic control systems with certain market value.

References

1. Shen, Z.: The Research on Performances of A Dispensing Control System in Microelectronics Encapsulation. Master's Thesis of Huazhong University of Science and Technology (2005)
2. Meng, L., Yang, Q.: The Realization of Mixing Programming of VB and MATLAB with COM Modules Development and Application of Computers, 24–26 (2008)
3. Jiang, L.: The Realization of COM Modules with MATLAB language. Microcomputer Applications, 275–277 (2007)
4. Liu, Z., Zhang, S.: The Detection of Screw Thread Based on Digital Image Processing Technologies, 66–68 (2006)
5. Chen, X., Zhang, X.: Measurements of Center Distances Sleeves, Balls and Chain-guides Based on Image Processing Technologies 36, 105–107 (2008)

Research of SOAP Message Security Model on Web Services

Shujun Pei and Deyun Chen

Computer Science and Technology
Harbin University of Science and Technology
150080 Harbin, China
peisj@hrbust.edu.cn, chendy@hrbust.edu.cn

Abstract. Based on .NET platform, the paper researches the security of Web services and presents the methods of implementation. A Web Services Security model is brought forward based on .NET platform with the use of its security mechanism and WS-Security specification. The methods of identification, digital signature, encryption and decryption, SOAP information authority are given, the problems of the end to end SOAP information security between applicants and offers are solved, and its secrecy, integrity, non-negation, identity identification and authority are ensured.

Keywords: End to End, SOAP Message, Web Services Security, .NET Platform.

1 Introduction

The rapid development of information technology requires higher security of information system. As the Internet has created an ideal space for information transmission, the security of network is becoming more and more important. Among them, for some special industries or important departments, their Web service security is a critical and complex problem. Their security system requires detailed planning, and the site administrators and programmers must have a clear understanding of how to ensure the security of the site and service.

For message-based architecture, the industry has got a set of ready-made and widely accepted transport-layer security mechanisms. The existing security mechanisms can not provide adequate security within the Web service model due to lack of end to end protection, non-repudiation, selective protection, flexible authentication and protection of message level. On the basis of .NET platform, this paper puts forward a Web service security model which is on .NET platform, giving the implementation methods by taking advantages of security mechanism and WS-Security specification of .NET platform.

S. Lin and X. Huang (Eds.): CESM 2011, Part I, CCIS 175, pp. 98–104, 2011.
© Springer-Verlag Berlin Heidelberg 2011

2   Status Analysis of Web Service Security

Key capability of Web service is to provide an integrated, comprehensive, interactive, and easily integrated solution. Currently, SSL (Secure Socket Layer) and TLS (Transport Layer Security) is used to provide Web services security in transport layer. SSL/TLS in point to point session can complete such requests, including auditing, data integrity, and confidentiality. IPSec in network layer is an important standard for Web service security. Similarly with SSL/TLS, it also provides host audit authentication, data integrity and data confidentiality functions. Since SSL/TLS is a point to point security transmission solving solution, while for the end to end security transmission solving solution, many standardization organizations, companies and research institutions home or abroad all research XML-based security standards of Web Services. Currently, the proposed XML security agreements are: XML Digital Signature, XML Encryption, SAML (Security Assertion Markup Language), XACML (Extensible Access Control Markup Language), XML Key Management Specification, SOAP security extensions, etc. Apart from these XML security protocols, the most authoritative and comprehensive security problem of Web service was Web service security specifications/WS-Security which was jointly put forward by Microsoft, IBM, and VeriSian Company in Apr. 2002. This is a mechanism that can guarantee the safe exchange of SOAP message. WS-Security particularly describes the enhancement to the existing SOAP information transmission, providing protection level by recognizing the application integrity of SOAP information, message confidentiality and single message authentication. These basic mechanisms can be combined in various ways to build multiple security models that used a variety of encryption technologies. WS-Security is primarily a standard in XML-based secure metadata container, having secure sockets layer SSL(Secure Socket Layer) , XML Encryption, XML Signature [1,2].

WS-Security specification itself neither proposes a new encryption algorithm or security model, nor provides a complete security solution, so WS-Security itself does not guarantee safety. It merely provides a framework; users are freely to combine Web service protocol, application layer protocol, a variety of encryption and security model to achieve message integrity, confidentiality and message authentication under Web service environment. Achieved WS-Security does not mean that an application system will not be attacked, nor means that security will not be threatened.

Therefore, factors that will possible affect the security of Web service are: how to identify the identification of communication parties (personal identification and verification); how to send message without seen by unauthorized person, or get (data confidentiality); how to ensure that the message received has not been modified (data integrity); how to ensure legitimate users to operate within a specified range (authorization and access control); how to ensure that the sender can not deny he send the message (undeniable).

3 Web Service Security Model Framework of .NET Platform

To ensure the security of Web service, the core is to ensure the security of transmitted information, the security of SOAP. Encrypt SOAP and having it digitally signature processed is a way to protect its safety. The appearance of WS-Security standard offers a good solution to the extension of SOAP information [3], the encryption of SOAP information, signature and carrying security token. Therefore, this paper put forward .NET platform-based Web service security model by security mechanism of .NET platform on the basis of WS-Security specification and extended SOAP standard protocol. The model is shown in Fig 1.

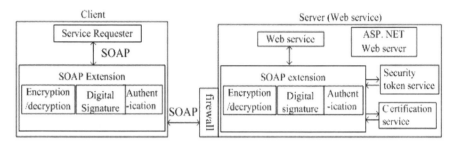

Fig. 1. Web Service Security Model Framework of .NET Platform

1) The Client adds to SOAP message extended head by encrypt SOAP message and digital signature;

2) SOAP message with encrypted data can be transmitted to server by any means of transmission; its security is independent of transmission protocol;

3) Server get the encrypted data from SOAP message to decrypt or digitally signature them to achieve message integrity, message confidentiality and single message authentication and other functions;

WS-Security specification describes enhancement function of SOAP messaging. These functions provide message integrity, message confidentiality, and single message authentication:

1) Authentication is provided by the security token in SOAP header. WS-Security specification dose not require the use of any particular type of token. Security tokens can include Kerberos tickets, X.509 certificate, or a custom binary token;

2) Secure communication is provided through digital signatures to ensure message integrity, and using XML encryption to ensure message confidentiality;

4 Implementation of Web Service Security Model Based .NET

There are many tools to achieve WS-Security specification, among which WSE (Web Services Enhancement) of Microsoft is the most excellent one. This chapter uses WSE2.0 development tool of Microsoft to achieve this security model on message level.

4.1 WSE2.0 Introduction

WSE is also the extension of supporting .NET Framework. It is used to create and use Web service, while WSE2.0 adopt new programming model. In the past, Web service support depends on Internet Information Server (IIS) as its host HTTP server; now, WSE 2.0 supports sending messages through TCP/IP or within the process [4,5]. In this way, you can send message from server to client through a peer, one-way, asynchronous method.

4.2 Implementation of Web Service Security Model

Using WSE to achieve the encryption and decryption of SOAP message and the signature principle; the encrypted SOAP message get to the server through transmission channel and decrypt and verify the signature there. Shown in Fig 2.

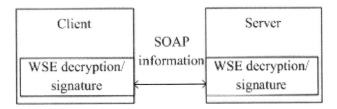

Fig. 2. Decryption and Signature of Soap Message

Implementation Method of Authentication with Username and Password. WS-Security defines a Username Token element, which provides the basic user name/password authentication method. It can send user name and password credentials in SOAP header information. Credentials are sent as a part of <Security> element in SOAP header. The client add Username-Token with a user name and password (clear text or encryption) in SOAP through SOAP extension and send it to Web server; after receiving the message, it also gets the user name and password from context through extension and then authenticate or doing other operations[6]. The following are the experimental procedures:
Client:

   1) Add Microsoft.Web.Services reference;
   2) Add Web reference to generate the local proxy class;
   3) Modify local proxy class generated from Web service reference, code of this class is in reference generation files. To open the Web service reference folder in solution explorer that lies at the right side of .NET development environment, opening up Reference. Map node, finding the Reference file and open it; to change the inherit parent of class into Microsoft.Web.Services.WebService Client Protocol at the statement of proxy class. Thus, proxy class can visit SOAP extension provided by WSE. If you update the Web service reference, you need to re-modify the inherit class;
   4) Add username and password through Username Token. Username Token belongs to Microsoft. Web.Services.Security. Tokens namespace;

Suppose a user name is Username, the user password is Userpwd, and then the code is as follows:

```
//generate the local proxy class instance dns Client
Localhost.DNSLookupService ();
//generate UsernameToken class instance, write the user
name,user password and the password sending means in
instances
Username Token untoken = new UsernameToken (Username,
Userpwd, PasswordOption.SendPlaintext);
//to set a term of validity for SOAP message to reduce
the possibility that the message is intercepted and used
by another user. Here it is set 60s, but we should pay
attention to the clock synchronization of different
system
DnsClient.RequestSoapContext.Security.Timestamp.TtlinSe
conds=60;
//to add the UsernameToken (the instance) into the
context of SOAP message
dnsClinet.RequestSoapContext,Security.Tokens.Add
(untoken);
//call the Web service, assuming the submitted domain
name is txtDNSName
String returnText= dnsClient.UsernameSay.Hello();
String          returnIPAddress=dnsClient.GetIPforHostname
(txtDNSName);
Server:
```

1) Firstly, add configured WSE element in configuration file Web.Config of Web service, this is the basic step of using WSE by the system developed by .NET platform. The following is the complete configuration file:

```
<Configuration>
<System.Web>
<WebServices>
<SoapExtensionTypes>
<addtype=Microsoft.Web.Services.WebServicesExtension,
Microsoft.Web.Services.Version=2.0.0.0,Culture=neutral,
PublicKeydtoken=3lbf3856ad364e350,priority=10,group=00>
</SoapExtensiontypes>
</WebServices>
</System.Web>
</Configuration>
```

2) Authentication action of configuration server.

The SOAP message sent from client has been added user's information; the work of server is to analyze it out, to compare and verify according to certain rules and return to result.

Method of SOAP Message Signature with Username and Password. The process mentioned above achieved the identification of Web service, but it can't guarantee that the SOAP message Web service received is the very one sent by declared user. Therefore, in practical use, the caller needs to signature on SOAP message and send the signature out together with message: after receiving the message, apart from authenticating the users, the server needs to do a certification to the signature, so as to make sure that the message has not been changed when transmitted, and the users be authenticated are those who signature on messages.

Client:

It only needs to add signature to the original SOAP message. The code is as follows:

```
DnsClient.RepuestSoapContext.Security.Tokens.Add
(untoken);
dnsClient.RepuestSoapContext.Security.Elements.Add(newM
essageSignature (untoken));
// call Web service
String return Text = dnsClient.UsernameSayHello();
String    returnIPAddress    =    dnsClient.GetIPforHostname
(txtDNSName);
```

The code mentioned above is a signature generated according to Username Token, and then to add the signature into SOAP message. Specifically, it is the SOAP header extended by WS-Security.

Server:

Firstly, server authenticates the username and password, then to authenticate the signature by using the username transmitted by Client and its password (WSE automatically obtained from the Windows Active Directory, or by the overloading the Authenticate Token). If the validation fails, it means that message is changed during transmission process or is not signed by the current calling user, returning to the corresponding error.

Methods of SOAP Encryption and Decryption with Username and Password. We've mentioned above, if the password of Username Token is express, then it is better to encrypt the Username Token. To change the code of client as follows:

```
dnsClient.RepuestSoapContext.Security.Tokens.Add
(untoken);
dnsClient.RepuestSoapContext.Security.Elements.Add
(newMicrosoft.Web.Services.Security.encryptedData
(untoken));
//call the Web service
String returnText = dnsClient.UsernameSayHello ();
 String   returnIPAddress   =   dnsClient.GetIPforHostname
(txtDNSName);
```

The code mentioned above is the user to encrypt the SOAP message according to Username Token and then add the cipher text in SOAP message, specifically, it is SOAP header extended by WS-Security.

The server automatically decrypts the message server. Server first validates the username/password and then decrypt data by using the username which delivered by server and the password (WSE automatically obtained from the Windows Active Directory, or by the overloading the Authenticate Token) it acquired. If failed, it returns the corresponding mistakes.

The Realization of SOAP Security Based on Role. The authority supports two security token: Username and Kerberos Token. When the server receives a SOAP message that signed with security token, WSE check this security token to determine the identity of the sender. If the check is passed, then create a Windows commission (Principal) authorization, and award the Token with the Principal attribute. Using Principal properties, code of Web service can determine whether the given role is qualified to execute all or part of the Web service method. The code is omitted.

5 Conclusion

In practical use, network complexity, variability and vulnerability of information system determines the security of Web service is of great significance of information transmission. To imitate implementation message-level Web service security model by using WSE, through a calling domain service instance. It gives the implementation method and data of digital signature, authentication encryption and authorization to SOAP message, and verifies the result of the experiment, thus ensures the confidentiality, integrity, non-reputation, authentication and authorization of the message under Web service environment.

References

1. IBM Corporation and Microsoft Corporation. Security in a web Services world: A Proposed Architecture and Roadmap-A joint security whitepaper from IBM Corporation (EB/OL) (2008), http://www-106.ibm.com/developerworks/library/ws-secmap/
2. WIKIPDIA. Public-keycryptography, http://en.wikipedia.org/wiki/Public-keycryptography
3. Benatallah, B., Casati, F.: Special issue on Web services. Distributed and Parallel Databases 12(2/3), 115–116 (2010)
4. Freier, A.O., Karlton, P., Kocher, P.C.: The SSL Protocol version3.0, Netscape Communications [EB/OL], http://www.wp.netscape.com/eng/ssl3/ssl-toc.html
5. Fensel, D., Bussler, C., Maedche, A.: Semantic web enabled web services. In: Horrocks, I., Hendler, J. (eds.) ISWC 2002. LNCS, vol. 2342, pp. 1–2. Springer, Heidelberg (2002)
6. Budak Arpinar, I., Zhang, R., Aleman-Meza, B., et al.: Ontology driven web services composition platform. Information Systems and E-Business Management 3(2), 175–199 (2009)

Application of Real Options Analysis for R&D Project Valuation in High-Tech Public Corporation

Kai Zhang

Institute of Policy and Management, Chinese Academy of Sciences,
Beijing, 100084, Ph.: (86) 10-68718932
zhangkai96@tsinghua.org.cn

Abstract. This paper addresses the theme of real options decision-making in R&D projects of High-Tech Public Corporation considering the characteristics of R&D projects (including high-risk, multi-stage, expandability, product life circle, etc.).The paper expanse traditional discounted Cash flow Analysis to the uncertain process, and presents the Black-Scholes formula for evaluating of the uncertainty. A solution algorithm which transforms the Black-Scholes equation into constant coefficient diffusion equation is developed. The expanded discounted Cash flow Analysis under uncertainty achieves investment decision-making optimality that is generally not well presented in traditional approaches for R&D projects.

Keywords: R&D, real option, Discounted Cash flow, Black-Scholes formula.

1 Introduction

Research and development (R&D) is vital to the development of enterprises, but How to evaluate R&D projects has been a difficult problem. Traditional discounted Cash flow (DCF) method, not considering the value of flexibility in decision-making, is unfit for the valuation of R&D projects with great uncertainty. Considering some characteristics of R&D projects (including high-risk, multi-stage, expandability, product life circle, etc.), real option theory is employed to build the model of valuation of the decisions.

Myers (1984) recognized the analogy between financial options and real world investments. For this relationship, he coined the expression real option. This term describes the cognition that, based on the resemblance mentioned above (R&D) investments can be valued similar to financial options. The scientific basis for this task is provided by the research of Black-Scholes and Merton who was awarded the Nobel Prize in1997.Real options account for management flexibility which delivers a significant value contribution in the presence of uncertainty. Therefore, real options analysis (ROA) was recommended several times to be more adequate than traditional discounted Cash flow (DCF) for judging R&D projects. In addition, following a real option's perspective on R&D projects in R&D intensive companies has a positive impact on both their R&D performance and their financial performance.

S. Lin and X. Huang (Eds.): CESM 2011, Part I, CCIS 175, pp. 105–111, 2011.
© Springer-Verlag Berlin Heidelberg 2011

This paper aims at investigating the application of real Options analysis of R&D projects in the High-Tech Public Corporation. The Black-Scholes formula is introduced to resolve the value of real option. Furthermore, we expanse the traditional DCF Analysis, and give a new method which considers the uncertainty and risk in the project. At last numerical example of valuation of R&D projects will be presented so as to explain the proposed solution method in the article.

2   An Overview of Real Options

Real options allow decision-maker to potentially amplify good decision or mitigate poor ones that can in loss to the project which add value to the R&D projects. Many complicated decisions must be made during the investment decision-making of an R&D project. For example, the decision-maker must account for many factors such as the character of the project, cost of the project, and the needs of the products. Each design parameter may provide flexibility which can be treated as real options embedded in the project. In this paper, we will focus on the following two real options:

(1)Expansion option

If the demand of products at research grows rapidly the decision-maker can exercise a real option which gives him an opportunity to expanse the R&D project.

(2)Abandon option

If the demand of products at research too small to cover the cost of the R&D project, decision maker has a real option which allows him to abandon the R&D project.

Note that the above real options are Europe-style options which only allow the decision maker emprise the option at the given time.

3   Formulations

3.1   Notation

B	benefit of the R&D project
r	risk free tate
μ	the drift term of the benefit
σ	the volatility of the benefit
B_{max}	the benefit can be awarded from the R&D project with the given planning
B_{min}	the benefit from patent transfer when stop the R&D project
T	the expiration time
t	any given time
V	value of the real option
V_{exp}	value of the expansion option
V_{aban}	value of the abandon option
P	the product demand
$N(d)$	the cumulative distribution function of d

3.2 Random Walk of the Benefit

The forecasted demand is inaccuracy and eventually become an underlined uncertainty for the R&D project in the decision-making process. Because of the wide variability of product over time, the demand P is random variable. And the benefits of the R&D project depend on the future demand P as follows:

$$B = \sum_{i=1}^{N} \frac{B_i(x)}{(1+r)^i} \tag{1}$$

Because the demand P is random variable, the benefit B is modeled as the following stochastic process:

$$dB = \mu B dt + \sigma B \sqrt{dt} \tag{2}$$

Where $\sqrt{dt}$ follows Wiener process.

3.3 The Black-Scholes Formula

To evaluate the option, we use Π denote the value of an investment portfolio; Δ denote the quantity of B, then:

$$\Pi = V(B,t) - \Delta B \tag{3}$$

The change in the portfolio is denoted as follows:

$$d\Pi = dV - \Delta dB \tag{4}$$

From Itô we have

$$dV = \frac{\partial V}{\partial t} dt + \frac{\partial V}{\partial B} dB + \frac{1}{2} \sigma^2 B^2 \frac{\partial^2 V}{\partial B^2} dt \tag{5}$$

Then

$$d\Pi = \frac{\partial V}{\partial t} dt + \frac{\partial V}{\partial B} dB + \frac{1}{2} \sigma^2 B^2 \frac{\partial^2 V}{\partial B^2} dt - \Delta dB \tag{6}$$

If we choose $\Delta = \dfrac{\partial V}{\partial B}$ \hfill (7)

Then the randomness is reduced to zero. Base on the no-arbitrage principle, we can write:

$$d\Pi = r\Pi dt \tag{8}$$

Substituting (6) (7) into (8) we find that

$$\frac{\partial V}{\partial t} + \frac{1}{2} \sigma^2 B^2 \frac{\partial^2 V}{\partial B^2} + rB \frac{\partial V}{\partial B} - rV = 0 \tag{9}$$

This is the Black-Scholes formula. In the expressway investment decision problem the final condition is:

$$V_{exp}= Max(S\text{-}E, 0) =Max\,(B\text{-}B_{max}, 0) \tag{10}$$

$$V_{aban}= Max\,(E\text{-}S, 0) =Max\,(B_{min}\text{-}B, 0) \tag{11}$$

3.4 The Expanded Cost-Benefit Analysis

Instead of the traditional discounted Cash flow (DCF), we can conclude that if a project satieties

$$B+V_{exp}+V_{aban}-C>0 \tag{12}$$

The investment is acceptable.

4 Numerical Studies

4.1 The Solution to the Black-Scholes Equation

We will transform the Black-Scholes equation into constant coefficient diffusion equation. First, we write

$$V(B,t)=e^{-r(T-t)}U(B,t) \tag{13}$$

$$\tau=T-t \tag{14}$$

$$y=\log B+(r-\frac{1}{2}\sigma^2)\tau \tag{15}$$

This takes the differential equation to:

$$\frac{\partial U}{\partial \tau}=\frac{1}{2}\sigma^2\frac{\partial^2 U}{\partial y^2} \tag{16}$$

which is a constant coefficient diffusion equation. Then we can solve this equation,

$$V_{exp}=BN(d_1)-Ee^{-r(T-t)}N(d_2) \tag{17}$$

$$V_{aban}=-BN(-d_1)+Ee^{-r(T-t)}N(-d_2) \tag{18}$$

Where

$$d_1=\frac{\log(B/E)+(r+\frac{1}{2}\sigma^2)(T-t)}{\sigma\sqrt{T-t}} \tag{19}$$

$$d_2=\frac{\log(B/E)+(r-\frac{1}{2}\sigma^2)(T-t)}{\sigma\sqrt{T-t}} \tag{20}$$

$$=d_1-\sigma\sqrt{T-t}$$

4.2 Algorithm Development

To resolve the stochastic partial differential equation, we develop an algorithm based on finite-difference methods. Let's introduce some notation. The time step will be δt and the benefit step δB, both of which are constant. Thus the finite-difference grid is made up of point at benefit

$$B = i\delta B \tag{21}$$

and times

$$t = T - k\delta t \tag{22}$$

where $0 \le i \le I$ and $0 \le k \le K$. We write the real option value at each of the finite-difference grid point as

$$V_i^k = V(i\delta B, T - k\delta t) \tag{23}$$

so that the superscript is the time variable and the subscript the benefit variable. We write (9) in a more general form as

$$\frac{\partial V}{\partial t} + a(B,t)\frac{\partial^2 V}{\partial B^2} + b(B,t)\frac{\partial V}{\partial B} + c(B,t)V = 0 \tag{24}$$

Furthermore, take the approximation to the derivatives, and put them into this equation:

$$\frac{V_i^k - V_i^{k+1}}{\delta t} + a_i^k \frac{V_{i+1}^k - 2V_i^k + V_{i-1}^k}{\delta B^2} + b_i^k \frac{V_{i+1}^k - V_{i-1}^k}{2\delta B} + c_i^k V_i^k = O(\delta t, \delta S^2) \tag{25}$$

Rearrange this difference equation to put all of the $k+1$ term on the left-hand side:

$$V_i^{k+1} = A_i^k V_{i-1}^k + (1 + B_i^k)V_i^k + C_i^k V_{i+1}^k \tag{26}$$

For the Black-Scholes equation the coefficient above simplify to

$$A_i^k = \frac{1}{2}(\sigma^2 i^2 - ri)\delta t \quad B_i^k = -(\sigma^2 i^2 + r)\delta t \quad C_i^k = \frac{1}{2}(\sigma^2 i^2 + ri)\delta t \tag{27}$$

If we know V_i^k for all i then (26) tell us V_i^{k+1}. This make us prescribe a relationship between the real option value at an end point and interior value.

The boundary conditions for expansion option is

$$V_0^k = 0 \tag{28}$$

$$V_I^k = I\delta B - Ee^{-rk\delta t} \tag{29}$$

The boundary conditions for abandon option is

$$V_0^k = Ee^{-rk\delta t} \tag{30}$$

$$V_I^k = 0 \tag{31}$$

4.3 Numerical Sample

The benefit follows random walk:

$$dB = 0.035Bdt + 0.2B\sqrt{dt}$$

Other parameters are:

$$r=0.035 \; B=6500 \; C=7000 \; B_{max}=8000 \; B_{min}=1000 \; T=1$$

We use (17) (18) to get the value of V_{exp} and V_{aban}:

$$V_{exp}=757 \qquad V_{aban}=60$$

Considering the value of the real option,

$$B+V_{exp}+V_{aban}-C = 6500+757+60-7000 = 317 > 0$$

Then the project is accepted. The relationship between option value and time, E is showed in Fig. 1.

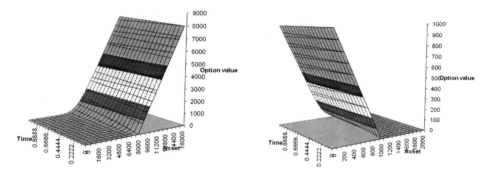

Fig. 1. The value of options

5 Conclusions

In this paper we have presented a stochastic model for decision making in R&D projects investment. Instead of traditional discounted Cash flow Analysis, the new method which uses real option theory considers numerous uncertainties in the investment. The Black-Scholes formula is introduced to computer the value of the real option. Numerical results indicate that the proposed model is helpful to the decision maker.

References

1. Baldwin, C.Y., Clark, K.B.: Modularity in design: An analysis based on the theory of real options. Harvard Business School (1994)
2. Kumaraswamy, A.: 1998. An organizational real options perspective of firms' R&D: Empirical evidence. Paper presented at the Second Annual Conference on Real Options, Theory Meets Practice Chicago (June 1998)

3. Hull, J.C.: Options, futures, and other derivative securities, 4th edn. Prentice Hall, Englewood Cliffs (1999)
4. Trigeorgis, L.: Real options: Managerial flexibility and strategy in resource allocation. MIT, Cambridge (1996)
5. Benaroch, M.: Managing investments in information technology based on real options theory. Journal of MIS 19(2), 43–84 (2002)
6. Teng, J.Y.: A multiobjective programming approach selecting non-dependent transportation investment alternatives. Transportation Research B (30), 291–307 (1996)
7. Kim, H.J., Weiss, M.B.H., Morel, B.: Real options and technology management: Assessing technology migration options in wireless industry. Telematics and Informatics 26, 180–192 (2009)
8. Brealey, R., Myers, S.: Principles of Corporate Finance. McGraw Hill, New York (2007)
9. Wilmott, P.: Paul Wilmott on quantitative finance, 2nd edn. Wiley, Chichester (2006)

A Fixed Point Theory for Quasi-Contractive Mappings in Ordered Sets

Jiawei Chen[1], Zhongping Wan[1], Zhanyi Ao[2], and Liuyang Yuan[1]

[1] School of Mathematics and Statistics, Wuhan University, Wuhan. Hubei, 430072, People's Republic of China
jeky99@163.com
[2] Department of Mathematics and Computer Science, Hebei Normal University of Nationalities, Chengde. Hebei, 067000, People's Republic of China
{zpwan-whu,zyiao,lyyuan}@126.com

Abstract. In this paper, the author presents a fixed point theorem for quasi-contractive maps in partially ordered sets, which extends corresponding results of [Nieto, J. J. and Rodriguez–Lopez, R.: Contractive Mapping Theorems in Partially Ordered Sets and Applicationsto Ordinary Differential Equations. Order, 22(2005), 223–239; Nieto, J. J. and Rodriguez–Lopez, R.: Existence and Uniqueness of Fixed Point in Partially Ordered Sets and Applications to Ordinary Dierential Equations, Acta Mathematica Sinica, English Series, 23 (2006), 2205–2212].

Keywords: Fixed point, partially ordered set, quasi-contractive map.

1 Introduction

Fixed point theory is an important content of nonlinear analysis that widely applied to optimization, computational algorithms, physics, building mathematical model, economics, variational inequalities, complementary problems, equilibrium problems, vector optimization problems, management science and so on (see, for example, [1-9]). Very recently years, considerable interest has been shown in developing various classes of fixed point under different maps, for instance, nonexpansive, constractive, quasi-constractive and pseudo-constractive mappings and so on, both for its own sake and for its applications.

In [1], some results on the existence of fixed points in partially ordered sets are presented. In [2] some results on the existence of a unique fixed point for nondecreasing mappings are applied to obtain a unique solution for a first order ordinary differential equation with periodic boundary conditions. In [3], the authors proved some fixed point theorems in partially ordered sets, providing an extension of the Banach contractive mapping theorem.

Inspired and motivated by above works, the purpose of this paper is to investigate that fixed point theorem for quasi-contractive maps is proved in partially ordered sets under certain assumptions, which extends corresponding results of [2,3].

S. Lin and X. Huang (Eds.): CESM 2011, Part I, CCIS 175, pp. 112–116, 2011.

2 Main Results

We first recall some necessary definitions, which are needed in our main results.

Definition 1. Let $(X,\leq)$ be a partially ordered set and $g : X \rightarrow X$ .We say that g is monotone nondecreasing if, for all $x, y \in X$,

$$x \leq y \Rightarrow g(x) \leq g(y).$$

g is monotone nonincreasing if, for all $x, y \in X$,

$$x \leq y \Rightarrow g(x) \geq g(y).$$

g is monotone if it is monotone nonincreasing or monotone nondecreasing.

Definition 2. Let $(X,\leq)$ be a partially ordered set. $f : X \rightarrow X$ is said to be quasi-contractive with constant r if there exists a constant $r \in (0,1)$ such that

$$d(f(x), f(y)) \leq rQ(x, y), \forall x \geq y \text{ or } x \leq y ,$$

where

$$Q(x, y) = \max\{d(x, y), d(x, f(x)), d(y, f(y)), d(x, f(y)), d(y, f(x))\} .$$

f is called to be contractive if it is quasi-contractive and satisfies that

$$Q(x, y) = d(x, y), \forall x \geq y \text{ or } x \leq y.$$

Theorem 1. Let $(X,\leq)$ be a partially ordered set and suppose that there exists a metric d in X such that (X,d) is a complete metric space. Let $g : X \rightarrow X$ be a monotone quasi-contractive map with constant $k \in (0, \frac{1}{2})$. Suppose that either g is continuous. If there exists $x_0 \in X$ with $x_0 \leq g(x_0)$ or $x_0 \geq g(x_0)$, then g has a fixed point. Furthermore, if x^* and y^* are fixed points of g with $x^* \geq y^*$ or $x^* \leq y^*$, then $x^* = y^*$.

Proof. If $g(x_0) = x_0$, then the proof is complete.

Suppose that $g(x_0) \neq x_0$. The proof is similar to that of Theorem 2.1 in [1].

For the completeness, we conclude it. Let $x_0 \in X$ with $x_0 \leq g(x_0)$ or $x_0 \geq g(x_0)$. Without loss of generality, suppose that $g^n(x_0) \neq g^{n+1}(x_0)$, i.e.,

$$d(g^n(x_0), g^{n+1}(x_0)) \neq 0, n = 0,1,2,...$$

Since g is monotone, $g^{n+1}(x_0)$ and $g^n(x_0)$ are comparable, for each $n = 0,1,2,...$. Then,

$$d(g^n(x_0), g^{n+1}(x_0))$$
$$\leq k \max\{d(g^{n-1}(x_0), g^n(x_0)), d(g^{n-1}(x_0), g^n(x_0)), d(g^n(x_0), g^{n+1}(x_0)),$$
$$d(g^{n-1}(x_0), g^{n+1}(x_0)), d(g^n(x_0), g^n(x_0))\}$$
$$\leq k \max\{d(g^{n-1}(x_0), g^n(x_0)), d(g^n(x_0), g^{n+1}(x_0)),$$
$$d(g^{n-1}(x_0), g^n(x_0)) + d(g^n(x_0), g^{n+1}(x_0))\}$$
$$\leq k(d(g^{n-1}(x_0), g^n(x_0)) + d(g^n(x_0), g^{n+1}(x_0))),$$

where $k \in (0, \frac{1}{2})$. It follows that

$$d(g^n(x_0), g^{n+1}(x_0)) \leq \frac{k}{1-k} d(g^{n-1}(x_0), g^n(x_0)). \tag{1}$$

Put $r = \frac{k}{1-k}$. Then $r \in (0,1)$. By induction from (1) one has, for $m > n$,

$$d(g^m(x_0), g^n(x_0))$$
$$\leq \left(r^{m-1} + r^{m-2} + \cdots + r^n\right) d(g(x_0), x_0)$$
$$= \frac{r^n - r^m}{1-r} d(g(x_0), x_0) \tag{2}$$
$$\leq \frac{r^n}{1-r} d(g(x_0), x_0).$$

Thus $\{g^n(x_0)\}$ is a Cauchy sequence in X . Since X is complete, there is $x^* \in X$ such that

$$\lim_{n \to \infty} g^n(x_0) = x^*.$$

Next, we prove that $x^* \in X$ is a fixed point of g . Note that d is continuous. If g is continuous, then letting $m = n+1$ in (2) allows to, as $n \to \infty$,

$$\lim_{n \to \infty} d(g^{n+1}(x_0), g^n(x_0)) = d(g(x^*), x^*), \tag{3}$$

and so

$$\lim_{n\to\infty}\frac{r^n}{1-r}d(g(x_0),x_0)=0.\tag{4}$$

Therefore, from (2),(3) and (4), we obtain

$$d(g(x^*),x^*)=0,$$

which implies that $x^* \in X$ is a fixed point of g.

Furthermore, assume that x^* and y^* are fixed points of g with $x^* \geq y^*$ or $x^* \leq y^*$, that is,

$$g(x^*)=x^*, g(y^*)=y^*.$$

Since g is monotone, one has

$$
\begin{aligned}
d(x^*,y^*)&=d(g(x^*),g(y^*))\\
&\leq kQ(x^*,y^*)\\
&= k\max\{d(x^*,y^*),d(x^*,g(x^*)),d(x,g(y^*)),d(y^*,g(y^*))\}\\
&= kd(x^*,y^*),
\end{aligned}
$$

which means that $d(x^*,y^*)=0$, i.e., $x^* = y^*$, where $k \in (0,1)$. This completes the proof.

3 Conclusions

In this paper, a fixed point theorem for quasi-contractive maps is established in partially ordered sets under certain assumptions. Further, we can discuss the common fixed point problem of a family of quasi-contractive maps, and apply the fixed point theory to study optimization, computational algorithms, management, building mathematical model, economics, variational inequalities, and complementary problems and so on.

Acknowledgments. The work is supported by the National Science Foundation of China (No. 70771080) and the Fundamental Research Fund for the Central Universities.

References

1. Ran, A.C.M., Reurings, M.C.B.: A Fixed Point Theorem in Partially Ordered Sets and Some Applications to Matrix Equations. Proc. Amer. Math. Soc. 132, 1435–1443 (2004)
2. Nieto, J.J., Rodriguez–Lopez, R.: Contractive Mapping Theorems in Partially Ordered Sets and Applicationsto Ordinary Differential Equations. Order 22, 223–239 (2005)

3. Nieto, J.J., Rodriguez–Lopez, R.: Existence and Uniqueness of Fixed Point in Partially Ordered Sets and Applications to Ordinary Dierential Equations. Acta Mathematica Sinica, English Series 23, 2205–2212 (2006)
4. Chen, J.W., Cho, Y.J., Kim, J.K., Li, J.: Multiobjective optimization problems with modified objective functions and cone constraints and applications. Journal of Global Optimization 49, 137–147 (2011)
5. Chen, J.W., Wan, Z.: Existence of solutions and convergence analysis for a system of quasivariational inclusins in Banach spaces (submitted)
6. Chen, J.W., Zou, Y.Z.: Existence of solutions of F-implicit variational inequalit problems with extended projection operators. Acta Mathmatica Sinica Chinese Series 53(2), 375–384 (2010)
7. Chen, J.W., Qi, Y.: Solvability of set-valued vector optimization problem. In: Proceedings of the 1st International Workshop on Education Technology and Computer Science, ETCS 2009, vol. 3, pp. 934–938 (2009)
8. Sun, H., Chen, J.W., Wan, Z.: Extended well-posedness for vector optimization problems with connected set constraint. In: 2010 International Conference on Computer Application and System Modeling, vol. 7, pp. 13–15 (2010)
9. Ao, Z., Chen, J.W., et al.: Duality for Multiobjective Programming with a Modified Objective Function. In: Proceedings of Third International Conference on Modelling and Simulation, Wuxi, P.R.China, June 4-6 (2010)

A New Optimization Approach for Grey Model GM(1,1)

Zhanyi Ao[1], Xiao-qing Ou[2], and Shaohua Zhu[2]

[1] Department of Mathematics and Computer Science,
Hebei Normal University of Nationalities,
Chengde. Hebei, 067000,
People's Republic of China
[2] Human Resources Department, Jihua 3509 Textile Co., Ltd.,
Hubei Hanchuan 431616, People's Republic of China
{469794021,724479775,108859099}@qq.com

Abstract. A new optimized approach is introduced by the exponential response of recuperating value of GM (1, 1) model, which has been strictly proved to have the white exponential superposition and the white coefficient superposition in theory. The normal exponential series and a practical example are also given to show that the new model has the very high simulation and prediction precisionn.

Keywords: GM(1, 1); Optimization; Background.

1 Introduction

Grey prediction model GM (1, 1) has been widely applied in many fields since it was introduced. In order to improve the precision of the model, literatures [3] and [4] derived the integral form of the background value from the white differential equation, which greatly improve the prediction precision. In literatures [5] and [6], the authors used the least square method to optimize coefficient, avoiding the error brought out by the initial condition. Due to the recuperating value of GM (1, 1) model has the homogeneous exponential form $\hat{x}^{(0)}(k) = ce^{-ak}$, therefore, if only working out a and c, we could obtain the recuperating value. According to the new background value derived in literature [4], we can work out development coefficient a ; according to the smallest principle that the difference quadratic sum between actual values and recuperating values, we could utilize the least square method to obtain c, thereby a new optimized GM(1, 1) method is presented in this paper.

2 Optimized Method and Its Properties

Lemma 1. Let $x^{(0)} = (x^{(0)}(1),\cdots,x^{(0)}(n))$ be the raw series, $x^{(1)} = (x^{(1)}(1),\cdots,x^{(1)}(n))$ be the 1- AGO series of $x^{(0)}$, $z^{(1)}(k)$ be background value. Let

S. Lin and X. Huang (Eds.): CESM 2011, Part I, CCIS 175, pp. 117–122, 2011.

$$Y = \begin{pmatrix} x^{(0)}(2) \\ x^{(0)}(3) \\ \vdots \\ x^{(0)}(n) \end{pmatrix}, \quad B = \begin{pmatrix} -z^{(1)}(2) & 1 \\ -z^{(1)}(3) & 1 \\ \vdots & \vdots \\ -z^{(1)}(n) & 1 \end{pmatrix}. \text{ Then}$$

A.   According to the least square method, we have $\hat{a} = (a,b)^{T} = \left(B^{T}B\right)^{-1}B^{T}Y$, and

$$\hat{a} = \frac{\sum_{k=2}^{n} z^{(1)}(k)\sum_{k=2}^{n} x^{(0)}(k) - (n-1)\sum_{k=2}^{n} z^{(1)}(k)x^{(0)}(k)}{(n-1)\sum_{k=2}^{n} z^{(1)}(k)^{2} - \left(\sum_{k=2}^{n} z^{(1)}(k)\right)^{2}} \tag{1.1}$$

B.   The time response of white differential equation $\dfrac{dx^{(1)}}{dt} + ax^{(1)} = b$ is

$$x^{(1)}(t) = \left(x^{(1)}(1) - \frac{b}{a} \right)e^{-a(t-1)} + \frac{b}{a}$$

C.   The time response of grey differential equation $x^{(0)}(k) + az^{(1)}(k) = b$ is

$$x^{(1)}(k) = \left(x^{(1)}(1) - \frac{b}{a} \right)e^{-a(k-1)} + \frac{b}{a}$$

D.   The recuperating value is

$$\hat{x}^{(0)}(k+1) = \hat{x}^{(1)}(k+1) - \hat{x}^{(1)}(k) = (1-e^{a})\left(x^{(0)}(1) - \frac{b}{a} \right)e^{-ak}, \quad k = 1, 2, 3, \cdots.$$

Let $c_{1} = \left(x^{(1)}(1) - \dfrac{b}{a} \right)$, $c_{2} = \dfrac{b}{a}$, then $x^{(1)}(k+1) = c_{1}e^{-ak} + c_{2}$ is the non-homogeneous

exponential form. Let $c = (1-e^{a})\left(x^{(0)}(1) - \dfrac{b}{a} \right)$, then $\hat{x}^{(0)}(k+1) = ce^{-ak}$ is the

homogeneous exponential form. Therefore, if only working out a and c, we could obtain the recuperating values. For the parameter a, we utilize (1.1) to obtain $\hat{a}$. Here it is also very important for selection of background value. This paper takes the new background value derived in literature [4], its derivation principle is based on the fact that $x^{(1)}$ has the non-homogeneous exponential form, where $x^{(0)}(k) = ge^{-a(k-1)}$ $(k = 1, 2, \cdots)$, i.e.,

$$x^{(1)}(k) = \sum_{i=1}^{k} x^{(0)}(i) = \sum_{i=1}^{k} ge^{-a(i-1)} = \frac{g}{1-e^{a}}e^{-a(k-1)} + \frac{ge^{a}}{e^{a}-1} = g_{1}e^{-a(k-1)} + g_{2}$$

Brief process as follows:

Firstly, calculate the integral of the white differential equation $\dfrac{dx^{(1)}}{dt} + ax^{(1)} = b$,

i.e., $\displaystyle\int_{k-1}^{k} \frac{dx^{(1)}}{dt}\,dt + \int_{k-1}^{k} ax^{(1)}\,dt = b \Rightarrow x^{(1)}(k) - x^{(1)}(k-1) + a\int_{k-1}^{k} x^{(1)}\,dt = b$,

then

$$z^{(1)}(k) = \int_{k-1}^{k} x^{(1)}\,dt = \int_{k-1}^{k}\left(g_1 e^{-a(k-1)} + g_2\right)dt = \frac{1}{a}\left(x^{(1)}(k) - x^{(1)}(k-1)\right) + d = \frac{x^{(0)}(k)}{a} + d.$$

Due to $\dfrac{x^{(0)}(k-1)}{x^{(0)}(k)} = \dfrac{ge^{-a(k-1)}}{ge^{-ak}} = e^{a} \Rightarrow a = \ln x^{(0)}(k-1) - \ln x^{(0)}(k)$, $x^{(0)}(k) = ge^{-a(k-1)}$

Then $g = x^{(0)}(k)e^{a(k-1)} = x^{(0)}(k)\left(\dfrac{x^{(0)}(k-1)}{x^{(0)}(k)}\right)^{k-1}$,

$$d = \frac{ge^{a}}{e^{a}-1} = \frac{x^{(0)}(k)\left(\dfrac{x^{(0)}(k-1)}{x^{(0)}(k)}\right)^{k-1}\dfrac{x^{(0)}(k-1)}{x^{(0)}(k)}}{\dfrac{x^{(0)}(k-1)}{x^{(0)}(k)}-1} = \frac{\left(x^{(0)}(k-1)\right)^{k}}{\left(x^{(0)}(k)\right)^{k-2}\left(x^{(0)}(k-1) - x^{(0)}(k)\right)}$$

Thus $z^{(1)}(k) = \dfrac{x^{(0)}(k)}{\ln x^{(0)}(k) - \ln x^{(0)}(k-1)} + \dfrac{\left(x^{(0)}(k-1)\right)^{k}}{\left(x^{(0)}(k)\right)^{k-2}\left(x^{(0)}(k-1) - x^{(0)}(k)\right)}$. (1.2)

Theorem 1. Taking (1.2) as the background value, grey model GM (1, 1) has the white exponential superposition.

Proof: Let $x^{(0)}(k) = ce^{-ak}$, then it suffices to prove $\hat{a} = a$ .Let

$$D = \sum_{k=2}^{n} x^{(0)}(k) = \sum_{k=2}^{n} ce^{-ak} = \frac{ce^{-a}}{e^{a}-1}\left(1 - e^{-a(n-1)}\right), \text{ and } \frac{x^{(0)}(k-1)}{x^{(0)}(k)} = \frac{ce^{-a(k-1)}}{ce^{-ak}} = e^{a}.$$

Therefore $z^{(1)}(k) = \dfrac{x^{(0)}(k)}{\ln(x^{(0)}(k)) - \ln(x^{(0)}(k-1))} + \dfrac{\left(x^{(0)}(k-1)\right)^{k}}{\left(x^{(0)}(k)\right)^{k-2}\left(x^{(0)}(k-1) - x^{(0)}(k)\right)}$

$$= \frac{x^{(0)}(k)}{\ln\left(\dfrac{x^{(0)}(k)}{x^{(0)}(k-1)}\right)}\left(\dfrac{x^{(0)}(k-1)}{x^{(0)}(k)}\right)^{k-2}\frac{x^{(0)}(k-1)\dfrac{x^{(0)}(k-1)}{x^{(0)}(k)}}{\left(\dfrac{x^{(0)}(k-1)}{x^{(0)}(k)}-1\right)} = \frac{ce^{-ak}}{-a} + \frac{c}{e^{a}-1} = \frac{c}{e^{a}-1}\frac{x^{(0)}(k)}{a}.$$

Let $C = \sum_{k=2}^{n} z^{(1)}(k) = \sum_{k=2}^{n}\left(\dfrac{c}{e^a-1}-\dfrac{x^{(0)}(k)}{a}\right) = \dfrac{c(n-1)}{e^a-1}-\dfrac{\sum_{k=2}^{n}x^{(0)}(k)}{a}$, then

$$C^2 = \left(\dfrac{c(n-1)}{e^a-1}-\dfrac{\sum_{k=2}^{n}x^{(0)}(k)}{a}\right)^2 = (n-1)^2\left(\dfrac{c}{e^a-1}\right)^2 - \dfrac{2c(n-1)}{a(e^a-1)}\sum_{k=2}^{n}x^{(0)}(k)+\dfrac{1}{a^2}\left(\sum_{k=2}^{n}x^{(0)}(k)\right)^2$$

$$E = \sum_{k=2}^{n} z^{(1)}(k)x^{(0)}(k) = \sum_{k=2}^{n}\left(\dfrac{c}{e^a-1}-\dfrac{x^{(0)}(k)}{a}\right)x^{(0)}(k) = \dfrac{c}{e^a-1}\sum_{k=2}^{n}x^{(0)}(k)-\dfrac{1}{a}\sum_{k=2}^{n}x^{(0)}(k)^2$$

$$F = \sum_{k=2}^{n} z^{(1)}(k)^2 = \sum_{k=2}^{n}\left(\dfrac{c}{e^a-1}-\dfrac{x^{(0)}(k)}{a}\right)^2 = (n-1)\left(\dfrac{c}{e^a-1}\right)^2-\dfrac{2c}{a(e^a-1)}\sum_{k=2}^{n}x^{(0)}(k)+\dfrac{1}{a^2}\sum_{k=2}^{n}x^{(0)}(k)^2$$

$$CD-(n-1)E = \dfrac{1}{a}\left((n-1)\sum_{k=2}^{n}x^{(0)}(k)^2 -\left(\sum_{k=2}^{n}x^{(0)}(k)\right)^2\right), \text{ and}$$

$$(n-1)F-C^2 = \dfrac{1}{a^2}\left((n-1)\sum_{k=2}^{n}x^{(0)}(k)^2 -\left(\sum_{k=2}^{n}x^{(0)}(k)\right)^2\right). \text{ From (1.1), we have}$$

$$\hat{a} = \dfrac{CD-(n-1)E}{(n-1)F-C^2} = \dfrac{\dfrac{1}{a}\left((n-1)\sum_{k=2}^{n}x^{(0)}(k)^2 -\left(\sum_{k=2}^{n}x^{(0)}(k)\right)^2\right)}{\dfrac{1}{a^2}\left((n-1)\sum_{k=2}^{n}x^{(0)}(k)^2 -\left(\sum_{k=2}^{n}x^{(0)}(k)\right)^2\right)} = a .$$

The above proof shows that it reaches precision of 100 percent to simulate the normal exponential series whether the development Coefficient a is large or small. However, it's not enough that the exponential series are of such characteristics. If the simulation precision of coefficient c is not high, it will also lead to a larger error. We can also fix the coefficient of the recuperating values by an appropriate way to realize that there is not error about the simulation of coefficient, thus there is not model error wholly for the normal exponential series. For the coefficient c , according to the smallest principle that the difference quadratic sum between actual values and recuperating values, we could utilize the least square method to obtain c .

At present, there are only two kinds of methods to verify the superiority of grey prediction model: one is to test the error size by normal exponential series simulation; another is to test the error size by the simulation about the data from actual production. In view of the fact that this paper already strictly proved that this new model has the white exponential law of coincidence, which guarantees that the error is not from the model but from the calculation process because of rounding, so we do not need to use the normal exponential series to illustrate, only need to give several examples to explain it. Example [4] The data of financial input in science and technology of 1997~2003 years of Jiangsu Province are given as follow:

Table 1. Data of Financial Input in Science and Technology of 1997~2003 Years

Year	1997	1998	1999	2000	2001	2002	2003
Data*	8.21	9.52	10.51	12.72	14.84	17.89	21.22

* Hundred million Yuan

Based on the data of 1997~2002 years, we establish *GM* (1, 1) model by the method in this paper and obtain the recuperating formula as follows:

$$\hat{x}^{(0)}(k+1) = 6.3544e^{0.1727k}, \quad k = 1, 2, \cdots$$

Finally we obtain the following results:

Table 2. Comparision of the Simulation Precision

Year	Actual value	Literature [4]		Method of this paper	
		Simulated value	Relative error(%)	Simulated value	Relative error(%)
1998	9.52	9.1162	4.2411	8.9757	5.7179
1999	10.51	10.835	3.0872	10.667	1.4975
2000	12.72	12.877	1.2307	12.678	0.3305
2001	14.84	15.304	3.1233	15.067	1.5330
2002	17.89	17.706	1.6652	17.907	0.0974

Table 3. Comparision of the Prediction Precision

Year	Actual value	Literature [4]		Method of this paper	
		Predicted value	Relative error(%)	Predicted value	Relative error(%)
2003	21.22	21.616	1.8662	21.2826	0.2827

From table 2 and table 3, we find that the method of this paper has higher simulation precision and prediction precision than Literature [4].

3 Conclusions

In this paper first of all, we choose (1.2) as the background value of the new model, then obtain development coefficient $\hat{a}$, and we have proved that it has no deviation between development coefficient $\hat{a}$ and the actual coefficient a for the normal exponential series under the new background value

After the development coefficient $\hat{a}$ was fixed, the parameter $\hat{c}$ in the recuperating values $\hat{x}^{(0)}(k) = \hat{c}e^{-\hat{a}k}$ $(k = 2,3,\cdots,n)$ is determined by (1.3). This method can guarantee that it also has no deviation between coefficient $\hat{c}$ and the actual coefficient c for the normal exponential series.

Thus we obtain a new model that has the white exponential superposition and white coefficient superposition. For the normal exponential series, the model has merely calculation error, no model error. Even if development coefficient a is bigger for the normal exponential series, the simulated values still reaches the precision of 100 percent. This optimized model has the feasibility and the obvious effect superiority in the example examination.

Acknowledgments. Thanks for the work of the authors of references.

References

1 Deng, J.: Grey Prediction and Grey Decision (Revision Edition). Press of Huazhong University of Science & Technology, Wuhan (2002)
2 Liu, S., Dang, Y., Fang, Z., et al.: Grey System Theory and Application, 3rd edn. Chinese Science Press, Beijing (1999)
3 Luo, D., Liu, S., Dang, Y.: The optimization of grey model GM (1, 1). Engineering Science 8, 50–53 (2003)
4 Wang, Z., Dang, Y., Liu, S.: An optimal GM (1, 1) based on the discrete function with exponential law. Systems Engineering Theory and Practice 2, 61–67 (2008)
5 Liu, B., Liu, S., Zhai, Z., Dang, Y.: Optimum Time Response Sequence for GM (1, 1). Management Science 4, 54–57 (2003)
6 Hu, D., Wei, Y., Shen, Y.: Optimization Integrated Background Value with Parameter for GM (1, 1) Combination Model. In: The 16th National Academic Conference on Grey System, Beijing, China (2008)
7 Dong, F., Tian, J.: Optimization integrated background value with original condition for GM (1, 1). Engineering and Electronic Technology 3, 464–466 (2007)
8 Chen, J.W., Cho, Y.J., Kim, J.K., Li, J.: Multiobjective optimization problems with modified objective functions and cone constraints and applications. Journal of Global Optimization 49, 137–147 (2011)
9 Chen, J.W., Wan, Z.: Existence of solutions and convergence analysis for a system of quasivariational inclusins in Banach spaces (submitted)
10 Chen, J.W., Zou, Y.Z.: Existence of solutions of F-implicit variational inequalit problems with extended projection operators. Acta Mathmatica Sinica Chinese series 53(2), 375–384 (2010)
11 Chen, J.W., Qi, Y.: Solvability of set-valued vector optimization problem. In: Proceedings of the 1st International Workshop on Education Technology and Computer Science, ETCS 2009, vol. 3, pp. 934–938 (2009)
12 Sun, H., Chen, J.W., Wan, Z.: Extended well-posedness for vector optimization problems with connected set constraint. In: 2010 International Conference on Computer Application and System Modeling, vol. 7, pp. 13–15 (2010)
13 Ao, Z., Chen, J.W., et al.: Duality for Multiobjective Programming with a Modified Objective Function. In: Proceedings of Third International Conference on Modelling and Simulation, Wuxi, China, June 4-6 (2010)

Approach of Web2.0 Application Pattern Applied to the Information Teaching*

GuangMin Li[1], Min Liu[2], GuoPing Li[1], ZiYun Wang[1,**], and WenJing Chen[3]

[1] College of Computer Science and Technology,
Hubei Normal University, Huangshi, Hubei
[2] College of Foreign Studies, Hubei Normal University, Huangshi, Hubei
[3] Huang Shi Productivity Promotion Center, Huangshi, Hubei
finesite@gmail.com, wziyun@hbnu.edu.cn

Abstract. This paper firstly focuses on the development and function of Web2.0 from an educational perspective. Secondly, it introduces the features and theoretical foundation of Web 2.0. Consequently, The application pattern used in the information teaching based on the introduction described above is elaborated and proved to be an effective way of increasing educational productivity. Lastly, this paper presents the related cases and teaching resources for reference.

Keywords: Web 2.0; Information Teaching; Blog; Wiki.

1 Introduction

Web2.0, the general term of the new generation for the Internet application, has been deeply rooted in people's daily life with its features: special personality, sharing (information sharing, the sharing of sources, sharing ideas and resources), openness, focusing on the customers' experience and emphasizing the interaction. The modern information technology education philosophy advocates creating an atmosphere which centers on "the students" instead of "the teachers, paying attention to the interaction and sharing during the process of study, cultivating the students' ability of independent innovation, solving the problem by oneself and coordinated cooperation. So the quintessence of Web 2.0 is identical with the idea of modern information teaching. Besides, it can provide powerful technical support and guarantee for its implementation.

2 The Main Features and Theoretical Foundation of Web 2.0

2.1 The Main Features of Web 2.0

Web 2.0 is the upgrading of Internet in the aspect of idea and ideology. There is a great change in the Internet system. The former one was top-down and in charge of the

---

* Supported by the Teaching Research Project of Hubei Normal University ,China(Grant No. 2009051).

** Corresponding author.

S. Lin and X. Huang (Eds.): CESM 2011, Part I, CCIS 175, pp. 123–127, 2011.

minorities intensively. Now it is transferred into from bottom to top and led by the collective wisdom and strength of the majority of the clients. Giving dominance to individuals is the intrinsic source of Web 2.0. In this way, it fully develops the individuals' enthusiasm. Then the impact and wisdom contributed by the majorities of individual, and the whole group's impact have taken the place of the impact brought by the minority. And it exploits the potentialities of individual creation and contribution, making the creativity be moved into a new level. The clients in the time of Web 2.0 don't have to have the circular motion around the portal site. They are the active information distributors instead of the passive information receivers. They can fully experience it and communicate and interact with each other.

From the information provided above, we can see that Web 2.0 is the process of transferring from one-way transmission to interactive one. The traditional teaching revolves round the teacher, classroom and the textbooks. Students are received the teachers' role as "propagate cardinal principles, impart professional knowledge, and resolve doubts" passively. There are many coincidences and similarities between the education reform of new type which takes the new curriculum reform as the clue and Web 2.0.From the idea of Web 2.0, the following table now presents the comparison between the new education and the traditional one :

Table 1. The comparison of the web2.0 education and the traditional education

Features	The Traditional Education Form	The Web 2.0 Education Form
The Main Role of Teachers	the source of knowledge	the source of knowledge and the administrator
The Tool and Content	the traditional material that was protected by copyright	The protected and free material is usually trans-system.
Learning Behavior	traditional: paper, assigned homework, test and group discussion in class	It turns to be more open and pay more attention on the cooperation in the learning process.
The Academic Institute	The exchange among the interdisciplinary was limited within campus; it was only taught, estimated and assigned a task by a certain subject	Pay more attention to the cooperation and coordination among the universities (international ones included)
How one studies	mainly received passively	take part in actively ; manifest the awareness of being master
The technical means	make use of electronic learning administering system; just get involved in one institute	It involves the other universities' E-learning cooperation, most part of which limited in the learning administering system, but can be collected with other system

From the table provided above, it is clear that the Web 2.0 education idea breaks the time and area limitation in teaching and learning, emphasizing on students to be the main body. The students will acquire the knowledge and build up their ability in relaxed harmonious circumstance. It also provides different plans for the student to make them interact and share with others, to experience the happiness of learning, to obtain something they are interested in by themselves, to increase the interaction and fully develop their subjective initiative. In that sense, the learners at the same time are the sharers.

2.2 The Main Theoretical Basis of Web 2.0

2.2.1 The Long Tail

The Long Tail is raised in October, 2004 in the passage named The Long Tail [1] by the chief editor of Wired Chris Anderson. In literal meaning, it refers to the commerce and economy pattern used in webs like Amazon and Netflix. That is, if the channel of store and circulation is as wide as possible, the market share taken by the low demand or not ideal sale products can be equal to or even more than the best-selling. To the clients, the value of internet is increased as the number of the new clients raised.

The application of Blog presents the thought of The Long Tail. Every Blog is different and of strong personality for their different focuses. Therefore, mostly the Blog will have obscure topics which caught little attention from the majority . But it satisfies the demand of a minority of people. Bolg gets the traffic from the long tail. Consequently, the increase of traffic will bring in people who have the same interests and income. (e.g.: putting advertisement in the blog)

2.2.2 The Strength of Weak Ties

The professor of Stanford MarkS.Granovetter put forward the Strength of Weak Ties in 1970s. He points out that one only will have a close relationship with the ones who have much in common. There is no difference in the information they have separately. On the contrary, because of the prominent differences, the ones who are estranged from each other may have more possibility to have the information which others don't have. So the weak ties relation is the necessary factor in being a part of the community. It can bring people unexpected information and chances[2].

In Web2.0, The Strength of Weak Ties reflects itself in Blog, SNS and so on. People having dissimilar social background and coming from different fields can provide the clients with various useful knowledge. For example, the teacher who writes something unfamiliar on the teaching Blog will help other teachers to know the brand-new but interesting area to them.

3 Approach of Web2.0 Application Pattern Used in the Information Teaching of University

Web 2.0 has fully affected trade, media and business world, not to mention the education . Teachers are exploring the potentials like Blog, media sharing service and other socialized software. These tools will make students acquire more knowledge and create exciting chances of learning.

3.1 Blog

Blog is the core member of Web 2.0, is the records made by individuals or group according to the order of time. It will be renewed regularly and called Network Logger. They can be divided into thematic and non-thematic. One of them is the educational

Blog, on which the famous educationists will publish the passage within the theme of education and show their opinions about the new field. There are also Blogs which record the process of their experiences. Blog has improved the sharing level from information to sources and ideas.

Blog occupies a crucial position. Not only does it remove the technical impediment appears in the on-line writing and giving out information software, but it also is the log which records the students' journey. Meanwhile, it is convenient by giving the readers important feedback and timely comment. The readers cover a wide range as teachers and colleagues. Suppose a teacher takes the course Software Program as the theme of his Blog. In it, he can show his opinions or quote copiously from a great variety of sources referring to the latest developing techniques and practice experience, so the students can have a wide range of knowledge. In the mean time, the students will put forward some new ideas on some of the viewpoints. The teacher will answer the questions, exchange the ideas and discuss them together. All of these will not be restricted within the time and space. The teacher and students will have more communications and interaction after class.

3.2 Wiki

Based on the idea of joint creation, Wiki is a hypertext system which supports collaborative writing and a pack of supplementary tools to support the writing. That is to say, everyone is able to browse, create, modify, present one's opinions or discuss and develop the common topics. The Wiki site will elaborate on the certain issues at some length, having relevance and showing common concern for subject.

Wiki has the irreplaceable advantage on the aspect of teaching resources' collaborative establishment or the college scientific research[4]. It can provide a common plat for all the teachers in the same teaching and research section. Each of the teachers can perfect their excellent teaching plan and courses to keep improving. What's more, Wiki controls the different versions and administering the modified versions in different stages. The application of Wiki avoids the repetitive research and work, improving the spreading of the fruit, arousing the enthusiasm of teamwork and enhancing the level of scientific research.

4   The Cases in Approach of Web2.0 Application Pattern Used in the Information Teaching of University

In view of Web 2.0 distinctive characters and powerful life-force, now many useful and meaningful education programs and education platforms with vivid Web 2.0 have been carried out, here are some examples:

Blog(http://edu2do.com/fanyi is the predecessor of Edu2Do.com. It was founded by English Teacher Rita Zhou. The source of translation came from Blog, aiming at help the readers to see the changes took place in the education field from different angle and at multi-level. It is fresh, convenient and rich. Over the one year, the group have translated hundreds of passages about the educational information, presented itself as the announcer of the frontier[5].

ElearnSpace(http://www.edu2do.com/elearnspace/) is the professional Blog of Canadian specialist George Siemens. He makes some brief comments on the latest international study development irregularly.

Journey East (http://www.jeast.net/teacher/jiahou) is Li Jiahou's blog. Professor Ni is the promoter at home on the advanced technology application. We are exposed to the frontier of the development in the educational world from his Blog.

References

1. Anderson, C.: The Long Tail. Wired (October 2004),
   `http://www.wired.com/wired/archive/12.10/tail.html`
2. Granovetter, M.S.: The Strength of Weak Ties. American Journal of Sociology 78(6), 1360–1380 (1973)
3. Travers, J., Milgram, S.: Experimental Study of Small World Problem. Sociometry 32(4), 425–443 (1969)
4. Liu, W.-c., Hu, Z. Approach of Teaching Pattern in University Based on Internet Web2.0. Technical Information, 15 (2007)
5. Education Technology Information [OL], `http://blog.donews.com/zhyujiang/`

Research and Analysis of TD-SCDMA Uplink Capacity[*]

Hao Chen[1,2], Tong Yang[3], Jian-fu Teng[1], and Hong He[4]

[1] School of Electronic and Information Engineering, Tianjin University, Tianjin 300072, China
[2] Computer Science and Information Engineering College,
Tianjin University of Science & Technology, Tianjin, 300222
[3] Tianjin Mobile Communications Co., Ltd., Tianjin 300052, China
[4] Tianjin Key Laboratory for Control Theory and Application in Complicated Systems,
Tianjin University of Technology, Tianjin 300384, China
heho604300@126.com

Abstract. In 3[th]G system network planning, the cell capacity calculation is a very important and critical issue. Assumed under the single-service of TD-SCDMA, this paper investigated the uplink cell capacities of the TD-SCDMA system and analyzed the relations between the user numbers and the required signal-to-noise ratios(SNR). Focusing the issue, firstly, we determined some several uplink cell parameters of TD-SCDMA cellular network based on the 3GPP specifications, such as SNR, processing gain, etc. Secondly, the equation of the uplink performance of TD-SCDMA was derived from two cases of a single cell and multiple-cell. It will provide a strong theoretical support for the future TD-SCDMA network planning and optimization.

Keywords: uplink capacity; processing gain; active factor.

1 Introduction

The third generation mobile communication system has started to comprehensively plan and commercially operate [1][2]. The 3[th]G consists of two modes, a frequency division duplex (FDD) mode [3] and a time-division duplex(TDD) mode [4]. TDD mode has two options, one is wideband TDD (WB-TDD) with chip rate of 3.84 Mcps and the other is low-chip rate TDD (LCR-TDD) with that of 1.28 Mcps. LCR-TDD is also called as TD-SCDMA (Time Division Synchronous CDMA) System. Most of the existing researches on capacity of cellular system are for FDD-CDMA systems. The single-cell and multi-cell uplink and downlink capacity formula has been derived .So far research on TD-SCDMA system capacity is little and limited to be derived. This paper is mainly to solve this problem, and it deduces the limit theory load capacity under the single-cell and multiple-cell conditions. In general, capacity analysis method has two kinds: One analysis method is from traffic statistical; another is derived from the view of interference. The paper chooses the latter. It mainly study

---

[*] The title selection is mainly originated from Tianjin science and technology innovation special funds project(10FDZDGX00400) "the research and development, demonstration and application of new generation mobile communication network coverage key technology".

S. Lin and X. Huang (Eds.): CESM 2011, Part I, CCIS 175, pp. 128–133, 2011.
© Springer-Verlag Berlin Heidelberg 2011

the relationship between capacity and bit energy-to-noise density ratio (E_b/N_0).When the uplink is studied, E_b/N_0 is ratio of received signal to noise arrived receiver. It is from the view of BS. So the study and analysis is not relevant to power of MS transmitter , path loss and transmission loss. We only think about the signal that has arrived at BS receiver. The paper are organized as follows. A single cell capacity function will be deduced in section 2. Multiple cells capacity function will be deduced in section 3. At last, conclusions are drawn in section 4.

2 Uplink Single Cell Capacity Analysis and Research

Capacity discussed in this paper is user capacity, that is, in the QoS requirements, per unit area and per bandwidth can accommodate the maximum number of users. Because single cell model is simple, this section start to analyze it in theoretical. It is assumed that only one base station in single cell and Omni-directional antenna[5] is used. The cell contains users.
The following symbolic meaning is interpreted

P_j is the j-th user power

I_{own} is all users power reaching base station.

N_o is the base station receiver thermal noise.

∂_{AF} is active factor.

I_{total} is that the whole power that is base station have received at all.

From the objective physical meaning, Equation (1) can be defined.

$$I_{own} = \partial_{AF} \times \sum_{j=1}^{N} P_j \tag{1}$$

According to Equation (1), Equation(2) can be drawn

$$I_{total} = \partial_{AF} \times \sum_{j=1}^{N} P_j + N_o \tag{2}$$

η_j is the uplink capacity percentage due to the j-th user added the single cell.

η is the uplink capacity percentage all users of the single cell

$$\eta_j = \frac{P_j}{I_{total}} \tag{3}$$

$$\eta = \sum_{j=1}^{N} \partial_{AF} \cdot \eta_j \tag{4}$$

G is processing gain. W is the rate of Spread Spectrum.

R is service rate. The function relation of the three parameters is following

$$G = \frac{W}{R} \tag{5}$$

If the received power of the j-th user is P_j, the ratio of signal to noise needed to demodulate the signal in Equation(6). G_j is the processing gain of the j-th user.

$$\left(\frac{E_b}{N_o}\right)_j = \frac{G_j \cdot P_j}{\partial_{AF} \times [\sum_{t=1}^{N} P_t - P_j] + N_0} \tag{6}$$

According to Equation (6), Equation (7) can be drawn

$$P_i = \frac{\left(\frac{E_b}{N_0}\right)_j \left[N_0 + \partial_{AF} \cdot \sum_{t=1}^{N} P_t\right]}{\left(\frac{E_b}{N_0}\right)_j \cdot \partial_{AF} + G_j} \tag{7}$$

When Equation (7) can be inserted Equation (3), Equation (8) can be arrived at

$$\eta_j = \frac{\left(\frac{E_b}{N_0}\right)_j}{\left(\frac{E_b}{N_0}\right)_j \cdot \partial_{AF} + G_p} \tag{8}$$

Equation (8) will be inserted in Formula(4), Equation (9) can be drawn

$$\eta = \sum_{j=1}^{N} \partial_{VF} \cdot \eta_j = \sum_{j=1}^{N} \frac{\left(\frac{E_b}{N_0}\right)_j \cdot \partial_{VF}}{\left(\frac{E_b}{N_0}\right)_j \cdot \partial_{AF} + G_j} \tag{9}$$

It is assumed that a single service rate is in the single cell, then all the parameters such as $\left(\frac{E_b}{N_0}\right)_j$ and G_j is constant to j. Equation (9) can be simplified to Equation (10)

$$\eta = \frac{\left(\dfrac{E_b}{N_0}\right) \cdot \partial_{VF} \cdot N}{\left(\dfrac{E_b}{N_0}\right) \cdot \partial_{VF} + G} \tag{10}$$

Network limit capacity is 100% load, that is $\eta = 100\%$. According to the Equation (10), Equation (11) can be obtained.

$$N = 1 + \frac{G}{\left(\dfrac{E_b}{N_0}\right) \cdot \partial_{VF}} \tag{11}$$

Equation (11) is important, the physical meaning can be demonstrated. When the number of users in a single cell will reach the limit capacity, high noise-rise[6][8] makes it difficult that BS(base station) demodulate the signal come from user. Thus the power control algorithm requires increasing transmitting power for each user. Whereas transmitting power increase of each user further improve the noise-rise. That is, the rate of single-user power-rise is lower than the rate of noise-rise since multi-users have increased transmitting power. So E_b / N_0 of demodulating the service will not become better due to single-user increasing transmitting power, but will be even worse [7]. It is cycled so as to power of MS (mobile station) reach to infinitely high. However, mobile station power is always limited in reality, inconstant noise-rise makes the mobile station power exhaust and still be unable to meet the E_b / N_0 requirements [9].

3 Uplink Multiple Cells Capacity Analysis and Research

In multiple cells conditions, to any cell, interference not only comes from self-cell, but also comes from adjacent cells .Some relevant parameters are as follows:

I_{own} is intra-interference. I_{other} is inter-interference.

F is actor of interference ratio. It can be defined

$$F = \frac{I_{other}}{I_{own} + I_{other}} \tag{12}$$

That is, in multiple cells, the base station receives the total interference power of multiple cells is more than single cell $\dfrac{1}{1-F}$ times, and the capacity of multiple cells also reduces $\dfrac{1}{1-F}$ times. In multiple cells capacity function can be drawn in Equation (13)

$$N_{multi} = \frac{N_{single}}{\dfrac{1}{1-F}} = N_{single} \cdot (1-F) \tag{13}$$

f is frequency multiplexing factor

$$f = 1 - F \tag{14}$$

Equation (13),(14) will be inserted Equation (11) , Equation (15) can be drawn.

$$N_{multi} = [1 + \frac{G \cdot}{(\dfrac{E_b}{N_o}) \cdot \partial_{AF}}] \cdot f \tag{15}$$

Result analysis: The limit capacity is relevant of many parameters of base stations such as demodulation abilities, service active factor, spread spectrum factor and multiplexing factor in a variety of channel conditions [9][10]. Higher is sensitivity of base station and Stronger is demodulation ability, lower E_b / N_0 requirements is acquired by base station. It can help to increase the coverage and increase capacity to base station [11]. Whereas in multiple cells environment, the frequency multiplexing means that interference will increase.

4 Conclusions

This paper analyzes the capacity of uplink transmission channel based on the several assumed parameters of the TD-SCDMA specifications and cell-loading concept. Neighbor cell interference is analyzed and limit load-capacity can be calculated with respect to the formula that has been deduced. Based on the analysis and evaluation of uplink capacity TD-SCDMA system, the equations can be utilized for establishing the effective cell planning and optimization scenario for TD-SCDMA system further deployment. What's more, it provides a theoretical basis and technical support for large-scale commercial operations.

Acknowledgment

The title selection is mainly originated from Tianjin science and technology innovation special funds project(10FDZDGX00400) and Tianjin Key Laboratory for Control Theory and Application in Complicated Systems, Tianjin University of Technology, Tianjin 300384, China. The name of the project is "the research and development, demonstration and application of new generation mobile communication network coverage key technology".

References

1 3GPP TR 36.942 V8, Evolved Universal Terrestrial Radio Access (E-UTRA); Radio Frequency (RF) system scenarios, 3rd Generation Partnership Project, Technical Specification Group Radio Access Networks, Technical Report (2008)

2 3GPP TR 25.942 V9, Universal Mobile Telecommunications System(UMTS); Radio Frequency(RF) system scenarios, 3rd Generation Partnership Project, Technical Specification Group Radio Access Networks, Technical Report (2010)

3 3GPP TR 25.945 V5, Universal Mobile Telecommunications System(UMTS); Radio requirements for low chip rate TDD option, 3rd Generation Partnership Project, Technical Specification Group Radio Access Networks, Technical Report (2007)

4 3GPP TR 25.951 V9, Universal Mobile Telecommunications System (UMTS); FDD Base Station(BS) classification, 3rd Generation Partnership Project, Technical Specification Group Radio Access Networks, Technical Report (2010)

5 3GPP TR 25.141 V9, Universal Mobile Telecommunications System (UMTS); Base Station(BS) conformance testing(FDD)," 3rd Generation Partnership Project, Technical Specification Group Radio Access Networks, Technical Report (2010)

6 3GPP TR 25.142 V9, Universal Mobile Telecommunications System (UMTS);Base Station (BS) conformance testing (TDD), 3rd Generation Partnership Project, Technical Specification Group Radio Access Networks, Technical Report (2010)

7 Li, B., Xie, D., Cheng, S., Chen, J., Zhang, P., Zhu, W., Li, B.: Recent Advances on TD-SCDMA in China. IEEE Communications Magazine 43, 30–37 (2005)

8 Kim, D.-h., Song, P.-j., Han, Y.-n., Choi, W.: The Capacity Analysis of an Embedded WCDMA FDD/TDD System sharing Allocation Frequency. IEEE VTC, 3044–3048 (Spring 2001)

9 Chen, J., Grace, D., Mitchell, P.: Capacity Analysis of Coexisting TD-SCDMA/WCDMA System. In: The 18th Annual IEEE International Symposium on Personal, Indoor and Mobile Radio Communications (PIMRC 2007) (2007)

10 Winters, J.H.: Optimum Combining in Digital Mobile Radio with Cochannel Interference. IEEE Journal on Selected Areas in Communications 2, 528–539 (1984)

11 Larsson, E.G.: Model-Averaged Interference Rejection Combining. IEEE Trans. on Communications 55, 271–274 (2007)

Simulation of Micro Stage System
Based on BP Neural Network Control[*]

Jianying Shen

College of Mechanical & Electrical Engineering, Jiaxing University,
314001 Jiaxing, China
zjjxsjy@163.com

Abstract. The transfer function of micro stage system is set up in the paper and the control algorithm combined PID control and BP neural network has been simulated with Matlab software. The simulation result indicates that there are no oscillation, no overstrike and smooth, and that the adjustment time is less than 0.05 second. So the control performance of PID controller is good and the control algorithm has achieved the expected effect.

Keywords: micro stage, BP neural network, simulation.

1 Introduction

With the development of science and technology, micro-displacement technology has been widely applied in many fields [1,2,3], such as aeronautics and astronautics, microelectronic engineering, butting optical fiber, ultra-precision machining, robot, bioengineering, nanotechnology, etc. High precision micro stage system is an important aspect of micro-displacement technology, and it is a key technology in advanced science and engineering. As an ideal micro-displacement actuator, piezoelectric actuator has many advantages: the small volume, high resolution, high precision, no noise and fast frequency response. But the displacement accuracy is affected by piezoelectric ceramic disadvantages [4], such as hysteresis, creep and nonlinearity. Therefore, the control measure should be adopted to improve displacement accuracy. In the paper the control algorithm combined PID control method with BP neural network is presented and simulated in the software Matlab.

2 Model Establishing of Micro-Stage System

2.1 Control Structure of Micro-Stage System

Micro-stage system is composed of computer, interface circuit, D/A converter, driving power, piezoelectric ceramics, micro-stage, displacement sensor, A/D data acquisition circuit, which is illustrated in Fig. 1.

---

[*] Supported by Key Foundation of Jiaxing University (No. 70110X06BL).

S. Lin and X. Huang (Eds.): CESM 2011, Part I, CCIS 175, pp. 134–138, 2011.
© Springer-Verlag Berlin Heidelberg 2011

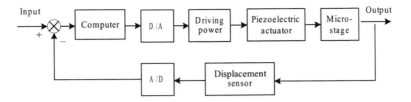

Fig. 1. Control diagram of micro-stage system

Through the interface circuit, D/A converter the digital signal from computer is amplified by driving power to produce a control DC voltage to control piezoelectric actuator and the micro stage produces the output of micro displacement driven by piezoelectric actuator. The micro displacement from micro stage is detected by a displacement sensor and it is returned to the computer through A/D data acquisition circuit. Then the closed-loop control for micro stage can be fulfilled by computer according to the deviation.

2.2 Transfer Function of Micro-Stage System

Piezoelectric actuator is equivalent to a capacitive component [5], which is a first-order inertial link. So its transfer function is given as follows:

$$G_1(s) = \frac{k_m}{Ts+1}.$$ (1)

where k_m is the coefficient of voltage to displacement, T is the time constant.

Micro-stage system can be simplified as mass-spring-damping second-order systems and its transfer function can be expressed by the following equation:

$$G_2(s) = \frac{k\omega_n^2}{s^2 + 2\xi\omega_n + \omega_n^2}.$$ (2)

DC driving power supply amplifies the analog voltage signal from D/A converter, which can control piezoelectric actuator, and its transfer function can be given as:

$$G_3(s) = k_v.$$ (3)

It can be seen from Fig. 1 that each part connects in series and an output of the former link is an input of the next link input. So according to the transfer functions established in every part, the open-loop transfer function of micro-stage system can be calculated as:

$$G(s) = \frac{k_n\omega_n^2}{(Ts+1)(s^2 + 2\xi\omega_n + \omega_n^2)}.$$ (4)

where $k_n = k_m k k_v$.

3 PID Control Method Based on BP Neural Network

The control functions of proportion, integral and differential should be properly adjusted to form a control relationship of mutual restriction and interdependence to achieve a good control effect for PID control method. This relationship is not a necessarily simple "linear combination" and the best relationship can be found from the boundless linear combination. Neural network can fully approximate any complicated nonlinear relationship with an ability of expressing arbitrary nonlinearity and of self adapting and self learning for complex uncertain systems and can fulfill the optimal PID control by learning the performance of the system. The error back propagation network (BP) is widely used in the neural network model and it is a kind of network which has hidden multilayer.

3.1 Control Principle

Self-learning PID controller can be created by adopting BP neural network, where the outputs of the neural network are proportional, integral and derivative gains. The control structure of PID controller based on BP neural network is shown in Fig.2, which is composed of two parts as follow:

(i) General PID controller

The controlled object can be directly controlled by general PID controller in a closed-loop manner where the three parameters KP, KI and KD are adjusted on line. The numerical PID control algorithm employed in the study is given by

$$u(k) = u(k-1) + K_P(e(k) - e(k-1)) + K_I e(k) + K_D(e(k) - 2(e(k-1) + e(k-2)).\qquad (5)$$

where K_P K_I and K_D are the proportional, integral and derivative gains, respectively.

(ii) Neural network

Neural network adjusts the parameters of PID controller in order to make some performance index optimize with respect to the operation condition of the controlled object. Through the self-learning and the adjusting of the weighting coefficients of neural network to get a certain optimal control law for PID controller the three adjustable parameters of K_p, K_i and K_D, which are the outputs of the neural network, are obtained.

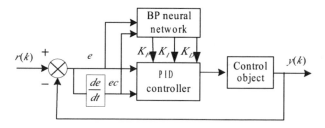

Fig. 2. Control structure of PID controller based on BP neural network

3.2 Simulation Stage

The simulation stage of the algorithm is given as follows:

(i) A three layered neural network based on the BP method used is shown in Fig.3. The initial values of weight coefficients in each layer are given while $k = 1$.

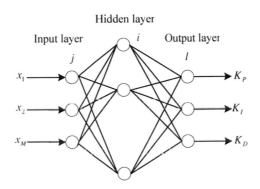

Fig. 3. BP network structure

(ii) The values of $r(k)$ and $y(k)$ are obtained by sampling and the error can be calculate by equation (6) at the moment.

$$e(k) = r(k) - y(k).$$ (6)

(iii) The inputs and outputs of neurons in each layer are calculated. The three adjustable parameters K_P, K_I and K_D of PID controller are the output of output layer of neural network.

(iv) The output $u(k)$ of PID controller is calculated by equation (5).

(v) The self-adaption adjustment of the control parameters in PID controller are achieved by learning and adjusting weight coefficients on line in neural network.

(vi) Let $k = k + 1$ and return to (i).

3.3 Simulation Results

The simulation is done using Matlab software according to the above control algorithm and the simulation result is shown in Fig. 4. It can be seen from the simulation curve in Fig. 4 that there are no oscillation, no overstrike and smooth, and that the adjustment time is less than 0.05 second. So the control performance of PID controller is good and the expected effect is achieved.

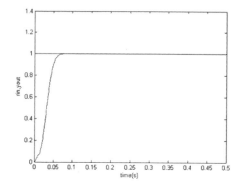

Fig. 4. Diagram of simulation curve

4 Conclusions

The closed-loop transfer function of micro-stage system has been theoretically established in the paper. Then the control algorithm combined PID control method with BP neural network has been simulated with the software Matlab. The simulation result illustrates that this algorithm has achieved the desired control effect.

References

1. Chang, S.H., Du, B.C.: A precision piezo-driven micropositioner mechanism with large travel range. Rev. Sci. Instrum 69(4), 1785–1791 (1998)
2. Nia, Z., Zhanga, D., Wub, Y., et al.: Analysis of parasitic motion in parallelogram compliant mechanism. Precision Engineering 34(1), 133–138 (2010)
3. Choia, K.-B., Leea, J.J., Hatab, S.: A piezo-driven compliant stage with double mechanical amplification mechanisms arranged in parallel. Sensors and Actuators A: Physical 161, 173–181 (2010)
4. Minase, J., Lu, T.-F., Cazzolato, B., et al.: Adaptive identification of hysteresis and creep in piezoelectric stack actuators. International Journal of Advanced Manufacturing Technology 46(9-12), 913–921 (2010)
5. Minase, J., Lu, T.-F., Cazzolato, B., et al.: A review supported by experimental results of voltage, charge and capacitor insertion method for driving piezoelectric actuators. Precision Engineering 34(4), 692–700 (2010)

Study on the Monolithic Muffler Acoustic Field Performance of the Train Air-Conditioning

Xuquan Li, Yaohua Wei, Minjie Gu, Gang Wang, and Songtao Hu

School of Environmental Municipal Engineering
Qingdao Technological University
Qingdao, China
lxuquan@163.com

Abstract. This article take the monolithic muffler which is commonly applied in the train air-conditioning duct as the study objection. Simulates the monolithic muffler acoustic field performance with SYSNOISE. Gets the internal acoustic pressure distribution. Measurements on the test-bed of train air-conditioning duct have done and verify the correctness and rationality of the simulation results. We get the monolithic muffler transmission loss was obtained by simulation. It provides the basis for the muffler performance further study.

Keywords: Train air conditioning; Monolithic muffler; Transmission loss, noise; Simulation.

1   Introduction

The noise which is generated by air conditioning unit come into the train room through the air conditioning duct, because the straight pipe, elbow, tee, reducer pipe exists the air conditioning duct, the noise will arise certain natural attenuation in the dissemination process [1]. As a lot of practices show, after the attenuation, the noise is difficult to come to the noise limit of train indoor, which requires certain measures to be taken on the air conditioning system for us to reduce noise, making the indoor noise is lower than the noise limits which stipulated in the GB/T12816-2006.

At present, the main method for reducing the noise of the train air conditioning duct is to install the duct silencers. On one hand, after installation of silencers, it is useful for reducing the noise in the duct, but on the other hand also will increases the resistance of air duct. So we should consider the requirement of the spot and the impact on the system resistance when design or select the silencers.

In this paper, we adopt the method that combines numerical simulation and experimental validation to study on the monolithic muffler acoustic field performance of the train air -conditioning duct [2][3]. The typical structure of the monolithic muffler is that fixes the sound-absorbing materials on the right and left wall and insert the silencer boards which are made up of sound-absorbing materials. The muffler is divided into a number of small uniform air flow channel, typically the thickness of the middle silencer boards is twice the size of the sound -absorbing material on both

S. Lin and X. Huang (Eds.): CESM 2011, Part I, CCIS 175, pp. 139–145, 2011.
© Springer-Verlag Berlin Heidelberg 2011

sides. The air and fiber inside the sound -absorbing materials of the monolithic muffler will vibrate when sound waves enter into the monolithic muffler. Because of the friction and viscous resistance, the part of the sound energy transform into heat and dissipate. As the sound wave transmit in the channel, the sound can continue to be absorbed by sound-absorbing materials. And its sound pressure decreases as the increasing of the transmission distance. Thus reduce the noise [4]. The length of muffler is 1.25m, and there is the glass-silk sound- absorbing material inside the muffler, and the entire muffler is divided into the four same channels by the three sound-absorbing material boards.

2   The Acoustic Field Simulation of the Monolithic Muffler

2.1   The Control Equations of the Monolithic Muffler

As a macroscopic physical phenomenon, the vibration of sound waves should satisfy the basic laws of physics, such as Newton's second law, law of conservation of mass and the state equation of description of temperature, pressure and density. We can descript the changing relations of sound pressure, particle velocity and density in the quantitative mathematical form and thus obtain and establish the changing relations of sound pressure over time and space, namely wave equation. when analysis the theories of acoustic wave movement, we makes the following basic assumptions about its transmission process [5][6]: (1) the medium is the uniform ideal fluid, which is no viscosity, (2) the acoustic transmission process is a adiabatic processes, that is, no heat exchange with the outside (3) what we descript is the small amplitude acoustic wave propagation, the change of state of the medium is linear.

The equations of motion

$$\vec{\nabla} p = -\rho_0 \frac{\partial \vec{v}}{\partial t} \tag{1}$$

$$\vec{\nabla} = \frac{\partial}{\partial x}\vec{i} + \frac{\partial}{\partial y}\vec{j} + \frac{\partial}{\partial z}\vec{k} \quad , \quad \vec{v} = v_x\vec{i} + v_y\vec{j} + v_z\vec{k}$$

Where: $\vec{\nabla}$ --the Laplacian,
P-- pressure of the particle, kPa;v -- velocity of the particle, m/s; ρ_0-- density of the medium, kg/m^3;

The equation of continuity

$$-\rho_0 \vec{\nabla}.\vec{v} = \frac{\partial \rho^{'}}{\partial t} \tag{2}$$

The equation of state

Because the sound waves transmit much faster than the speed of heat, we can assume that the process of sound transmission is adiabatic process. Thus equation of the adiabatic state of a certain quality of an ideal gas is as follow:

$$\frac{\partial p}{\partial t} = c^2 \frac{\partial \rho}{\partial t} \tag{3}$$

Acoustic wave equation

$$\overline{\nabla}^2 \overline{p} = -\frac{1}{c^2} \frac{\partial^2 \overline{p}}{\partial t^2} \tag{4}$$

2.2 The Sub-grid Model of the Acoustic Fields

Because SYSNIOSE pre-treatment functions are weak, we should create a finite element model of the muffler at the proportion of 1:1 in ANSYS, and create two ducts model whose length both are125mm at the opening and the entrance of the finite element model. We also mesh the model according to "each wave length with 6 units" rule after modeling in ANSYS:

$$f_{max} = \frac{c}{6\Delta L} \tag{5}$$

The highest frequency we analysis and calculate is 4322Hz. Figure 1 shows the finite element model after the model is imported into the SYSNIOSE.

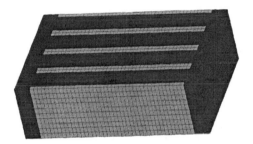

Fig. 1. Mesh model after imported into the NIOSE

2.3 Boundary Conditions and Material Properties Setup of the Acoustic Field Model

After the model is imported into the SYSNIOSE, we should define boundary conditions and material properties, and the boundary conditions of the acoustic field include in the inlet, outlet and wall settings. Table 1 is boundary conditions, Material properties setup is as follow: Fluid density is 1.225 kg/m^3, Sound wave velocity is 340 m /s, Impedance is 12000pa.s/m^2, the structure coefficient is 4, Porosity is 0.4.

Table 1. Boundary conditions setup

Position	Boundary types	Value
Inlet	Unit speed	-1
Outlet	All sound-absorbing export	416.5
Muffler wall	Rigid wall	Default

3 Validation and Performance Analysis of the Muffler Acoustic Field Simulation

3.1 Tests on the Muffler Sound Field Performance

In order to verify the correctness and rationality of the muffler sound field model, we do the measurement on the test-bed of train air-conditioning duct. Fig. 2 shows test-bed schematic diagram. Testing instruments is as follow:

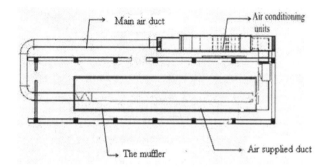

Fig. 2. Test-bed schematic diagram

(1) The polyhedron sound sources, it is the sound source without directivity which adopts electric speakers and it is usually used in the architectural acoustics test as point source. In the 100-10000Hz frequency range, the sound power of center frequency of all 1 / 3 octave changes within the 12dB and the sound power level of the center frequency of the two adjacent 1 / 3 octave changes within ± 3dB.(2) The microphone, its function is to convert acoustic signals into electrical signals. (3)The dual-channel acoustic real time analyzer, it is a digital frequency line display device, it can display simultaneously the input signal within its measure range in a very short period of time, it connects microphone probe by two channels interface, and can real-time measure A, B, C weighted sound level in octave band and 1 / 3 octave Zones, and shows the obtained data in order to facilitate to analysis further. (4) The sound calibrators, it is a sound source that can produce a constant level value for 94dB under the frequency of 1000HZ ,and can be used to calibrate the absolute sound pressure sensitivity of the microphone. We must calibrate the microphone before and after the measurement. (5) The power amplifier.

Firstly open air conditioning unit, and adjust the air supply fan for 3800m³/h to test the flow field, including the upstream and downstream flow of the muffler, static pressure, dynamic pressure and temperature tests. Turn off air conditioning unit After the flow field test, open the acoustics test instrument and debug the acoustic power amplifier, while ensure the interior noise value of the train greater 10dB than background noise value, then may begin the acoustic test.

3.2 The Evaluation Indexes of the Muffler Acoustics Performance

The sound deadening capacity usually is used to evaluate the quality of the muffler acoustics performance, according to the different test method, the evaluation index of the muffler acoustics performance include in transmission loss, insertion loss, transmission sound pressure level differential and insertion sound pressure level differential, this paper apply the transmission loss as the evaluation index.

The muffler transmission loss LTL is the difference of the sound power level of the muffler inlet and export. It is in terms of the sound insulation of the components to reflect the sound deadening capacity of the muffler with the transmission loss. The formula is as follow:

$$L_{TL} = 10\lg\left(W_1 \big/ W_2\right) = L_{W_1} - L_{W_2} \tag{6}$$

where: L_{TI}—The transmission loss ,dB,W_1—The entrance sound power,W,W_2—The exit sound power,W,L_{W1}—The entrance sound power level,dB,L_{W2}—The exit sound power level, dB. The transmission loss is an intrinsic feature of the muffler. It is little subject to the impact of the sound source and the environmental. Because the sound power levels is difficult to measure directly in the practical engineering tests. So usually by measuring the average level of the cross-section before and after the muffler, and then calculated as follows:

$$L_{w1} = L_{P1} + 10\lg S_1 \tag{7}$$

$$L_{w2} = L_{P2} + 10\lg S_2 \tag{8}$$

Where: L_{P1}—Average sound pressure level of the muffler entrance,dB, L_{P2}—Average sound pressure level of the muffler exit,dB,S_1—Cross-sectional area of the muffler entrance,m^2, S_2—Cross-sectional area of the muffler exit,m^2.

3.3 The Analysis of Test Results and Simulation Results of the Sound Field

The test values and simulation values under the center frequency of the 1/3 octave are just as Table 2.

Table 2. Test and simulation values of the transmission loss by A weighted

Test	value	Simulation values	Deviation
Inlet	Outlet		
91.8dB	63.7dB	26.7dB	5.24%
28.1dB			

Table 2 shows that the test value of the muffler transmission loss by A-weighted is 28.1dB, and the deviation compared with simulation value is 5.24%. It indicates that the simulation model is reasonable, and provides a good way for the muffler further research.

Figure 3 shows the size of the test value and simulation value of each frequency in 1/3 octave band, what can be seen from Figure 3 is as follows: (1) The attenuation frequency of the monolithic resistive muffler is very wide and the attenuation effect is obvious, especially for the middle and high frequency sound wave, but to low frequency sound wave, its effect is little. This trend fits well with the monolithic muffler characteristics.(2)The change trend of the simulation results and test results of sound deadening capacity under each frequency are basically identical, which indicates that the software SYSNOISE can play a better guiding role in analysis and design of the muffler. But numerical simulation is different form measured value under specific frequency.

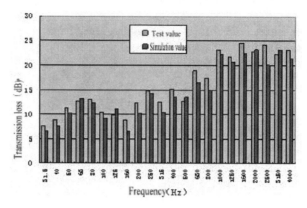

Fig. 3. Test values of transmission loss compared with the simulation value

The measured value is higher than the simulation under the same frequency. It is mainly due to the following reasons:(1) .simplification is too idealized in the simulation calculation, for example, take the exit of the muffler as the full absorption surface, but in the actual testing process, because the muffler connect the duct directly, so it will produce a certain disturbance to the sound wave transmission at the variable cross-section, and inevitably have some impact on the sound deadening capacity of the muffler; furthermore, take the muffler wall as the rigid wall in the calculation and overlook the transmission effect of the muffler wall in the practice.(2) In the actual test, background noise will be inevitably affected by the surrounding environment.

4   Analysis of Simulation Results of the Muffler Sound Field

Fig. 4 shows the sound deadening capacity of the muffler under each frequency. It can be seen from the figure that the monolithic muffler is weak for the noise under the medium and low frequency, size of the sound deadening capacity is 8dB-12dB. But to the high frequency, the muffler have a greater impact, the peak volume of the sound deadening capacity is 2400Hz, 3700Hz and 4100Hz. In general, to the frequency of 600Hz - 2200Hz, the sound deadening capacity is 15dB, to the frequency of 2200Hz-4300Hz, the sound deadening capacity is 20dB around.

Fig.5 shows the internal sound pressure nephogram of the muffler under the frequency of 1000Hz.It can be seen from the figure, with the acoustic transmission in the muffler, due to itself attenuation and the effect of the sound-absorbing material. The sound pressure of the sound wave show a step decrease, and the reduction in the sound-absorbing material is significantly greater than in the air, which indicates that sound-absorbing material play a very important role in the silencing effect of the muffler.

By software calculating, we get the transmission loss value under each frequency, and calculated the sound deadening capacity by A- weighted is 26.7dB.

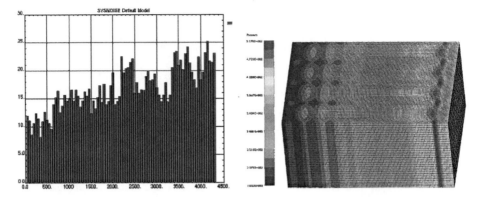

Fig. 4. Simulation of the transmission loss under each frequency

Fig. 5. Internal sound pressure nephogram of the muffler under the 1000Hz

5 Conclusion

In this paper, we take the monolithic muffler applied on the train air conditioning duct as the study objection, and simulates numerically the monolithic muffler acoustic field performance with the acoustic analysis software SYSNOISE, and do the experiment test for verifying the correctness and rationality of the simulation. The main conclusions are as follows: (1) the analysis result of the muffler by the software SYSNOISE is consistent with the test result. It is feasible for simulating the acoustic field characteristics of the monolithic muffler by the SYSNOISE. It provides a basis for the study on the performance of the muffler. (2)The attenuation frequency of the monolithic resistive muffler applied in the train duct is very wide and the attenuation range is mainly the middle and high frequency sound wave. The attenuation effect is obvious. (3)The sound-absorbing material of the monolithic resistive muffler applied in the train duct play a very important role in the silencing effect of the muffler.

References

[1] YouMa, D.: Noise and Vibration Control Engineering Manual. China Machine Press, 9 (2002)

[2] Ma, J.: Reserch on the Properties of the Flow Field and Acoustic Field internal the Muffler. Master Thesis of Jilin University (2005)

[3] Shen, B.: Design of the Monolithic Muffler and Application in Environmental Noise Control. Shantou University (1995)

[4] Yu, Y.: Design of the Central air conditioning system. Southeast University Press (2007)

[5] Du, G.: Basic of Acoustics. Nanjing University Press (2001)

[6] Liu, B., Maeno, M., Hase, S., Wakamatsu, S.: A Study of a Dual Mode Muffler. SAE paper 2003-0 1-1 647

Cell Status Diagnosis for the Aluminum Production on BP Neural Network with Genetic Algorithm

Shuiping Zeng, Jinhong Li, and Lin Cui

North China University of Technology, Beijing, 100144
zshp@ncut.edu.cn

Abstract. To diagnose the status of aluminum production cell, we set up a diagnosis system. This system was based on BP neural network with 10 inputs and 3 outputs. It used frequency energy of cell resistance as characteristic vectors. Also genetic algorithm was used to optimize the initial weights and threshold value of BP network. After designed and tested this software system, three kinds of status were successfully diagnosed, which are anode lesion, liquid aluminum fluctuation and normal condition. As a result, by sampling data on site, the status diagnosis accuracy is larger than 83%.

Keywords: Aluminum production cell, Genetic algorithm, BP neural network.

1 Introduction

Aluminum is produced by electrolysis, with alumina as raw material, cryolite-alumina melts as solvent, carbon block as anode and liquid aluminum covered on the carbon as cathode. Direct current is injected. After the electrolytic reaction, carbon dioxide mixed with carbon monoxide is produced at anode and aluminum at cathode. The analysis and diagnosis of aluminum production cells status is important to the aluminum production industry. It is also a bottleneck for this industry to improve the automation [1].

Aluminum production cell is the major equipment for aluminum production, which status of is not only related to the economic technical indexes, but also affecting the cells life and daily production. Aluminum production cell is a nonlinear, more coupling, time-varying and large delay process. In this process, the material balance and energy balance are constantly changing, influencing and restraining each other, so that some status maybe happen, such as anode effect, anode lesion, cold cell, hot cell, etc. Once some of them happen, large economic losses will be caused. It has been an urgent problem to reduce the energy consumption of aluminum electrolysis, to increase cell age, and to reduce the economic loss [2].

Cell status or Fault diagnosis technology in aluminum production mainly deal with the fuzzy expert system, neural network, wavelet transform and the combination of other technology methods. Good results have been achieved in some extent from the papers. But systems with good performance in industry process are not reported. The intelligent diagnosis research of the aluminum production cells has great progress in theory but most of the research remains in the laboratory [3-5].

S. Lin and X. Huang (Eds.): CESM 2011, Part I, CCIS 175, pp. 146–152, 2011.
© Springer-Verlag Berlin Heidelberg 2011

2 System Design

2.1 Classification of Aluminum Production Cells Status

Because of the situation of anode and cathode are mainly considered in the process, this system primarily diagnoses three cell conditions: anode lesion, liquid aluminum fluctuation and normal condition.

The structure of aluminum production cells status analysis has been shown in the *Figure 1*.

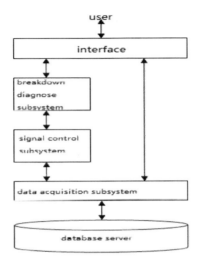

Fig. 1. System structure

From the figure 1, the general structure of the system can be divided into three levels. The top is man-machine interface, namely interface layer, including all sorts of man-machine interface, menus, command buttons, graphic display, etc. The middle layer is the body of signal analysis, slot status diagnosis algorithm and various parameters computing, namely logic layer, including various parameters computing, realization of cell status diagnosis algorithm, parameters setting and online data acquisition, etc. The low level is the database server, namely the data layer, storing various online data on site, etc.

3 Cell Status Diagnosis System Design

3.1 Selection of Input and Output Characteristic Vectors

Literature [6] collected and discussed the cell resistance signal under the normal and abnormal circumstance. The cell resistance signal was sampled and treated by frequency analysis. According their results, we find that the three kinds of status mentioned above behave different in their resistance signal frequency and the amplitude of spectrum. The characteristic of different kinds of cell status are shown in the *table 1*.

On the basis of literature 6, cell status samples are established with the frequency energy as the characteristic vectors. The input characteristic vectors are P0, P1, P2, P3, P4, P5, P6, P7, P8, P9. They represent the total energy with the frequency respectively between *0~0.01Hz*, *0.01~0.02Hz*, *0.02~0.03Hz*, 0.03~0.04Hz, 0.04~0.05Hz, 0.05~0.06Hz, 0.06~0.07Hz, 0.07~0.08Hz and 0.08~0.09Hz.

We take three kinds of cell status as the network output characteristic vectors. The following forms can represent them. *Y*1: （1 0 0） donates the cell status is normal; *Y*2: (0 1 0) donates the liquid aluminum is fluctuating; *Y*3: （0 0 1） donates the anode is abnormal.

Table 1. Characteristic of aluminum production cells under the diffident status

Cell status	characteristic			
	Frequency energy	Low-frequency (< 0.01Hz)	Intermediate-frequency (0.01~0.1Hz)	High-frequency (>0.1Hz)
Normal	Low	A control signal	No obvious law	No obvious peak value
Liquid aluminum fluctuation	High	A control signal	An obvious peak value at the frequency of 0.02~0.03Hz	No obvious peak value
Anode abnormal	High	A control signal	Tow obvious peak value at the frequency of 0.03~0.04Hz and 0.06~0.07Hz	No obvious peak value

3.2 Determining the Nodes

Neurons at the input layer are determined by the dimensions of input characteristic vectors. By referring to the discussion above, the dimensions are 10. That is to say the nodes are also 10. Neural nodes at the output layer are determined by the different kinds of status. In this paper we mainly talk about three circumstances. As a result, the nodes of output layer are 3. According to the rule of determining the hidden nodes under 3 layers of BP neural network, taking the number of hidden nodes for 8. After repeated experiments, the learning rate was selected as 0.08 and expectative error as 0.005.

3.3 Establishing the Neural Network Model

According to the analysis above, we establish a BP neural network model with 10 input neurons, 3 output neurons and 8 hidden neurons. Here we assume that the BP neural network has three layers: input layer (I), hidden layer (H) and output layer (O). Among them I_i is the output of *ith* node at input layer, H_j is the output of *jth* node at hidden layer, O_k is the output of *kth* node at output layer. WIH_{ij} is the weight between the *ith* node of input layer and the *jth* node of hidden layer, WHO_{jk} is the weight between the *jth* node of hidden layer and the *kth* node of output layer, h_j is the threshold value of *jth* node at hidden layer, O_k is the threshold value of *kth* node at output layer. Where $1 \leq i \leq 10$, $1 \leq j \leq 8$, $1 \leq k \leq 3$.

The structure of BP neural network is shown in the *Figure 2*.

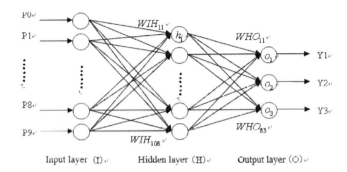

Fig. 2. BP neural network

4 Optimizing the BP Neural Network by Genetic Algorithm

4.1 Optimization

1. Parameters initialization. Setting some parameters: initial population G is 30, maximum genetic algebra T is 100, crossover rate $P_{crossover}$ is 0.6, mutation rate $P_{mutation}$ is 0.09. The fitness function f_i is realized by the software MATLAB.

2. Coding and generating initial population. We code any weight and threshold value with real. Then construct a code chain. Every chain is a collection of weight and threshold value in the BP neural network. Finally an initial population which contains 30 individuals is generated randomly.

3. Computing the Adapter value of every individual according to the fitness function. Judging whether it meets the requirements or not. If not, conducting the genetic operation and comes out the new individuals. Then we compute the sun of error squares of the artificial neural network. If the result does not reach the expectation, where the expectation value ε_{GA} is 5.0, the genetic operation went on. If it satisfies certain condition within 100 times operation, we will finally get the optimal solution.

4. Decomposing the optimal solution into the weight and threshold value of BP neural network.

The flowchart of genetic algorithm is shown in Figure 3.

We use genetic algorithm to optimize neural network weight and threshold value. Then conduct the neural network learning with *BP* algorithm. The software MATLAB is used for programming in the design. After 2571 times training, the neural network will reach the expected precision, where expected precision ε_{BP} is 0.005.

The result is $TT =$
0.9832 0.9952 0.9855 0.0091 0.0162 0.0126
0.0199 0.0108 0.0102 0.0147 0.0106 0.0142
0.9925 0.9895 0.9813 0.0116 0.0162 0.0130
0.0185 0.0072 0.0144 0.0119 0.0095 0.0188
0.9838 0.9858 0.9902

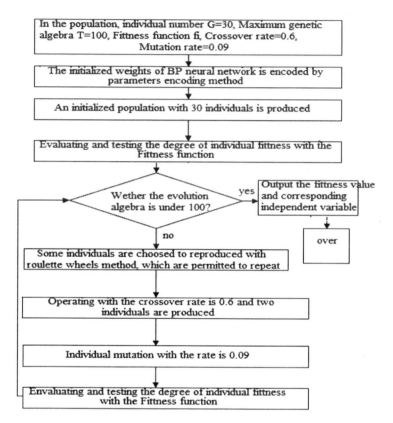

Fig. 3. Genetic algorithm flowchart

The ideal output, where T donates it, is:
1 1 1 0 0 0 0 0 0
0 0 0 1 1 1 0 0 0
0 0 0 0 0 0 1 1 1
Obviously after 80 times operation, we get the expectation.

4.2 System Application

Aluminum production cells status diagnosis system can detect the parameters of the cell online, including voltage, electric current, alumina concentration and temperature. Also this system could accomplish the status diagnosis during the electrolytic process.

Figure 4 is the components of the system. We use the 30 sets of data acquired on site to test the well-trained BP neural network. As a result, 25 sets of them could diagnose the status correctly. That is to say the accuracy rate could reach 83% The accuracy of this cell diagnosis model is verified.

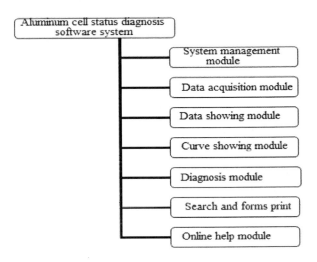

Fig. 4. System function module chart

5 Conclusion

1. According to the characteristics of the aluminum production cells status and the production system at present, we accomplish an overall design for the system.
2. Neural network is used to establish the cell status diagnosis model. Also genetic algorithm is applied to optimize the initial weights and threshold value of the BP neural network.
3. After testing this system with the actual production data. We can find that the diagnosis result is consistent with the actual situation.

Acknowledgment. Project supported by the National Natural Science Funds (Based on the Six Sigma and Trend of Sequential Pattern of Aluminum Cell Condition Forecasting Model and Algorithm for Research, Funding: 51075423).

References

1. Liu, Y., Li, J.: Modern Aluminum Production. The Metallurgical Industry Press, Beijing (2008)
2. Zeng, S., Li, J.: Model Predictive Control of Superheat for Prebake Aluminum Production Cells. Light Metals (2008), TMS Annual Meeting (March 2008)

3. Zeng, S., Li, J.: The Fuzzy Predictive Control of the Aluminum Electrolytic Cell Electrolyte Molecular Ratio. In: The seventh Global Intelligence Control and Automation Conference, pp. 1229–1233 (June 2008)
4. Banta, L., Dai, C., Biedler, P.: Noise Classification in the Aluminum Reduction Process, Light Metals, pp. 431–435 (2003)
5. Li, H., Zhi, M., Tang, Q., et al.: The Aluminum Production Cell Status Diagnosis on the Fuzzy Neural Network. Journal of System Stimulation 18(2), 482–484 (2006)
6. Ding, L.: 350kA Aluminum Production Cell Fault Diagnosis System Research (Master degree thesis). North China University of Technology, Beijing (2006)

The Application of Project Isomerization Teaching Method in Database Course Design

Qin Liu

Department of Information Science and Technology
East China University of Political Science and Law
Shanghai 200042, China
liuqin@ecupl.edu.cn

Abstract. We propose a teaching method taking project as the main theme and isomerization as the soul by the long-term teaching practice of database course design. This method emphasizes taking the project as center in the process of course design, organizing teaching according to the organization method of real project, and stresses the factors such as subject isomerism, personnel isomerism and grading isomerism in the process of teaching. Practice proves that this method can provide some help for students to improve their abilities in creation, independence and cooperation, and be useful to other sectors of practice teaching.

Keywords: Teaching method; Course design; Database; Project isomerization.

1 Introduction

Today, the database technology has become a necessary part of modern engineering application, a research branch in the area of computer science, and almost all students majoring in computer in the universities study database course, and many universities offer database course as an elective course for students whose major is not computer. Under both of the two situations, universities usually require students to make database course design, or complete a term project with similar aim or conduct a comprehensive experiment at the end of course to enable them to master relevant knowledge. The course design is a comprehensive design in large scale which students should make when they finish their courses..It is very important for students to improve their abilities of hand-on practice, and it is a summarization of study and basis of graduation project, and an important method to improve students' abilities in resolving problems and innovation. So, the database course design plays a great role in teaching.

The project isomerization teaching method is a scheme which can efficiently organize course design proposed on the basis of experiences in the practice, namely a teaching scheme taking project as the main theme and isomerization as the soul. This teaching method can enable students to master the essential of course by the greatest degree in limited time and with limited teaching resource, and it combines theory with practice teaching organically, exploits the independent innovation ability of students

S. Lin and X. Huang (Eds.): CESM 2011, Part I, CCIS 175, pp. 153–158, 2011.

sufficiently, enhances their comprehensive ability in resolving practice problems. This paper introduces the project isomerization teaching method firstly, and then illustrates its application process and result in the teaching.

2   The Project Isomerization Teaching Method

The project isomerization teaching method is a teaching activity performed through actualizing a complete project, and teachers finish their teaching task step by step and designedly in the whole teaching activity, they take project as the main theme and isomerization as the soul. The teaching activity has five basic steps including project proposing, project planning, project implementing, showing results and project evaluating, and the idea of isomerism mainly is embodied in the aspects of task isomerism, personnel structure isomerism and evaluation system.

2.1   The Basic Steps

1) Project proposing
In this stage, the tutors will propose the aim, steps and demands of whole database course design, and advance the name of project, name of sub-projects or sub-task, the characteristics of each sub-project and the abilities from which students could obtain. Here, it should be explained especially that we divide the project into several parts, and the requests and emphasis of cultivating abilities in each part aren't the same completely, hence, each sub-project has its own characteristics, and students can select some projects and sub-projects fitting to them according to their knowledge level and interests, of course, students can also set the topic by themselves after being affirmed by the tutors. The students are supervised in groups; three or four students are put into one group, and one of them serve as project leader, students in the group responsible for different work cooperate with others; and they complete design and development task together.

2) Project planning
This part of work is completed mainly by students who fill in the planning leaflet and make the plan. The teachers instruct and evaluate the project plans, help students to control the time schedule to enable students to implement the project more efficiently.

3) Project implementing
This is the key step of whole teaching activity, and can be divided into five main steps including demand analysis, concept structure design, logical structure design, physical structure design, implementing, coding.
There into, the demand analysis requires that students should track down the related reference by various ways and methods in the libraries, network, or relevant organizations, departments, enterprises according to background and reference information provided by teachers; analyze and dispose the data combining their own experiences, draw the data flow charts of various layers and compile detailed data dictionary. The teachers instruct students and evaluate the demand analysis reports. The demand analysis is the basis of whole project, but we must understand that most of course designs aren't entity project because of restriction of many objective

conditions, and there aren't requestors, so it is difficult to carry on demand analysis commonly, most of demand analysis come from experiences or existing information. With limited condition at present, it is very important that tutors should instruct students to complete demand analysis reports. The concept structure design requires students to design E-R model, describe attributes of entities and the relation of entities, and eliminate unnecessary redundancy on the basis of demand analysis. The logical structure design can realize the transformation from E-R chart to relation model, and normalize the relation model, define the primary key, foreign key and view. The physical structure design is selecting index and cluster group. Implementing and coding means the implementing, running and maintaining of database, include program and debugging of application system.

4) Showing results
When students complete the design and development of project with the mode of project group, the project leaders of various groups demonstrate the program and show the results. We can also regard this stage as pre evaluation, and students will improve their own works further according to the amending suggestions proposed by classmates and teachers and using the advantages of others for reference.

5) Project evaluating
The project evaluating is divided into two parts mainly, which include self rating and teacher rating. At the stage of showing results, students have known the situations of their own works and others, and they will describe the advantages and disadvantages of their own projects literally without grading in the part of self rating. In the part of teacher rating, teachers will grade step by step, namely grade each item according to key steps in the process of database course design mentioned above.

2.2 The Isomerism Factors

In the process of implementing course design, we stress the feature of isomerism, and do our best to exercise the special talents of each student by the isomerism of subject, personnel and evaluation system in order to improve the action of course design.

1) Subject isomerism
The subjects can be divided into three types including classical cases, special areas and distinctive projects. The subjects of classical cases type, such as teaching management system and books management system, have so many reference information students could find, so they can be implemented easily. The subjects of special areas type, such as case management system, document movement system, have their own application area, and most of students haven't contacted with them, so they need some kind of practical environments to obtain the demands. The subjects of distinctive projects type include the management system of evidence collecting, and the computer evidence collecting is a distinctive major of our college at present, a great number of data obtained through evidence collecting need to be organized efficiently through database. These kinds of subjects are difficult to some extent. There are many differences between these types of subjects in the aspects of applied areas, demands of practice environment, knowledge quantity. The isomerism between subjects is useful to cultivating students in different levels or with different characteristics.

2) Personnel isomerism

The personnel composition in one project group should be an advantage combination of different knowledge backgrounds and majors. For example, for the subject of management system of evidence collecting, because the persons designing this system should know about laws knowledge if they want to do it well, so we organize the students taking law course as the second major and those learning same program design language to compose the project group. The isomerism in professional knowledge of personnel will enable different persons to exert their own professional advantages for mutual benefit and learn each other to finish the course design better.

3) Evaluation isomerism

Because the difficulties of various types of projects are different, for example, the subjects of classical cases type are easier; more people will choose this type of subjects and the chances of communication or learning each other are much more, so this type of subjects are completed better. While the projects of special areas type and distinctive projects type have characteristics such as limited practice environment, difficult demand analysis and shortage of successful systems which can be used for reference. Hence, there exists isomerism to some extent in the process of evaluating projects. The emphases of evaluation are function improvement for the projects of classical cases type, and demand improvement and reasonable database design for the projects of other types.

3 Teaching Example

We take the distinctive project such as management system of evidence collection for example, and introduce how to embody the teaching characteristic that is taking project as the main theme and project as the soul.

The evidence collection management system stores evidences obtained with the mode of large object and selects parts of feature data as attribute of relation. This kind of management system requires students should have some knowledge in theory of laws to develop it, and know the business flow and justice tradition of computer evidence collection, at the same time master the knowledge of project management and database development. The process of project development should follow five steps described in section 2.1. In the five steps, the contents of project planning stage are the same to those of showing results stage, so we only give priority to introducing the key steps and teaching link with feature of isomerism which are project proposing (personnel isomerism), project implementing, project evaluation (evaluation isomerism) to avoid redundancy.

3.1 Project Proposing (Personnel Isomerism)

We design the sub-project (sub-task) and arrange personnel from the aspects of demand analysis, development and design, coding and testing according to the flow of project development. The emphasized ability of each task obtained by students will be different, and the requirements to knowledge background are different too. In the stage of demand analysis, students should know judicature practice to some degree and master some knowledge in theory of laws, so we must pay attention to put students selecting some law courses and those who don't select law courses but have sound computer professional knowledge into one group. We are a law university, and many students whose major is not law have learned some knowledge in law to some extent, so it can be handled to arrange and assign personnel.

At the same time, in order to manage project group conveniently, a leader will be designated in each group, who will take charge of developing project completely. And each number will take part in development of all sub-tasks, but exert different advantage and dominate different sub-task in the process of development. For example, students who are good at judicature practice and master rich knowledge in theory of laws can dominate the task in the stage of demand analysis; students who don't know knowledge in laws but master knowledge in computer can dominate the coding work. In this stage, we emphasis the difference in personnel structure to exert and mobile the independence and enthusiasm of students fully.

3.2 Project Implementing

Like all of database course design, the management system of evidence collection is divided into five key steps including demand analysis, concept structure design, logical structure design, physical structure design, implementing and coding.

We implement demand analysis by investigating, because the management system of evidence collection isn't a traditional project, and there isn't much information to use for reference, so we lead our students to do this kind of projects in our own practice base, and communicate with judicature expertise personnel to understand the business flow. In the demand analysis, students are required to draw the data flow charts, use case diagrams and other documents regularly according to knowledge in software engineering. In the stage of concept structure design, students will design E-R model on the basis of demand analysis with the modeling knowledge learned in the database course; they will design the local model firstly, and then integrate the global model after eliminating redundancy and different meanings. Students will realize the transformation from E-R chart to relation model in the stage of logical structure design, moreover, standardize the relation model and define the primary key, foreign key and view. Students will chose index and cluster group in the stage of physical structure design. They will implement, run and maintain database in the stage of implementing and coding, such as programming and debugging of application system.

3.3 Project Evaluating (Evaluation Isomerism)

As mentioned above, the management system of evidence collection is a project of distinctive project type which is difficult than projects of other types in aspects of design and knowledge quantity, so when teachers evaluate it, the standards are whether demand analysis is complete, whether it can describe a process of data query, amending and increasing evidence collection, whether it can accomplish a judicature practice completely, whether the database design accord standardization rules, whether the design is reasonable. And the demands in the detail, integrity and innovation of function model are simple. That means, we will provide different evaluating standards for projects of different types.

4 Conclusions

The course design is used for bridge connecting theory knowledge and practice ability in the higher education teaching works, have arose increasing attention from all students and teachers, and study and implementing a good set of teaching mode in course design has been the goal pursuing by students and teachers together. This paper proposes a teaching method taking project as the main theme and project as the soul aiming at the database course design, and put forward different isomerism strategies in the aspects of determining subject, arranging personnel and evaluation system according to the features of titles. This teaching method is very useful to students in the aspects of mobilizing the study interests and independence of them fully, training the cooperation spirit and others. It is the new development of traditional teaching mode, the teaching effect is obvious, and adapts to be extended into other course design teaching with more powerful practice.

References

1. Yulin, T.: Considerations about Strengthening the Computer Technology Training in University. SCI/TECH Information Develpment & Economy 14(5), 20–24 (2004)
2. Stock, G.: The Impact of Extrinsic Factors on the Success of Group-based Assignments in Undergraduate Courses. In: The Proc. of International Technology, Education and Development Conference, Valencia (March 2009)
3. Qiao, L., Gejian, D.: Projected Experimental Teaching Method of Database Course Design. Research & Exploration in Laboratory 28(4), 131–132 (2009)
4. Maoxiang, A.: Exploration and Practice of Cultivating Undergraduate Students' Innovation Ability on Database System and its Application. Science and Technology Management Research 30(14) (2010)

Use of Anaerobic Sludge for Manufacturing Light Ceramsite

Hui Li

Ji Lin Institute of Architecture and civil Engineering,
Changchun 130118 China
Lihui2380@163.com

Abstract. As byproducts derived from the regular activities of wastewater treatment plants,it is necessary to implement an adequate disposal of sludges.On the basis of introducing the study on using sewage sludge from sewage treatment plant as a source to produce a new kind of buildingmaterial-light ceramsite both at home and abroad,the application prospect of the technology on aspect of preparation technologym,technical feasibility analysis and the economic and environmental profits are discussed.

Keywords: sewage sludge; light ceramsite; feasibility analysis.

As the sewage treatment plant scale expands unceasingly and processing level enhances unceasingly, excess sludge emissions are getting more serious. The sludge emissions of a secondary biological wastewater treatment plant is $0.3\% \sim 0.5\%$(volume fraction). At present the total emissions of wastewater is about 400 million tons in our country. How to reasonably dispose of sludge has become a urgent task. Sludge treatment methods included landfill, burn, composting methods at home and abroad. These methods can dispose lots of sludge, is the effective ways of sludge treatment, but there are also many problems. At the present stage resource recovered technology is aimed at organic component of sludge, lack of use of inorganic composition. Therefore, seeking economic and effective reduction, harmless and recycling sludge treatment technology have the important meaning.

Ceramsite as a kind of lightweight aggregate, with its light, heat preservation, environmental protection and other characteristics has the good application value. The production mainly is clay ceramsite in our country, but most of the clay source from farmland, do not accord with sustainable development. Therefore use sludge as main raw materials, made a kind of light ceramsite after the decarburization and firing inflation, this method can consume lots dewatering sludge, not only the cost significantly lower than sludge incineration, and also avoid secondary pollution, especially fits our reduction, harmless and recycling solid waste treatment, will have broad development prospects [1].

S. Lin and X. Huang (Eds.): CESM 2011, Part I, CCIS 175, pp. 159–162, 2011.

1 Application and Development of Lightweight Ceramsite

1.1 Overview of Lightweight Ceramsite

Lightweight ceramsite is one variety of ceramsite, Chinese industry standard《lightweight ceramsite and pottery sand》JC 487-92 defined it as stacking density less than 500 kg/m3 ceramsite. According to the stacking density is divided into 200 and 300, 400 and 500 four grade. According to its maximum grain size is divided into 10 mm and 20 mm. According to its quality index points is divided into superior quality(A), first-class(B), qualified (C) [2].

Lightweight ceramsite use high quality clay, shale or fly ash as the main raw material, made of high temperature firing and expanded through rotary kiln and it is a good light-weight aggregate. It has excellent properties, such as low density, compression strength, high porosity, high coefficient of softing, great freezing resistance: 耐冻性；抗凝固性；抗冻性, good ARR etc, because of its internal cellular structure. Using ceramsite these superior performance, it could be widely used in building material, gardening, food and beverage, thermal insulation material, chemical industry, oil industry, its application field is still continues to expand.

1.2 The Research of Sludge–Ceramsite at Home and Abroad

1.2.1 Overseas Research Status

The Overseas sludge disposal and resource start earlier, 1994 Wisconsin company built the world's first using municipal sludge (main raw material is fly ash) to produce ceramsite factory, the annual output is approximately 10 million m^3, because the product's good quality to get government and sewage treatment plants 'subsidies, enterprise economic and social comprehensive benefits is better. To the end of 2002, the United States has completed six ceramsite factories, In Japan, they use burned sludge powder as main raw materials and adding combustible powder, according to the need of GCV deployment into mixture, add water for prilling, made light weight aggregate which burned in the chain sintering machine. The sludge–ceramsite's sintering temperature is 1000~1100℃, sintering time is 25~30 min, compression strength is 3~4 Mpa, waster absorption is 16%~18%。

Nakouzi S, used reusing dye sludge as pottery grains of pottery-making composition, instead of the original land landfill disposal method which has obtained certain economic benefits, and it solves the problem sludge disposal [3].

1.2.2 Domestic Research Situation

Chinese scholars such as ChiChangJiang used sludge as main raw materials and mixed with clay and little solid fuel, produced sludge ceramsite [4]. HuaSui ceramsite factory(Guangzhou, China) used sludge as accessory material (main materials is clay or silt) produced lightweight ceramsite, daily production has reached 300t/d. The high temperature calcination, it can eliminate the various harmful substances in sludge, effective to protect the ecological environment, water resources and land resources, and ceramsite has good performance economic benefits and social benefits of good, future development prospects are bright.

1.3 Production Process of Sludge Ceramsite

According to calcination process, production process shown in Table 1.

Table 1. Production process of sludge ceramsite

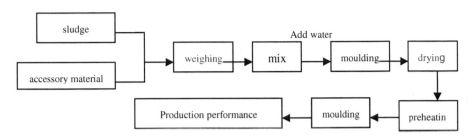

The lightweight ceramsite performance test can basis of the People's Republic of China national standard "lightweight aggregate test method" (GB 2842-81) and the People's Republic of China building material industry standard "Lightweight ceramsite and ceramic sand" (JC 487-92).

2 The Prospect

2.1 Technical Availability Analysis

Sludge is one biological solid which separated from sewage, The main inorganic component is SiO_2, Al_2O_3 and Fe_2O_3, such as clay.

The main factors of ceramsite's expansion is chemical composition of raw materials. According to their effect can be divided into three groups: one is ceramic, it contains SiO_2, Al_2O_3 and Fe_2O_3, the quality of raw material is 3/4; Second is the cosolvent, it contains Na_2O, K_2O, FeO, MgO; Third is producing gas material which produced gas under high temperature, such as H_2O, O_2, CO_2, CO, H_2. According to research [5], to made high quality ceramsite products, raw material chemical composition must meet the following requirements:

SiO_2: 48%~79%, Al_2O_3: 8%~25%, Fe_2O_3: 3%~12%, CaO+MgO: 1%~12%, K_2O+Na_2O: 0.5%~7.0%.

Because of dewatering sludge has low SiO_2 content and high loss on ignition, contract after calcination, do not have expand performance. So in order to produce high quality ceramsite, we should take kaolin, black clay and chromium residue as raw materials. Kaolin can enhance raw ball SiO_2 and Al_2O_3 proportion; Chromium residue, has high content of CaO, MgO, K_2O, Na_2O, can increases the cosolvent content. If the materials of chemical composition can control in the above range, then can burn out of a certain intensity ceramsite.

2.2 Economic Benefit

The ceramsite concrete -hollow blocks and partition board is one of excellent properties new wall materials, which use ceramsite instead of gravel. According to calculate, ceramsite concrete used in high-rise buildings, can reduce weight 30%, reduce labor intensity 20%, reduce cost 10%.

2.3 Environmental Benefits

The sludge ceramsite, will greatly reduce the severe sludge treatment problems, In the process of calcining Large numbers of bacteria be killed and heavy metal is fixed in ceramsite which Avoid heavy metals from agricultural products to enter the food chain, and finally to enter the body. Especially fits our reduction, harmless and recycling solid waste treatment.

3 Conclusion

Ceramsite as a kind of lightweight aggregate can replace common sand to placing lightweight aggregate concrete, ceramsite as a kind of lightweight aggregate, with its light, heat preservation, environmental protection and other characteristics has the good application value. So using sludge produced ceramsite, not only can solve of wastewater treatment of sludge outlet problem, but also can obtain certain economic returns.

References

1. Jun, H.: Use of Sewage Sludge for Manufacturing Light Ceramsite. Urban Environment & Urban Ecology 16(6), 13–14 (2003)
2. JC 487-92, Ultralight Ceramsite and ceramic sand
3. Nakouzi, S.: A Novel Approach to Paint Sludge Recycling. Journal of Material Research 13(1), 53–60 (1998)
4. Jiang, C.: Manufacturing method of junk ceramsite and sludge ceramsite, China: 95101220, 11-10) (1995)
5. Yun, L., Li, X.: Experiment on Producing Ceramisite with River Sediment. Journal of Donghua University. Natural Science 29(4), 81–83 (2003)

The Application Research on Anti-counterfeiting of Fractal Graphics in Color Printing Based on Newton Iteration and Escape Time Algorithm

Fucheng You and Yujie Chen

Information & Mechanical Engineering School
Beijing Institute of Graphic Communication
Beijing, 102600, China
youfucheng@yahoo.com, chenyujie0311@163.com

Abstract. The anti-counterfeiting printing which is a branch of feature printing is an anti-counterfeiting technology. Anti-counterfeiting printing technology is a measure which is used to prevent somebody unwarranted from copying, counterfeiting and imitating. Fractal graphics is applied to color printing anti-counterfeiting in this paper because of its protean shape and unpredictable color. The detailed analysis of Julia set escape time algorithm of Newton iterative method shows that the method of color printing anti-counterfeiting combined with fractal graphics has prefect anti-counterfeiting functions. No one can get the same graphics with original picture by common methods of duplicating, scanning, photographing and other measures.

Keywords: printing anti-counterfeiting, fractal graphics, Newton iterative algorithm, escape time algorithm.

1 Introduction

In real life, to obtain illegal revenues, some unscrupulous traders always deceive consumers by copying others packaging pictures. Anti-counterfeiting technologies date to Classic Age, it is particularly important in this rapid development economic world. It is high sense of social responsibility. Anti-counterfeiting printing is an anti-counterfeiting means of special printing technology. Such as high-precision version pattern printing technology, chemical anti-counterfeiting ink, laser holograph anti-counterfeiting printing technology, and so on. These new technologies bring layers of obstructions and resistances to fakers [1].

New theory and high-tech will be applied to anti-counterfeiting to achieve better and more effective anti-counterfeiting results in the future. They are hotspots of research and application of current society. And fractal anti-counterfeiting is one of them.

Newton iteration is one important method of fractal theory [2]. Fractal graphics created by Newton iteration are beautiful extremely and with countless changes. In fractal graphics generation system, different fractal graphics are mainly controlled by the parameters of color scheme and iterative coefficients [3].

S. Lin and X. Huang (Eds.): CESM 2011, Part I, CCIS 175, pp. 163–169, 2011.

2 Julia Set Escape Time Algorithm Based on Newton Iterative Algorithm

2.1 The Basic Theory of Escape Time Algorithm

Supposing there is an integer N, and it is big enough, when iterative number of an initial point α in un-escape area M is less than N, the initial point arrives at the boundary of un-escape area M and even goes beyond the boundary, then, the initial point is thought escaping. Otherwise, we think the initial point is a point of convergent area A. Boundary graphics of A can be drawn by this method. It is the basic idea of escape time algorithm.

　　Obviously, the value of N affects quality of drawing directly. If the value of N is too small, only smaller points can escape, then, the points which do not belong to convergent area A are kept, and the graphics we got is rough and not exact. Contrarily, if the value of A is too big, some points on A will escape, the graphics will be fuzzy. Appropriate value of A depends on debugging over times and experimental accumulation [4].

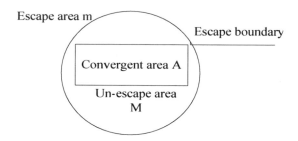

Fig. 1. The schematic diagram of escape time algorithm

2.2 Julia Set Escape Time Algorithm Based on Newton Iterative Algorithm

Newton iteration is proposed in seventeen century by Newton, it is a method to get root of equation which depends on easy calculation.

　　If we know x_0 is the approximate root of function $f(x) = 0$, it closes to the real root of the function. So, $f(x_0) = 0$ and $f'(x_0) = 0$ can be calculated easily. Because, x_0 is closes to the real root x, so derived function $f'(x_0)$ can be replaced approximately. Because $f(x) = 0$, so,

$$f'(x_0) = \frac{-f(x_0)}{x - x_0}$$
(1)

So,

$$x - x_0 = -\frac{f(x_0)}{f'(x_0)}$$
(2)

Then, the approximate solution of amendment is given by:

$$x_1 = x_0 - \frac{f(x_0)}{f'(x_0)} \qquad (3)$$

If this process is repeated, the subsequence x_n will be got, and it will converge to the real root x.

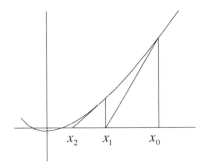

Fig. 2. The schematic diagram of extracting a root using Newton iteration

If it is complex plan, the formula of Newton iteration can be given by:

$$z_{n+1} = z_n - \frac{f(z_n)}{f'(z_n)} \qquad (4)$$

Most initial points iteration can converge on one root of equation, but few initial points can not, they are emanative. Therefore, we can set a bigger iterative number N, when real iterative number exceeds N, the point is not convergent, it escapes. Because the iterative number is limited, all convergent points are not always converging on the real roots. So, there is no harm in setting a small value e which is used to representative the error between convergent point and the real root. If the error is smaller than e, it is thought convergent.

The steps of Julia set escape time algorithm based on Newton iteration are described as follows [4]:

(1) Setting parameters: window size i×j, iterative number N, error e;
(2) Every point of window do N iterations;
(3) In iterative process, if the distance between iterative point and root is smaller than e, the current parameter location is colored. Then, next point goes on. If the distance is bigger than e, next point goes on still, but, current point is not colored.
(4) Until all points of window are done, the process is over.

3   Analysis of Anti-counterfeiting Theory

The computer graphics created by fractal theory has extremely irregular and unsmooth shape and extremely abundant color. Fractal graphics which can not be designed by general graphics design software has self-similarity, and graphics created by general graphics design software are set with classical Euclidean geometry algorithm, and it can not generate colorful fractal graphics. The dimension of fractal graphics is fraction, and it belongs to nonlinear technology [5]. If the parameter has small change, there will be big changes on the fractal graphics. Using these features of fractal graphics, it is a very effective anti-counterfeiting printing means with fractal graphics. As long as parameters are not revealed, no one can generate same or similar fractal graphics. At the same time, fractal graphics have infinite fine details, so they can not be got by common ways of copying, scanning or photographing by low-end camera and other means.

3.1   The Anti-counterfeiting Space of Color RGB

The above two fractal graphics are created by Newton iteration. During the process, the program adopts random function. Every pixel creates random gray-scale values of R, G, B three color components, and every component value is between 0 and 255. Then, three components are put together to create a color scheme. In color RGB anti-counterfeiting space, the size of the space also depends on the size of image. So, the size of color RGB anti-counterfeiting space is $2^8 \times 2^8 \times 2^8 \times M \times N$ (M×N is size of fractal graphics). Therefore, fakers can not create the same picture with original under the condition of unknown the color scheme.

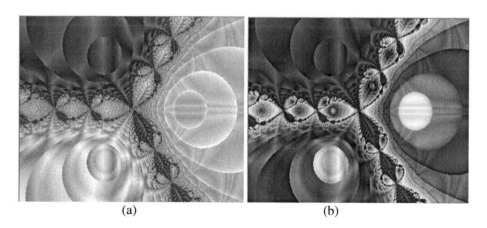

(a)   (b)

Fig. 3. Fractal graphics drawn by Newton iteration

3.2   The Anti-counterfeiting Analysis of Shape

The dimension of fractal graphics is fraction. Therefore, if the parameters have small changes, there will be big changes on the fractal graphics.

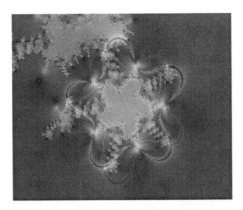

Fig. 4. Fractal graphics created by $f(z) = \dfrac{z \times (1 + z^A)}{1 - z^A} = R$ using Newton iteration

In the formula, parameter A=5, R is a plural, its real part is 5 and imaginary part is 5. Parameters A, real part and imaginary part of R can be set Double type. In Visual Basic system, the precision of Double type is 15 bit. Therefore, the search precision of the formula is $10^{15} \times 10^{15} \times 10^{15}$. In color spare, if we do not know the color scheme, the search precision is $10^{15} \times 10^{15} \times 10^{15} \times 2^8 \times 2^8 \times 2^8 \times M \times N$. The parameter A mainly controls the numbers of petal, and its anti-counterfeiting function is not very well (Fig.5 shows an example). But, if the anti-counterfeiting function of A is excepted, the search space is $10^{15} \times 10^{15} \times 2^8 \times 2^8 \times 2^8 \times M \times N$, it is very big still. The real part and imaginary part of Parameter R have perfect anti-counterfeiting function, they change little, very big changes will generate on the fractal graphics (Fig.6 shows an example). The differences can be detected by eyes and other image processing technologies.

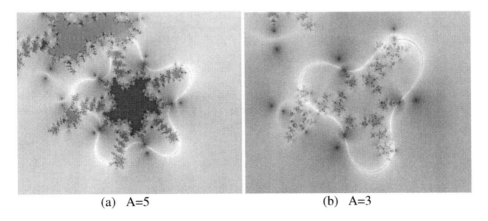

(a)   A=5   (b)   A=3

Fig. 5. Different fractal graphics created by different A and the same R

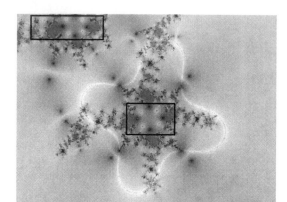

(a) A=4, real part of R is 5 and imaginary part is 5

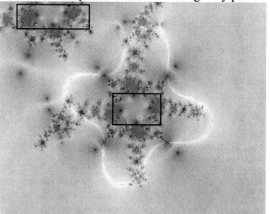

(b) A=4, real part of R is 5.5 and imaginary part is 5

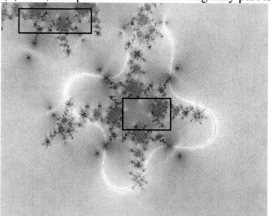

(c) A=4, real part of R is 5 and imaginary part is 5.7

Fig. 6. Different fractal graphics created by different parameters

4 Conclusion

In this paper, fractal graphics is applied to color printing anti-counterfeiting. This method can bring some big resistances to fakers for protecting the benefits of merchants and customers well. The experiment indicates that, the fractal graphics created by escape time algorithm of Newton iteration has protean shape and unpredictable color. No one can obtain the same picture with original image. Therefore, fractal graphics is applied to product package, and it has very good anti-counterfeiting functions.

Acknowledgements. This paper is supported by Project for Beijing Municipal Party Committee Organization Department (No. 10000200118) and the Funding Project for Academic Human Resources Development in Institutions of Higher Learning under the Jurisdiction of Beijing Municipality (No. 10000200118 PXM2010_014223_095557 and PHR201108349).

References

1. Gao, H.: Research and application of fractal graphics in anti-counterfeiting printing technology. Xian University of Science and Technology (2006)
2. Yu, B., Zhang, Y.: Jacquard Pattern Design Based on Triangle Function and Newton Iterative. Silk Monthly 08, 7–9 (2009)
3. Wu, Y., Li, Y.: Create fractal graphics using Newton-overlapping method. Journal of Xian University of Science and Technology 25(3) (September 2005)
4. Sun, B.: Fractal and design of program—Visual Basic. Science Press, Beijing (2004)
5. Chen, L.: The application of fractal graphics based on escape time algorithm. Computer Knowledge and Technology 6(15), 3976–3977 (2010)

Rainfall Infiltration Influence to Asphalt Concrete Pavement

Jilei Hu, Xiaochu Wang, and Rendong Guo

School of Constructional Engineering, Shenyang University, 110044, P.R. China
ray_1986@163.com

Abstract. The adverse impact of rainfall infiltration to asphalt concrete pavement structure should not be ignored. Based on the theory of unsaturated seepage theory, in this paper we analyze the progress and rules of pavement infiltration in rainfall condition, put forward some measures to prevent damage of asphalt concrete pavement, and provide reliable basis for drainage design of asphalt concrete pavement.

Keywords: asphalt concrete pavement; rainfall infiltration; prevention measures.

1 Introduction

Water is an important natural factor of causing highway damage. Water seepage action accelerates the pavement performance deterioration, and shortens the using life of asphalt concrete pavement [1]. In fact, asphalt concrete pavement is pervious, even has a strong permeability. When the asphalt pavement cracks, the small cracks have a greater ability to transport water, and they can change the local pavement moisture content to larger extent, reduce pavement strength, finally destruct roads and reduce transport capacity of roads. Based on the unsaturated seepage theory, in this paper we analyze the progress and rules of pavement infiltration in rainfall condition, and put forward some effective measures to prevent damage of asphalt concrete pavement.

2 Mechanism of Asphalt Concrete Pavement Infiltration

The difference between asphalt concrete pavement infiltration and soil infiltration is that in the asphalt concrete pavement surface porosity is larger than soil, but it is very thin, in addition, the road surface materials conduction water ability will change with different water content. Therefore, the asphalt concrete pavement infiltration and soil infiltration are distinguishing [2].

In rainfall process, the rainwater can enter and be detained in the pores of asphalt concrete pavement surface layer, and the speed of seepage will be very slow to the outside, it needs several weeks or months to gradually remove the rainwater. The whole pavement structure is similar to be placed in a closed slot, the water is sealed in the

S. Lin and X. Huang (Eds.): CESM 2011, Part I, CCIS 175, pp. 170–173, 2011.
© Springer-Verlag Berlin Heidelberg 2011

pavement structure will soak in the layers of pavement structure materials, it can make pavement intensity drop and increase the deformation, thereby, it makes the bearing capacity of the pavement structure reduce. In the end, it results in pavement damage. In large quantity and fast driving conditions, part of asphalt concrete will become loose. If the rainwater enters and is detained in the asphalt concrete pavement, free water in pavement will produce a lot of pressure and it will erode fines in the surface layer of pavement, this produces mortar, finally, the mortar will be pressed into the road surface. In the case of the large number of mortars, the pavement may produce holes. In the case of the small number of mortars, the Pavement somewhere produces shaped crack or deformation. If the pavement produces shaped crack, deformation or holes, the rainwater will more easily penetrate into it, and form a vicious cycle, finally it lead to road damage.

3   Rainfall Infiltration Process and Rule Analysis

3.1   The Process of Rainfall Infiltration

Saturated seepage theory considers that the soils are saturated soil below the groundwater, and they are dry above the groundwater. In fact, the regions above the groundwater level are unsaturated. Infiltration of rainwater is essentially water movement in the soil aeration zone. It is a type of two-phase flow process, which is very intense along with the change of time and space [3]. When the rainfall intensity exceeds soil infiltration capacity, the pavement will emerge runoff or water accumulation, and form the expanding saturated zone, at this time, the water movement in soil is saturated-unsaturated flow. When the rainfall intensity is lower than infiltration capacity, infiltration process will be affected by water supply capacity. Rainfall infiltration process can be divided into the following three processes [4]:

(1) Infiltration process. The infiltration is the process which the moisture enters into the soil, this process is mainly affected by capillarity and matrix suction.

(2) Moisture redistribution process. Moisture redistribution process is after infiltration, moisture movement is affected by capillarity and gravity. In this process, moisture absorption and moisture desorption are exist at the same time, between moisture absorption process and moisture desorption process the soil - water characteristic curve is dissimilar, and their curves are also dissimilar because of different initial moisture content.

(3) Drainage process. Drainage process is mainly the moisture infiltrates to the deep zone, and eventually supply to groundwater.

3.2   Rainfall Infiltration Rule

Rainfall infiltration water and underground water are interrelated, and it can make the underground water level is greatly raised in a short time. In addition, the supply of water by rainfall infiltration can increase the saturation of the soil, thus reduce the shear strength of soil and the performance capability.

(1) Infiltration rule transient flow analysis during the rainfall. In the initial rainfall period, road surface volume water content will gradually increase, with the infiltration of rainwater, the surface material's matrix suction achieves the water filling values, and its volume water content will rapidly increase until the saturated state. The rainwater does not infiltrate into the basic course, so the volume water content of the basic course still maintains invariable.

(2) Drainage transient flow analysis after the rainfall. The road surface water supply is zero after the rain stop. The situation of road surface enters into unsaturated drainage stage from the saturated state. At this time, the road surface volume water content is still increasing in a short time, but with the rain is expelled outside pavement structure by graded crushed stone of base course, the surface course volume water content will decrease rapidly. The permeability coefficient of the surface materials is very small, and the infiltration time from surface course to basic course is too long, therefore, the increase of basic course volume water content is very small after the rain stop.

4 Prevention and Control Measures

In recent years, the development of highway is very rapid, so we have put forward some higher requirements to strength and stability of subgrade and pavement. But the existing pavement drainage systems are often only concerned about the surface water expel outside the road, think little of expelling the perched water of the pavement structure. In the not setting effective pavement internal drainage system situation, the perched water is very dangerous, it can make the mechanical properties of subgrade and pavement change, affect the strength and stability of the road. It is one of the important reasons which cause subgrade and pavement early destruction in a part of highway. Therefore, rainfall infiltration in subgrade and pavement destruction of prevention and control measures are having quite important significance.

(1) Consummating the pavement drainage system. We should handle both the drainage system of road edge and the drainage system of drainage layer, add expel seepage gravel layer in the shoulder, this is beneficial to reduce the residence time of seepage.

(2) Coat a new-style waterproof material in pavement, the material will form a layer of impermeable film on the pavement, so that the residence time of seepage is declined, the road surface water is expelled outside as soon as possible, thus it can greatly reduce the road damage.

(3) Between surface course and basic course set lower seal coat to enhance the impermeability and surface water stability of basic surface.

(4) Improving the design and construction of surface course and basic course. In the construction process, we should improve the standard of compaction machine, rolling should be uniform, from light to heavy, from slow to fast, it is not only necessary to ensure the smoothness of the pavement, but also ensure the compaction of the pavement, thus, it can increase the adhesion of asphalt aggregate, and reduce the damage of asphalt concrete pavement.

5 Conclusions

Through analyzing the asphalt concrete pavement failure influencing factors and rainfall infiltration process and rule, we can draw the following several conclusions:

(1) In rainfall conditions, the rain continuously penetrates into surface course and basic course, the volumetric water content of surface course will gradually increase until saturation. After the rain stopped, infiltration water is constantly expelled outside pavement structure from basic course, the volumetric water content of basic course will decrease rapidly, at this time, the road surface volumetric water will continue to increase in a short time, but then it will gradually decrease.

(2) The design method based on saturated seepage theory cannot objectively reflect the real situations of rainwater infiltration to pavement structure, we should take the unsaturated seepage theory into pavement design, this will help us better understand the rain infiltration rule.

(3) Control infiltration of asphalt concrete pavement is a comprehensive work, so we should seriously pay more attention to it. In aspect of the design and construction, we should take effective measures to reduce the damage of road, and ensure the performance and service life of road.

References

1. John, S., Zhou, S.: Improving Pavement Sub-Surface Drainage Systems by Considering Unsaturated Water Flow (2001)
2. Fu, J.: Permeability Performance and Its Decay Law of Drainage Asphalt Concrete Pavement. Road, 6 (2010)
3. Lei, Z., Yang, S., Xie, S.: Soil Water Dynamics, pp. 34–38. Tsinghua University Press, Beijing (1988)
4. Tan, X., Chen, S., Yang, M.: Slope Saturated-unsaturated Seepage Analysis under Rainfall. Rock and Soil Mechanics 24, 381–383 (2003)
5. He, Y.: Rainfall Conditions in The Pavement Structure of Unsaturated Seepage and Drainage Performance Assessment (MS Thesis). pp. 44-48. South University, Nanjing (2009)
6. Ministry of Communications standards. JTG D50-2006. Roadbed Design. China Communications Press, Beijing (2006)
7. Sha, Q.: Early Failure of Asphalt Pavement and Prevention. People Communications Press (2000)

The Research on Anti-counterfeiting of Fractal Graphics in Color Printing Based on Escape Time Algorithm of Julia-set

Fucheng You and Yingjie Liu

Information & Mechanical Engineering School, Beijing Institute of Graphic Communication, Beijing, 102600, China
youfucheng@yahoo.com.cn, liuyingjiea@hotmail.com

Abstract. Fractal graphics based on escape time algorithm of Julia-set are studied in the paper for the application of anti-counterfeiting in color printing. Different parameters of Julia-set make anti-counterfeiting space difficult to search. Therefore anti-counterfeiting in color printing based on Julia-set is implemented. A novel approach of anti-counterfeiting space based on color and shape is proposed for anti-counterfeiting in color printing. This approach is applied to analyze anti-counterfeiting capacity of fractal graphics based on Julia-set. Firstly, anti-counterfeiting space of RGB color is estimated from fractal graphics of Julia-set. Anti-counterfeiting space is generated on basis of RGB color and graph size. Then, anti-counterfeiting space of shape which is generated by parameters changing enlarges anti-counterfeiting space based on fractal graphics of Julia-set. Different parameters lead to different shape of fractal graphics to a great extent. Experimental results demonstrate that higher anti-counterfeiting capacity of color printing can be achieved with the proposed approach.

Keywords: Julia-set; escape time algorithm; fractal graphics; anti-counterfeiting in color printing.

1 Introduction

In recent years, development of anti-counterfeiting technology in color printing prevents unscrupulous businessmen or individuals to obtain illegal benefits by counterfeit in legal ways, thereby protect the interests of legitimate businessmen. However, emergence of color printers and scanners with higher precision makes faking color printing products appear more and more in many fields. Therefore, more efficient technologies of anti-counterfeiting in color printing are extremely expected by legitimate businessmen to protect their benefits. The key point of anti-counterfeiting in color printing is to design graphics which are difficult to copy and imitate. Fractal graphics based on escape time algorithm of Julia-set are studied in the paper for the application of anti-counterfeiting in color printing.

Fractal theory mainly researches the irregular shape and graphics with similarity in non- linear system [1]. Fractal theory can construct fractal graphics with complicated

S. Lin and X. Huang (Eds.): CESM 2011, Part I, CCIS 175, pp. 174–179, 2011.
© Springer-Verlag Berlin Heidelberg 2011

texture and shape, which are extremely difficult to imitate. Thereby large space of anti-counterfeiting in color printing can be generated by fractal graphics [2].

Under this background, an anti-counterfeiting approach based on escape time algorithm of Julia-set is proposed in the paper for improving anti-counterfeiting capacity in color printing. By setting different parameters of fractal graphics, anti-counterfeiting space can be generated, which is large enough and very difficult to search, then anti-counterfeiting in color printing is implemented. After many experiments with the proposed algorithm, anti-counterfeiting space generated by RGB color, graph size, shape and adjusting parameters makes imitation more difficult.

2 Fractal Theory Based on Julia-set

Basic function of Julia-set is shown in (1), in which Z and C are all complex numbers. Different initial C has great influence on fractal graphics of Julia-set. Let x denote the real part of Z, and y denote the image part of Z. Let p denote the real part of C, and q denote the image part of C. Then $Z = x + yi$ and $C = p + qi$ can be obtained. Different p and q can generate very different fractal graphics of Julia-set [3].

$$F(Z) = Z^2 + C \qquad (1)$$

2.1 Escape Time Algorithm

Escape time algorithm is an effective theoretical algorithm of constructing fractal graphics. The key of this algorithm lies in the construction of escape time function, $y = f(x)$. If x_0 denotes initial x, then corresponding y can be obtained, i.e. $y = x_1 = f(x_0)$. Let x_1 denote new x, then new y can be written as $y = x_2 = f(x_1)$. After repeated and iterative computation for n times, i.e. $y = x_{n+1} = f(x_n), n = 0,1,2\cdots$, the sequence of $x_0, x_1, x_2, \cdots, x_n \cdots$ can be obtained. Some points of the sequence are limitary, that is, tracks of these points can not exceed a certain range. But other points of the sequence are limitless, that is, these points can escape to the infinite. If the different points are displayed on computer screen with different colors, then fractal graphics are obtained. That's the basic idea of escape time algorithm [4].

2.2 Escape Time Algorithm Based on Julia-set

Julia-set is an iterative process with complex numbers by $Z \rightarrow Z^2 + C$. From the point of escape time algorithm, the interior of Julia-set is convergent for one or several points, and the exterior of Julia-set is emanative to the infinite with escape time. Escape bound is Julia-set. Escape time algorithm based on Julia-set can generate complicated fractal graphics in complex plane [5].

Let $a \times b$ denote the resolution of fractal graphics, i.e. graph size. $K + 1$ types of colors can be displayed, which are denoted as $0, \cdots, K$. Let t denote the escape time.

Let $C = p + qi$, $x_{min} = y_{min} = -1.5$ and $x_{max} = y_{max} = 1.5$. Then Δx and Δy are shown by (2) and (3).

$$\Delta x = (x_{max} - x_{min})/(a-1) \tag{2}$$

$$\Delta y = (y_{max} - y_{min})/(b-1) \tag{3}$$

Let (n_x, n_y) denote the point of fractal graphics. For $n_x = 0,1,2,\cdots,a-1$ and $n_y = 0,1,2,\cdots,b-1$, implement circulated steps as follows.

Step 1. Make $x_0 = x_{min} + n_x \times \Delta x$, $y_0 = y_{min} + n_y \times \Delta y$ and $t = 0$.

Step 2. Compute (x_{t+1}, y_{t+1}) by (x_t, y_t) according to iterative process shown as (4) and (5).

$$x_{t+1} = x_t^2 - y_t^2 + p \tag{4}$$

$$y_{t+1} = 2x_t y_t + q \tag{5}$$

Step 3. Compute $r = x_t^2 + y_t^2$.

If $r > t$, select color t and then go to step 4.

If $t = K$, select black color and then go to step 4.

If $r \le t$ and $t < K$, then go to step 2.

Step 4. Make point (n_x, n_y) display color t and then transfer to next point.

3 Analysis on Anti-counterfeiting Principle

Some anti-counterfeiting technologies of color printing can not prevent imitation efficiently. The main reason lies in the ineffective anti-counterfeiting space. Fractal graphics based on escape time algorithm of Julia-set have great anti-counterfeiting space which is very difficult to search for purpose of imitation. A little bit changing of parameters can lead to very different shape changing of fractal graphics. Therefore, fractal graphics based on escape time algorithm of Julia-set can be applied in anti-counterfeiting of color printing and can provide higher anti-counterfeiting capacity for color printing due to great anti-counterfeiting space.

3.1 Anti-counterfeiting Space of RGB Color

Random function is adopted during the implementation process of fractal graphics based on escape time algorithm of Julia-set. Every pixel of fractal graphics can generate gray value which has three random colors, i.e. R, G and B. The range of every random color is from 0 to 255. Therefore, random color for every pixel can generate different fractal graphics with same shape and different colors as shown in Fig. 1.

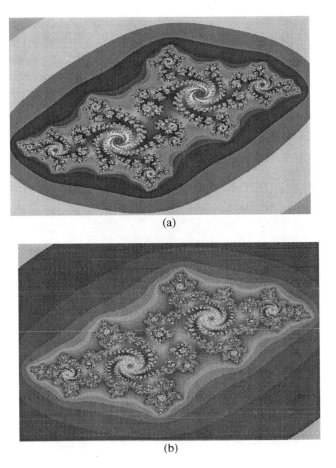

(a)

(b)

Fig. 1. Fractal graphics of Julia-set with same shape and random colors

Anti-counterfeiting space of RGB color is also related with the size of fractal graphics. Let $M \times N$ denote the size of fractal graphics. Then anti-counterfeiting space of fractal graphics is shown in (6). For so great anti-counterfeiting space, it is very difficult to search when imitator do not know the random color. Thereby, it is impossible to imitate the fractal graphics with same colors.

$$S = 256 \times 256 \times 256 \times M \times N = 2^{24} \times M \times N \qquad (6)$$

3.2 Anti-counterfeiting Space of Shape

Due to the dimension of fractal graphics is fractional type, it is great changing in shape and texture of fractal graphics based on escape time algorithm of Julia-set, when adjusting the real and image parts of initial C of Julia-set. Make this advantage applied in anti-counterfeiting of color printing can achieve higher anti-counterfeiting capacity.

Set the real part p and the image part q of initial C of Julia-set as double type during programming. The precision of double data is 15 bits. Thereby the size of search space for one random color in fractal graphics is $10^{15} \times 10^{15}$. If random RGB color is unknown, then the anti-counterfeiting space can be enlarged to $10^{30} \times 10^{30} \times 10^{30} \times 2^{24} \times M \times N$.

Difference can be generated in fractal graphics of Julia-set when adjusting the real and image parts of initial C of Julia-set a little, as shown in Fig. 2. The difference is marked by white rectangles in Fig. 2. It can be seen that the width of texture in white rectangle is different.

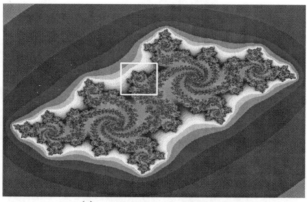

(a) $p = -0.463$, $q = 0.5651$

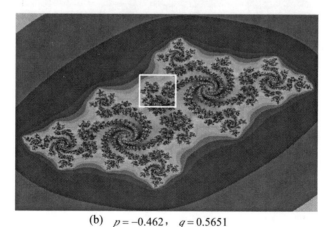

(b) $p = -0.462$, $q = 0.5651$

Fig. 2. Fractal graphics of Julia-set with different real and image parts of initial C

4 Conclusion

An anti-counterfeiting approach based on escape time algorithm of Julia-set is proposed in the paper for improving anti-counterfeiting capacity in color printing. By setting different parameters of fractal graphics, anti-counterfeiting space can be generated, which is large enough and very difficult to search, then anti-counterfeiting in color printing is implemented. After many experiments with the proposed algorithm, anti-counterfeiting space generated by RGB color, graph size, shape and adjusting parameters make imitation more difficult. Fractal graphics based on escape time algorithm of Julia-set have great anti-counterfeiting space which is very difficult to search for purpose of imitation.

Therefore, fractal graphics based on escape time algorithm of Julia-set can be applied in anti-counterfeiting of color printing and can provide higher anti-counterfeiting capacity for color printing due to great anti-counterfeiting space.

Acknowledgement

This paper is supported by Project for Beijing Municipal Party Committee Organization Department (No. 10000200118) and the Funding Project for Academic Human Resources Development in Institutions of Higher Learning under the Jurisdiction of Beijing Municipality (No. 10000200118 PXM2010_014223_095557 and PHR201108349).

References

1. Zhang, L., Liu, H.: Research and Application of Fractal Art in Anti-counterfeiting of Product Information. Information Technology 1, 111–113 (2007)
2. Mei, H.: Application of Fractal Graphics in Packaging Anti-counterfeiting. China brand and Anti-counterfeiting 1, 60–62 (2008)
3. Sun, B.: Fractal Algorithm and Program Design-Visual C++, pp. 105–113. Science Press, Beijing (2004)
4. Spehar, B., Colin, W.G., Ben, R.: Universal aesthetic of fractals. Computers & Graphics (7), 813–820 (2003)
5. Xu, S., Li, C.: Research on Algorithms of Generating Fractal Image. Microcomputer Development 15(9), 4–6 (2005)

On Virtual Expert of Knowledge Management an Extenics Oriented Ontology

Feng Liu

Dept. of E-Commerce, School of Information,
Xi'an University of Finance and Economics,
710100 Xi'an, China
liufeng49@sina.com

Abstract. Based on intensive investigation of Chinese classics the paper presents a novel ontological frame for management of seemingly incompatible knowledge to serve wisdom infrastructure. With the unity-contradiction model, the paper finds that existence of knowledge is defined by the identity property in a contradiction, its extensibility lies in the equilibrium property of identity aspect. By changing the equilibrium pattern one can resolve the incompatibility or inconsistency. The paper indicates that KM expert is dependent on cognition and communication manner basically tacit, in which extensibility plays the primary role. It also suggests an oriental approach above logic layer to codify knowledge behavior.

Keywords: Knowledge management, expert, tacit, explicit, contradiction, identity, eight trigrams.

1 Introduction: Knowledge(k) ≠ Knowledge(k)

What is the virtual expert of knowledge management system (KMS)? Does virtual expert mean the human expert who manages KMS? No, neither consultant. Hereby I refer to the virtual agent comprises knowledge grid, KMS, KM managers workers and human experts, consultant, users. Thus it is crucial to make an extenics based oriental approach to the meta level ontology of such agent.

In his paper "To be or not to be, A multidimensional logic approach" Carlos Gershenson has generalized proofs on: (a) Everything is and isn't at a certain degree. (b)Nothing can be proved (that it exists or doesn't) (author: relative to our current intelligence). (c) I believe, therefore I am. (i.e., I take it true, because I believe so) [1]."(I am the true author of the full text. In fact Prof. Smarandache knows nothing of Chinese and cannot investigate the referenced Chinese classics. Due to the philosophical responsibility, I didn't agree the immediate publication of the paper, therefore under his name.) There is Also self-negating property. Take an example of circle, it negates itself: it can be a cake, a dish, a bowl, a balloon..., even the moon, the sun ... in different scenarios. In this sense circle is a varying concept, but in fact few believes bowl = circle, etc. – self negating effect, because more one believes

S. Lin and X. Huang (Eds.): CESM 2011, Part I, CCIS 175, pp. 180–185, 2011.

something as circle, less he believes as anything else, e.g., a bowl. Dao De Jing shows that: "The Tao that can be expressed is not the eternal Tao; the name that can be defined is not the unchanging name…"

1.1 Belief Comes Up as the Result of a Sophisticate Process – Identity in a Contradiction

A knowledge representation K is viewed differently in different scenarios, as in the circle example above. Even in the same scenario, person 1 to person i perceive K as K_1 to K_i as different mental reflections. They are regarded same but meanwhile not, since they are viewed in both identity and contradictory perspectives. Apart from the similarity in language or name and expression, it is reflected with different images or rules serving different goals and performances, and perceived by different consciousnesses, understandings with different experiences, even in different instances of time that count. Therefore knowledge exists dependently on cognition model and cognition procedure, or in general, reference frame, otherwise it has no meaning. This is the contradictory aspect. In this aspect, *70 year old (p) $\neq$ 1 year old (p)*. But on the other side regarded equal which supports the existence of knowledge K, expressed as *70 year old (p) = 1 year old (p)*. The general concept of the person is gathered from all the possible appearances and signifies the *identity* of all the instances if there is, as (*CM* for cognition model)

$$\int \sum K_i \cdot d(CM\ i) \tag{1}$$

as the relatively more general representation of knowledge, its limit is defined:

$$expert(K) = Lim_{n \to \infty} \int \sum_{i=1\ to\ n} K_i \cdot d(CM\ i) \tag{2}$$

as the most general model, or *expert knowledge*, which should be recognized as the identity.

However does it converge? Never mind, since it signifies the multidimensional cognition procedure on a common belief, and K_i acts as a particular case in cognition model i, one may confirm that he will eventually find the ultimate reality of the multidimensional appearances. How can it come?

Let's consider:

$$d(CM\ i) = d(CM\ i)/\ d(CM\ C) \cdot d(CM\ C) \tag{3}$$

where cognition model C denotes the ultimate common reference frame or reference system, and have

$$expert(K) = Lim_{n \to \infty} \int \sum_{i=1\ to\ n} K_i \cdot d(CM\ i) \tag{4}$$

$$= Lim_{n \to \infty} \int \sum_{i=1\ to\ n} K'_i \cdot d(CM\ C) \tag{5}$$

where $K'_i = K_i \cdot d(cognition\ model\ i)/\ d(cognition\ model\ C)$, i.e., knowledge K_i in the ultimate common reference frame C's respective.

The point: The existence of such a common reference frame - seemingly a unified field theory which science is not able to prove. However based on my persistent investigation on oriental classical culture I believe that the mutual ultimate common reference frame exists in everyone's hidden consciousness, and everyone can realize the genius to see the ultimate truth in the ultimate world (e.g., the Pure Land).

This expression carries the means of knowledge K in broad sense, or the identity in different scenarios.

With extenics one can turn incompatible knowledge into resoluble. In Chinese idiom "Prince Caochong weighing elephant" where the goal and condition are incompatible at ancient time, he reaches the wisdom by changing the equilibrium in the identity process (as weighing equal weight of rocks on a boat):

$$weighing\ elephant = measuring\ weights = weighing\ rocks \qquad (6)$$

which implies a precondition:

$$weighing\ elephant \neq weighing\ elephant \qquad (7)$$

i.e., he remains unsticking to (unabsorbed in, not adhering to) knowledge K therefore reaches the extension of knowledge K.

2 Virtual Expert

In the sense of my personal approach of extenics, expert is in fact the extensibility of knowledge. I propose the imaginary part in description as in number theory:

$$Lim\ expert(K) = imaginary\ part(K) \qquad (8)$$

in the sense that more general in expertise, more tacit aspect in knowledge that seemingly hidden, latent [2]. According to my personal understanding of yinyang philosophy of Chinese (Book of Changes), tacit character is intrinsic to every piece of knowledge, as can be a future branch of this issue. E.g., knowledge is always represented in domain specific, scenario specific, process specific, action specific, or individualized data, with individualized manner, belief, default habit or culture, which I call conditioned or constrained appearances, if one assumes an integration of these differentials existing independent of scenario or conditions, I find no way to represent, as Dao De Jing shows: *"The Tao that can be expressed is not the eternal Tao; the name that can be defined is not the unchanging name..."*

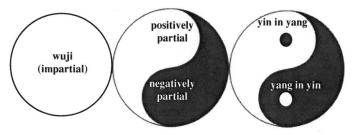

In this way knowledge is redefined as the unity (like an integral) of real part and imaginary part, in which explicit knowledge relates more to the former,

Fig. 1. Wuji and Taiji: Wuji as impartial reference implies far more sophisticated philosophy in Dao De Jing, commonly taken as supernatural mind, or in metaphor, god. But habitually man manually discriminates verbal truth and false, good and bad and in this way looses the permanent truth and integrity. For example, as one loves something he simultaneously hates something else from his love. Therefore even for a kind person there is fault in him and vice versa, merit in evils.

and tacit to the latter. They are not transformable in character but one can continuously mine for explicit character of tacit, or yin in yang of fig. 1, and vice versa. As to completeness, one can apply:

$$\int Positive\ image \cdot d(\ positive\ CM) + Negative\ image \cdot d(\ negative\ CM) \qquad (9)$$

from smaller scenarios to the more general scenarios to the endless recursion (fig. 2).

The philosophy implies that to reach a more general extension of knowledge, one needs to abandon his absorption in the current reference frame and thus reestablishes his mental equilibrium.

- Even though one sees identity, contradiction, unknown properties etc. but never sticks to, never asserts anything. He remains peace and quiet

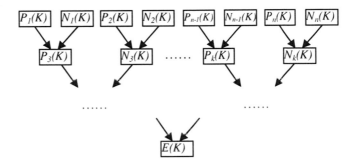

Fig. 2. Communication ontology. *P*: positive; *N*: negative; *E*: extension.

undisturbed, and in this way he relies on his deepest instinct to meditate, to touch the hidden forms of existence, and finally toward a kind of freedom, instead of logical means of truth or false. In other words: never arbitrarily assert anything (any *K*) before the endless purification (escape from illusion in [3]).

3 Property

Confirmative extension: new equilibrium tends to reinforce the identity property, to discover life-force or vigor of belief *K*. In extenics words it would be transformations of constraints (in my words adjusting equilibrium state, choice of value, reevaluation) that turns incompatible problems soluble, or a persistent realization.

Negative extension: that reinforces the contradiction property, to discover anti-life force of belief *K*.

Contradiction extension: a bidirectional extension that discovers characteristic and essence of belief *K*. Extenics is designed to conduct this. Chinese classics are most apt to this issue. E.g., A dialect reader is ready for both directions, pros and cons, or in simultaneous parallelism, seemly neutral but not stand – He stands on no background, sticks to no logic (right or wrong), and therefore impartial.

Unknown extension: one fails to reach a satisfactory goal but reserves the belief for future extension.

4 Implementation Issue

This ontology calls for a knowledge grid arranged in a geographical knowledge space, like knowledge geography, equipped with knowledge mining philosophy, e.g., clustering, to conduct bidirectional match: from knowledge seeker to consultant, and vice versa, taking account of common reference frames. The habitual pattern of such reference manner constitutes a weighted map, like a tourist map with frequency or priority marked on each road specific to a site (tourist spot). Thus in this assumption the issue turns into the equilibrium state problem, like neural networks.

- In fact, relent domains of knowledge is often interlinked to form a virtual society.
- But remember, knowledge expert in this definition is the integration of man and tools, therefore I concern more about meta-operations.

To resolve geography oriented issues, I prefer Book of Changes as the primary guideline, therefore I proposed an eight dimensional model in 2009 from the congenital eight trigrams (Fuxi Ba-gua) [2], to figure out the grid arrangement pattern. A properly arranged structure should be far easier to conduct knowledge match.

The metaphor of congenital eight trigrams shows that: "Heaven and earth received their determinate positions; mountains and collections of water interchanged their influences; thunder and wind excited each other the more; and water and fire did each other no harm. Among these eight symbols there was a mutual communication." The metaphor to my inspiration suggests the uncertainty of knowledge. According to tutorials, knowledge is true justified belief. However through investigation [3] I show that there is no unchangeable authorized knowledge although believed valid (let's avoid religious aspect). However is there anything that permanently holds true? There should be, but not in our common logic, but a character, which is denoted by yang.

The metaphor is "Heaven" that signifies the extremity of tacit communication, as the highest level. For example, religious communication. Chinese culture integrates big philosophies within single words called idioms that need sophisticated tacit experience to understand. But in IT environment, it can be regarded as the extensibility, the varying perspective mining for the insight that penetrates the constraint appearances. And in extenics, as a virtual representation of the integral, holograph or universal form of knowledge I call imaginary part that relates to extension of knowledge via transformations in condition, content, scenario, etc. to the flexibility of application, or artificial wisdom. But in my personal approach, to the change of equilibrium state established with rebalanced situations.

Comparatively, the static aspect of knowledge is normally regarded as explicit character. This character maintains knowledge logically valid, i.e., to codify experience, and formalize into some content, e.g. context, semantic relations, believed true, but note that it is activated only with the impetus (yang) that endows knowledge with vigor, e.g., a call for a specific scenario (e.g. a process solution). This agent has the character of "Earth".

Accordingly, more characters as "Mountain", "Collection of water", "Thunder", "Wind", "Water" and "Fire" need to illustrate. More general in the forthcoming paper, "Four Flows of Knowledge Communication - An extenics oriented knowledge ontology toward wisdom".

From the above metaphor I mainly describe the constitution of knowledge. As operational approach, I need to figure out another metaphor, the acquired eight trigrams (Wenwang Ba-gua) of Book of Changes. According to the original metaphor: "God comes forth in Zhen (to his producing work); he brings (his processes) into full and equal action in Xun; they are manifested to one another in Li; the greatest service is done for him in Kun; He rejoices in Dui; he struggles in Qian; he is comforted and enters into rest in Kan; and he completes (the work of the year) in

Gen", my inspiration suggests that:

- When one initializes a learning project (something abnormal that shakes the previous balance, as process Zhen), he refers (as with Xun) to tutorials and match sources knowledge with his experience, and, by assembling the fragment matches from these reference models, he reaches a general sketch of belief pattern to which fragments attach (as to Li), as hypothesis to be verified and implemented in the forthcoming steps, toward the proved realization as learned knowledge. The hypothesis needs to be nurtured and to grow up (as with Kun) in the specific scenario. When the hypothesis is mature enough, it needs to be represented (as with Dui), and to expand and contradict with influence of older knowledge (new balance is reached by vigorously breaking the previous balance, as with Qian), e.g., to make update, renovation, reformation or even revolution in knowledge, and in this way the new thought is verified, modified and substantialized. When the novel thought takes the principal role (dominant position) in the conflict the learner should have a rest (in Kan) to avoid traps of superstition (to stick to what he knows). Finally the end of learning cycle (as with Gen). The process can be in recursion.
- More in the forth coming paper, "Toward Learning Wisdom - An extenics oriented learning ontology".

5 Final Remarks

Tacit manner plays the primary role that defines man's character. I don't agree the assertion that experience can be learned from symbols, figures etc. because road map and signpost are not equal to destination, and the Bible not equal to heaven. But knowledge management can facilitate and help with further experience.

Beyond human cognition, toward a god perspective, can one find the right route (see Dao De Jing Chp. 28): *"Who knows his manhood's strength (the known, my note), Yet still his female feebleness maintains (the unknown, humility); As to one channel flow the many drains (knowledge), All come to him, yea, all beneath the sky(the ultimate reality). Thus he the constant excellence retains (unchanging self-nature); The simple child again, free from all stains (original purity)."*

References

1. Smarandache, F.: Toward Dialectic Matter Element of Extenics Model (2010), http://vixra.org/pdf/1004.0006v1.pdf
2. Liu, F.: The Eight Dimensions of Knowledge Management. In: Proc. of the 8th Wuhan International Conference on E-business. Alfread University Press (2009)
3. Liu, F.: Wisdom and Knowledge Communication. In: Proc. of the 4th International Conference on Wireless Communications, Networking and Mobile Computing (ISM 2008) (2008)

The Study on College Sports Education Reform Based on the Learning Organization Theory

Li Gang

Huaiyin Normal University

Abstract. Presently, P.E. Major Teaching in China's institutes of higher learning exist a lot of disadvantages, for example, teaching methods are single and outmoded, course contents break away from practice and teaching arrangements lack the links of practices, etc, the cause of which is that students lack the study enthusiasm and therefore the teaching effect is not that favorable. However, the Learning Organization Theory has a strong objective, which, specifically, can not only enable the teachers to become the organizer, guider, regulator, decider, instructor and participator instead of the role as an authority in an activity so that teacher objectively treats students' individual difference and teaches them according to their aptitude, but also stimulate students' learning enthusiasm and initiative to better excavate students' potential so that students constantly break limitation of ability to improve their learning efficiency.

Keywords: sports education, learning organizational theory, teaching.

1 Theoretical Base on Setting Up Colleges and Universities Sports Training Learning Organization

Currently, educational reform and innovation are the hot topics in colleges and universities. During the process of educational reform, not a few teachers borrow teaching ideas from higher education and educational psychology, getting the good teaching achievement. But, in fact, the experiences and theories on educational reform we can use are not only limited in the fields of education. The learning organization theory in the field of management caters to the improvement of students' passive and objective role in the traditional classroom teaching and the need of improvement of teaching efficiency. It also supplies an effective way on how to train students' teamwork consciousness and ability, as well as the sustainable development in learning ability. The theory of learning organization appeared in western scholar Hutchins's *Learning Society*, published in 1968 at the earliest and then finally was formed in *The Fifth Discipline---Art and Trend of The Learning Organization*, written by American managerialist Peter M. Senge. The five disciplines of learning organization refer to personal mastery, improvement of mental models, building shared vision, teamwork learning and system thinking. The personal mastery means organization is made up of several individuals engaging in the continuous creations.

S. Lin and X. Huang (Eds.): CESM 2011, Part I, CCIS 175, pp. 186–191, 2011.

The shared vision means to unite the different people with different personalities through the shared will, value and mission, gradually breaking through the toplimit in organization members' personal ability growing in order to make progress for the shared aim. To improve mental models is to breach the traditional thinking patterns to the disadvantage of the development of organization and to overcome all factors influenced organization activities efficiency. Instead, it aims to improve organization activities efficiency by use of new ideas and ways, methods in favour of its development. The feature of teamwork learning breaks through the individual's being enclosed learning state and organizes the active discussion in members for the purpose of making progressing together. The system thinking requires the notice of the interaction among all factors. It requires one should not take link between the learning organization and other organizations one-sidedly, regarding the links in learning organization activities as the isolated states. It is a kind of beneficial attempt to apply the learning organization to colleges and universities' educational reform especially to the teaching reform in sports major.

2 Analysis of Applicability of Learning Organization in the P.E. Major Teaching among Institutions of Higher Learning

In modern society, the need for the talents specialized in P.E. is not limited to the professionals of a single sport, on the contrary, those versatile talents who have a better understanding of the expertise and possess related organizational abilities are really favored by the society. Therefore, for students who are specialized in P.E., it's equally important to foster the creative and organizational ability as well as the teamwork spirit besides leaning professional skills and theoretical knowledge.

2.1 Students' Physical and Mental Characteristics are Conductive to Carry Out the Learning Organization Theory

Students of P. E. major in universities an colleges are a special group, as art students, the mark of their college entrance examination is the combination of the mark of their academic courses and the mark of their P. E. examination, therefore, the general academic level of students of P. E. major is relatively low. Their temperament type mostly belongs to sanguine temperament and choleric temperament, and their main psychological characteristics include: Students belong to sanguine temperament are living, active, vigorous, expressive, with changeable and alternative moods, quick and smart languages and behaviors, optimistic, amiable but impulsive; while students with choleric temperament are energetic, with changeable and enthusiastic moods, quick and uncontrollable languages and behaviors, demonstrative, straightforward, warm but moody, rash, courageous and resolute. Meanwhile, students of P.E. major also have the general character of modern students, that is, their body and psychology are close to maturity and stability, and their logical thinking and creative thinking are also gradually mature. The most striking characteristics of learning organization is "learning as a whole" and "team learning", emphasizing the cooperative learning among organization members and group's organization intelligence development.

Therefore, if such organization can be build up, it can make up the defects in bad cultural performance for P.E. students. Also, it can help them to overcome the individual character weakness in favor of collective intelligence development, learning together and making progress together. In this way, students' learning initiative must be driven.

2.2 Particularity of P.E. Teaching Is Beneficial to Operation of Learning Organization Theory in Teaching

Particularity of P.E. lies in: first, the P.E. major courses are divided into two parts: theory and practice lesions with the majority in practice lessons. Second, the learning combines static and dynamic and the former gives priority to the latter. Third, it takes the physical exercise as the principle thing in learning content and it has less extracurricular work. Thus, there is abundance of free time. At present, the teaching from, the two-classes successively is used in colleges and universities' P.E. teaching. Within the limited 90 minutes, students can only get sports training and physical exercises, but the training for their cooperation, creativity and consciousness is relatively rare. If some practice lessons are properly arranged to students, it is good for students' realization to teaching content improvement from perceptual level to the rational level. If some practicable operations such as match, holding the post of judge and teaching practice and organized for students in teaching process, it can make students experience the whole process in which theory knowledge and techniques are applied to the practice. It will get the incomparable effect beyond the simple lecturing. It is urgent affairs to take a way to combine the class and extracurricular lessons, individual and community lessons. Once such organization which has cooperative, focus on teamwork learning and shared knowledge is set up, the whole teaching process becomes the process of collective exploration and studying on the basis of mutual inspiration and thinking. It can bring up a kind of relation that teaching benefits teachers as well as students. This process can benefit for the product of innovative thinking.

2.3 The Modern Teaching Development Provide the Convenient Conditions for Carrying Out Learning Organization Theory

The application of the multi-media in teaching can widen teachers and students' knowledge vision and can provide them with rich and teaching-related information source and learning materials, saving time for their material and information searching. At the same time, it can supply an exchange platform between students and teachers, students and students so that the exchange can not be limited in space and time. As a result, people can learn from each other and solve their common problems in groups, breaking down the bounds between class and outside of classroom. After the building up of learning organization, teachers, just as students, become the members in the organization. Thus, teachers can change their identity in thinking and can realize what students really want in teaching, making their teaching objective more directed to demand students' need in learning. In addition, their teaching efficiency can be improved greatly. These fit into the modern teaching theory.

3 Application of Learning Organization in Teaching of P.E. Major in Universities and College

3.1 Cultivating Cooperative Consciousness and Summarizing and Improving Teaching Method

Combined with the first practice—personal mastery, the teacher should firstly propagate the advantage of learning organization and mobilize students to join the organization. Competition in class, election of the representatives of subjects, comparing and appraising of groups, setting up progress award and other activities should be held. Its purpose is to place students in dynamic environment and to make the members of class, representatives of subjects; groups and organizations surpass themselves and progress constantly. The second purpose is to make the members of organization process collective honor and the achievement and pride of conquering themselves. The third purpose is to give students inexhaustible motive of study by continuous self-motivation and stimulation of external condition. What's more, by combining the second practice to improve the mental model, physical education teachers' traditional managing modes and teaching ideas should be alter in studying-type class. The theory of learning organization focuses on giving full play to the positivity, initiative and creativity of the members. It also emphasizes humanism, because human is both the production factor and the factor different from other material form, highlighting that people are a kind of living elements. Teacher as the organizer and guides of the organization is the supervisor of executing the decision and provides the time and space guarantee for organization learning. Teacher should ensure that the information of organization learning is unblocked, try to communicate with students, develop the communication among students and timely praise progressive students. Teacher and students should be together to question the problem in P.E. teaching and investigate and find the solutions.

3.2 Defining the Learning Goals and Establishing Shared Vision of Teachers and Students

Shared vision is an important feature of learning organization. The goal of learning organization refers to that the learning subject should specially describe the goal he or she wants to realize. It is not an external standard, but the internal forming. It is the common vision of both parties of teacher and students. When processing the common vision, the members of origination will strive for the common goal.

Concerning with teaching practice of PE major, establishing the corporate vision actually requires teacher to formulate the teaching goal of applying to the teaching features of PE major, combining the different demands and the physical and mental features of every students. PE major students have the strong desire performance and yearn for the recognition and approval of college and teachers. At the same time, PE major students' self-consciousness and independence formed in the competition are more obvious than students' of other majors. They will affect the character formation of modesty and tolerability. Thus, as long as they meet the problems, they will have the improper actions and destroy the harmonious development of class under the influence of self-consciousness. Therefore, to make students establish the clear learning goals and plans is good for students, who can have guide to action. Thus, students can work hard toward the common goal that includes both short-term and long-term goals. The long-term goal covers the curriculum goal of PE major, the goal of academic year and the goal of semester. The short-term goal refers to the goal of every unit, the goal of every class and the special activity goal of group and its members in every class. It is essential to help students to define the orientation of long-term goal and to and make student earnestly practice the special short-term goal. By this method, every student can have his or her own target system, combining the long-term goal with the short-term goal, the individual goal and the common goal, the personal goal and the class goal. Thus, every student can define their goal and understand the goal and hope the class wants to finish. Hence, students should improve their learning efficiency by the definite object in view. The goal will be achieved through the common effort of teacher and students in a community and the mutual help among students.

3.3 Reorientation of Relationship between Teachers and Students to Establish Team Learning Model

Team learning is a process that members of team work hard and actively and coordinate with each other to realize the goal of team under the guidance of common vision and that all the members change the common vision into its individual ideal. Learning organization focuses on stimulating members to create new knowledge by learning ability of collective intelligence, based on group learning to pool collective wisdom and rational communication and assistance to share the learning experience. Thus, the efficiency of individual learning is much poorer than group learning.

To build mode of group learning requires the new orientation of role of teacher and students. In traditional teaching mode, teacher is the only subject and students are just the objects to learn passively. Thus, students can not study initiatively and there is not enough communication between teacher and students and among students. At present, the classes of college and university are typical individual learning and leaning efficiency is low. Therefore, in the process of building organization learning, teacher should be not the subject of teaching and students not the object of teaching. Traditional relationship between teacher and students should be changed to be more equal like the members in a group. Through the role transformation, teacher should be the guider and partner of students in the process of class teaching. Namely, both teacher and students should be the subjects of class teaching. Thus, teaching method in class is not to emphasize teacher' lecture but to concern with students' discussion and practice in line with such requests. In class, teacher should not just encourage students to express their opinions, but also guide them to obtain actively truth from their practice. In the entire stage of learning, teachers should pay attention to grasping the overall situation and coordinating relation. In physical activity, students' bodies and minds are excited so that the little thing may cause the great conflict. Teacher should use aptly the conflict and guide students to change the conflict into inflection and discussion of skills and actions. Thus, conflict can become the learning motivation and a chance to increase the friendship of students.

4 Conclusion

Teaching target will be more reasonable. In addition, it also makes teacher and students to learn communication, cooperation, sharing and creating so as to cultivate the ability of communication and corporation and team spirit. In the united and positive collective atmosphere, teacher and students can gain positive emotional experience and produce innovative thinking in the interaction. The learning organization theory is a relatively new and strange theory system and its application is still at the embryonic stage of exploration. To use learning organization theory in teaching of PE of college and university aims to find a new idea by the theory and to make it lay the foundation for the further teaching practice.

References

1. Senge, P.M.: The Fifth Discipline—Art and Trend of the Learning Organization. Shanghai San Lien Book Store (1998)
2. Senge, P.M.: The Fifth Discipline—Strategies and Methods of Establishing Learning Organization. Orient Press (2002)
3. Chen, H.: Analysis on Learning Organization's Value of Improving Teaching Quality in Colleges and Universities. Suzhou S&.T University Journal (Social Science Edition) (April 2004)
4. Tu, J.: Practice Strategy of Constructing Learning Organization with Analysis of Class Teaching Cases as the Carrier. Jiangsu Education (January 2004)
5. Meng, F.: Constructing Learning Organization of Modern Schools. Research on Comparative Education (January 2002)
6. Zhang, S.: How to Create Learning Organization. Beijing University Press, Beijing (2004)

The Implementing and Researching of BIT in Airborne Computer

Xinyu Tian[1,2], Xiaolin Zhang[2], Haitao Wu[1], and Ying Yao[1,3]

[1] National Time Service Center, Chinese Academy of Sciences Lintong,
Shaanxi, 710600, China
[2] No 365 Institute Northwestern Polytechnical University, Xi'an 710065, China
[3] Department of Electronic and Information Engineering, Xi'an
University of Post and Telecommunications, Xi'an 710121, China

Abstract. BIT (Built - in Test) is an important ways to improve the performance of testing and maintenance in the airborn computer. But the widespread use of BIT is hindered by the high false alarm rate. A new BIT design strategy and arithmetic for airborn computer is proposed in this paper to reduce the false alarm rate. And some BIT solutions of key technologies in airborn computer are given in this paper, such as digital I/O channels, A/D channels, D/A channels and serial interface. It is proved by practice that the BIT design strategy proposed in this paper can improve the test cover rate to 90%, reduce the false alarm rate to 35%, make the reliability and maintainability of the airborn computer increasing obviously.

Keywords: BIT, Airborne, Reliability, Maintainability.

1 Introduction

BIT(Built In Test) is a new technology for system testing or fault diagnose and isolation, it become more and more important in the reliability and maintainability design of the aviation electronic equipment. The more complex the airborn computer is, the more important the system's BIT technology is [2]. The BIT technology effect the healthy rate of combat equipment, the task executing and the system or device's function and state report giving directly. So BIT technology can shorten the maintenance time, debase the maintenance fare [3].

It can achieve the high cover rate and low false alarm rate in BIT testing and improve the reliability and security of airborn computer by designing special circuit and soft ware in airborn computer.

2 The Design and Realization of System BIT

The excellent BIT system can test each part function of the system, diagnose and isolation the system's fault correctly, improve the reliability, viability and MTBF (mean time between failure, MTBF) of the system. The fault testing rate, the fault

S. Lin and X. Huang (Eds.): CESM 2011, Part I, CCIS 175, pp. 192–198, 2011.
© Springer-Verlag Berlin Heidelberg 2011

isolating rate and the false alarm rate are the important performance figures in the BIT system design, and the false alarm rate is the key figure for the BIT performance evaluation. The false alarm rate is near to 20% in most aviation electronic equipment. And the phenomena that the fault can't be recur and the function is normal when re-testing appear frequently. So inducing the false alarm rate is the key problem to improve the BIT system performance .

The BIT system can be expressed by math as follow:

$$y(t) = f \{ x (t) , u (t) , m (t) , n (t) \} \tag{1}$$

x (t): the system input.

y (t): the system output.

n (t): the process noise of the system.

u (t): the state variable of testing object.

m(t): the model parameter of the dynamic process.

x(t) and y(t) can get by sensor. u(t) is a state variable, some can be test and some can't. The model parameter m(t) can't be test directly, it can be calculated only by the model suppose, state estimate or parameter distinguish. The process noise of the system, n(t) can't be test directly for its incertitude and instantaneous.

Formula (2) can get by predigesting formula (1).

$$y(t) = f\{ x(t) , m(t) \} \tag{2}$$

y(t): the output of BIT system.

x(t): the input of BIT system.

m(t): the uncertainty input of the BIT system.

The input of BIT system is composed by two parts, the certainty input and the uncertainty input. The uncertainty input is the main reason for the false alarm appearance in the BIT system.

The uncertainty input is composed by all kinds of system noise, uncertainty and instantaneous, just as temperature noise, humidity noise and signal burr and so on. The noises produce the false alarm, reduce the correct rate of the BIT testing. The important solution for this question is the self-adapt filter of testing passageway, wiping out the influence of noise or interferential. It is the important way to reduce the false alarm rate and assure the system's performance testing and fault diagnosing intelligently.

The fault rate of BIT circuit influenced the reliability of system directly. The fault rate of system is influenced little by the BIT circuit of lower fault rate. Otherwise the high fault rate of BIT circuit would produce the high false alarm of system. Then the BIT test can't get a confidence result, the security and reliability of the system will reduced mostly.

In the BIT test process, the data that from the single test point or once test can't ensure the accuracy and integrality of the test, for the test result can only reveal the situation of the test object partly and be influenced by all kinds of noise easily. The test data got by many test point can reduce the influence of noise and reveal the actual situation of system, reduce the fault rate of BIT circuit mostly.

Suppose the false alarm rate of BIT circuit fault produced by single test point is $P(\lambda_m)$, satisfied (0, 1) distribution and each of the test points is separate. $P(\lambda)$ is the final false alarm rate of BIT circuit fault. Taking the minimum false alarm rate of the BIT circuit as the optimized objective, the optimized formula is as follow:

$$P(\lambda) = P(\lambda_1)\ P(\lambda_2)\ _{...}\ P(\lambda_m) \tag{3}$$

m: The maximal number of the test point in BIT circuit.

It can obtain from formula (3) that m is inversely proportional to $P(\lambda)$. So the more test point the lower false alarm rate produced by BIT circuit fault.

Formula (3) can be express as follow:

$$P(K) = P(K_1)\ P(K_2)\ _{...}\ P(K_m) \tag{4}$$

m: The maximal number of the test point in BIT circuit.

$P(K)$: the false alarm rate of BIT circuit.

$P(K_m)$: the false alarm rate of single test point in BIT circuit.

Because $P(K_m) < 1$, it can be obtain by formula (4) that $P(K)$ is inversely proportional to m, the lager m is, the false alarm rate is lower.

So the more test point designed in the system, the higher rate of fault test and fault isolation is. The system is more reliability. But the BIT test system need realized by special hardware circuit, so the more BIT test system induce the totality system is more complex. The totality system is less reliability and bigger cubage. So the number of BIT test system or the value of m should not be raised, when the rate of fault test, fault isolate and false alarm is satisfied the system demand. The number of BIT test system designed in this paper is less or equal to 3, and the data from different test point should be information fusion for improve test validity and reduce the conflict of the data from different test point.

It can be get from formula (4) that reducing m can raise false alarm rate, raising m can reduce false alarm rate. When raising m, the system will be more complex, weight, bigger, and less reliability. The conflict can be resolve by analyzing formula (4), $P(K)$ is proportionate to $P(K_m)$. When m is definite, reducing $P(K_m)$, $P(K)$ is decreased too. For $P(K_m) < 1$, formula (5) can be got as follow:

$$P(K) = P(K_1)^n \, P(K_2)^n \dots P(K_m)^n \qquad (5)$$

n: the repeat test number of single test point.

In formula (5) , for $P(K_m) < 1$, $P(K_m)^n \ll P(K_m)$. But the more lager the repeat test number is, the test software is more complex and the time expended on test is longer. In this paper, n assigned 3. The flow chart of the BIT system in the airborn computer is show as follow:

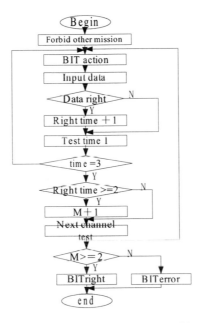

Fig. 1. The flow chart of the BIT system in the airborn computer

3   The BIT Method and Fault Isolation of Partial System

BIT test need special hardware, the test circuit for different partial system test is different. The basic test need executed in the airborn computer include: digital I/O channel test, A/D, D/A channel test, serial interface test, and the test methods is discussed as follow.

3.1   Digital I/O Channel Test and Fault Isolation

The airborn computer digital I/O channel is used for digital signal input and output. Generally there are many digital I/O channel in airborn computer. If each channel test by special test circuit, the BIT system would be complex and big size, and the reliability of the system would reduced. So a circle test method is proposed below. This method designs a BIT test circuit for special digital I/O channel and special software working together with the test of each I/O channel.

In output channel test, setting the digital value exporting though output channel first, the output digital value should be read though BIT input channel, then comparing the read data with the setting value. Though the circle test program, the BIT test result of the output channel can be got. In input channel test, a group setting data output though the BIT output channel, then reading the data though input channel, compare it with the setting value. Though the circle test program, the BIT test result of the input channel can be got. If the data output and input is same with the setting data, the channel is normal. Otherwise the channel is fault and should be isolation from the system. The BIT system block diagram of digital I/O channel test is show as fig 2.

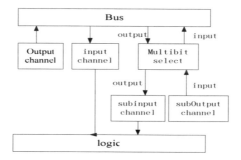

Fig. 2. The flow chart of the digtial I/Ochannel test

3.2 A/D, D/A Channel Test and Fault Isolation

The analogy signal is input and output though A/D, D/A channel in airborn computer. The BIT test method of A/D channel is as follow. The A/D channel of airborn computer is connected with the reference voltage. Though running the special A/D test program, the reference voltage is collect though the A/D channel. Comparing the collect value with the reference value, if the difference is lower to the error tolerance, the A/D channel is normal, otherwise send out the fault report. For example, the reference voltage outside is +5V, 0V and -5V separate, the collected result though A/D channel in airborn computer would be compared with FFFH, 7FFH and 0H. If the compare result $|\Delta| \leq n$ bit (n is the allow error tolerance of the system, n determined by system's precision), the A/D channel is normal. Otherwise the channel is default, should be isolation from the system.

D/A channel test method is reference voltage method. The particular test step of the method is as follow. When the aerocraft is in ground test state, the airborn computer output settlement data, and the assistant A/D channel collect the signal. Comparing the collect data with the settlement data, if the difference is lower to the error tolerance, the D/A channel is normal, otherwise send out the fault report. For example: the airborn computer output FFFH, 7FFH and 0H three data. Using the assistant A/D channel collect the signal, then comparing the collected data with the settlement data, if the compare result $|\Delta| \leq$ n bit (n is the allow error tolerance of the system, n determined by system's precision), the D/A channel is normal. Otherwise the channel is fault, should be isolation from the system.

The system block diagram is show as fig 3 :

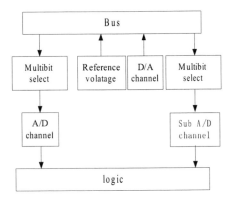

Fig. 3. The flow chart of A/D, D/A channel test

3.3 The Serial Interface Test and Fault Isolation

The serial interface BIT test method is send & receive circle test method. In the sending channel test, the settlement data would be sent by the serial interface, and the data should be read by assistant BIT serial interface. Comparing the data read by BIT circuit with the settlement data, according to the rule of the minority subordinated to the majority, the interface can be judged to be normal or fault. If the interface is fault, it should be reported and isolation from the system.

In the receive channel test, using the assistant BIT interface read the data at the same time, according to the rule of the minority subordinated to the majority, the interface can be judged to be normal or fault. If the interface is fault, it should be reported and isolation from the system.

The system block diagram is show as fig 4 :

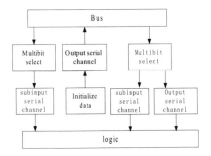

Fig. 4. The flow chart of serial channel test

4 Conclusion

In the BIT design of modern airborn computer, the high false alarm rate blocks the improving of BIT performance seriously. It is proved by practice that the BIT design strategy proposed in this paper can improve the test cover rate about to 90%, reduce the false alarm rate to 35%, and improve the reliability and maintainability of the airborn computer with lower price of software and hardware.

References

[1] Benvenga, C., Murray, D.: Embedding model-based diagnostics into a complex instrument to improve reliability through self diagnosis. In: Agilent Technical Conference (2007)
[2] Smith, J.: Built in Test - Coverage and Diagnostics, 978-1-4244-4981-1/09/2009 IEEE
[3] Woell, J.J.: ATCS, IMTC 2005– Instrumentation and Measurement Technology Conference Ottawa, Canada, May 17-19 (2005)
[4] Chen, P., Xu, H.-c.: Aviation Electron System BITSummary. China Water Transport (Academic Version) 6(2), 108–110 (2002)
[5] Woell, J.J.: Application of Trend Analysis Methodologies on uilt-in-Test (BIT) (and non-BIT)Systems in a Operational U.S. Navy Fighter/Attack Squadron, 2005. In: IMTC–Instrumentation and Measurement Technology Conference Ottawa, Canada, May 17-19 (2005)

Existence of Periodic Solution for Fuzzy Cellular Neural Networks with Time-Varying Delays

Qianhong Zhang[1,*], Lihui Yang[2], and Daixi Liao[3]

[1] Guizhou Key Laboratory of Economics System Simulation,
Guizhou College of Finance and Economics, Guiyang, Guizhou 550004, P.R. China
Tel.: +86 851 6902456
[2] Department of Mathematics, Hunan City University, Yiyang, Hunan 413000,
P.R. China
[3] Basic Science Department, Hunan Institute of Technology,
Hengyang, Hunan 421002, P.R. China
zqianhong68@163.com, ll.hh.yang@gmail.com,
liaodaixizaici@sohu.com

Abstract. In this paper, by employing continuation theorem of coincidence degree, and inequality technique, some sufficient conditions are derived to ensure the existence of periodic solution for fuzzy cellular neural networks with time-varying delays. These results have important leading significance in the design and applications of neural networks.

Keywords: Fuzzy cellular neural networks, Periodic solution, Coincidence degree, Time varying delays.

1 Introduction

It is well known that fuzzy cellular neural networks is first introduced by Yang and Yang [1]. Researchers have founded that FCNNs are useful in image processing, and some results have been reported on stability and periodicity of FCNNs(see, for example,[1]-[10]). However, to the best of our knowledge, few author investigated the existence of periodic solution for fuzzy cellular neural networks with time-varying delays. In this paper, we investigate the following system

$$x_i'(t) = -c_i(t)x_i(t) + \sum_{j=1}^{n} a_{ij}(t)f_j(x_j(t)) + \bigwedge_{j=1}^{n}\alpha_{ij}(t)f(x_j(t-\tau_{ij}(t))) + I_i(t)$$

$$+ \bigvee_{j=1}^{n}\beta_{ij}(t)f_j(x_j(t-\tau_{ij}(t))) + \bigwedge_{j=1}^{n}T_{ij}(t)u_j(t) + \bigvee_{j=1}^{n}H_{ij}(t)u_j(t) \quad (1)$$

$i = 1, 2, \cdots, n,$ where n corresponds to the number of neurons in neural networks.

---

* Corresponding author.

S. Lin and X. Huang (Eds.): CESM 2011, Part I, CCIS 175, pp. 199–206, 2011.

For $x_i(t)$ is the activations of the i th neuron at time t, $c_i(t)$ denotes the rate with which the i th neuron will reset its potential to the resting state in isolation when disconnected from the network and external inputs; $\wedge$ and $\vee$ denote the fuzzy AND and fuzzy OR operations. $a_{ij}(t)$ denotes the strengths of connectivity between cell i and cell j at time t. $\alpha_{ij}(t)$, $\beta_{ij}(t)$, $T_{ij}(t)$ and $H_{ij}(t)$ are elements of fuzzy feedback MIN template and fuzzy feedback MAX template, fuzzy feed-forward MIN template and fuzzy feed-forward MAX template between cell i and j at time t. $\tau_{ij}(t)$ corresponds to the time delay required in processing and transmitting a signal from the j th cell to the i th cell at time t. $u_j(t)$ and $I_i(t)$ denote the external input, bias of the i th neurons at time t, respectively. $f_j(\cdot)$ is signal transmission functions.

Throughout the paper, we give the following assumptions

(A1) $|f_j(x)| \leq p_j |x| + q_j$ for all $x \in R$, $j = 1, 2, \cdots, n$, where p_j, q_j are nonnegative constants.

Let $\tau = \max_{1 \leq i, j \leq n} \sup_{t \geq 0} \{\tau_{ij}(t)\}$, For continuous functions φ_i defined on $[-\tau, 0]$, $i = 1, 2, \cdots, n$, we set $\Psi = (\varphi_1, \varphi_2, \cdots, \varphi_n)^T$. Assume that system (1) is supplemented with initial value of type

$$x_i(t) = \varphi_i(t), \quad -\tau \leq t \leq 0.$$

Lemma 1. [11] If $\rho(K) < 1$ for matrix $K = (k_{ij})_{n \times n} \geq 0$, then $(E - K)^{-1} \geq 0$, where E denotes the identity matrix of size n.

Lemma 2. [2] Suppose x and y are two states of system (1), then we have

$$\left| \bigwedge_{j=1}^{n} \alpha_{ij}(t) f_j(x) - \bigwedge_{j=1}^{n} \alpha_{ij}(t) f_j(y) \right| \leq \sum_{j=1}^{n} |\alpha_{ij}(t)| |f_j(x) - f_j(y)|,$$

and

$$\left| \bigvee_{j=1}^{n} \beta_{ij}(t) f_j(x) - \bigvee_{j=1}^{n} \beta_{ij}(t) f_j(y) \right| \leq \sum_{j=1}^{n} |\beta_{ij}(t)| |f_j(x) - f_j(y)|.$$

The remainder of this paper is organized as follows. In Section 2, we will give the sufficient conditions to ensure the existence of periodic oscillatory solution for fuzzy cellular neural networks with time-varying delays. In Section 3 we will give a general conclusion.

2 Periodic Oscillatory Solutions

In this section, we will consider the periodic oscillatory solutions of system (1), we give the following assumption.

(A2) $\tau_{ij} \in C(R,[0,\infty))$ are periodic functions with periodic ω for $i, j = 1, 2, \cdots, n$.

(A3) $c_i \in C(R,(0,\infty)), a_{ij}, \alpha_{ij}, \beta_{ij}, T_{ij}, H_{ij}, u_j, I_i \in C(R,R)$ are periodic functions with common periodic ω and $f_j \in C(R,R), i, j = 1, 2, \cdots, n$.

We will use the coincidence degree theory to obtain the existence of an ω-periodic solution to system (1).

Lemma 3. [12] Let L be a Fredholm mapping of index zero and let N be L-compact on Ω. Suppose that

(a) for each $\lambda \in (0,1)$, every solution x of $Lx = \lambda Nx$ is such that $x \notin \partial\Omega$.

(b) $QNx \neq 0$ for each $x \in \partial\Omega \cap KerL$ and $\deg\{JQN, \Omega \cap KerL, 0\} \neq 0$.

Then the equation $Lx = Nx$ has at least one solution lying in $DomL \cap \bar{\Omega}$.

To be convenience, in the rest of paper, for a continuous function $g:[0,\omega] \mapsto R$, we denote

$$g^+ = \max_{t\in[0,\omega]} g(t), \; g^- = \min_{t\in[0,\omega]} g(t), \; \bar{g} = \frac{1}{\omega}\int_0^\omega g(t)dt$$

Theorem 1. Under assumptions (A1); (A2) and (A3), $k_{ij} = (\frac{1}{c} + \omega)(|\bar{a}_{ij}| + |\bar{\alpha}_{ij}| + |\bar{\beta}_{ij}|)p_j$, $K = (k_{ij})_{n\times n}$. Suppose that $\rho(K) < 1$, then system (1) has at least an ω-periodic solution.

Proof. Take $X = Z = \{x(t) = (x_1(t), x_2(t), \cdots, x_n(t))^T \in C(R,R^n) : x(t+\omega) = x(t)\}$. and denote $\|x\| = \max_{1\leq i\leq n} \max_{t\in[0,\omega]} |x_i(t)|$. Equipped with the norm $\|\cdot\|$, both X and Z are Banach space. For any $x(t) \in X$, it is easy to check that

$$\Theta(x_i,t) := -c_i(t)x_i(t) + \sum_{j=1}^n a_{ij}(t)f_j(x_j(t)) + \bigwedge_{j=1}^n \alpha_{ij}(t)f_j(x_j(t-\tau_{ij}(t))) + I_i(t)$$

$$+ \bigvee_{j=1}^n \beta_{ij}(t)f_j(t-\tau_{ij}(t))) + \bigwedge_{j=1}^n T_{ij}(t)u_j(t) + \bigvee_{j=1}^n H_{ij}(t)u_j(t) \in Z$$

Let

$$L:DomL = \{x \in X : x \in C(R,R^n)\} \ni x \mapsto \dot{x}(\cdot) \in Z. \; P:X \ni x \mapsto \frac{1}{\omega}\int_0^\omega x(t)dt \in X$$

$$Q: Z \ni z \mapsto \frac{1}{\omega}\int_0^\omega z(t)dt \in Z, \quad N: X \ni x \mapsto \Theta(x,\cdot) \in Z$$

Then system (1) can be reduced to operator equation $Lx = Nx$. It is easy to see that $KerL = R^n, \mathrm{Im}\,L = \{z \in Z : \frac{1}{\omega}\int_0^\omega z(t)dt = 0\}$, which is closed in Z. $\dim KerL = co \dim \mathrm{Im}\,L = n < \infty$, and P, Q are continuous projectors such that $\mathrm{Im}\,P = KerL, KerQ = \mathrm{Im}\,L = \mathrm{Im}(I-Q)$. It follows that L is a Fredholm mapping of index zero. Furthermore, the generalized inverse (to L) $K_p : \mathrm{Im}\,L \mapsto KerP \cap DomL$ is given by

$$(K_p(z))_i(t) = \int_0^t z_i(s)ds - \frac{1}{\omega}\int_0^\omega \int_0^s z_i(v)dvds$$

Therefore, applying the Arzela-Ascoli theorem, one can easily show that N is a L-compact on $\overline{\Omega}$ with any bounded open subset $\Omega \subset X$. Since $\mathrm{Im}\,Q = KerL$.we take the isomorphism J of $\mathrm{Im}\,Q$ onto $KerL$ to be the identity mapping. Now we need only to show that, for an appropriate open bounded subset, applying the continuation theorem corresponding to the operator equation $Lx = \lambda Nx, \lambda \in (0,1)$. Let

$$x_i'(t) = \lambda\Theta(x_i,t), i = 1, 2, \cdots, n. \tag{2}$$

Assume that $x = x(t) \in X$ is a solution of system (2) for some $\lambda \in (0,1)$. Integrating (2) over the interval $[0, \omega]$, we obtain that

$$0 = \int_0^\omega x_i'(t)dt = \lambda \int_0^\omega \Theta(x_i,t)dt \tag{3}$$

Hence

$$\int_0^\omega c_i(t)x_i(t)dt = \int_0^\omega \{\sum_{j=1}^n a_{ij}(t)f_j(x_j(t)) + \bigwedge_{j=1}^n \alpha_{ij}(t)f_j(x_j(t-\tau_{ij}(t))) + \bigwedge_{j=1}^n T_{ij}(t)u_j(t)$$

$$+ \bigvee_{j=1}^n \beta_{ij}(t)f_j(x_j(t-\tau_{ij}(t))) + \bigvee_{j=1}^n H_{ij}(t)u_j(t) + I_i(t)\}dt$$

Noting assumption (A1), we get

$$|x_i|\_\overline{c_i} \le \sum_{j=1}^n (|\overline{a}_{ij}| + |\overline{\alpha}_{ij}| + |\overline{\beta}_{ij}|)p_j|x_j|^+ + \sum_{j=1}^n (|\overline{a}_{ij}| + |\overline{\alpha}_{ij}| + |\overline{\beta}_{ij}|)q_j$$

$$+ \bigwedge_{j=1}^n |\overline{T}_{ij}| \|u_j\|^+ + \bigvee_{j=1}^n |\overline{H}_{ij}| \|u_j\|^+ + |\overline{I}_i| \tag{4}$$

It follows that

$$|x_i| \leq \frac{1}{c_i} \sum_{j=1}^{n} (|\overline{a}_{ij}| + |\overline{\alpha}_{ij}| + |\overline{\beta}_{ij}|) p_j |x_j|^+ + \frac{1}{c_i} \sum_{j=1}^{n} (|\overline{a}_{ij}| + |\overline{\alpha}_{ij}| + |\overline{\beta}_{ij}|) q_j$$

$$+ \frac{1}{c_i} \{ \bigwedge_{j=1}^{n} |\overline{T}_{ij}| \|u_j|^+ + \bigvee_{j=1}^{n} |\overline{H}_{ij}| \|u_j|^+ + |\overline{I}_i| \} \tag{5}$$

Note that each $x_i(t)$ is continuously differentiable for $i = 1, 2, \cdots, n$; it is certain that there exists $t_i \in [0, \omega]$ such that $|x_i(t_i)| = |x_i(t_i)|_-$. Set $F = (F_1, F_2, \cdots, F_n)^T$

where

$$F_i = (\frac{1}{c_i} + \omega) \{ \sum_{j=1}^{n} |\overline{a}_{ij}| + |\overline{\alpha}_{ij}| + |\overline{\beta}_{ij}|) q_j + \bigwedge_{j=1}^{n} |\overline{T}_{ij}| \|u_j|^+ + \bigvee_{j=1}^{n} |\overline{H}_{ij}| \|u_j|^+ + |\overline{I}_i| \}$$

In view of $\rho(K) < 1$ and Lemma 1, we have $(E - K)^{-1} F = h = (h_1, h_2, \cdots, h_n)^T \geq 0$

where h_i is given by $h_i = \sum_{j=1}^{n} k_{ij} h_j + F, i = 1, 2, \cdots, n$. Set

$$\Omega = \{ (x_1, x_2, \cdots, x_n)^T \in R^n : |x_i| < h_i, i = 1, 2, \cdots, n \} \tag{6}$$

Then, for $t \in [t_i, t_i + \omega]$, we have

$$|x_i(t)| \leq |x_i(t_i)| + \int_{t_i} D^+ |x_i(t)| \, dt \leq |x_i(t)|_- + \int^{+\omega}_{t_i} D^+ |x_i(t)| \, dt$$

$$\leq \frac{1}{c_i} \sum_{j-1}^{n} (|\overline{a}_{ij}| + |\overline{\alpha}_{ij}| + |\overline{\beta}_{ij}|) p_j |x_j|^+ + \frac{1}{c_i} \{ \sum_{j-1}^{n} (|\overline{a}_{ij}| + |\overline{\alpha}_{ij}| + |\overline{\beta}_{ij}|) q_j$$

$$+ \bigwedge_{j=1}^{n} |\overline{T}_{ij}| \|u_j|^+ + \bigvee_{j=1}^{n} |\overline{H}_{ij}| \|u_j|^+ + |\overline{I}_i| \} + \int^{+\omega}_{t_i} D^+ |x_i(t)| \, dt$$

$$\leq (\frac{1}{c_i} + \omega) \{ \sum_{j=1}^{n} (|\overline{a}_{ij}| + |\overline{\alpha}_{ij}| + |\overline{\beta}_{ij}|) p_j |x_j|^+ \} + (\frac{1}{c_i} + \omega) \{ \sum_{j=1}^{n} (|\overline{a}_{ij}| + |\overline{\alpha}_{ij}|$$

$$+ |\overline{\beta}_{ij}|) q_j + \bigwedge_{j=1}^{n} |\overline{T}_{ij}| \|u_j|^+ + \bigvee_{j=1}^{n} |\overline{H}_{ij}| \|u_j|^+ + |\overline{I}_i| \}$$

$$\leq \sum_{j=1}^{n} k_{ij} h_j + F_i = h_i$$

Clearly, $h_i, i = 1, 2, \cdots, n$, are independent of λ. Then for $\forall \lambda \in (0, 1), x \in \partial\Omega$ such that $Lx = \lambda Nx$. When $u = (x_1, x_2, \cdots, x_n)^T \in \partial\Omega \bigcap KerL = \partial\Omega \bigcap R^n$. u is a constant vector with $|x_i| = h_i, i = 1, 2, \cdots, n$: Note that $QNu = JQNu$, when $u \in KerL$. it must be

$$(QN)u_i = -\bar{c}_i x_i + \sum_{j=1}^{n}(\bar{a}_{ij} + \bar{\alpha}_{ij} + \bar{\beta}_{ij})f(x_j) + \bigwedge_{j=1}^{n}\bar{T}_{ij}\bar{u}_j + \bigvee_{j=1}^{n}\bar{H}_{ij}\bar{u}_j + \bar{I}_i$$

We claim that

$$\left\|(QN)u_i\right\| > 0, i = 1, 2, \cdots, n. \tag{7}$$

On the contrary, suppose that there are some i such that $\left\|(QN)u_i\right\| = 0$, namely

$$\bar{c}_i x_i = \sum_{j=1}^{n}(\bar{a}_{ij} + \bar{\alpha}_{ij} + \bar{\beta}_{ij})f(x_j) + \bigwedge_{j=1}^{n}\bar{T}_{ij}\bar{u}_j + \bigvee_{j=1}^{n}\bar{H}_{ij}\bar{u}_j + \bar{I}_i$$

Then we have

$$h_i = |x_i| = \frac{1}{\bar{c}_i}|\sum_{j=1}^{n}(\bar{a}_{ij} + \bar{\alpha}_{ij} + \bar{\beta}_{ij})f(x_j) + \bigwedge_{j=1}^{n}\bar{T}_{ij}\bar{u}_j + \bigvee_{j=1}^{n}\bar{H}_{ij}\bar{u}_j + \bar{I}_i|$$

$$\leq \frac{1}{\bar{c}_i}\{\sum_{j=1}^{n}(|\bar{a}_{ij}| + |\bar{\alpha}_{ij}| + |\bar{\beta}_{ij}|)p_j h_j + \sum_{j=1}^{n}(|\bar{a}_{ij}| + |\bar{\alpha}_{ij}| + |\bar{\beta}_{ij}|)q_j$$

$$+ \bigwedge_{j=1}^{n}|\bar{T}_{ij}|\|u_j|^+ + \bigvee_{j=1}^{n}|\bar{H}_{ij}|\|u_j|^+ + |\bar{I}_i|\}$$

$$\leq (\frac{1}{\bar{c}_i} + \omega)\{\sum_{j=1}^{n}(|\bar{a}_{ij}| + |\bar{\alpha}_{ij}| + |\bar{\beta}_{ij}|)p_j|h_j|^+\} + (\frac{1}{\bar{c}_i} + \omega)\{\sum_{j=1}^{n}(|\bar{a}_{ij}| + |\bar{\alpha}_{ij}| + |\bar{\beta}_{ij}|)q_j$$

$$+ \bigwedge_{j=1}^{n}|\bar{T}_{ij}|\|u_j|^+ + \bigvee_{j=1}^{n}|\bar{H}_{ij}|\|u_j|^+ + |\bar{I}_i|\}$$

$$= \sum_{j=1}^{n}k_{ij}h_j + F_j \tag{8}$$

Which is a contradiction. Therefore (7) holds and $Lu = Nu$

$$QNu \neq 0, u \in \partial\Omega \bigcap KerL = \partial\Omega \bigcap R^n \tag{9}$$

Consider the homotopy $\Phi : (\Omega \bigcap KerL) \times [0,1] \mapsto \Omega \bigcap KerL$ defined by

$$\Phi(u, \mu) = \mu diag(-\bar{c}_1, -\bar{c}_2, \cdots, -\bar{c}_n)u + (1 - \mu)QNu$$

Note that $\Phi(\cdot, 0) = JQN$, if $\Phi(u, \mu) = 0$, then we have

$$|x_i| = \frac{1-\mu}{\overline{c}_i} |\sum_{j=1}^{n} (\overline{a}_{ij} + \overline{\alpha}_{ij} + \overline{\beta}_{ij}) f(x_j) + \bigwedge_{j=1}^{n} \overline{T}_{ij} \overline{u}_j + \bigvee_{j=1}^{n} \overline{H}_{ij} \overline{u}_j + \overline{I}_i|$$

$$\leq \frac{1}{\overline{c}_i} \{ \sum_{j=1}^{n} (|\overline{a}_{ij}| + |\overline{\alpha}_{ij}| + |\overline{\beta}_{ij}|) p_j h_j + \sum_{j=1}^{n} (|\overline{a}_{ij}| + |\overline{\alpha}_{ij}| + |\overline{\beta}_{ij}|) q_j$$

$$+ \bigwedge_{j=1}^{n} |\overline{T}_{ij}| \|u_j|^+ + \bigvee_{j=1}^{n} |\overline{H}_{ij}| \|u_j|^+ + |\overline{I}_i| \}$$

$$\leq (\frac{1}{\overline{c}_i} + \omega) \{ \sum_{j=1}^{n} (|\overline{a}_{ij}| + |\overline{\alpha}_{ij}| + |\overline{\beta}_{ij}|) p_j |h_j|^+ \} + (\frac{1}{\overline{c}_i} + \omega) \{ \sum_{j=1}^{n} (|\overline{a}_{ij}| + |\overline{\alpha}_{ij}| + |\overline{\beta}_{ij}|) q_j$$

$$+ \bigwedge_{j=1}^{n} |\overline{T}_{ij}| \|u_j|^+ + \bigvee_{j=1}^{n} |\overline{H}_{ij}| \|u_j|^+ + |\overline{I}_i| \}$$

$$= \sum_{j=1}^{n} k_{ij} h_j + F_j \qquad (10)$$

Therefore $\Phi(u, \mu) \neq 0, (u, \mu) \in (\Omega \bigcap KerL) \times [0,1]$.

It follows from the property of invariance under homotopy that

$$\deg\{JQN, \Omega \bigcap KerL, 0\} = \deg\{\Phi(\cdot, 0), \Omega \bigcap KerL, 0) = \deg\{\Phi(\cdot, 1), \Omega \bigcap KerL, 0)$$
$$= \deg\{diag(-\overline{c}_1, -\overline{c}_2, \cdots, -\overline{c}_n)\} \neq 0$$

Thus, we have shown that Ω satisfies all the assumptions of Lemma 3. Hence, $Lu = Nu$ has at least one ω-periodic solution on $DomL \bigcap \overline{\Omega}$. This completes the proof.

3 Conclusion

In this paper, we have studied the existence of the periodic solution for fuzzy cellular neural networks with time-varying delays. Some sufficient conditions set up here are easily verified. The obtained criteria can be applied to design periodic oscillatory fuzzy cellular neural networks.

Acknowledgement

This work is partially supported by the Doctoral Foundation of Guizhou College of Finance and Economics (2010), the Scientific Research Foundation of Guizhou Provincial Scientific and Technological Department, and the Scientific Research Foundation of Hunan Provincial Education Department (10B023).

References

1. Yang, T., Yang, L.B.: The global stability of fuzzy cellular neural networks. IEEE Trans. Circ. Syst. I 43, 880–883 (1996)
2. Yang, T., Yang, L.B., Wu, C.W., Chua, L.O.: Fuzzy cellular neural networks: theory. In: Proc. IEEE Int. Workshop Cellular Neural Networks Appl., pp. 181–186 (1996)
3. Yang, T., Yang, L.B., Wu, C.W., Chua, L.O.: Fuzzy cellular neural networks: applications. In: Proc. IEEE Int. Workshop on Cellular Neural Neworks Appl., pp. 225–230 (1996)
4. Huang, T.: Exponential stability of fuzzy cellular neural networks with distributed delay. Phy. Lett. A 351, 48–52 (2006)
5. Huang, T.: Exponential stability of delayed fuzzy cellular neural networks with diffusion. Chaos Solitons and Fractals 31, 658–664 (2007)
6. Zhang, Q., Xiang, R.: Global asymptotic stability of fuzzy cellular neural networks with time-varying delays. Phy. Lett. A 371, 3971–3977 (2008)
7. Zhang, Q., Luo, W.: Global Exponential Stability and Periodic Solutions of FCNNs with Constant Delays and Time-varying Delays. In: Proc. of 2009 International Joint Conference on Computational Sciences and Optimization, vol. 2, pp. 659–662 (2009)
8. Yuan, K., Cao, J., Deng, J.: Exponential stability and periodic solutions of fuzzy cellular neural networks with time-varying delays. Neurocomput. 69, 1619–1627 (2006)
9. Liu, Y., Tang, W.: Exponential stability of fuzzy cellular neural networks with costant and time-varying delays. Phy. Lett. A 323, 224–233 (2004)
10. Huang, T.: Exponential stability of delayed fuzzy cellular neural networks with diffusion. Chaos, Solitons and Fractals 31, 658–664 (2007)
11. Berman, A., Plemmons, R.J.: Nonnegative Matrices in the Mathematical Science. Academic Press, New York (1979)
12. Gaines, R.E., Mawhin, J.L.: Coincidence Degree, and Nonlinear Differential Equations. Springer, Berlin (1977)

A Simulation and Experiments of Rapeseed Logistics Supply System Based on Flexsim Software

Dejun liu[1], Guangsheng Zhang[2,*], Xiurong Zhao[1], and Claus Age Søresen[3]

[1] College of Engineering, Shenyang Agricultural University,
Shenyang, 110866, China
[2] College of Economic Management, Shenyang Agricultural University,
Shenyang, 110866, China,
Ph.: 0086-13002444896
gshzhang@163.com
[3] Department of Bio-system Engineering,
Agricultural faculty of Aarhus University, 8800, Denmark

Abstract. An important aspect of rapeseed logistics supply system is to manage the processes of harvesting and transporting from the different rural fields to the processing plants. This paper applies Flexsim simulation techniques to build the simulation model to solve a problem that vehicles coordinate with harvesters and other plant facilities, analyzing the performance of the system in varied configurations and policies for its operations. Studies proved the effectiveness of the methods to increase harvest logistics efficiencies as well as facilities implement. The studies are also useful for other agro plants with similar supply system.

Keywords: Rapeseed, Logistics Supply System, Simulation.

1 Introduction

An important aspect of logistics supply system in agro industries is to manage the process of harvesting and transporting raw materials, from the rural fields to the processing plants (Iannoni et al., 2006). There are many studies and related work that uses simulation models to analyze agricultural products supply chain in agro industries such as sugarcane (Le Gal et al.,2009); cotton (Ravula et al.,2008); cotton-stalk(Tatsiopoulos et al.,2003) and other biomass supply chain issues(Rentizelas et al.,2009; Sokhansanj et al.,2006) etc. The rapeseed harvest logistics include the process from the harvesting to unloading rapeseed or straw in the cranes or conveyors of company. Therefore, trucks or tractors once arriving at the company go through several operations such as net weighing on a scale, sampling tests to determine content quality, unloading on intermediary storage areas or on the cranes and conveyors. The longer waiting times maybe delayed the return of the trucks to the harvesting fields, thereby reducing their availability to transport rapeseed to the company, as well as causing machine and worker idleness in the field (Iannoni et al., 2006).

---

* Corresponding author.

S. Lin and X. Huang (Eds.): CESM 2011, Part I, CCIS 175, pp. 207–212, 2011.
© Springer-Verlag Berlin Heidelberg 2011

The purpose of this paper is to analyze the rapeseed harvesting logistics processes and investigate optimal configurations and policies for their operations so that the machine efficiency maximized, harvesting and transport coordinated and costs of rapeseed supply chain minimized. Due to several sources of uncertainty and the operational complexity in these systems, the method of analysis is based on discrete simulation techniques of Flexsim software. The paper describes the methods developed to identify opportunities for increased harvest logistics efficiencies as well as the process intended to facilitate implementation.

2   The Framework of Modelling Simulation in Case Study

There are two methods of rape harvest: multiple-step harvest and single-step harvest. Trucks of different types from different fields arrive at the weighing location in the processing plant, where data is collected and the net weight is recorded. After receiving a dispatching instruction at the dispatching location, the vehicle proceeds to the assigned unloading line to unload the rapeseed. The dispatching instruction takes into account not only the queuing state of the unloading lines, but also the truck type, the state of the intermediary storage and the quality of rapeseed. In order to avoid congestion and idle of unloading warehouse, an appropriate decision is necessary.

The operating of modelling simulation is determined by time consumption. Generally only if the rapeseed accumulated a certain quantity that transportation start otherwise trucks have to stand idle, so firstly transportation determined by harvesting time, once trucks leave to plants, harvesting have to performed continuously for the next arrival of trucks. If the reception takes too long to delay the return of the trucks to the rural fields, it may cause machine and workers idleness in the fields. As soon as a vehicle finishes the unloading process, it returns to the rural field to be reloaded, and the cycle begins again. The cycle time includes the time spent in the company's reception area until unloading, the travel time back to the field, the time spent in the field until loading is complete, and the travel time back to the company.

3   Simulation of the System

3.1   Description of Modelling Simulation

The company in case study has 100 vehicles including 3 types and average 25 farmers' fields operated at the same time every day in the harvest season. According to the proportion the simulation simplified to 40 vehicles and 10 fields every day while the regulations are maintained. In the model the whole process from harvesting at different 10 fields, transporting to the company and unloading them at the different warehouse. There is only one kind of flow-item named rapeseed in the model, but it is processed at the different field with different harvester, so we define 10 item-types represented different rapeseed in the 10 fields. There are ten different types flow-items entered the model at the source that will arrive based on a normal distribution. Item-types will be uniformly distributed from 1, 2 to 10. As flow-items arrive they will be placed in a corresponding queue and wait to be harvested. The unit of flow-item is defined tonne; once a tonne of rapeseed is harvested it will be stored in queue until reach the capacity of the vehicle, and then transported to the company. The time consumption of transportation determined by speed and distance based on normal distribution. When the vehicle arrive at company it must be weighed to get net weight of rapeseed, and then it is dispatched based on the type of trucks and quality of rapeseed at the dispatching location, finally it is unloaded in the warehouse. The process of unloading is carried out by corresponding processor at the end of the unloading processer the flow-item will be sent to a sink where it will exit the model.

3.2 Setting of Parameters

In the model the rape field is described Fixed-Resource that handles flow-items in a certain way. They receive flow-items through their input ports, and then release the flow-items to be sent on through their output ports. The harvesters as processor receives exactly one kind of flow-items and do something to those flow-items, then release it to the next queue where only the quantity reached the capacity the flow-items are transported by vehicles. The different processor time is determined by real-life statistics and calculation. 4 type of harvester process time are 10.07, 7.08, 8.67, 7.58 min respectively in random assortment. The transporter 23-33 process times determined by type of vehicle (speed1, speed2 and speed 3; capacity 1, capacity 2 and capacity3), distance (5-30km) and other traffic conditions in random assortment. The model parameters sets and components are listed in the table 1.

Table 1. The main parameters of the objects and components of the model

Model elements	System elements or function	Parameters or remarks
Source1	Generating flow-items, define item-type	Statistical distribution: exponential(0,1,1)
Flow-item	Rapeseed	Productivity according tons per minutes
Queue 2	Sending item-type1-10 to processer 3-12	Maximum content to 1000, by expression /get item-type
Processers 3-12	Harvester in different fields	Statistical distribution: normal distribution according productivity
Queue 13-22	Accumulating flow-item to capacities of vehicles	Maximum content to 30 or 60
Network node NN1-NN11	Defining the distance of transporter	Random distribution according real world within 5-30km-80km
Transporter 23-33	Vehicle to transport rapeseed	
Dispatcher 34	Dispatching vehicles to corresponding fields	
Processer 35	Weighing	Statistical distribution: normal(5,2)
Processer 36	Dispatching transporters to unload line	Statistical distribution: normal(5,2)
Queue 37-40	Waiting line	Maximum content to 1000
Processer 41-44	unload	Statistical distribution: normal(3,2)
Sink 45	Intake flow-items	

4 Results and Discussion

Analyses focused on number of vehicles, idle, processing, busy, blocked rate of the vehicles and processors. The simulation run for 600 min (10h) and initiate the variables. Figure 1 shows that the harvester is busy that processing time is more than idle time and the weighing location is idle most of time, and the checking quality is basically same leisure and working time, so it is considerable to combine the weigh location and checking quality. The unload location idle time is more than processing time due to there are four unloading location in the company which means four warehouse doors used.

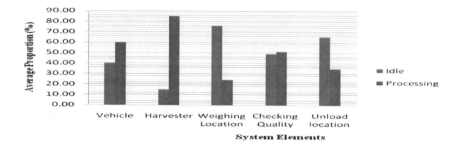

Fig. 1. The average time proportion of vehicle, harvesters, and company working lacation

The productivity of loading is grown in the experiments by changing the loading time from normal (10, 2) to normal (5, 1), which is available by using advanced loading equipments. Figure 5 shows the idle rate variety with the reducing number of trucks.

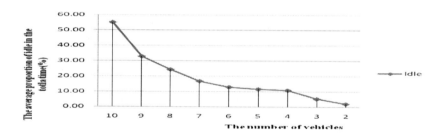

Fig. 2. The idle rate variety with the reducing number of trucks

Figure 2 shows that the proportion of idle in the total time reduced sharply when the method of transportation changed from one vehicle charge one field to dispatcher managing vehicles, the idle rate drop from 55.05 to 32.8. Whereas in the model running process the vehicle working time are imbalanced, that one start to transport only when the other vehicle is busy working, so continue to reduce the number of vehicles. When the number of vehicle reduced to four all the vehicle run at the same time and the idle rate is 10.86%. When the number of vehicle reduced to 3 there is flow-item blocked occurred. So there are 4 trucks appropriate configuration for company to transport rapeseed from 10 different fields. According this proportion, 10 trucks can meet the transport requirement of 25 contract farmers of the plant located within 30km.

Figure 3 shows that there is no big difference in idle rate before and after combine, that means it is available to combine processor 36 and processor 37 into a multi-processor 36, so combine system elements weighing location, checking quality and dispatcher into a multi-function working booth, where weighing, checking quality and dispatching vehicle to unload in 4 warehouse by two people. Because the worker has 45.22% leisure time, the dispatching vehicles to fields also should be combined into this working group. After simulation the working group idle and processing rate are 67.57% and 32.43%, so this optimization is reasonable. In the real world the dispatcher needs to access to the information of harvesters in different fields timely to make decision to dispatch vehicle to suitable farmer fields.

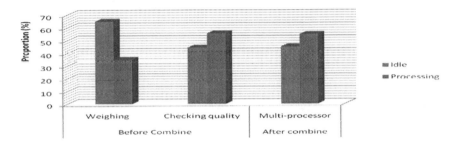

Fig. 3. The results of idle and processing proportion before and after combine weighing checking and dispatching

With the operation of system there maybe have other new contract farmers to join and some farmers may withdraw from the production of rapeseed. So the number of contract farmers should change yearly and the distance from the fields to company should also changed yearly. Suppose the distance ranges varied in the case of the number of farmers the same, Figure 4 shows the vehicles idle rate varying the average distance from farm location to company.

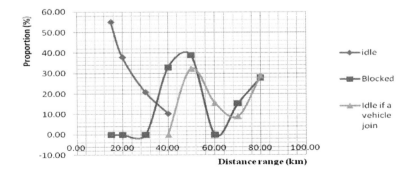

Fig. 4. The average idle rate of vehicles varying the average distance from farm location to company

Figure 4 shows that the average idle rates reduce with the increasing distance rage and there is a blockage occurred when the distance ranges reach 40km and the blocked rate occurred 38.87%. When a new truck joined the average idle rate of vehicles back to 32.89%, then continue to increase the distance range and the average idle rate reduce again. The new blockage occurred again until the distance range get to 70km and the blockage rate reach to 28.87% when the distance range is 80km.

According to the real world the contract farmers are different every year and the locations change too. So the number of contract farmers and the distance ranges change at the same time. So the experiments of this issue remain to be further studied.

5 Conclusion

Studies show that Flexsim simulation techniques can be efficiently used to model complex agricultural products logistics supply systems. Particularly it illustrates how the simulation experiments of different scenarios can detect efficiencies of facilities and bottlenecks of processes. The analysis of the present study has wider applicability for the similar supply systems.

References

1. Caputo, A.C., Palumbo, M., Pelagagge, P.M., Scacchia, F.: Economics of biomass energy utilization in combustion and gasification plants: effects of logistic variables. Biomass and Bio-energy 28, 35–51 (2005)
2. Gunnarsson, C., Lena, V., Per-Anders, H.: Logistics for forage harvest to biogas production-Timeliness, capacities and costs in a Swedish case study. Biomass and Bio-energy 32, 1263–1273 (2008)
3. Hobson, R.N., Bruce, D.M.: Seed loss when cutting a standing crop of oilseed rape with two type of combine harvester header. Bio-systems Engineering 81(3), 281–286 (2002)
4. Iannoni, A.P., Morabito, R.: A discrete simulation analysis of a logistics supply system. Transportation Research Part E 42, 191–210 (2006)
5. Kurt, A., Rosentrater, E.K.: Modeling the effects of pelleting on the logistics of distillers grains shipping. Bio-resource Technology 100, 6550–6558 (2009)
6. Le Gal, P.Y., Le Masson, J., Bezuidenhout, C.N., Lagrange, L.F.: Coupled modeling of sugarcane supply planning and logistics as a management tool. Computers and Electronics in Agriculture 68, 168–177 (2009)
7. Rentizelas, A.A., Tolis, A.J., Tatsiopoulos, I.P.: Logistics issues of biomass: The storage problem and the multi-biomass supply chain. Renewable and Sustainable Energy Reviews 13, 887–894 (2009)
8. Ravula, P.R., Robert, D.G., John, S.C.: Cotton logistics as a model for a biomass transportation system. Biomass and Bio-energy 32, 314–325 (2008)
9. Sokhansanj, S., Kumar, A., Anthony, F.T.: Development and implementation of integrated biomass supply analysis and logistics model(IBSAL). Biomass and Bio-energy 30, 838–847 (2006)
10. Tatsiopoulos, I.P., Tolis, A.J.: Economic aspects of the cotton-stalk biomass logistics and comparison of supply chain methods. Biomass and Bio-energy 24, 199–214 (2003)

Roll Stability Performance Simulation of Tractor-Semitrailer Based on ARCSIM

Xiaomei Liu[1], Jun Li[2], and Jianrong Zhou[2]

[1] Jiangxi Changyun Motor Vehicle Inspection Center, Nanchang 330001, China
[2] East China Jiaotong University, Nanchang 330013, China
ljecjtu@yahoo.com.cn

Abstract. The simulation of vehicle performance will help to improve the design quality and shorten product development cycle. In this paper, ARCSIM software is employed to simulate the roll stability performance of the tractor-semitrailer. To analysis, "lane-changing" condition and "steering and braking" condition are selected, by means of ARCSIM, the critical speed when overturning and other results can be obtained. It will provide theoretical guides to decide better design parameters of the vehicle.

Keywords: tractor-semitrailer, roll stability, simulation.

1 Introduction

General layout of vehicle, vehicle design parameters and matching relationship between them has a critical influence on performances. Simulation analysis of vehicle performance will contribute to optimize vehicle design and match parameters reasonably. So the design quality can be enhanced and the development cycle can be shortened [1].

Trailer truck, as one way of road freight transport, has been in extensive use. Especially in recent years, in order to improve transport efficiency and capacity of roads, trailer truck plays an important role in the carriage of goods. At present, the tractor-semitrailers occupy the high scale in the number of trailer trucks in China. With the number of tractor-semitrailers increasing, the safety of their running becomes more and more important. In order to enhance the design quality of the tractor-semitrailer and protect the vehicle running safety, performance simulation for them has great practical significance [2].

2 Simulation Software and Simulation Object

ARCSIM is demonstration software from the Automotive Research Center (ARC), which is a center of excellence funded by The U.S. Army TARDEC. The ARC is headquartered at The University of Michigan.

ARCSIM is an easy-to-use integrated set of computer tools for simulating and analyzing the braking and handling behavior of a six-axle tractor-trailer combination.

S. Lin and X. Huang (Eds.): CESM 2011, Part I, CCIS 175, pp. 213–218, 2011.
© Springer-Verlag Berlin Heidelberg 2011

ARCSIM performs virtual tests, replacing an instrumented test vehicle with a computer model. It solves the equations of motion numerically for a mathematical model to predict 3D motions of a vehicle in response to braking and steering inputs [3].

In this paper, by means of ARCSIM software, research work has been done on roll stability simulation of tractor-semitrailer. So the method of simulation analysis is gained in order to provide reference for product design. Simulation object is selected as follows: tractor is CA4188P11K2CT1 truck of the FAW Group and trailer is SGG9370TJZ FAW-trailer which's gross deadweight is 40 tons. The basic size of FAW tractor CA4188 is shown in Figure 1.

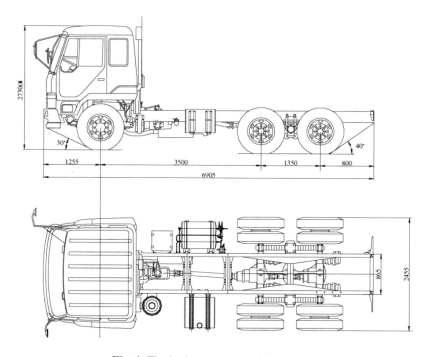

Fig. 1. The basic parameters of the tractor

3   Simulation Analysis of Roll Stability

3.1   Simulation of Lane-Changing Condition

First simulation case of roll stability is taken as: "lane-changing" condition, full load, the running speed is set from 96.56km/h to up. When simulation, the speed is divided by several grades, the steering wheel angle step input signal is applied, and then response data is analyzed. Further, the roll stability in different structural parameters and motion parameters is studied [4,5].

When the tractor-semitrailer runs at the speed on 96.56km/h, the simulation results are shown in Fig.2.

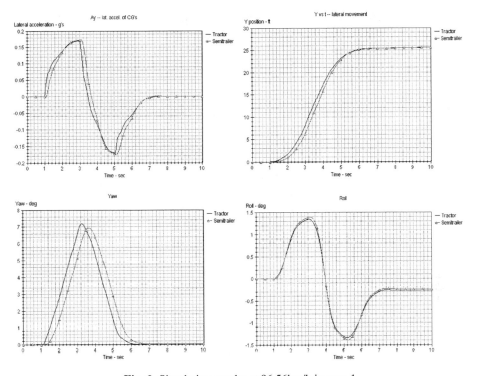

Fig. 2. Simulation results at 96.56km/h in case 1

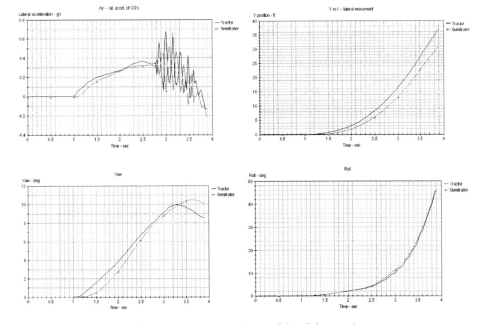

Fig. 3. Simulation results at 126km/h in case 1

Fig.2 shows lateral accelerations, lateral movements, yaw angles and roll angles of tractor and semitrailer respectively at 96.56km/h speed. It is can be noted that the response data of semitrailer is close to the response data of tractor. So the performance of roll stability of the vehicle is good at this speed. Also we can see the yaw degree of semitrailer delay that of tractor. It meets the practice when the vehicle is changing lane.

When the tractor-semitrailer's speed is up to 126km/h, from Fig.3 we can see lateral accelerations of tractor and semitrailer occur great fluctuation. It means the vehicle will roll, so 126km/h is the threshold of roll in this condition.

3.2   Simulation of Steering and Braking Condition

This simulation case is assumed as: "steering and braking" condition. Same with the case one, the vehicle is full load and the running speed is set from 96.56km/h to up. When simulation, the speed is divided by several grades, the steering wheel angle step input signal is applied too.

Taking the running speed 96.56km/h as a starting point, the simulation results in different speeds should be gotten. Figure 4 shows the changes of simulation test indicators with time. It can be seen that the semitrailer is almost synchronous with the tractor. The case is stable.

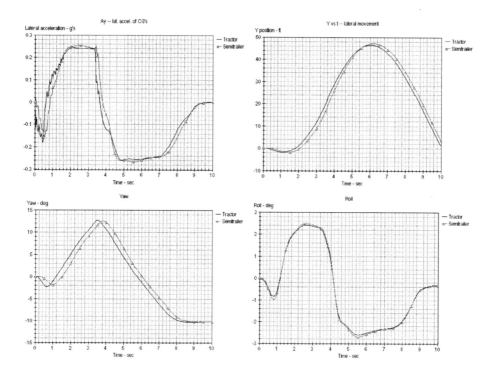

Fig. 4. Simulation results at 96.56km/h in case 2

When the speed is up to 112.65km/h, from Fig.5 we can see lateral accelerations of tractor and semitrailer occur great fluctuation. It means the vehicle will roll, so 112.65km/h is the threshold of roll in steering and braking condition.

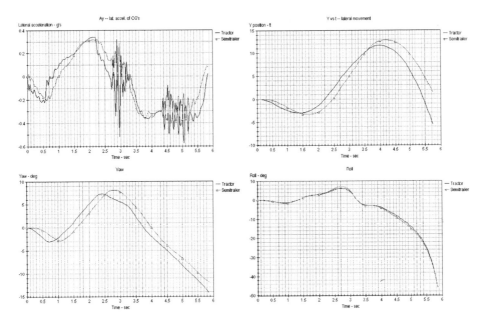

Fig. 5. Simulation results at 112.65km/h in case 2

4 Conclusion

In this paper, tractor semitrailer CA4188P11K2CT1 of FAW Group Corporation is taken as an example. Its roll stability performance is analyzed by means of ARCSIM simulation software. Two running conditions are selected. One is "lane-changing" condition and another is "steering and braking" condition. According to simulation test data of two conditions, we can conclude:

1) The relative values of lateral acceleration, lateral displacement, yaw angle, yaw angle between the tractor and the semitrailer is smaller, the roll stability performance is better.

2) As to this tractor semitrailer under full load, it will roll at 126km/h when it change lane and roll at 112.65km/h when it steer and brake meanwhile.

3) We can increase the speed threshold of roll and enhance the roll stability through optimizing design parameters of the tractor semitrailer.

4) One suggestion is that the orthogonal test can be used to analysis main effects on performance of design parameters.

Acknowledgments. The work is supported by the Department of Transportation of Jiangxi Province (2010T0048).

References

1. Huang, C.S., Kui, H.L., Wu, Z.X.: A Simulation Study on the Dynamics of Tractor-Semitrailer Combination. Auto. Eng. 27, 744–750 (2005)
2. Guan, Z.W.: Stability Analysis about Steering Wheel Angle Step input Controllability Based on Simulation Tractor-Semitrailer. Chinese Agricultural Mechanization (1), 88–91(2006)
3. Ma, W.H., Peng, H.: Worst-Case Vehicle Evaluation Methodology-Examples on Truck Rollover/Jackknifing and Active Yaw Control Systems. Vehicle System Dynamics (32), 389–408 (1999)
4. Nalecz, A.G., Bindemann, A.C., Brewer, H.K., et al.: Dynamic analysis of vehicle rollover. In: Proceedings of the 12th International Technical Conference on Experimental Safety Vehicles, Gottenburg, Sweden, pp. 803–819 (1989)
5. Jamie, G.: Simulation of Dynamic Rollover Threshold for Heavy Trucks. SAE International (2004)

A Class of Hybrid Projection Methods with Perturbations

Meixia Li

School of Mathematics and Information Science
Weifang University
Weifang, Shandong Province, China
limeixia001@163.com

Abstract. In this paper, a new kind of method which are called hybrid projection methods with perturbations are proposed and nonmonotone line search technique is employed. At the same time, global convergence of these methods is proved only in the case where the gradient function is uniformly continuous on an open convex set containing the iteration sequence.

Keywords: Hybrid projection method; Perturbation; Global convergence.

1 Introduction

We consider the unconstrained optimization problem

$$\min\{f(x) : x \in R^n\}, \tag{1.1}$$

where R^n denotes the n dimensional *Euclidean* space and $f : R^n \to R$ is a continuously differentiable function. There are many iterative schemes for solving (1.1). Among them the line search method has the form

$$x_{k+1} = x_k + \lambda_k d_k, k = 0,1,2,\ldots, \tag{1.2}$$

where d_k is a descent direction of $f(x)$ at x_k and λ_k is a step size. Denote x_0 the initial point and x_k the current iterate at the k th iteration. Generally, we denote $f(x_k)$ by f_k, $\nabla f(x)$ by $g(x)$, $\nabla f(x_k)$ by g_k and $f(x^*)$ by f^*, respectively. And the set that consists of all the stationary points of problem (1.1) is denoted by Ω^*, that is, $\Omega^* = \{x \in R^n | g(x) = 0\}$. The search direction d_k is generally required to satisfy

$$g_k^T d_k < 0. \tag{1.3}$$

There are many methods for solving (1.1), for example, gradient method, conjugate gradient method, Newton method, quasi-Newton method, trust region method, *et al* (see [1,7,8]). In line search methods, if the search direction d_k is given at the k th

S. Lin and X. Huang (Eds.): CESM 2011, Part I, CCIS 175, pp. 219–225, 2011.
© Springer-Verlag Berlin Heidelberg 2011

iteration then the next task is to find a step size α_k along the search direction. The ideal line search rule is the exact one that satisfies

$$f(x_k + \alpha_k d_k) = \min_{\alpha > 0} f(x_k + \alpha d_k). \tag{1.4}$$

In fact, the exact step size is difficult or even impossible to seek in practical computation, and thus many researchers constructed some inexact line search rules, such as Armijo rule, Goldstein rule, Wolfe rule and nonmonotone line search rules(see [1,4,7]).

Since Grippo, Lampariello and Lucidi proposed the nonmonotone line search rule for Newton methods, the new line search approach has been studied by many authors (e.g. [2-4]). Although it has many advantages, especially in the case of iterates trapped in a narrow curved valley of objective functions, the nonmonotone line search rule has some drawbacks(see [6]). Therefore, Shi and Shen proposed a new nonmonotone line search for general line search method, which is described as follows.

New nonmonotone line search (NNLS): Let M be a nonnegative integer. For each k, let $m(k)$ satisfy

$$m(0) = 0, 0 \leq m(k) \leq \min[k-1, M], \forall k \geq 1. \tag{1.5}$$

Given $\beta \in (0,1), \sigma \in (0, \frac{1}{2})$ and $\delta \in [0.5, 2)$, B_k is a symmetric positive definite matrix that approximates the Hessian of $f(x)$ at the iterate x_k and

$$s_k = -\frac{\delta g_k^T d_k}{d_k^T B_k d_k}.$$

Choose α_k to be the largest α in $\{s_k, s_k \beta, s_k \beta^2, \ldots\}$ such that

$$f(x_k + \alpha d_k) - \max_{0 \leq j \leq m(k)} f_{k-j} \leq \sigma \alpha [g_k^T d_k + \frac{1}{2} \alpha d_k^T B_k d_k]. \tag{1.6}$$

The new line search is a novel scheme of the nonmonotone Armijo line search and allows one to find a larger accepted step size and possibly reduces the function evaluations at each iteration.

In this paper, we propose a kind of hybrid projection method with perturbations (see Algorithm 2.1). In the algorithm, we employ the new nonmonotone line search technique. We prove the iteration sequence $\{x_k\}$ generated by the algorithm satisfies either $f_k \to -\infty$ or f_k converges to finite value and $g_k \to 0$ only in the case where $g(x)$ is uniformly continuous on an open convex set containing the iteration sequence $\{x_k\}$. In doing so, we remove various boundedness conditions such as boundedness from below of $f(\cdot)$, boundedness of x_k, etc.

2 Hybrid Projection Methods with Perturbations

In this paper, the algorithms have the following iterative scheme

$$x_{k+1} = x_k + \alpha_k d_k,$$

$$d_k = s_k + \omega_k.$$

In the above-mentioned two formulae, the main direction s_k satisfies the following conditions.

(H_1) $\|s_k\| \le c_1 \|g_k\|$.

(H_2) $\langle g_k, d_k \rangle \le -c_2 \|g_k\|^2$.

Perturbation term ω_k satisfies

$(H3)$ $\|\omega_k\| \le \gamma_k (q + p\|g\|)$ and $\gamma_k > 0$ satisfies

$(H4)$ $\sum_{k=1}^{\infty} \gamma_k^2 < +\infty,$

where c_1, c_2, q and p are positive constants.

Let $N = \{1,2, \quad \}, I = \{k \in N \mid \langle g_k, s_k + \omega_k \rangle \ge 0\}$ and $J = N \setminus I$.

The hybrid projection methods with perturbations are described as follows.

Algorithm 2.1. Given a nonnegative integer $M \ge 1$, $x_0 \in R^n$, $\beta \in (0,1)$, $\sigma \in (0, \frac{1}{2})$ and $\delta \in [0.5,2)$, μ_0, μ_1, $\gamma \in (0,1)$ and a symmetric positive definite matrix B_0. Set $k := 0$.

Step 1. If $g_k = 0$, then stop. x_k is a stationary point. Else, goto step 2.

Step 2. If $k \in I$, then let $x_{k+1} = x_k + \gamma_k d_k, k = k+1,$ return to step 1. Else, goto step 3.

Step 3. Let $\alpha_k = \gamma^{m_k}$, where m_k is the smallest nonnegative integer satisfying

$$\langle g(x_k + \alpha_k d_k), d_k \rangle \le \mu_0 \langle g_k, d_k \rangle \tag{2.1}$$

and

$$\langle g(x_k + \alpha_k d_k), d_k \rangle \ge \mu_1 \|g(x_k + \alpha_k d_k)\|^2 \tag{2.2}$$

Step 4. Set $\delta_k = x_{k+1} - x_k, \gamma_k = g_{k+1} - g_k$ and modify B_k as B_{k+1} by using BFGS or DFP formula or other quasi-Newton formulae.

Step 5. Let $y_k = x_k + \alpha_k d_k$, $v_k = g(y_k)$, $P_k = -\dfrac{\langle v_k, x_k - y_k \rangle}{\|v_k\|^2} v_k$. $i >$

$- P_k^T B_k P_k / \|P_k\|^2$, $B_k = B_k + iI$. $x_{k+1} = x_k + \lambda_k P_k$, where λ_k is defined by the NNLS.

Step 6. Set $k = k+1$, return to step 1.

In the following, we prove the convergence property of Algorithm 2.1. We first assume that $\{x_k\}$ is an infinite sequence generated by Algorithm 2.1. The following assumptions are satisfied.

(H$_5$) The objective function $f(x)$ has a lower bound on R^n.

(H$_6$) The gradient $g(x)$ is uniformly continuous on an open convex set D that contains $\{x_k\}$.

(H$_7$) There exists $m > 0$, for any k, $P_k^T B_k P_k \geq m\|P_k\|^2$.

The assumption (H$_5$) is very mild. Because the objective function $f(x)$ can be replaced by $e^{f(x)}$, if the assumption is not satisfied.

According to the related reference, we have the following Lemma.

Lemma 2.1 [5]. Suppose that (H$_2$), (H$_3$) and (H$_4$) hold for s_k, ω_k and γ_k. Then when $k \in I$ is sufficiently large, we have

$$\|g_k\| \leq c_3 \gamma_k,$$

where $c_3 > 0$ is a constant.

Analogous to the proof of the corresponding Lemmas in [5], we can obtain the following Lemmas.

Lemma 2.2. Let $\{x_k\}$ be an infinite iteration sequence generated by Algorithm 2.1. If $g(x)$ is uniformly continuous on an open convex set D containing $\{x_k\}$, then there exists a constant $\sigma_1 > 0$ such that $\{f_{l(k)} + \sigma_1 T_k\}$ is monotone and non-increasing. Further, the sequence $\{f_{l(k)}\}$ is convergent (which converges to a finite value or $-\infty$).

Without loss of generality, we assume that $\lim\limits_{k \to \infty} f_{l(k)} = f^*$.

Lemma 2.3. Let $\{x_k\}$ be an infinite iteration sequence generated by Algorithm 2.1. If $g(x)$ is uniformly continuous on an open convex set D containing $\{x_k\}$ and $\lim\limits_{k \in K_{i-1}, k \to \infty} f_k = f^* (0 \leq i \leq M-1)$, then we have

(1) $\lim\limits_{k \in K_{i-1}, k \to \infty} g_k = 0$

(2) $\lim\limits_{k \in K_i, k \to \infty} f_k = f^*$.

Proof. Now we show that (1) holds in two cases.

Case 1: When $I \cap K_i$ is an infinite index set, it follows from Lemma 2.1 that

$$\lim\limits_{k \in I \cap K_i, k \to \infty} g_k = 0.$$

Case 2: When $J \cap K_i$ is an infinite index set, suppose, on the contrary, that there exist an infinite subset $\overline{K}_i \subseteq J \cap K_i$ and $\varepsilon_0 > 0$ such that

$$\|g_k\| \ge \varepsilon_0, \forall k \in \overline{K}_i. \tag{2.3}$$

Utilizing (2.1),(2.2),(H$_2$),(H$_3$) and (2.3), we have

$$
\begin{aligned}
-\langle g_k, P_k \rangle &= \frac{\langle v_k, x_k - y_k \rangle}{\|v_k\|^2} \langle g_k, v_k \rangle \ge \mu_1 \langle v_k, x_k - y_k \rangle = -\mu_1 \alpha_k \langle g(y_k), d_k \rangle \\
&\ge -\mu_0 \mu_1 \alpha_k \langle g_k, d_k \rangle = -\mu_0 \mu_1 \alpha_k [\langle g_k, s_k \rangle + \langle g_k, \omega_k \rangle] \\
&\ge \mu_0 \mu_1 \alpha_k [c_2 \|g_k\|^2 - \|g_k\|\|\omega_k\|] \\
&\ge \mu_0 \mu_1 \alpha_k [c_2 \|g_k\|^2 - \gamma_k \|g_k\|(q + p\|g_k\|)] \\
&\ge \mu_0 \mu_1 (c_2 - \gamma_k p - \gamma_k q/\varepsilon_0) \alpha_k \|g_k\|^2
\end{aligned}
\tag{2.4}
$$

for $k \in \overline{K}_i$.

On the other hand, by Algorithm 2.1, (H$_1$), (H$_3$) and (2.3), we have

$$
\begin{aligned}
\|P_k\| &= \frac{\langle v_k, x_k - y_k \rangle}{\|v_k\|} \le \|x_k - y_k\| = \|\alpha_k d_k\| \\
&\le \alpha_k (c_1 \|g_k\| + \gamma_k (q + p\|g_k\|)) \\
&\le \alpha_k (c_1 + \gamma_k p + \gamma_k q/\varepsilon_0) \|g_k\|
\end{aligned}
\tag{2.5}
$$

for $k \in \overline{K}_i$.

Note that for every $k \in \overline{K}_i$, there exists an integer k' such that $k = l(k') - i - 1$, that is, $k + 1 = l(k') - (i-1) - 1 \in K_{i-1}$.

Therefore by (1.6), for $\forall k \in \overline{K}_i$, we have

$$
\begin{aligned}
f_{l(k)} - f_{k+1} &\ge -\sigma \lambda_k g_k^T P_k - \frac{1}{2} \sigma \lambda_k^2 P_k^T B_k P_k \\
&\ge -\sigma \lambda_k g_k^T P_k - \frac{1}{2} \sigma \lambda_k s_k P_k^T B_k P_k \\
&= -\sigma \lambda_k g_k^T P_k - \frac{1}{2} \sigma \lambda_k \frac{-\delta g_k^T P}{P_k^T B_k P_k} P_k^T B_k P_k \\
&= -\frac{\sigma(2-\delta)}{2} \lambda_k g_k^T P_k,
\end{aligned}
\tag{2.6}
$$

which, together with (2.4) and $\sigma > 0, \delta < 2$, implies that

$$f_{l(k)} - f_{k+1} \ge -\frac{\sigma(2-\delta)}{2} \lambda_k g_k^T P_k \ge -\frac{\sigma(2-\delta)}{2} \mu_0 \mu_1 (c_2 - \gamma_k p - \gamma_k q/\varepsilon_0) \alpha_k \lambda_k \|g_k\|^2. \tag{2.7}$$

Taking limits on the both sides of the above inequality as $k \in \overline{K}_i, k \to \infty$, according to $\lim\limits_{k \in K_i, k \to \infty} f_k = f^* = \lim\limits_{k \to \infty} f_{l(k)}$, we obtain

$$\lim_{k \in K_i, k \to \infty} \alpha_k \lambda_k \|g_k\| = 0. \tag{2.8}$$

By (2.3), we have

$$\lim_{k \in K_i, k \to \infty} \alpha_k \lambda_k = 0. \tag{2.9}$$

It follows from (2.9), Armijo rule and NNLS that if $\psi_k = \dfrac{\alpha_k}{\gamma}$ and $\psi'_k = \dfrac{\lambda_k}{\gamma}$ at least one of the following three inequalities holds for $k \in \overline{K}_i$ sufficiently large.

$$\langle g(x_k + \psi_k d_k), d_k \rangle > \mu_0 \langle g_k, d_k \rangle.$$

$$\langle g(x_k + \psi_k d_k), g_k \rangle < \mu_1 \|g(x_k + \psi_k d_k)\|^2.$$

$$f(x_k + \psi'_k P_k) > \max_{0 \le j \le m(k)} f_{k-j} + \sigma \psi'_k [g_k^T P_k + \frac{1}{2} \psi'_k P_k^T B_k P_k].$$

But whichever holds, similar to the proof of Lemma 2.4 in [5], by using (2.3),(2.8) and (2.9), we can obtain the corresponding $\mu_i \ge 1 (i = 0,1), \sigma > \dfrac{1}{2}$, which is a contradiction. Therefore we have

$$\lim_{k \in K_i, k \to \infty} g_k = 0.$$

(2) Similar to the proof of (2) in Lemma 2.4 [5], we can obtain the conclusion easily.

Analogous to the proof of Theorem 2.1 in [5], it is easy to prove the following theorem.

Theorem 2.1. Suppose that $\{x_k\}$ is an infinite iteration sequence generated by Algorithm 2.1. If there exists an open convex set D containing $\{x_k\}$ such that $g(x)$ is uniformly continuous on D, then either $\lim\limits_{k \to \infty} g_k = -\infty$ or $\{f_k\}$ converges to a finite value and

$$\lim_{k \to \infty} g_k = 0.$$

By Theorem 2.1, the following corollary is obvious.

Corollary 2.1. Suppose that the assumption conditions of Theorem 2.1 hold. If the infinite iteration sequence $\{x_k\}$ generated by Algorithm 2.1 has cluster point x^*, then $x^* \in \Omega^*$.

Acknowledgments. This research is supported by the National Natural Science Foundation of China (10901096) and the Natural Science Foundation of Shandong Province (ZR2009AL019) and the Project of Shandong Province Higher Educational Science and Technology Program (J09LA53).

References

[1] Bertsekas, D.P.: Nonlinear Programing. Athena Scientific, Belmont (1995)

[2] Bertsekas, D.P., Tsitsiklis, J.N.: Neuro-Dynamic programming. Athena Scientific, Belmont (1996)

[3] Gaivoronski, A.A.: Convergence properties of backpropagation for neural nets via theory of stochastic gradient methods. Part 1, Optim. Methods Software 4, 117–134 (1994)

[4] Grippo, L., Lampariello, F., Lucidi, S.: A nonmonotone line search technique for Newton's method. SIAM J. Numer. Anal. 4, 707–716 (1986)

[5] Li, M., Wang, C.: Convergence property of gradient-type methods with non-monotone line search in the presence of perturbation. Appl. Math. Optim. 174, 854–868 (2006)

[6] Shi, Z., Shen, J.: Convergence of nonmontone line search method. J. Comput. Appl. Math. 193, 397–412 (2006)

[7] Wang, Y., Xiu, N.: Nonlinear Programming Theory and Algorithms. Shanxi Science and Technology Press (2004)

[8] Yuan, Y., Sun, W.: Optimization Theory and Algorithms. Science Press, Beijing (1997)

A Research into "PRAMs" Mode of Orders Education

Hanyu Guo, Xiujuan Yan, and Jianfeng Hu[*]

Jiangxi Blue Sky University
Nanchang, Jiangxi 330098, China
ghy0791@gmail.com, jxyxj1220@qq.com, huguess@21cn.com

Abstract. The implementation of the orders education in vocational colleges has an important impact in personnel training. In course of educating, we should adhere to the PRAMs features, which includes a way of Part-time work, namely arranging students to participate in work and study of learning after they receiving theoretical education, to enhance students job awareness and gain appropriate compensation, to stimulate enthusiasm for learning; an environment of Real swords and spears to make students complete the actual project or task and enhance the practical ability; an advance education which enterprises and colleges Advance of enhancing the depth of training of students, making students be trained for jobs that enterprises require; we focus on matching students' attributes and job characteristics, training students to achieve human-job Matching, and ultimately makes enterprises, colleges and students feel Satisfaction at the orders education.

Keywords: Orders Education, PRAMs, Human-job matching, Vocational education.

1 Introduction

Orders education, the characteristic of higher vocational education, is a new model of cooperation between colleges and enterprises in students training. The implementation of the orders education takes a positive action in training versatile students of higher vocational college. It trains the required students for enterprise, providing a reference for the reform of higher education, and playing an active role in promoting student employment.

As the stability and development of economic in China, lacking of jobs is no longer the bottleneck of students' employment. Yet the adaptability and stability of employment have become a new problem troubled enterprises and colleges. Therefore, we should keep reforming and improving the ways of orders education, making the special training mode adapt better to social and economic development changes and meeting the enterprises' needs to the students, and guiding the personnel training in higher vocational colleges. Meanwhile, in the process of cooperation with enterprises, taking the advantage of enterprises' resources to help students better understand their

---

[*] Corresponding author.

S. Lin and X. Huang (Eds.): CESM 2011, Part I, CCIS 175, pp. 226–231, 2011.

characteristics effectively and the requirements of enterprises. And strengthen the practical education and improve students' competitiveness. It also can build a good platform of career development to the students and enhancing their adaptability and stability.

2 Current Problems of Orders Education

Orders education is a new personnel training mode of higher vocational education. It means that the college and the enterprises draw up the training programs by consultation, and cooperating with each other in forming classes, setting courses, teaching management and job evaluation. Vocational Colleges attach great importance to the "orders education ", although orders education have some flexibility, but there are still some problems in practice, common problems are the following: First, students do not understand the post in future, the colleges don't form an effective mechanism to guide and encourage students to participate in the orders education; Second, students is still in school-based, can only grasp the basic theoretical knowledge and simple training skills, they are often not enough attention to the practice areas, there is no perceptual knowledge of the situation of enterprises, and they aren't clear to the professional skills learned in the future application and development of enterprises. Third, the time of the orders education is short, usually only three or four months or so, the ability of professional practice and the professionalism is not enough; fourth, in the selection of student, more focus on students' Profession, considering less about the matching of student's personal characteristics, career interests, career planning and the features of industry, enterprises, jobs. What these lead, the practical ability of students is not strong enough, the cognition to position is not clear, the stability of post-employment is not high, the effect of personnel training units can not meet the requirements of enterprises.

3 "PRAMs" Mode of Orders Education

The previous orders education' form was that colleges draw up teaching programs with enterprises, focusing on practical teaching and have some flexibility. But in actual operation, it just increases a slightly proportion of experimental training on the basis of theoretical knowledge. And the practical teaching is more of a simulation and the students still need a long time to adapt to.

On the basis of original character of orders education, in order to deepen the educational reform model and enhance the ability of students to adapt to social needs. It aims to achieve collaboration between colleges and enterprises, engagement in internal training and external training, integration of theoretical teaching and practical projects. It's proposed that orders education enable students to understand better the workflow through *part-time work*; contact with the product through *real swords and spears*, making students factually involve in the environment of producing, managing, marketing and servicing. And at the same time, in order to let students to know the work roles better; orders education makes students not only master theory, but also *advance* to enhance skills and develop good professional qualities through depth education.

Orders education makes the students understand better of the prospects of profession, industry and career by various training, and as a result, to achieve **human—job matching**. Orders education trains the personnel which have solid theory, strong skills, and ability to adapt to the application quickly. Lastly making the enterprises, colleges and students all fell **satisfactory**.

3.1 P: Part-Time Work

The explanation of Work—integrated Learning by Association for World Education said is, combining the classroom learning with work integrated learning, and the students apply the theory to the practical relevant work, render a service for the true employer and usually get paid. Then take challenges encountered in the work and growth of knowledge back to the classroom which could help them to analyze in the learning process and think.

Therefore, orders education arranges a time for students to work and study in the enterprises cooperating with college, This way not only to make students understand the profession's role in the future work, but also to obtain remuneration, stimulate students interest in learning, and achieve a sense of accomplishment. In the process of part—time work, enterprises can also be targeted to arrange jobs and training, selecting professional and technical staff to get skills counseling, which is based on the actual situation. For example, during the collaboration of Jiangxi Blue Sky University and HanDa Technology Group, they specially arrange three months for students to work in the enterprises. The students return to school and learn that they not only understand the actual situation of enterprises, but also strengthen the practical ability and enhance the learning thirst for knowledge, and understand better the requirements of course developed by enterprises and colleges. It makes students to promote competitiveness and adapt the requirements of the enterprise. For example: students who are from "HanDa mechanical & electrical engineer Class", not only are arranged to produce in enterprise, but also train with special content which are targeted for engineers.

3.2 R: Real Swords and Spears

Orders education trains personnel basing on the employment standards. Enterprises put forward specific requirement and take part in drawing up teaching program and courses syllabus. In the light of post character, Students study knowledge, master skills and enhance ability. How to make students enhance quality and apply the learning and adapt to the requirement when they study professional skills is a focus of orders education. Therefore, students not only have practical ability, but also have innovative consciousness and capacity, organization and mission capability, exchanges and cooperation, learning and thinking, resistance to pressure and responsibility. These capabilities stressed not just a special professional ability and career skills, but for different occupational adaptation and creativity. Thus, personnel are practical. To this end, during the process of orders education, how to make students connect with real product in the training process, participate in the real workplace by *Real swords and spears,* it is an important means to enhance the professionalism of students and mature students of personality. Therefore, the implementation of school-enterprise cooperation in the orders education, conditional cooperation projects can build a practice base on campus or introduce the product into campus, such as training marketing talent, we can be in the form of practical projects to enable students to carry out product marketing activities, enable students to enter the job role. For example, the cooperation with Jiangxi Blue Sky University and Shanghai Hotsales Network Technology Co., Ltd, which introduce production into campus, encourage students to develop the marketing action, students share the realization, which enhances the students ability to adapt to the workplace.

Enterprises need personnel who have real swords and spears which they are conducive to the development of enterprises. Thus, practical teaching with real swords and spears enable students to adapt to social needs, and they can be appreciated in the course of employment, laying a good foundation for more development opportunities in future.

3.3 A: Advance

Short-term orders education usually goes on only 3-4 months and it only trains students' cognitive abilities of the future. For enterprises, personnel is targeted, having technical skills and can be used when they graduate which could achieve students' talent and will not result in wasting of human resources. Training personnel who can meet the needs of the various types, are not only with strong professional knowledge and practical ability, and also has good professional qualities. We should advance to give students depth training during the students at the school.

To strengthen the affection of orders education, we must focus on achieving professional settings link to industry needs, professional theory link to work and study, the student's link to individual needs and requirements of the posts, the normal curriculum linked to open hook. According to the characteristics of students, we infiltrate professional knowledge, professional skills, professional ethics and culture into the students on different stages from low grade students. We also arrange students to participate in internships and other social practice. With personnel training for junior students, students have a deeper understanding of industry and enterprises in the future. They can experience real work and life situations in advance, and then they can enhance learning initiatively and consciously, and improve their comprehensive ability. And at the same time, to do a good groundwork for entering the job market successfully. For example: Jiangxi Blue Sky University cooperate MiTAC Computer Co., Ltd. to open an orders education. To develop a "computer programmers" talent, they choose students from sophomore to organize a "MiTAC programmers Class", require them master Oracle and ERP applications, SFCS system developing, Office, Workflow, Automation applications. The training content includes basic common course, professional courses, internships (item practice), theoretical study, and project training and so on. It greatly enhances students Capacity in practical work.

3.4 M: Human—Job Matching

Student employment stability has become a problem which trouble enterprises. Lots of college students do not understand themselves and their chosen profession, occupation. They found that they are unsuitable or not suited to the position after employment, so they turnover frequently. Colleges and enterprises are paying a lot of power, material and financial resources for developing orders education. Therefore, the students serve enterprises better and realize their own value. To achieve "human-job matching" is a factor we should think about in the implementation of orders education. "Human—job matching" theory suggests that personality structure is different, different personality is fit for different occupations. People should find suitable career to achieve the Human—job matching based on their own personalities, and then meet the individual needs and interests to maximize their potential.

To achieve the purpose of school education and promote the healthy development of students, promoting students to have better career stability and serve enterprises well, orders education should pay attention to the following factors. Firstly, helping students to understand themselves and their career interests, personality, values and then establish awareness of career planning and career development. Secondly, the enterprises select students not only access expertise, but focus more on the interest, personality traits, career planning, and follow the intention of the students development of the industry; selecting the appropriate object through vocational assessment. Thirdly, enterprises should help students to understand the industry and occupational requirements in future by the way of corporate culture introduction, job descriptions, internship and other methods combine with the characteristics of the industry. For example: Jiangxi Blue Sky University and Luen Thai Metropolitan Life in Shanghai develop a class training "call center outsourcing services" talent, where students are selected through the "professional assessment", interviews and "leaderless group discussion Approach", evaluating the personality traits of students, career development planning, communication skills and stress resistance, and several other aspects, to select students matching to the enterprises' requirement. After theoretical teaching, and internship training, from business-to-student feedback after 1 year, it posts that these students for employment in enterprise have more than 98% of the stability, and the performance has also been recognized.

3.5 S: Satisfactory

Orders education makes enterprises, colleges and students share resources, so that the tripartite satisfaction and achieve win. For enterprises, through participation in personnel training, applying management theory and methods to the training mode, to make enterprises management link with colleges' management, it is in favor of training personnel enterprises need. Through cooperation with colleges, enterprises attract more talents, priority attain staff needed for producing, saving human cost. For colleges, they can make full use of enterprises' resources, improving the educational level and accumulating teaching experience. And colleges can find deficiencies in school teaching and management, to reform and promote the development of schools. At the same time, to promote student for employment, build schools brand and enhance the competition. For students, orders education let them know what enterprises require while studying at the college, being aware of professional development, improving their professional interests, which make learning more focused and effective, and further enhance the employment competition, and reduce the employment pressure.

4 Summary

PRAMS Orders education, fully embodies the concept of vocational education, which is "Employment-oriented and capacity-building as the core". By "PRAMS" order in education, enterprises reserve talents, improving the quality of staff. Colleges train talents that are needed by enterprises. Students not only solve the problem of employment, enhance employability, earn what are usable and realize the value of life, but also improve the quality and stability of employment.

Acknowledgments

This study was supported by 2010 Humanities and Social Science Foundation of Ministry of Education of China (10YJC880048) and Teaching Reform Project of Jiangxi Educational Committee (JXJG-08-19-11). The authors are grateful to the anonymous reviewers who made constructive comments. They would also like to thank Wang D. and Liu S. for various helps and suggestions.

A New Method of Sound Travel-Time Measurement in Stored Grain

Guannan Chen, Hua Yan, Yinggang Zhou, and Lijun Liu

School of Information Science and Engineering, Shenyang University of Technology,
Shenyang 110870, China
chenguannan99@163.com,
yanhua_01@163.com

Abstract. The measurement of sound travel-time in grain bulk was researched for monitoring grain temperature by the acoustic method. A measurement system of sound travel-time in stored grain based on the virtual instrument was built. A time-delay estimation method using triple correlation with wavelet transform is proposed for solving the problem of sound attenuation in grain bulk. Sound travel-time in soybeans was measured by the proposed method, cross-correlation method, and cross-correlation with wavelet transform method. The results show that the proposed method is best in measurement stability and accuracy. Thus it is expected to be used in an actual acoustic temperature monitoring system for stored grain.

Keywords: Acoustic temperature measurement; Stored grain; Wavelet transform; Correlation; Virtual instrument.

1 Introduction

Stored grain is destroyed by fungi, insects and moisture. That could be reflected by temperature of grain [1]. Grain is the poor conductor of heat, temperature monitors must have higher spatial resolution for detecting hot spot earlier. Presently, temperature measurement of stored grain is usually realized by contact method, and the space resolution of temperature measurement is very low, the hot spot can't be detected when it exist far away from contact sensors. Compared with contact method, non-contact method is much better for stored grain temperature monitoring [2].

Acoustic temperature measurement [3] has advantages of non-contact, wide range and large area. Sound is transmitted principally through the gas in the passageways between the grain kernels [4]. Therefore, the research on acoustic temperature measurement in stored grain could be available.

Sound travel-time measured accurately is very important for acoustic temperature measurement in stored grain. As a consequence of acoustic reflection and viscosity caused by grain kernels, the sound attenuation related to frequency obviously occur during the propagation in grain bulk [4]. It makes the sound signal distorted that increases the difficulty to measure the sound travel-time accurately in stored grain.

S. Lin and X. Huang (Eds.): CESM 2011, Part I, CCIS 175, pp. 232–237, 2011.
© Springer-Verlag Berlin Heidelberg 2011

In this paper, a time-delay estimation method using triple correlation with wavelet transform was proposed. A measurement system of sound travel-time in stored grain based on the virtual instrument was built. Sound travel-time in soybeans was measured by the proposed method, cross-correlation method, and cross-correlation with wavelet transform method. The stability and accuracy of three methods were compared by experimental data.

2   Theory of Sound Travel-Time Measurement in Stored Grain

If sound travel time t from location A to location B is measured, average temperature T of the sound propagation path is calculated by follow [3]

$$T = \left(\frac{l}{t \cdot Z} \right)^2 .$$
(1)

where l is the distance from A to B; Z is acoustic constant confirmed by composing of gas, especially 20.045 for air. For making the equation (1) available in stored grain, a parameter λ called grain porosity influence factor is introduced in the paper. And the model of acoustic temperature measurement in stored grain could be

$$T = \left(\frac{l \cdot \lambda}{t \cdot Z} \right)^2 .$$
(2)

λ is affected by sound frequency, composition of gas and the average spacing between the grain kernels. As sound frequency and composition of gas are fixed, λ principally depend on average spacing between the grain kernels. Therefore, the value of λ could be variety in different spatial locations of the grain bulk, and it need to calibrate in practice.

Supposed, t_1 and t_2 are sound travel-time between location A and B measured respectively at temperatures of T_1 and T_2 in stored grain. With equation (2), we have

$$\frac{t_2}{t_1} = \sqrt{\frac{T_1}{T_2}} .$$
(3)

Use the equation (3), the stability and accuracy of sound travel-time measurement could be evaluated easily without calibration of λ.

3   The System of Sound Travel-Time Measurement

The system shown in Figure 1 includes that, a cubic tank (2m×0.6m×0.6m) filled with soybeans; a computer installed LabVIEW, and the computer generates a 200~1500Hz chirp signal which emitted by speaker as the sound signal; a fixture made to hold a speaker and three microphones with preamplifiers (MIC1~MIC3); a signal conditioner used to supply power for microphones and its preamplifiers; a data acquisition module used to collect signal from MIC1~MIC3 simultaneously, its sampling rate was 100kHz, each channel of module collected 30000 samples of signal.

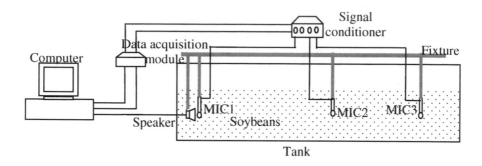

Fig. 1. System of sound travel time measurement

4 Time-Delay Estimation Method Using Triple Correlation with Wavelet De-noise

4.1 Cross-Correlation (CC)

Supposed, $x_1(n)$ and $x_2(n)$ are the signals measured by location A and B respectively, and they can be written in the form

$$x_1(n) = s(n) + n_1(n) \, , \, x_2(n) = \alpha \cdot s(n-D) + n_2(n) \, . \tag{4}$$

where $s(n)$ is the available signal、D is time-delay of signal transmitted from A to B、$n_1(n)$ and $n_2(n)$ are additive noise、α is the attenuation factor of signal.

The cross-correlation [5] of $x_1(n)$ and $x_2(n)$ is expressed as

$$
\begin{aligned}
R_{x_1 x_2}(m) &= E\left[x_1(n)x_2(n+m)\right] = E\left[\left(s(n)+n_1(n)\right)\left(\alpha \cdot s(n+m-D)+n_2(n+m)\right)\right] \\
&= \alpha \cdot R_{ss}(m-D) + \alpha \cdot R_{n_1 s}(m-D) + R_{s n_2}(m) + R_{n_1 n_2}(m) \, .
\end{aligned}
\tag{5}
$$

According to the properties of auto-correlation, it can be known that $|R_{ss}(m-D)| \leq R_{ss}(0)$. And $m=D$, $R_{x_1 x_2}(D)=\max[R_{x_1 x_2}(m)]$ is the time-delay estimation between $x_1(n)$ and $x_2(n)$ with cross-correlation.

4.2 Cross-Correlation with Wavelet Transform (WT-CC)

Mallat decomposition and reconstruction algorithm of wavelet transform is used to de-noise the signal of $x_1(n)$ and $x_2(n)$. It includes three steps:

(1) Fix the wavelet mother function. Decompose the one-dimensional digital signal with wavelet transform. In this paper, db18 is fixed as mother function of wavelet based on experiment analyses. (2) Fix the scale of decomposition j. If the bandwidth of sampling signal is f_k, after Mallat decomposition in the scale of j, the low frequency coefficient of signal $a_k^{(j)}$ is obtained, and the range of bandwidth of $a_k^{(j)}$ is $0 \sim f_k/2^j$ [6]. Therefore, if the upper limit of available bandwidth of signal is f, the scale j must be appropriate to make $f_k/2^j$ approached to f. In this paper, the sampling frequency of the system is 100kHz, according to Nyquist sampling theory, the bandwidth of sampling

signal f_k is 50kHz. Decomposing $x_1(n)$ and $x_2(n)$ in the scale of $j=5$, the range of bandwidth of $a_k^{(5)}$ is 0~1562.5Hz, that is very suitable for 200-1500Hz chirp signal. (3) Signal de-noise and reconstruction. The $a_k^{(j)}$ include the whole available information of signal, and the noise is mainly set to 0. Reconstruct $a_k^{(j)}$ with the Mallat reconstruction algorithm (inverse of Mallat decomposition) to generate de-noise signals $x'_1(n)$ and $x'_2(n)$.

The cross-correlation of $x'_1(n)$ and $x'_2(n)$ is expressed as

$$R_{x'_1 x'_2}(m) = E\left[x'_1(n)x'_2(n+m)\right] = E\left[\left(s'(n)+n'_1(n)\right)\left(\alpha \cdot s'(n+m-D)+n'_2(n+m)\right)\right] \tag{6}$$
$$= \alpha \cdot R_{s's'}(m-D)+\alpha \cdot R_{n'_1 s'}(m-D)+R_{s'n'_2}(m)+R_{n'_1 n'_2}(m) \ .$$

4.3 Triple Correlation with Wavelet Transform (WT-TC)

The triple correlation with wavelet transform is proposed for improving the stability and accuracy of time-delay estimation in stored grain.

The auto-correlation [7] of de-noise signal $x'_1(n)$ is expressed as

$$R_{x'_1 x'_1}(m) = E\left[x'_1(n)x'_1(n+m)\right] = E\left[\left(s'(n)+n'_1(n)\right)\left(s'(n+m)+n'_1(n+m)\right)\right] \tag{7}$$
$$= R_{s's'}(m)+R_{n'_1 s'}(m)+R_{s'n'_1}(m)+R_{n'_1 n'_1}(m) \ .$$

In the equation (6) and (7), $R_{s's'}(\bullet)$ can be considered as the available signal, and the others can be considered as the noise. For simplifying the calculation, new expression is shown

$$y_1(m) - R_{x'_1 x'_1}(m) - R_{s's'}(m)+\omega_1(m) \ , \ y_2(m) - R_{x'_1 x'_2}(m) = \alpha R_{s's'}(m-D)+\omega_2(m) \ . \tag{8}$$

From equation (8), it can be seen that, the available signal of $y_2(m)$ is the delay and attenuation of the available signal of $y_1(m)$, and the time-delay of them is also equal to D. The cross-correlation of $y_1(m)$ and $y_2(m)$ can be expressed as

$$R_{y_1 y_2}(\tau) = E\left[y_1(m)y_2(m+\tau)\right] = E\left[\left(R_{s's'}(m)+\omega_1(m)\right)\left(\alpha \cdot R_{s's'}(m-D+\tau)+\omega_2(m+\tau)\right)\right] \tag{9}$$
$$= \alpha \cdot R_{RR}(\tau-D)+\alpha \cdot R_{\omega_1 R}(\tau-D)+R_{R\omega_2}(\tau)+R_{\omega_1 \omega_2}(\tau) \ .$$

In the equation (9), $\tau=D$, $R_{RR}(D) = \max[R_{RR}(m)]$ is the time-delay of $x_1(m)$ and $x_2(m)$ estimated by triple correlation with wavelet transform.

5 Experiment of Sound Travel-Time Estimation in Stored Grain

During the experiment, MIC1 is 0.08m away from speaker, the distance l between MIC1 and MIC2 is 1.2m, and that is 1.8m between MIC1 and MIC3. Fill the tank with soybeans at three different times, make the depth h of microphone in soybeans be 0.3m, 0.4m and 0.5m respectively, and totally get six sound paths of different locations and distances. The sampling signals received simultaneously by MIC1, MIC2 and MIC3 can be estimated the sound travel-time of each sound path by CC,

WT-CC and WT-TC. A group of power spectrum density (PSD) of measured signal at the sound path of h=0.5m, l=1.8m is shown in Figure 2. $x_1(n)$ and $x_2(n)$ are measured signal of MIC1 and MIC3.

From Figure 2, it can be seen that, sound signal is obviously attenuated after propagating for a distance, and the higher the frequency is, the more sound signal attenuated; after wavelet transform de-noise, the signal its frequency higher than 1500Hz is attenuated about 20dB, and its PSD curve becomes smooth, but the signal its frequency lower than 1500Hz is not attenuated; $y_1(m)$ and $y_2(m)$ are both attenuated 70dB based on de-noise signal $x'_1(n)$ and $x'_2(n)$ as the frequency higher than 1500Hz, nevertheless, only 20~30dB attenuation as the frequency lower than 1500Hz.

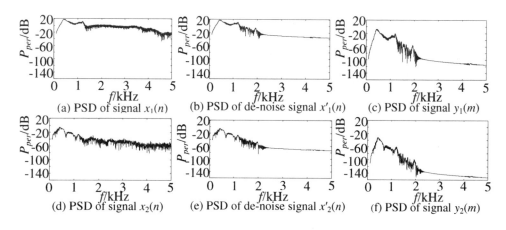

Fig. 2. PSD of measured signals

As the temperature of soybeans is T_1=300K and T_2=291K respectively, three sound travel-time estimation methods were used to measure sound travel-time of six sound paths in stored grain for 100 times. $\overline{t_1}$ and $\overline{t_2}$ are the average values of measured data at different temperature of stored grain. The stability and accuracy of sound travel-time measurement in stored grain are evaluated by follow

$$v_1 = \frac{s_1}{t_1} \times 100\% \ , \ v_2 = \frac{s_2}{t_2} \times 100\% \ , \ r_e = \frac{\left| \overline{t_2}/\overline{t_1} - \sqrt{T_1/T_2} \right|}{\sqrt{T_1/T_2}} \times 100\% \ . \tag{10}$$

where s_1 and s_2 are the standard deviation of $\overline{t_1}$ and $\overline{t_2}$; v_1 and v_2 are the coefficient of variance of $\overline{t_1}$ and $\overline{t_2}$; r_e is the relatively error of the ratio of sound travel-time at different temperature in stored grain.

Shown in Table 1, v_1 and v_2 of WT-TC are much smaller than the other two methods. The maximum of r_e of WT-TC, WT-CC and CC are 0.16%, 0.35% and 0.64% respectively. Therefore, the stability and accuracy of WT-TC are better than the other methods.

Table 1. The stability and accuracy of three sound travel-time estimation methods

Sound paths in stored grain	CC			WT-CC			WT-TC		
	$v_1(\%)$	$v_2(\%)$	$r_e(\%)$	$v_1(\%)$	$v_2(\%)$	$r_e(\%)$	$v_1(\%)$	$v_2(\%)$	$r_e(\%)$
l=1.2m,h=0.3m	0.25	0.18	0.17	0.25	0.19	0.35	0.09	0.06	0.12
l=1.8m,h=0.3m	0.32	0.19	0.09	0.22	0.13	0.11	0.07	0.03	0.13
l=1.2m,h=0.4m	0.27	0.31	0.64	0.20	0.21	0.23	0.10	0.08	0.05
l=1.8m,h=0.4m	0.08	0.12	0.01	0.07	0.11	0.02	0.01	0.01	0.07
l=1.2m,h=0.5m	0.11	0.08	0.12	0.10	0.07	0.02	0.09	0.03	0.16
l=1.8m,h=0.5m	0.07	0.01	0.05	0.07	0.03	0.09	0.06	0.02	0.02
Average	0.183	0.148	0.180	0.152	0.123	0.137	0.070	0.038	0.092

6 Conclusion

Measuring sound travel-time accurately is the key of acoustic temperature measurement for stored grain. The triple correlation with wavelet transform proposed in the paper can certainly improve the SNR of sound signal by wavelet transform denoise and multiple correlation. The result of experiment shows that, the stability and accuracy of WT-TC are much better than WT-CC and CC for sound travel-time estimation in soybeans. Therefore, WT-TC is expected to use in an actual acoustic temperature monitoring system for stored grain.

Acknowledgements. The work is supported by Natural Science Foundation of China (60772054), Specialized Research Fund for the Doctoral Program of Higher Education (20102102110003) and Shenyang Science and Technology Plan (F10213100).

References

1. Cao, J.R., Cao, Z., Hu, Z.S.: Temperature-humidity examine and control system inside corn. J. Beihua Univ. 8, 454–457 (2007)
2. Manickavasagan, A., Jaya, D.S., White, N.D.G., et al.: Thermal imaging of a stored grain silo to detect a hot spot. Appl. Eng. Agric. 22, 891–897 (2006)
3. Fonakoshi, A., Mizutani, K., Nagai, K., et al.: Temperature distribution in circular space reconstructed from sampling data at unequal interval in small numbers using acoustic computerized tomography. Jpn. J. Appl. Phys. 39, 3107–3111 (2000)
4. Hickling, R., Wei, W., Hagstrum, D.W.: Studies of sound transmission in various types of stored grain for acoustic detection of insects. Appl. Acous. 50, 263–278 (1997)
5. Gao, S.W., Cong, D.N., Yang, L.J.: Locating algorithm for leakage point of gas pipeline. J. Shenyang Univ. Technol. 31, 691–694 (2009)
6. Zeng, X.W., Zhao, W.M., Sheng, J.Q.: Corresponding relationships between nodes of decomposition tree of wavelet packet and frequency bands of signal subspace. Acta. Seismologica Sinica 30, 90–96 (2008)
7. Li, Y.B., Yue, X., Yang, X.Y.: Estimation of sinusoidal parameters in powerful noise by multi-layer autocorrelation. J. Harbin. Eng. Univ. 25, 525–528 (2004)

ILOG and MAS Based Framework of Job-Shop Scheduling System

LiZhi Qin and QingSong Li

School of Transport and Automotive Engineering, Xhu University,
610039 Chengdu Sichuan
liqs73@163.com

Abstract. Job-Shop Scheduling Problem (JSSP) is a problem of resources assignment with the goal of satisfying the tasks and constrains. For efficiency and practicality of actual Job-Shop Scheduling System, (JSSS), a synthetic method was used in our research. A framework was designed to take advantage of Multi-Agent System, (MAS) and ILOG, which is a powerful calculation platform in field of optimization. Interactive models between MAS and ILOG, among agents in MAS were also devised. Prototype of this JSSS represents some more convenient and flexible scheduling plan in test by engineer of an automobile factory.

Keywords: JSSP, framework, MAS, ILOG.

1 Introduction

JSSP (Job-Shop Scheduling Problem) is a class of resource distribution to meet requirements of task configuration and order constraints. As JSSP in the actual production involved of raw materials, equipments, manpower, funds and so on, and it is complex, random, and more targeted, shop scheduling problems have become complex. A good Job-Shop Scheduling System is particularly necessary.

2 Research Status of Job-Shop Scheduling Problem

Job-Shop Scheduling Problem mainly balances the logistics and information in the shop. It is an interface between the management and processing. Existing research on JSSP mainly consists of two aspects, which are system on theory of various algorithms and system on multi-agent. A highly efficient hybrid genetic algorithm has been applied to the JSSP, from which you can get a better answer in a more complex environment [1]. Application of bacterial foraging algorithm to optimize JSSP can greatly improve the efficiency of plant [2]. JSSP on theory also includes putting ant colony algorithm into job-shop scheduling, theory of TOC into job-shop scheduling and so on. All these systems were verified better in solving scheduling problems. A Multi-Agent System is more popular for its high degree of flexibility, quick responsiveness, intelligence and compatibility to data and knowledge uncertainty.

S. Lin and X. Huang (Eds.): CESM 2011, Part I, CCIS 175, pp. 238–242, 2011.

Researchers has done further study on MAS so as to make Multi-Agent System to be closer to the actual JSSP and better to solve practical scheduling problems. For example, optimizing the contract net protocol (CNP) can solve conflicts caused by the pursuit of maximizing their own interests among agents [4]. Gather the advantages of genetic algorithm and ant colony algorithm and put them into the Multi-Agent Systems, the system we got can be more closed to the actual production scheduling problems and of course a better scheme for decision.

This paper aims to combine advantages of ILOG and Multi-Agent Systems, and design a Job-Shop Scheduling System which can get a better scheduling project in the actual job-shop scheduling.

3   Frame Designing of Job-Shop Scheduling System Based on ILOG and MAS

In order to finish a task, a Job-shop Scheduling System has some features. (1) Decision making. The feature of this part is receiving assigned tasks and feeding back arrangements to the decision makers. (2) Shop scheduling. In this part what should you do is task allocation and then assigning it to each workshop. (3) Arranging part. Do reasonable arrangements to the gotten tasks from shop scheduling, insuring that one task matching one machine. (4) Resources (including machinery and equipment). This section should include the utilization of machinery. When getting a new task, each machine should make reasonable arrangements for the new tasks without delay the other tasks. Therefore the Job-Shop Scheduling System based on ILOG and MAS in this paper consists four agents: Decision Agent、 Shop Scheduling Agent、 Task Agent and Resources Agent. All agents perform their duties, cooperate together to complete the task shop scheduling.

The following Fig. 1. is the framework of Job-Shop Scheduling System based on MAS and ILOG. This kind of structure allows each module to complete their tasks independently without the influence of other modules, and can guarantee the system to run efficiently.

When getting the tasks from Decision Agent, Shop Scheduling Agent will decompose the tasks using ILOG. Each sub-task will be generated corresponds to a Task Agent. Each Task Agent completes its tasks independently, and it takes information exchange with Resource Agent through the communication interface to achieve distributions from sub-tasks to various machines and equipment.

4   Interactive Mode of Job-Shop Scheduling System Based on ILOG and MAS

The proposed Job-Shop Scheduling System based on ILOG and MAS is as shown in Figure 2.

The system contains five modules as Decision Agent, Shop Scheduling Agent, Task Agent, Resource Agent and workshop capacity library .Compared with Figure 1, there is a workshop capacity library in the system.

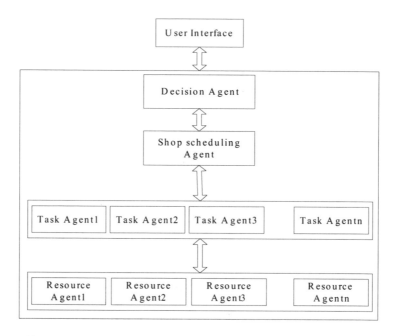

Fig. 1. Frame of Job-Shop Scheduling System based on ILOG and MAS

In Fig. 2.each agent has the knowledge base, human-machine interfaces and communication interfaces, even a management decision-making in decision agent. Each agent's function is marked in Fig. 2.

Some agents in the system mainly are as follows:

(1) Decision Agent. Decision Agent is responsible for receiving tasks, and then tests the capacity of the workshop through workshop capacity library. If yes, Decision Agent assigns tasks to the Shop Scheduling Agent. Decision Agent is also responsible for receiving feedback from the Shop Scheduling Agent, and presents generated production tasks to decision makers for reference.

(2) Shop Scheduling Agent. When getting a new task, Shop Scheduling Agent will decompose it using ILOG, and generate some sub-task automatically. Each sub-task will be generated corresponds to a Task Agent. In this Task Agent, there will be process list, product delivery, performance indicators, and the number of requirements and so on.

(3) Task Agent. After receiving the tender, Task Agent will calculate their existing processing time, processing costs on machines, and send message to Resources Agents to ask if they will accept each task. After receiving answers from resources agents, Task Agents will take into account processing time, cost and other factors to choose satisfied Resource Agents. At last Task Agents will send the results of feedback to the Shop Scheduling Agent and Resource Agent.

(4) Resource Agent. Resource Agent will do some calculation referring processing time, equipment utilization to decide if it is capable to bid. Satisfied resources should get the Task Agent known of its bender.

If each agent at last gets the conclusion that there is no bidding, it means that the shop cannot finish the task on the premise of meeting the constraints. Decision makers should cancel or postpone the production task. Workshop capacity library in figure 2 is used to determine whether the receiving task is in the production range. If they meet, the task was assigned; if not met, exit and display on the window that the task is not in production range.

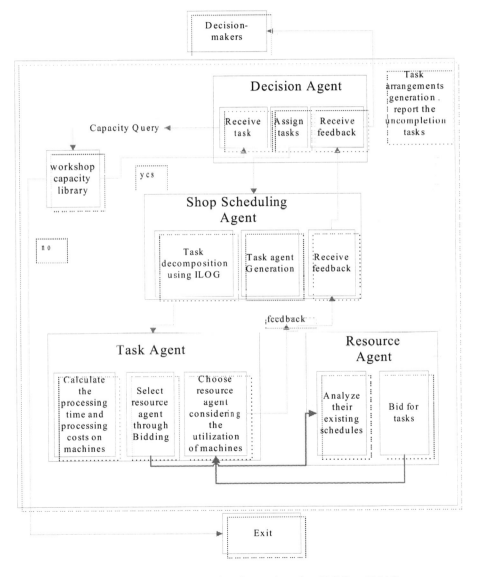

Fig. 2. Job-Shop Scheduling System based on ILOG and MAS

5 Conclusions

Nowadays development in information technology is rapid, the old mode of production cannot meet the needs of modern manufacturing systems. Job-Shop scheduling as the core of the entire manufacturing system, directly affects the production of finished products, production cycle, core competitiveness. A good Job-shop Scheduling System is the key to improve enterprise efficiency. Prototype of this JSSS we designed represents some more convenient and flexible scheduling plan in test by engineer of an automobile factory.

Acknowledgment

This is one part of the work, *Research on Dynamic Job Shop Scheduling Problem in Auto-mobile Industry Based on Multi-agent Method*, financially supported by Sichuan Youth Sci. & Tech. Foundation, Number 08ZQ026-009. Thanks for their kindness assistance. It also is funded by Construction Foundation of *Xihua University Transportation Planning and Management Key Subject*, Number XZD0816-09-1.

References

1. Lee, H., Kim, S.: Integration of Process Planning and Scheduling Using Simulation Based Genetic Algorithms. The International Journal o f Advanced Manufacturing Technology, pp. 586–589 (2001)
2. Mishra, S.: A hybrid least square- fuzzy bacteria foraging strategy for harmonic estimation. IEEE Trans. Evol. Computer, 1–3 (2005)
3. Fox, M.: Constrain: Directed search: A case study of job shop scheduling (Dissertation). Carnegie-Mellon University, Pittsburgh (1983)
4. Zhengwen, D., Zhang, A., Wu, I.: An agent-based approach for e- manufacturing and supply chain integration. Computer & Industrial Engineering, 340–352 (2006) (in Chinese)
5. Feng, L., Ma, H., Song, Z.: Development and Application of Spare Part Management System of Decision Making. Metallurgical Equipment, 36–38 (2006)
6. Nello, C., John, S.-T.: An Introduction to Support Vector Machines and Other Kernel-based Learning Methods. Cambridge University Press, Cambridge (2000)
7. Tang, X.-p., Wang, W.-t.: Research on Support Vector Machine for Pattern Classification. Modern Computer (2007) (in Chinese)
8. Yuan, K., Zhu, J.: Improved genetic algorithm for the flexible job-shop scheduling with multi-object. Chinese Mechanical Engineering, 150–158 (2007) (in Chinese)

The Infiltration Numerical Simulation for Several Kinds of Unsaturated Soil under Rainfall Condition

Dongfang Tian

College of Hydraulic & Environmental Engineering, China Three Gorges University
Yichang, Hubei 443002, China
Tdf_2005@163.com

Abstract. The research of infiltration numerical simulation for unsaturated soil is of great significance in the fields such as soil science, hydrology and water resources etc. In this paper, based on the numerical couple model of infiltration and runoff, the infiltration processes of silt, silt clay and clay column are simulated. The couple model is based on Richards' equation and kinematic wave model. The calculation results show that the infiltration in clay soil is most slow and wetting front is sharpest. This paper has some guiding significance to the research of infiltration process.

Keywords: rainfall, unsaturated soil, infiltration, numerical simulation.

1 Introduction

The stability problem of rock and soil engineering caused by rainfall is very important in literature. The key to solve the problem is to deepen the evolution of the state, moisture and water potential of unsaturated soil during infiltration processes under rainfall condition [1]. The infiltration processes contains two stages [2]: one is free seepage, another is pressure infiltration. In free seepage stage, the surface soil is dry; the infiltration rate is lager than rainfall intensity, all the rainfall infiltrates into soil. While in pressure infiltration stage, surface soil is saturated, and the infiltration rate is close to the saturated conductivity of soil.

With the rapid development of Computer Technology and algorithm, many numerical methods are brought out to simulate the seepage of unsaturated soil under rainfall condition. A representative numerical model is the couple model of infiltration and runoff [3]. The couple model is based on Richards' equation and kinematic wave model. Furthermore, the couple model could solve the seepage and runoff simultaneously.

In order to seek for the evolution of infiltration processes, four kinds of soils such as silt, silt clay and clay are simulated in this paper. The soil-water characteristic curves of four soils are Fredlund model. Based on the couple model, the infiltration processes of different soils under rainfall condition are compared.

S. Lin and X. Huang (Eds.): CESM 2011, Part I, CCIS 175, pp. 243–247, 2011.
© Springer-Verlag Berlin Heidelberg 2011

2 Analysis Methods

The FEM model is presented as follows:

$$[M]\frac{\partial\phi}{\partial t}+[N]\phi=\{Q\} \tag{1}$$

$$[M]=[S]+n_3[A] \tag{2}$$

$$[N]=[D]-[B_1^*]-[B_2^*] \tag{3}$$

$$\{Q\}=\{Q_1\}+\{Q_2\}+\{Q_3\} \tag{4}$$

While, in eq.(1), ϕ is potential function; t is time; $[M]$ and $[N]$ is coefficient matrixes respectively; $\{Q\}$ is column vector; the calculation methods of $[M]$, $[N]$ and $\{Q\}$ are shown in eq.(2)~(4). In eq.(2), $[S]$ is the superposition of $[S]^e$, $[S]^e=\int CN_iN_jd\Omega$, e means element, C is water capacity of e, N_i is shape function of e, $i,j\in[1,nnode]$, $nnode$ is element knots, Ω is region of e; $[A]$ is the superposition of $[A]^e$, $[A]^e=\int N_iN_jdS$, S is slope surface border of e; n_3 is the cosine of the angle between the outer normal vector and Z axis. In eq.(3), $[D]$ is the superposition of $[D]^e$, $[D]^e=\int[B_i]^T[k][B_j]d\Omega$, $[B_i]^T=[\frac{\partial N_i}{\partial x},\frac{\partial N_i}{\partial y},\frac{\partial N_i}{\partial z}]$, $[k]$ is conductivity matrix; $[B_1^*]$ is the superposition of $[B_1]^e[\lambda_x]^e$, $[B_1]^e=\int N_i\frac{\partial N_j}{\partial x}dS$, $[\lambda_x]^e=diag(\lambda_{xi})$, $\lambda_{xi}=\frac{1}{n}h_i^{5/3}$ $\frac{f_{xi}}{(f_{xi}^2+f_{yi}^2)^{1/4}(z_i+h_i/n_3)}$, n is Manning roughness, h_i is water depth of node i, z_i is z coordinate of node i, f_{xi} and f_{yi} are slope gradients along x and y directions of node i ; $[B_2^*]$ is the superposition of $[B_2]^e[\lambda_y]^e$, $[B_2]^e=\int N_i\frac{\partial N_j}{\partial y}dS$, $[\lambda_y]^e=diag(\lambda_{yi})$, $\lambda_{yi}=\frac{1}{n}h_i^{5/3}\frac{f_{xi}}{(f_{xi}^2+f_{yi}^2)^{1/4}(z_i+h_i/n_3)}$.

In eq.(4), $\{Q_1\}$ is the superposition of $\{Q_1\}^e$, $\{Q_1\}^e=\int N_iq_1dS_1$, q_1 is the normal boundary flux on S_1 of element which does not contain slope surface; $\{Q_2\}$ is the superposition of $\{Q_2\}^e$, $\{Q_2\}^e = -\int N_i q_2 d\Gamma$, q_2 is the normal boundary flux on Γ of runoff element; $\{Q_3\}$ is the superposition of $\{Q_3\}^e$, $\{Q_3\}^e = \int N_i q_3 dS$, q_3 is rainfall intensity. If water depth is less than 0, it does not need to calculate $[A]$, $[B_1^*]$ and $[B_2^*]$.

3 Analysis Model

Based on the couple model, the infiltration processes of a soil column with 8.75cm width, 8.75cm length and 61 cm height are simulated. The soil columns are silt, silt clay and clay respectively, which are homogeneous and isotropic. The densities (ρ) and saturated conductivities (Ks) of soils are listed in Table 1.

Table 1. The parameters of soils

Soil type	Silt	Silt clay	Clay
ρ(g/cm3)	2.00	1.95	1.80
Ks(*10⁻²cm/min)	0.69	0.35	6.9×10-3

The soil-water characteristic curves is described by Fredlund model as eq.(5).

$$S_e = \frac{1}{\{\ln[e + (\frac{h}{a})^n]\}^m} \qquad (5)$$

The fitness parameters of Fredlund model for four soils are shown in Table 2 [4].

Table 2. Parameters in soil-water characteristic curve

Soil type	a(Kpa)	n	m
Silt	68	1.189	0.796
Silt clay	186	0.594	0.482
Clay	109	0.728	0.556

Suppose the initial volume water content is 0.10, the top boundary is rainfall, and the other boundary is impervious. The rainfall intensity and duration will be given in next section.

4 Numerical Simulation Results and Analysis

4.1 Infiltration Process of Silt Column

The rainfall intensity is given as 5.0cm/h, and the rainfall duration is 180minutes. Calculation results show that the soil suctions decrease rapidly at the beginning, then

246   D. Tian

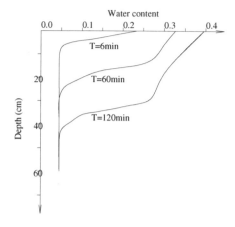

Fig. 1. Evolution with time of bulk water along depth direction

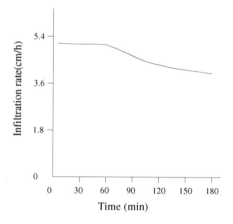

Fig. 2. Evolution with time of computed infiltration rate

decrease slowly soon after. Water accumulation appears at about 60min. Evolution with time of bulk water along depth direction is shown in Fig.1. The evolution of wetting front could also be seen from this figure.

Evolution with time of computed infiltration rate is shown in Fig.2. It could be seen that the infiltration is 5.0cm/h, and it is consistent with rainfall intensity.

4.2 Infiltration Process of Silt Clay and Clay Column

The rainfall intensity is given as 5.0cm/h, and the rainfall duration is 180minutes. Calculation results show that the soil suctions decrease rapidly at the beginning, then decrease slowly soon after. Water accumulation appears at about 30min. Evolution with time of bulk water along depth direction is shown in Fig.3. The evolution of wetting front could also be seen from this figure. It could be seen that wetting front is sharper than silt clay column. The Infiltration process of clay column is similar with Fig.3, but wetting front is sharpest of them.

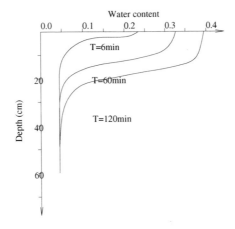

Fig. 3. Evolution with time of bulk water along depth direction

5   Conclusions

In this paper, based on the couple model, the infiltration processes of different soils under rainfall condition are compared. As calculation results show, the infiltration in clay soil is most slow and wetting front is sharpest. This paper has some guiding significance to soil science, hydrology and water resources etc.

References

1. Zhu, W., Cheng, N., Chen, X.: Some fundamental problems of unsaturated seepage. Journal of Geotechnical Engineering 28(2), 235–240 (2006) (in Chinese)
2. Wang, J., Wang, E., Wang, S.: Potential description of rainfall free infiltration phase. J. Tsinghua Univ (Sci. & Tech.) 50(12), 1920–1924 (2010) (in Chinese)
3. Kollet, S.J., Maxwell, R.M.: Integrated surface–groundwater flow modeling: A free-surface overland flow boundary condition in a parallel groundwater flow model. Advances in Water Resources 29, 945–958 (2006)
4. Wang, D.: Experimental study on volume change of unsaturated soil and its application to estimation of subsidence. Dalian University of Technology (May 2007)

The Research and Exploration of Project Course Developmental Evaluation in Higher Vocational Colleges Software Major

Gang Teng[1] and Qian Wu[2]

[1] Department of Computer Engineering, Suzhou Vocational University,
Suzhou, Jiangsu 215014, China
[2] Office of Academic Affairs, Suzhou Vocational University,
Suzhou, Jiangsu 215014, China
{fixxxer,sunniwu}@163.com

Abstract. Higher Vocational Education should foster and improve student's professional ability, and concentrate on student overall growth and the continued development of their career. The developmental direction of Higher Vocational Education model is the Higher Vocational Project Course, which will effectively perform the guiding role of evaluation mechanisms in project course. This paper starts with the connotation of the project course developmental evaluation in the Higher Vocational Education, and then discusses the methodology and construction of the developmental evaluation of the project course.

Keywords: Higher Vocational Education; Project Course; Developmental Evaluation; Evaluation Methodology; Evaluation Mechanism.

1 Introduction

The critical factor for Higher Vocational Education to foster highly skilled personnel is to develop and improve the professional competence of students. Nowadays, the project course model based on working process becomes the orientation of the Higher Vocational Education reformation. For software major, curriculum is inclined to start with the "do". In the specified projects, let student to learn professional knowledge, skills. Therefore, the project course plays an important role in fostering software major students.

However, due to the current implement of the project course still in the exploratory stage, especially for the evaluation of the project course still in the research stage. As the evaluation method has leadership function in the process of curriculum design and implementation, instead of using the traditional curriculum evaluation methods, it is critical to introduce new evaluation methods suited to the project course.

S. Lin and X. Huang (Eds.): CESM 2011, Part I, CCIS 175, pp. 248–252, 2011.
© Springer-Verlag Berlin Heidelberg 2011

2 The Connotation of the Project Course Developmental Evaluation in the Higher Vocational Education

2.1 The Inherent Requirements of the Project Course Evaluation in the Higher Vocational Education

The project course is the course mode which is to select, organize course content according to task, and to complete the career job as learning mode. In order to make the project course can meet the target, there must be suitable evaluation mechanisms running through each stage of the curriculum like design, implement, etc. The evaluation mechanisms will ensure the well alignment between course standards and professional qualification standards, and the excellent inosculation among theoretical courses, practical contents and technology contents. [1].

Therefore, the evaluation of the project course in Higher Vocational Education needs to emphasis the occupational, applied and practical features, and starts with professional ability, adhere to the principle -- "ability-based education where theory and professional are both important" [2]. Through the collection and use of information, to assess the rationality, scientificity, curriculum implementation conditions and implementation effect of the professional course in the Higher Vocational Education. Meanwhile, keep seeking the ways to improve the curriculum mechanism.

2.2 The Connotation of Course Developmental Evaluation

Developmental evaluation is one kind of concepts, which accelerate the continuous improvement in course. It is formed gradually in the development of course evaluation. The fundamental meaning of developmental evaluation is introspection, in which the process of course exploitation is rethought profoundly. By rethinking and evaluating each stage of course development, to ensure the course reformation sticks to the original plan. Therefore, the connotation of course developmental evaluation is to appreciate the formative ability which regards reformation as the main characteristic.

Secondly, the developmental evaluation of course considers the improvement of students' and teachers' ability as the core objectives. The evaluation carries out among students and teachers, and evaluates the development of course itself. Therefore, evaluation of developmental course is the inherent requirement in the Higher Vocational Education.

3 The Methodology of the Developmental Evaluation of Software Major Project Course

There are several fields in the course evaluation methodology. Since the project course and working assignment are closely related, so the completeness and fitness is an important criterion for the evaluation of project course. [3] In practice, the principle to choose the right method of the developmental evaluation of project course needs to follow many requirements which are able to represent the characteristics of the developmental evaluation of project course and its methods. Specifically include the following three aspects:

3.1 The Principle of Perceptiveness

The Principle of Perceptiveness is the important principle of the course evaluation, which requires using understanding vision to re-examine the evaluation. Perceptiveness includes the understanding to the object of evaluation, the understanding to the information of evaluation and the mutual understanding between the objects. The evaluation based on perceptiveness principle will be better to conform to the real situation of the object of evaluation, to well grasp the information of the object of evaluation, and deeply understand the meaning behind the object of evaluation.

3.2 The Principle of Diversity

The meaning of the principle of diversity is not the default standard or delineation of scope, but in the correct understanding of the characteristics of various methods, considering about the difference phenomenon in courses, based on the specific characteristics of the evaluated object, rationally use various methods, promote the integrated use of different types of method to finally obtain the comprehensive evaluation of the object information. The principle of diversity evaluation concerns the students' ability, attitude and emotional assessment, and the training of fostering the student ability. The purpose is to make students with individual differences, to develop the personal characteristic in each student.

3.3 The Principle of Actuality

The meaning of the principle of actuality is that the evaluation of the course around the purpose of evaluation, based on the actual situation of the evaluated object and the specific circumstances of the participants, design and organize the evaluation method realistically. From the principle of actuality, the real excellent evaluation is not necessarily a good looking at all aspects of the evaluation, but through the evaluation process, the participants involved in the evaluation program can have a better understanding the characteristics of themselves, which can really improve themselves. This is also what the function of development of the course evaluation requires for.

4 The Construction of the Developmental Evaluation of the Software Major Project Course

The software major project course in our college is the study process mainly based on student study, supplied by teacher instruction, highlights the student learning activities.

Learning content is not the traditional academic disciplines, but based on software technology activities analysis, according to the software design activities, horizontally integrated knowledge and skills. In the requirement of teaching objectives classification, to create the project course which will foster the software design ability. There are three components which are independent but also closely related in the system of developmental evaluation of project course. They are: the Evaluation of Course Construction, the Evaluation of Course Implementation and the Evaluation of Course Performance.

4.1 The Developmental Evaluation of Project Course Construction

The development evaluation of project course construction is to investigate if the project course focuses on training student design ability in software development. The evaluation content should include: The relevancy between the project course content and the requirement from software design job; the consistency between the interests and development of student; the harmony between the project course content and the course resources acquired from college; the rationality of the course setting; whether the teachers have the will, knowledge and ability to set the project course; whether the project course meets the students' interests and needs; whether the project course objectives are clear; whether the project course can meet the needs of students in different level; whether choose the appropriate project contents; whether the organization of the course content is reasonable and so on.

4.2 The Developmental Evaluation of the Implementation of the Project Course

The main content of the implementation of the project course is that: through continuous understanding the behavior of teachers, students and course manager, to detect the difficulties and problems appearing in the process of curriculum implementation, in order to effectively control the progress of the project course. The evaluation contents should mainly include: whether the teaching model meets the requirements of project course and the guidance of the advanced theory of the Higher Vocational Education; whether learning solutions follows the basic discipline that the way for student to acquire knowledge and learn abilities; how the effectiveness of the learning situation and the professional situation; whether teaching methods is suitable for the functional requirements of project courses; the integrity of course documents; whether teaching team members can trace and feedback in time in the process of implementation, appropriately adjust the finishing status of projects, achieve the aim of the project course and so on.

4.3 The Developmental Evaluation of the Performance of Project Course

The developmental evaluation of the performance of project course is the evaluation that assess the objectives of course study and the execution of student personalized objectives. Good program performance is one of the purposes of course reform. The evaluation contents should include: whether achieve the intended objective in the certain implementation phase of the project course; whether there have been some unforeseen problems; how to develop the next step of course implementation and reform and so on. Personnel who are in charge of develop and implement courses or who are related to manage courses concern to the performance of courses. Comprehensive understanding of program effectiveness is the key part to build and reform course, and also the problem needed to be answered and solved.

5 Conclusion

The mechanism of developmental evaluation captures the people-oriented principle and continuously improves this principle, which is the foundation and guarantees of the formation of project course in the Higher Vocational Education. The establishment of effective and reasonable developmental course evaluation has clear practical value and theoretical significance in improving current project courses in the Higher Vocational Education and promoting the training level of high application type skilled personnel.

References

1. Zhou, Q.: The Evaluation to Project Curriculum in Higher Vocational Colleges Under the Guidance of Scientific Concept of Development. Vocational Education Research (May 2010)
2. Wang, H.: Development Curriculum Evaluation in use of University Courses Evaluation. Helongjiang Education (Higher Education Research & Appraisal) (March 2008)
3. Gao, J.: The Construction and Exploration of the Project Course Evaluation System of Higher Vocational Colleges. Chinese Vocational and Technical Education (May 2010)
4. Dai, S.: Curriculum Teaching Reform of Vocational Education. Tsinghua University Press, Beijing (2007)

Bidirectional Matching Algorithm for Target Tracking Based on SIFT

Zhenxing Wu, Jingling Wang, Chuanzhen Li, Yue Yan, and Chen Chu

Information Engineering School, Communication University of China,
Beijing, 100024, China
{Wzx,wjl,lichuanzhen}@cuc.edu.cn, yanyue3736@126.com

Abstract. The SIFT is mainly used to detect the feature points of an image, and achieve a match between two images. Because of its stable ability in matching, it often gets an excellent performance on images match. This paper is mainly to study the performance of the SIFT on moving target tracking, we propose a bidirectional algorithm based on SIFT, and make it automate select the best template when there are many templates in the data base. Our results of the experiments show that the bidirectional matching algorithm we proposed here is more accuracy and stable than the previous unidirectional matching algorithm.

Keywords: SIFT, Scale-space, feature detecting, bidirectional matching, template selecting.

1 Introduction

Because of the stable matching performance of SIFT, and it can keep invariant to the change of the light and the scale, it is widely used in Face Recognition, Images Match and Synthesis. But it is rarely used in target tracking, this is mainly because its match is usually dependent on its template. Most of the time, however, it is very hard to achieve much when the target deformation happens [1]. This article is mainly to study the performance of the SIFT on moving target tracking.

In the article, we propose a kind of bidirectional algorithm under SIFT features, by doing this, we can avoid the situation when two or more points in one image both match with one point that in the other image, and the quantity of the right matched points are not decrease too much. At the same time, because the SIFT features can keep invariant to the change of the light and the scale, and it not need to know too much about the target that you want to track, it will have a good performance in target tracking .

This paper is organized as following: In section 2, we briefly describe how to extract SIFT features from an image. In section 3, we propose the bidirectional matching algorithm. Section 4 is the results of the experiment and the analysis. Section 5 is the conclusion of the paper.

S. Lin and X. Huang (Eds.): CESM 2011, Part I, CCIS 175, pp. 253–258, 2011.

2 The Extracting of the SIFT Feature

2.1 The Building of the Scale-Space

To detect the keypoints in the scale-space effect, SIFT use the gauss function to build the scale-space.

$$D(x,y,\sigma)=(G(x,y,k\sigma)-G(x,y,\sigma))\times I(x,y)=L(x,y,k\sigma)-L(x,y,\sigma) \qquad (1)$$

In the last formula the $G(x,y,\sigma)$ is the gauss function, the $I(x,y)$ is the image function [2].

2.2 Keypoint Detect

To find the extreme points of one image in the scale-space, the centre sampling point will be compared with the eight points that are around it in the same scale and the eighteen points that are in the up scale and the next scale, as shown in the Figure 1.

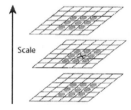

Fig. 1. keypoints detect [3]

2.3 Descriptor Representation

These samples are accumulated into orientation histograms summarizing the contents over 4×4 subregions, as shown on the right. This figure shows a 2×2 descriptor array computed from an 8x8 set of samples, whereas the experiments in this paper use a 4×4×8 = 128 element feature vector for each keypoint [4].

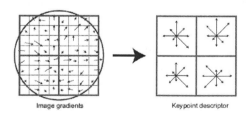

Image gradients   Keypoint descriptor

Fig. 2. The creation of a keypoint descriptor

3 Target Matching and Tracking

3.1 Target Match

3.1.1 Matching Improvement

There is an improvement on the match of the SIFT features in the article. Take the example of matching two images, the original match is calculating all the Euclidean distance between a definite feature in image one and every feature in image two, as shows in figure 3,if the nearest distance is shorter than 0.6 times of the second nearest then we accept this match, but we have a problem here is that there could be two or more points in image one are matched with one point in image two at the same time, obviously, there are wrong matched points in image one [5].To avoid the appearing of this kind of circumstance, we have a reverse match in the base of the original match in this article, as shows in figure 4. The result of the experiment shows that it can remove the wrong matched points efficiently. Although it cuts down the quantity of the matched points, it makes the match more accuracy and stable.

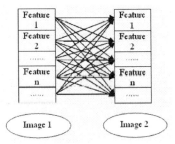

Fig. 3. The original features match

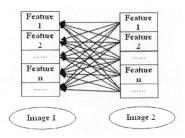

Fig. 4. The reverse features match that added

3.1.2   The Description of the Bidirectional Matching Algorithm

Take the example of the quantity of features in image 1 is m, and n in image two.D1(i,j) is the distance between the i'st feature in image 1 and the j'st feature in image 2.D2(j,i) is the distance between the j'st feature in image 2 and the i'st feature in image 1.t1(i) and t2(j) is the i'st feature in image 1 and the j'st feature in image 2.

First, calculate the Euclidean distance of every feature in image 2 between a definite feature in image 1. Take the first feature in image 1 for example:

$$D1(1, j) = \sqrt{\sum (t1(1) - t2(j))^2} \quad j = 1.2...n \tag{2}$$

If there is a match between the ist feature point in image 1 and the jst feature point in image 2,then we mark this as match1(i)=j.

Second, calculate the Euclidean Distance of every feature in image 1 between a definite feature in image 2. Take the first feature in image 2 for example:

$$D2(1, i) = \sqrt{\sum (t2(1) - t1(i))^2} \quad i = 1.2..m \tag{3}$$

If there is a match between the k'st feature point in image 1 and the h'st feature point in image 2,then we mark this as match1(h)=k.

Third, if match1(match2(j))=j, then we accept this match or we drop it.

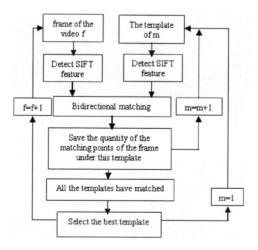

Fig. 5. Program structure

3.2 Target Tracking

We take a man as the moving target in this article, because man is non-rigid object, the body of the man will deform when the man is walking, it is difficult to track .But the gesture of a man will repeat, so we select several gestures of the man to be the templates then we match all the templates with every frame of the video, the program will select the template that has the most matching points to be the best template of the frame, by doing this, we can tracking the target efficiently.

4 The Experiment and Result

First we select seven gesture of the man from 30 frames of the video to be the templates, as shows in figure 6.

Fig. 6. Seven templates

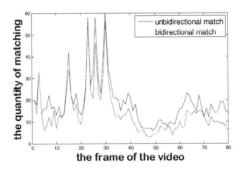

Fig. 7. The comparison of the quantity of matching

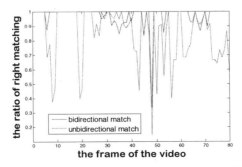

Fig. 8. The comparison of the ratio of right matching

From the result of the experiment we can see that, it removes the wrong matching points effectively under the bidirectional matching algorithm. There are eighteen frames could not find their best frame in the totally eighty frames under the original matching way ,the ratio of right matching is 78% by statistics, but when using the bidirectional matching algorithm, there are only seven frames fail to find their best template, the ratio of right matching is 92%.

5 Conclusions

The article uses the bidirectional matching algorithm that under SIFT to track the target. The result of the experiment shows that the match is more stable when using the bidirectional matching algorithm than original matching way, and it have a good quantity of the matching points, so it has important significant in actual world using. But it takes too much time from detecting to find the best template for each frame, it can not meet real-time need. We can find a way to update the template automatic, then the time of template selecting will be reduced, and it can meet the real-time need.

References

1. Cao, X., Wang, W.: Improved Image Matching Based on SIFT Algorithm. Department of Information Science and Engineering, Shanghai Maritime University 200135
2. Ji, H., Wu, Y., Sun, H., Wang, Y.: SIFT feature matching algorithm with global information. Optics and Precision Engineering 17(2) (2009)
3. Lowe, D.G.: Distinctive Image Features from Scale-Invariant Keypoints, January 5 (2004)
4. Chen, Z.: The SIFT Research and Implementation Based on the Image Registration (2008)
5. Zhang, S., Song, H., Xiang, X., Zhao, Y.: Fast SIFT Algorithm for Object Recognition. Computer Systems & Applications (06) (2010)

The Design and Implementation of a Kind of Simple and Easy Access to Database Framework

Pin Yuan, Jia Chen, and Xi'an Lou

Dalian Maritime University
Management Science and Engineering, China
yuan_pin_yp@yahoo.cn, chen_jia8008@sina.com,
lou_xi_an@126.com

Abstract. Architecture is one of the important methods of simplifying system development process, and design patterns are summary of good software design experience, this article introduces the process of designing of a simple database access mechanism structure by the use of certain design patterns and adopting control inversion technique, this architecture simplifies the programmer's job, make the programmers will energy from technology transfer to business, so the operations on data will be safer, complete, and suitable for various system .It has some practical value.

Keywords: architecture , design pattern , database, control reversed.

1 Introduction

With the development of information technology, the programmer's workloads become harder and harder, in hard work, the programmer due to the technical requirements usually neglect business requirements, in order to solve this problem, in recent years people have put forward architecture, architecture is one of the problems which are mentioned in the systems development process, good architecture can simplify the development process, make programmers during development, focusing on business rather than merely in technical, it can accelerate the development process and reduce repeated work, reduce routine testing, and reduce the debate on procedural details, make development output can be expected, the behavior can be controllable.

Architecture itself is a "intermediate" and a configurable, clear abstract way.

2 Application Background and Demand

Cargo_track system has realized comprehensive management on complete process of food from production to sales, it at any time can find the current food production time, place and its production intermediate process, and after its sales because of the management needs, we will integrate the previous data, and make a comparison and forecasting.

S. Lin and X. Huang (Eds.): CESM 2011, Part I, CCIS 175, pp. 259–265, 2011.

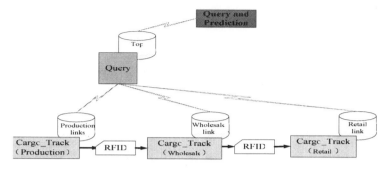

Fig. 1. Integral structure of Tracing system

This tracing system installed respectively in the production process, wholesale, retail link links, and in every link , it all involved operation in the database, in the inquiry platform, it is a system that different from the bottom, only provides function of inquiry prediction , also want to do the database operation. In the production process and wholesale and retail link are linked with card to connect, which store in the link with the basic information of the cargo, enabling us to in the inquiry platform be traced back to the cargo from the production to sales of the entire process, at the bottom and top database, it involves operations on data, and in two systems, the existing data transfer function, therefore, it improves the function of data processing the request.

For instance in the underlying database contains the database tables as follows: daily purchasing information table, sales information table, etc., and the top of the table, contains tables as follows: purchasing information table, sales information table, etc. Although the tables in the top and bottom name of some form and structure are the same, yet its storage of data is not the same.At the bottom of deposit is daily sales records, and on the top floor contains a related information collection, it makes search analysis be more efficient and accurate, when we use the inquiry platform to inquiry ,we need to integrate data of several months or even years, for management, but in the meanwhile, database query data in constantly update, this makes programmers in processing, must spend a lot more in technic, such ability make data inquiried out more accurate, the results predicted is more credible.

As is known to all, now Microsoft for the vast number of users and programmers provides powerful data access architecture, as below:

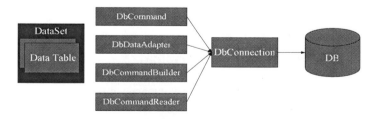

Fig. 2. Microsoft's data access architecture

However, because Microsoft provides powerful data access in architecture, in data processing, efficiency has decreased, for example, when we connect to the database, we should write a class alone, it will be connected data available statements written in, and then, every time you have access to database, it generates this object, and it do the database connections, then make database operation. Due to the existence of inquires that it might appear in different platforms simultaneously data manipulation phenomenon, also add transaction, that is to say, when we do a data access, we will write about 20 lines of code, which not only makes code amount increases, but also increases the rate that the data in the process may go wrong. Make the programmers to put most energy in technology, in the object-oriented, customer-oriented era, if we want to try to meet customer demand, it demands that energy is put in business, and non-technical issues. Therefore, we design simple database access mechanism framework.

3 Design Thought

3.1 Inversion of Control

Inversion of Control is one of the important of object-oriented programming methodologies for cutting of the computer program coupling problem. IoC is also called Dependency Injection.

IoC could be seen as the distillation of the factory model , and it also could be seen as a big factory, which is just to create objects that are defined is in XML documents. And then useing Java "reflection" programming, corresponding objects are created according to the class name which is given in XML . Judging from the realization, IoC changes the code which is fixed written in the factory method object to be defined in XML file. That is to say, the factory is separated from object generated, so as to improve flexibility and maintainability.

3.2 Design Patterns

Design patterns are composed of a group of particular relationship class or object. The special relationship between class and object refers to the calls, communication (events), collaboration and dependencies. It also determines the classes and examples it contained, their roles, collaborative approach and responsibilities distribution. Its naming and abstraction determines the major aspects in the structure, and formed reusable object design. Design patterns focuses on specific object design problems or points, describes its environment, constraint condition, effect, and processes itself according to the specific problem.

3.3 Design and Implementation

The file app.Config is the core configuration file in the entire database access framework , which can be embed the boot file app. config.
Main structure is as follows

```
     <add key="tablename" value="test" />
      <add key="TableDef_test"
value="AA,key,System.String,DbType.String,0,0,True;BB,sec
ond, System.String, DbType.String ,1,50, false;CC,third,
   System.Integer,DbType.Int16,2,0,false" />
<add key="TableDef_test1"
value="id1,key1,System.Integer,DbType.Int16,1,0,true" />
      <add
key="TableDef_test2"value="id2,key21,System.interger,
DbType.Int16,1,0,true; id3,key22,System.Integer,
DbType.Int16,2,0,true;desc2,explain,System.String,
DbType.String ,1,S45,false" />
     <addkey="TableDef_test3"          value="id3,key31,System.
Integer,DbType.Int16,1,0,true;desc3,explain,System.String,
DbType.String,1,45,false" />
     <add key="TableDef_test4" value="id4,key41,System.
Integer,DbType.Int16,1,0,true;id3,foreignkey1,System.
Integer,DbType.Int16,1,0,false;desc4,explain,System.Strin
g,DbType.String,1,45,false" />
     <add key="DBConnectionString" value="server=localhost;
user id={0};password={1};database=test;pooling=false" />
     <add key="DataDllInfo"
value=",System.Data,Version=2.0.
0.0,Culture= neutral,PublicKeyToken=b77a5c561934e089" />
<add key="ConnTypeStr"value=
"System.Data.SqlClient.SqlConnection" />
```

4   Implementation

This simple data access framework not only achieved the purpose of regulating development, but also has the independent controllability and small scale characteristic. It realized the characteristics of dependence of injected, and used a variety of design patterns, such as factory model, a single example mode, reflection mechanism, etc.

The main structure of simple and easy access to database framework design is shown below:

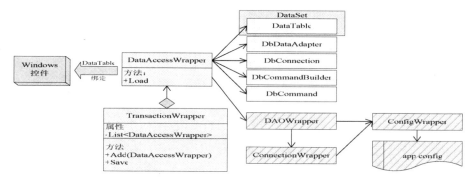

Fig. 3. static class

As shown in figure of static class, the operation for database is unified in background. The only programmers should do is to create a DataAccessWrapper objects, and use Load methed. Because the class DataAccessWrapper didn't have Save method, if the operate is needed to save, create a TransactionWrapper object is necessary. The class TransactionWrapperis used to execute transactions, which ensure the data's integrity and consistency. And the structure can also save with multiple changes, that is to say, create more than one DataAccessWrapper object, after changing the table and joining to TransactionWrapper objects, and then execute Save method , the changes can be saved according to the joined order.

The main DataAccessWrapper implementation code is as follows:

```
Public Overrides Sub Load()
      Me.SelectCommand =DAOWrapper.GetInstance.NewDbCmd
(Me.QueryString, Me.Connection)
           Me.Adapter =
DAOWrapper.GetInstance.NewDataAdapter(Me.SelectCommand)
           Me.CommandBuilder =
DAOWrapper.GetInstance.NewCmdBuilder(Me.Adapter)
           Me.DataTable = fillData(Me.DataSet, Me.Adapter,
Me.TableName)     Me.IsLoaded = True End Sub
      Private Function fillData(ByRef aDataSet As
DataSet, ByRef adapter As Common.DbDataAdapter, ByVal
tableName As String) As DataTable
   Dim rtn As DataTable = Nothing
         Try
   MyDebugger.Log(Me).Println(Me.SelectCommand.CommandText)
      adapter.Fill(aDataSet, tableName.ToLower)
      rtn = aDataSet.Tables(tableName.ToLower)
   If rtn Is Nothing Then
     Throw New NullValueOrRefException("get errors when to
fill Dataset according to the data table")      End If
         Catch e As Exception
       Throw New LoadFailedException(" Fail to create
data according to DataTable query", e)
   End Try
      Return rtn
   End Function
```

5 Application Conclusion

This Cargo_Track System uses c # language development. In database access, a database connection statements are written in the config file app.config, while inversion technology is direct used to connect the database, in the class DataAccessWrapper. The only programmers could do is according to table to query string to get DataTable object (subset of database table), in the class DataAccessWrapper's objects, which is only suitable for single table operation to return to a subset of the database tables with the primary key. At the same time, this Subset table (DataTable) can be updated. This class didn't explicit provide Save method, so if persistent is needed, this class object must be submitted to TransactionWrapper objects to realize transaction to guarantee data persistent. If users get DataTable, they can relize DataTable as data sources which is used to bound to the Windows visual control,to relize the data automatic updates.

When connecting database, the constructor DataAccessWrapper with four parameters is direct calede with the user name and password for the database, which not only connected to the database, and it provided DataTable to operate database table directly. The class DataAccessWrapper did not provide Save method, so the class TransactionWrapper had to be used. This will add it to the transaction to realize the data integrity. Below is the operation implementation on the database CargoTrack:

```
TransactionWrapper tw = new TransactionWrapper();
  DBHelper.DataAccessWrapper      daw      =      new
DataAccessWrapper("sa","","*", "CargoTrack");
     daw.Load();
   DataTable dt = daw.DataTable;
   dt.Rows[0].Delete();
    tw.Add(daw);
  DBHelper.DataAccessWrapper      daw1      =      new
DataAccessWrapper("sa","", "*","CargoTrack");
   daw1.Load();
 DataTable dt1 = daw1.DataTable;
   DataRow dr = dt1.NewRow();
   dr[0]   =   (Convert.ToInt32(dt1.Rows[dt1.Rows.Count   -
1][0])) + 1;
    daw1.DataTable.Rows.Add(dr);
    tw.Add(daw1);
 tw.Save();
```

Above is two operations performed for table CargoTrack. Execute save method, and the operation on the database can be kept.

This simple database access architecture makes access to database and modification to table more easily. Programmers in the design process could cost more time in business, instead of in thinking access to database and modification to table. This database access framework is not only used in Cargo_Track system, but in other systems. If the file app.config is midified in Server address, username, password, database, use type of database, such as SQL Server Mysql information, it can be used in other systems to realize the database access.

6   Conclusion

This framework encapsuled over databases operation. Using the technology such as reflection and control reverse, this custom data access architecture not only achieved rapid development purpose, but really turned programmers attention from technical to business. Of course, any one of the proposed framework is not perfect. This simple data access structure still have some disadvantages, for example, because of bad encapsulation, it make learning cost taller, performance lower, etc.

References

1. Malarvannan M.: Design better software with the inversion of Control pattern [EB/OL] (March 18, 2005), http://www.devx.com/Java/Article/27583/0/page/1
2. Head First Design patterns Eric Freeman, Elisabeth Freeman, Kathy Sierra&Bert Bates China (2007)

A Brief Study on the Theory and Application of Interactive Simulation

F.Y. Ma[1], Jinguo Li[2], Weiwei Wu[1], Lijun Cai[1], and Wei Li[1]

[1] College of Automobile Engineering, Shanghai University of Engineering Science,
Shanghai 201620, China
[2] Department of Product Development, Xinfu Motorcycle Co., Ltd. of SAIC, Shanghai, China
mafuyin@163.com

Abstract. There are difference types of simulation software should be used in some problems like noise analysis, fatigue analysis, optimization, and so forth. A new definition should use to general designation this technology as interactive simulation. More and more very complexity engineering problems and a problem which depends on other value will be solving through this concept. This paper mainly introduces the theory and application of interactive simulation and it will useful to the computer simulation engineers and technicians.

Keywords: Interactive simulation, Document Interface, Simulation Platform.

1 Introduction

These years, there exist all kinds of simulation software in our society, CAD software like UG, Catia, Pro/E, Solidworks, AutoCAD, CAE software like Nastran, Abaqus, Ansys, Hyperworks, and CAM software like MasterCAM, and so forth. These pieces of software have different features from each type, CAD software should be used to build the model of products [1], CAE software should to analysis the motion, stress, strain, vibration, fluid flow [2] etc. and CAM software should simulate the process of NC machining [3].

First assume the school or corporations have the right to use some different software. And a complexity engineering problem should be solving by interactive simulation easier than use unique software or maybe some problem couldn't solved by unique software [4]. A preliminary definition to interactive simulation may express as use some different software or different modules to solve a problem which hard to solve or can't solve by unique software or modules. Based on this technology some primary engineers and technicians may solve some complexity engineering problem by basic skill and it means some senior engineers should to do other more value work. Cycle time of product development would be shortage at the same time and this was promoted in our society especially these years. At present this technology always has been used to solve following problems:

(1) Build an analysis model by different software through interactive simulation.
(2) Pre-treatment and post-processing of analysis by these pieces of software interactive with analysis software [5].

S. Lin and X. Huang (Eds.): CESM 2011, Part I, CCIS 175, pp. 266–272, 2011.

(3)The analysis depends on previous analysis like NVH analysis [4], fatigue analysis [6] and optimization [7].

(4)Part of analysis need supported by some user definition programs from FORTRAN [8] or other computer language like VC++ [9].

(5)Simulation platform is building in these years [10] and it will become the final form of interactive simulation.

2 Build Model by Interactive Simulation

Maybe there are three typical applications in simulation the engineers or scholars always like to use. Firstly, if someone get a two-dimension plane drawing has been drew by AutoCAD software or CAXA software, three-dimension solid model should get more convenient by this technology than to draw it directly. Secondly, build fluid model always based on build the container model and through interactive simulation to get the fluid model from other software. Thirdly, by use some user definition programs to build some complexity model. There are many papers have used these methods before and following examples have been introduced by author to illustrate these applications [9, 11].

2.1 Plane Drawing to Solid Model

Most engineers like to draw two-dimension plane drawing by AutoCAD software or CAXA software. It is a widely habit in engineering whether Mechanical Engineering or other engineering. But if someone should solve the motion or other relation that three-dimension solid model should be built for later analysis. And the engineer will hope to build the solid model depends on size relationship of plane drawing directly. It should reduce many works and save some time of production developing.

Fig.1a is a plane drawing of Hydraulic impactor that get from AutoCAD software. Now if you want to get the three-dimension solid model you should export this program as .dwg form and import it into Solidworks or other software you used to build solid model. When import the plane drawing into Solidworks software some features should be deleted and only reserve a few features. And a three- dimension solid model of piston has got by Solidworks very easy like fig.1b. An important point is that before import other analysis software you should save the three-dimension solid model as .step form best.

2.2 Fluid Model Build

The shape of all flow fluid is depends on the shape of container that contact with fluid. So we should build the fluid model through container model indirect. In this

(a)   (b)

Fig. 1. Schematic diagram of plane drawing to solid model

step the Boolean subtraction function of CAD software or pre-treatment module of CFD software like Gambit in Fluent software should been used.

Some CFD simulations need to analysis the hydromechanics behavior in engineering and these works almost base on fluid model. CAD engineers can provide the components to you and you should use the interactive simulation technology to build the CFD analysis model very easy. It allows the CFD engineers haven't CAD drawing skill too much and can reduce many works also.

Fig.2a is a CFD analysis model for hydraulic impactor has got from Gambit module in fluent software based on figure.1a and a cylinder model through Boolean subtraction function. Fig.2b is the result of fluid velocity solved by fluent software. It is only an example to illustrate this method and there are some other applications for engineering.

(a)   (b)

Fig. 2. CFD analysis model for hydraulic impactor

2.3 Build Model by User Definition Programs

There are so many examples that engineers have used to build model by user definition programs. Some CAD software like UG contain own Grip language or interface to other language as C++, FORTRAN, Basic, C#, .net and so forth. And other software also provides this function more or less.

There are some program-packages have always been integrated in these software and use the user definition programs to achieve your ideas will very easy. Sometimes build a complex model would only by little simple program sentences or commends. This method suit the model that has a clear mathematics expression or could convert by some commends. Universal software unable contains all features the user wants to achieve, so this method is very important and wide used in engineering.

3 Pre-treatment & Post-processing

Pre-treatment & post-processing is the earliest and most mature form in interactive simulation. The earliest universal FEM analysis software, Nastran (1966), is using this method earliest. Because the Nastran software is only solver software and the user should define the mesh or boundary conditions by pre-treatment software, and it also should use the post-processing software to show the analysis result like cloud map.

The later FEM analysis software like Marc, Ansys, and Abaqus have become contain the pre-treatment & post-processing module. Nowadays, there exist much excellent pre-treatment & post-processing software, FEM analysis software, CFD analysis software and other type in our society. Although most analysis software contain pre-treatment & post-processing module themselves, the functions are less convenient than the special pre-treatment & post-processing software. For example, if you want to get structural hexahedral mesh for a complex model, it is more hard use the pre-treatment & post-processing module of analysis software than use the special pre-treatment & post-processing software. It is well known by most engineers and this paper only to summary these theories and methods.

When you import the model was showed in Figure.3a into the MSC.Marc software to mesh, you can't get the structural hexahedral mesh by mentat module directly. There exist at least two methods for to solve this problem that uses the interactive simulation ideal. One is use the pre-treatment & post-processing software like MSC.Patran, Hypermesh or ANSA to mesh it through cut the model. The other method is after the model has been imported into MSC.Marc software you should delete all features except a main surface. The structural mesh of this main surface was showed in figure.3b and the solid mesh was got from surface mesh by same sizes expand like figure.3c. Use this method will best valid to mesh the gear or gerotor especially.

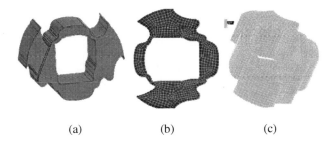

(a)   (b)   (c)

Fig. 3. Complex model to get structural mesh

One most important point should to introduce in this part is changing the models between CAE software and CAD software same time. Through this method you should change the analysis model in CAD software and keep other conditions unchanged in CAE software. By this feature you should save some time to redefine the analysis conditions. For example, in general nonlinear FEM analysis software Aqaqus6.9 version, you should change the analysis model in UG software same time and in Aqaqus6.10 version you also should change the model in Catia software, too.

4   Analysis Depends on Previous Analysis

NVH analysis, fatigue analysis and topology optimization through interactive simulation have been introduced in this part. These analysis all have a same characteristic that the analysis would depends on previous analysis.

There are at least two types of NVH analysis in engineering, one is aeroacoustics analysis interactive between CFD analysis software like Fluent to solve the fluid flow and sound analysis software like Sysnoise to solve the sound [12], the other one is structural acoustics analysis interactive between FEM software like Nastran to solve the vibration and analysis software to solve the sound.

Vibration and noise of the car or parts should be solve and analysis when you want to evaluate the comfort of a car. Of course, you may test it by laboratory equipment, too. But if you want to solve it by theory or simulation method not test, you should first to solve the vibration frequency and through this result to solve the sound pressure. For example, you may solve the vibration frequency by Nastran software and get a result file as .op2 form, and read this file into Sysnoise software the sound pressure should be solved through you define some conditions and solve it.

Another example is to solve the aeroacoustics by this method. You should solve the air flow or water flow near a car, an aircraft or a submarine by Fluent software and read these results into Sysnoise to solve the sound pressure. This is a most useful method to solve the sound which caused by fluid flow.

Difference from NVH analysis that fatigue analysis and topology optimization should first to solve the stress-strain relationship of a part and read these results into corresponding software to solve the life circle or optimization result. You may choose any FEM software to solve the stress-strain relationship like Nastran, Abaqus, Ansys, Marc, etc. And there also exist some software to solve the fatigue like MSC.Fatigue and so forth.

5 Secondary Development

Sum up the secondary development of engineers always use there maybe exist two typical types should be classified or defined from it. I -Secondary development and II - Secondary development should be separately nominated by this paper.

I -Secondary development is a method that the user should project some program sentences depend on pure numerical algorithm to achieve some functions. This method indicates the process was derived by strict mathematics relationship like user may define the concentration force followed boundary conditions for MSC.Marc software [8] or dynamic mesh for Fluent software [13]. In other words, most of examples previous paper should be classified to this type. Through this method you may define some complex material constitutive relations, complex boundary conditions to develop the solve ability for software.

II - Secondary development is the method that user should connect some software through some ports and to achieve truly interactive simulation. This method indicates the interface between software and software. Pre-treatment & post-processing and call some commands in a software like Visual C++ or Visual Basic from another software like MATLAB are the most usually used at present. This method will not involve the mathematics relationship and only some ports to active the function of software have contained itself. One example is you define the solve conditions in Hypermesh software for MSC.Nastran software to solve and you should set some code variables for MSC.Nastran along. Another example is you should call the magic function in Visual C++ from MATLAB software to easily solve any order magic square by a simple command.

It is maybe very clear to realize the secondary development from this classified. And as of these expressions you may have an overall realization to interactive simulation and development of simulation at present. Based on these expressions an initial concept of simulation platform or simulation system should be built in your mind and it maybe the latest development at present.

6 Simulation Platform

Most ultimate and aspiration form of interactive simulation may be nominated as simulation platform. It is a new concept advancing and developing in these years.

However, there are some preliminary concepts were existing long time as Pre-treatment & post-processing software and optimization software. But these forms lack of intelligent and we should develop more intelligent form to realize a truly simulation platform. The simulation platform should be defined as the platform based on internet and you should submit your job list to it and this system may choose the programs to solve by itself. This platform would not only to simplify your analysis work but also to concentrate the resources and the utilization should be improved significantly.

There are some more successful software should develop to simulation platform like Ansys, LMS.Virtual.Lab, Hyperworks and so forth. These pieces of software always contain some modules like Pre-treatment & post-processing, nonlinear dynamic analysis, standard analysis, CFD analysis, motion analysis, fatigue analysis or sound analysis. And some scholars are building the simulation platform based on internet these years and we confirm that the advanced simulation platform will build no longer.

7 Conclusion

A systematic summary to development of computer simulation technology have been done and a new interactive simulation concept was introduced in this paper. Some example for build model by interactive simulation, Pre-treatment & post-processing, Analysis depends on previous analysis, Secondary development and simulation platform were explained from some engineering projects. Besides, the secondary development were also separately nominated and the initial definition of I -Secondary development and II - Secondary development were introduced by author. From this paper the reader may get a system concept to numerical simulation and some useful inspirations to solve the engineering programs.

Acknowledgments

The author wishes to thank the Shanghai Municipal Education Commission scientific research and originality Project (10YZ174) for providing research fund and all colleagues who previously provide technical support.

References

1. Lorenzo-Yustos, H., Lafont, P., Diaz Lantada, A., et al.: Towards-completeproduct development teaching employing combined CAD - CAM - CAE technologies. Computer Applications in Engineering Education 18(4), 661–668 (2010)
2. Liu, J.-h., Guo, G., Xu, Z.-j., et al.: Application and Prospect of Computer-Aided Engineering. Journal of Chongqing University (Natural Science Edition) 24(6), 113–116 (2001)
3. Kotani, T., Nakamoto, K., Ishida, T., et al.: Development of CAM system for multi-tasking machine tools. Nihon Kikai Gakkai Ronbunshu 75(757), 2589–2595 (2009) (in Japanese)
4. Abdallah, A.A., Avutapalli, B., Steyer, G., et al.: Effective NVH analysis and optimisation with CAE and computer experiments. International Journal of Vehicle Noise and Vibration 3(1), 1–26 (2007)

5. Yuan, J., Chen, S., Huang, H.: Engineering applications of structural optimization system based on Patran/Nastran. Journal of Beijing University of Aeronautics and Astronautics 32(2), 125–129 (2006) (in Chinese)
6. Cha, S.-W., Ha, E.-J., Lee, K.-W., et al.: Development of fatigue durability analysis techniques for engine piston using CAE. SAE International Journal of Engines 2(1), 403–408 (2006)
7. Körtélyesi, G., Erdos-Sélley, C.: A transformation technique for efficient shape optimization in CAD/CAE environment. Periodica Polytechnica, Mechanical Engineering 52(1), 19–23 (2008)
8. Chen, H., Xue, X.: Secondary development guide of MSC.Marc. Science Press, Beijing (2004)
9. Zou, Q., Xiong, N., Zou, S., et al.: Dijkstra optimization and CAD based on VC lowest cost process. In: 2009 1st International Conference on Information Science and Engineering, ICISE 2009, Nanjing, China, pp. 3760–3763 (2009)
10. Li, B.-h., Chai, X.-d., Hou, B.-c., et al.: Networked Modeling & Simulation Platform Based on Concept of Cloud Computing—Cloud Simulation Platform. Journal of System Simulation 21(17), 5292–5299 (2009) (in Chinese)
11. Zhang, Z., Sun, Y., Xiao, X., et al.: Sanitary Ceramic Products CAD System Based on Application Development of Unigraphics. Journal of Computer-Aided Design & Computer Graphics 19(6), 764–768 (2007) (in Chinese)
12. Zhou, C.-s., Ma, W.-p.: Simulation of aerodynamic noise of automobile on sysnoise. Technological Development of Enterprise 28(3), 58–60 (2009)

Evaluation on Chinese Defense Expenditures from 1978–2009—From View of International Comparison

Ling Li, Yu Wang, and Sheng Zhou

Department of Military Finance, Military Economics Academy
Luojiadun No.122, 430035, Wuhan, China
stonelee9@yahoo.com.cn

Abstract. This paper attempts to measure the burden of Chinese defense expenditures. We design a system of indexes from three angles, which are macroeconomy, public finance, and the governmental preference. A conclusion is drew that although the nominal defense expenditures mounted up at high speed from 1989, their real relative scale just began rising in 1997, and converted into decreasing tendency in 2003. In addition, the paper deduces that in the future Chinese government should give more priority to the development of education and healthcare, not the enhancement of military power.

Keywords: China, defense expenditures.

1 Introduction

Chinese defense expenditures began to rapidly increase from 1989.The growth rate is more than 10% each year in name except 2010, which is 7.5% because of the influence of global finance crisis. However, Chinese defense expenditures reached 532.1 billion CNY in 2010, which was 21.8 billion CNY in 1988. The fast growth rate of Chinese defense expenditures intensified the opinion of China's Threat, and the dispute about China's peaceful rise. However, China hasn't realized the modernization of defense. For China, it is meaningful to evaluate the level of her defense expenditures for the future decision.

The studies on the evaluation of China's defense expenditures have experienced three periods. The first period began in the early 1980s. Those literatures emphasized that defense should be in obedience to and serve the development of national economy, so the defense expenditures should be cut down. The second period started in 1990s. After several years of defense expenditures being cut, the gap between the defense demand and the effective supply was exposed obviously. The reasons of the gap and its influence attracted many researchers (Sun Xiude & Huang Chenglin, 1997[1]; Wan Gongcheng[2], 1998; Liu Liegui, 2000[3]). The third period began in the 21st century, researchers began to pay more attention to the economic effect of rapid growth of Chinese defense expenditures, and discuss the appropriate level of defense expenditures (Huang Ruixing, 2007[4]).

With respect of the methods to evaluate the level of defense expenditures, there are two main methods. One method is the ratios comparison (Li Guoting, 2004[5]), the

S. Lin and X. Huang (Eds.): CESM 2011, Part I, CCIS 175, pp. 273–279, 2011.

other is the econometric analysis (Hao Wanlu & Sun Zhaobin, 2007[6]). Hao Wanlu and Sun Zhaobin (2007) analyzed the relationship of defense expenditures among China and other countries, and got the conclusion that China's defense expenditures were lower than the equilibrium level under the circumstance of military game among China and foreign countries. Concerning with the ratios comparison, the existent literatures used the traditional ratios, such as the absolute scale of defense expenditures, the ratio of defense expenditures to GDP, the ratio of defense expenditures to public expenditures.

The level of defense expenditures is determined by safety demand and capacity of economy supply. The exclusive angle of military competition overlooked the limits of economy. Those traditional ratios analysis ignored the difference among economic bodies, such as public financial systems, multi-objects of government and so on. That ignorance deduced incorrect evaluation about the appropriate of defense spending one nation.

Thus, this paper establishes a system of various ratios from the view of combining military competition with economic capacity, in order to analyze Chinese defense expenditures since 1978. In addition, we evaluate the defense expenditures under the circumstance of multi-objects of governance and forecast the possibility of the growth of defense expenditures in the future.

2 Method of Analyzing Defense Expenditures

2.1 Theory about Demand and Supply of Defense

The fundamental reason for defense is the awareness of outside threat. Defense provides safety for nation. If there is no alternative safeguard method, the more threat one nation is aware of, the more demand for defense.

Concerning the methods of safeguard, different theories of international relationship hold different opinions. Realists think that international society is in a state of anarchy. The competition among nations is a zero-game. Each nation pursues its relative power, but not the absolute power. Military power is an important part of comprehensive national strength, the growth of other nations' military power is equal to the decline of domestic defense capacity. Furthermore, because of the state of anarchy, the relative power based on military capacity is more helpful than diplomacy to ensure the national benefits. Thus, realist's basic judgment about anarchy state deduces that other nations' defense expenditures determine domestic defense expenditures. In the meanwhile, neo-liberal school thinks that the reality of economic relationship among nations and the development of international systems can bring out win-win result. Thus, the international co-operation can substitute defense to some extent to improve the safety. Constructivism thinks that culture, religion, ideology and etc. are all parts of national strength. The difference of culture is one source of international conflict. It is possible to resolve the international conflict by formation of the common culture.

There is no consensus of theory about the solution to international conflict. However, few nations and districts hold zero defense spending. Thus, even if the realism couldn't explain all the behaviors of nation, it is rather persuasive to explain the demand for defense. Based on that, it is meaningful that we compare some nations' defense spending in the same period, which will lead to the evaluation of level of domestic defense spending.

Except for the awareness of threat, the defense expenditures are limited by the following economic factors in general. Firstly, the national economy development forms the vital limit. In any period, defense is the most expensive public goods, and represents the most advanced technology. In the course of new military revolution, it is evident that defense depends on capital and technology more and more. Secondly, capability of fiscal revenue forms the direct limit. Defense is provided by government, especially by the central government. So the governmental fiscal revenue, rather than GDP, is the direct constraint for defense. If one nation is rich, whereas the capability of fiscal revenue is weak, the government is hard to establish a strong army. Thirdly, the priority sequence of the governmental multi-objects influences the investment in defense. In democratic society, government always pursues not only strong military power but also advanced education, good health care and so on. Thus, the priority with regard of the sequence of public goods determines its respective public spending.

2.2 Measurment and Method of Analysis

Based on the above analysis and the reference to Gulay Gunluk-Senesen (2001) [7], we can design three sorts and five items of indexes to measure the defense expenditures in all-around views of point as possible as we can.

Indexes with regard to GDP:
  Index 1:

$$DEG = \frac{Defense\ Expenditures}{Gross\ Domestic\ Production}. \tag{1}$$

  Index 2:

$$DEAG = \frac{Defense\ Expenditures}{Adjusted\ Gross\ Domestic\ Production}. \tag{2}$$

AGDP infers Adjusted Gross Domestic Production. We define that:

$$AGDP = GDP - Living\ Cost. \tag{3}$$

For China,

$$Living\ Cost = Urban\ Population \times Urban\ Living\ Cost + Rural\ Population \times Rural\ Living\ Cost \tag{4}$$

Indexes with regard to Public Finance:
  Index 3:

$$DEP = \frac{Defense\ Expenditures}{Public\ Expenditures} \tag{5}$$

  Index 4:

$$DECG = \frac{Defense\ Expenditures}{Public\ Expenditures\ of\ Central\ Goverment} \tag{6}$$

Index with regard to Governmental Preference:
Index 5:

$$DEEHR = \frac{Defense \ Expenditures}{Public \ Expenditures \ in \ Education, Healthcare, R \& D} \tag{7}$$

DEG is a widely-used traditional index. A kind government pursues not only the strong defense but also the improvement of standard of people's living, therefore the rest of GDP minus the necessary demand of people's living is more appropriate for standing for the resources for defense.

We also analyze two indexes with public finance: one is the ratio of defense expenditures to public expenditures, and the other is the ratio of defense expenditures to central governmental expenditures. Because the governmental system is generally of multilevel and the defense is provided by the central government, the ratio of defense expenditures to central public expenditures is more suitable to reflect the defense spending from government.

The last but not the least, the ratio of defense expenditures to public expenditures in education and health care and R&D reflects the priority of government's objects.

We analyze China's defense spending from two points of view. One is the historical analysis in time series. The other is the comparison between China and other countries. The comparison between China and other countries is helpful to forecast the highest limits of China's defense expenditures, and the structural hinder to the rise of Chinese defense expenditures.

According to international politics and military relationship, we choose 8 nations as the objects compared with China, which are the U.S.A., the U.K., France, Germany, Russia, Japan, Korea and India.

2.3 Data

We studies the data of China from 1978-2009. There are two reasons for that. The first reason is that China has been focusing on economy growth since 1978. The second reason is that the peace has been lasting since 1978 on the whole in China, although armed conflicts broke out from 1978 to 1988 between China and Vietnam. That consistence of peace and economic development makes the ratios comparability.

3 Positive Analysis of China's Defense Expenditures

3.1 Indexes with Regard to GDP

Tendency of China
Having a close relationship with macro-economy, China's defense expenditures saw three periods. The first period is from1978 to 1996 when the defense expenditures continued falling until DEG reached the least level of 10.6% in 1996. The second period is from 1997 to 2002, this ratio began to rise. However, DEG in China has been falling again from 2003, yet still beyond the level of 1996. Thus, it is from 1997 that the real relative scale of defense activities expanded, not from 1989 when the absolute scale defense expenditures raised at the speed of morn than 10%. But this rising period is

very short, lasting only 6 years. Therefore, the opinion of China's Threat just focused on the rising of absolute scale defense expenditures, ignoring the declining of DEG and DEAG.

International Comparison
Limited by the availability of data, we can only calculate DEG of each nation.

From Fig.2, we can see even using the data of SIPRI, China's DEG isn't higher than other countries. Moreover, China's DEG varied similarly with other countries in the period of 1988-2008. The variation track is like "U". With the ending of the cold war, each nation's DEG declined rapidly. And from the end of 1990s, each nation's DEG has been rising. Because of the similarity between China and other nations, there isn't clear evidence to prove the view of China's Threat.

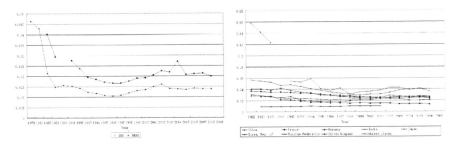

Data: Chinese Statistic Yearbook1980-2010.   Data: Database of World Bank and SIPRI

Fig. 1. China's DEG and DEAG   **Fig. 2.** Other Nations' DEG

3.2   Indexes with Regard to Public Finance

Tendency of China
China's DEP has been declining since 1980, from the level of 15% to 6.6%. The decrease reveals that more and more public financial revenue has been invested in other public goods than defense, which proves the argument that defense development must submit to economy development. China's DECG saw a "W" track. The "W" track resulted from not only the variation of defense expenditure but also the change of Chinese public finance systems in 1994. Before 1994, the revenue capability of the central government was quite poor, in other words, the ratio of central governmental revenue to the whole revenue was less than 50%. Thus DECG showed a increasing tendency. In 1994, a new tax sharing system put into use. As a result, the central government revenue has improved greatly since 1994, and has become much more than the local government revenue. Therefore, DECG fell down. But as the defense expenditures increased to a large extent from the end of 1990s, DECG started to rise again.

International Comparison
Due to the availability of data, we just compare the DECG internationally. We find there are two kinds of nation. One kind of nation has rather low level of DECG, such as Germany, France, and the U.K., whose DECG is about 4-7%. The other kind of

nation has high level of DECG, such as the U.S.A., China, India, Russia and Korea, whose DECG is higher than 10%. In the U.S.A., DECG is the highest at 19%. China, India and Russia rank after the U.S.A. with the level of 16-17%.The common reason for the low DECG of European nations lies in that the governments spend lots of public revenue on social security.

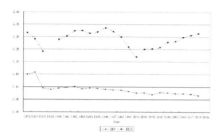

Data: Chinese Statistic Yearbook1980-2010.

Fig. 3. China's DEP and DECG

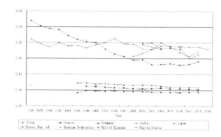

Data: Database of World Bank and SIPRI

Fig. 4. Other Nations' DECG

3.3   Index with Regard to Governmental Preference

Tendency of China
From 1978 to 2009, China's DEEGR continued falling, which means that its defense expenditures increased less than public expenditures in education, health care and research & development. Thus, we can confer that Chinese government pursues development of economy and society firstly, not of the military power.

International Comparison
Due to the availability of data, we only calculate the ratio of defense expenditures to public education and health care expenditures. That ratio in China and the U.S.A. are beyond 1, the other nations are less than 1 to a large extent, especially in Germany this ratio is just 10%, which means the Germany government pays more attention to public education and health care than other governments.

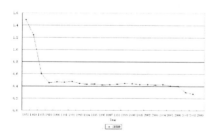

Data: Chinese Statistic Yearbook1980-2010.

Fig. 5. China's DEEHR

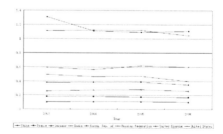

Data: Database of World Bank and SIPRI

Fig. 6. Other Nations' Governmental Preference

4 Conclusion and Policy Suggestion

We design a system of indexes to appraise the level of Chinese defense expenditures from various angles such as macro-economy, public finance and multi-objects of government. By the analysis of ratios comparison, we find that it is not wise to claim the level of Chinese defense expenditures was high or not. In fact, Chinese defense spending had double characteristic. From the view of macro-economy, China had a low level of defense expenditures, but from the view of the government's multi-objects, the defense sector had expended much public revenue. In the future, China will pay more attention to the social security, education, technology research and development. As a result, the increase of Chinese defense expenditures has to depend on the expansion of public finance. If the space of this expansion is baffled, then a great pressure to adjust the structure of defense expenditure will be brought about so as to improve the effective performance of military power.

Acknowledgments. This paper is sponsored by Chinese Postdoctoral Research Fund. The name of the project is Research on Defense Policy with China's Strategy of Peaceful Development.

References

1. Sun, X., Huang, C.: Study on Macro Adjust of Defense Expenditures. Military Economics Study 5, 3–8 (1997)
2. Wan, D.: The Appropriate Zone of Defense Expenditures. Military Economics Study 5, 28–33 (1998)
3. Liu, L.: Research on Effect of Surpport of Chinese Military Expenditures. Military Economics Study 6, 22–23 (2000)
4. Huang, R.: The Compensative Character of Chinese Military Expenditures Growth. Military Economics Study 11, 5–7 (2007)
5. Li, G.: Some Quantity Research on China's Defense Expenditures. Management Academic 11, 309–316 (2004)
6. Hao, W., Sun, Z.: Positive Research on Equilibrium and Causality of Chinese Defense Expenditures. In: Defense Economics of China, 2006, pp. 93–110. China Financial and Economy Publish House (2007)
7. Gunluk-Senesen, G.: Measuring the Extent of Defense Expenditures: the Turkish Case with Turkish Data. Defense and Peace Economics 12, 27–45 (2001)

Construction of Exact Traveling Wave for KP-Type Equation Based on Symbolic Computation

Qingfu Li[1,*] and Ruihua Cheng[2]

[1] School of mathematics and information science, Pingdingshan University,
Pingdingshan 467000, China
[2] Department of mathematics and information science,
Henan University of Finance and Law, Zhengzhou, 450002, China
wjm1261@sohu.com

Abstract. The (2+1)-dimensional KP-type equation arising from the soliton hierarchy associated with new spectral problem is studied, it is the compatible condition of Lax triad. With the aid of symbolic computation system Mathematica, theta function periodic solutions for the (2+1)-dimensional KP-type equation are constructed by the auxiliary equation method.

Keywords: Riemann-Theta function, the (2+1)-dimensional KP-type equation, auxiliary method.

1 Introduction

There are many mathematical models described by nonlinear partial differential Equation (NLPDE), especially some basic equations in physics and mechanics, To investigate the exact solutions for these NLPDE plays an important role in the study of nonlinear physical phenomena. In recent years, direct search for exact solutions to NLPDE has become more and more attractive partly due to the availability of computer symbolic systems like Maple or Mathematica which allows us to perform some complicated and tedious algebraic calculation on computer, and helps us to find new exact solutions to NLPDE, such as Homogeneous balance method[1], tanh-function method[2], sine-cosine method[3], Jacobi elliptic functions method[4], F-expansion method[5,6] and so on. In this paper, we apply auxiliary equation method [7] to seek exact theta function periodic solutions for (2+1)-dimensional KP-type equation:

$$\omega_t = \frac{3}{4}\partial_x^{-1}\omega_{yy} + \left(\frac{1}{16}\omega_{xx} - \frac{3}{2}\omega^2\right)_x . \tag{1}$$

By taking full advantages of elliptic equation:

$$F'(x) = A + BF^2(x) + CF^4(x) . \tag{2}$$

* This work has been supported by the Basic and advanced technology projects of Henan Province (No.102300410262) and the National Science Foundation of Henan Province (No.2010A110001).

S. Lin and X. Huang (Eds.): CESM 2011, Part I, CCIS 175, pp. 280–285, 2011.
© Springer-Verlag Berlin Heidelberg 2011

and get some traveling wave solutions in terms of theta functions with the aid of symbolic computation for the first time. The (2+1)-dimensional KP-type eqation (1) arises from the soliton hierarchy associated with spectral problem [8]:

$$\phi_x = U\phi, \ U = \begin{pmatrix} -\lambda + u & 2v \\ 2(\ln v + r_1)/v & \lambda - u \end{pmatrix}$$ (3)

where $\phi = (q, p)^T$, r_1 is constant.

This paper is arranged as follows. In section 2, we shall illustrate the auxiliary equation method; In section 3, we apply auxiliary method [12] to seek exact solutions of (2+1)-dimensional KP-type equation; Some conclusions are given in section 4.

2 Method of Solution

For the elliptic equation (2), the following fact is needed to realize the aim of this paper.

Proposition: If we take $C = -A = -\vartheta_2^2(0)\vartheta_4^2(0)$ and $B = \vartheta_2^2(0) - \vartheta_4^2(0)$, then $F(z) = \vartheta_1(0)/\vartheta_3(0)$ satisfies the elliptic equation (2), where theta functions are defined as following

$$\vartheta\begin{bmatrix}\varepsilon \\ c'\end{bmatrix}(z|\tau) = \sum_{n=-\infty}^{\infty} \exp\{\pi i \tau (n + \frac{\varepsilon}{2})^2 + 2(n + \frac{\varepsilon}{2})(z + \frac{\varepsilon'}{2})\}$$

$$\vartheta_i(z) \triangleq \vartheta_i(z|\tau) = \vartheta[\varepsilon_i](z|\tau),$$

$$\varepsilon_1 = \begin{bmatrix}1 \\ 1\end{bmatrix}, \varepsilon_2 = \begin{bmatrix}1 \\ 0\end{bmatrix}, \varepsilon_3 = \begin{bmatrix}0 \\ 0\end{bmatrix}, \varepsilon_4 = \begin{bmatrix}0 \\ 1\end{bmatrix}$$

$i = 1, 2, 3, 4$.

In the following, we seek traveling wave solution in the formal solution for the equation (1)

$$u(\xi) = a_0 + \sum_{i=1}^{N} a_i F^n(\xi) \quad (a_N \neq 0)$$ (4)

by taking

$$u(x_1; x_2; \cdots; x_l; t) = u(\xi),$$
$$\xi = x_1 + k_2 x_2 + \cdots + k_l x_l + \lambda_t.$$ (5)

where $k_1, k_2, \cdots, k_l, \lambda$ are constants to be determined, and a_i, A, B, C are constants to be determined, $F(\xi)$ satisfies elliptic equation (2).

Step 1: Inserting (4) into (1) yields an ODE for $u(\xi)$:

$$P(u; u'; u''; \cdots) = 0. \tag{6}$$

Step 2: Determine N by considering the homogeneous balance between the governing nonlinear term(s) and highest order derivatives of $u(\xi)$ in (6).

Step 3: Substituting (4) into (6), and using (2), and then the left-hand side of (6) can be converted into a finite series in $F^k(\xi)$ $(k = 0, 1, \cdots, M)$.

Step 4: Equating each coefficient of $F^k(\xi)$ to zero yields a system of algebraic equations for a_i $(i = 0, 1, \cdots, N)$.

Step 5: Solving the system of algebraic equations, with the aid of Mathematica or Maple, a_i, k_i, λ can be expressed by A, B, C (or the coefficients of ODE (6)).

Step 6: Substituting these results into (4), we can obtain the general form of travelling wave solutions for equation (1).

Step 7: From propositon, we can give theta function periodic solutions for equation (1).

3 Exact Solutions

In this section, we will make use of the auxiliary equation method and symbolic computation to find the exact solutions to the (2+1)-dimensional KP-type equation.

We assume that (1) has travelling wave solution in the form

$$u(x; y; t) = u(\xi), \xi = \alpha x + \beta y + \omega t. \tag{7}$$

Substituting (7) into (1), then (1) is transformed into the following form:

$$\left(\frac{3}{4}\beta^2 - \alpha\omega\right)U'(\xi) + \frac{\alpha^4}{16}U'''(\xi) - 3\alpha^2 U(\xi)U'(\xi) = 0 \tag{8}$$

According to step 2 in section 2, by balancing $U'''(\xi)$ and $U(\xi)U'(\xi)$ in (8), we obtain $n = 2$, and suppose that Eq. (8) has the following solutions:

$$U(\xi) = a_0 + a_1 F(\xi) + a_2 F^2(\xi), \tag{9}$$

Substituting (9) along with Eq. (2) into (8) yields a polynomial equation in $F(\xi)$. Setting their coefficients to zero yields a set of algebraic equations for unknown parameters a_0, a_1, a_2, ω. Solving these equations, we can get the following solutions:

$$a_1 = 0, \quad a_2 = \frac{\alpha}{4}C, \quad \omega = (3\beta^2 - 12\alpha^2 a_0 + a^3 B)/4\alpha. \tag{10}$$

and a_0, A, B, C are arbitrary constants.

The traveling wave solution of the KP-type equation are given by

$$U(\xi) = a_0 + \frac{\alpha C}{4}F^2(\xi),$$

where $\xi = \alpha x + \beta y + \omega t$, A, B, C, α, β are arbitrary constants, and a_2, ω are given in (10).

From the proposition, if we choose $C = -A = -\vartheta_2^2(0)\vartheta_4^2(0)$ and $B = \vartheta_2^2(0)$ $-\vartheta_4^2(0)$, we can get the solution to the KP-type equation in terms of theta functions:

$$u(x, y, t) = a_0 + \frac{\alpha C}{4}\frac{\vartheta_1^2(\xi)}{\vartheta_3^2(\xi)}, \tag{11}$$

where, A, B, C, α, β are arbitrary constants, and a_2, ω are given in (10).

To grasp the characteriste of solutions of (1), we dipict the figure of the solution $u(x, y, t)$ by using the mathematica, their properties and profiles are displayed in figures (1)-(4) under chosen parameters:

$a = 3, c = d = 1$, $\alpha = 1, \beta = 8, \gamma = 0$, $C = -1$ and $t = 2$ for 2D figure (3), $x = 2$ for 2D figure (4).

From figures (1)-(4), it is easy to see that the solution $u(x, y, t)$ is periodic wave solution.

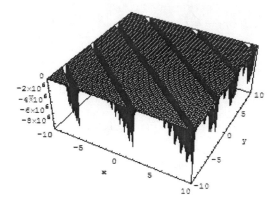

Fig. 1. Perspective view of the wave $u(x, y, t)$

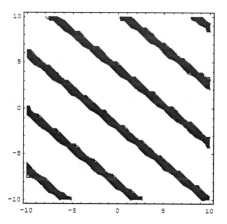

Fig. 2. Overhead view of the wave $u(x, y, t)$

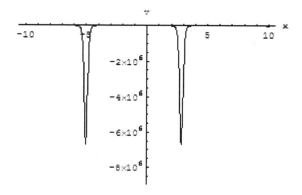

Fig. 3. The propogation of the wave along x -axis

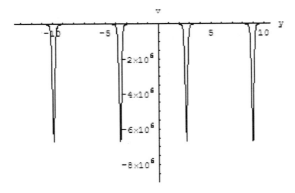

Fig. 4. The propogation of the wave along y -axis

4 Conclusions

In this paper, we have studied the KP-type equation. By using auxiliary equation method, some traveling wave solutions in terms of theta functions are successfully obtained with the aid of symbolic computation for the first time, they should be meaningful to explain some physics phenomena. It is shown that the auxiliary equation method is a very effective and powerful mathematical tool for solving nonlinear evolution equations in mathematics and physics. Moreover, with the aid of computer symbolic systems (Mathematica or Maple), the method can be conveniently operated.

References

1. Wang, M.L., Zhou, Y.B., Li, Z.B.: Application of a homogeneous balance method to exact solutions of nonlinear equations in mathematical physics. Phys. Lett. A. 216, 67–75 (1996)
2. Fan, E.G.: Extended tanh-function method and its applications to nonlinear equations. Phys. Lett. A. 277, 212–218 (2000)
3. Yan, C.T.: A simple transformation for nonlinear waves. J. China Uni.of Sci.and Tech. 224, 77–84 (1996)
4. Fu, Z.T., Liu, S.D., Liu, S.K., Zhao, Q.: New exact solutions to KdV equations with variable coefficients or forcing. Applied Mathematics and Mechanics 25, 73–79 (2004)
5. Liu, J.B., Yang, K.Q.: The extended F-expansion method and exact solutions of nonlinear PDEs. Chaos, Solitons and Fractals 22, 111–121 (2004)
6. Yomba, E.: The extended F-expansion method and its application for solving the nonlinear wave, CKGZ,GDS, DS and GZ equations. Phys. Lett. A. 340, 149–160 (2005)
7. Cai, G.L., Wang, Q.C., Huang, J.J.: A Modified Fexpansion Method for Solving Breaking Soliton Equation. International Journal of Nonlinear Science 2, 122–128 (2006)
8. Cao, C.W., Geng, X.G.: C Neumann and Bargmann systems associated with the coupled KdV soliton hierarchy. Journal of Physics A: Math. and Gen. 23, 4117–4125 (1990)

Comparison and Application of Time-Frequency Analysis Methods for Nonstationary Signal Processing

Qiang Zhu, Yansong Wang, and Gongqi Shen

College of Automotive Engineering, Shanghai University of Engineering Science,
Shanghai, 201620, China

Abstract. Most of signals in engineering are nonstationary and time-varying. The Fourier transform as a traditional approach can only provide the feature information in frequency domain. The time-frequency techniques may give a comprehensive description of signals in time-frequency planes. Based on some typical nonstationary signals, five time-frequency analysis methods, i.e., the short-time Fourier transform (STFT), wavelet transform (WT), Wigner-Ville distribution (WVD), pseudo-WVD (PWVD) and the Hilbert-Huang transform (HHT), were performed and compared in this paper. The characteristics of each method were obtained and discussed. Compared with the other methods, the HHT with a high time-frequency resolution can clearly describe the rules of the frequency compositions changing with time, is a good approach for feature extraction in nonstationary signal processing.

Keywords: Nonstationary signal, Short-time Fourier transform, Wavelet transform, Wigner-Ville distribution, Hilbert-Huang transform.

1 Introduction

Many signals in engineering are time-varying. And the frequency features of the signals are very important and can usually be used to distinguish one signal from the others. The Fourier transform and its inversion play important roles in establishment of the relationship between time and frequency domains. They are defined as follows:

$$X(f) = \int x(t)e^{-j2\pi ft} dt \tag{1}$$

$$x(t) = \int X(f)e^{j2\pi ft} df \tag{2}$$

Based on the Fourier transform, the description and energy distribution of a signal in frequency domain can only reflect its frequency features. As the Fourier transform and its inversion are global transform, the signals can only be described entirely in time domain or frequency domain. In practical applications, the Fourier transform is not the best tool, due to most of signals encountered in engineering are nonstationary and time varying, such as the signals of engine noises and vibrations. In order to study the

S. Lin and X. Huang (Eds.): CESM 2011, Part I, CCIS 175, pp. 286–291, 2011.

nonstationary signals, the time-frequency techniques are introduced. Figure 1 shows three descriptions of a chirp signal: (a) is the description in time domain which loses the frequency information, (b) is the description in frequency domain which loses the time information, and (c) is the time-frequency representation which shows the signal energy flowing in a time and frequency plane.

The basic idea of time-frequency analysis is to design a joint function, which can describe the characteristics of signals on a time-frequency plane [1]. Studies of the time-frequency analysis have become an important research field; and many time-frequency representation methods are presented. In this paper, five time-frequency techniques, i.e., the short-time Fourier transform (STFT), wavelet transform (WT), Wigner-Ville distribution (WVD), pseudo-WVD (PWVD) and Hilbert-Huang transform (HHT) are investigated and compared.

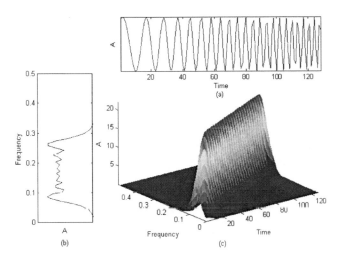

Fig. 1. Three description methods of a chirp signal in (a) time, (b) frequency and (c) time-frequency domains

2 Theory Background

2.1 Short-Time Fourier Transform

The short-time Fourier transform (STFT) presented by Gabor in 1946 is to intercept the signals by using a window function. The section in the window which can be regarded as stationary signal is processed by the Fourier transform to find its frequency components. The entire frequency information over time can be obtained by moving the window function along the time axis [2]. The STFT of a signal $x(t)$ can be described as:

$$STFT_x(t,f) = \int_{-\infty}^{+\infty} x(\tau)g^*(\tau-t)e^{-j2\pi f\tau}d\tau. \tag{3}$$

2.2 Wavelet Transform

In 1980s, the wavelet transform (WT) was developed by Morlet and Grossmam, et al. In recent years, the WT has become a very popular method and is introduced into the analysis of sound and vibration signals in engineering. Due to the high efficiency and superiority in multiresolution analysis of the WT, the analyzed signals can be observed from coarse to fine [3]. The WT of the signal $x(t)$ can be described as:

$$WT_x(a,b) = \int_{-\infty}^{+\infty} x(t)\varphi_{a,b}^*(t)dt = \frac{1}{\sqrt{a}}\int x(t)\varphi^*(\frac{t-b}{a})dt \quad . \tag{4}$$

2.3 Wigner-Ville Distribution

The Wigner-Ville distribution (WVD) was presented by Wigner in the research of quantum mechanics in 1932 and applied to signal processing by Ville later. The WVD of the signal $x(t)$ can be described as:

$$WVD_x(t,f) = \int_{-\infty}^{+\infty} x(t+\tau/2)x^*(t-\tau/2)e^{-j2\pi f\tau}d\tau \quad . \tag{5}$$

If the signal has two components x_1 and x_2, the WVD can be expressed as:

$$WVD_x(t,f) = WVD_{11}(t,f) + WVD_{22}(t,f) + WVD_{21}(t,f) + WVD_{12}(t,f) \quad . \tag{6}$$

Here $WVD_{11}(t,f)$ and $WVD_{22}(t,f)$ are self terms of the WVD, while $WVD_{12}(t,f)$ and $WVD_{21}(t,f)$ are cross terms. The cross terms are involved due to that the WVD belongs to quadratic analysis. To suppress influences of the cross terms, the pseudo-WVD (PWVD) as an equivalent smoothed WVD was developed. The PWVD of $x(t)$ can be expressed as:

$$PWVD_x(t,f) = \int_{-\infty}^{+\infty} h(\tau)x(t+\tau/2)x^*(t+\tau/2)e^{-j2\pi f\tau}d\tau \quad . \tag{7}$$

2.4 Hilbert-Huang Transform

A new time-frequency analysis method called Hilbert-Huang transform (HHT) was presented by Norden E. Huang et al in 1998. The HHT contains two important parts: empirical mode decomposition (EMD) and Hilbert transform. First, the EMD is used to obtain the intrinsic mode function (IMF). Then Hilbert transform may be applied to obtain a three-dimensional (time-frequency-amplitude) distribution, i.e., the Hilbert spectrum of the signals. A great contribution of HHT is that it can obtain the instantaneous frequency feature of the nonstationary signals from the Hilbert spectra [4, 5]. Essentially, the EMD is used for smoothing the nonstationary signals and decomposing them into a set of data sequences with different scale characteristics, i.e., IMFs. The target signal $x(t)$ can be expressed as the sum of IMF c_i (i=1,2,3,...,n) and the residue component r_n after the EMD. i.e.,

$$x(t) = \sum_{i=1}^{n} c_i + r_n \quad . \tag{8}$$

Imposing Hilbert transform on each IMF component, the Hilbert spectrum of $x(t)$ can be obtained by taking the real part of the sum of the Hilbert transform results. Thus, the instantaneous frequency representation of the signal is,

$$x(t,f) = \text{Re} \sum_{i=1}^{n} a_i(t)e^{j\theta_i(t)} = \text{Re} \sum_{i=1}^{n} a_i(t)e^{j\int f_i(t)dt} \qquad (9)$$

In the expression (9), r_n is ignored; Re denotes the real part of the complex signals.

3 Simulation and Comparison of Time-Frequency Analysis

To compare the characteristics of the above mentioned time-frequency methods, a typical nonstationary signal $x(t)$ is designed as that in equation (10). Note that the $x(t)$ is a multi-component signal constituted with a cosine component (frequency: 50Hz), a linear frequency modulation component (fundamental frequency: 200Hz) and a sine frequency modulation component (fundamental frequency: 100Hz, modulation frequency: 15Hz). The $x(t)$ in time domain and its frequency spectrum are showed in Figures 2 and 3, respectively.

$$x(t) = 1.5\cos 100\pi t + 2\sin(400\pi t + 100\pi t^2) + \cos(200\pi t + \sin 30\pi t) \qquad (10)$$

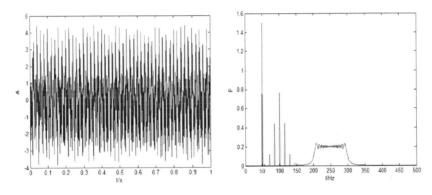

Fig. 2. The designed signal $x(t)$ **Fig. 3.** Frequency spectrum of $x(t)$

The STFT, WT, WVD and PWVD are performed to analyze the nonstationary signal $x(t)$, and the time-frequency maps are shown in Figure 4. It can be seen that, the STFT can recognize the linear frequency component and the cosine component, but the time and frequency resolutions are low. The WT with multiresolution characteristic can improve the resolutions; it has a good frequency resolution in the low frequency region and a good time resolution in the high frequency region. However, the STFT and WT can't exactly recognize the sine frequency modulation component. In contrast, the WVD has higher resolution and can describe the sine frequency modulation, but there are a lot of cross terms appeared in the distribution. The useful informations in the distribution are disturbed seriously by the cross terms. Although the PWVD can suppress the cross terms to a certain extent, it can not eliminate the cross term completely. Meanwhile, the PWVD reduces the resolution and disrupts many mathematical properties in WVD.

Compared with the STFT, WT, WVD and PWVD methods, the HHT which has adaptive characteristic is based on the signal itself. As shown in Figure 5, the signal x(t) was decomposed into five IMF components and one residue component by the EMD. As the EMD decomposes signal from high frequency, the c_1, c_2 and c_3 represent the linear frequency modulation, sine frequency modulation and cosine components, respectively. The c_4 and c_5 are trend terms, and r_5 represents the residue component.

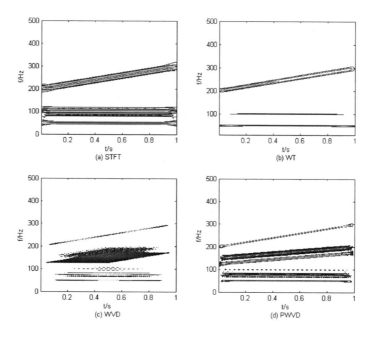

Fig. 4. Comparison of time-frequency analysises of the signal $x(t)$

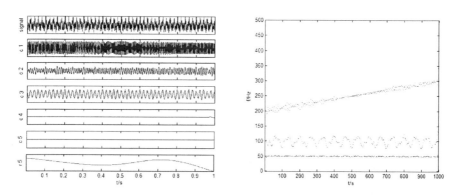

Fig. 5. The EMD of $x(t)$ **Fig. 6.** Hilbert time-frequency spectrum

The Hilbert time-frequency spectrum of $x(t)$ shown in Figure 6 can be obtained by performing Hilbert transform to the IMF components, following equation (9). Compared with the time-frequency maps in Figure 4, the Hilbert time-frequency spectrum with good time-frequency resolution can reflect all frequency components of the signal $x(t)$ and give a clear rule of these components changing with time axis. Thus, in the view of applications, the HHT may be a better method for time-frequency analysis of nonstationary signals.

4 Conclusions

In this paper, five time-frequency analysis methods, i.e., the STFT, WT, WVD, PWVD and HHT, were compared and discussed in nonstationary signal processing. The advantages and shortcomings of each method were investigated. Among the five methods in discussion, the HHT which has adaptive characteristic can exactly express the local information of nonstationary signals in a high time-frequency resolution. It overcomes the irreconcilable contradiction between the time-frequency aggregation and cross term. A conclusion can be drawn that, since the HHT can exactly reflect instantaneous frequency components, it is quite suitable for nonstationary signal analysis in engineering.

Acknowledgments

This work was supported by the NSFC (grant no. 51045007), the Program for Professor of Special Appointment (Eastern Scholar) at Shanghai Institutions of Higher Learning, and partly supported by graduate student scientific innovation project of SUES (grant no. A-0530-10-15).

References

1. Zhang, X.: The analysis and processing of nonlinear signals. National Defence Industry Press, Beijing (1998)
2. Hu, G.: Modern signal processing course. Tsinghua University Press, Beijing (2004)
3. Mallat, S.: A Theory for Multi-Resolution Signal Decomposition Wavelet Representation. IEEE Trans. on Pattern Analysis and Machine Intell. 11(7), 674–693 (1989)
4. Huang, N.E., Shen, Z.: The empirical mode decomposition and the hilbert spectrum for non-linear non-stationary time series analysis. Proc. R. Soc., London (1998)
5. Huang, N.E.: A new view of nonlinear waves: the hilbert spectrum. Annual Review of Fluid Mechanics 31(5), 417–457 (1999)

Design of Adaptive Filter Based on Matlab and Simulink

YanPing He[1] and HaiDong Zhang[2]

[1] School of Electrician Engineering, Northwest University for Nationalities
[2] School of Mathematics and Computer Science, Northwest University for Nationalities,
730030, Lanzhou Gansu, P.R. China
he_yanping@126.com, lingdianstar@163.com

Abstract. The paper introduces the principle and structure of adaptive filter based on least mean square algorithm, studies a design scheme of a single frequency adaptive notch filter, and simulates its working procedure by Matlab programming and Simulink modeling. The simulation results show that the adaptive notch filters by two methods have filtered noise from noise added signal in the appropriate parameter.

Keywords: LMS Algorithm, Matlab Simulation, Simulink Simulation, Adaptive Notch Filter.

1 Introduction

Adaptive filter has an extremely important position in the field of signal processing, and has been used widely in communication, radar, navigation system and industrial control, etc. We can not achieve optimal filtering signal with a fixed coefficient filter in some occasions of unpredictable signal and noise characteristics, and have only a solution that is to introduce adaptive filter [1]. Matlab language has some incomparable advantages with other high-level languages, such as writing simple, programming with high efficiency, easy to learn understand, etc. Simulink is one of Matlab toolkits, whose modeling is the more intuitive and simple than general program modeling. We don't have to remember usage of all kinds of commands and parameters, and can complete very complicated work with the mouse [2]. In this paper ,we will carry out quickly and efficiently adaptive filter analysis, design and simulation in Matlab and Simulink, change parameters at any time in the design in order to achieve optimization filter, and observe and compare the filters of two methods design.

2 The Principle of Adaptive Filter Based on LMS Algorithm

The difference of adaptive filter and ordinary filter is that it can dynamically change parameters varying with outside signal characteristics, and maintain optimal filtering state. How to adjust parameters according to the change of outside signal is decided by adaptive algorithm. So adaptive algorithm will influence directly on filtering effect [3]. LMS(Least Mean Square) algorithm is a kind of fast search algorithm of using gradient

S. Lin and X. Huang (Eds.): CESM 2011, Part I, CCIS 175, pp. 292–297, 2011.

estimate instead of gradient vector, and has been widely used in many electronic systems because of simple structure, stable performance, small calculated amount and easy realization, etc [4]. The basic idea of LMS algorithm is that it makes mean-square error be minimum between the output signal of filter and desired signal by adjusting the weights parameters of filter.

Adaptive filtering usually includes two basic processes: filtering process and the parameters adjustment process of filter that are composed of a feedback loop, as shown in Fig. 1 [5], where $X(n)$ are N filtered input signal and can be expressed as follows:

$$X(n) = [x_1(n), x_2(n), \cdots, x_N(n)]^T . \tag{1}$$

$W(n)$ are N filter weights and can be expressed as follows:

$$W(n) = [w_1(n), w_2(n), \cdots, w_N(n)]^T . \tag{2}$$

$y(n)$ is filtered output signal, $d(n)$ is reference signal, and $e(n)$ is error signal between $y(n)$ and $d(n)$. Error signal $e(n)$ controls adaptive filter coefficients.

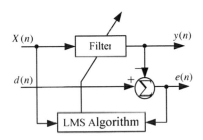

Fig. 1. The principle diagram of adaptive filter based on LMS algorithm

Then filtered output signal can be written as follows:

$$y(n) = \sum_{i=1}^{N} w_i(n)x_i(n) = X^T(n)W(n) . \tag{3}$$

and estimate error signal can be written as follows:

$$e(n) = d(n) - y(n) = d(n) - X^T(n)W(n) . \tag{4}$$

According to the rule of least mean-square error, the parameters of optimal filter should make performance function—mean-square error $E[e^2(n)]$ be minimum. Because the following equation hold that

$$E[e^2(n)] = E[(d(n) - y(n))^2] = E[(d(n) - X^T(n)W(n))^2] \tag{5}$$

which is the quadratic equation of weight coefficient $W(n)$ and has only a minimum, we can use the steepest gradient method to repeatedly search least mean-square error $E_{\min}[e^2(n)]$ corresponding optimal weights. At this time, we can obtain the iterative equation of weights:

$$W(n+1) = W(n) - \alpha \cdot e(n) \cdot X(n). \tag{6}$$

where α is a parameter of controlling stability and convergence rate, called step factor. Equation (6) is called LMS algorithm. The smaller α value makes convergence rate the slower, and the bigger α value leads to divergence.

Definitions of input signal, output signal and reference signal are determined by specific application requirements when we use filter based on LMS algorithm as shown in Fig.1. Adaptive notch filter can carry out notch to input signal by adopting the above adaptive algorithm and filter single frequency signal from input signal. We will regard input signal $x(n)$ that is a single-frequency signal as local reference signal for single-frequency adaptive notch filter in Fig.1, and regard desired signal as input signal. Task of adaptive notch filter is to filter single frequency signal from input signal. Filter weights can be reduced to two because reference signal has only single-frequency component. So one weight is in-phase component, and another is orthogonal component. We give the principle diagram of adaptive filter as shown in Fig.2.

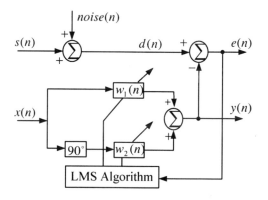

Fig. 2. The principle diagram of adaptive notch filter

3   The Simulation of Adaptive Notch Filter in Matlab and Simulink

In the simulation experiment, assume that input signal is composed of speech signal and gaussian noise, we take desired signal as input signal according to Fig.1, e.g. $d(n) = s(n) + noise(n)$, where $s(n) = A \cdot \sin(2\pi f_s t + \theta_0)$, A is signal amplitude, θ_0 is initial phase, and f_s is frequency of single frequency signal; $noise(n) = B\sin(2\pi f_n t)$, B is noise signal amplitude. Let $s(n)$ frequency $f_s = 2Hz$, $A = 10$, $\theta_0 = 0$, $noise(n)$ frequency $f_n = 50Hz$, and $B = 3$. Assume that reference signal $x(n) = \sin(100\pi ft)$, we can filter noise signal *noise(n)* from input signal by adaptive notch filter.

In Fig.2, we make output signal $y(n)$ approximate $d(n)$ in least mean square error by adjusting adaptively filter weights w_1 and w_2. At this time, error signal $e(n)$ is output signal of adaptive notch filter.

(1) The simulation of adaptive notch filter in Matlab

```
%main
...
s=10*sin(4*pi*t)+3*sin(100*pi*t);
...
x1= sin(100*pi*t);
x2= sin(100*pi*t+pi/2);
...
for k=1:50
    y(k)= w1(k)*x1(k)+ w2(k)*x2(k);
e(k)=s(k)-y(k);
w1(k+1)=w1(k)+2*0.1*e(k)*x1(k);
w2(k+1)=w2(k)+2*0.1*e(k)*x2(k);
end
...
```

(2) The simulation of adaptive notch filter in Simulink

We can establish the corresponding Simulink simulation model according to the principle diagram of adaptive notch filter of Fig.2, as shown in Fig. 3.

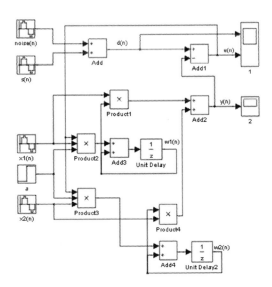

Fig. 3. The simulation model of adaptive notch filter based on LMS algorithm

In Fig.3, $x_1(n)$ is in-phase signal of $x(n)$, $x_2(n)$ is signal of phase shifting $90°$, and a is α in the equation (6). We suppose that $a = 0.1$ in the experiment. Because reference signal is a single frequency signal, the number of filter weights can be simplified to two. At this time, the iterative equation of equation (6) weights can be rewritten as follows:

$$w_1(n+1) = w_1(n) + a \cdot x_1(n) \cdot e(n)$$
$$w_2(n+1) = w_2(n) + a \cdot x_2(n) \cdot e(n) \qquad (7)$$

So we can obtain output signal and error signal. That is, the following equations hold that

$$y(n) = w_1(n) \cdot x_1(n) + w_2(n) \cdot x_2(n). \qquad (8)$$

$$e(n) = d(n) - y(n). \qquad (9)$$

4 Simulation Results

We know that adaptive notch filter based on LMS algorithm can filter very well noise from noise added sinusoidal signal by setting proper parameter a whether using Matlab language programming to realize or using Simulink direct modeling to realize. Further, we can observe a influence on filter performance by choosing different a values in the model.

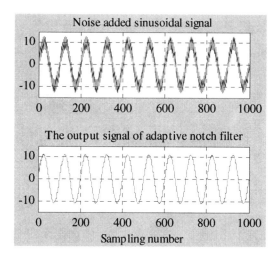

Fig. 4. The simulation results in Matlab

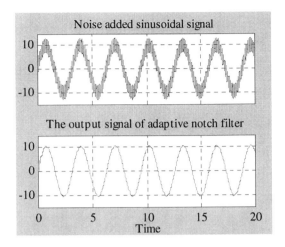

Fig. 5. The simulation results in Simulink

5 Summary

We design a kind of simulation scheme of adaptive notch filter by introducing how to use Matlab tool software to simulate adaptive algorithm. Simulation results show that adaptive notch filter designed by Matlab language programming and Simulink modeling has very good effect and performance. We can verify the correctness of Simulink modeling by Matlab language programming. Because Simulink modeling is the more intuitive and simple than Matlab programming, we don't have to remember usage of all kinds of commands and parameters, can complete very complicated work with the mouse, and modify parameters easily.

References

1. Chen, L., Li, Y., Yao, S.: Design of Adaptive Filter Based on LMS Algorithm in Matlab. Journal of North China Institute of Water Conservancy and Hydroelectric Power 29, 51–53 (2008)
2. Zhang, D.: MATLAB Communication Engineering Simulation. China Machine Press, Beijing (2010)
3. Xianda, Z.: Modern Signal Processing. Tsinghua University Press, Beijing (2002)
4. Zou, Y., Gao, Y.: Adaptive filter algorithm overview. Journal of Guangzhou University 1, 44–48 (2007)
5. Zhao, Z., Liu, S.: Digital Signal Processing Experiment. Zhejiang University Press, Hangzhou (2007)
6. Yubin, S.: MATLAB/Simulink Communication Systems Modeling and Simulation Case Analyse. Tsinghua University Press, Beijing (2008)
7. Changxin, F.: Communication Principles. Publishing House of Electronic Industry, Beijing (2007)

Research on an Improved Method for Maximum Power Point Tracking of Photovoltaic

Bin Wang[1,2], Chunfu Gao[2], Xinsheng He[2], and Zhiyong Luo[1,2]

[1] School of Mechanical and Electronics Engineering, Lanzhou Jiaotong University
730070 Lanzhou, China
[2] College of Engineering, Zhe Jiang Normal University
321004 Jinhua, China
{computerwangbin,onliday}@163.com,
{cfgao2007,xsh}@zjnu.cn

Abstract. In order to improve the efficiency of photovoltaic, it is necessary to track the maximum power point(MPP) all the time. After studying various algorithms, a new algorithm was presented based on online short-circuit current, open-circuit voltage, and variable step of perturbation and observation method. This algorithm could track MPP change rapidly and accurately without the disturbance of photovoltaic system, and also can reduce the power oscillation around MPP and the light mutation of the false judgement phenomenon. The simulation results show that the algorithm has a good dynamic and steady-state performance.

Keywords: MPPT, short-circuit current, open-circuit voltage, perturbation and observation method, variable step.

1 Introduction

The output of photovoltaic (PV) has obvious characteristics of non-linear, which is effected by the external environment. In order to make the power output of PV maximize, the output of PV requires the maximum power point tracking (MPPT). There are many techniques that have been proposed for tracking the MPP of PV: open-circuit voltage method, short-circuit current method, perturbation and observation (P&O) method, incremental conductance (INC) method, and fuzzy control method [1]. Open-circuit voltage and short-circuit current method offer a simple and low-priced way to acquire the maximum power. Nevertheless, they have a larger steady-state error and low energy conversion efficiency. P&O method is widely applied in the MPPT controller due to its simplicity and easy implementation, but its accuracy in steady-state is low and when the insolation is changed rapidly, the P&O method probably failed to track MPP. INC method has the advantage of fast tracking and dynamic stability, but which is difficult to determine the appropriate steps. Fuzzy control method does not need to study the specific characteristics of PV, but determining the shape of membership functions needs more experienced designers [2]. According to the characteristics of PV and various control algorithms, a new MPPT

S. Lin and X. Huang (Eds.): CESM 2011, Part I, CCIS 175, pp. 298–304, 2011.

control algorithm was proposed. Through the simulation experiments, the results show that the algorithm has good dynamic and steady-state performance.

2 Tracking Principle of PV MPP

Maximum power point tracking is a self-optimizing process, namely, by controlling the PV terminal voltage U, the battery under a variety of sunlight and temperature conditions can intelligently output maximum power, which is the MPPT principle of PV. Output power of PV are greatly influenced by the external environment, ambient temperature, sunlight intensity, and output voltage. The relationship of PV output current and voltage [4] are:

$$I = I_s - I_0 \left\{ \exp(\frac{qU}{AkT}) - 1 \right\} .$$

(1)

I ,U is output current and voltage of PV cell respectively; I_s is short-current under the condition of 25℃ and 1000w/m^2;I_0 is reverse saturation current of PV; T is the temperature of PV;k is Boltzmann's constant (k=1.38×10^{23}J/K);q is electronic charge (q =1.6×10-19C); A is diode characteristic factors (T=300K, A is approximately equal to 2.8).

Figure. 1 shows the output power characteristics of P-U curve [5]. P-U curve is a single convex curve. When the cell voltage is less than the maximum power point Umax, the output power increases with the increasing U; when the operating voltage is greater than the maximum power point voltage Umax, the output power decreases with the increaseing U.

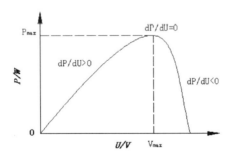

Fig. 1. PV output power characteristics of P-U curve

3 Improved MPPT Control Strategy

Traditional P&O method is a commonly method in the MPP tracking.The thought of controlling algorithm is: measuring the current power output of photovoltaic cells P1, then at the initial output voltage U adding a small Δu , the output power will be changed to P_2, comparing P_2 with P_1. If the power increases, it will continue to use the initial disturbance. If the power is reduced, it will change the direction of the initial disturbance. This method is simple and easy to be implemented, but there will be oscillation around MPP, resulting in a energy loss, and the tracking accuracy and speed of response could not be taken into account [1]. To solve the above problems, this paper proposes an improved algorithm.

3.1 The Basic Ideas of Improvement

Figure 1 shows that dP/dU curve has the following characteristics.

$$\frac{dP}{dU} > 0, \quad left \ of \ MPPT,$$

$$\frac{dP}{dU} = 0, \quad at \ MPPT, \tag{2}$$

$$\frac{dP}{dU} < 0, \quad right \ of \ MPPT.$$

Therefore, tracking algorithms could be divided into three sections. On the left of the MPP short-circuit current method is used, around MPP variable step P&O method is used, and on the right of the MPP open-circuit voltage method is used. The test steps are followed as below:

(1) Detection of short-circuit current

Figure 2 shows the whole process of the search algorithm. It could be seen from the figure dP/du decreases monotonically with the PV cells output voltage increasing. The curve of photovoltaic cells is in the short circuit condition at A point, the battery output current is zero, dP/du is equal to the battery's short circuit current. With the increase of output voltage, dP/du value is slowly declined which could be seen that the value is approximately equal to the short-circuit current in the AB Interval [6].

As the I_{mpp} and I_s have a approximate linear relationship, therefore, the output power of PV under the method can not reach the MPP and only work around the MPP. By this design, the algorithm could accelerate initial speed and rapidly approaching MPP.

(2) Variable step P&O method-- gradual approximation search

The tracking algorithm could be realized by variable step P&O method around MPP which is carried out by the idea of gradual approximation step search [7].The algorithm has a high precision and small fluctuations in a steady state. First, a larger step is used to search in the region where the maximum power is and then go on to search by narrowing it to half step, by this moment, searching area will be reduced to the half and the precision will be doubled till to the MPP.

(3) Detection of open-circuit voltage

It could be seen from the figure.2, dP/di increases monotonically with the PV output current increasing. The curve of PV is in a open state at D point , the battery output current is zero, dP/di is equal to the absolute value of the battery's open circuit voltage. With the battery output current increasing, dP/di value is slowly rises which could be seen that the value is approximately equal to the open circuit voltage in the DC Interval [8].

Open-circuit voltage method could make the right of MPP rapidly return to the MPP. As it is an approximate point, which can only work around MPP.

Based on the above analysis, when the system is worked on the left of MPP (AB section), short-circuit current method could be used to control, when worked around MPP(BC section), variable step P&O method could be used, searching the step by the idea of gradual approximation, when worked on the right of MPP(CD section), open-circuit voltage method could be used to control. In the AB and CD section, dP/du and dP/di are respectively constant which are approximately equal to the short circuit current and open circuit voltage, only around MPP the two values will be significantly changed. With the short circuit current and open circuit voltage, the far away point from the left and right could be made soon to return to the MPP. Thus the interfering with the system under the normal operation by the traditional short-circuit current method and open-circuit voltage method is avoided.

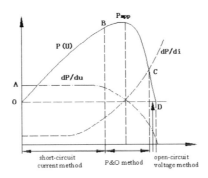

Fig. 2. The whole process of the search improved algorithm

3.2 Algorithm Flow

Flow chart of the improved algorithm is shown in Figure 3.

Specific process: (1) Calculate the output power of PV at time t and compare it to the time t-1, judging whether the system is working in the current source or voltage source mode;(2) If the system is working in current source mode, then it can be calculated that $I_t = dP_t/dU_t$ at time t and $I_{t-1} = dP_{t-1}/dU_{t-1}$ at time t-1 by output voltage and current, then compared to I_t and I_{t-1}. If the absolute difference between the two is less than ε (ε is a very small value), thus I_t could be realized that is equal to short circuit current; (3) If $U_t = dP_t/dI_t$ at time t and $U_{t-1} = dP_{t-1}/dI_{t-1}$ at time t-1 of the absolute difference value less than ε, thus U_t can be as a open circuit voltage;(4) If neither in the short-circuit current nor open circuit voltage state, it could be infered that the system works around MPP. MPPT controlling method is achieved by the variable step P&O method which is adopted the ideal of gradual approximation method. Assumed that the system operating point is at the left of MPP, step will be Δu to search. Where m and n are expressed dP/dU direction, m means the last direction, n means this direction, then compare the P_{t-1} and P_t, until up to $P_{t+1}<P_t$. At this time, the operating point is at the right of MPP, it should be changed the search direction, then reduced to $\Delta u/2$, the precision will be doubled, and continue to search until the search direction changed secondly. Then continue to reduce the step to $\Delta u/4$, the precision will be doubled again. And so on, until the MPP is searched. Using this variable step P&O method is the mainly control target of stability around MPP. The perturbation step size is selected by the requirements of MPP stability. As the step is much smaller than the traditional P&O method, therefore, the system can effectively eliminate oscillation at steady-state around MPP.

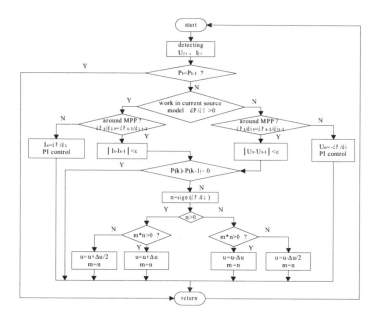

Fig. 3. Improved Algorithm flow chart

4 Simulation Experiment

A block diagram of the main circuit system is shown in Fig. 4. Controlling algorithm of the entire system is achieved by the MCU. The system is consisted by photovoltaic modules, DC-DC converter and load.

Photovoltaic modules will adopt solar panels,its parameters: open-circuit voltage U_{oc} = 21.0 V; short-circuit current I_s = 0.33A; maximum power corresponding to the output voltage U_{mpp} = 17.0 V; maximum power corresponding to the output current I_{mpp} = 0.29A; the maximum output power P_m= 5.0W.Then according to the PV output voltage, temperature, illumination intensity, short-circuit current and open circuit voltage temperature coefficient calculate the output current. The traditional P&O

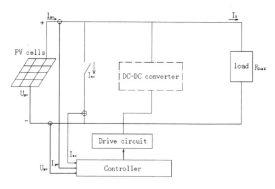

Fig. 4. The main circuit diagram of the system

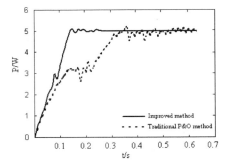
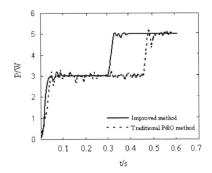

Fig. 5. Comparison of two algorithms for output power

Fig. 6. Light mutation of two algorithm for output power

method and improved method was simulated to verify the validity of the algorithm. The curves of obtaining the PV output power are shown in Figure.5 and Figure.6. Figure.5 shows the output power between traditional P&O method and improved method at 1000W/m² and 25℃. Figure. 6 shows the comparison chart of output power about the two algorithms due to solar insolation change from 600 W/m² to 1000W/m².

As can be seen from Figure 5, traditional P&O method's power oscillates at the beginning of the process. After a period of time, the waveform gradually stabilized and oscillated in a small area. It will reach maximum power about 0.35s and oscillate largely around the MPPconversely, the power of improvement has a small oscillation at the outset and achieves MPP about 0.15s. It could be drawn that the improved algorithm has a quick tracking speed, high precision, small fluctuations around the MPP. Figure 6 shows that the power of illumination intensity mutates from 600 W/m² to 1000W/m² which the traditional P&O method has a poor tracking accuracy, larger fluctuations and a bad responson when the light suddenly changes. Nevertheless, the improved algorithm has a rapid responson to light mutated, and be quickly stabilized at MPP. It is proved that the improved algorithm has a better stability and high efficiency in different illumination conditions.

5   Conclusion

The paper analysed the characteristics of the PV power system and proposed a new MPPT control algorithm by combining with various control algorithms. The voltage and current could be calculated by the open-circuit voltage, short-circuit current online testing, thus the disturbance of PV system with traditional detection method. In order to reduce the power oscillation around MPP and the "false judgement" phenomenon, variable step P&O method was adopted by the idea of gradual approximation method to search step, so the MPP could be rapidly and accurately tracked. Through the curve two algorithms in PV output power, the simulation results demonstrate that the improved algorithm could quickly track the change of external environment, also avoid the power fluctuation and have a good practical value.

References

1. Cheng, Q., Cheng, Y.: Survey on MPPT Methods of Photovoltaic Cells. J. Journal of Shanghai University of Electric Power 25(4) (2009)
2. Chen, J., Zhao, Z.: Comparison of maximum power point tracking technologies for photovoltaic power systems. J. Tsinghua Univ. (Sci.&Tech.) 50(5) (2010)
3. Su, J., Yu, S., Zhao, W.: Investigation on engineering Analyticalmodel of Silicon Solar Cells. J. Acta Energiae Solaris Sinica 4, 409–412 (2001)
4. Zhao, G., Wang, Q.: Research on Realization Means and Principle of Maximum Power Point Tracing. J. Acta Energiae Solaris Sinica 127(10) (2006)
5. Zhang, C., He, X.: Short-current Combined With Perturbation and Observation Maximum power point Tracking Method for Photovoltaic Power Systems. J. Proceedings of the CSEE 26, 98–102 (2006)
6. Xue, J.: Principles and Methods of Optimization. Metallurgical Industry Press, BeiJing (2008)
7. Sugimoto, H., Dong, H.: A new scheme for maximum photovoltaic power racking control. In: Power Conversion Conference, Nagaoka (1997)

Application of RBF Neural Network Model on Forecasting Tourists Quantity in Hainan Province

HuaiQiang Zhang and JingBing Li[*]

School of Information Science and Technology, Hainan University, Haikou 570228, China
zhq0319@163.com, Jingbingli2008@hotmail.com

Abstract. Tourist quantity is an important factor deciding economic benefits and sustainable development of tourism. Thus tourist quantity prediction becomes the important content of tourism development planning. Based on the tourist quantity of Hainan province for more than twenty years, this paper establishes tourist quantity prediction model according to RBF neural network [1], in which the principle and algorithm of RBF neural network is used. And this paper also predicts the future tourist quantity of Hainan province. The Matlab emulational result of RBF neural network model shows based on RBF neural network tourist quantity prediction model can exactly predict the future tourist quantity of Hainan province, thus providing a new idea and mean for tourist quantity prediction.

Keywords: RBF neural network, International Tourism Island, Tourists quantity, Forecast.

0 Introductions

With the development of Hainan international tourism island strategy[2], Hainan Province travel services will have a new period of development. During this period, the number of tourism will continue to increase in Hainan which will cause some damages to the Hainan Provincial Tourism landscape resources and the environment. Therefore, in the Hainan international tourism island development planning and feasibility study process, Hainan tourism scale is the scientific basis for forecasting tourism development, establishing tourism management decisions, reasonable controlling visitors scale, realizing the sustainable development of Hainan tourism.

Artificial neural network (ANN) modeling method is an effective analysis method for forecasting, which can well reveal the correlation of nonlinear time series in delay state space. So ANN can achieve the purpose of prediction. The Kolmogorov continuation theorem in neural network theory ensures the prediction feasibility of the neural network which is used for time series from the view of mathematics[3]. The number of visitors is decided by many objective factors. The forecast of tourist number

---

[*] Corresponding author.

S. Lin and X. Huang (Eds.): CESM 2011, Part I, CCIS 175, pp. 305–311, 2011.
© Springer-Verlag Berlin Heidelberg 2011

has not good ways now. As the number of visitors has a good nonlinear characteristic and the RBF neural network is better used to handle nonlinear problems, the RBF neural network can apply to forecast the number of tourisms. The article establishs prediction model and predictes the number of tourisms .The result of experiment proves that the prediction model has good prediction effect.

1   The Principle, Structure and Algorithm of RBF Neural Network

1.1   The Principle of RBF Neural Network

RBF neural network is the abbreviation of radial basis function neural network, which is a kind of feed-forward neural network. Its construction is based on the function approximation theory. The distance ‖dist‖ between weight vector and threshold vector is used to independent variable of the transfer function of the network "adbas". The ‖dist‖ is got through the product of input vector and weighted matrix's row vector. Each hidden layer neurons transfer function of RBF neural network makes up a base function of a fitting plane, so RBF neural network gets the name.

1.2   The Structure of RBF Network

RBF radial basis network is a three-layer feed-forward neural network, which includes an input layer, a hidden layer with radial basis function neurons and an output layer with linear neurons. As shown in figure 1 [4].

Hidden layer is usually using radial basis function as excitation function and the radial basis excitation function is commonly gaussian function, which is usually expressed as:

$$R\left(x^{q}-c_{i}\right)=\exp\left[-\left(\left\|w1_{i}-X^{q}\right\|\times b1_{i}\right)^{2}\right] \tag{1}$$

Where $\left\|w1_{i}-X^{q}\right\|$ is the Euclidean distance, c is the center of gaussian function. $X^{q}=(x_{1}^{q},x_{2}^{q},...,x_{j}^{q},...,x_{m}^{q})$ is the qth input data.

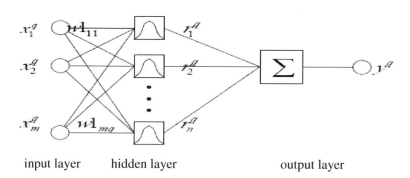

input layer   hidden layer   output layer

Fig. 1. The structure of RBF neural network

The distance between the weight vector $W1_i$, connected to the inputting layer and in the every neuron in the hidden layer, and the input vector X^q is multiplied by the threshold $b1_i$, which is considered as its own input. As figure2 shows:

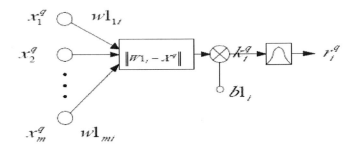

Fig. 2. The input and output of RBF neural network hidden layer neurons

Thus we get the ith input of hidden layer neuron which can be expressed as k_i^q:

$$k_i^q = \sqrt{\sum_j \left(w1_{ji} - x_j^q \right)^2} \times b1_i \qquad (2)$$

The ith output of hidden layer neuron can be expressed as r_i^q:

$$r_i^q = \exp\left(\sqrt{\sum_j \left(w1_{ji} - x_j^q \right)^2} \times b1_i \right) \qquad (3)$$

The output of RBF neural network is the weighted summation of each hidden layer neurons's output and the excitation function is using pure linear function, so the qth output layer neurons's output which is corresponding to the qth input can be expressed as y^q:

$$y^q = \sum_{i=1}^{n} r_i^q \times w2_i h \qquad (4)$$

1.3 The Learning Algorithm of RBF Neural Network

RBF neural network learning process can be divided into two stages [5]: first stage, self-organizing learning phase, this phase is the unsupervised learning process, solving the center and variance of the hidden layer base functions; second stage, tutor learning phase, this phase is solving weights which is between the hidden layer and output layer.

2   The Construction and Forecast of RBF Model on Forecasting Tourists Quantity

2.1   RBF Neural Network Input Variables and Output Variables

Input variable selection is an important task before the RBF neural network modeling, whether to choose a set of input variables which can best reflect the reason for desired output changes is directly related to the performance of neural network prediction. The number of tourist is restricted by many factors, for example, geography, environment, culture, government policy, etc. If all these factors are considered, it will bring a lot of inconvenience to predict. Tourists quantity every five years as the neural network input variables is the innovation of the article, so Input samples can be determined by the input variable. We can select the sixth year number of tourists after every five years as the neural network output variable.

2.2 Input Samples Pretreatment

Since the implicit function of RBF neural network is Gaussian function, which general requires for input value between 0 and 1, do normalize on the number of Hainan province tourists from 1988 to 2008. Normalization is basically the same way to statistical data normalization, generally using the following form:

$$\bar{X} = \frac{X - X_{min}}{X_{max} - X_{min}} \tag{5}$$

Where X is the actual value of sample; X_{max} takes a large value, ensuring forecast year is less than the value; X_{min} takes a sample of data is less than the minimum value to ensure normalized value is not close to 0. After the pretreatment of data completes the training, do process data (inverse transform) to get the actual value.

Table 1. The actual number of visitors of Hainan Province in 1988 to 2008

Years	1988	1989	1990	1991	1992	1993	1994
Tourists quantity(million)	118.54	88.05	113.46	140.61	247.37	274.41	289.60

Year	1995	1996	1997	1998	1999	2000	2001
Tourists quantity(million)	361.01	485.82	791.00	855.97	929.07	1000.76	1124.76

Year	2002	2003	2004	2005	2006	2007	2008
Tourists quantity(million)	1254.54	1234.11	1402.88	1516.47	1605.02	1873.78	2060.00

Note: Table 1 Data from the Hainan Provincial Bureau of Statistics.

2.3 Determining Training Samples and Test Samples

From the above we can determine the number of input neuron of RBF neural network is 5, and the number of output neurons is 1. Treating the samples as follows [6]: Input neuron P=[p(t-5),p(t-4),p(t-3),p(t-2),p(t-1)]; Output neurons T=[p'(t)]. Where, t = 1993, 1994 ... ... 2008, P (t) denote the normalized number of tourism at t year. In this method, we can obtain the training samples and test samples.

3   RBF Neural Network Training and Prediction

Creating a precise neural network by Newbe function, this function creates RBF network, automatically select the number of hidden layer and make the error to 0. MATLAB codes are as follows [7]:

```
SPREAD=1;
net=newrb(p,tt.err_goal, SPREAD,200,1);
```

Training sample, shown in Figure 3.

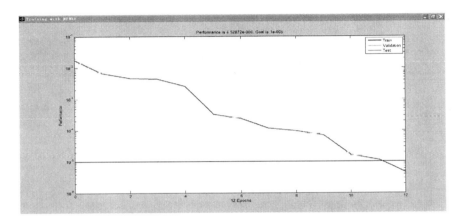

Fig. 3. RBF neural network learning and training curve

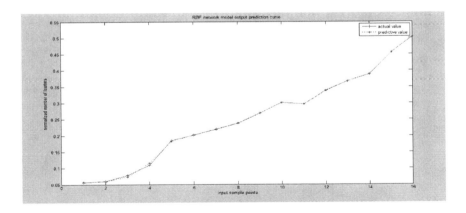

Fig. 4. RBF network model output prediction curve

Where, p is the input vector, tt is the target vector. SPREAD is the density of basis functions, SPREAD is larger the function is smoother, where selecting SPREAD = 1.Then testing the neural network and verifying the prediction performance. MATLAB codes are as follows:

$$y=sim(net,P\_test)$$

Where, P_test is the network test samples. The results are as follows:

$$y= 0.3666 \quad 0.3887 \quad 0.4560 \quad 0.5024$$

After training and testing the network, the network output values obtained through inverse transform are compared with the actual values to check whether it meet the requirements of their error, as shown in table 2.

Table 2. RBF neural network analysis table accuracy

Year	Actual value(million)	Fittedvalue(million)	Absolute error
2005	1516.47	1516.40	0.07
2006	1605.02	1604.80	0.22
2007	1873.78	1874.00	-0.22
2008	2060.00	2059.6	0.4

We can see from Table 3, RBF neural network can reach 99.99% accuracy. it meets the prediction requirements.This provides an accurate basis for predicting tourists quantity in the future.

Enter the actual value from 2004 to 2008, we can obtain the normalized predicted value in 2009.Similarly, after a multi-step iterative, we can get the normalized predicted value from 2010 to 2018, as shown in table 3.

Table 3. The normalized predicted value of tourists quantity from 2009 to 2018

year	2009	2010	2011	2012	2013
Predictive value	0.58336	0.63658	0.67832	0.72896	0.76542
year	2014	2015	2016	2017	2018
Predictive value	0.81986	0.83942	0.84738	0.85106	0.86256

Then after inverse transform, the predicted value can be obtained from 2009 to 2018, as shown in table 4.

Table 4. Predictive value of tourists quantity from 2009 to 2018

Year	2009	2010	2011	2012	2013
Predictivevalue(million)	2373.44	2586.32	2753.28	2955.84	3101.28
Year	2014	2015	2016	2017	2018
Predictive value(million)	3279.41	3397.68	3437.52	3442.24	3486.24

As can be seen from Table 4, after a slow growth phase from 2009 to 2015, tourists quantity in Hainan Province will be gradually stabilized, in between 34 million to 35 million.

4 Conclusion

This paper has presented a tourists prediction method based on RBF neural network.Through RBF neural network adaptive, self-organization and self-learning function, making tourists quantity every 5 years as the RBF neural network's input, we can predict tourists quantity in the sixth year. After MATLAB training, forecasting, simulation, this method achieves a good prediction effect. The use of this method provides a new way of thinking for simulating and predicting tourists quantity in Hainan province, provides a reference for the construction of Hainan International Tourism Island.

Acknowledgements

This work is partly supported by Hainan University Graduate Education Reform Project (yjg0117), and by Natural Science Foundation of Hainan Province (60894), and by Education Department of Hainan Province project (Hjkj2009-03).

References

1. Wei, H.-k.: Neural network structure design theory and method. National Defence Industry Press, Beijing (February 2005)
2. International Travel Hainan Island,
   http://baike.baidu.com/view/3139516.htm?fr=ala0_1_1
3. Sun, Y.-p., Zhang, L., Lv, R.-y.: Tourist quantity forecast by using neural network. Human Geography 17(6), 50–52 (2002)
4. Liu, X.-q., Wang, X.-y., Yu, R.-d.: Study on traffic accidents prediction model based On RBF neural network. Computer Engineering and Applications 45(17), 188–190 (2009)
5. Zhang, D.-f.: MATLAB Neural Network Application Design. Mechanical Industry Press, Beijing (January 2009)
6. Li, J.-b., Zhang, H.-q.: Application of BP neural network model on forecasting the number of tourists in Hainan province. In: Computer and Communication Technologies in Agriculture Engineering (CCTAE) (2010)
7. Zhang, D.-f.: MATLAB Neural Network Simulation and Application. Electronic Industry Press, Beijing (June 2009)

A Set of Algorithm to Simulate the Dynamics of Land System

Xiangzheng Deng[1,2] and Xin Wen[3]

[1] Institute of Geographic Sciences and Natural Resources Research,
Chinese Academy of Sciences, Beijing, 100101, China
[2] Center for Chinese Agricultural Policy, Chinese Academy of Sciences,
Beijing, 100101, China
dengxz.ccap@igsnrr.ac.cn
[3] China University of Geosciences, Beijing, 100083, China
wx0410@Gmail.com

Abstract. A set of algorithm stored into the Dynamics of Land System (DLS) model is a collection of program that simulates pattern change of land uses by conducting scenario analysis of the area of land use change. In this paper we show that the model analyzes causes of the dynamics of land use pattern, simulates the process of land use changes and assists land use planning and land management decisions. We introduce the main procedures of DLS including framework, parameter configuration, function modules and results output.

Keywords: Algorithm, Simulate, Parameter configuration, DLS.

1 Framework

The DLS model fully considers the links between related models of nature, ecology and economy. It also extracts decision-making reference information used in land use planning, environmental planning and management of natural resources by designing different scenarios of changing regional land use area [1, 2]. Users of the DLS model can input nonlinear demand change, different conversion rules and driving factors at different pattern changes of land uses to simulate and analyze the complex changes of regional land use patterns. The DLS model also considers the influence of macroscopic factors such as topography, environment, trade and institutional arrangement and land management policies to more accurately simulate possible scenarios of pattern changes of land uses.

2 Function Modules

The DLS model is based on quantitative analysis of land use pattern changes at the pixel level, interactions among driving factors and spatial-temporal distribution of land use pattern change [3]. It simulates the pattern changes of regional land uses by analyzing

S. Lin and X. Huang (Eds.): CESM 2011, Part I, CCIS 175, pp. 312–316, 2011.

the driving forces of land distribution at the grid scale and allocation of changing land use areas [4]. Analyzing both the driving forces behind land distribution and the spatial allocation of land use change is the important component of the DLS model.

Mechanism analysis of the DLS model aims to estimate the statistical relationship between the pattern changes of land uses and its driving factors. Theoretically, mechanistic analysis provides a reaction function of each land use type. Corresponding weights are given to all driving factors according to principles that can be assumed to be fixed for a short period, but driving factors change over time. With the reaction function determined, reasons for differences between simulated and observed distribution of land use types can be summarized as follows: values of some driving factors have changed, such as population growth or temperature; competition exists among different land use types; and restrictions occur between local historic conditions and current demand. Driving factors include natural environmental conditions, socioeconomic factors and land use management policies, all of which are closely linked to pattern changes of the land uses. Driving factors behind land use pattern can be analyzed with the explanatory linear model of land use pattern (ELMLUP) and explanatory nonlinear model of land use pattern (ENMLUP) built at the pixel level.

3 Explanatory Linear Model

Linear regression is the model most commonly used in researching driving mechanisms of land use patterns as it explores driving factors at wide ranges and with high spatial resolution. The explanatory linear model of land use pattern at the pixel level, or ELMLUP, contains a demanding and a distribution module. The target variable of the ELMLUP is the proportion of the area of land use type k ($k=1, 2... M$) in grid i ($i=1, 2...$ n) at time t abbreviated as Q_i^{kt}. The explanatory variable of the model is a covariant vector of driving factors composed of a series of natural environmental conditions and socioeconomic factors that are tightly related to the pattern changes of land uses (with a significance level of 5%):

$$X_i^t = (x_{i1}^t, x_{i2}^t, ..., x_{il}^t, ..., x_{iL}^t)^T.$$

(1)

To measure the impact of spatially autocorrelated land use types, several variables, including $\hat{Q}_i^{kt}$ and $\hat{X}_i^t$, are defined in the ELMLUP. The quantitative relationship between $\hat{Q}_i^{kt}$ and $\hat{X}_i^t$ is developed through the following multiple linear regression model:

$$\hat{Q}_i^{kt} = a_0^k + a^k \hat{X}_i^t.$$

(2)

where $a^k = (a_1^k, a_2^k, ..., a_L^k)$ is the coefficient matrix of $\hat{X}_i^t$, and a_0^k is a constant term. Regarding grid i at time t, the result $reg(\hat{Q}_i^{kt})$ estimated by the model is naturally employed to reflect the average proportion of area of land use type k under natural and socioeconomic conditions $\hat{X}_i^t$.

4 Explanatory Nonlinear Model

The driving force analysis model for land use pattern in nonlinear form is built based on land use area percentage grid data. Percentage data was first proposed by Ferrers (1866) and is becoming increasingly important in statistical analysis. It is usually expressed as the following vector set:

$$S = \left\{ (s_1, s_2, \cdots, s_m)^T \in R^m \mid \sum_{i=1}^{m} s_i = 1, 0 < s_i < 1 \right\}, \tag{3}$$

$$s_i = S_i \Big/ \sum_{j=1}^{m} S_j . \tag{4}$$

where s_i is the ith element of the percentage data, and S_i is the original observed value of s_i, or the area of cultivated land and the area of developed land.

Area percentage data is derived from grid data at a certain grid pixel scale. Area percentage data is constrained by two restriction conditions as follows:

$$\sum_{i=1}^{m} s_i = 1, 0 < s_i < 1, \tag{5}$$

$$\sum_{i=1}^{m} S_i = \Omega. \tag{6}$$

where Ω is constant and represents the area of the grid pixel.

The grid area percentage data is then obtained for land use categories:

$$Y = \left\{ (y_1, y_2, \cdots, y_p)^T \in R^p \mid \sum_{j=1}^{p} y_j = 1, 0 < y_j < 1 \right\} \tag{7}$$

Where y_j is the area proportion of the jth land use category in the total area of grid pixels.

Symmetric log-ratio transformation is conducted after the grid is percentage data are treated to stretch the values of area percentage data from $(0, 1)$ to $(-\infty, +\infty)$:

$$Z = (z_1, z_2, \cdots, z_p)^T , \quad z_j = \ln \left(y_j \Big/ \sqrt[p]{\prod_{i=1}^{p} y_i} \right), \quad j = 1, 2, \cdots, p . \tag{8}$$

where $z_j \in (-\infty, +\infty)$. Let $s_j = z_j - z_p, j = 1, 2 \ldots p\text{-}1$, and through the inverse transformation we can get Eq (9):

$$y_j = \frac{e^{s_j}}{1 + \sum_{i=1}^{p-1} e^{s_i}}, \quad y_p = \frac{1}{1 + \sum_{i=1}^{p-1} e^{s_i}}, \quad j = 1, 2, \cdots, p-1 . \tag{9}$$

Symmetric log-ratio transformation not only solves the essential zero problem and the problem of constrained total land area, but also linearizes the non-linear relationships between land use patterns and their driving factors.

5 Spatial Allocation

The input parameters used in the module for spatially allocating changes in land use area reflect local, regional and historical characteristics of the pattern changes of regional land uses [5]. Specific steps are shown in the following figure.

(i) If a certain land use type existed in the previous simulation year, and its stability is less than 1, the spatial allocation module will calculate the distribution probability, sum of the compensation factor and stability factor, which are used as the allocation probability:

$$L_{i,k} = P_{i,k} + C_k + S_k. \tag{10}$$

where $L_{i,k}$ is the allocation probability of the kth land use type in grid i; $P_{i,k}$ is the distribution probability of the kth land use type in grid i; C_k and S_k are the compensation and stability factors, respectively.

(ii) When the compensation factor C_k is nearly 0, $L_{i,k}$ consists of the distribution probability $P_{i,k}$ and compensation factor C_k as follows:

$$L_{i,k} = P_{i,k} + C_k. \tag{11}$$

(iii) Within each spatial allocation step, DLS excludes those pixels with a decreasing trend for a certain kind of land use type from obtaining new area of that kind of land use type [6]. If the spatial allocation does not allow the configuration of stability, then the land use type with the largest $L_{i,k}$ is allocated to grids without enough area of land use types.

6 Summary

DLS is a software tool developed based on the DLS model for the dynamic simulation of the land use pattern changes. This paper introduces the main procedures of DLS including framework, parameter configuration, function modules and results output. It can measure the influence of driving factors that are closely associated with changes in the land use pattern, including natural conditions, socioeconomic factors and even land use management policies. It can simulate the spatial-temporal process of pattern changes of land uses and export maps of pattern changes of land uses with high spatial and temporal resolution by setting conversion rules of land use types and designing change scenarios.

Acknowledgements. This research was supported by the National Key Programme for Developing Basic Science (2010CB950904), the Chinese Academy of Sciences (KZCX2-YW-326-1), National Scientific Foundation of China (40801231), and the Ministry of Science and Technology of China (2008BAK50B06).

References

1. Deng, X., Su, H., Zhan, J.: Integration of multiple data sources to simulate the Dynamics of Land Systems. Sensors 8(2), 620–634 (2008)
2. Deng, X., Jiang, Q., Lin, Y., Han, J.: Simulation of Changes of soil organic carbon stock of cropland in China. Geographical Research 29(1), 93–101 (2010a)
3. Burgi, M., Hersperger, A.M., Schneeberger, N.: Driving forces of landscape change-current and new directions. Landscape Ecology 19, 857–868 (2004)
4. Li, L., Zhang, P.Y., Hou, W.: Land Use/Cover Change and Driving Forces in Southern Liaoning Province since 1950s. Chinese Geographical Science 15(2), 131–136 (2005)
5. Deng, X., Huang, J., Rozelle, S., Uchid, E.: Economic Growth and the Expansion of Urban Land in China. Urban Studies 47(4), 813–843 (2010)
6. Liu, X.H., Wang, J.F., Liu, M.L., Meng, B.: Spatial heterogeneity of the driving forces of cropland change in China. Science in China Series D-Earth Sciences 48(12), 2231–2240 (2005)

Computer-Based Estimation System for Land Productivity

Xiangzheng Deng[1,2], Qunou Jiang[1,3], and Xin Wen[4]

[1] Institute of Geographic Sciences and Natural Resources Research,
Chinese Academy of Sciences, Beijing, 100101, China
[2] Center for Chinese Agricultural Policy, Chinese Academy of Sciences,
Beijing, 100101, China
dengxz.ccap@igsnrr.ac.cn
[3] Graduate University of the Chinese Academy of Sciences, Beijing, 100049, China
jiangqo.dls@163.com
[4] China University of Geosciences, Beijing, 100083, China
wx0410@Gmail.com

Abstract. Land productivity generally refers to the overall productivity related to various combinations of the natural characteristics of the land and socioeconomic factors. Structural change and pattern succession in land systems undoubtedly leads to changes in the suitability and quality of different kinds of land types and directly influences agricultural productivity. In this paper we describe the processes, parameters needed and methods of data preparation, which will improve the ability of readers to use this model and provide a foundation for its wide application.

Keywords: Land productivity, Parameter configuration, ESLP.

1 Principles

The land resource is a multifunctional natural resource, which is in continuously growing demand under a background of rapid population growth and fast economic development [1]. This is especially the case in China, where the economy is developing rapidly and land use patterns are undergoing unprecedented change due to pressure from these demands [2]. Structural change and pattern succession in land systems undoubtedly leads to changes in the suitability and quality of different kinds of land types and directly influences agricultural productivity.

The Estimation System for Land Productivity (ESLP) is a collection of several applications, including land suitability assessment, and the evaluation of land productivity, and some advanced applications which use the stock of land resources as fundamental input information. The outputs from the ESLP include agro-ecological zoning maps, land suitability assessment maps, and attribute data such as cropping area and crop production.

2 Parameters

The growing period for crops, influenced by seasons, is one of the important parameters in the ESLP. As a comprehensive indicator of changes to the agro-ecological

S. Lin and X. Huang (Eds.): CESM 2011, Part I, CCIS 175, pp. 317–321, 2011.
© Springer-Verlag Berlin Heidelberg 2011

conditions, the growing period is defined as the period from the time when moisture and temperature conditions are suitable for crop growth until the crops mature [3, 4, 5]. The thermal zone is one of the important parameters in agro-ecological zoning. It indicates the total heat available during the growing period which can usually be represented by the heat available for the crop during each day of the growing period.

The soil property information is the basis of soil mapping. Soil types are classified as different soil genus or soil species. Soil properties are influenced by the soil quality, land management and even the habits of the planted crops. The land resource stock is characterized by the combined status of land use types, and constitutes the basis of agro-ecological zoning. The climate parameters under different scenarios are useful to simulate and predict the spatial-temporal changes in land productivity under different scenarios, which can be extended with climate parameters. An effective way to increase productivity is to raise the input levels, which can include the financial investment by governments, collectives or individual farmers in fixed and current assets. The ESLP can estimate and simulate changes in land productivity for different input levels [6].

3   Function Modules

The ESLP estimates land productivity through an iterative method. The calculation procedure includes five steps as following.

The potential photosynthetic productivity is the potential land productivity as determined solely by the photosynthetically active radiation, based on the assumption that the temperature, water, soil, breeds and other agricultural inputs are all in optimal condition. It is calculated as:

$$Y_1 = Cf(Q) = K\Omega\varepsilon\phi(1-\alpha)(1-\beta)(1-\rho)(1-\gamma)(1-\omega)$$
$$\cdot(1-d)sf(L)(1-\eta)^{-1}(1-\delta)^{-1}q^{-1}\sum Q_j. \tag{1}$$

Where Y_1 is the potential photosynthetic productivity, with the unit kg/ha; C is the unit conversion factor; K is the area coefficient; $\sum Q_j$ is the total solar radiation during the growing period (MJ/m^2); Ω is the crop solar radiation utilization efficiency; ε is the percentage of effective radiation in the total radiation; Φ is the photon conversion efficiency; α is the reflectivity of the plant groups; β is the transmittance of the luxuriant plant groups; ρ is the proportion of radiation intercepted by non-photosynthetic organs of plants; γ is the proportion of the light that exceeds the light saturation point; ω is the proportion of respiration in the photosynthate; d is the crop leaf abscission rate; s is the economic crop coefficient; $f(L)$ is the corrected value of the crop leaf area dynamics; η is the moisture content of the ripened grain; δ is the percentage of ash; and q is the heat content of the dry matter (MJ/kg).

The potential thermal productivity, the upper limit of irrigated agricultural production, refers to the land productivity determined by the natural thermal condition when water, soil, breeds and other agricultural inputs are all in optimal conditions. It is calculated from the following formula:

$$Y_2 = f(T)\cdot Y_1. \tag{2}$$

where Y_2 stands for the potential thermal productivity, in units of kg/ha; $f(T)$ is the temperature revision function for crop photosynthesis. $f(T)$ is identified from three cardinal temperatures for major crop plants at which crops can grow and high yield can be achieved and used as a benchmark in this study. $f(T)$ is calculated using the following equations:

$$f(T) = \frac{(T-T_1)(T_2-T)^B}{(T_0-T_1)(T_2-T_0)^B},$$ (3)

$$B = (T_2-T_0)/(T_0-T_1).$$ (4)

where T is the average temperature for one period, which is an asymmetric parabolic function in the range of 0-1 determined by T_1, T_2 and T_0 which are the lower, upper and optimum temperatures for crop growth and development, respectively. In this study, the crop growth period is divided into five stages: seedling, vegetative, nutrition and reproduction, nutrition and grain-filling, and maturity stages. $f(T)$ is calculated separately for each stage.

The potential climate productivity is calculated by further revising the water indicator based on the potential thermal productivity, which is calculated from the following formula:

$$Y_w = Y_T \cdot f(W)(1-I_r) + Y_2 \cdot I_r.$$ (5)

where I_r is the irrigation coefficient; Y_2 is the potential thermal productivity; Y_W is the potential climate productivity. The study of the potential thermal productivity can be summed up as research on the function of water. There are no authoritative models for the water calculation at this time, so the model recommended by the United Nations Food and Agriculture Organization is used here:

$$f(W) = 1 - K_y \times (1 - Pe/ET_m),$$ (6)

Where K_y is the reactive yield coefficient; ET_m is the maximum evapotranspiration (mm); Pe is the effective precipitation, which can be calculated from the model designed by the US Department of Agriculture Soil Conservation Service:

$$Pe = R/125 \cdot (125 - 0.2 \cdot R) \quad \text{(If R<250mm),}$$ (7)

$$Pe = 125 + 0.1 \cdot R \quad \text{(If R>250mm).}$$ (8)

where R is the total precipitation; and ET_m is the maximum evapotranspiration during the crop growing period, which can be calculated from:

$$ET_m = K_1 \cdot ET_0.$$ (9)

where K_1 is the crop coefficient, which is related to the season, the crop breed and the crop colony structure; ET_0 is the reference evapotranspiration, which is calculated using the improved Penman-Monteith model:

$$ET_0 = \frac{0.408\Delta(R_n - G) + \gamma\dfrac{900}{T+273}u_2(e_s - e_a)}{\Delta + \gamma(1 + 0.34u_2)}.$$ (10)

where Δ is the slope of the saturated vapor pressure-temperature curve (kPa°C^{-1}); R_n is the net radiation from the crop canopy surface (MJm^{-2}h^{-1}); G is the soil heat flux (MJm^{-2}h^{-1}); γ is the hygrometer constant; T is the daily average temperature (°C); u_2 is the wind speed at 2 m height; e_s is the saturation vapor pressure (kPa); e_a is the actual vapor pressure; the soil heat flux G is calculated from the following formula:

$$G=0.1*R_n. \tag{11}$$

The potential land productivity can be obtained from the potential climate productivity (Y_w) and the validity coefficient for soil:

$$Y_L = f(s) \cdot Y_w. \tag{12}$$

Twelve factors that influence soil properties are selected and their weighting coefficients (W_i) are determined by establishing a comparison matrix based on their relative importance to soil effectiveness, soil properties and soil nutrients. The ESLP calculates the soil effectiveness coefficients using the following formula:

$$f(s) = \sum_i A_i \cdot W_i. \tag{13}$$

The ESLP uses the Cobb-Douglas function to estimate land productivity influenced by fundamental inputs and conventional production inputs as follows:

$$Y=AK_1^{\alpha}K_2^{\beta}YL^{\gamma}. \tag{14}$$

where Y is the land productivity; A is the scaling parameter of the Cobb-Douglas function; K_1 is the fundamental input for improving land conditions; K_2 is the routine productive input for specific production processes; YL^{γ} is the potential land productivity; α, β and γ meet the following conditions:

$$\alpha+\beta+\gamma=1. \tag{15}$$

The total investment is allocated between the fundamental inputs and conventional production inputs based on the profit maximization principle. Assuming that the total investment amount is M, then

$$M=K_1P_1+K_2P_2. \tag{16}$$

where P_1 and P_2 are the prices of fundamental inputs and productive inputs, respectively. So the allocation of the total investment between the fundamental inputs and productive inputs satisfies the optimum condition:

$$\text{MAX } W=AK_1^{\alpha}K_2^{\beta}YL^{\gamma}P- K_1P_1- K_2P_2. \tag{17}$$

where W is the production profit, and P is the product price. The optimum investment program is found by solving the equations above, so that:

$$K_1 = \left(\frac{1}{Y_L^{\gamma}}\right)^{\frac{1}{\alpha+\beta-1}} \left(\frac{P_1}{\alpha}\right)^{\frac{1-\beta}{\alpha+\beta-1}} \left(\frac{P_2}{\beta}\right)^{\frac{\beta}{\alpha+\beta-1}}, \tag{18}$$

$$K_2 = \left(\frac{1}{Y_L^{\gamma}}\right)^{\frac{1}{\alpha+\beta-1}} \left(\frac{P_1}{\alpha}\right)^{\frac{\alpha}{\alpha+\beta-1}} \left(\frac{P_2}{\beta}\right)^{\frac{1-\alpha}{\alpha+\beta-1}}. \tag{19}$$

The estimation of land productivity is found by substituting K_1 and K_2 into the land productivity calculation formula.

4 Summary

Land productivity is one of the important indices in the assessment of effects of the dynamics of land system change. The ESLP is a collection of several application programs, including land suitability assessment, the evaluation of land productivity, and some advanced applications which use the stock of land resources as the fundamental input information. The ESLP involves numerous parameters in the process of land productivity estimation, and the calculation processes are lengthy and complex. This chapter describes the processes, parameters needed and methods of data preparation, which will improve the ability of readers to use this model and provide a foundation for its wide application.

Acknowledgements. This research was supported by the National Key Programme for Developing Basic Science (2010CB950904), the Chinese Academy of Sciences (KZCX2-YW-326-1), National Scientific Foundation of China (41071343), and the Ministry of Science and Technology of China (2008BAK50B06).

References

1. Deng, X., Huang, J., Rozelle, S., Uchida, E.: Cultivated land conversion and potential agricultural productivity in China. Land Use Policy 23(4), 372–384 (2006)
2. Deng, X., Jiang, Q., Zhan, J.: Scenario analyses of land productivity in China. Ecology and Environment 18(5), 1835–1843 (2009)
3. Fischer, G., Sun, L.X.: Model based analysis of land—use development in China Agriculture. Ecosystem and Environment 85(1-3), 163–176 (2001)
4. Foley, J.A., De Fries, R., Asner, G.P., Barford, C., Bonan, G.: Global Consequences of Land Use. Science 309, 570–575 (2005)
5. Veldkamp, A., Verburg, P.H.: Modelling land use change and environmental impact. Journal of Environmental Management 72(1-2), 1–3 (2004)
6. Fischer, G., Van Velthuizen, H., Nachtergaele, F.O.: Global agro-ecological zones assessment: methodology and results. Interim Report IR-00-064. Luxemburg, Rome, IIASA (2000)

An Algorithm to Simulate the Equilibrium of Land Use Structures

Xin Wen[1] and Xiangzheng Deng[2,3]

[1] China University of Geosciences, Beijing, 100083, China
wx0410@Gmail.com
[2] Institute of Geographic Sciences and Natural Resources Research,
Chinese Academy of Sciences, Beijing, 100101, China
[3] Center for Chinese Agricultural Policy, Chinese Academy of Sciences,
Beijing, 100101, China
dengxz.ccap@igsnrr.ac.cn

Abstract. The structure of regional land use is influenced by socioeconomic factors, including industrial structure, trade environment, economic policies and institutional arrangements, and these multi-dimensional factors should be taken into consideration by different departments as part of an open, balanced economic system. In this paper we show that an equilibrium algorithm packed into a Computable General Equilibrium of Land Use Change (CGELUC) model uses the framework of the Computable General Equilibrium (CGE) to analyze the factors that influence regional land use types. The analysis is based on macroscopic quantitative analysis and reveals relationships between the land use structure of cultivated land, economic forest, meadow for grazing, and economic development.

Keywords: Land use, Equilibrium algorithm, CGELUC, CGE.

1 The CGELUC Model

Generally, the CGELUC model is divided into two parts when simulating structural changes in regional land use, including a thematic quantitative analysis section and an equilibrium analysis section of regional land area supply and demand. The two parts are linked by feedbacks from a series of relevant parameters. These are then put into the equilibrium analysis section, in which supply and demand of regional land areas are input as exogenous variables. The equilibrium analysis section of regional land use structure mainly simulates the relationship between land use structure and economic activity [1].

Thematic quantitative analysis is mainly used to simulate and predict total changes in developed, water, grassland, woodland and unused land regions. Changes in these land use areas are then exported under specific scenarios to the equilibrium analysis section of land area supply and demand, and the influence of exogenous factors (such as land policy and planning) on regional land use structure is then analyzed. Macroeconomic variables such as production volume, price index and land rent are used as

S. Lin and X. Huang (Eds.): CESM 2011, Part I, CCIS 175, pp. 322–326, 2011.

land policy parameters, and the total economic output, employment rate and energy consumption are used as characteristic variables that indicate industrial development of land-consumption sectors [2, 3]. Analysis of the influence of land policies can be used to make corresponding baseline hypotheses and calculations according to the current amount of land use and land use characteristics. The analysis is based on results of government investments, technical progress of sectors consuming land, structural changes in product consumption and the impacts of macroeconomic policies on the economic variables are then included in the equilibrium analysis section of land area supply and demand [4, 5]. This section estimates and quantifies product demand, economic development and land use efficiency.

Land plays a key role in the CGELUC model. On one hand, land is involved in production activities and is traded in the factor market as a commodity. Alternatively, land uses change with changing human activities, such as farmland returning to forest or grassland, reclaiming wasteland and clearing forest for farmland expansion. Change in land property is generally called land use conversion [6]. The computer-based CGELUC model is constructed based on CGE theory, the areas of five land use types and the connection between economic development and land use structure of developed, economic forest and grassland areas. It consists of production, demand, price, trade, income distribution and macroeconomic closure modules. On the other hand, agricultural, forest and livestock products produced directly on the land are land output products, while other products are non-land output products. The difference between the two is that non-land output products consider the land as an input factor, and land output products consider the land as a commodity. Here, the module equations associated with land use structure are highlighted, and other equations are similar to the equation of the general CGE model.

2 The SAM

The Social Accounting Matrix (SAM) dataset serves as the basis for running the CGELUC model, the construction of which facilitates parameter estimation of the model. The structural change in regional land use is analyzed by expanding the traditional SAM dataset and adding factors and commodities of several land use types balanced among sectors and regions in the CGELUC model. The SAM dataset complements and expands the input-output tables because it indicates interdependence of production activities, income distribution factors and income distribution of different sectors. It also determines expenditure patterns of different sectors.

The economic meaning of each land factor in the SAM table is briefly explained below. Macroscopic SAM in the CGELUC model generally describes the economic cycle of production, distribution and consumption in the economic system starting from commodities.

2.1 Preparation of SAM Parameters

The prices of products and factors are generally set to the same unit since the transaction values involved in the SAM dataset of the CGELUC model are expressed as values. Most of the parameters in the model can be calculated by incorporating equations of the CGELUC model, and the few parameters that cannot be calculated in this way are determined with the quantitative analysis module.

2.1.1 Proportion Parameters of the Product Production Module

The consumption coefficients of products $ax_{d,c}$ and $al_{1,c}$ can be directly obtained from the ratios of the intermediate input of commodities and land factor input and the total department output in the SAM $al_{1,c} = LK_{1,c}/Z_c$. The parameter $al_{1,c} = t_{4,1}/COL1$ is calculated with data in the SAM table mentioned above.

The share of factor f in the production process of the intermediate product c is $\beta_{f,c}(t)$ can be determined from the ratio of the proportion of the quantity of factor f input into the quantity of all factors in the production process of product c in the SAM matrix.

The production scale coefficient of the intermediate product c, or $b_c(t)$, can be calculated with the following formula:

$$b_c(t) = \left. Y_c(t) \middle/ \prod_f Fc_{f,c}(t)^{\beta_{f,c}(t)} \right. \tag{1}$$

In the integrated products of domestic sales, the share parameters of imported products $\delta m_c(t)$ and locally produced products $\delta d_c(t)$ can be determined by the ratio of the quantity of imported and locally produced products and the total quantity of domestic sales. The elasticity of substitution $\eta_c(t)$ between the locally produced product c and imported product c cannot be directly obtained through the SAM. These need to be estimated with econometric methods; the setting of these parameters is further described in the following text. After obtaining $\delta m_c(t)$, $\delta d_c(t)$ and $\eta_c(t)$, the scale parameter of the Armington function, $\gamma_c(t)$, can be determined with the following formula:

$$\gamma_c(t) = \left. Q_c(t) \middle/ \left(\delta m_c(t) M_c(t)^{\eta_c(t)} + \delta d_c(t) DK_c(t)^{\eta_c(t)} \right)^{1/\eta_c(t)} \right. \tag{2}$$

Relevant parameters of the total quantity of domestic products mainly include the share parameter $\xi e_c(t)$ of the export c, share parameters $\xi d_c(t)$ of product c produced and sold at home, the elasticity of conversion $\Phi_c(t)$ between the domestic product c and exported product c and the scale parameter $\theta_c(t)$ of the transfer function. These parameters are calculated based on processes and approaches similar to those of the integrated products sold at home.

2.1.2 Proportion Parameters of the Land Use Conversion Module

In the CGELUC model, land use conversion participates in economic activities as an independent sector similar to other commodity productions. Relevant parameters mainly include the consumption coefficient $axl_{c,zl}(t)$ of the intermediate product c in the land use conversion zl, consumption coefficient $ayl_{zl}(t)$ of other types of land, share of the factor $f\beta l_{f,zl}(t)$ in the production process of intermediate products in land use conversion zl and scale parameter $bl_{zl}(t)$ of the zlth newly-increased land. The calculation is similar to that of $ax_{d,c}(t)$, $al_{1,c}(t)$, $\beta_{f,c}(t)$ and $b_c(t)$.

2.1.3 Proportion Parameters of the Demand Module

The proportion parameters of the demand module mainly involve the consumption demand for different products, investment demand, land demand and demand for other factors of economic entities (government and residents). Government consumption should strictly conform to the implemented financial budget in the model. $\mu_c(t)$ is the proportion of the expense of the product c account in total government expenditures, and $\alpha_c(t)$ is the proportion of the expense of consumer good c in total household expenditures.

2.1.4 Parameters of the Product Price Module

The price of the product is directly related to the type of production function selected in the production module. In the top-level nest of the CGELUC model, the Leontief linear production function is adopted. The amount of intermediate inputs in the final products will directly affect the price of the final product.

2.2 Subdivision of the Macroscopic SAM

The macroscopic SAM is subdivided into subaccounts. The setting of the subaccounts often differs in countries and has no standard form. This is because (i) the statistical bases and availability of data differ in countries, and (ii) the purposes of policy analysis and forms of established economic models vary, which results in different requirements for subdivision levels.

There is a method always available to subdivide an account. The first is to subdivide the entire economic class into unit classes. The activity account and the product account are first subdivided according to industrial and product sectors, respectively, which stand for the input-output relationship of production. Consequently, some regard the SAM as an extension of an input-output table. After the activity and product accounts are subdivided, the factors are then subdivided into labor, capital and land. The business account is then subdivided. Finally, the enterprises are subdivided into state-owned enterprises, shareholding enterprises and foreign-owned enterprises according to ownership, or large-scale enterprises, medium-scale enterprises and small-scale enterprises according to size.

In the compilation of SAM, a disaggregated SAM is obtained by combining the two methods, subdividing the industrial activity and kinds of products and incorporating the macroscopic economic data with the subdivided data of relevant institutions.

The disaggregated SAM, which includes the relationships between product activities and transactions among sectors at the sector level, is ideal to describe mid-level economic flows and can provide large amounts of valuable data for policy analysis and model building.

3   Summary

Economic activities are the main driving factors behind structural changes in land use and are also constrained by the structure of regional land use. The CGELUC model analyzes factors that influence the types of regional land use based on macroscopic quantitative analysis, reveals relationships between economic variables and changes in area of cultivated, economic forest and pasture lands and then constructs mechanism-based models to analyze dynamic laws for the succession of land use structure at the regional scale. The CGELUC model selects the framework of CGE to analyze the influence of socioeconomic factors in an equilibrium economic system such as the industrial structure, trade environment, economic policies and institutional arrangements on the structure of regional land use.

Acknowledgements. This research was supported by the National Key Programme for Developing Basic Science (2010CB950904), the Chinese Academy of Sciences (KZCX2-YW-326-1), National Scientific Foundation of China (70503025), and the Ministry of Science and Technology of China (2008BAK50B06).

References

1. Deng, X., Jiang, Q., Lin, Y., Han, J.: Simulation of Changes of soil organic carbon stock of cropland in China. Geographical Research 29(1), 93–101 (2010a)
2. Haberl, H., Batterbury, S., Moran, E.F.: Using and shaping the land: a long-term perspective. Land Use Policy 18(1), 1–8 (2001)
3. Gelan, A.: Trade liberalisation and urban-rural linkages: a CGE analysis for Ethiopia. Journal of Policy Modeling 24(7–8), 707–738 (2002)
4. Lehtoner, H., Aakkula, J., Rikkonen, P.: Alternative agricultural policy scenarios, sector modelling and indicators. A sustainability assessment. Journal of Sustainable Agriculture 26(4), 63–93 (2005)
5. Wong, G.Y., Alavalapati, J.R.R.: The land-use effects of a forest carbon policy in the US. Forest Policy and Economics 5(3), 249–263 (2003)
6. Deng, X., Huang, J., Rozelle, S., Uchida, E.: Growth, Population and Industrialization and Urban Land Expansion of China. Journal of Urban Economics 63(1), 96–115 (2008)

An Evacuation Simulation Based on Boltzmann Distribution

Hao Lian, Ang Li, Yang Tian, and Ying Chen

No 10, Xi Tu Cheng Road, Haidian District
Beijing University of Posts and Telecommunications
100876 Beijing China

Abstract. The exited popular ways of evacuation simulation can't satisfy us in the computational efficiency and the calculation accuracy at the same time. In order to get acceptable efficiency and accuracy, we applied the related concept of statistical physics to the specific circumstances of evacuation and built an evacuation model based on Boltzmann Distribution. We also came up with the exit attraction function and direction judging principles to depict people's exit choosing and obstacles avoiding behaviors. At last, we proved our model is applicable and reasonable by comparing the classical models with ours.

Keywords: Evacuation, Boltzmann distribution, Exit Attraction Function.

1 Introduction

When the accidents (such as fires) happen in the large buildings nowadays, the location design of the emergency exits and peoples' escaping routes both have crucial influence on the final evacuation time. If we analyze the evacuation data from the simulation to find the choke point of the evacuation process, then we can evaluate the buildings' design quality and put forward the improvement suggestions.

The classical evacuation models either go against engineering applications because of large amount of calculation (such as Social Force Model [1]-[6]), or can't provide reliable evacuation results because of lacking authenticity (such as Cellular Automata model [7]-[13]). Thus, how to balance the accuracy and the time of the simulation has already been the main trend of the evacuation study.

We try to use a totally new method (the Boltzmann Distribution way) to handle the evacuating problems and our goal is to make the efficiency and the accuracy both reach an acceptable range.

2 The Evacuation Model Based on Boltzmann Distribution

2.1 Attraction Indicators

In many classical models, people are seen as particles in a specific space and the influence of emergency exits and the people around are treated as a kind of attractions

S. Lin and X. Huang (Eds.): CESM 2011, Part I, CCIS 175, pp. 327–334, 2011.
© Springer-Verlag Berlin Heidelberg 2011

or exclusions. These influences decide a person's speed and direction of escaping. In fact, the space with attractions is similar to the "field" in classical physics. In the field, a particle will present different kinds of moving states as the result of the influence of the field. We define the influence generalized applied force F_i. In physics, the random motion can be seen as a kind of thermal motion. Although the bulk movement of the people has some what a trend, the specific moving state isn't regular and somewhat disordered. Thus it is reasonable to introduce the concept of the statistical physics. We introduce the influence factor —— the attractive potential energy, which can also be called Attraction Indicators:

$$G_i = \frac{F_i}{\overline{F}}$$

Where $\overline{F} = \frac{\sum F_i}{N}$. We introduce $\overline{G} = \frac{\sum G_i}{N}$ to present the average value of the indicator. If everyone is at the same location (of course it will never happen in the real case), then the force F_i is the same, which leads to $G = 1$. Here G can be seen as the ground state energy which can also be called the minimum energy.

2.2 The Boltzmann Distribution

If the evacuation is treated as the thermo logy behavior of a particle in a field, then we can introduce the Boltzmann Distribution of the statistical physics [14]. That is, in a specific energy level, the amount of the particles $a_l = w_l \cdot e^{-\alpha - \beta \varepsilon_l}$, where w_l is degeneracy. Though a specific person in the space has N kinds of states, different people can't be at the same location. That means the evacuation of the people should be in agreement with the no-degenerate conditions, which leads $w_l = 1$. So an individual state which a person occupies can be seen as an energy level of this system. ε_l is the specific energy of a level and $\beta = \frac{1}{kT}$ (k is the Boltzmann constant).

The total amount of particles satisfies the following equation:

$$N = \sum_l a_l = \sum_l w_l \cdot e^{-\alpha - \beta \varepsilon_l} \tag{1}$$

From the view of the classical statistics, the probability of a particle at a certain energy level is:

$$P_l = \frac{a_l}{N} = \frac{w_l \cdot e^{-\alpha - \beta \varepsilon_l}}{\sum_l w_l \cdot e^{-\alpha - \beta \varepsilon_l}} = \frac{w_l \cdot e^{-\beta \varepsilon_l}}{\sum_l w_l \cdot e^{-\beta \varepsilon_l}} \tag{2}$$

Then the probability of a person at a certain state in the space should be similar to equation (2).

2.3 The Probability Distribution of People

Based on the Attraction Indicators in the real circumstances and the Boltzmann Distribution, we make the following analogy:

$$\frac{1}{G} \to \beta, G_i \to \varepsilon_i, P_i \to P_l \tag{3}$$

So in the "attractive field" which is equivalent in the evacuation, the probability distribution of the ith person is:

$$p_i = \frac{w_i \cdot e^{\frac{G_i}{G}}}{\sum_i w_i \cdot e^{\frac{G_i}{G}}} \tag{4}$$

Where $w_i = 1$:

$$p_i = \frac{e^{\frac{G_i}{G}}}{\sum_i e^{\frac{G_i}{G}}} \tag{5}$$

The equation (5) is the probability distribution in the "attractive field", we can approximately consider the distribution is also available in the specific evacuation space.

2.4 The Specific Description of the Evacuation Model

We treat the specific area of the evacuation as an attractive field, in which the potential energy decides the speed and direction of people's moving. In the real case, there are two means factors which lead the people's moving, one is the attractive force of the exits and the other is the influence the other people because of the group psychology. Based on the Boltzmann Distribution mentioned above, we come up with a probability vector $P = (P_1, P_2)$ to describe the next moving state of the ith people:

$$P_1^i = \frac{e^{\frac{l_i}{l_c}}}{\sum_i e^{\frac{l_i}{l_c}}} \qquad P_2^i - \frac{e^{-\kappa \frac{l_i}{l_c}}}{\sum_i e^{-\kappa \frac{l_i}{l_c}}} \tag{6}$$

P_1^i represents the influence of the exits on the ith person, P_2^i represents the influence from the other people. l_c represents the bar centric coordinates of the person at one moment. l_{ci} represents that bar centric coordinates all the other people.

As the coordinates of the exits will not change as time goes by, so the influence of the exits can be seen as an absolute influence and the influence of the people is a relativistic influence. So we introduce the parameter K to differ P_2^i from P_1^i. In fact, K represents the intensity of the attractiveness. We call it the indicator constant, so the intensity will increase if K increases, and vice versa.

From the above, the moving direction of the ith person is the direction of $\max\{P_1, P_2\}$, and the value of the speed is the maximum a person can reach.

As congestion will happen near the exits, so there will be very serious overlap situations if we keep the people's speed to be their maximum all the time. So we introduce a distance indicator ε to represent the extent of the people's congestion. In the range of ε, we give the person who has the minimum distance to the exit the largest speed, while the other people a smaller speed. In the real simulation, we find out that this method can make the congestion near the exits very visible.

When taking the obstacles into consideration, the simulation should show the people's prejudgment behavior when they have to avoid the obstacles, which means the moving path of a person should be in compliance with the real circumstances. This requires the simulation should have a direction judging principles for all people.

In our simulation, we set up a constant distance d, we forcibly make the speed component vertical to the obstacle $v_{\perp} = 0$, and the other speed components will not change when the distance between the person and the obstacle is smaller than d. In this way, the simulation can guarantee the people move in the "tangential direction" of the obstacle. Figure 1 shows the specific process of a person avoiding an obstacle:

The initial distribution of the people	People choose their path at the beginning	The process of avoiding an obstacle	Run away from the exits
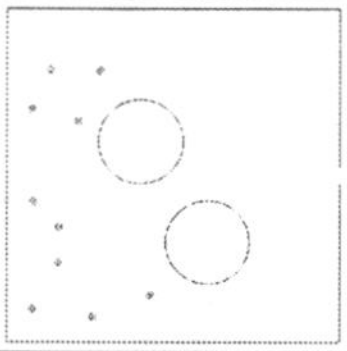	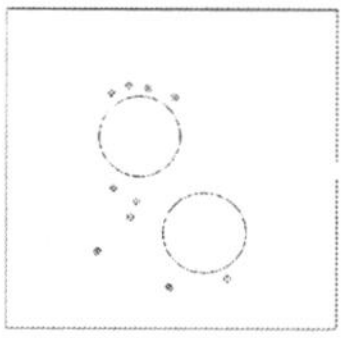	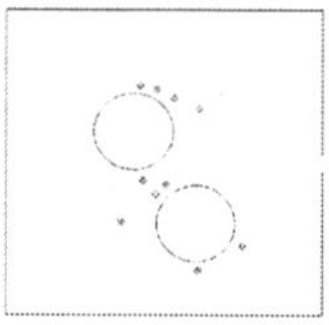	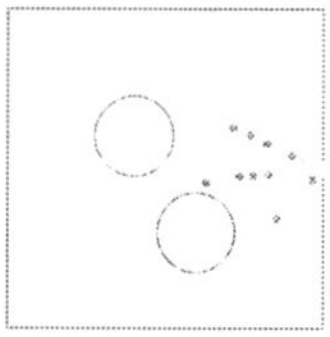

Fig. 1. The specific process of a person avoiding an obstacle

When there is more than one exit in the area, choosing the suitable obstacle is important for the people. The classical models always make people run to the nearest exit without considering the congestion near that exit. This method doesn't take the people's psychology of avoiding running to the crowed people into consideration and the simulation can't totally represent the real circumstance.

In the real case, the people will always choose their escaping path based on the distance to the exits and the congestion extent near the exit. Thus, we introduce the exit attraction function f_i:

$$f_i = e^{k_1(S-S_i)} \cdot e^{k_2(l_{max}-l_i)}$$

Where to one person, S represents the total amount of people in his sight. S_i represents the real amount of the people between this person to the ith exit. l_{max} represents the largest distance among all the distances between the exits and the person. l_i represents the real distance between the ith exit and the person. We choose the exit with the largest f_i to be the person's escaping exit. Figure 2 show the circumstances of people's choosing different exits:

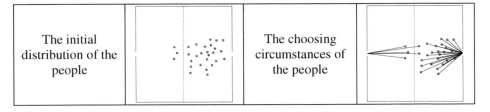

Fig. 2. The circumstances of people's choosing different exits

We need to determine some parameters in our model, such as the k_1, k_2 in the exit attraction function and these parameters directly influence the results of the simulation. However, there isn't a standard in the real circumstances. What we can do is to summarize an experiential standard by ways of watching some evacuation videos and so on. Therefore, we do many times of simulation and make the parameter values of the simulation which we consider is the most close to the real case.

3   Compare to the Classical Models

In order to test the rationality of our model, we apply the classical Social Force Model, Cellular Automata Model and our model to the same initial evacuation conditions and then compare the results of different models.

In a square room with the edge length 20m, we assume there is a huge obstacle at the center of the room which has an area of about 28 square meters. At the very beginning, the people are in the left side of the obstacle and the exit is in the right side of the obstacle. The results of the three models are shown in Figure 3:

Cellular Automata Model	Social Force Model	Our Model
Initial People Distribution		
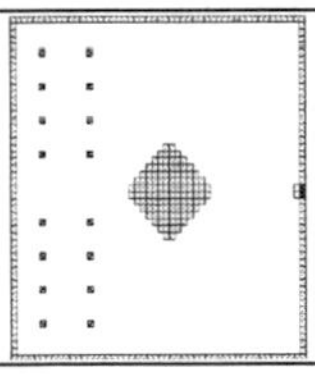	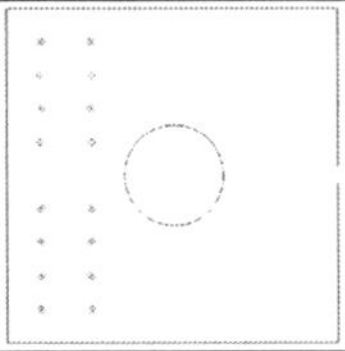	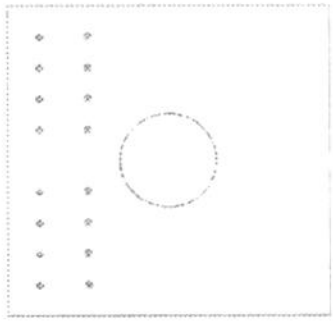
The path of avoiding the obstacle is not ideal	The people are able to avoid the obstacle	The people are able to avoid the obstacle in the tangential direction
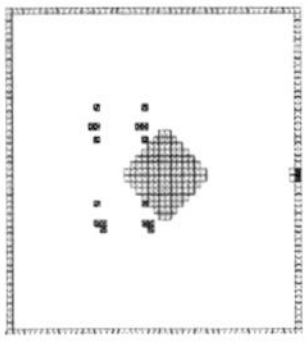	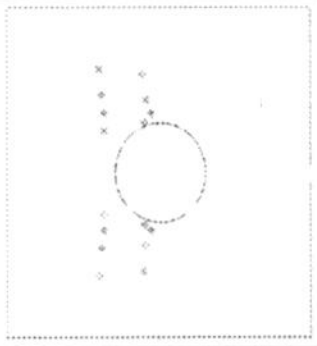	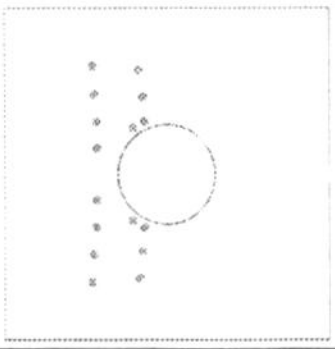

Fig. 3. The comparison of the results of the three models

The people will avoid the obstacle only when they are near to the obstacles.	The people will change their moving directions once their escaping path isn't kept back by the obstacle	The people will change their moving directions once their escaping path isn't kept back by the obstacle
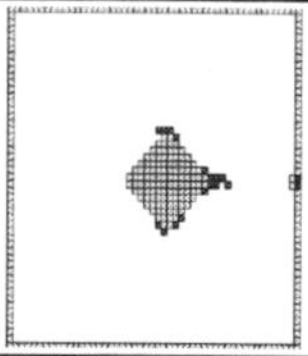	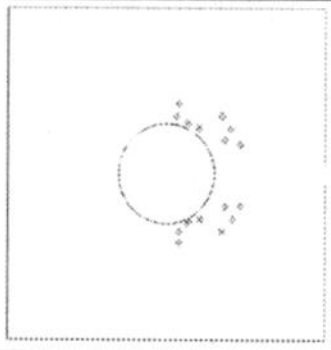	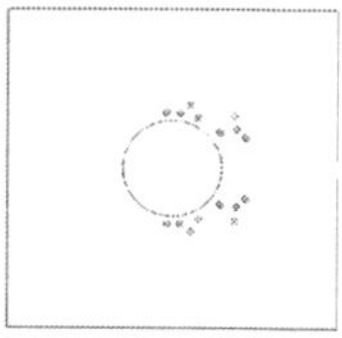
We can hardly see the congestion near the exit	There is significant congestion near the exit	There is significant congestion near the exit
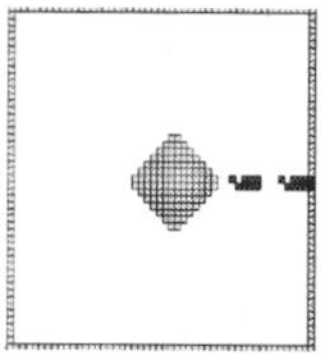	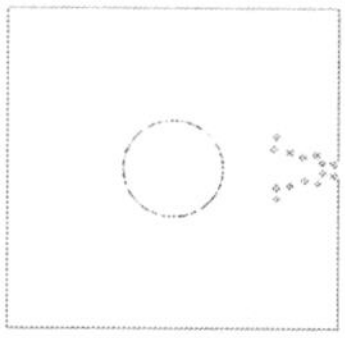	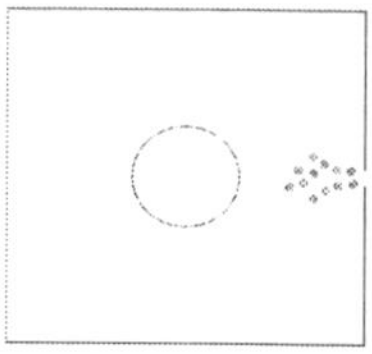

Fig. 3. (*Continued*)

It is obvious that everything is treated as a small grid in the Cellular Automata Model, which limits the true extent of its simulation. It can't represent the ideal avoiding obstacle path. However, it is of the most efficiency among the three models.

Compared with the Cellular Automata Model, the Social Force Model can represent the process of avoiding the obstacle and the congestion near the exit better. But the calculating efficiency is very low.

Our model has nearly the same accuracy with the Social Force Model. In the aspect of the congestion near the exit our model seems does better. What's more, our efficiency is less than half of the Social Force Model (in the same calculating conditions, the Social Force Model needs to calculate 2089 times, while our model needs 1018 times).

Then we can get the data comparison as Table 1:

Table 1. The data comparison among three models

The Model	Congestion near the exit	The path avoiding the obstacle	Times need to calculate
Social Force Model	It can reflect	Avoid once the person finds it	2089 times
Cellular Automata Model	It can hardly reflect	Avoids along the edge of the obstacle	48 times
Our Model	It can reflect	Avoid once the person finds it	1076 times

From the above analysis, we can arrive at the conclusions that our model has nearly the same simulation accuracy with the Social Force Model and the efficiency is just half of it. We have made a useful attempt on the evacuation problem and the results satisfy us to a certain extent

4 Conclusions

We put aside the method of depicting the moving state of everyone intensively in the classical models and come up with the Boltzmann Distribution evacuation model based on the thoughts of the trend of bulk movement. Through comparing our model to the classical models, we get some conclusions shown as followings:

- Up to now, the best model of depicting moving state intensively is the Social Force Model and our model has nearly the same intensive extent with it. Of course our model depicts much better than the Cellular Automata Model. The efficiency of our model is nearly half of that of the Social Force Model.
- We also come up with the Exit Attraction Function to simulate the choosing conditions when there are different exits and the avoiding principles which make people go along a curve path to avoid the obstacles.

Our model consider the possible moving trend as a whole instead of intensively depicting everyone's moving state which is totally a new way in the evacuation simulation study. Based on the results, the simulation effect seems acceptable, which provides a valuable direction in the future in similar questions

Acknowledgment

We should show our gratitude to the research innovation fund for college students of Beijing University of Posts and Telecommunications.

Also, we should extend our thanks to the Bupt mathematic and physics innovation laboratory for the lab conditions. What's more, professor Zuguo He helped us a lot.

References

[1] Helbing, D., Farkas, I., Vicsek, T.: Simulating dynamical features of escape panic. Nature(S0020-0836) 407(1), 487–490 (2000)
[2] Helbing, D., Farkas, I.J., Molnar, P., et al.: Simulation of pedestrian crowds in normal evacuation situations. Pedestrian and Evacuation Dynamics, 21–58 (2002)
[3] Helbing, D., Molnar, P.: Social force model for pedestrian dynamics. Pys. Rev. E 51(5), 4282–4286 (1995)
[4] Helbing, D., Farkas, VIcsek, T.: Simulating dynamical features of escape panic. Nature 407(6803), 487-490 (2000)
[5] Helbing, D., Keltsch, J., Molnar, P.: Modelling the evolution of human trail systems. Nature 388(6637), 47–50 (1997)
[6] Helbing, D., Schweitzer F'KeltSch, J.:

[7] Muramatsu, M., Irie, T., Nagatani, T.: Jamming transition in pedestrian counter flow. Physica A 267, 487–498 (1999)

[8] Muramatsu, H., Nagatani, T.: Jamming transition in two-dimensional pedestrian traffic. Physica A 275, 281–291 (2000)

[9] MuramatSu, M., Nagatani, T.: Jamming transition of pedestrian traffic at a crossing with open boundarie. Physica A 286, 377–390 (2000)

[10] Tajima, Y., Nagatani, T.: Clogging transition of pedestrian flow in T-shaped channel. Physica A 303, 239–250 (2002)

[11] Tajima, Y., Nagatani, T.: Scaling behavior of crowd flow outside a hall. Physica A 292, 545–554 (2001)

[12] Tajjma, Y., Takinoto, K., Nagatani, T.: Scaling of pedestrian channel flow with a boltleneck. Physica A 294, 257–268 (2001)

[13] Nagatani, T.: Dynamical transition and scaling in a mean-field model of pedestrian now at a bottleneck. Physica A 300, 558–566 (2001)

[14] Wang, Z.: Statistic and Thermodynamic Physics, 190–218 (2008)

On Self-adaptability of the Higher Vocational Education

Guanlong Luo, Jianjun Yun, and Jie Tang

Department of Mechatronics Engineering
Applied Technical College of Jilin University, China
{Luogl,Yunjj,Tj}@jlu.edu.cn

Abstract. The higher vocational education bears the dual-task of transmitting the human survival culture and development culture. And its educational characteristics make it have to adjust its teaching management, content, method and objective and other items in the teaching as soon as possible so as to adapt to the employment pressure on the students from the career along with the economic development and change in the progress of science. The discussion about the self-adaptability of higher vocational education aims at making the teaching catch up with the development of economy and science and technology, shorten the gap between the vocational education and vocational demand and replace the educational mode with rapid and active self-adaptive change for the educational mode with traditionally passive change with a view to really make the higher vocational education play a due role in the development of national economy.

Keywords: vocational education; self-adaptability; non-written assessment.

Introduction

Various experience and conclusions that the human beings write down are culture. Contextualizing the essence of the human activities is an important basis for the human development, because it can make people possibly do something for the human development in their short life based on the effective learning of previous culture.

1 Higher Vocational Education

The vocational education belongs to the category of survival cultural education and it is a means of transmitting culture with the technology culture as the major educational content. And the higher vocational education is a means of transmitting culture with the modern technology culture as the major educational content and the so-called modernization here refers to the high technology of vocational purpose and the mode of production with high yield and high efficiency. This mode must be the vocation based on the modern science and technology. And it is based on the new materials, new methods, mew processes and new theories and is also the concentrated embodiment of non-traditional vocations. Besides, it is also different from the traditional vocational education with a slow updating based on the manual labor in the non-higher vocational education.

S. Lin and X. Huang (Eds.): CESM 2011, Part I, CCIS 175, pp. 335–340, 2011.

The higher vocational education focuses on the "teaching", with the main purpose of providing applied talents in the modern production for the society and it is the basis for the development of national economy.

Because the vocational education concerns the factors in various aspects, such as society, school, enterprise and students, it is a complicated systems engineering and their general relationships are as follows:

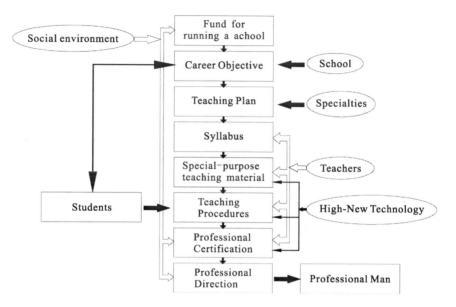

Fig. 1. Flow Chart of Relationships between the Vocational Education and Other Factors

In Figure 1, the square frames stand for the procedure items while the round frames stand for the external influencing factors.

The modern science and technology develops so rapidly that we even can use explosion to describe its expansion speed and the development of science and technology directly affects the economic development. It does not only can speed up the updating and upgrading of traditional careers, but also can create many new careers, which brings huge challenges for the higher vocational education, namely, how to adjust the education direction to adapt to the modern higher vocational education.

2   The Self-adaptability at School Level in the Higher Vocational Education

The self-adaptability generally refers to the stress reaction of organisms to the environment and the organisms adjust their own various states with a view to adapt to the change of environment and survive.

2.1 Self-adaptability of Specialty Setting

The self-adaptability of specialty setting is the location result of career objective group in the vocational education and its location does not only need to meet the requirement of current occupation, but also should consider the sustainable development of the students, namely, having certain ability of career transition and development. Because the higher vocational education takes the post adaptability as the basic connotation, along with the social and economic development and the progress of science and technology, the division of labor in society is more and more specialized and the division of labor at post is finer and finer. Therefore, it becomes the objective development requirement to adapt to the vocational needs of different post groups, to make targeted necessary setting of specialty and discipline adjustment according to the characteristics of specialties and disciplines and to establish the post ability-oriented curriculum system. This post adaptability which sets courses based on s the posts and educates people by posts becomes the basic connotation of self-adaptability of higher vocational education. There should be specialists who make follow-up study on the typical professional posts so as to provide basic information about adjustment for the self-adaptability of specialty.

2.2 Self-adaptability of Teaching Process in the Higher Vocational Education

Due to the particularity of vocational education, the major influencing factor of its teaching process is the self-adaptability of syllabus, special-purpose teaching material and teaching methods and so on.

2.2.1 Self-adaptability of Syllabus

Syllabus is the guidance document for the courses and is the reflection of knowledge requirements in the specialty objective for vocational groups in the teaching process. Because the vocational education in China started late, the setting of its course mainly follows the undergraduate teaching materials. And the content of undergraduate teaching materials pays much attention to the completeness of theoretical framework of the courses, so the major problem of the self-adaptability of syllabus of the same course in the vocational education is to weaken the completeness of theoretical framework of the courses, to strengthen the application content of the course and to pay attention to the pervasiveness of content for the vocational group and guidance of it for the selection and preparation of teaching materials. Its purpose is to save the time to learn the courses and make the students get more applied knowledge in a limited time, which is also an inevitable result of time limitation in the vocational education, because the knowledge explosion does not make the human lifespan increase obviously and there is a law for people to understand the knowledge they acquire. Therefore, to raise the learning efficiency is a problem that should be solved in the process of people learning culture.

2.2.2 Self-adaptability of Teaching Materials

The self-adaptability of theoretical teaching materials focuses on using the modern scientific method to complete the theoretical validation content. For example, we can use the computer to verify the correctness of the theories, which does not only can guarantee the completeness of the original theory courses, but also can save time. There is a lot of work to do. Because the teachers in the current vocational education are mainly the students of certificate education, it is unavoidable that the certificate education finds its way in the process of preparing the teaching materials and the teaching process. Then, it is necessary to prepare the special theoretical teaching materials for the vocational education and widely apply the modern instrument of computer in the teaching process so as to raise the teaching efficiency.

The self-adaptability of technical teaching materials focuses on solving the problem of technical obsolescence. Because of the limitation of the teaching materials' editors and their insufficient knowledge of the modern technology, the problem of lagged technical teaching materials is not solved for a long time. This requires that there should be special professional technology researchers make the teaching materials about the same technology catch up with the development of technology application as much as possible through a lot of survey and researches and with the cooperation of professional and technical personnel. If possible, they should make proactive technical prediction to arouse the interest of student to explore.

Because the sources of theoretical basis for the technical teaching materials is diversified and the technologies in the same specialty are greatly related, the content studying on the relevance of various technologies and integrating them into the teaching materials can make the teaching yield twice the result with half the effort.

The self-adaptability of teaching method: The modern teaching method is an effective means adapting to the modern education. The traditional teaching method is the most effective means which is proved in the constant teaching practices and its mainstream aspect is beyond a shadow of a doubt. Because the teaching methods also constantly updates along with the development of modern technology, especially the updating speed of vocational education is faster than other types of education, the updating of its teaching method focuses on the teaching improvement and innovation on the self-adaptability of modern students and the specific rules of vocational technical teaching.

2.2.3 Self-adaptability of Theoretical Teaching
The self-adaptability of theoretical teaching is mainly embodied in simplifying the theories and getting rid of the stale ones while taking in the fresh ones. It talks the theories with a relatively large influence on the modern technology as much as possible, simplifies the theories with a relatively indirect influence on the modern technology; and taking the case-based technologies of theory application as the destination of theoretical conclusions, with the description about the guidance of complete theories for the practice, it guides the students to find correct theoretical basis when applying the new technology so as to enhance the ability of practical application under the guidance of theories.

2.2.4 Self-adaptability of Practice Teaching
The practice teaching is a characteristic teaching method in the vocational education and its major ways include experiment, training, fieldwork, on-the-job training, technique contest, design competition, making competition, debate, collective report, speech, survey and oral defense and so on.

Among them, the experimental teaching focuses on verifying the correctness of classroom theories and it belongs to confirmatory teaching and is the continuation of theoretical teaching. Besides guiding the students to verify the theories, the experiment in this teaching process should take the practical application cases of theories as the experimental items so as to guide the ability of students in integrating theory with practice.

The training is mainly to make designed and purposeful practice of a vocational skill, with view to make the students close to the professional man in the vocational skill, at least obviously different from the ordinary people. Because this practice is a uniform training of human thinking and body movements and it is a relatively boring repeated work, a good external environment should be provided for the practice and certain incentive mechanism should also be given so as to make the trainee complete the training objective with a relatively happy feeling.

The fieldwork is to make professional training through the practice methods of simulation career or actually going on duty. It should provide actual professional training for the students as many as possible and if there is no professional training opportunity, it should provide the simulated professional training for the students. And its major purpose is to make the students obtain working experience from the practice teaching process and make the practice teaching be the bridge of students to the career.

2.3 Self-adaptability of Assessment in the Higher Vocational Education

The written (test-oriented) assessment is an important component of modern education. It makes huge contribution to the modern high efficient and standardized education and is the major test means in the modern education process. Its major method is that the students answer the questions on paper in writing and the teachers test the learning effect of the students through judging whether the answers on paper are correct or not.

In the vocational education, the written examination is still the major assessment method, but should not be the only method, which is determined by the characteristics of the vocational education. That's because the major objective of vocational education is the education of professional skills and the assessment is to test the ability of the students in applying the science and technology. And the learning effect of the students in professional skill can not be fully tested by the written examination, so it is necessary to introduce the non-written assessment methods into the assessment of vocational education.

There are many non-written assessment methods and their standards vary from the testing purposes. They make the assessment through evaluating the preparation of experiment report, result of training test, effect of fieldwork, result of on-the-job training, technique contest, design competition, making competition, effect of debate, quality of special report, effect of speech, ability of survey and research and correctness of oral defense and so on and the above assessment method can not be completed by written examination. But they can the effective method which can relatively correctly test the practical operation, research and resilience of the students. And the their scoring method is also difference from the scoring method in written examination, namely, its scoring result is not as consistent as the scoring in written examination.

2.3.1 Assessment Method of Theory Courses

The assessment of theory courses is based on the written examination and the non-written assessment methods can be introduced, such as course summary, professional application design, assumption of related professional applications, paper writing, solution and application of the related subjects on computer and so on, which can make up the problems that the initiative of the students can not be sufficiently mobilized in the written test.

2.3.2 Assessment Method of Practice Course

The assessment of practice courses is based on the non-written examination.

The experimental courses should be mainly tested by preparing the experiment report, whose content include the design of experiment, method of operation, test report, error analysis, application assumption, questions and solutions, attentions, utilization of test instrument and so on; and the operation can be test at any time in the experiment process.

The training courses are assessed by the result of actual operation skill. For testing the actual operation ability according to the objective and requirement of training, there are two indexes and they are the requirement for quality of the operation result, namely, the operation process or the soundness of result, and the requirement for quantity, namely, the test for the operation efficiency.

Because the fieldwork has the closest relationship with the career, if possible, it can be replaced by the direct on-post practice. And its assessment method mainly includes two aspects: one is the comprehensive evaluation of the employing units; the other is the evaluation on practice report of the students.

References

1. Liu, B.: Tradition and Reform of Ideas of Universities. Educational Science Publishing House (2004)
2. Liu, B.: Tradition and Reform of Ideas of Universities. Educational Science Publishing House (2004)
3. National Center for Education Development Research. Green Paper on Education in China. Educational Science Publishing House (2004)

Design and Implementation of Middle Layer for Off-line Query Based on JSF and Hibernate Framework

Zheqiong Yan, Jia Chen, and Minggang Wang

Dalian Maritime University, Dalian 116026, Liaoning, China
yanzheqiong@gmail.com

Abstract. The J2EE hierarchical framework of enterprise level makes software development very difficult and low-level efficiency. For this reason, in the small and medium web systems, it will be more convenient with JSF and Hibernate Integration Framework. But there is still not a standard about how to transfer data between JSF and Hibernate, so in this paper, a Middle Layer for off-line query based on JSF and Hibernate integrate framework will be proposed and its architecture and principle will be analyzed in detail combined with practical examples.

Keywords: JSF, Hibernate, off-line query, Middle Layer.

1 The Necessary of Middle Layer

1.1 The Necessary of Integrating JSF and Hibernate

According to the knowledge of JSF and Hibernate, it's clear that JSF framework based on MVC design pattern isolate the sources program and business processes by controlling the configuration file, thus system is easy to be maintained and modified.

Though stand out in the view layer, JSF still leaves much to be desired in the model layer. Compared with JSF, Hibernate has many advantages in model layer, it's basically an ORM tool used for OR mapping which allows you to perform database activates without bothering about the Database change. But if only develop system using Hibernate, the logic of system is still confused, the process and view don't be separated effectively, as a result, the coupling degree isn't be decreased.

As a solution, integrating JSF and Hibernate is proposed. JSF, the infrastructure of whole system, is in charge of implementing the MVC pattern, and Hibernate is used to support the persistence layer. Thus, the coupling degree can be deceased by JSF and Hibernate is responsible for reducing the difficulty of processing business and accessing database, so that it's convenient to interactive with database. Based on this, the integrating framework can be useful and convenient in theory, but how to integrate two framework and transfer data between them in practice is becoming a main issue. The Middle Layer is to solve this problem. As the initial aim of integrating is to simplify the process of accessing database while sticking to decrease the coupling degree and definitude multilayer framework, so the Middle Layer is a MVC-based design.

S. Lin and X. Huang (Eds.): CESM 2011, Part I, CCIS 175, pp. 341–346, 2011.

1.2 The Traditional Query Mode

In the traditional query mode, the query conditions need to be transferred from web layer to business object, and then the business object constructs select statements by listing out the conditions. It is traditional to use Map as a container of conditions. However, the Map can only transfer the name and value, not deliver the logic of conditions that is conditional expressions, thus, the business object has to involve many conditional expressions. So once the logic of conditions change, the business object must be modified accordingly, and it's prone to much error.

1.3 The Off-line Query Based on Middle Layer

To solve the above problem, this paper used another query mode; called DetachedCriteria. DetachedCriteria is an off-line query mode, used to build up Criteria outside the scope of a session. DetachedCriteria can purity the DAO, so that DAO can concentrate on accessing database. In this case, it's not need to add conditions in the DAO, instead all of query conditions are encapsulated into a detached object, and then the detached object is transferred to DAO without having to using any data transfer objects. You can later on reattach the detached object to another session. Choosing Detachedcriteria query mode, the codes of program can be reduced and the boundary of every layer is also delimited. The working way of Detachedcriteria between the JSF and Hibernate is shown in Figure 1:

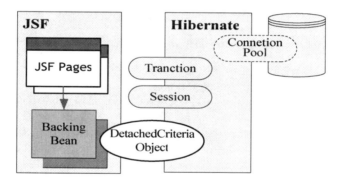

Fig. 1. The working way of Detachedcriteria between the JSF and Hibernate

None the less, Detachedcriteria object is still exposed to the web layer. It isn't good to divide the front and back labors. The web programmer has to learn some knowledge of Detachedcriteria. So it's necessary to design a middle layer to encapsulate Detachedcriteria object, thus the details of Detachedcriteria is transparent to the web programmer. In this way, the JSF and Hibernate are really separated. The whole framework after adding the Middle Layer is shown in Figure 2:

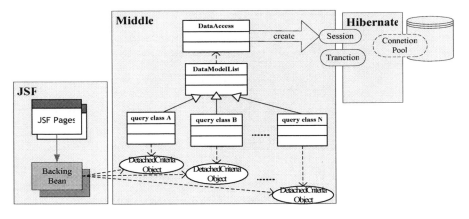

Fig. 2. The whole framework after adding the Middle Layer

In order to further understand the working principle of the Middle Layer, one example will be analyzed in detail.

2   The Implantation of Middle Layer

2.1   Background

Food safety is a topic drawing prior attention of the society. As we all know, substandard food can cause the serious harm to the human body. With this in mind, Food Traceability System can track food information "from the origin to mouse". The core of Food Traceability System is tracing, identifying, and linking the information flow and real logistics to make all aspects of food traceable and identifiable.

In the food traceability system, due to regional differences in various aspects of the circulation, the distributed database should be considered. So, the top-level database and the underlying database are designed. The underlying database set at various supermarkets and other retail outlets is responsible for managing the purchasing-selling-stocking data; while the top-level database is in charge of summarize data from each underlying database for inquiring, aggregating and analyzing in the future.

In this paper, the query platform is built on the top-level database. If you feed a source tracing code in, the system will show the detail information and every aspects of this food's circulation information, in other words, one operation involves two actions: query detail information and circulation information.

2.2   Working Principle

First of all, the focus is the Middle Layer's working principles. In order to explain the working principle more clearly, we should analyze the class diagram. The class diagram of Middle Layer is shown in Figure 3:

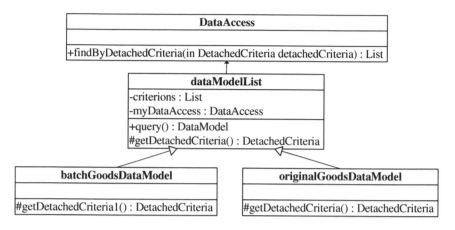

Fig. 3. The class diagram of Middle Layer

Middle Layer can be divided into three layers in concept: data access layer; core layer and query layer. The data access layer includes DataAccess class, which is the interface with Hibernate. In DataAccess, the parameter DetachedCriteria received from core layer will be processed in a Hibernate session opened in DataAccess. The key codes are as follows:

```
public static List findByDetachedCritria(DetachedCriteria detachedCriteria){
List list=null;
try {session = HibernateUtil.currentSession();
tx = session.beginTransaction();
list=detachedCriteria.getExecutableCriteria(session).list();   tx.commit();
}catch (HibernateException e) {
e.printStackTrace();tx.rollback();
}finally{HibernateUtil.closeSession(session); }
return list; }
```

The core layer is just what the name implies: the key of Middle Layer. In the layer, an abstract class named DataModelList is involved. The major tasks of DataModel-List have two points: return different DetachedCriteria object to DataAccess with the idea of polymorphism, secondly, encapsulate dataset returned by DataAccess as DataModel, which can be used by JSF's components as data source, such as DataTable. The key codes are as follows:

```
public abstract class dataModelList {
private DataAccess myDataAccess=new DataAccess();
private DataModel dataList=new ListDataModel();
private List<Criterion> criterions=new ArrayList<Criterion>();
protected abstract DetachedCriteria getDetachedCriteria();
final public DataModel query(){
try { dataList.setWrappedData(myDataAccess.
findByDetachedCriteria(getDetachedCriteria()));
```

```
}catch (Exception e) {
e.printStackTrace();}
return dataList;}}
```

Last layer is query layer, the interface with JSF, which includes specific query classes. All query classes are inherited from the abstract class DataModelList; they are instantiated in the JSF's backing Bean according to different purposes, one instance of query class is a DetachedCriteria object. In the food traceability system, there are two query actions, so its need to design two query classes named batchGoodsDataModel and originalGoodsDataModel. The key codes are as follows:

```
@Override
protected DetachedCriteria getDetachedCriteria() {
DetachedCriteria detachedCriteria =
DetachedCriteria.forClass(TableReceive.class);
for(int i=0;i<criterions.size();i++){
detachedCriteria.add(criterions.get(i)); }
return detachedCriteria; }
```

In the JSF framework, the Backing Bean collects the data from the JSF pages referenced on Backing Bean, So Bean can be seen as the logic part of the JSF.

As the requirement is relatively simple in the food traceability system, two query pages share a common Backing Bean named QueryBean. Meanwhile, the interaction with the Middle Layer is implemented in QueryBean.When a user clicked the query button, the method queryAction () defined in QueryBean will be called. The major task of queryAction () is creating a batchGoodsDataModel object, actually, that object is a DetachedCriteria object encapsulating query values in the JSF pages.After collecting all query conditions, the method query () of batchGoodsDataModel object is called to return the results from DataAccess in the form of DataModel, thus, the component DataTable can use result as data source directly, without transforming. The key codes are as follows:

```
batchGoodsDataModel batchDataModel=new batchGoodsDataModel();
if(this.batchNo==null || this.batchNo.isEmpty()){
return "NullInput";}
if(this.batchNo.length()<10){return "noRecords";}
String batchLast=this.batchNo.substring(0, 10);
String goodsNo=this.batchNo.substring(10);
Criterion criterion1=Restrictions.like("batchNo","%"+batchLast);
Criterion criterion2=Restrictions.eq("goodsNo",goodsNo);
batchDataModel.getCriterions().add(criterion1);
batchDataModel.getCriterions().add(criterion2);
```

2.3 The Advantage of Middle Layer

Using polymorphism, an important feature of the object-oriented programming, in abstract class DataModelList to return different off-line objects under the complicated application has many benefits. It can build a multi-layer Middle Layer with high reliability, maintainability, expansibility and reuse.

If the need of application is expanded, requiring to query more information, what we just need to do is to add a new query class inheriting from abstract class DataModelList, the new query class has to override the abstract method getDetachedCriteria (),then it can be used as the already existing query classes. The reason is the query logic is completely alike, except the query conditions. The key of Middle Layer is extracting the same code and logic to abstract class so that it can achieve maximum code reuse. A parallel case, if the query logic need to be modified, just change the implementation of the abstract class method, then test one query class, if one query class can be debug successfully, with the same way, other query classes can be adjusted thus, it really relent the programmers's modify task.

3 Summary

Nowadays, there is a prevalent trend of framework-based programming. Under this back ground, how to use framework flexibility and how to integrate different frameworks effectively have already become the major problems faced by programmers.

As a solution, this paper proposed a design of Middle Layer used in off-line query platform based on JSF and Hibernate framework. The Middle Layer applies the idea of multi-layer and polymorphism, so that it can be more reliability, more maintainability and more expansibility. in other off-line query application, the Middle Layer can be modified to adapt to complicated application.

References

1. Zhou, J., Liu, G.-y., Zhang, G.-p.: Developing Web Interface Using JSF. Journal of East China Jiaotong University (February 2007)
2. Zhang, C., Li, C.-p.: Improvement of search based on O/R MAPPING technology. Journal of Computer Applications (February 2006)

Reliability Analysis of Real-Time Multitasking Software Based on Neural Network

Xiang Chen[1], Wei Hou[1], and Yong Zhang[2]

[1] School of Civil Engineering, Xi'an Technological University,
710032 Xi'an, China
[2] Wuhan University of Science and Technology,
430071 Wuhan, China
{xichen0801,houwei75}@163.com, appserver@yahoo.cn

Abstract. Real-time multitasking software is core of large scale real-time system in industrial control. Characteristics of real-time system determine that it laid high requirements on software reliability. Based on analyzing on characteristics of real-time multitasking software, the paper modeled and researched on reliability of real-time multitasking software according to module mode based on neural network and established neural network model of real-time multitasking software. Simulation results based on application example shows that the proposed model introduced running time of each task mode into reliability model, which adapt to characteristic of real-time multitasking software and is more accurate than the method that does not based on task modules.

Keywords: real-time multitasking, reliability, neural network.

1 Introduction

Real-time system is widely used in industrial control, the core of which is real-time multitasking software. For characteristics of real-time system itself, it laid high requirements on software reliability, especially real-time systems as large-scale oil processing system. As to these complex real-time systems, the core real-time multitasking software is a kind of complex software with complex control relationships, high computation speed and rigid processing order. Error of system software may lead to failure and even disastrous consequences [1]. Software reliability can be measured by various parameters, such as reliability, failure rate, failure intensity, Mean Time To Failure (MTTF) and etc, which can be interchangeable each other. Real-time multitasking software can also be measured by these reliability indexes. In order to quantitatively analyze on its reliability, it must clear that real-time multitasking software also obey reliability increase rule for it has inherent characteristics of general software firstly. Secondly, there are restrictions in different aspects between real-time multitasking software and traditional software in many cases, which will affect its reliability. Finally, reliability of hardware will also impact on reliability of whole system.

According to above analysis, we can know that analyzing on reliability of real-time multitasking software can not follow traditional methods and models of ordinary

S. Lin and X. Huang (Eds.): CESM 2011, Part I, CCIS 175, pp. 347–352, 2011.
© Springer-Verlag Berlin Heidelberg 2011

software, we should establish its reliability model according to characteristics of real-time and multitask. By analyzing on characteristics of such kind of software, neural network was used to model and research its reliability in module manner. The paper is organized as follows. Section 2 gives evaluation model of real-time multitasking system. Neural network models to evaluate reliability of general software and real-time multitasking software are compared in section 3. Specific example is used to test performance of proposed real-time multitasking software reliability model based on neural network and section 5 concludes our work.

2   Real-Time Multitasking Evaluation Model

At any time t, actual running time t_{exe} of the task A_i is

$$t_{exe} = \begin{cases} t_{i1}, & t \le t_{unit} \\ t_{i1} + t_{i2} = t_i, & t_{unit} < t \le t_{rel} \\ t_i + p_i(t - t_{rel}), & t > t_{rel} \end{cases} \tag{1}$$

We can see that actual running time t_i of A_i is used to estimate parameter B_{xi} and b_i. At any time t ($t > t_{rel}$) after software was delivered, the task A_i may not run in time interval $[t_i, t_{rel}]$ and $[(1-P_i)(t-t_{rel}), t]$, so the system will not fail, and then t can not be used to estimate reliability of A_i directly. Based on the model, we can determine mean of failure number $m_i(t)$, failure intensity $\Phi_i(t)$ and running time ratio P_i. As to task set $S = \{A_1, A_2, \ldots, A_n\}$ at t, there is

$$m(t) = \sum_{i=1}^{n} m_i(t) \tag{2}$$

and

$$\Phi(t) = \sum_{i=1}^{n} \Phi_i(t). \tag{3}$$

In some time interval $[t_s, t]$ $(t_s \ge t_{rel})$, the Mean Time Before Failure (MTBF) is

$$MTBF = \frac{t - t_s}{\int_s^t \sum_{i=1}^{n} \Phi_i(t)}. \tag{4}$$

It we use T to represent the time from time 0 to software failure, the software reliability $R(t)$ is

$$R(t) = \exp(\int_0^t -\Phi(t)dt) = \exp(\int_0^t -\sum_{i=1}^{n} \Phi_i(t)dt). \tag{5}$$

Time t obeys the distribution of t_{exe}. If $t > t_{rel}$, (5) can be re-wrote as

$$R(t) = \exp(\int_{rel}^{t_i + p_i(t - t_{rel})} (-\sum_{i=1}^{n} \Phi_i(t)dt)) .$$ (6)

3   Reliability Model of Real-Time Multitasking Software

3.1   Neural Network Model of General Software Reliability

With method combined Halstead theory [2] and G-O model [3], we can know that reliability index currently can be arrived according to software code line number B_s, software test time T_s, failure number in test N_s and running time T. Good approximation capability of RBFNN can be used to establish its reliability analyzing model. The parameters B_s, T_s. N_s and T are input of RBFNN and reliability index is its output. Here failure rate Φ is selected. Structure of RBFNN is shown in Fig. 1. Failure rate can be used to describe software reliability. RBFNN was trained with actual measured data. After the success of network training, the trained network can be used to analyze its reliability index with some new specific inputs.

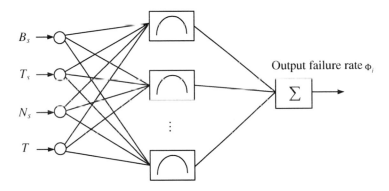

Fig. 1. Neural network model of general software reliability

3.2   Neural Network Model of Real-Time Multitasking Software Reliability

Each task module of real-time multitasking software has relatively independent functions. Real-time was scheduled by operation system with some scheduling strategy to occupy CPU resource. Each task module has its own independent reliability. Based on structural and modular idea of Littlewood, we can independently analyze on reliability of each task module, and then to draw reliability of whole software. For difference of running period and execution time, the proportion P_i of each module $i(i=1,2,\ldots,n)$ account for overall running time is different. Task module that occupies larger proportion of overall running time may have greater impact on system reliability. So P_i is an important factor to determine software reliability [4]. $P_i = C_i / t_i$, where C_i is task execution time and t_i is period of task. The parameters C_i and t_i are determined by designers before development, which are known before test.

Neural network model to evaluate reliability of real-time multitasking software can be established based on its characteristics. Improvements should be conducted on above mentioned neural network model. Firstly it needs to substitute B_s, T_s and N_s with code number B_i, test time T_i and failure number N_i of each task module. Secondly add P_i as input of neural network. RBFNN of real-time multitasking software is shown in Fig. 2, which presents reliability model of a task module. P_i, B_i, T_i, N_i and T are inputs of network and module failure rate Φ_i is the output. As modules of software are developed in same environment, we can train neural network based on test data in software module test report, and then to analyze reliability of other modules with trained neural network. The failure rate of whole system is the sum of all modules' failure rate.

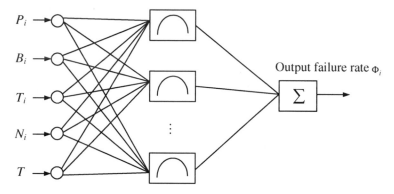

Fig. 2. Neural network model of real-time multitasking software reliability

4   Case Study

Test report of some real-time multitasking software is shown in Table 1 [4]. The software was divided into 14 task modules. DS model method [5] was used to compute failure rate of each module after 10 days operation. DS model algorithm is currently accepted method to study reliability of real-time multitasking software, the computation result of which has considerable accuracy. As module number of the software is relatively little and there is little data for training, so it have relatively poor network computing accuracy. To address this problem and expand training data, neural network simulation method was used to produce data with same statistical principle based on original data to expand sample number [6, 7]. The former 12 group of reliability data was expanded. Then expanded data was used to train neural network model of general software and real-time multitasking software. Two trained network was then sued to perform simulation computation on remaining two group data, the results of which are shown in Table 2. We can know from simulation results that the proposed model reduced error greatly and improve accuracy significantly compared with that of general software neural network model.

Table 1. Real-time multitasking software test report

Task module	P_i	Test Failure B_i	Test Time T_i	Code Number N_i	Failure Rate with DS Φ_i
1	0.1566	5	3	470	0.125988
2	0.1364	7	2	405	0.034529
3	0.099	5	2	396	0.09049
4	0.2227	38	10	1783	0.211092
5	0.0922	13	4	738	0.095572
6	0.0495	17	3	792	0.029602
7	0.0420	22	4	672	0.042815
8	0.0503	14	3	807	0.089472
9	0.0222	12	2	440	0.028256
10	0.0584	20	6	1169	0.091465
11	0.0501	19	3	1002	0.100794
12	0.0528	32	11	1267	0.043711
13	0.0282	21	3	848	0.057195
14	0.0309	16	4	928	0.054471

Table 2. Analyzing result comparison

Result with DS	Result of original neural network	Relative error of original neural network	Result of improved neural network	Relative error of improved neural network
0.057196	0.061472	7.5%	0.058447	2.1%
0.054471	0.058793	7.9%	0.053373	1.7%

5 Conclusion

Characteristics of real-time determine that it laid high requirements on software reliability. Based on analyzing on characteristics of real-time multitasking software and highlight its distinguish with reliability with general software, a kind of neural network analyzing model of real-time multitasking software was presented. The model introduced running time of each task module into reliability model to meet features of real-time multitasking software, which is more accurate than methods not according to task module. It can analyze reliability of real-time multitasking software well and solve shortcoming of large error of general model, which also has good scalability. Example study shows its effectiveness and superiority.

References

1. Broklehurst, S., Chan, Y.P., Littlewood, B.: Recalibrating Software Reliability Models. IEEE Transaction on Software Engineering 16, 458–463 (1990)
2. Lipow, M.: Number of Faults Perline of Code. IEEE Trans Software Engineering 7, 437–439 (1982)
3. Song, X.-q.: Analysis on Characteristics of Software Reliability G-O Model. Computer Engineering and Design 17, 55–57 (1996)
4. Lei, H., Xiong, G.-z.: The Reliability Evaluation Model of Real-time Multitasking Software. Computer Applications 20, 9–14 (2000)
5. Lei, H., Xiong, G.-z., Liu, J.-d.: A Real-time Multitasking Software Reliability Model. Journal of Applied Science 16, 1–5 (1998)
6. Wang, J.-c., Chen, Z.-l., Zeng, J.-y.: Study of Neural Network Simulating and Extending Reliability Data. Electronic Product Reliability and Environmental Testing 19, 2–6 (2001)
7. Wang, J.-c., Wang, L.-s., Sun, X.-m.: Study of Neural Network Simulating and Extending Reliability Data. Systems Engineering and Electronics 23, 90–92 (2001)

Construction of Distance Education System Based on Online Game Operation Mode

Xiang Chen[1], Xue-feng Zhou[1], and Yong Zhang[2]

[1] School of Civil Engineering, Xi'an Technological University,
710032 Xi'an, China
[2] Wuhan University of Science and Technology,
430071 Wuhan, China
xichen0801@163.com, zxf0311@126.com, appserver@yahoo.cn

Abstract. Modern distance education is not simple supplement to traditional education mode, but a new exploration and innovation. Popular online game operation modes were analyzed and the design idea of virtual world online game was introduced to distance education to construct more attractive education system. General process and main development tool were also described. System architecture to construct online game distance education was analyzed and designed according to modular principle for server and client. A general implementation program for distance education software design based on online game engine was given finally.

Keywords: distance education, online game, virtual world game, modular design.

1 Introduction

Modern distance education is product of traditional education combing with technologies of computers and network, which is not merely supplement to traditional education, but a new exploration and innovation. Game, especially online game is very attractive to players for its special interactive, participatory and social. As to part of school-age players, a negative social evaluation emerged for excessive indulgence into online games [1]. As to education distance, students are in an isolated Internet client far away from campus environment. Autonomous learning can be greatly improved in that we can study at any time and any place, which also have some problems [2]. Without monitoring manners of naming and examination in campus and communication channel among students, it is difficult for learners to put lasting passion to complete an online course [3, 4]. Referring to design idea of online games, design and deployment pattern of distance education software were explored and overall architecture to construction online game distance education system was given. The paper is organized as follows. Section 2 introduces basic mode and common editing tools of online games. Section 3 gives overall architecture of distance education system based on online game operation mode and section concludes our work.

S. Lin and X. Huang (Eds.): CESM 2011, Part I, CCIS 175, pp. 353–358, 2011.

2 Basic Game Mode and Common Editor Tools

According to characteristics, currently various popular online games can be divided into four types according to operation mode, namely real-time strategy, first person shooter, virtual world or role playing and card games. The role in games of different mode has different behaviors. For example, in real-time strategy game, the role has behaviors of movement in all directions, patrolling, defense, attack, picking up things, upgrade and add some other acts. In the first-person shooter, there are behaviors of forward, backward, left and right shift, jump, switch weapons, run, walk, buy weapons, fire and 360-degree angle conversion. In the card games, the role has behaviors of waiting and acting. In the virtual world games, the role has behaviors of move around, 360-degree angle conversion, jump and talk with other players, trading, upgrades, building equipment, and other acts. In these basic modes, behaviors of role in virtual world games not only includes basic behaviors of former three types, but also has broad social participation to best meet people's emotional needs. So it is the most attractive game mode. Therefore, design idea of virtual world game can be introduced into distance education to construct more attractive online knowledge learning system.

A successful game edition involves many aspects. It not only needs wonderful plot and level design by game planners, but also role and scene design by art staff. It also needs program developers to design based on game engine. Completion of game needs many tools.

(1) Scene editor to create game scenarios to accommodate interaction of players. Tools as SceneEditor, 3DMAX, ShadowEditor, MagicGearEditor3D, Photoshop CS are used to create, place or modify natural terrain such as mountains, rivers, or man-made terrain such as housing, roads, or other similar things, such as space in the game like planets.

(2) Task editor. Task is also called barriers or risks, which includes a series of works to achieve a target. Task editor usually needs to set task return conditions, design traps and NPC triggers when players try to complete the task as well as that used for tracking time-limited tasks. The task editor includes Pitrunner, Blade of Darkness and so on.

(3) Sound Editor. Tools as Audioblast 1.6.3, Adobe Audition, Goldwave are used to insert sound into action trigger or edit background sound. Any places need sound will be completed by trigger.

(4) Script editor. Tools as Seraph are used to create or debug game mechanism that has not been written as hard code. The editor is used to assist improving performance of games.

(5) Props or article editor. The tool as ShadowEditor is used to create or edit things can be got by players, such as interactive thing.

3 Overall Architecture of Distance Education System Based on Online Game

Based on above analysis, we can create a society-oriented non-campus distance education system based on Internet with network technology and multimedia technology referring to design idea of virtual world games. The system provide support services of various game education software to gradually form various micro-community of types theme, so as to complete the accumulation of game-based educational software and ultimately constitute a sound knowledge learning system.

3.1 Architecture Analysis of Online Game Knowledge Learning System

To simplify system development cycle and reduce costs, communication framework and basic database with existing engine were selected to simplify system development. The principle of selection is open, real-time, ease of use and the ability to work in the Internet environment. So C/S structure was selected as basic communication platform.

C/S is client and server structure. It makes full use of advantage of hardware environment on both ends and rationally allocates tasks to the client and the server side to implement, reducing the system communication overhead. Most application software is two-layer structure with form of Client/Server. As software application system now is developing to distribute Web applications. Web and Client/Server applications can perform same business processing and use different modules sharing logic components. All users of C/S structure are connected to a central server. Communication between clients is forwarded through the server. Management information can be stored on the server. The structure also has a simple programming model.

Construction of online game knowledge learning system is a complex large scale software project. An excellent performance, maintainable, extensible system framework is vital to development of online game knowledge learning system. The modular design idea can be used. As to the structure, services provided by system can be divided into series of loosely coupled components according to functions and logic relationship. Interfaces are established among components. The mechanism can isolate component modules in function to achieve freedom assembly and component separation [5]. The system can also be better maintainability and scalability. Thus, developers of education system only need to concern about business in related problem fields using this framework, which greatly reduce workload of developers.

Online game distance education system is not simply established on distributed system with C/S structure, which also has its own characteristics. Server does not merely complete simple services, but to provide a service component factory. The factory is responsible for producing application services that created for specific applications and all students. All these services are reflected as components, the structure of which was shown in figure 1.

Where, login service component is used for build connections for clients to provide login service. Account service component is responsible for user account registration, login, verification, destruction, access, delete, find, and statistics. Control service component is used to initiate or terminate some services. Forward service component is responsible for direct communication among services.

In this modular assembly architecture, fixed interfaces among modules can be costumed and module itself can be replaced or upgraded. Modules can also operate on different operating system platform. Thus, the architecture of whole system has scalable and portable performance advantages.

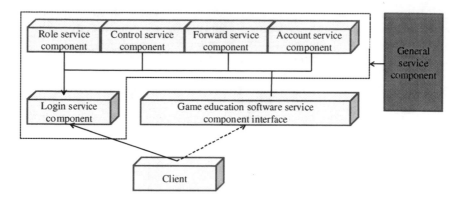

Fig. 1. Server component in distance education system based on online game

On the client, business process can be divided into multi-layer structure according to different event handling logic as shown in figure 2.

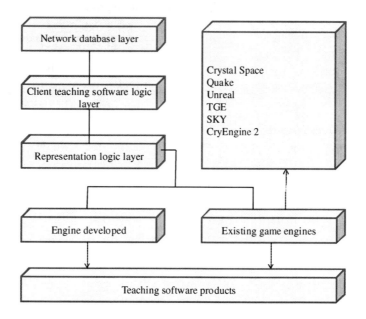

Fig. 2. Client structure of distance education system based on online games

Functions of each layer are as follows:

(1) Network database layer provide functional implementation for network connection of server and client. It also provides encryption service for transmitting information to ensure information security of the whole system.

(2) Client teaching software logic layer is part of teaching software logic existed on client. Compared with server, it is only a little part. It keeps pace with teaching logic on server through network connection.

(3) Presentation logic layer is responsible for map logic objects and presentation objects, such as processing manner, images and sound. It also implements some detail requirements of client itself.

(4) Engine layer is divided into existing game engine and engine developed. In the existing game engine, Unreal and Quake as shown in the figure has widely usage.

The client also uses modular assembly architecture, which can replace specific representation engine to produce game teaching software with different manners.

3.2 System Design Program Based on Existing Engines

Game engine mainly includes engine kernel, graphic processing module, sound processing module, network processing module and interaction processing module. In the specific implementation to construct knowledge learning system based on online games, existing game engines can be utilized to produce teaching software of different disciplines. Thus, developers do not need to program software from the underling layer. They can design appropriate script, build corresponding entity model, design various roles and determine scenario and transformation calling related API functions to complete programming of teaching software. In this way, complex software programming process can be transferred into related simple special teaching data organization process, which can be refined to graphic file, sound file, input and network information as shown in figure 3.

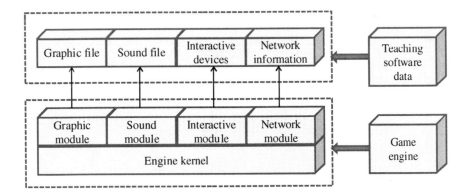

Fig. 3. Common implementation schema to design teaching software based on game engine

As to graphics rendering, tools mentioned above can be used to build needed teaching models, and then transferred into required internal format with appropriate plugins. Graphics system of game engine can then be called to plot scenarios. In the aspects of sound, sound module of game engine can be utilized to achieve vivid sound, which usually uses existing sound API as DirectSound and OpenAL for implementation. As to interaction, input sub-system was set in the interaction module. So it is easy to obtain unified behaviors with different input devices. Network processing module of engine can achieve network interaction between server and client as well as among clients.

4 Conclusion

Referring to design mode of games, network teaching software based on C/S structure can be designed with design framework and opening-source engines of games. With teaching software service interfaces on server, sound organization can be achieved with general account and role services to accumulate game education software for different disciplines, and then gradually form various micro-community of types theme, so as to complete the accumulation of game-based educational software and ultimately constitute a sound knowledge learning system.

References

1. Ji, X.-k., Liu, W.-t.: Affect of Online Games on Students in Network Era. Modern Education Formula 8, 16–17 (2010)
2. Premslu, M.: Digital Game-Based Learning. McGraw-Hill, New York (2001)
3. Ma, H.-l., Li, X.-w.: Integrating the Social Responsibilities into Educational Online Games. Modern Educational Technology 10, 102–105 (2010)
4. Hui, Z., Li, C.-f., Liu, X.-x.: A Virtual Exhibition Scheme Based on 3D Game Engine. Microcomputer Development 15, 93–95 (2005)
5. Chu, X.-j., Wang, S.: The Application of Game Elements on Network Experimental Teaching. Journal of Jilin Teachers Institute of Engineering and Technology 26, 46–48 (2010)

Modeling and Optimization Algorithm of FMS Logistics System Based on Petri Nets and PSO

Wei Yang[1,2], ZhiGang Bing[1,2], GuiPing Yi[1], and QuanLi Li[1]

[1] Tianjin University of Technology and Education, 300222, Tianjin, China
[2] Tianjin Key Laboratory of Information Sensing and Intelligent Control,
300222 ,Tianjin, China
yangwei851123@163.com

Abstract. Flexible manufacturing system (FMS) is one of the main production modes of the advanced manufacturing industry. As an important part of FMS, logistics system impact on the overall system performance directly. A small FMS logistics system is modeled by Petri net, and its working process simulation and optimization using the particle swarm optimization, PPS-PPR encoding method is studied. The results showed the algorithm can improve the efficiency of the logistics system compared with traditional genetic algorithm, can use shorter working hours and improve equipment utilization, and improve the productivity of the entire FMS.

Keywords: FMS logistics system, Petri nets, Modeling, PSO, PPS-PPR encoding.

1 Introduction

Manufacturing industry is an important pillar of the modern national economy and national comprehensive power. Flexible Manufacturing System (FMS) is an important advanced manufacturing technology. FMS organically integrate automation equipment in the factory production activities. FMS consists of three parts: processing systems, logistics systems and control system. Logistics subsystem includes warehouse and automatic guided cart (AGV). AGV automatically run in the FMS, conveys materials to various work sites. Operation process composed by the following steps: call of the operating point, the central control room scheduling, AGV traveling and material exchange [4]. The operation mode is shown in Figure 1 and Figure2. Logistics system directly impact on the performance of the flexible manufacturing system.

Therefore, reasonable optimization of logistics equipment operation order has a very important significance for FMS. Huogen Chen [1] adopt mixed integer programming approach to model logistics distribution center vehicle scheduling problem with time constraint, exact methods were used to analyze and solve the complexity of such problems, and a solving method was proposed that genetic algorithm combined with heuristic algorithm. Xiaofeng Li [2] put forward one method that tabu-search combined with priority rule, in accordance with mixed flow-shop system's maximum

S. Lin and X. Huang (Eds.): CESM 2011, Part I, CCIS 175, pp. 359–365, 2011.
© Springer-Verlag Berlin Heidelberg 2011

completion time minimization scheduling problem. In addition, the ant colony opti-mization algorithm [3] and immune algorithm were applied to optimize the schedul-ing problem, and achieved a better optimization results. Particle swarm optimization (PSO) has the advantages ,such as easy achieving, high precision and fast conver-gence speed.

Fig. 1. Block diagram of FMS   **Fig. 2.** Operation mode of FMS logistics system

On the other hand, in order to ensure the FMS in the production process has effi-ciency and high stability, accurate modeling and simulation of its work before produc-ing is meaningful. Petri net modeling approach is an ideal graphical modeling tool. In this paper, it takes a small FMS logistics system as an example, using Petri nets to model it and optimize the work process with the particle swarm optimization, which uses the PPS-PPR encoding method.

For large high-tech flexible manufacturing systems, automatic storage and AGV are often identified as the structural unit. Researching on FMS logistics subsystem control methods, improving the efficiency of the logistics process, are essential for achieving coordinated operation of the FMS system and improve of the production efficiency [5].

2   Modeling of Logistics System Based on Petri Net

2.1   Petri Net

Petri net is a mathematical models of studying information systems and their relation-ship. Petri net can express the static structure and dynamic changes of discrete event dynamic system well, and use the form of network diagram to simulate discrete event systems simply and intuitively. It's the most promising real-time control system mod-eling tools set with system modeling, analysis, production planning and scheduling, design and control.

The structure of Petri nets is a directed graph described by five elements:

$$PN=(P,T,I,O,M_0)$$

Annotation: (1)$P=(P_1 P_2...P_n)$ is the finite set of place, n is the number of place and $n>0$;(2)$T=(T_1 T_2...T_m)$ is the finite set of transition, m is the number transition and $P \cap T=\Phi$;(3)$I:P \times T->N$ is the input function. It defines the set including the repeated number of directed arc or the right from P to T, and $N=\{0,1,...,\}$ is a non-negative integer;(4)$O:T \times P->N$ is the output function, which defines the set including the re-peated number of directed arc or the right from T to P;(5) M_0 is the initial state that initially identified markers.

2.2 FMS Logistics Subsystem Model

The prototype FMS (Figure 3)is designed and produced

Fig. 3. FMS prototype

In the warehouse unit of logistics system, the processing flow chart of warehousing request [10] is shown in Figure 4 (left), and the processing flow chart of ex-warehousing request is similar.

According to the flow chart showing and the rules of Petri net modeling ,the Petri net model of the storage unit is established and shown in Figure 4(right).

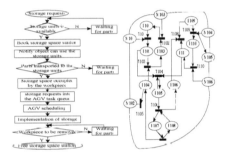

Fig. 4. Processing flow chart request and the Petri model of warehouse

The meaning of some symbols in the figure as follows. M104: storage request from the delivery objects; M105: allowing delivery object into the storage unit; M106: workpiece has been transported to the storage unit.; T104: applying AGV to perform tasks; T106: AGV begins to perform the tasks; T107: AGV finished the tasks; T108: workpiece on storage unit is removed by AGV, the station is released; T109: booking storage space station, allowing the delivery object into the storage units; T110: arrival on the storage unit. The processing flow chart of one AGV and its Petri model were shown in Figure 5.

The meaning of some symbols in the figure as follows:M10:AGV requested to provide transport services queue; M11:AGV in the delivery state; M12:AGV is in wait or idle state; P08:AGV receives transportation requests; P11:AGV sent storage requests to the warehouse object; P12:AGV receives the feedback message from the warehouse; T8:requesting AGV to transport workpiece; T9:AGV convery parts; T10:AGV finished transporting the workpiece; T11:responses received from the warehouse.

With VS2008. AGV class , storage class and algorithms are established. The logistics system simulation interface is shown in Figure 6.

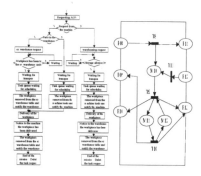

Fig. 5. The processing flow chart of one AGV and its Petri model

Fig. 6. Simulation interface of FMS logistics system

System optimization method is POS, which is discussed as follows.

3 Application of PSO

3.1 Description of Issue

In logistics system, there are some assignment and scheduling problems of multiple AGVs to a number of transport-tasks, which need to be ordered by scheduling rules. Therefore, after more than one tasks were applied and about to enter AGV waiting queue, these tasks should be scheduled. The scheduler should reasonable and arrangements for each AGV task to improve the efficiency of all. Scheduled task assigned to each AGV's waiting queue and to be executed in turn [6].To solve this problem, Particle swarm optimization (PSO) [7] is used to optimize the proposed model above.

3.2 Algorithm Description

Assuming in a n-dimensional goal-search space, there is a group consist of N particles, of which the i- particle represents a n-dimensional vector $x_i = (x_{i1}, x_{i2},...,x_{in})$, $i = 1, 2, ..., N$, and the position of each particle is a potential solution. The flight speed of i-particle is also a n-dimensional vector, denoted as $v_i = (v_{i1}, v_{i2},..., v_{in})$. The best location of the i-particle searched so far is recorded as $p_i =(p_{i1}, p_{i2}, ..., p_{in})$, and the best location of the entire population of particles is recorded as $p_g = (p_{g1}, p_{g2}, ..., p_{gn})$, ω is the weight. Formula (1) and (2) are often referred to as the standard equation of PSO algorithm:

$$v_i^{(t+1)} = wv_i^{(t)} + c_1r_1(p_i^{(t)} - x_i^{(t)}) + c_2r_2(p_g^{(t)} - x_g^{(t)}) \qquad (1)$$

$$x_i^{(t+1)} = x_i^{(t)} + v_i^{(t+1)} \tag{2}$$

The working flow chart of PSO is shown in Figure 7:

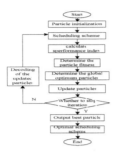

Fig. 7. The working flow chart of PSO

3.3 Algorithm Achieving

Encoding and decoding
The particle's position can't be directly used to represent the solution of scheduling problem. Reference [6] proposed three-dimensional particles encoding method which is based on the particle position sequence (PPS) and the particle position round (PPR). In this paper the method's application field is changed and applied on AGV scheduling of FMS logistics system. It is referred to as particle encoding method based on PPS-PPR.

Table 1. Vector representation method about the ith partical

Machine number	1	2	3	⋯	M
Application order	m_{i1}	m_{i2}	m_{i3}	⋯	m_{iM}
AGV allocation	n_{i1}	n_{i2}	n_{i3}	⋯	n_{iM}

In the table1, N is the total number of a scheduling task, the total number of AGV is J, M is the number of particle swarms, $i \in [1, M]$. The first line means the task number of AGV application; The second line means the order of the N tasks, when decoding, sort the whole column of vector particles to the tasks which belong to the same AGV by the value of $m_{i\,(1\sim N)}$; The third line means AGV assignment, when the upper and lower limit of particles initialization were given, and $n_{i\,(1\sim N)} \in [1, J + 1)$, by taking the operation INT (n_{ij}) get the natural number between1 to J, after value decoded corresponding the AGV number. Therefore, during the algorithm initialization each dimension vector can be set a range, to some degree it equivalent to the feasible region range of the algorithm. For example, the first dimension range is 1 ~ N, the second dimension range is 1.0 ~ 10.0, the third dimension range is 1~J +1 (If the number of AGV is J). However, the range must be coordination with the algorithm step selected, otherwise, the phenomenon that particle standing still may appear.

The objective function

With the purpose of achieving the shortest time, considering the uniform of multiple AGV tasks, so set the maximal AGV task time as the objective function while iteration, then make the overall operating efficiency optimal [8].Objective function as follows [9]:

$$\min F_{fit} = \max(\sum_{n=1}^{N} A_{mnij} + B_{mnjk}, m = 1,2,3,\ldots, \text{ J}) \quad s.t. \quad A_{mnij}, B_{mnjk} \geq 0, \sum_{m=1}^{J} n_m = N$$

The delivery time of task n contains two parts: the time that AGV reaching the current position of the task from the current position, and the time that from the current position of the task to the target location. A_{mnij} means the task n moving time from its current location i to location j by AGV m; B_{mnjk} means time from current position of the task j to the task target location k. System initialization can set the initial AGV position in the warehouse, after executing a mission it stops at the target location k, AGV continue to execute the next task, the new task's AGV starting position is last task's target location, Viz. $i_{n+1} = k_n$.

The algorithm's objective function is calculated as follows: in each group of task queue, first process velocity - displacement calculation according to the encoding of the particle, and then decoding the new position of particles that calculated by the method which proposed in 3.3. After decoding, according to each AGV number that corresponding to the task order to determining start and end of each task, then cumulative running time of the corresponding AGV, which is the total running time of the AGV. Then compare the total run time of all the AGV, in order to get the shortest running time of FMS and for each AGV run time uniform, select a maximum time as the objective function of the iteration.

4   Simulation and Analysis

The actual system is a small FMS consist of four machine tools, an automated warehouse, two AGV, and a buffered station. To facilitate for analysis, simulate on multi-procedure processing of 6 work piece, the simulation result is shown in Table 2:

Table 2. Optimization results in the different PSO parameters

$\omega/c_1/c_2$	iterations	AGV1	AGV2	Time/s
1.2/2/2	50	1260	1480	1542
0.9/2/2	50	1402	1400	1474
0.6/2/2	50	1442	1318	1506
0.3/2/2	50	1282	1510	1558

It can be seen from the simulation result, when c1 = 2, c2 = 2 and ω = 0.9, the optimization result is better, so finally select this set parameters as the PSO parameters to simulate. To demonstrate the strongpoints of this algorithm, comparing with optimization result of the genetic algorithm(GA). The result is shown in Table 3.

Simulation result shows that the two AGV task get better match after optimization, the working time is shorted, PSO has higher efficiency and better uniformity than the GA algorithm's task distribution.

Table 3. Simulation result comparison about PSO and GA

Optimization algorithm	iterations	AGV1	AGV2	Time/s
GA	50	1300	1454	1562
GA	100	1419	1396	1478
PSO	50	1402	1400	1474
PSO	100	1358	1352	1418

5 Conclusion

In this paper, under the premise of referencing to the literature [8], the PSO application area is transferred, it is used in discrete space optimization, a modified POS is came up with. After comparing with previous algorithm, a better result is obtained.

Acknowledgements. This work has been supported in part by the Tianjin City High School Science & Technology Fund Project No. 20090704.

References

1. Chen, H., Ding, H., Cheng, Y.: Logistics Distribution Vehicle Scheduling Model and Genetic Algorithm Designing. Journal of Zhejiang University (Engineering Science) 37(5), 512–516 (2003)
2. Li, X.: Simplified Tabu Search Programs to Solve the Mixed FlowShow Scheduling. Journal of Shanghai Jiaotong University 37(4), 234–238 (2003)
3. Silva, C.A., Sousa, J.M., et al.: Schedulin. In: Manufacturing Systems Using The Ant Colonies Optimization Algorithms
4. Liu, Y.: Flexible Manufacturing Automation Introduction. Huazhong University of Science and Technology press, Wuhan (2008)
5. Zhang, H.: Modeling and Simulation Of FMS Logistics System Based on Petri Nets. Xi'an University of Technology, Xian (2007)
6. Liu, Z.: Research and Application of Particle Swarm Optimization in Scheduling Problem. Wuhan University of Technology, Wuhan (2005)
7. Kennedy, J., Eberhart, R.: Particle swarm optimization. In: Proceedings of the 4th IEEE International Conference on Neural Networks, pp. 1942–1948. IEEE Service Center, Piscataway (1995)
8. Bian, P.: Modeling: Simulation and Real-time Scheduling Optimization for FMS Logistics System. Xi'an University of Technology, Xian (2009)
9. Lei, K.: Research on Particle Swarm Optimization and Its Application. Southwest University, Chongqing (2006)
10. Mao, Y., Han, W.: Research and Implementation of FMS Scheduling Based on Petri Nets. Journal of Chinese Computer Systems 31(5), 1001–1005 (2010)

Variable Fuzzy Sets and Its Application in Flood Disaster Loss Evaluation

Qiong Li

School of Mathematics and Physics, Huangshi Institute of Technology, Huangshi, Hubei, China

Abstract. In order to test the grade criterions of flood disaster loss and resolve the non-uniformity problem of evaluation results of disaster loss indexes, and to raise the grade resolution of flood disaster loss, a new method—variable fuzzy sets(VFS) is suggested for evaluating the grade model of flood disaster, where the disaster loss grade is continuous real number. The method can scientifically and reasonably determine the relative membership functions of disquisitive indexes at level interval that relating to flood, also it can fully use one's experience and knowledge, qualitative and quantitative information of index system to obtain weights of indexes for operating comprehensive evaluation. The numerical example of floods in Henan Province has shown that the proposed method is feasible and effective, and it provides a new theory for flood loss evaluation.

Keywords: variable fuzzy sets, flood disaster, loss, evaluation.

1 Introduction

Flood disasters are more and more frequent in our country, and about two-thirds of the area face the test of different types and degrees of flood disasters. The theory of variable fuzzy sets (VFS) was established by author Chen([1]). Comprehensive evaluation of variable fuzzy sets (VFS) can effectively solve influence of border fuzzy and monitor error of estimation standard to evaluation result. The method can scientifically and reasonably determine membership degrees and relative membership functions of disquisitive objectives (or indexes) at level interval that relating to flood, also it can fully use one's experience and knowledge, qualitative and quantitative information of index system to obtain weights of objectives(or indexes) for operating comprehensive evaluation of flood([1],[2],[3]).

In this study we propose a loss evaluation model based on variable fuzzy sets and it is then applied to the flood loss evaluation in Henan province successfully.

2 Model Introduction

2.1 Variable Fuzzy Sets

To define the concept, let us suppose that U is a fuzzy concept, A express characteristic of attactability and A^c states repellency. Hence, to any elements u ($u \in U$),

$\mu_A(u)$ and $\mu_{A^c}(u)$ are relative membership degree (RMD) function that express degrees of attractability and repellency respectively. We have $\mu_A(u) + \mu_{A^c}(u) = 1$. Here $0 \le \mu_A(u) \le 1, 0 \le \mu_{A^c}(u) \le 1$.

Let $D(u) = \mu_A(u) - \mu_{A^c}(u)$, Where $D(u)$ is defined as relative difference degree of u to A. Mapping $D: u \to D(u) \in [-1,1]$ is defined as relative difference function of u to A. Then $D(u) = 2\mu_A(u) - 1$, or $\mu_A(u) = 1 + D(u)/2$ .Let

$$V_0 = \left\{ (u, D) \middle| u \in U, D(u) = \mu_A(u) - \mu_{A^c}(u), D \in [-1,1] \right\}$$

$$A_+ = \left\{ u \middle| u \in U, 0 < D(u) < 1 \right\}$$

$$A_- = \left\{ u \middle| u \in U, -1 < D(u) < 0 \right\}$$

$$A_0 = \left\{ u \middle| u \in U, D(u) = 0 \right\}$$

Here V_0 is defined as variable fuzzy sets(VFS), A_+, A_-, and A_0 are defined as attracting sets, repelling sets and balance boundary or qualitative change boundary of VFS V_0.

2.2 Methods of Relative Difference Function

We suppose that $X_0 = $ [a, b] are attracting sets of VFS V on real axis, i.e. interval of $\mu_A(u) > \mu_{A^c}(u)$, $X' = $ [c, d] is a certain interval containing X_0, i.e. $X_0 \subset X'$.

According to definition of VFS we know that interval [c, a] and [b, d] are all repelling sets of VFS, i.e. interval of $\mu_A(u) < \mu_{A^c}(u)$. Suppose that M is point value of D(u)=1 in attracting sets [a, b]. x is a random value in interval X', then if x locates at left side of M, its difference function is

$$\begin{cases} D(x) = (\dfrac{x-a}{M-a})^\beta & x \in [a, M] \\[2mm] D(x) = -(\dfrac{x-a}{c-a})^\beta & x \in [c, a] \end{cases} \tag{1}$$

$$\text{or} \quad \begin{cases} \mu(x) = 0.5[1 + (\dfrac{x-a}{M-a})^\beta] & x \in [a, M] \\[2mm] \mu(x) = 0.5[1 - (\dfrac{x-a}{c-a})^\beta] & x \in [c, a] \end{cases} \tag{2}$$

And if x locates at right side of M, its difference function is

$$\begin{cases} D(x) = (\dfrac{x-b}{M-b})^{\beta} & x \in [M,b] \\[2mm] D(x) = -(\dfrac{x-b}{d-b})^{\beta} & x \in [b,d] \end{cases} \tag{3}$$

$$\text{or} \quad \begin{cases} \mu(x) = 0.5[1 + (\dfrac{x-b}{M-b})^{\beta}] & x \in [M,b] \\[2mm] \mu(x) = 0.5[1 - (\dfrac{x-b}{d-b})^{\beta}] & x \in [b,d] \end{cases} \tag{4}$$

Where β is index bigger than 0, usually we take it as $\beta=1$, viz. (1) and (3) become linear functions which equal Equations (2) and (4).

3   VFS for Comprehensive Evaluation of the Flood Degree-Taking Henan Province for Examples

According to the 41 years' practical series material from 1950 to 1990 in Henan province([6]), we take disaster area- $x(1, j)$ and direct economic loss- $x(2, j)$ as the disaster degree's indicator and by frequency analysis we classify it into four levels: small, medium, large and extreme (see Table 1).

Table 1. Henan flood disaster rating standard

Disaster level	Inundated area (hm^2)	Direct economic losses (Billion yuan)	Grade number
small flood	0~46.7	0~9.5	1
medium flood	46.7~136.7	9.5~31.0	2
large flood	136.7~283.3	31.0~85.0	3
extreme flood	283.3~	85.0~	4

According to Table 1 and Chen ([2]), we set up values matrix of parameters for calculating difference function of VFS:

$$I_{[a,b]} = \begin{bmatrix} [0,46.7] & [46.7,136.7] & [136.7,283.3] & [283.3,1000] \\ [0,9.5] & [9.5,31.0] & [31.0,85] & [85,300] \end{bmatrix}$$

$$I_{[c,d]} = \begin{bmatrix} [0,136.7] & [0,283.3] & [46.7,1000] & [136.7,1000] \\ [0,31.0] & [0,85] & [9.5,300] & [31.0,300] \end{bmatrix}$$

$$M = \begin{bmatrix} 0 & 76.7 & 234.4333 & 1000 \\ 0 & 16.6667 & 67 & 300 \end{bmatrix}$$

Based on matrixes $I_{[a,b]}, I_{[c,d]}$ and M, we judge that evaluating index x locates at left side or right side of point M, and according these to select (1) or (2) for calculating difference function $\mu_h(u_{ij})$ of indexes to standards. Here h is grade number and $h = 1$, 2, 3, 4; i is indexes number and i = 1, 2; j is the sample number and $j = 1, 2 \cdots 32$.

When $i = 1$, its attracting matrix [a, b], interval matrix [c, d] and point values matrix M respectively are

$$[a, b] = ([0, 46.7] [46.7, 136.7] [136.7, 283.3] [283.3, 1000])$$

$$[c, d] = ([0, 136.7] [0, 283.3] [46.7, 1000] [136.7, 1000])$$

$$M = (0\ 76.7\ 234.4333\ 1000)$$

For sample 7, when $i = 1, j = 7$, the first index value $x(1,7) = 97.60$, it locates in the interval of degree 2 [46.7,136.7], $c_{12} = 0, a_{12} = 46.7, b_{12} = 136.7, d_{12} = 283.3$. It is obtained that $M_{12} = 76.7$ by $M_{ih} = \dfrac{c-h}{c-1}a_{ih} + \dfrac{h-1}{c-1}b_{ih}$ (5) (chen 2009), then we can see that index value (97.60) locates at right side of point M_{12} and belongs to interval $[M_{11}, b_{11}]$, so we select equation $\mu(x) = 0.5[1 + (\dfrac{x-b}{M-b})^\beta]$ in Eq. (4). Substituting β=1 and other relevant parameters into this equation then we obtain $\mu(X_{12}) = 0.8258$. Analogously, we get relative membership function $\mu(X_{ih})$ of each single index under i = 1, 2 to degrees h = 1, 2, 3, 4 as:

$$\mu^0(X_{ih}) = \begin{bmatrix} 0.2172 & 0.8258 & 0.2828 & 0 \\ 0.2163 & 0.8244 & 0.2837 & 0 \end{bmatrix} \tag{5}$$

And according to ([6]) we obtain weights of two evaluation indexes as: $w' = (0.7388, 0.6739) = (w_i')$. Then normalized weights vector of indexes is: $w = (0.5230\ 0.4770) = (w_i)$.

To get synthetic RMD of each index, we use variable fuzzy recognition model presented by Chen ([1]) as follows,

$$u_h'(x_j) = \left\{ 1 + \left[\dfrac{\sum_{i=1}^m [w_i(1-\mu(x_{ij})_h]^p}{\sum_{i=1}^m [w_i\mu(x_{ij})_h]^p} \right]^{\frac{\alpha}{p}} \right\}^{-1} \tag{6}$$

$$H=(1,2,3,4)* u_h(x_j) \tag{7}$$

here h=1,2,3,4, x_j represent sample j, x_{ij} is sample j's ith index value. Therefore we may use variable fuzzy recognition model (14) to calculate synthetic RMD of sample 7. With Formula (7) we obtain synthetic RMD of each index for flood, after normalizing them that we get normalized synthetic RMD of each index. Here w_i is the above index weight ; m is number of recognition indexes; α is rule parameter of model optimization, p is distance parameter.

When taking rule parameter of model optimization $\alpha =1$ distance parameter $p =1$ and substituting relative data into model (6) we get synthetic RMD $u_h'(x_j)$. After normalized it is $u_h(x_j)$ .Using Formula (7) we get disaster degree of sample 7 as H=2.046. In the same way, we can calculate the disaster degree values of all the 32 samples as shown in Table 2, and Figure 2 shows the scatter plots of calculated values of test samples by VFS and projection pursuit (PP) model ([6]). The disaster degree values agree with the estimated degree values using PP ([6]).

Table 2. The disaster degree values during the 32 years in Henan province

sample	degree value	Judgement Result	experiential judgment	sample	degree value	Judgement Result	experiential judgment
i	x_i			i	x_i		
1	1.415	1	1	17	2.685	3	3
2	1.411	1	1	18	3.5	3	3.5
3	1.343	1	1	19	3.404	3	4
4	1.259	1	1	20	3.823	4	4
5	1.390	1	1	21	3.781	4	4
6	1.5	1	1.5	22	3.644	4	4
7	2.046	2	2.0	23	3.863	4	4
8	1.699	2	2.0	24	1.708	2	2
9	2.189	2	2.0	25	2.277	2	2
10	1.644	2	2.0	26	2.685	3	3
11	1.910	2	2.0	27	2.517	3	3
12	2.5	2	2.5	28	3.556	4	4
13	3.288	3	3.0	29	3.157	3	3
14	2.953	3	3.0	30	3.039	3	3
15	3.468	3	3.0	31	3.532	4	4
16	3.135	3	3.0	32	2.853	3	3

Due to the standard of four grades, so we have([4]):

(a) If $1.0 \leq H \leq 1.5$,then desertification degree belongs to small (1 grade).

(b) If $1.5 < H \leq 2.5$,then it belongs to medium (2 grade).

(c) If $2.5 < H \leq 3.5$, then it belongs to large (3 grade).

(d) If $3.5 < H \leq 4$, then it belongs to extreme (4 grade).

Hence we judge that comprehensive desertification evaluation (2.046) belongs to 2 grade, the rest can be obtained in the same way. The results are showed in Table 2 in comparision with traditional experiential judgment.

4 Conclusion

Floods occur frequently in China and cause great property losses and casualties. In order to implement a compensation and disaster reduction plan, the losses caused by flood disasters are among critically important information to flood disaster managers. This study develops a method of flood loss evaluation model based on variable fuzzy sets method, and it can be easily extended to other natural disasters. It has been tested that the method is reliable and the results are consistent with the real values.

References

1. Chen, S.Y.: Engineering Fuzzy Set Theory and Application, pp. 1–221. National Defence Industrial Press, Beijing (1998)
2. Chen, S.Y.: Fuzzy recognition theory and application for complex water resources system optimization. Jilin University Press, China (2002)
3. Chen, S.Y.: Theory and model of engineering variable fuzzy sets - mathematical basis for fuzzy hydrology and water resources. Journal of Dalian University of Technology 45(2), 308–312 (2005)
4. Chen, S.Y.: Theory and model of variable fuzzy sets and its application. Dalian University of Technology Press, Dalian (2009)
5. Palm, R.: Multiple-step-ahead prediction in control systems with Gaussian process models and TS-fuzzy models. Engineering Applications of Artificial Intelligence 20(8), 1023–1035 (2007)
6. Jin, J.L., Zhang, X.L., Ding, J.: Projection Pursuit Model for Evaluating Grade of Flood Disaster Loss. Systems Engineering-Theory & Practice 22(2), 140–144 (2002)

An Improved Algorithm for PAPR
Reduction of OFDM Systems

Yazhen Li, Xinhui Zhou, and Jing Guan

Communication Engineering Department of
Northeastern University, Qinhuangdao
lyzlyz699@163.com

Abstract. To reduce peak-to-average power radio (PAPR) of orthogonal frequency division multiplexing (OFDM) system, a hybrid algorithm is proposed. It
based on the DFT property of the time domain circular convolution (TCM) and a
linear companding transform (LCT) methods. The algorithm has reduced system's PAPR through lower twice the PAPR of OFDM signal at the transmitter. A
number of simulation results demonstrate that the proposed algorithm can enjoy
an improved performance and has a low complexity cost.

Keywords: OFDM, PAPR, optimization.

1 Introduction

OFDM system has great advantages of having simple equalization and capability of
transmitting high data bit rates over frequency selective channels and has been widely
used modulation technique for wireless communication. One of its main drawbacks is
the large peak-to-average power ratio (PAPR) of the time-domain transmit signal. To
reduce the high PAPR of OFDM systems, many algorithms [1], [2] have been proposed
in recent years, such as clipping, scrambling and coding techniques. As a scrambling
technique, partial transmit sequence (PTS) is known to achieve high PAPR reduction
with a small amount of redundancy. However, PTS requires multiple inverse fast
Fourier transforms (IFFT), and the big issue of finding the optimal phase combination
for PTS sequence is complex and difficult when the number of subcarriers is increased,
which results in high computational complexity for practical system [3],[4]. In this
paper, a novel PAPR reduction algorithm is proposed by combining TCM [5] with LCT
[6] methods. The simulation results show that the algorithm has the better ability of
PAPR reduction than two algorithms.

2 Basic Idea of Hybrid Algorithm

Account for the shortage of the existing methods, based on the study of methods to
reduce PAPR, the proposed hybrid algorithm has been presented. The basic idea [7] is
as follows: Firstly, the OFDM signal is processed via TCM algorithm, and is selected
the sequence with the minimum PAPR for transmission in order to complete PAPR

S. Lin and X. Huang (Eds.): CESM 2011, Part I, CCIS 175, pp. 372–378, 2011.

reduction of OFDM signal. Secondly, via LCT algorithm, the PAPR of OFDM signal is reduced again. After two lower PAPR implementing, the PAPR of the OFDM signal has been substantially improved. In the receiver, through the anti-compression and expansion transform, the transmit signal is restored, and then through the auxiliary information received, the original signal is obtained.

By means of DET time-domain circular convolution theorem, using the special phase sequence designed, TCM only use an IFFT algorithm to achieve the PAPR reduction of the OFDM signal, and then can effectively reduce the system PAPR. The different amplitudes of signals are reduced by the LCT algorithm with compression and expansion of two inflexion points [8]. By combining the two above methods, the system has a good balance between the PAPR reduction and BER performance. Therefore, in this paper, the novel algorithm based on the DFT property of TCM and LCT algorithms can reduce PAPR of the OFDM signal.

3 Simulation Analysis

We can use MATLAB as simulation software, for the random number generator, serial-parallel switching and IFFT transform can be completed by the function of complex matrix operation in the simulation system. In addition, MATLAB has powerful graphics generation capabilities, and data processing capabilities for simulation results of the system. The experiments prove that the proposed algorithm can reduce PAPR of the OFDM signal effectively. Now description of details involved in the simulation are as follows:

In this paper, the study is to reduce peak average power ratio of the OFDM signal, and mainly on study of the novel algorithm, by combining the DFT property of the time domain circular convolution (TCM) and the linear companding transform with two inflexion points (LCT). Some experiments are presented. Because of the processing is done at the transmitter, whether the PAPR of the signal is reduced is known after OFDM modulation. We can observe the effect of various PAPR reduction methods at the transmitter. Considering the AWGN channel the BER performance of OFDM modulation is shown in this paper.

The signal modulation uses 4 kinds of modulation, namely BPSK, QPSK, QAM, 16QAM. There are 4 choices 64, 256, 512, and 1024 for the number of subcarriers, respectively. The oversampling technique is used, and the oversampling factor is 4. In the TCM algorithm, the random phase sequence P of length L can be arbitrary [9],

$P = \exp\{ j2\pi[0:L-1]/(2L)\}$ .The PAPR reduction performance is evaluated by using the complementary cumulative distribution function (CCDF) of the PAPR, which indicates the probability that the PAPR of an OFDM sequence may exceed the threshold level $PAPR_0$.

For the focus of this paper is to reduce the signal peak average power ratio, all the presented algorithms are based on the equivalent complex baseband OFDM signal. So the simulations are carried out in the digital domain and the transmitter and the receiver of the signal processing module are involved.

4 Simulation Results

We can compare and analyze the simulation results from signal amplitude, complementary cumulative distribution function, L value, the modulation mode, the number of subcarriers and BER.

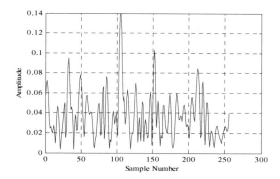

Fig. 1. The amplitude of the original OFDM symbol

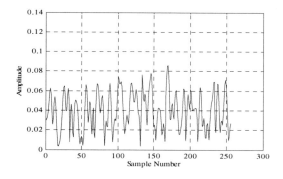

Fig. 2. The amplitude of the OFDM symbol with TCM algorithm

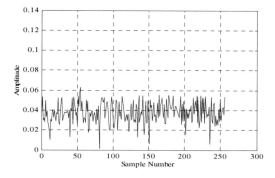

Fig. 3. The amplitude of the OFDM symbol with LCT algorithm

4.1 The OFDM Signal Amplitude Comparison

The sampling points are 256, and modulation type is QPSK. The OFDM signals are compared by the original OFDM, TCM algorithm, LCT algorithm and the proposed hybrid algorithm.

From Fig.1, Fig.2, Fig.3 and Fig.4, we can observe that OFDM signal has higher signal amplitude and has reduced significantly by using the hybrid algorithm as compared with TCM and LCT algorithms.

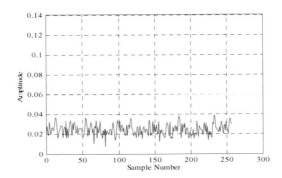

Fig. 4. The amplitude of the OFDM symbol with the combining algorithm

4.2 CCDF Comparison of the Algorithms

The simulation conditions are assumed that the signal type is QPSK and the number of subcarriers is 64. The OFDM signal is oversampled and the factor is 4. In this system, 100000 randomly symbols are generated. Figure 5 shows the PAPR performance of the conventional OFDM, TCM algorithm, LCT algorithm and hybrid algorithm. From Figure 5, it is clear that the threshold of hybrid algorithm, LCT algorithm and TCM algorithm are 4.2dB, 4.5dB and 6.5dB respectively, when $CCDF = 10^{-3}$. So the performance of hybrid algorithm is better than TCM algorithm and LCT algorithm. The hybrid algorithm can effectively reduce the peak to average power ratio.

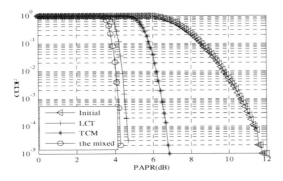

Fig. 5. Comparison of PAPR performance

4.3   L Value Comparison

The PAPR performance of hybrid algorithm is displayed in fig. 6. The simulation result is presented when the subcarriers is 64 and the modulation mode is QPSK for L=4, 8, 16 and 32.

From the Fig. 6, it can be seen the performance of algorithm can gradually improve with increasing L value, for $CCDF = 10^{-4}$, when L=4, 8, 16 and 32, and the threshold $PAPR_0$ are 4.50dB, 4.43dB, 4.33dB and 4.25dB, respectively. But with continuous increasing L, the system performance improvement is not obvious.

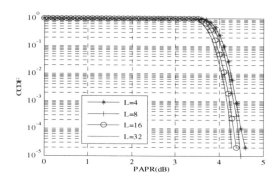

Fig. 6. Comparison of PAPR performance with different value of L

4.4   The Modulation Mode Comparison

Considering the different modulation modes, the performance of hybrid algorithm is shown in Fig. 7, which shows the CCDF performance of the OFDM system using BPSK, QPSK, QAM and 16QAM, respectively.

From Fig. 7, it is clear that PAPR performance of the hybrid algorithm is almost the same with different modulation modes. It is that the choice of modulation has little effect on the PAPR value. Without considering other factors, we can choose subcarrier modulation mode with freedom and consider the data transmission rate.

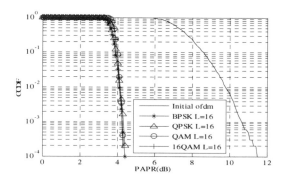

Fig. 7. Comparison of PAPR performance with different modulation

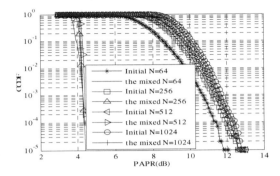

Fig. 8. Comparison of PAPR performance with different subcarriers

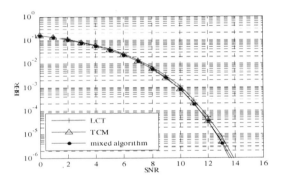

Fig. 9. Comparison of BER performance

4.5 The Number of the Subcarriers Comparison

Considering different number of subcarriers, the performance of hybrid algorithm is shown in Fig. 8, which shows the different performance of the system using hybrid algorithm when the number of subcarriers is 64, 256, 512 and 1024 for $L = 16$, respectively. It can be seen from the figure in different number of subcarriers PAPR of OFDM signals can obviously be reduced. When we consider 1024 subcarriers and $CCDF = 10^{-3}$, the threshold of the hybrid algorithm signal is 7.4dB lower than the conventional OFDM signal. But the difference of PAPR performance is small when the number of subcarriers is different. It can be shown that the choice of the number of subcarriers has little effect on the PAPR values, and hybrid algorithm can be applied to any number of subcarriers.

4.6 BER Comparison

We assume that signal modulation is QPSK and the subcarriers are 64. 100000 randomly symbols are generated with Gaussian noise channel (AWGN). From the Figure 9, it is demonstrated that BER of the hybrid algorithm is close to the BER of TCM algorithm and LCT algorithm.

5 Conclusions

In this paper, the novel hybrid algorithm is proposed based on TCM and LCT algorithms. We discussed respectively the PAPR performance of the hybrid algorithm, TCM algorithm and LCT algorithm. The simulation results have shown that the proposed algorithm can reduce PAPR effectively, and take an excellent tradeoff between PAPR reduction and BER performance.

References

1. Seung, H.H., Jae, H.L.: An overview of peak-to-average power ratio reduction techniques for multicarrier transmission. J. IEEE Wireless Communications 12, 56–65 (2005)
2. Wu, Y., Zou, W.Y.: Orthogonal frequency division multiplexing: a multi-carrier modulation scheme. J. IEEE Trans. Consumer Electronics 41, 392–399 (1995)
3. Chen, H.S., Liang, H.Y.: Combined selective mapping and binary cyclic codes for PAPR reduction in OFDM systems. J. IEEE Trans. Wireless Communications 6, 3524–3528 (2007)
4. Gao, J., Wang, J.K., Wang, B.: Suboptimal partial transmit sequence algorithm to reduce the PAPR in OFDM systems. In: ICCDA, vol. 4, pp. 500–503 (2010)
5. Lu, G., Shaochao, Z.: Novel distortion less PAPR reduction scheme for OFDM system. J. China: Journal of Communication 26, 51–56 (2005)
6. Aburakhia, S.A., Badran, E.F., Mohamed, D.A.E.: Linear Companding Transform for the Reduction of Peak-to-Average Power Ratio of OFDM Signals. J. IEEE Transactions on Broadcasting 5, 155–160 (2009)
7. Kim, D., Stuber, G.L.: Clipping Noise Mitigation for OFDM by Decision-Aided Reconstruction. J. IEEE Communications Letters 3, 4–6 (1999)
8. Tarokh, V., Jafarkhani, H.: On the Computation and Reduction of the Peak-to-Average Power Ratio in Multicarrier Communications. J. IEEE Trans. Communication 48, 37–44 (2000)
9. Saeedi, H., Sharif, M., Marcasti, F.: Clipping Noise Cancellation in OFDM Systems Using Oversampled Signal Reconstruction in multicarrier communications. J. IEEE Communications Letters 6, 73–75 (2002)

The Design and Realization of Experiment Platform in Airborne Equipments

Ying Gao, Tao Jiang, Lei Lei, and Shuxia Guo

School of Marine Technology, Northwestern Polytechnical University, 710072 Xi'an, China
jt5270@sina.com, gaoying@nwpu.edu.cn

Abstract. In view of the actual requirement of piloting aircraft of EW and the use of virtual reality technology and visualization technology, we establish a platform for virtual simulation system and analyze the main function of the various modules in the system. And then make use of certain methods and steps to implement the system, and introduce the methods that using the OpenGL function to implement the description of electromagnetic signal. In the last, the article implements the system function by using the computer program.

Keywords: Electronic Warfare, Virtual Scene System, Visualization, Vega, OpenGL Function.

1 Foreword

Currently, virtual reality technology is widely used, the use of virtual reality and simulation technology to develop virtual test simulation system of airborne equipments, can improve the quality of testing, training and data analysis. Therefore, in the process of developing and testing equipments carried by aircrafts, both domestic and foreign attach great importance to the function of computer simulation technology in development of models, from the beginning of the model design to the whole development process in the factory, according to the requirements of different stages, complete different experiments of the digital simulation[1].

"Simulation experiment platform of airborne fire control equipments" is a specific application using the virtual reality technology and visualization technology in the semi-physical missile test. A carrier plane is imitated as virtual equipments launch platform which will carry out the entire fight flow path's simulation.

2 Overall System Design

"Simulation experiment platform of airborne fire control equipments" is developed to simulate a carrier plane as the virtual equipments launch platform, carry on certain control training, and it can be also used as a node in the closed-loop of the missile's guidance and control system which go through the half-material distributed simulation of the overall system. In the simulation process, the release of aircraft and airborne fire control equipments combat missions and the real-time dynamic display for

S. Lin and X. Huang (Eds.): CESM 2011, Part I, CCIS 175, pp. 379–384, 2011.
© Springer-Verlag Berlin Heidelberg 2011

radar target detection, identification information will be realized, and, the simulation of process for attacking target is finished [2]. The main function of system components is shown in Fig.1.

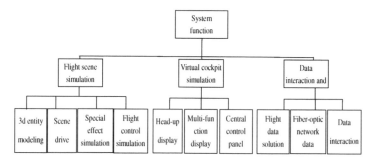

Fig. 1. System functional components

3 System Implementation Plan

Software development environment is VC ++2003, Creator is selected as the modeling software, graphics management software is Vega Prime, GL Studio is used in the part of virtual instrument, and network transmission is using a reflective fiber memory (RFM network). The basic framework of system is shown in Fig.2.

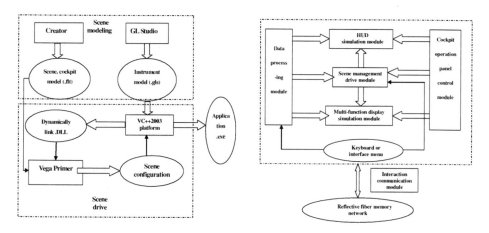

Fig. 2. The basic framework of the system   **Fig. 3.** Relationship of system function

4 Realization of the System Function Modules

Simulation system has mainly realized the flight visual simulation, cockpit display and control simulation and data processing functions. Flight visual simulation achieves a carrier aircraft flight simulation with six degrees of freedom and drives the point of view and aircraft model move in the scene by using the parameters obtained;

meanwhile, cockpit display and control simulation realized the simulation of a virtual head-up display, multifunction display and the central control panel. The operator by controlling the simulated flight, according to a variety of multi-function display and instrument information icons offered by virtual cockpit, can carry on the simulation process [3].

There are six modules totally in the system. The relationship between various modules is shown in Fig.3.

4.1 Realization of the Virtual Scene Outside Cockpit

In the "simulation experiment platform of airborne fire control equipments", Vega Prime software environment is used for visual simulation of the battlefield. Visual management driver module ultimately achieves three-dimensional effect, including scene roaming, the target model transferring, the definition of movement pattern, viewpoint management, loading and management of large terrain, the change of weather in battlefield environment, the process of transformation for observing view-point in battlefield scene and special effects after hitting the target, which makes combat simulation effect more apparent. Simulation results are shown in Fig.4.

Fig. 4. The missile's attacking the target   Fig. 5. The effect of the virtual cockpit

4.2 Realization of the Virtual Cockpit Function

Function modules in cockpit contain head-up display, multi-function display (MFD), and the central control panel. The three all complete an independent development and debugging firstly in the professional development of software named GL Studio, then use the vpGLStudio provided by Vega Prime to embed the cockpit and instrument system into the virtual scene system. Virtual cockpit effect is shown in Fig.5.

4.3 Implementation of Data Communications

Software receives commands through the network, then determine the working status of entire flight simulation system, adjust the system display interface following the instructions; and receives simulation data through the network, including the target and missile status parameters, and according to Simulation mode shows the corresponding graphics, characters and parameters; through the network the software will send the parameters set by this node to the simulation of the total console; finally with the network connection status of self-test, confirms the connection status conditions between many of the system and other subsystems of the network. The effect is shown in Fig.6.

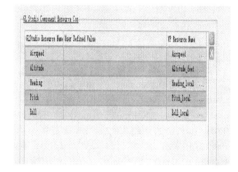

Fig. 6. Real-time controlling missile's flight by fiber-optical network

Fig. 7. vpGLStudio module parameters that can be transmitted

5   Key Technologies to Achieving System

5.1   Flight Simulation Control by Using the Interpolation

There are two concepts, simulation step time and frame time, involved in the system. In the "airborne fire control equipments simulation platform", the simulation step is identified during the master control and all other nodes in the network communication, while the frame time is the time that Vega Prime in visual system complete a rendering. Simulation step time and frame time is inconsistent, so there is a problem here, that is when the simulation runs, during each simulation time step, the host computer send the new position of the target and to the virtual simulation system, while the missile flight path should be updated according to the frame, otherwise it is impossible to achieve a smooth track, which can not meet the needs of visual simulation. To solve this problem, we need to use inter-thread communication technology to work on the interpolation of the track data and the calculation of war unit stance, in the case of ensuring data access security [4].

Analyzing the track data (x, y, z) of needed interpolation, and using the linear or parabolic interpolation between data and step length data or data on the two step, then the number of the data points of interpolation can be identified by the ratio between the simulation time step and the frame time. After calculating the location of aircraft at each point, then according to the location of the interpolation point and the next interpolation point, we can calculate the stance of the point (x, y, z, h, p, r), to ensure that the stance of the war unit at the point is always pointing to the next point's position. After completion of interpolation, the member function Unlock () is called to release the critical section. In thread of the visual display, the data interpolated is used to update position and stance.

5.2 Two-Way Data Transmission between VP and GL Studio

1. DATA TRANSFERRING FROM VP TO GLS

First, activate the vpGLStudio optional module in the Vega Prime, and create a virtual instrument instance. Then load and generate a dynamic link library files *.dll in the instance, and enter the class name. The plug-in named vp GLStudioPlugin supported by GL Studio, can have the dynamic-link library files (DLL) compiled from the code generated by the GL Studi3.2 loaded directly into the Lynx Prime editor [5].

In the vpGLStudio module editor of Lynx Prime, users can choose a variety of parameters to transfer the current incoming data to GLS component, as shown in Fig.7, the parameters provided by the VP include free speed, altitude, heading, pitch angle roll angle and so on. But the choice of the parameters is limited in VP Resource Name and they can not be added and modified.

Therefore, for certain special parameters of the node, such as the relative coordinate value or the control instruction of the simulation, they can not be associated with the instrumentation through this simple method, and need to change the instrumented initial value to achieve association. For instance, distance between carrier aircraft and target, while relative position relationship are not found correspondingly in VP Resource Name, so, it is need to obtain the value calculated, then assign values to the corresponding variables of the GL Studio Resource Name, which can make instrument indicating change depending on different value. Development steps are as follows:

1)Add following code:
vpGLStudioComponent*Cockpit=vpGLStudioComponent:: find ("Cockpit");
//define instrument instance and an instance of the instrument
char buf [50]; // define a character string array Sprintf (buf, "% 3f", Value);
//assign needed data to be transferred to a string array
cockpit-> addAttribute ("VPValuePassToGLS", buf,);
//pass the value into the interface function called VPValuePassToGLS.

2) Write the response function code into the components created by GL Studio, such as VPValuePassToGLS ().

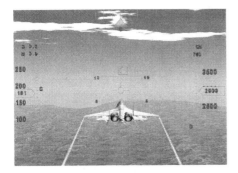

Fig. 8. Position relationships between carrier aircraft and target in the virtual scene

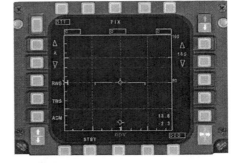

Fig. 9. The relationship between carrier aircraft and target location in MFD

Fig.8 and 9 show the effect of data transmission, the relative position relationship between the carrier aircraft and the locked target (in the square and diamond frame) in the VP is calculated out, then the value is transferred into the multi-function display developed by GL Studio, in a simulated radar screen relative position relationship between the carrier aircraft and target is shown.

2. GLS COMPONENT DATA IS TRANSFERRED INTO THE VP

In simulation process, it involves data's transferring from GLS components to Vega Prime, and in the vpGLStudio VP module that provided function of data's transferring from VP to GLS components, but transmission does not provide the reverse.

In the process of development, by means of global variables exported in the generated DLL from the components, data sharing between GLS components and VP can be implemented. Steps are as follows:

1) Declaration in the header file of GLS component: _declspec (dllexport) int GlobalData; so that other components can access the global variables GlobalData.
2) Generate the *.dll and. Lib file and it is need to use global variables GlobalData components to complete the configuration process.
3) The declaration in the VP code: extern_declspec (dllimport) int GlobalData; and the generated *.dll files are copied to the component folder. So that GlobalData data in terms of global variables is imported into the VP.

In addition, this method can be used in transferring data from GLS components to VP, also in transferring data between components.

6 Conclusion

The Implementation of "simulation experiment platform of airborne fire control equipments" system involves a large number of functional modules, which is a simulation software developed home with the combination of semi-physical, also is the simulation software of a carrier aircraft fire equipments with more complete feature, and offers a standard application program interface, efficient integrated environment and a rich graphical display feature. It can improve the sense of reality, real-time and degree of visual data of visual simulation systems; what is more, it will become a new simulation method for the rich semi-physical simulation experiment.

References

1. Wang, G.: Missile flight virtual reality simulation system, 1, 1–5, Harbin Engineering University, Master thesis (2007)
2. Li, L.: Virtual Display and Control System in developing a modular. Manufacturing Information 2, 103–104 (2009)
3. Yang, Z.: Software for aircraft flight visual simulation and cockpit display. University of Electronic Science and Technology, Vol 3, 54–57 (2009)
4. Zhang, P., Gao, Y.: A virtual battlefield environment and visualization of electromagnetic signals. System Simulation 21(13) (2009)
5. Tian, Y., Tong, D., Ling, H., et al.: The application of GLStudio and VegaPrime in the ship's virtual simulation system. Ship & Ocean Engineering 5, 130–132 (2008)

Considerations of the Subject Teaching Method Applying in the Information Technology Course

Yaqing Shi[*], Meijuan Wang, and Tingting Zhang

Institute of Science, PLA Univ. of Sci. & Tech., 211101 Nanjing Jiangsu, China
qingyashi_blue@sina.com

Abstract. "Information technology" is a basic course of computing. It is foundation of many following courses. Taking educational reform as the turning point, considering military academy students' specific demands, and combing new personnel training plan, the author proposed the application to enhance the students' information accomplishment by integrating the subject teaching method in "Information technology" course.

Keywords: Subject teaching method, Information technology, Information accomplishment.

1 Introduction

"There are methods in teaching, but there isn't fixed method in teaching". Teaching needs to begin with the reality, and it exhibits differently according to different people or different time. It should not fix to one teaching method. Introducing the subject teaching method to the teaching of information technology course can stimulate the students' study interest and bring student's initiative. It makes the students study the course heart and soul, thus it enhances student's Information Literacy. It meets the demand of education for all-around development.

Actually, teaching is influenced by many factors. How to grasp the "subject" of subject teaching method? Can the subject which is novel, interesting and stimulating student's interest be taken as the subject? Will it mislead understanding of students like this? Combining characteristics of subject and information technology course teaching, this article analyzes how to apply subject teaching into information technology course and proposes suggestions about subject's designing.

2 Characteristics of Subject Teaching Method and Information Technology Course

2.1 Understanding of Subject Teaching Method

The effective teaching improves the quality of teaching. Bao Ritchie, American teaching potency expert, proposed that there are five essential behaviors to achieve

---

[*] Corresponding author.

S. Lin and X. Huang (Eds.): CESM 2011, Part I, CCIS 175, pp. 385–391, 2011.

effective teaching in "Effective Teaching method". There are clear teaching, diverse teaching, driving task, guiding students into process of studying, guaranteeing ratio of success.

The subject teaching method is an effective teaching method. According to the goal of teaching and actual situation of students, it establishes the subject in the teaching process. Then it designs corresponding teaching steps and activities according to "subject". Simultaneously this teaching method attempts to establish a kind of situation or approach similar to the scientific research. It makes students choose and confirm related subject from study, life and social practice under the teachers' guidance. It makes students explore, discover and experience on their own with the similar way of scientific research or experiment. At the same time, it makes students be capable of collecting, analyzing and estimating about information, and it enhances students' elaborative faculty and creativity and trains student's innovative spirit and practical ability from achieving and applying knowledge, and resolving problems [1].

The subject teaching method has much superiority which traditional teaching methods don't have. It is why we apply it in the information technology course:

First, it is uniting of teaching and studying. The subject teaching method is a kind of teaching to the teacher, but is a kind of studying to the student. Uniting the both sufficiently about" subject" incarnates the principle of unifying about teaching and studying.

Second, it embodies students' subject status fully. The subject teaching method takes the subject as the center, and it is for the purpose of stimulating the students' enthusiasm to study, promoting students' inspirit of innovating, enhancing students' ability of thinking and practicing. It stresses that students are the main body of study. It thinks much of bringing up students' inspirit of exploring, ability of practicing and consciousness of cooperation.

Third, it is further extensions of teaching material, and it is grasping knowledge system in the round. The teaching material has the indispensable status in the teaching, but any teaching material is impossible to include all discipline elementary knowledge and newest research results. The subject teaching method can maximize stimulate students using the rich extra curricular resources, such as network, the library, the life practice and so on. It can unearth the teaching material knowledge thoroughly, and grasp foreland theoretical knowledge with some depth and breadth comprehensively.

Fourth, it is further enhancement of knowledge and accomplishment. The subject teaching method usually requests the student complete the subject duty through cooperating in the implementation stage. The student has mastered the knowledge, learned the contact, strengthened the sense of collective honor and the sense of responsibility and realized further enhancement of the knowledge and the accomplishment in the collective cooperation and studies together.

2.2 Characteristics of Information Technology Course

A key character of information society is the circulation and the accumulation of information. It is the essential requirement proposed to education that trains the student to have the good information consciousness and information ability. The information technology course is an important component of the university computer teaching. On the one hand, there is the foundational characteristic in the curriculum content, such as the computer elementary knowledge, the data algorithm, the software function introduction and so on. And it trains the students' interest and consciousness of using computer, and enables the student to understand and master the elementary knowledge and skills of information technology. Also it has the practical characteristic. It makes students understand the profound influence that the development and application to the human daily life, and enables the student to follow close on the development step of the times. It is the course with doughty utility and the operational. On the other hand, it may raise the students' good information accomplishment and makes the information technology as the support to lifelong studying and the cooperation studying and so establishes the essential foundation for the adaptation to study, work and live in information society.

The information technology course not only enables the student to master a technique and it is more important to enhance students' comprehensive accomplishment under the guidance of modern teaching theories and the theory of learning. Reforming and the attempting in the teaching method, paying attention to the information technology' samalgamation with other curriculum knowledge, using many kinds of modern teaching method which can fully manifest the students' main body status, creating the environment of independently studying and development with cooperation for the student, using the dynamic nimble evaluation criteria and method, raising students' innovative idea, enhancing the students' ability to gain, retrieve, analyze and process information, and all these are purpose of the information technology course.

This course's educational model was formerly unitary and the teaching method was unable to stimulate students' interest to study. More teachers use the teaching method of indoctrinating and pay great attention to the tendency of the knowledge imparting. In this situation. Students study by the way of accepting and memorize mechanically. Students' interest of study is neglected .The initiative to study is constrained. All these do not favor in raising students' spirit of innovative and the ability of practice.

The teaching practice in recent years proved that the teaching establishing basis of the subject teaching method conforms to the information technology course characteristic and can fully mobilize students' initiative and raise their ability of exploring initiatively and make them become the main body of information processing, the initiative constructor of knowledge significance. Simultaneously it can enhance students' ability of information technology application in a short time and can raise students ability of information technology innovation and solving problems to enhance students' information literacy.

3 Analyzing with Subject Teaching Method

In the information technology course teaching, we usually use the way of teaching which is traditionally taking the knowledge as the standard, namely we teach strictly bases on the knowledge system of teaching materials and accentuate the integrity of knowledge and take excessively more time into tuition of knowledge and goals such as method and emotion were still neglected. In the process of teaching each part of knowledge, we teach according to the principle of "propose-explain-cite". And this is a kind of typical educational model whose teaching and studying is controlled by the teacher. Its merit lies in fully manifesting teachers' guidance function, and the short-coming lies in students' main body activity to be restricted. Continuously for a long time hence, the sense of participation and the study effect of students are able to come under the influence.

In view of the shortcoming of traditional, we apply the subject teaching method to the information technology course and attempt to design good teaching steps and the learning activity by introducing this method under the premise of exert teachers' introductory function. It enables students exert main body activity extremely and study and construct their own knowledge system according to the frame which the teacher have built. Compared with the traditional teaching which is completely controlled by the teacher, the difference lies in the content and the advancement of study dominated independently by the student.

Otherwise, while adopting the above teaching method, it is certainly to pay great attention to create an independent and cooperative study environment for the students basis of fully exert teachers' instruction function, Such as bringing up students' ability of initiative exploring and cooperating though using the network resource reasonably. In this process, the teacher plays the role of helping, promoting and guiding: on the one hand, the teacher provides some excellent websites for the student and instructs them how to search and use the resources correctly; on the other hand, when the student meets the problem, the teacher can provide help timely and reasonably evaluate the activity achievement when students finish their learning activity; furthermore, the teacher is the organizer of the entire learning process, and plays the role of supervising.

The process of applying subject teaching method into the information technology topic which is proposed by us shows in the following Fig.1:

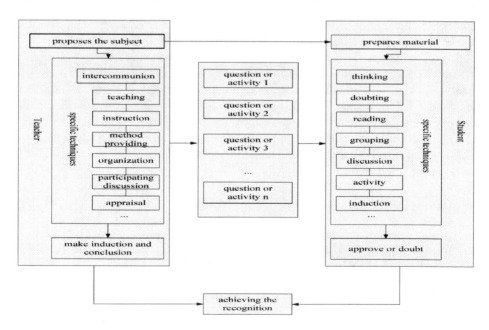

Fig. 1. Application process of the subject teaching method

We apply subject teaching method in the information technology course with circum fusing the teaching subject and the ultimate objective is to realize recognition between the teachers and students to this subject.

Firstly, the teacher "proposes subject". This is the most essential step in subject teaching method. The quality of the subject proposed immediately influences the enthusiastic of students participating in following steps and the course content progressing and the teaching schedule. The subject cannot be oversized or too small, and also cannot be too difficult or too simple. The subject teaching method requests the teacher to establish the special subject according to the teaching goal and the students' actual situation and then arrange the subject to the student before attending class. We will introduce the point need to pay attention to about proposing subject in the information technology course in the third part.

Secondly, it is the foundation that the student "prepares material". The students can only use teaching material, tutorial book, Internet such tools and so on before the class according to the subject proposed by the teacher, and try their best to collect content related to the subject, and then they can build the foundation for the future "thinking", "discussion", "activity", "induction" as well as the "intercommunion" with the teacher. Simultaneously it doesn't need to prepare all the material related to the subject in the material preparation step. It needs pertinence and selection. And this requests the student to read the teaching material under the subject arranged by the teacher and take the teaching material as the original version and determinate the subject's emphasis according to the teaching material and reduce the scope of materials target-oriented and discard the dross and select the essential and choose the subject most related and closed to content. This step is also actually the process of student self-ponder and the self study.

After finishing above two steps, the subject teaching method really starts. The teacher must adopt "intercommunion", "teaching", "instruction", "method providing", "organization", "participating discussion" and the "appraisal" such concrete method and so on to guide the student to carry on "thinking", "doubting", "reading", "grouping", "discussing", "campaigning" and "inducting". The concrete process is as follows: the teacher must carry on the preliminary exchange with the students after proposing the subject of the course. This kind of exchange both includes the overall introduction to the subject and includes the entire design of the whole class. The design must let the student clearly know the direction of following class but not how to do specifically step by step. The goal is to let the students think how to go out their own new step in the big frame designed by the teachers and raise the students' ability of independent thinking and design. Certainly this kind of exchange will probably assist corresponding teaching, and make the subject's stress embodiment with opposite traditional teaching. The students will have certain doubts about the former exchange and teaching more or less. The doubts with regard to the subject's content, the material preparation and carrying on following study are so-called questions and this is the beginning of alternation between students and teachers. When the students have questions, the teacher can use many kinds of ways to instruct and guide the students to return to the books with questions and read with pertinence. In this process the teachers have many methods to provide. According to teachers' instruction, the students group according to whether or not their self-viewpoint is consistent and forms each discussion group and simultaneously thoroughly discuss about subject. The goal of current discussion is farther refining subject content and here needs the teachers join at the suitable time and discuss together. The exchange in classis the activity which needs all members to participate anticipated. When the discussion among students goes to the certain extent, teachers' involvement may achieve the goal of teaching very well and deepen students' impression. Finally through all kinds of activity to students can clearly understand and grasp the subject. At last the teacher works out the appraisal and this kind of appraisal needs to serve the goal of teaching and pay great attention to the appraisal to the students' participation. The teacher commonly uses the multi-dimensional appraisal in the topical study and evaluates the students' achievements from multi-dimensional. The teachers can assign several targets in the learning process and inspect from aspects of the material value, rationality of grouping activity design, innovation and comprehensive and effectively applying knowledge and so on. Certainly the students also make the final induction. This kind of induction includes the induction to the course and the subject content and the induction to individual and the group, namely self-appraisal and mutually appraisal with certain extent.

After completing above all, the teacher needs to "make induction" about this course and this subject and draw the final "conclusion" which is "approved or doubted" by the student. And "achieving the recognition" between teachers and students is the final target.

4   Several Suggestions to Design Subject

The subject design is not only a skill but also an art. The subject, while considered the pertinence, must have the strong ductility. Namely, the subject doesn't purely aim at some concrete practical operation case, but must be refined to the core concept which covers some type question with the research value .The subject is the organic unification of practicality and the theory. And it also makes the student obtain cognition with the universal value by researching the typical questions in the study, namely the subject has extrapolated potential [2]. We give several suggestions to the subject design as follows:

(1) Basis of the teaching material. According to the teaching content, holding the basic concept and the elementary knowledge, threading up teaching materials' center, key and difficulty, and proposing the subject ingeniously, all these is necessary in designing subject. But basis of the teaching material is not along a prescribed path, it must break the original teaching materials' fetter like class, section and frame. It must reorganize and integrate the teaching material content appropriately to refine the subject.

(2) Select and abandon properly. Designing subject not only needs to consider the goal and the content of teaching but also needs to generally consider the students' characteristic, students' existing cognition level as well as the existing teaching environment and the actual operation difficulty and so on. When some factors cannot simultaneously be satisfied, it should select and abandon properly.

(3) Designing the subject with a clear goal. This is the precondition of success or failure about the subject design. The subject design should serve the educative purpose and the duty. While design the teaching, we must consider repeatedly to aspects about the goal, scope, degree, angle as well as language description of subject and so on and grasp the difficulty, the breadth and the depth of the subject.

(4) Level clearly. While designing subjects, it should design the scientific, gradient and stratified subject as far as possible. The subject needs to be small and concrete and avoid be empty and abstract. Decomposing certain difficulty subject to several small subjects with inner relations will deepen the students' understanding to the knowledge.

References

1. Zhang, L.: Teacher authority's modern reforming. Education Research, 11 (2003)
2. Dai, J.: The teaching method analyzes of subject research. Kapok Institute Journal, 19 (2002)

Research on Localization Technology in Wireless Sensor Networks

XingHua Ma[1,2], ZhiGang Bing[1,2], and YuQiu Tang[1]

[1] Automation and Electrical Engineering College, Tianjin University of Technology and Education, 300222, Tianjin, China
[2] Tianjin Key Laboratory of Information Sensing and Intelligent Control, 300222, Tianjin, China
happyboymxh_19@126.com

Abstract. Localization is one of the mainly topic of wireless sensor networks. Localization algorithm in wireless sensor networks can be divided into two types: range-based localization algorithm and range-free localization algorithm. LDV-HOP algorithm, based on range-based localization algorithm, is presented in this paper. The local positioning accuracy is improved by cycling the localization result under the small amount of low-power conditions. The simulation of the algorithm is carried out in the NS2 platform to verify correctness and feasibility. At last, the algorithm is employed in the physical experiments to further validate the good accuracy in the practical application.

Keywords: Wireless sensor networks, Location algorithm, DV-Hop, LDV-Hop.

1 Introduction

Wireless sensor networks (WSNs) in recent years are widely concerned by the international academic and industrial researchers. WSNs are widely used in the industrial, military, environmental and other fields [1]. WSNs are arranged in the monitoring area by large number of sensor nodes through wireless communication to form a multi-hop's self-organizing network, which aims to collaborate perception, acquisition and processing of network coverage area to be monitored object information, and send to observer [2]. GPS is currently the most mature of the most widely used positioning system with high positioning accuracy, real time, anti-interference ability, etc., but the positioning was only suitable for outdoor environment without shelter. Meanwhile the user nodes of GPS have many disadvantages such as high energy consumption, the big volume, high cost and infrastructure-needed to fix and so on. WSNs nodes are improved rapidly in working around the clock indoor and outdoor and low consumption of cost and power. WSNs node localization is the key supporting technologies and research focus. The localization of sensor network is essential for system monitoring to determine the location of the incident or to obtain information. WSNs localization is one of the most basic functions, and plays a key role in effective of sensor network applications [3].

S. Lin and X. Huang (Eds.): CESM 2011, Part I, CCIS 175, pp. 392–398, 2011.

2 WSNs Framework and Sensor Nodes

The sensor network structure of WSNs is composed of sensor node, sink node, and manager station. The sensor nodes are deployed randomly in the monitoring area with self-organization to get, transmit and process the monitoring data by multi-hop. The data is transmitted to the sink node, and finally arrived via the Internet or satellite management station. Sensor node is usually a micro embedded system, and its processing power, storage capacity and communication capacity is relatively weak with limited energy. The processing power, storage capacity and communication capacity of sink node is relatively strong. It connects the sensor network and Internet and other external networks, communicates between the two protocol stack protocol conversion, and releases management node monitoring tasks, and to collect data forwarded to the external network.

Sensor node include sensing unit, communications unit and processing unit, energy unit and other components [4], shown in Fig. 1.

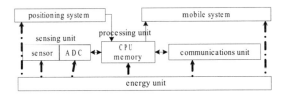

Fig. 1. Structure of sensor node

CC2430/CC2431, firstly produced by TI, is the perfect combination of excellent performance with the leading CC2420RF transceiver core and an enhanced 8051 controller. CC2430/CC2431 chip with past CC2420 chip architecture, integrate in a single chip ZigBee radio frequency (RF) front end, memory and microcontroller.

The difference between CC2430/CC2431 is the location tracking engine of CC2431 and CC2430-free location tracking engine. Fig. 2 (a) shows the wireless communication module consisting of CC2430 WSNs node hardware chart. Shown in Fig. 2 (b) is an extension of the network board with a CC2430 module coordinator communication module.

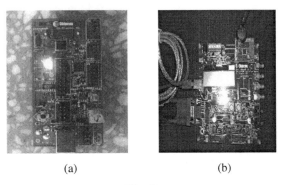

(a)   (b)

Fig. 2.

3   Localization Technologies in WSNs

Currently, localization algorithm in WSNs can be divided into two types: range-based localization algorithm and range-free localization algorithm. Range-free localization algorithm using received signal strength or wireless connections between nodes to determine the distance to neighbor nodes and achieving localization [1]. Range-based localization algorithm include RSSI [5], TOA [6], TDOA [7], AOA [8], and range-free localization algorithm include DV-HOP [9], centroid algorithm [10], convex programming method [11] and so on.

Range-free localization technology which is not need node's absolute distance or orientation has been proposed. It has reduced the requirements of the node hardware. Meanwhile, range-free localization algorithm is simple and easy to achieve, distributed local calculation, small communication load and good at scalability. So it is widely using in the location algorithm.

3.1   DV-HOP Algorithm Analysis

Distance Vector-Hop algorithm is proposed by D. Niculescu and B. Nath [9], its location principle is that calculate the minimum number of hop between positioning nodes and reference nodes at first. Then, estimating the distance of average hop, the minimum number of hops multiplied by the distance of average hops can get the estimating distance between positioning node and reference node. Last, triangular measurement method or maximum likelihood estimation method is used in estimation coordinates of the node positioning.

3.2   LDV-HOP Algorithm Description

In DV-HOP algorithm, the sum of hop distance is instead of actual distance. Accumulation error will be increased for the addition of number of hop. If the receiver node is just accepted the scope of local reference node information, which is in a small amount near of positioning node. This will reduce the accumulative error and help to improve positioning accuracy and reduce the whole of network communication load. Conclusion what have been mentioned, limit DV-HOP(LDV-HOP)algorithm was proposed. LDV-HOP has divided local processing into three stages.

First, the minimum number of hops has been computed among positioning nodes and reference nodes with limited number of hops. Reference nodes broadcast its position information to the neighbor nodes. Positioning node record what it have received the minimum number of hops about reference nodes, and the larger number of hops which come from the same reference node should ignore. Finally, all the nodes have recorded the minimum number of hops to each reference node. Second, the count of hops distance has been computed among positioning nodes and reference nodes with the limited number of hops. According to record information that is location information and the number of hops about the other reference nodes, each reference node estimated the actual distance of average jump following the formula (1), and broadcast the result to the network.

$$HopSize = \frac{\sum_{j \neq i} \sqrt{(x_i - x_j)^2 + (y_i - y_j)^2}}{\sum_{j \neq i} h_j} \qquad (1)$$

In formula 1, (x_i, y_i), (x_j, y_j) is the coordinates of reference node i and j, h_j is the number of hops among node i and j ($j \neq i$). Third, using triangular measurement method or maximum likelihood estimation method calculate their position.

It is easy to estimate the rough position of positioning node coordinate through LDV-HOP positioning technology, then, weighted least squares method with triangular measurement method can be used to calculate new coordinate, achieve refinement cycle,. There are two characteristics in this refinement cycle.

First, adding the value of a property right for estimating position of the node. Using weighted least square method to implement positioning calculate, which make nodes with large position error have smaller influence on positioning calculating. Second, node with low connectivity which cause large positioning error was prevented them from participating in the refinement cycle process in order to eliminate their effect.

Comparing with DV-HOP algorithm, LDV-HOP with the circulation refinement link obtain positioning information within the local area, it reduce the localization energy consuming, improve the positioning accuracy and reduce communications volume. LDV-HOP algorithm with increase circulation refinement link can meet the low power requirements and simply node of WSNs.

4 Experiment and Simulation

4.1 Simulation and Analysis of Algorithm

Using the Network Simulator version 2 (NS2) in simulation experiment to test the performance of the LDV-HOP algorithm which increased the refinement cycle.

First decompress the installation package NS2 in the host machine with the Windows operation system which installs Linux OS in VMware virtual machines, then configure and install, finally set the environment variable. The simulation takes the MAC type with IEEE802.15.4 protocol, the AODV route protocol. 30 nodes distribute in the 400m*400m square region, and each node randomly moved with direction and velocity which the maximum velocity of movement is 50m/s, and the scene continues 50s set by setdest tool. Using the cbrgen current capacity tool to complete the following, the current capacity is cbr, the speed of 30 nodes are 1.0 m/s.

The entire simulation process includes the network topology and the process of the data sending and receiving defined in the tcl script. The actual content is as followed: 1) Define the scenario parameters; 2) Configure the node parameters; 3) Record the tracking data of simulation process; 4) To create 20 mobile nodes; 5) Define the conclusion of process. To open the "nam" animation analog picture with the simulation NS2 and the executive command after producing the tcl script.

Finally analyzed and processed of data which recorded in the simulation experiment. When the reference node occupies the total nodal point number is certain (20%), compared the position error and the communication load of the different connection between the DV-HOP algorithm(D) and LDV-HOP algorithm after increasing the circulation refinement link(L). The simulation experiment results under the different connectivity of network show in the table 1.

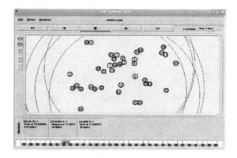

Fig. 3. Communicate between nodes

Table 1. Location error and packets under different connectivity

connectivity		3	4	5	6	7
Location error% of	D	100	92	84	76	64
radio range	L	67	58	49	40	40
Quantity of sending	D	400	1100	1810	2590	2990
packets	L	360	500	680	860	1410

Table 1 listed the comparisons of the position error and the communication load in the different connectivity between the DV-HOP algorithm and LDV-HOP algorithm after increasing the circulation refinement link. When the reference node's percentage is certain (e.g.20%), the connectivity is relatively small, the position error of the LDV-HOP algorithm after increasing the circulation refinement link is smaller than DV-HOP algorithm obviously, the communication load increases along with the connectivity is lower than the DV-HOP algorithm. Therefore, the LDV-HOP algorithm after increasing the circulation refinement cycle can effectively improve the positioning accuracy and reduce the amount of data packets.

4.2 Application of Physics Experiment

The planning of experiment scene: In an area of 50m*50m spacious outdoor plane domain, taking the CC2430 module with wireless radio function as the node of WSNs. The stochastic deployment of WSNs was shown in Fig. 4 (a). Let the marked label 0, 1, 2 nodes as the reference node, which occupied 10% of the total nodes, and the others are unknown nodes. Fig. 4 (b) shows the orientation of distribution of WSNs position which the red circled round are reference nodes, and the yellow circle are localization nodes, in process of orientation, through the wireless communication transfer the gathering data to the coordinator part, and the coordinator communicated with the host computer through the serial port, finally analyzed the gathering data and drew the conclusion.

Experimental procedures: First installed IAR Embedded Workbench on PC, then according to the localization process, node own function and the receiving and dispatching information and so on, developed the application procedure in IAR, and downloaded the program through the USB line to the CC2430 module. Similarly, develop the application procedure which can meet the sending and receiving data of the coordinator, communication protocols and the serial commands. Then download through USB to the experiment plane, finally, to control the positioning process by the defined serial port commands.

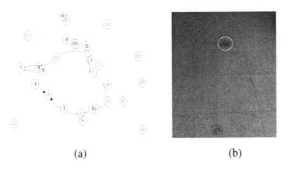

(a)   (b)

Fig. 4.

Localization experiments, any part of the nodes selected as research the localization object, the experimental results were shown in Table 2. The experiment separately takes the DV-HOP algorithm(D) and the increasing circulation refinement link's LDV-HOP(L), the part unknown node estimate coordinate and the error listed in Table 2. The "actual coordinate" is the real(x, y) coordinate of the node; and the "measurement coordinate" is the estimated coordinate through the DV-Hop algorithm and after increasing the circulation and refinement links' algorithm, the error calculated by the following formula (2)

$$err = \sqrt{\left(x_{Rval} - x_{Eval}\right)^2 + \left(y_{Rval} - y_{Eval}\right)^2} \qquad (2)$$

LDV-HOP with increasing circulation refinement link which is localization method with the limited jumps, through setting a threshold hop count N, the number data packet of threshold limit is bigger. The node receives the fewer of hop count due to reduce the communication load of overall network. Meanwhile, the sum of jump

Table 2. Measurement data

Node ID	Actual coordinate	Measurement coordinate D/L	Error D/L	Number of hops away from reference node 0, 1, 2 D/L
3	(31.7,12.8)	(46.3,43.7)/(37.3,23.9)	34.15/12.46	(4.3.7)/(4.3.5)
6	(37.5,13.9)	(46.3,43.7)/(41.8,33.9)	31.01/20.44	(4.3.7)/(4.3.6)
7	(20.5,12.8)	(57.8,48.1)/(40.7,32.0)	51.33/27.86	(6.5.9)/(6.5.3)
11	(27.5,9.7)	(52.0, 45.9)/(34.4,19.7)	43.71/12.07	(5.4.8)/(5.4.4)
18	(15.1,19.6)	(82.3,107.4)/(23.3,29.9)	110.53/13.2	(3.4.10)/(3.4.2)
23	(32.9,12.8)	(46.3,43.7)/(38.6,24.3)	33.68/12.87	(4.3.7)/(4.3.5)
28	(28.6,7.4)	(52.0, 45.9)/(35.9,19.3)	45.06/13.04	(5.4.8)/(5.4.4)

distance is instead of the actual distance, the error is reduced because of the decreasing the number of jumps, however, the cycle of refinement to results of positioning reduces the influence of the pointing accuracy which caused by higher node deviation and the lower connectivity, finally achieves the purpose of improving the positioning accuracy.

5 Conclusion

This paper has analyzed range-based and range-free positioning technology, and token most focus on DV-HOP and LDV-HOP positioning technology. And the circulation refinement link has been added to LDV-HOP. The simulation result and the physical applications have proved that LDV-HOP algorithm which has been increased cycle refinement link is more applicability and superiority in the local orientation. It also have reduced location error, and delayed the communication load. For the requirements of low power WSNs, the purpose of positioning can be achieved effectively.

Acknowledgements. This work has been supported in part by the Tianjin City High School Science & Technology Fund Project No. 20090704.

References

1. Yu, N., Wan, J., Wu, Y.: Localization Algorithm in Wireless Sensor Networks. J. Chinese Journal of Sensors and Actuators 20, 187–192 (2007)
2. Akyildiz, F., Su, W., Sallkarasubramaniam, Y., et al.: A Survey on Sensor Networks. J. IEEE Communications Magazine. 40, 102–114 (2002)
3. Rabacy, J.J., Ammer, M.J., da Silva Jr., J.L., Patel, D., Roundy, S.: Picorodio Supports Ad Hoc Ultra-low Power Wireless Networking. Computer 33, 502 (2000)
4. Bing, Z., Dang, Q., Hao, M., et al.: Steel Cylinder Comprehensive Supervision System Based on RFID and WSNs. J. Computer Engineering 04, 277–279 (2009)
5. Girod, L., Bychovskiy, V., Elson, J., et al.: Loeating Tiny Sensors in Time and Space: A case study. In: Proceeding of the 2002 IEEE International Conference on Computer Design: VLSI in Computers and Processors, Freiburg, Germany, pp. 214–219 (2002)
6. Harter, A., Hopper, A., Steggles, P., et al.: The Anatomy of A Context-aware Application. Wireless Networks 8, 187–197 (2002)
7. Girod, L., Estrin, D.: Robust Range Estimation Using Acoustic and Multi Modal Sensing. In: Proceeding of The IEEE/RSJ International Conference on Intelligent Robots and Systems(IROS01), Maui, pp. 1312–1320 (2001)
8. Nieuleseu, D., Nath, B.: Ad Hoe Positioning System(APS) Using AOA. In: Proceeding of The IEEE INFOCOM 2003, San Francisco, pp. 1734–1743 (2003)
9. Niculescu, D., Nath, B.: DV-based Positioning in Ad Hoc Networks. J. Telecommunication Systems 22, 267–280 (2003)
10. Bulusu, N., Heidemann, J., Estrin, D.: CPS-less Low Cost Outdoor Localization for Very Small Devices. IEEE Personal Communications Magazine 7, 28–34 (2000)
11. Doherty, L., Pister, K.S.J., Ghaoui, L.E.: Convex Position Estimation in Wireless Sensor Net works. In: Proceeding of The IEEE INFOCOM 2001, Anehorage, USA, pp. 1655–1663 (2001)

Development of a Catastrophe Model to Assess the Allocation Efficiency of Competitive Sports Resources in China

Qian Wang[*]

College of Physical Education, Huaiyin Normal University, Jiangsu, China
wqstudy@yahoo.cn

Abstract. High allocation efficiency of competitive sports resources is key for building powerful sports nations. In this regard, there is considerable need for methods and indicators to diagnose the allocation efficiency of competitive sports resources for adjusting the allocation mode, management and regulation. A catastrophe assessment model for allocation efficiency of competitive sports resources was developed in this paper. The assessment indices were divided into hierarchical subsystems under the "input-output" framework. These indices were combined by suitable membership degree functions, such as cusp, fold, swallowtail and butterfly model. Aided by a geographic information system, this model was applied to evaluate comprehensively the spatiotemporal dynamics of allocation efficiency of competitive sports resources in China between 2003 and 2008, taking the administrative division as the assessment unit. Results showed that the allocation efficiency of competitive sports resources in China generally descended from east to west. The allocation efficiencies of the eastern coastal regions were significantly higher than those of the central and western regions. Given the temporal trends, the allocation efficiency of competitive sports resources in most provinces remained low and stable. Specifically, the allocation efficiency of competitive sports resources in central and western provinces remained low across the years. The catastrophe model not only reduces the weight of the subjectivity of the assignment, and can reduce the subjective evaluation criteria to determine the uncertainty of the calculation process. Being simple and operational, it is thus believed to provide an alternative approach to multi-attribute assessment in sports modeling and simulation.

Keywords: multi-attribute assessment, catastrophe theory, allocation efficiency, competitive sports resources, spatiotemporal dynamics, China.

1 Introduction

After several decades of development, China has made remarkable achievements in its competitive sports and has been among the ranks of powerful sport nation. Recalling its development process, it is not difficult to find that reasonable and effective

---

[*] Corresponding author.

S. Lin and X. Huang (Eds.): CESM 2011, Part I, CCIS 175, pp. 399–404, 2011.
© Springer-Verlag Berlin Heidelberg 2011

allocation of competitive sports resources is foundation and premise for the brilliant achievements. The so-called competitive sports resources is the sum of all the input resources for competitive sports activities, including human, financial and material resources, as well as some tangible and intangible resources like training techniques, physical fitness, moral laws, customs and culture [1]. With human development, social progress, economic system transition and transformation of social institutions, the original sports resource allocation pattern has shown many limitations and drawbacks. How to adjust the allocation mode of competitive sports resources in China should be given priorities. In this regard, there is considerable need for methods and indicators to diagnose the allocation efficiency of competitive sports resources for adjusting the allocation mode, management and regulation.

As a kind of multi-attribute assessment, the evaluation of the allocation efficiency of competitive sports resources is conducted mainly through the use of proxy indicators. These indicators are then aggregated into a composite index by certain weight determination procedure. The indices aggregation procedure is a continuous process of optimization, the transition of the equilibrium state from instability to stability [2]. The analytic hierarchy process (AHP) has been used widely for determining weights of indices in multi-attribute assessment studies [3-4]. However, the weight determination procedure of AHP is treaded as a discontinuous process, given that the importance of the indicators is divided into certain grades [2]. Despite its popularity and simplicity in concept, this method is often criticized for its inability to adequately incorporate the inherent uncertainty and imprecision associated with quantifying decision maker's perceptions using discrete (crisp) values [5-6].

Thom (1975) [7] proposed the catastrophe theory (CT), a mathematical model studies systems that, under particular conditions, show sudden changes in the steady equilibrium state as a consequence of small changes in the value of certain input parameters [8]. Due to its dialectic characteristics and advantages as a simple mathematical construct with clear physical meaning, the catastrophe theory has recently found home in multi-attribute assessment studies [2, 9]. The catastrophe-based assessment model considers the whole problem as a particular catastrophic behavior, a small and gradual change in the steady equilibrium state of a sub-system can rapidly cause the whole system to reach the crush state [2]. This thus serves to avoid the disadvantages associated with the weight determination procedure. Given the characteristics of competitive sports resources and the advantages of catastrophe-based assessment models, this paper aims to propose a catastrophe model for the assessment of allocation efficiency of competitive sports resources in China.

2 Development of a Catastrophe Assessment Model

2.1 Indices Selection

From the view of system theory, China's competitive sport resources system is an open giant system, and relates tightly with the environment through a wide range of resources inflow and outflow. The optimal allocation of competitive sport resources is to improve the use and allocation efficiency of competitive sport resources, at a certain time and space scales, with the minimum consumption of human, financial resources and material resources, and with the maximum outputs. Under such circumstances, the "input-output" evaluation framework for resource allocation efficiency assessment, proposed by Woidasky (2009) [7], was chosen as the basis for defining indices to assess the allocation efficiency of competitive sports resources. Besides, indices selection in this study was guided by the principles of integrity, simplicity, dynamic response, geographical accuracy, and data availability and the "three-step" method proposed by Su et al. (2010) [6]. We referred to previous studies and the framework as well as the principles explained above to generate a set of assessment indices. Initially, a set of 60 indices was developed. Subsequently, we established a three-round Delphi Process from which 18 indices were selected and 2 indices were added. After performing principal component analysis to reduce data dimensionality, a total of 7 indices were generated: Input (Funding amount for competitive sports, Total number of full-time coaches, Total area of sports venues) and Output (Gold metals at national level and above level, Number of persons doing regular physical activities, Total output of sports patent, Sports lottery sales).

2.2 Data Source and Standardization

Statistical data between 2003 and 2008, obtained from "China Statistical Yearbook", "China Sports Yearbook", "State Patent Database" and "China Statistical Database", were used in this paper. Given the different dimension and distribution of indices, it was difficult to directly compare or operate among them. Data standardization was thus performed to make the original data of indices dimensionless using the following equations:

$$x_i' = \frac{x_i - x_{i\min}}{x_{i\max} - x_{i\min}} \tag{1}$$

Where i is the index, xi is the original value of i, x_{imax} and x_{imin} are respectively the maximum and the minimum value of i.

2.3 Application of Catastrophe Theory

Catastrophe theory uses mathematical models to describe, predict qualitative changes of natural phenomena and social activities. Catastrophe theory focuses on the potential function [V = V (x, u)], which describes the system behavior using the state variables x and the external control parameter u. When the state variable is one dimensional, there exist four catastrophe models [8] (Table 1). The assessment index system can be divided into hierarchical sub-systems. If the index at higher level (response variable) contains two lower level indices (control variable), it can be assumed as a cusp system. The relative importance of these two control variables should be determined (u_1, important; u_2, less important), and control variable can then be obtained from the membership function. Similarly, when the index at higher level contains one, three or four lower level indices, it can be respectively calculated based on fold, swallowtail and butterfly membership function. The catastrophe assessment model for China's allocation efficiency of competitive sports resources was therefore developed following such approach.

Table 1. Summary description of catastrophe models [8]

Category	Dimension of control variables	Potential function	Bifurcation set	Normalization formula
Fold	1	$V(x) = x^3 + u_1 x$	$u_1 = -3x^2$	$X_{u_1} = \sqrt{u_1}$
Cusp	2	$V(x) = x^4 + u_1 x^2 + u_2 x$	$u_1 = -6x^2, u_2 = 8x^3$	$X_{u_1} = \sqrt{u_1}, X_{u_2} = \sqrt[3]{u_2}$
Swallowtail	3	$V(x) = \frac{1}{5}x^5 + \frac{1}{3}u_1 x^3 + \frac{1}{2}u_2 x^2 + u_3 x$	$u_1 = -6x^2, u_2 = 8x^3,$ $u_3 = -3x^4$	$X_{u_1} = \sqrt{u_1}, X_{u_2} = \sqrt[3]{u_2},$ $X_{u_3} = \sqrt[4]{u_3}$
Butterfly	4	$V(x) = \frac{1}{6}x^6 + \frac{1}{4}u_1 x^4 + \frac{1}{3}u_2 x^3 + \frac{1}{2}u_3 x^2 + u_4 x$	$u_1 = -10x^2, u_2 = 20x^3,$ $u_3 = -15x^4, u_4 = 4x^5$	$X_{u_1} = \sqrt{u_1}, X_{u_2} = \sqrt[3]{u_2},$ $X_{u_3} = \sqrt[4]{u_3}, X_{u_4} = \sqrt[5]{u_4}$

2.4 Score Transformation

The synthetic values of catastrophe assessment are generally high and the differences are not obvious and it is difficult to determine the actual level directly using the results obtained by catastrophe assessment [9-10]. Usually, the synthetic values of multi-attribute assessment are divided into five grades and the allocation efficiency of competitive sports resources accordingly can be divided into five grades: 0.2 (low), 0.4 (relatively low), 0.6 (middle), 0.8 (relatively high) and 1.0 (high). The problem is how to find a way to transform the results obtained by catastrophe assessment into the ordinary-used synthetic values. This paper used the method proposed by Su et al. (2011) [2] for score transformation as follows: Suppose the relative membership degree for all indices equals n, then the relative membership degree for higher level indices should also equal n. Consequently, the synthetic membership degree can be obtained by applying suitable catastrophe model. The catastrophe value for each secure grade was thus calculated (Table 2).

Table 2. Corresponding values between assessment results of catastrophe model and ordinary-used values at different levels

	Low	Relatively low	Middle	Relatively high	High
Relative membership degree obtained by catastrophe model	<0.799	0.799-0.879	0.879-0.930	0.930-0.969	>0.969
Corresponding ordinary-used values	<0.2	0.2-0.4	0.4-0.6	0.6-0.8	>0.8

3 Results and Discussion

Spatial patterns of allocation efficiency of competitive sports resources in China between 2003 and 2008 were displayed in Fig.1. The allocation efficiency of competitive sports resources in China generally descended from east to west. The allocation efficiencies of the eastern coastal regions were significantly higher than those of the central and western regions. Specifically, Guangdong, Shandong, Jiangsu, Beijing and other powerful sports provinces exhibited higher level of allocation efficiency of competitive sports resources. Four explanations can be forwarded for the spatial variations in allocation efficiency of competitive sports resources in China. First, funding for the development of competitive sports in eastern provinces was much higher than other ones. Second, sports science research institutes are mainly concentrated in eastern areas. The high output of innovative knowledge and human resources laid solid base for the optimal allocation of competitive sports resources. Third, the development of sports industry and sports consumption was much faster in eastern regions than the counterparts, increasing the allocation efficiency of competitive sports resources. Last, the historical dual "urban-rural" division not only imbalanced the development of urban and rural, but also highlighted the low allocation level of competitive sports resources in western areas. Given the temporal trends, the allocation efficiency of competitive sports resources in most provinces remained low and stable. Specifically, the allocation efficiency of competitive sports resources in central and western provinces remained low across the years. Sichuan, Hubei and Zhejiang provinces witnessed increases in the allocation efficiency of competitive sports resources. These can be attributed to the increased sports funding, transformation of sports industry development mode and introduction of talents.

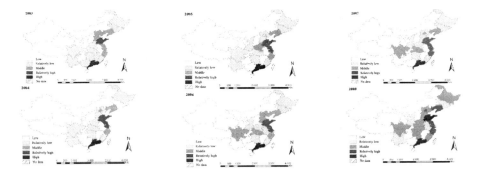

Fig. 1. Spatiotemporal dynamics of allocation efficiency of competitive sports resources in China between 2003 and 2008

The catastrophe model combined the hierarchical indices system using the catastrophe fuzzy membership functions, rather than weights assigned by the users. Such operation is thus believed to reduce subjectivity and uncertainty [2]. The whole calculation, mainly depending on suitable membership degree functions (cusp, fold, swallowtail and butterfly model), requires a relatively low level of technical expertise, making the modeling procedures simple and operational. In addition, the data requirements in this study were low, since all the data were publicly available. It is found that the assessment results approximated reality quite well by reflecting the allocation efficiency of competitive sports resources in China across time and space. As a result, the catastrophe model presented in this paper is applicable enough to other nations. Of importance is to realize that the allocation mode, management and regulation of competitive sports resources, as well as social expectations, may be quite different in other nations. Besides, indices in the "input-output" framework are dynamically linked. In these cases, indices of the assessment model should be modified according to those certain conditions.

4 Conclusions

This paper developed a catastrophe model to assess the allocation efficiency of competitive sports resources in China. Results showed that the allocation efficiency of competitive sports resources in China generally descended from east to west. Those of the eastern coastal regions were significantly higher than those of the central and western regions. Given the temporal trends, the allocation efficiency in most provinces remained low and stable. Specifically, the allocation efficiency of competitive sports resources in central and western provinces remained low across the years. Results of the model were found reliable, and the catastrophe model was thus regarded as simple, quick and easy to handle. Given its characteristics of being simple and operational, the catastrophe model thus believed to provide an alternative approach to multi-attribute assessment in sports modeling and simulation.

References

1. Hu, P.: China's competitive sports resources: Allocation and adjustment. Ph.D thesis of Harbin Engineering University (2009) (in Chinese with English abstract)
2. Su, S., Li, D., Yu, X., Zhang, Z., Zhang, Q., Xiao, R., Zhi, J., Wu, J.: Assessing land ecological security in Shanghai (China) based on catastrophe theory. Stoch Environ. Res. Risk Assesst (in press), doi: 10.1007/s00477-011-0457-9
3. Vaidyaa, S.O., Kumar, S.: Analytic hierarchy process: An overview of applications. Eur. J. Oper. Res. 169, 1–29 (2006)
4. Bryson, N., Mobolurin, A.: An approach to using the analytic hierarchy process for solving multiple criteria decision making problems. Eur. J. Oper. Res. 76, 440–454 (1994)
5. Li, T., Huang, H.: Applying TRIZ and Fuzzy AHP to develop innovative design for automated manufacturing systems. Expert Syst. Appl. 36, 8302–8312 (2009)
6. Su, S., Chen, X., DeGloria, D.S., Wu, J.: Integrative fuzzy set pair model for land ecological security assessment: a case study of Xiaolangdi Reservoir Region, China. Stoch. Environ. Res. Risk Assess. 24, 639–647 (2010)
7. Woidasky, J., Schweppe, R., Hirth, T.: Resources and Energy efficiency. Chem. Ing. Tech. 81, 1711–1719 (2009)
8. Woodstock, A.E.R., Poston, T.: A geometrical study of the elementary catastrophes. Springer Lecture Notes in Math, vol. 373. Springer, New York (1974)
9. Poston, T., Ian, S.: Catastrophe theory and application, Lord, Pitman (1978)
10. Schreiber, F.A., Baiguera, M., Bortolotto, G., Caglioti, V.: A study of the dynamic behaviour of some workload allocation algorithms by means of catastrophe theory. J. Syst. Architect. 43, 605–624 (1997)

MPCS: A Wireless Communication Protocol for Ubiquitous Industrial Environment

Yuhuang Zheng

Department of Physics, Guangdong University of Education
510303 Guangzhou, China
zhyhaa@126.com

Abstract. This paper describes a MPCS communication protocol developed to solute the problem of different Programmable Controllers communication in ubiquitous industrial environment. The MPCS protocol can overcome the disadvantages of MODBUS polling mechanism, and achieve higher throughput, lower average message delay and less average message dropping rate in wireless communication. The experimental result of a wireless network in industrial environment also is reported. It illustrates that the MPCS protocol can perform well in industrial application.

Keywords: Wireless networks, Ubiquitous Computing, Programmable Controller (PLC).

1 Introduction

Wireless networks have been under rapid development during recent years. Types of technologies being developed to wireless personal area network for short range, point-to multi-point communications, such as Bluetooth and ZigBee. [1] The application of wireless technology for industrial communication and control systems has the potential to provide major benefits in terms of flexible installation and maintenance of field devices and reduction in costs and problems due to wire cabling. [2]

Wireless communications from machine to machine greatly enhance automation of an industrial system. Ubiquitous industrial environment is coming and allows the engineers to acquire and control the real-time data of wireless networks of the factory at anytime anywhere. [3]

A key issue currently limiting ubiquitous industrial environment development involves compatibility among components in industrial environment from different suppliers, generally referred to as interoperability. Full compatibility among components would also provide end users with the flexibility to connect highly specialized, high-end sensors with best-in-class wireless interface devices. [4]

Interoperability in ubiquitous industrial environment means wireless communication protocol and the protocol of monitoring and controlling industrial equipments are interoperable. Interoperable wireless protocols are making or have appeared by some international organizations and alliances, such as ISO, WINA, ZigBee, etc. Most industrial equipments have their special monitoring and controlling protocols. PLC is

S. Lin and X. Huang (Eds.): CESM 2011, Part I, CCIS 175, pp. 405–410, 2011.

the most important controller in industrial application, but different brands almost have different inherent monitoring protocols. For example, Siemens PLC S7-200 uses PPI, Siemens PLC S7-300 uses MPI, A-B PLC Micrologix and SLC series uses DF1, MITSUBISHI PLC FX2N has different inherent protocols. It is common for a factory to using different kinds of PLCs in their product lines. How to make these different PLCs can communicate with each other is a key problem.

This paper addresses the MPCS protocol to solute this problem. MPCS is the abbreviation of MODBUS for Producer/Consumer Services. MPCS protocol applies ZigBee as wireless protocol among wireless nodes. The core of MPCS is to use the MODBUS protocol without polling to carry industrial equipments protocol. MODBUS protocol is applied to an electronic controller on the lingua franca. The most important is the protocol also must be supported by typical PLCs. But most of the industrial monitoring systems adopt fixed period polling with less consideration about dynamic period in using MODBUS. So in ubiquitous industrial environment, the MODBUS protocol cannot satisfy the latency requirement of wireless protocol and it cannot guarantee the real-time monitoring of industrial environment conditions. And the polling method of MODBUS adds extra loads and burdens the wireless channel. The MPCS protocol changes the polling mechanism of MODBUS and the slave equipments can send the messages by themselves periodically without receiving query command from the master equipment.

MPCS protocol applies ZigBee as wireless protocol among wireless nodes and MODBUS with sending message periodically as industrial monitoring protocol. Experiment shows that the combination of MPCS and ZigBee is a good way to solute the interoperability in ubiquitous industrial environment. MPCS has the advantages in saving bandwidth and lightening servers' load and enhances the real-time performance of industrial wireless sensor networks.

This paper first introduces the experiment system. Secondly ZigBee and ZigBee gateway are discussed. Thirdly it introduces MPCS protocol in different PLCs. There is an experiment to test MPCS protocol in this section. Finally it is a conclusion.

2 System Overview

Wireless sensors provide the network with the ability to reconfigure on the fly without being tied down by signal cables. The goal of the system is to implement such a network using PLCs connected by Zigbee transceivers to a central computer that interfaces with a database accessible. The three major components consist of different brands of PLCs, CC2530 Low Power Transceivers for ZigBee, and the SCADA software hosted on the central computer. A block diagram of the high level design is provided in Fig 1 below.

There are PLCs in this system, including Siemens PLC S7-224 and XINJIE PLC XC3-24RT-E. S7-224 uses PPI protocol and XC3-24RT-E uses MODBUS protocol. PLCs collect data from the industrial machinery and transmit them in MODBUS format to ZigBee gateway in which data are processed. ZigBee gateway packed data according to the ZigBee protocol, and transmitted them to via radio. Finally, data are transmitted to ZigBee gateway of the central computer. At the central computer, incoming data from ZigBee gateway of it are received and processed by the SCADA software which is developed in Kingview. [5]

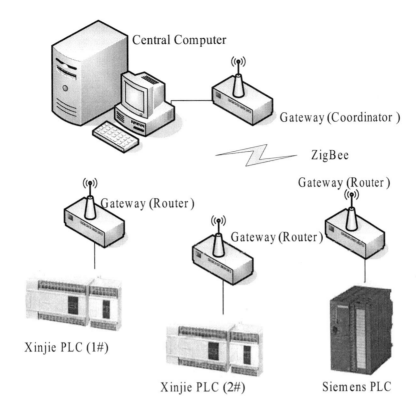

Fig. 1. System Architecture of System

3 ZigBee

3.1 ZigBee in Industrial Environment

There are thousands of devices in a factory, such as, PLC, HMI, IPC, smart sensor, and so on. ZigBee is focused on control and automation. ZigBee standards have a characteristic of "three low" of low electricity consumption (year's cell life), low cost (less than $5) and low data rate (250 Kb/s). [6-7] ZigBee works with small packet devices and supports a larger number of devices and a longer range between devices than other technologies. ZigBee devices can form mesh networks connecting hundreds to thousands of devices together. Devices use very little power and can operate on a cell battery for many years. In timing critical applications, such as industrial application, ZigBee is designed to respond quickly. ZigBee is a good wireless technology in industrial application.

3.2 ZigBee Gateway Designation

The ZigBee gateway is based on the CC2530 System-on-Chip, which combines a RF transceiver with an industry-standard enhanced 8051 MCU, in-system programmable

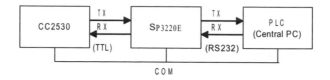

Fig. 2. A ZigBee Gateway

flash memory, 8-KB RAM, and other powerful peripherals. Fig 2 is a ZigBee gateway. The gateway consists of CC2530, SP3220E devices, battery and some interfaces.

Because PLC has a UART interface and the interface usually is RS-232. But UART of CC2530 is TTL, so RS232-TTL conversion is done with a SP3220E chip.

ZigBee gateway allows device containing UART to communicate via radio with other devices. Each device connects to ZigBee gateway. In this system, the four ZigBee gateways provide the radio communication link.

When the ZigBee gateway is used in an application, it is assumed that a permanent power source will be available at both ends of the wireless link. This means the on-chip radio can always be active, eliminating the need to synchronize the transmission/reception of data. The link is designed to operate at up to 19200 baud.

The ZigBee gateway of PC must act as a PAN Coordinator. The PAN Coordinator is responsible for starting the network and allocating an address to the other gateway, which acts as a Router. Fig 3 is the program flow chart of PAN Coordinator.

The ZigBee gateway of PLC acts as a router device. The router device scans the radio channels, looking for the PAN Coordinator. Once it has found the Coordinator, it associates with it. Data transfer between radio and the on-chip UART is identical to that described above. Data received via the radio is output to the connected device using the on-chip UART, and data received by the on-chip UART from the device is transmitted over the radio. This process is repeated every 20ms. Fig 4 is the program flow chart of Router.

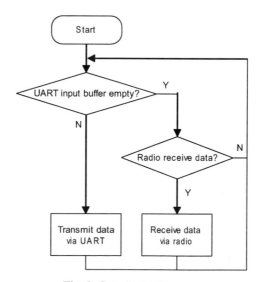

Fig. 3. Coordinator Program

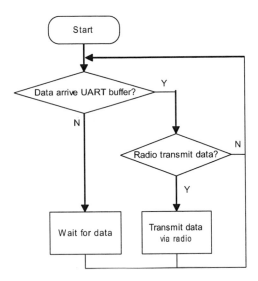

Fig. 4. Router Program

4   MPCS Protocol

MPCS is important to have a protocol at the application layer that allows PLCs to take advantage of producer/consumer services. Using producer/consumer, the data "producer" which is a PLC, puts the PAN Coordinator ID at the front of each packet. The message is then sent out of the network and the Coordinator screens the ID to determine if the data is for its consumption. If so, the Coordinator becomes the "consumer." As a result, multi-cast communication happens naturally and efficiently in a producer/consumer service.

MODBUS is designed for source/destination communication or master/slave model. MPCS, however, joins forces with producer/consumer technology to offer a superior message-delivery mechanism of MODBUS. MPCS supports all of the major communication relationships of MODBUS. MPCS is a flexible protocol and results in efficient use of bandwidth.

MODBUS-compliant devices are common in industrial application. Users can achieve MODBUS by device's internal standard, direct interface and external converter. Internal standard means MODBUS is the basic protocol that PLC uses for parsing messages, such as Modicon and XINJIE controllers. Some PLCs have their internal standard protocols, but these PLCs also provide MODBUS communication interface and MODBUS communication instruction. For example, The MicroLogix controller family of Rockwell Automation supports RS-485, direct interface to MODBUS RTU master-slave networks without an external electrical interface converter. These PLCs are internal support MODBUS. In order to use MODBUS protocol, some PLCs must add some external electrical interface converter, such as Siemens S7-300 and S7-400.

In this experiment system, MODBUS is internal standard of XINJIE controller. Microwin 4.0, which is. the program software of S7-224, provides MODBUS

Communication Instruction Library. With the MODBUS instruction, the S7-224 can use MODBUS via its programmable UART interface.

To verify the performance and interoperability of MPCS protocol, we did a test of the system in section 2. The monitoring period of controlling center is 1 second. The PLCs used are distributed among 30 meters distance. Table 1 shows the result of the test. One Siemens PLC of S7-224 and two Xinjie PLCs of XC3-24RT-E send 3000 packets relatively and the central computer records these packets. Basically, the test results are satisfied, and the MPCS protocol are suitable in non-critical industrial environment.

Table 1. Test Result

PLC	S7-224	XC3-24RT-E(1#)	XC3-24RT-E(2#)
Transmit Packets	3000	3000	3000
Receive Packets	2860	2827	2831
Successful Rate	98.66%	94.23%	97.7%

5 Conclusion

MPCS communication protocol is developed for industrial monitoring system. The results show the performance and interoperability for the wireless networks are good enough for some monitoring and non-critical instrument systems.

References

1. Wang, N., Zhang, N., Wang, M.: Wireless Sensors in Agriculture and Food Industry—Recent Development and Future Perspective. Computers and Electronics in Agriculture 50(14), 1–14 (2006)
2. Bonivento, A., Carloni, L.P., Sangiovanni-Vincentelli A.: Platform-Based Design of Wireless Sensor Networks for Industrial Applications. In: Proceedings of Design, Automation and Test in Europe, pp. 1–6. IEEE Press, New York (2006)
3. Low, K.S., Win, W.N.N., Er, M.J.: Wireless Sensor Networks for Industrial Environments. In: International Conference on Intelligent Agents, Web Technologies and Internet Commerce, pp. 271–276. IEEE Press, New York (2005)
4. Industrial Wireless Technology for the 21st Century,
   http://www1.eere.energy.gov/industry/sensors_automation/pdfs/wireless_technology.pdf
5. Xi, X., Tao, C., Fang, X.: A Health Care System Based on PLC and ZigBee. In: International Conference on Wireless Communications, Networking and Mobile Computing, Shanghai, China, pp. 3063–3066 (2007)
6. Li, Z.: ZigBee Wireless Sensor Network in Industrial Applications. In: International Joint Conference, Busan, Korea, pp. 1067–1070 (2006)
7. Gungor, V.C., Hancke, G.P.: Industrial Wireless Sensor Networks: Challenges, Design Principles, and Technical Approaches. IEEE Transactions on Industrial Electronics 54(10), 4258–4265 (2009)

Study on Throughput of Network with Selfish Nodes Based on IEEE 802.15.4

Haiping Li, Jianlin Mao, Ning Guo, and Bin Zhang

Haiping Li, Kunming University of Science and Technology, 650000 Yunnan, China
lhping3@126.com

Abstract. CSMA/CA mechanism in 802.15.4 protocol provides a contention mechanism and has been widely used in wireless sensor networks. But some nodes may disobey the backoff algorithm and behave selfishly in order to obtain more bandwidth share. In this paper, we study the selfish behavior of nodes which minimize their BE (Backoff Exponent) once sense the channel state is busy. Finally, NS2 is used to simulate the CSMA/CA mechanism and the simulation result indicates that the network packet loss rate is decreased, the fairness is affected and the throughput is reduced due to the introduction of selfish node.

Keywords: selfish node, CSMA/CA, NS2.

1 Introduction

Over the last few years, wireless sensor networks (WSN) develops very quickly. It has become the predominant medium responsible for the wireless internet access in many environments. WSN is constituted by a large number of low energy consumption and small size sensing nodes, which are capable of dealing with data and identifying the current network. Based on the above mentioned, WSN technology have come to pervade every aspect of our lives, especially wireless remote monitoring system. IEEE802.15.4 is a simple and low rate Media Access Control (MAC) standard, which is applied to the transducer and other low energy consumption equipments. IEEE802.15.4 utilizes the contention based MAC based on CSMA/CA (Carrier Sense Multiple Access/Collision Avoidance). Due to the advent of programmable radios, different MAC protocol parameters can be manipulated in various ways to gain an unfair share of the wireless channel resources and that leads to the birth of the selfish behavior. In practice, protocol parameters such as transmission power and carrier sensing threshold can be easily adjusted [1].For example, a higher CCA threshold can effectively disable carrier sensing. Thus, the selfish node gains more transmission opportunities. The authors in [2] [3] propose a routing misbehavior. The selfish nodes participate in the route discovery and maintenance processes but refuse to forward data packets. Li Dan and Wu jianping[4] survey the recent research trends in this area, and classify the research into three categories according to the working steps of ALM protocols, that is ,the selfishness in maintenance of control structure, the selfishness in collection of node information, and the selfishness in construction of

S. Lin and X. Huang (Eds.): CESM 2011, Part I, CCIS 175, pp. 411–417, 2011.
© Springer-Verlag Berlin Heidelberg 2011

data structure. Similarly, setting the back off window smaller provides an unfair advantage by backing off for a shorter interval on average. To design robust and trustworthy 802.15.4 protocols, it is necessary to study the selfishness. In this paper we keep the minimum BE (Backoff Exponent) of the selfish nodes. Then analyze the result of simulation and find out the impact of selfish nodes on the network.

1.1 Introduction of IEEE 802.15.4 CSMA/CA

WSN is constituted by numerous sensing nodes; every node needs to compete to access the channel in the operation of network. The Carrier Sense Multiple Access/Collision Avoidance (CAMA/CA) mechanism provides an effective method. In the mechanism, if one node that wants to send data, it should first listen to the channel. If the channel is idle and this state last longer than Distributed Inter Frame Space (DIFS), then the node permit to send Require to Send (RTS) frame. If the channel is busy, backoff mechanism should be taken to avoid conflicts with other nodes. If one node starts the back off mechanism, a random number will be generated between [0, CW]. If the idle state of the channel lasts as long as DIFS, the random number will subtract one. Only when the random number reduces to zero then the node begin to send data. The picture of mechanism principle is as follows.

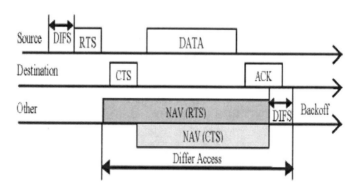

Fig. 1. Data transmission mechanism

In a network of a time running, a source station has some information to send to a destination station, the source station listens to channel and in this moment, the channel is idle, the source station sends a RTS to the destination station. On receiving the RTS from the source station, the destination station replies CTS after a SIFS (Short Inter-Frame Space). The source station sends data after receive the CTS. Then the destination station replies an ACK to source station after receiving the data from the source station. so, the sending process is over .When the source station is sending a RTS frame, there is another station has data to send to the same destination station, according to the back off mechanism, the new source stations start back off mechanism to avoid collision. The new source stations begin to send data only when the random number reduces to zero.

2   CSMA/CA Mechanism Simulation

As open source network simulation software, NS2 provides strong support for simulating and studying of wired and wireless networks. In the CSMA/CA mechanism, the size of the CW affects nodes contend to the channel. The smaller the CW is, the more opportunity to obtain channel resources.

In order to research the impact of selfish nodes on network, we design 5 groups of simulation experiment.

2.1   Throughput Analysis

We simulate the network exists selfish nodes and does not exist selfish node. A super frame has 16 intervals, and there are 21 nodes in the network, the No.0 node is destination node, and the No.1--20 nodes are source nodes. We adopt TCP protocol in agent layer and FTP in the application layer and the packet size is 1500 bytes. The structure of the network is illustrated in Fig. 2.

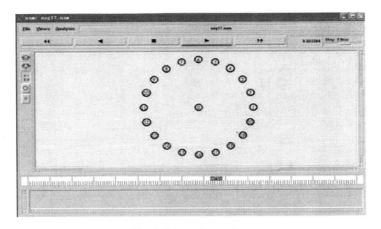

Fig. 2. Network topology

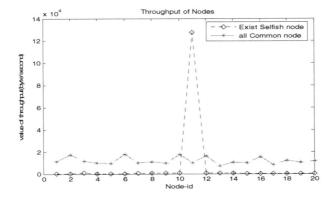

Fig. 3. Throughput of nodes

In this paper, the selfish nodes minimize their BE once they sense the channel state is busy while the common nodes increase their BE respect the backoff mechanism. Therefore, the selfish nodes dramatically increase the probability to obtain the channel resource.

Analyzing the result of simulation, we get the throughput of each node, as illustrated in Fig. 3.

In Fig. 3, the throughput of each node is roughly the same when the nodes are all common nodes. But when the network exist one selfish node, like the No.11 node, the majority of the channel resources are occupied by the selfish node.

2.2 Different Network Size Simulation

For the further study of the impact of selfish nodes on the network, we change the network size, and analyze the throughput and the packet loss rate. The number of nodes in the network is increasing from 3 to 20. Fig. 4 illustrates the throughput of selfish node and common nodes while increasing the network size. Fig. 5 respectively illustrates the throughput of network exists selfish nodes and does not exist selfish node.

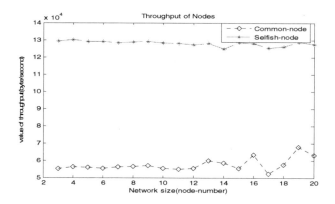

Fig. 4. Throughput of selfish node and common node

As shown in Fig. 4, when only 3 nodes exist in the network, this is, one selfish source node, one common source node and one destination node, the selfish node receives a great number of data packets, nearly occupy all the network resources, while the common node only receives one data packet. With the increasing of the common nodes in the network, the throughput of common nodes shows an upward trend. When the number of the common nodes amounts to 19, the throughput of them amounts to 2000 bytes, however, the throughput of the selfish node is 8,000 bytes. With continuing increase network size, the throughput of the common source nodes changes little. Therefore, when a selfish node exists in the network, with the network size increasing, the throughputs of the common nodes increase but far from that of the selfish node. The selfish node occupies the majority of the channel resources.

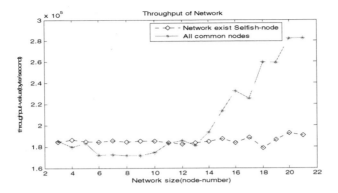

Fig. 5. Throughput of network

As shown in Fig. 5, along with the network size increasing from 3 to 20, the throughput of network increasing when none selfish node exist in the network. However, when there is one selfish node, the throughput hold steady.

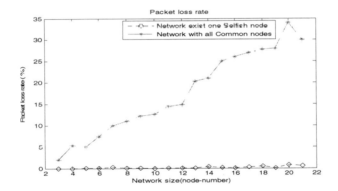

Fig. 6. Packet loss rate

In Fig. 6, when none selfish node exist, the packet loss rate show an upward trend and amounts to 34% when the nodes amounts to 20. But when a selfish node exists, along with the network size increasing, the packet loss rate change little, and always keep in 1%.

2.3 Different Selfish Level Simulation

In this experiment, we analyze the impact of different selfish level on the network. We define the ratio of the selfish behavior frequency to the backoff frequency in a simulation as the selfish level and we introduce parameter P use to measure the selfish level. When P=0, it means the process of simulation does not appear selfish behavior; When P=1, it means the nodes are all selfish nodes which set their own BE as system minimum value once sense the channel state is busy. There are 21 nodes in the network, the No.0 node is destination node, and the No.1--20 nodes are source nodes. We adopt TCP protocol in agent layer and FTP in the application layer and the packet size is 1500 bytes. As selfish level increases from 0 to 1, network throughput analysis results as shown in figure 7.

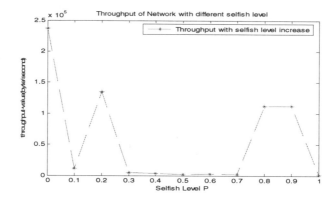

Fig. 7. Network throughput with different selfish level

As shown in Fig. 7, When no selfish node exist (P=0), network throughput is reach 238680 byte, but with P increasing, the throughput appear in large fluctuations, when P=1, the network throughput reduce to 1304 byte.

3   Conclusions

In this paper, we analyze the impact of selfish behavior on network. Although the selfish node seriously affects the fairness of the network and occupies the majority of the channel resource and also reduces the throughput, it greatly decreases the packet loss rate.

Our future work will focus on the model and improvement of the protocol since the throughput of the network is greatly decreased due to the introduction of selfish node. In order to use well in practical application, we also plan to take measures in the protocol to against and handle selfish behavior.

References

1. Eunho, Y., Jaehyuk, C., Sunglim, L.: On Selfish Behavior using Asymmetric Carrier Sensing in IEEE 802.11 Wireless Networks. In: 33rd IEEE Conference on Montreal, Local Computer Network, LCN (2008)
2. Paul, U., Das, A.R.: Detecting elfish Carrier-Sense Behavior in Wi-Fi Networks by Passive Monitoring. In: 2010 IEEE/IFIP International Conference on Dependable Systems & Networks, Chicago, June 28-July 1 (2010)

3. Chen, L.: Research on Selfish Behavior of Nodes in Mobile Ad hoc Network Using IEEE 802.11 Protocol. J. Computer Era (3) (2010)
4. Li, D., Wu, J., Cui, Y.: Study on Selfishness in Application-Layer Multicast. Journal of Software 3(18), 625–635 (2007)
5. Sundararajan, T.V.P., Shanmugam, A.: Modeling the Behavior of Selfish Forwarding Nodes to Simulate Cooperation in MANET. J. International Journal of Network Security & Its Application 2(2) (April 2010)

Attraction for Stochastic Cellular Neural Networks

Li Wan[1] and Qinghua Zhou[2]

[1] Department of Mathematics and Physics, Wuhan Textile University, Wuhan 430073, China
[2] Zhaoqing University, Zhaoqing 526061, China

Abstract. The aim of this paper is to establish new results and sufficient criteria on weak attractor for stochastic cellular neural networks with delays. By using Lyapunov method and Lasalle-type theorem, sufficient conditions ensuring the weak attractor for stochastic cellular neural networks are established. The almost surely asymptotic stability is a special case of our results. Our criteria are easily tested by Matlab LMI Toolbox. An example is given to demonstrate our results.

Keywords: Stochastic cellular neural networks, Weak attractor, Delays.

1 Introduction

Cellular neural networks have been extensively studied in past years and found many applications for solving a number of problems in various scientific disciplines. Such applications heavily depend on the dynamical behaviors. In recent years, considerable attention has been paid to investigate the dynamics of stochastic neural networks since stochastic disturbances are mostly inevitable owing to thermal noise in electronic implementations. Some results on stochastic neural networks with delays have been reported in [1-9] and references therein. However, these literatures only consider the stability of stochastic neural networks with delays. In fact, except for stability property, dynamical behaviors include uniform boundedness, attractor, bifurcation and chaos. To the best of our knowledge, so far there are few results on the attractor for stochastic cellular neural networks with delays.

Motivated by the above discussions, the objective of this paper is to establish new results and sufficient criteria on the weak attractor for the following stochastic cellular neural networks with delays:

$$dx(t) = [-Cx(t) + Af(x(t)) + Bf(y(t))]dt + [Px(t) + Qy(t)]dw(t) \quad (1)$$

with the initial condition $x(t) = \phi(t)$, $-\tau \leq t \leq 0$, where $x(t) \in R^n$ is the state vector, $y(t) = (x_1(t-\tau_1), \cdots, x_n(t-\tau_n))^T$; $C = diag(c_1, \cdots c_n) > 0$ represents the rate with which the ith unit will reset its potential to the resting state in isolation when being disconnected from the network and the external stochastic perturbation; $f(x(t)) = [f_1(x_1(t)), \cdots, f_n(x_n(t))]^T$ represents the neuron activation function with

S. Lin and X. Huang (Eds.): CESM 2011, Part I, CCIS 175, pp. 418–422, 2011.
© Springer-Verlag Berlin Heidelberg 2011

$f(0) = 0$; $A \in R^{n \times n}$ and $B \in R^{n \times n}$ represent the connection weight matrix and the delayed connection weight matrix, respectively; $P \in R^{n \times n}$ and $Q \in R^{n \times n}$ are the diffusion coefficient matrix; $w(t)$ is a one-dimensional Brownian motion defined on a complete probability space with a natural filtration; $\tau = \max\{\tau_i\}$, $\phi(t) \in C([-\tau, 0], R^n)$ is measurable and bounded random variable.

2 Preliminaries

The notation $A > 0$ (respectively, $A \geq 0$) means that matrix A is symmetric positive definite (respectively, positive semi-definite). A^T and A^{-1} denote the transpose and inverse of the matrix A. Let $C^{2,1}(R^n \times R^+; R^+)$ denote the family of all nonnegative functions $V(x,t)$ on $R^n \times R^+$ which are continuously twice differentiable in x and once differentiable in t. Let $F(x(t), y(t)) = -Cx(t) + Af(x(t)) + Bf(y(t))$, $G(x(t), y(t)) = Px(t) + Qy(t)$. Define an operator $LV \in C(R^n \times R^n \times R^+; R)$ by

$$LV(x, y, t) = V_t(x,t) + V_x(x,t)F(x, y) + \frac{1}{2} trace\{G^T(x, y)V_{xx}(x,t)G(x, y)\}.$$

Throughout this paper, we always assume that there exists $L = diag(l_1, \cdots, l_n)$ such that

$$0 \leq \frac{f_i(u) - f_i(v)}{u - v} \leq l_i, u, v \in R. \tag{2}$$

From (2), it follows that system (1) has a unique solution $x(t)$ [10]. Moreover, $F(x(t), y(t))$ and $G(x(t), y(t))$ are locally bounded in (x, y).

Lemma 1. (Lasalle-type theorem, [11]) Assume that system (1) has a unique solution $x(t)$. Moreover, $F(x(t), y(t))$ and $G(x(t), y(t))$ are locally bounded in (x, y). Assume that there are $V \in C^{2,1}(R^n \times R^+; R^+)$ and $W_1 \geq 0$, $W_2 \geq 0$ such that $\lim\inf_{|x| \to \infty, t \geq 0} V(x,t) = \infty$,

$$LV(x, y, t) \leq -W_1(x) + W_2(y), W(x) = W_1(x) - W_2(x) \geq 0,$$

Then $KerW = \{x \in R^n : W(x) = 0\}$ is nonempty and

$$\lim_{t \to \infty} \inf_{y \in KerW} \|x - y\| = 0, a.s. \tag{3}$$

3 Main Results

Formula (3) shows that the solutions $x(t)$ will be attracted by $KerW$ eventually. So we may say that $KerW$ is a weak attractor for the solutions of system (1).

Theorem 1. Assume that there exist matrix $M > 0$ and diagonal matrices $U_i = diag(u_{i1}, \cdots, u_{in}) \geq 0(i = 1,2)$ such that $H_1 \geq H_2 \geq 0$, where

$$H_1 = \begin{pmatrix} MC + CM - MBM^{-1}B^T M - 2P^T MP & -MA - LU_1 \\ (-MA - LU_1)^T & 2U_1 \end{pmatrix},$$

$$H_2 = \begin{pmatrix} 2Q^T MQ & LU_2 \\ (LU_2)^T & M - 2U_2 \end{pmatrix},$$

Then $KerW = \{x \in R^n : W(x) = 0\}$ is nonempty and formula (3) holds, where $W_i(x) = z^T(x)H_i z(x), z(x) = (x^T, f^T(x))^T$. In particular, if $H_1 > H_2 \geq 0$, then $KerW = \{0\}$ and the solution of system (1) will tend to zero asymptotically with probability 1.

Proof. Let $V(x) = x^T(t)Mx(t)$. Then one obtains

$$LV(x, y, t) = 2x^T(t)MF(x(t), y(t)) + trace\{G^T(x, y)MG(x, y)\} \quad (4)$$

$$\leq 2x^T(t)M[-Cx(t) + Af(x(t))] + x^T(t)MBM^{-1}B^T Mx(t)$$

$$+ f^T(y(t))Mf(y(t)) + 2[x^T(t)P^T MPx(t) + y^T(t)Q^T MQy(t)].$$

On the other hand, one obtains

$$0 \leq -2\sum_{i=1}^n u_{1i}[f_i(x_i(t)) - l_i x_i(t)]f_i(x_i(t)), \quad (5)$$

$$0 \leq -2\sum_{i=1}^n u_{2i}[f_i(y_i(t)) - l_i y_i(t)]f_i(y_i(t)). \quad (6)$$

Thus, one derives

$$LV(x, y, t) \leq -W_1(x(t)) + W_2(y(t)),$$

in which $W_i(x) = z^T(x)H_i z(x), z(x) = (x^T, f^T(x))^T$. From Lemma 1, one obtains (3).

4 One Example

For system (1), taking $U_2 = 0$, $L = diag(1,1,1)$, $C = diag(1.5,1.5,1.4)$, $Q = diag(0.1,0.1,0.1)$,

$$A = \begin{pmatrix} 0.2 & 0.1 & -0.2 \\ 0.3 & -0.1 & 0.1 \\ -0.1 & 0.1 & 0.3 \end{pmatrix}, \quad B = \begin{pmatrix} -0.3 & 0.2 & 0.2 \\ 0.1 & 0.3 & -0.3 \\ 0.2 & -0.1 & -0.2 \end{pmatrix},$$

$$P = \begin{pmatrix} 0 & 0.1 & 0.2 \\ 0.1 & 0 & 0.2 \\ 0.1 & 0.1 & 0 \end{pmatrix}.$$

One computes $U_1 = diag(13.4497,13.6833,13.3997)$,

$$M = \begin{pmatrix} 4.2058 & -0.3947 & 0.2864 \\ -0.3947 & 4.7899 & -0.1674 \\ 0.2864 & -0.1674 & 4.0809 \end{pmatrix}.$$

Therefore, $H_1 \geq H_2 \geq 0$, and the solution of such system will approach $KerW$ asymptotically with probability 1.

Acknowledgments. This work was supported   by the National Natural Science Foundation of China (No: 10801109, 10926128 and 11047114), Science and Technology Research Projects of Hubei Provincial Department of Education (Q20091705) and Young Talent Cultivation Projects of Guangdong (LYM09134).

References

1. Chen, W.H., Lu, X.M.: Mean Square Exponential Stability of Uncertain Stochastic Delayed Neural Networks. Physics Letters A 372, 1061–1069 (2008)
2. Huang, C., Cao, J.: Almost Sure Exponential Stability of Stochastic Cellular Neural Networks with Unbounded Distributed Delays. Neurocomputing 72, 3352–3356 (2009)
3. Huang, C., Cao, J.: On pth Moment Exponential Stability of Stochastic Cohen-Grossberg Neural Networks with Time-varying Delays. Neurocomputing 73, 986–990 (2010)
4. Huang, C., Chen, P., He, Y., Huang, L., Tan, W.: Almost Sure Exponential Stability of Delayed Hopfield Neural Networks. Applied Mathematics Letters 21, 701–705 (2008)
5. Huang, H., Feng, G.: Delay-dependent Stability for Uncertain Stochastic Neural Networks with Time-varying Delay. Physica A 381, 93–103 (2007)
6. Huang, C.X., He, Y.G., Huang, L.H., Zhu, W.J.: pth Moment Stability Analysis of Stochastic Recurrent Neural Networks with Time-varying Delays. Information Sciences 178, 2194–2203 (2008)

7. Huang, C., He, Y., Wang, H.: Mean Square Exponential Stability of Stochastic Recurrent Neural Networks with Time-varying Delays. Computers and Mathematics with Applications 56, 1773–1778 (2008)
8. Rakkiyappan, R., Balasubramaniam, P.: Delay-dependent Asymptotic Stability for Stochastic Delayed Recurrent Neural Networks with Time Varying Delays. Applied Mathematics and Computations 198, 526–533 (2008)
9. Sun, Y., Cao, J.: pth Moment Exponential Stability of Stochastic Recurrent Neural Networks with Time-varying Delays. Nonlinear Analysis: Real World Applications 8, 1171–1185 (2007)
10. Mao, X.R.: Stochastic Differential Equations and Applications. Horwood Publishing, England (1997)
11. Mao, X.R.: A Note on the LaSalle-type Theorems for Stochastic Differential Delay Equations. Journal of Mathematical Analysis and Applications 268, 125–142 (2002)

Designing on a Special Algorithm of Triple Tree Based on the Analysis of Data Structure

Min Wang and Yunfei Li

Computer Science Department, Weinan Teachers University, Weinan, Shanxi, China
wntcwm@126.com

Abstract. This paper introduces in detail the design and analysis of the algorithm of computing the number of descendant nodes of each node in the triple tree based on analyzing the special storage structures of triple tree. The recursive algorithm description in C is introduced subsequently after the design ideas, the implementation methods, and the concrete steps of the algorithm were given. Finally, the algorithm is evaluated from the two aspects of time complexity and space complexity.

Keywords: Triple tree; Descendant; The triple tree preorder traversal; Recursive algorithm; Time complexity; Space complexity.

1 Introduction

Data structure and Algorithms are important and basic subjects in computer science, and they are an indivisible whole. The procedure of computer solving problem follow such steps that inputting the initial data, processing by the computer, and then outputting the information. For a given problem, it is essential to decide how to organize the initial data, how to store them in the computer, and how to choose and design appropriate algorithms for it. To solve a particular problem, it needs to analyze the problem at first, and then combine organically the data structure and algorithms. To solve the problem effectively, algorithms must adopt suitable data structures [1].

This paper will design the algorithm of computing the number of descendant nodes of each node in the triple tree, analyze in detail the approaches and steps for problem solving by analyzing the basic data structure of the triple tree, give the recursive algorithm description in C, and analyze and evaluate the algorithm time complexity and space complexity.

2 Problem Description of the Triple Tree

The problem to be solved is described as follow:

Known that the triple tree T has a special triple list storage structure, and each node of it includes four fields, that are *lchild*, *mchild*, *rchild* and *DescNum*. Where, fields *lchild*, *mchild* and *rchild* are point respectively the left, the middle and the right child node of this parent node; while the field *DescNum* is a non-negative integer that

S. Lin and X. Huang (Eds.): CESM 2011, Part I, CCIS 175, pp. 423–427, 2011.

represents the number of descendants of this parent node. The initial value of field *DescNum* in each node is 0. It needs to compute the number of descendant nodes of each node in the triple tree, and store the numbers into the field *DescNum* in each node.

3   Data Structure Definition

According to the meaning of problems, the node structure of the triple linked list is shown as Fig.1.

DescNum	Lchild	Mchild	Rchild

Fig. 1. The node structure of the triple linked list

The node type can be defined in C as follows:

```
typedef struct TriNode{
    unsigned DescNum;
    struct TriNode *Lchild,*Mchild,*Rchild;
} TriNode, *TripleTree;
```

Since the triple tree adopted the specified storage structure mentioned above, the algorithm below will be designed based on it.

4   Algorithm Design and Implementation

To imagine the triple tree is an inverted tree, and the root node locates in the first layer, then the descendants of a certain node are all the nodes of the subtree of this node.

4.1   Algorithm Design Ideas

The algorithm of computing the number of descendant nodes of each node in the triple tree can be implemented through the procedure of triple tree preorder traversal. The triple tree preorder traversal can be described as follows:

    (1) If the triple tree is empty, the algorithm will terminate and return;
    (2) Otherwise, follow these steps to visit the tree nodes:
        ① Visit the root node of the triple tree;
        ② Preorder traverse the left subtree of the root node while the left child of the root node exists;
        ③ Preorder traverse the middle subtree of the root node while the middle child of the root node exists;
        ④ Finally, Preorder traverse the right subtree of the root node while the right child of the root node exists.

The design ideas of computing the number of descendant nodes of each node in the triple tree using the preorder traversal procedure aforementioned are as follows:

The procedure starts from the root node, and terminates when the tree is NULL. If it wasn't terminated, it then needs to determine whether the root node has a left child. The field *DescNum* of root node will be increased by one if the answer is yes, and then a new procedure which computes the number of descendant nodes will start from the left subtree of the root node. This procedure uses the same method to modify field *DescNum* of the root node of the left subtree. Next, the same way used to determine the middle subtree and the right subtree of the root node of the original triple tree, and modify the *DescNum* fields of the root nodes of the two subtrees. Finally, the number of descendant nodes of the root node eaquals to the sum of the modified *DescNum* field of the root node and the other three *DescNum* fields of the root nodes of the subtrees of the root node.

The concret steps of the algoritnm are as follows:

(1) If the triple tree is empty, the algorithm will terminate and return;
(2) Otherwise, follow these steps to continue:

   ① If the left child of the root node exists, the *DescNum* field of the root node will be increased by 1. Then, starting from the root node of the left subtree, the recursive preorder traversal procedure will be executed to compute the number of descendant of the left child of the root node;

   ② If the middle child of the root node exists, the *DescNum* field of the root node will be increased by 1. Then, starting from the root node of the middle subtree, the recursive preorder traversal procedure will be executed to compute the number of descendant of the middle child of the root node;

   ③ If the right child of the root node exists, the *DescNum* field of the root node will be increased by 1. Then, starting from the root node of the right subtree, the recursive preorder traversal procedure will be executed to compute the number of descendant of the right child of the root node;

   ④ Finally, the *DescNum* field of the root node adds the three *DescNum* fields of its children (left, middle, and right nodes).

4.2 Algorithm Description in C

Suppose that the triple tree adopts the triple linked list storage structure *TripleTree* mentioned before, and the root pointer points to it. The recursive design ideas of this algorithm can be described in C is as follows:

```
void NumberofChildren(TripleTree *root)
  { if(!*root)   return;        //Return when the tree is empty
    if((*root)->Lchild)
    {  NumberofChildren(&((*root)->Lchild));
       (*root)->DescNum++;   }//End_if
    if((*root)->Mchild)
    {  NumberofChildren(&((*root)->Mchild));
       (*root)->DescNum++;   }//End_if
    if((*root)->Rchild)
    {  NumberofChildren(&((*root)->Rchild));
```

```
    (*root)->DescNum++;    }//End_if
   (*root)->DescNum+=(*root)->Lchild->DescNum;
   (*root)->DescNum+=(*root)->Mchild->DescNum;
   (*root)->DescNum+=(*root)->Rchild->DescNum;
}//End
```

4.3 Algorithm Evaluation

The returned result of each recursive calling does not be saved, so it must be computed once more whenever needed, this leads to the time complexity of recursive functions actually depend on the times of recursive calling [4-6].

This paper adopted the recursive function *NumberofChildren()* to describe the algorithm, the first calling begin with the root of the triple tree. Since this function includes three recursive calling statements, the times of recursive calling is actually the sum of the number of nodes in the forest and the number of null pointers. An n nodes triple linked list has $3n$ pointers, where there are $n_0=2n+1$ null pointers, and then the total number of recursive calling is $3n +1$ times [6]. Regarding the number (n) of nodes in the forest as the scale of the problem, and with the gradually increase of problem scale, the algorithm time complexity is nearly $T(n)=O(3n+1)$.

In addition to the storage space used by the function itself and the tree nodes, function *NumberofChildren()* introduced no assistant space, so the algorithm space complexity is constant order, that is $S(n)=O(1)$.

5 Conclusion

The procedure of analyzing and designing the algorithm of computing the number of descendant nodes of each node in the triple tree based on the data structure was introduced in detail in this paper. After the recursive algorithm description in C had been given, the algorithm was evaluated from the two aspects of time complexity and space complexity. Therefore, this work plays a guiding role in teaching the relevant chapters in "Data Structure" curriculum.

Acknowledgments. This work is supported by Research Fund of Weinan Teachers University (No. 11YKS014) and Graduate Special Fund of Weinan Teachers University (No. 09YKZ012).

References

1. Wang, W.: Data Structure Learning guidance. Electronic Science and Technology University Press, Xi'an (2004)
2. Yan, W., Wu, W.: Data Structures(C language edition). Tsinghua University Press, Beijing (2002)
3. Geng, G.: Data Structure—C Language description. Electronic Science and Technology University Press, Xi'an (2005)

4. Wang, M., Li, J.: Analysis of Time Efficiency in Recursion Algorithm. Journal of Weinan Teachers University 18(5), 61–62 (2003)
5. Wang, M.: Non-Recursive Simulation of the Recursive Algorithm for Searching the Longest Path in Binary Tree. J. Science Technology and Engineering 10(6), 1535–1539 (2010)
6. Wang, M.: The Recursive Algorithm of Converting the Forest into the Corresponding Binary Tree. In: CSIE 2011 (in press, 2011)

Application of Wireless Communication in Temperature Measurement

Dejie Song, Boxue Tan, and Wenfeng Liu

School of Electrical and Electronic Engineering
Shandong University of Technology, SDUT
Zibo, Shandong, 255049, China
s_dj@sina.com

Abstract. Because a seed rod always rotates in the process of crystal growth, it is difficult to measure the crystal temperature in the crystal growth process. In order to solve this problem, applying wireless communication approach, we designed a meter using Micro Control Unit (MCU) AT89S52 and PT2262/2272, and realized the wireless measurement for the crystal growth process temperature. Measurement result can be recorded and stored in computer in time. It lays the good foundation for analyzing the crystal growth blemish and quality.

Keywords: PT2262/2272; Thermocouple; wireless measure; MCU; seed rod.

1 Introduction

In resent years, along with Cadmium Zinc Telluride (CdZnTe) crystal is widely used, growth of high-quality CdZnTe has become pursued unceasingly goal for tens of thousands of scientific researchers, but it is rather difficult to obtain high quality single crystals of CdZnTe. The first, its melting point is higher; and its chemical composition is not easy to control exactly [1]. The second, its thermal conductivity is so low that substantial concavity is usually present in the entire crystal growth process. The third, theoretical study shows that suitable temperature gradient in the crystal growth process and appropriate crucible rotation mode can improve the crystal growth quality. However, what are appropriate is that people have been looking for the target. In order to obtain single crystals of good quality, firstly, want to design and manufacture the crystal growth equipments. Secondly, want to repeat test repeatedly under the theory guide. Thirdly, to measure accurately temperature of solid-liquid interface is a key. At present, CdZnTe single crystal growth equipments are mostly composed of Accelerated Crucible Rotation Technique (ACRT) and Vertical Bridgman Method (VBM). Because crucible is rotating in crystal growth process, to measure accurately temperature of solid-liquid interface is difficult. In order to look for the measurement method of temperature of solid-liquid interface, applying wireless communication techniques test solid-liquid interface temperature obtain success in this paper.

In temperature measurement of various rotating systems, because of inconvenient wiring, the temperature measurement method usually has following 2 kinds now: one is through electric brush to fetch out temperature signal. Then use measuring device

S. Lin and X. Huang (Eds.): CESM 2011, Part I, CCIS 175, pp. 428–433, 2011.

to measure. Disadvantage of this method is the slide contact, the credibility is bad, the interference is big, need usually to replace and maintain it. This other is through non-contact temperature sensor to measure (such as infrared, then color etc.) But this method can not use to measure the temperature of closed system, and the accuracy is low, the anti-interference ability is bad, the cost is big, the application is restricted. In order to overcome above disadvantage, has designed a wireless temperature measuring device. Install it on rotating seed rod; through transceiver transmit the measure data to display. Solve measure device power-supply and anti-interference problem. This designs low cost, easy to use and reliable. It has obvious advantage and good promotion value in the particular situation of the inconvenient wiring.

2 The Hardware Design of Temperature Measuring Devices

2.1 The Design of Temperature Measuring Transmitting Circuit

Fig. 1 is the hardware structure chart of measuring device Installed on a rotating seed rod; it is composed of Micro Control Unit (MCU), the wireless transmitter, the thermocouple and peripheral circuit. In this design chooses 51 series MCU and PT2262 wireless transmitter.

As the seed crystal in the high-temperature furnace and rotating state, and the growth process longer (about 21 days). In order to solve the problem of the electric circuit power supply, make use of hand dynamo principle, has designed a set of generating electricity device, and installed it on the seed rod. Make use of the seed rod rotation to generate electricity, charge the storage battery. Ensure temperature measure device to use electricity power for a long time.

For economizing energy, MCU works at the sleep or work state. The time ratio of two states can be set through the DIP switch of measure meter. Before MCU enters a sleep state, it turns off all peripheral power to economize system power supply. When MCU is asleep it can be awaked by timer interrupt into work state. Complete temperature measurement and send out measurement data to receiver.

After transmitter is initialized, MCU turn on the peripheral device power switch. Thermocouple signal processing by amplification is send to ICL7135. The ICL7135 is four and a half bits AD converter. Its advantage is high-accuracy, low-price, anti-interference ability strong, converting rate moderate etc. The data processing as follows: first, MCU reads a converting value of ICL7135, and return to the voltage value (mV) of the thermocouple, and use K degree to process it linearly, gets at present temperature measured CT(n), gets CT value with CT=[CT(n)+CT(n-1)]/2 linear filter.

Suppose that the cold end's temperature is CL at present, then actual temperature is CN=CT+CL, and through PT2262 and 315MHz transmit a Cn value and completes a transmitting process. Last MCU turns off peripheral power. Return to sleep state. When sleep time arrive after, MCU turn on peripheral power switch, repeat above process.

2.2 The Design of Temperature Measuring Device Receiving Circuit

Receiving circuit hardware structure is shown Fig. 2.

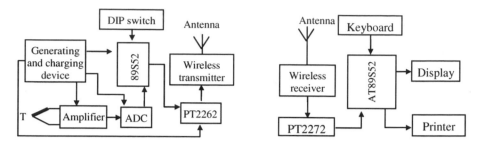

Fig. 1. Temperature measure block diagram   **Fig. 2.** Temperature display and print block

It is composed of the power circuit, MCU, wireless receiver, recorder, key and display etc. its main function is receiving signal from temperature measuring device, and save the temperature value in memorizer, and show and record the data. If received the data exceed setup range, measurement device can also give an upper and lower limit alarm. It includes four LED display, a micro-printer, four-setup keys, PT2272 and wireless receiving module. Passing the keys can set alarm temperature for upper and lower limit.

2.3 The Temperature Measurement Wireless Communication Principle

The design uses wireless transceiver encoding/decoding chip set PT2262/2272. It is Taiwan Princeton Technology Corp.'s low-power, wide voltage (2.6V-15V) universal codec chip. It makes up of a wireless transmit/receive circuit matching with 315MHz module. It is 18-pin package, mainly have address coding, receive/dispatch control and the data input/output pin etc. Since only measure temperature, therefore, can use a single wireless correspondence method. (Namely temperature measurement device sends out data, display device receives data.)

Encoding signal sent out by PT2262 is composed of address code, data code and synchronous code. Pin 14 (TE) is a code to start end of the data encoding for multi-launch, low is effective, controlled by the MCU P1.0.Pin 17 (DOUT) is code exportation, output serial data signal. That MCU sends 4-bit data to PT2262 send to the wireless transmitter module through pin 17.During pin 17 is high 315 MHz high-frequency transmitter starts oscillation and transmits high- frequency-amplitude signals. During pin 17 is low 315 MHz high-frequency oscillator to stop oscillation. So high-frequency oscillator is completely controlled by pin17 output's digital signals of PT2262, completes amplitude shift keying(ASK) modulation to make, is equivalent to 100% modulation of amplitude. When pin 14 is high, stop coding output, so that 3 I5MHz high-frequency oscillator do not work [2].

The data-received electric circuit is composed of PT2272 and 315MHz wireless received module, PT2272 of pin14 (DIN) is serial data input, receive data signal come from a wireless received module.pin17 (VT) is an output of the decoding effective [3]. Usually low, decoding effectively translated into high. When PT2272 received the signal, pin 17 become high after its address code checked twice is correct. At the same time the corresponding four data output pin is also valid data. When AT89S52 queries that pin17 is high, receive data, and then save, show and print this data.

3 Wireless Temperature Measure Software Design

In order to ensure the credibility of wireless communication, use mold 64 rectifying code, and request to launch the data twice. Only when mold 64 rectifying code is all right and two temperature values is homology, think correspondence success. PT2262/2272 coded communication is carried out by a half-byte mode. The data package is composed of the header E, 8 BCD code, temperature values and check code.

The correspondence data package format as follows:

E	BCD0	BCD1	BCD2	BCD3	BCD4	BCD5	BCD6	BCD7	CRC

Header checksum module 64 requests the sum of 12 half-byte. When the result of 5 low-bits is zero and BCDi=BCDi+4(i=0, 1, 2, 3), think correspondence success, and update temperature data.

3.1 The Design of Temperature Measurement Transmitting Program

Interrupt service flow chart is shown in Fig. 3. After system is initialized, MCU turns on external device power switch, go into temperature measure process, then repeat transmitting temperature measurement data twice and get into sleep state. In sleep mode MCU can be waked by timer interrupt. Interrupt once, the interrupt counter plus 1, and re-enter the sleep mode. When the timer has risen to the setting numbers, then jumps to the main program start position and turn on external equipments power switch and again go to measurement temperature and data transmitting progress, again and again.

3.2 The Design of Receiving Temperature Program

Receive program include main program and interruption service sub-program two parts. Interrupt service program frame diagram such as Fig. 4 show. Receive data with

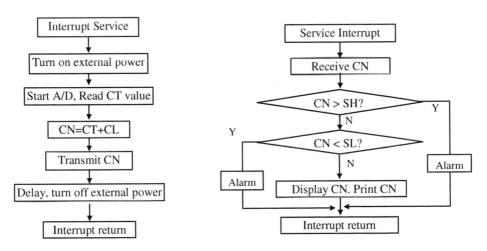

Fig. 3. Interrupt transmit flow chart   **Fig. 4.** Interrupt receive flow chart

interruption method. When PT2272 receives data, sends an interrupt request to MCU, MCU responds to interrupt and receives data. When the temperature measuring value is outside setting scope, send out respectively an alarm. When the temperature measuring value is inside setting scope, save, show and print the receiving data.

4 Experiment Analytical

Table I is temperature test list. Test equipment installed in the rotating seed rod, using standard potentiometer simulates K thermocouple. An ambient temperature of 25℃, temperature range of 0-1300℃.So reality temperature should be the sum of measurement temperature and cold end temperature. From table I it can be seen that this device accuracy is high and the absolute error ≤2℃, the opposite error ≤0.2%), satisfy accuracy requests in industry.

Table 1. The Wireless Temperature Test List

Test No.	Voltage (mV)	Theory Value ℃	Display Value ℃	Absolute Error ℃	Relative Error %
1	0.000	25	25.2	0.2	0.80
2	4.095	125	125.6	0.6	0.48
3	8.137	225	226.2	1.2	0.53
4	12.207	325	323.9	-1.1	-0.34
5	16.395	425	425.3	0.3	0.07
6	20.640	525	525.9	0.9	0.17
7	24.902	625	625.2	0.2	0.03
8	29.128	725	723.8	-1.2	-0.17
9	33.277	825	825.7	0.7	0.08
10	37.325	925	925.8	0.8	0.09
11	41.269	1025	1026.3	1.3	0.13

The tests have proved that the design satisfy the request of self-supplying power if each 20 seconds send out data once. Emission instrument communicate with receiving communication within 100 meters range is credibility. Slightly improvement can be applied to other occasions of inconvenient wiring. Or apply to the technique reformation of equipments. The practice has proved that the system is reliable, easy to use, and has low cost. As a result, it has more wide applied value.

5 Conclusions

Applying the design to the crystal growth furnace obtain success. The various indexes have achieved all design requests through the test. Use the design to grow out CdZnTe single crystal through 21 days as in Fig. 5 shown. By means of cutting, rubbing and polishing the CdZnTe single crystal produced, test its spectrum and volt-ampere characteristic, them are consistent with emulation result. Behind changes control parameters produced a few crystal again, and obtain result basic consistent with theories. Certainly also there is different in some index [4]. These places need yet further discussion hereafter from two aspects of the theories and practice. It laid the groundwork for further exploring the law of single crystal growth and mastering the optimal control parameters. The test proved that the control system runs well on the crystal growth furnace, the function is stable, the work is dependable, and the operation and usage are convenient.

Fig. 5. CdZnTe single crystal

Acknowledgments. This work's funds were provided by Natural Science Foundation of China (NSFC), Grant No. 50372036.

References

1. Li, Q.-f., Zhu, S.-f., Zhao, B.-j., et al.: Growth and properties of high resistivity Cd0.8Zn0.2Te single crystals. Chinese Journal of Semiconductors 23(2), 157–160 (2002) (in Chinese)
2. Princeton Technology Corp. Remote Control Encoder PT2262 (V3.8), Taiwan (September 2008)
3. Princeton Technology Corp. Remote Control Decoder PT2272 (V3.7), Taiwan (June 2008)
4. Liu, J., Song, D., Zhang, H., Zhai, S.: Optimization of control parameters of cadmium zinc telluride Bridgman single crystal growth. J. Crystal Research and Technology 42(8), 741–750 (2007)
5. Song, D.-j., Liu, J.-c.: Control system of ball screw on growing crystal stove. Microcomputer Information 24(22), 58–59 (2008) (in Chinese)

Study of the Supply Chain Finance Operational Risk[*]

Di Wang[1] and Baosen Wang[2]

[1] Student ID 0994042240
School of Business Beijing Wuzi University
Beijing, China
wangbaosen2006@sina.com
[2] School of Economics Beijing Wuzi University
Beijing, China
wangbaosen2006@sina.com

Abstract. The purpose of this study is to establish a reasonable and systematic evaluation system for supply chain finance Operational risk. It is to determine the supply chain finance operational risk assessment index which features for supply chain operations and structure, and to establish a supply chain finance Operational risk model based on fuzzy comprehensive evaluation. This paper aims to provide some theoretical support for supply chain finance Operational risk management and provide reference and guidance for study of the finance Operational risk which faces many supply chain member companies.

Keywords: Supply Chain Finance Operational risk, AHP, The Fuzzy Comprehensive Evaluation Introduction.

Today supply chain becomes more and more complex, It's more like a network rather than a chain in many cases. The vulnerability of supply chain in the study of the Cranfield University is defined as: "an exposure of the severe disturbance caused by both internal and external risk of the chain" (Martin Christopher, 2002) Because of the uncertainty factors, the finance Operational risk is always accompanied with all member companies of supply chain and leads to vulnerability in the entire supply chain operation. When operating in an interdependent environment, The supply chain must bear the influence of the expanding of strategy and strategic role, which faces all enterprises now. That issues and risks in operational and strategic level make supply chain become weaker and weaker, so it has become the major obstacle in supply chain management. However, based on the condition of our own country, the related knowledge and research remains rare, thus concerning about finance Operational risk has became an unavoidable topic in supply chain management.

1 The Meaning of Supply Chain Finance Operational Risk

As the junction of the finance Operational risk theory and supply chain risk, the research of the risk of the chain just began and has not developed into a integrated

---

[*] Project of Beijing Wuzi University research base, No. WYJD200903.

S. Lin and X. Huang (Eds.): CESM 2011, Part I, CCIS 175, pp. 434–440, 2011.
© Springer-Verlag Berlin Heidelberg 2011

theoretical system at the present time. We can define supply chain finance Operational risk as followed: The risk which may cause potential loss because of errors or omissions in Control, system and operational processes in all links of Supply chain operational processes and the external environment which member companies are situated. Internal management of supply chain goes wrong, for example, compensation or damages must be made as failure to supply the contract on time; some people exploit the flaw of legal instruments; insiders steal and outsider deceive; communications, power failure because of electronic systems hardware and software breaking down; earthquakes, floods, fires, terrorist attacks and so on. All of these do harm to the supply chain operations and are collectively referred as finance Operational risk.

We must correctly understand two points of the supply chain finance Operational risk meaning. Firstly, Supply chain finance Operational risk does not exist in processes. According to the Definition, Finance Operational risk does not only include operational errors, offense and ultra vires which are caused by personal factors, but also the un-strict execution of the process. Secondly, all supply chain finance Operational risk events aren't independent but interrelated. Many people regard finance Operational risk as unexpected events. They think it can't meet Statistical distribution and can't be measured by risk measurement methods.

2 Basic Principles and Steps of Fuzzy Comprehensive Evaluation

Fuzzy evaluation method was appeared in 1965, and made by the automatic control L.A.Z experts Chad is proposed for the first time. It's a method from fuzzy mathematics and used in the quantification of some poorly circumscribed and not easily quantifiable factors, then carry on composite evaluation. Therefore, it's one of the most normal methods in fuzzy decision theory to solve the evaluation or evaluation problems which involve multivariate or multiple indicators. Moreover it's most major characteristic may be that we could deal with the problems of complicated and fuzzy in a much more relaxed way.

Assuming $U = \{U_1, U_2, \cdots U_n\}$ is n kinds of indicators of the objects, and supposing $V = \{V_1, V_2, \cdots V_m\}$ is the evaluation set which is made up of m kinds of indicators. These are two classes of fuzzy sets, one is that $K = (K_1, K_2, \cdots K_n)$ reflects weight of the Kth judges in factor set U; the other is fuzzy relations of $U \times V$ that manifest as the fuzzy matrix R. we can carry fuzzy operation on the two classes of fuzzy sets and obtain fuzzy set $B = (b_1, b_2, \cdots b_m)$ in V. The fuzzy comprehensive evaluation can be expressed as the following steps:

1) Constructing the factor set and evaluation set
Determining the factors set of $U = (U_1, U_2, \cdots, U_n)$ $i = (1, 2, \cdots, n)$,

$$U_i = \{U_{i1}, U_{i2}, \cdots, U_{iq}\}, j = 1, 2, \cdots, q \cdot$$

Determining the evaluation set of $V = \{V_1, V_2, \cdots V_m\}$, V_k is assessment, $k = 1, 2, \cdots, m$.

2) Constructing the fuzzy evaluation matrix R_i

Determining membership degree that Factors correspond with every assessment level, which calculate evaluation matrix R_i of U_i by fuzzy mapping $f : U \to V$.

Evaluation matrix R can be show as the following: $R_i = (r_{ijk})_{q \times m}$. In the formula, r_{ijk} show membership degree of index u_{ij} which correspond with k level reviews V_k.

The value of r_{ijk} can be determined by $r_{ijk} = t_k \Big/ \sum\limits_{t=1}^{m} t_k$ (t_m show the V_m level reviews).

3) Constructing the index weight at all levels

$K = (K_1, K_2, \cdots K_n)$ Show weight vector of the index. There are a great number of methods to confirm the index weight, such as rough set, entropy weight method, AHP method e.g. The weight of evaluation set plays an important role in the comprehensive evaluation. In this article, using the AHP method construct the index weight.

4) Setting up the comprehensive evaluation

Firstly, based on AHP method described in the above content, we can figure out the second-lever index weight coefficient vector K_i. The composition B_i can use the matrix's multiplication, that is $B_i = K_i \times R_i = (b_{i1}, b_{i2}, \cdots, b_{im})$.

Secondly, the result of the evaluation is B_i and it is the U_i's evaluation. Now, we can obtain matrix of degree of membership by following:

$$R = \begin{pmatrix} B_1 \\ B_2 \\ \vdots \\ B_n \end{pmatrix} = \begin{pmatrix} b_{11} & b_{12} & \cdots & b_{1m} \\ b_{21} & b_{22} & \cdots & b_{3m} \\ \vdots & \vdots & \ddots & \vdots \\ b_{n1} & b_{n2} & \cdots & b_{nm} \end{pmatrix}$$

For R, we use following get the comprehensive evaluation result B:

$$B = C \times R = (c_1, c_2, \cdots c_n) \times [B_1, B_2, \cdots B_n]^T = (b_1, b_2, \cdots b_m)$$

5) Determining the assessment results

According to the maximum degree of membership principle, The maximal element b_m belongs to an especial evaluation grade in the ultimate result vector $B = (b_1, b_2, \cdots b_m)$. Namely, it is the final evaluating consequence. With the formula expressed as: $b^* = \max\{b_1, b_2, \cdots b_m\}$.

3 Supply Chain Operations Risk Assessment Based on Fuzzy

Supply chain is a dynamic network alliance which is built around the enterprise, so the risk management lacks original data and can't show the objective probability distribution. Fuzzy comprehensive evaluation is a relatively mature theory, besides the fuzziness of supply chain data determines the applicability of this method, but the determination of the weight is more subjective. In order To solve this problem, this article will combine AHP theory and fuzzy theory and build supply chain finance Operational risk assessment model based on fuzzy comprehensive evaluation which determines weight use AHP.

In this article, we will Take a simple retailers Industry supply chain as example. We will employ all the knowledge above for case study and test the feasibility of theory or method.

3.1 The Establishment of Index System

The assessment of retail supply chain finance Operational risk is a multi-level and multi-factor assessment, so we must build an evaluation index system to make a large number of interrelated and mutually restraining factors get layered and well organized. As supply chain finance Operational risk is interdependent and mutual influenced, the establishment of index system should be related to other supply chain risk in order to be more accurate. Therefore, the evaluation index of supply chain finance Operational risk includes 6 terms of main indicators and 21 secondary indicators.

The first-lever factor set can set $U = (U_1, U_2, U_3, U_4, U_5, U_6)$ and it can be divided into four subsets which are classified by different secondly-attributions. $U_1 = \{u_{12}, u_{12}, u_{13}\}$, $U_2 = \{u_{21}, u_{22}, u_{23}\}$, $U_3 - \{u_{31}, u_{32}, u_{33}, u_{34}, u_{35}\}$, $U_4 - \{u_{41}, u_{42}, u_{43}\}$, $U_5 = \{u_{51}, u_{52}, u_{53}\}$, $U_6 = \{u_{61}, u_{62}, u_{63}, u_{64}\}$.

The evaluation set can set $V = \{V_1, V_2, V_3, V_4\} - \{A, B, C, D\}$.

3.2 Setting Up Weight Matrix by AHP

1) Set up judgment matrix of paired-comparisons
In order to carry out paired-comparisons on different indexes by using the 1-9 scale method that is proposed by professor T.L. Satty, Then construct judgment matrix $A = (a_{ij})_{n \times n}$, in which is the total number of the evaluation indexes. We obtain the matrix of paired-comparisons above by the questionnaire survey of the supply chain finance Operational risk of retail industry.

$$K = \begin{bmatrix} 1 & 1/4 & 1/4 & 2 & 1 & 1/2 \\ 4 & 1 & 1/2 & 5 & 3 & 3 \\ 4 & 2 & 1 & 5 & 3 & 3 \\ 1/2 & 1/5 & 1/5 & 1 & 1/2 & 1/2 \\ 1 & 1/3 & 1/3 & 2 & 1 & 1/2 \\ 2 & 1/3 & 1/3 & 2 & 2 & 1 \end{bmatrix} \quad K_1 = \begin{bmatrix} 1 & 2 & 1 \\ 1/2 & 1 & 1/2 \\ 1 & 2 & 1 \end{bmatrix} \quad K_2 = \begin{bmatrix} 1 & 1/3 & 2 \\ 3 & 1 & 4 \\ 1/2 & 1/4 & 1 \end{bmatrix}$$

$$K_3 = \begin{bmatrix} 1 & 2 & 3 & 5 & 6 \\ 1/2 & 1 & 1 & 4 & 5 \\ 1/3 & 1 & 1 & 4 & 5 \\ 1/5 & 1/4 & 1/4 & 1 & 2 \\ 1/6 & 1/5 & 1/5 & 1/2 & 1 \end{bmatrix} \quad K_4 = \begin{bmatrix} 1 & 1/2 & 1/3 \\ 2 & 1 & 1/2 \\ 3 & 2 & 1 \end{bmatrix}$$

$$K_5 = \begin{bmatrix} 1 & 1/2 & 1 \\ 2 & 1 & 2 \\ 1 & 1/2 & 1 \end{bmatrix} \quad K_6 = \begin{bmatrix} 1 & 1 & 3 & 1/2 \\ 1 & 1 & 3 & 1/2 \\ 1/3 & 1/3 & 1 & 1/4 \\ 2 & 2 & 4 & 1 \end{bmatrix}$$

2) Calculate the largest characteristic root and eigenvector
On the basis of judgment matrix A, we can identify the largest characteristic root $\lambda_{max} = 6.007$ and its corresponding eigenvector $W = (0.085, 0.281, 0.354, 0.055, 0.093, 0.132)^T$ Therefore, we get the weight sorting of the relative importance on the indexes of the same level relative to the indexes of level above.

3) Carry out consistency test to judgment matrix

In order to testing the consistency of judgment matrix A, it is required to calculate the consistency index $C.R. = C.I/R.I$, and it is considered that the judgment matrix must be satisfied consistency when the random consistency ratio $C.R. < 0.10$ .Otherwise need to adjust the judgment matrix in order to get satisfied consistency.

Carry out $C.R = 0.0011 < 0.10$ of judgment matrix A, so there is good consistency. At the same time, we examine all judgment matrix with the same way and obtain good result.

4) determine index weight

Carry out weight set of each factors classes and each factor by the above method:

$$K = (K_1, K_2, K_3, K_4, K_5, K_6) = (0.085, 0.281, 0.354, 0.055, 0.093, 0.132)$$

$$K_1 = (K_{11}, K_{12}, K_{13}) = (0.4, 0.2, 0.4)$$

$$K_2 = (K_{21}, K_{22}, K_{23}) = (0.240, 0.623, 0.137) \quad K_3 = (K_{31}, K_{32}, K_{33}, K_{34}, K_{35}) = (0.396, 0.240, 0.240, 0.074, 0.05)$$

$$K_4 = (K_{41}, K_{42}, K_{43}) = (0.164, 0.297, 0.539) \quad K_5 = (K_{51}, K_{52}, K_{53}) = (0.25, 0.5, 0.25)$$

$$K_6 = (K_{61}, K_{62}, K_{63}, K_{64}) = (0.239, 0.239, 0.089, 0.433)$$

3.3 Setting the Comprehensive Evaluation

Evaluation results indicated that with the fuzzy evaluation matrix $R_i(i = 1, 2, \cdots 6)$, the evaluation results of $U_i(i = 1, 2, \cdots, 6)$ can be show with $B_i(i = 1, 2, \cdots, 6)$ .Then evaluating first-Level indicators, In which the fuzzy evaluation matrix is $R = (B_1, B_2, B_3, B_4, B_5, B_6)^T$.

Finally, it obtained comprehensive assessment results $B = C \cdot R = (b_1, b_2, \cdots b_m)$. The evaluation matrix of first-level indicators as follows:

$$R_1 = \begin{bmatrix} 0.6 & 0.4 & 0 & 0 \\ 0.8 & 0.2 & 0 & 0 \\ 0.4 & 0.5 & 0.1 & 0 \end{bmatrix} \quad R_2 = \begin{bmatrix} 0.3 & 0.6 & 0.1 & 0 \\ 0.2 & 0.7 & 0.1 & 0 \\ 0.2 & 0.8 & 0 & 0 \end{bmatrix}$$

$$R_3 = \begin{bmatrix} 0.3 & 0.7 & 0 & 0 \\ 0.1 & 0.6 & 0.3 & 0 \\ 0.7 & 0.3 & 0 & 0 \\ 0.5 & 0.5 & 0 & 0 \\ 0.6 & 0.4 & 0 & 0 \end{bmatrix} \quad R_4 = \begin{bmatrix} 0.7 & 0.3 & 0 & 0 \\ 0.3 & 0.5 & 0.2 & 0 \\ 0.1 & 0.6 & 0.3 & 0 \end{bmatrix}$$

$$R_5 = \begin{bmatrix} 0 & 0.5 & 0.4 & 0.1 \\ 0.2 & 0.7 & 0.1 & 0 \\ 0.1 & 0.5 & 0.4 & 0 \end{bmatrix} \quad R_6 = \begin{bmatrix} 0.5 & 0.5 & 0 & 0 \\ 0.1 & 0.6 & 0.3 & 0 \\ 0 & 0.7 & .0.2 & 0.1 \\ 0 & 0.1 & 0.3 & 0.6 \end{bmatrix}$$

$K_1 = (0.400, 0.200, 0.400)$ $K_2 = (0.240, 0.623, 0.137)$

$K_3 = (0.396, 0.240, 0.240, 0.074, 0.050)$ $K_4 = (0.164, 0.297, 0.539)$ $K_5 = (0.250, 0.500, 0.250)$

$K_6 = (0.239, 0.239, 0.089, 0.433)$

According to $B_i = K_i \cdot R_i$, the calculation method for the primary evaluation is as follows:

$B_1 = K_1 \cdot R_1 = (0.560, 0.400, 0.040, 0)$

$B_2 = K_2 \cdot R_2 = (0.224, 0.6897, 0.0863, 0)$ $B_3 = K_3 \cdot R_3 = (0.3778, 0.5502, 0.072, 0)$

$B_4 = K_4 \cdot R_4 = (0.2578, 0.5211, 0.2211, 0)$ $B_5 = K_5 \cdot R_5 = (0.125, 0.6, 0.25, 0.025)$

$B_6 = K_6 \cdot R_6 = (0.1434, 0.3685, 0.2194, 0.2687)$

Carried on fuzzy comprehensive evaluation, we draw the calculation as follows:

$$R = (B_1, B_2, B_3, B_4, B_5, B_6)^T = \begin{bmatrix} 0.560 & 0.400 & 0.040 & 0 \\ 0.224 & 0.6897 & 0.0863 & 0 \\ 0.3778 & 0.5502 & 0.072 & 0 \\ 0.2578 & 0.5211 & 0.2211 & 0 \\ 0.125 & 0.6 & 0.25 & 0.025 \\ 0.1434 & 0.3685 & 0.2194 & 0.2687 \end{bmatrix}$$

$$C = (0.085, 0.28, 0.354, 0.055, 0.093, 0.132)$$

The results of comprehensive evaluation:

$$B - C \cdot R = (0.289018, 0.555679, 0.117510, 0.037793)$$

Final evaluation results shows: the second-scale membership degree value (55.6%) is the largest value of this vector. Therefore the evaluation result that we can consider is B-level. Judging from the evaluation process, the supply chain finance Operational risk is comparatively largely influenced by laws, regulations, industry policies and the extent of government intervention; the self-serving behavior affects performance reliability and fair competition partly intervenes the distribution of profits; economic growth, the market's seasonal demand is important to the operation of the supply chain; fluctuation of demand will lead to increasing risk; the rationality of supply chain structure, corporate strategic planning, safety of target software system can effectively improve the operation of the supply chain; logistics chain, which is complicated and involves a wide range of things, is the key element of the whole finance Operational risk management.

4 Conclusion

Supply chain is composed by a number of member companies, which are all independent economic entities and have operation and management of independent power; the contradictions exists between the overall effectiveness optimization of the supply chain and own efficiency optimization of single enterprise in supply chain and the rights dominated between core business and non-core businesses and so on; all of these increase the risk of supply chain operations within limits. The study of supply chain finance Operational risk can lower the variation of supply chain value distribution and increase supply chain value.

Building a supply chain finance Operational risk assessment model can make it more comprehensive and systematic, when investigating the issues of supply chain risk management; it can effectively improve the efficiency of the supply chain and establish a rational system of supply chain finance Operational risk management; it can also provide a program for enterprises to effectively identify, assess and manage supply chain risk.

References

1. Zsidisin, G.A.: Managerial Perceptions of Supply Risk. The Journal of Supply Chain Management 6, 14–25 (2003)
2. Jordan, J., Rosegren, E.: Using Loss to Quantify Operational Risk(DB/OL), vol. 4 (2003), http://www.chicagofed.org
3. Svensson, G.A.: Conceptual Framework for the Analysis of Vulnerability in Supply-chain. International Journal of Physical Distribution & Logistics Management 30(9), 731–749 (2000)
4. BCBS. The (2002), loss data collection exercise for operational Risk: Summary of the DataCollected(EB/OL), Switzerland, http://www.bis.org/bcbs/,2003-06-30
5. Jiang, X., Chen, F.: Risk analysis and assessment in supply chain network. Journal of Southeast University (Natural Science Edition) 2 (2007)
6. Hang, X.-y., Yang, M.-c.: The Risk Pooling and Profit Sharing Mechanism in Supply Chain Management. Journal of Huazhong University of Science and Technology Edition of Social Sciences 5, 94–97 (2004)
7. Liu, D., Wang, C.: Evaluation of Multi-Risk Combination of Supply Chains and Its Risk Management. Journal of Wuhan University of Technology (Information & Management Engineering) 8, 110–111 (2006)
8. Ding, W.: Study on Risk of Supply Chain. China Safety Science Journal 13(4), 64–66 (2008)
9. Han, L., Wang, P.:The Aplications of Fuzzy Math, vol.1. Beijing Capital University of Economics & Business Press (1998)

Stability Faults Detecting and Quality Attributes Assessing of Network Information

Sheng Qi Li

College of Economics & Management, Zhe jiang Agriculture and Forest University
Lingan City, 311300, China
sqli65@163.com

Abstract. This paper proposes an approach that can be used to test the stability and other related attribute of Network information, and that can be easily enhanced to assess other quality attributes. The framework is based on rules for test case generation that are designed by, firstly, analyzing WSDL document to know what faults could affect the stability quality attribute of Network information, and secondly, using the fault-based testing techniques to detect such faults. A proof of concept tool that depends on these rules has been implemented in order to assess the usefulness of the rules in detecting stability faults in different Network information platforms.

Keywords: SOAP, Testing Approach, Quality Attributes, Assessing, generation rules.

1 Introduction

Network information [6] are considered a new paradigm in building software applications based on the Internet and open standards. This paradigm has changed the way we look at the Internet from being a repository of data into a repository of Services. By using Network information, companies can ensure that their applications will communicate with those of their business partners and customers even if they are using different programming language or platforms.

A problem that limits the growth of Network information is the lack or trustworthiness by the Service Requesters because they can only see the WSDL document but not the implementation or source code.

Testing can be used to solve this problem; by assessing the quality attributes of a Web Service under test, the confidence or the trustworthiness of the requesters increase or decrease according to the test results. This will also help requesters to choose between Network information that are doing the same task.

However, Network information testing still face many problems like the unavailability of the source code to the Service Requesters and that the traditional testing technique do not cope with the new characteristics introduced by Network information standards. This paper introduces an approach that can participate in solving these problems. This approach is based on analyzing WSDL documents in order to generate

S. Lin and X. Huang (Eds.): CESM 2011, Part I, CCIS 175, pp. 441–446, 2011.
© Springer-Verlag Berlin Heidelberg 2011

test cases to test the stability quality attribute of Network information depending on fault-based testing techniques.

The trustworthiness requirements include security, reliability, safety, survivability, interoperability, availability, and fault tolerance, in order to increase Service Requesters trustworthiness of Network information, all these requirements must be addressed by researchers and practitioners. Stability is a sub attributes of reliability [1], so assessing and increasing the stability of Network information will contribute to the increasing the reliability and hence the trust worthiness of Network information.

The stability quality attribute of Web Services affects other quality attribute such as the fault tolerance to wrong input and security, the test cases design using this paper approach will explain what exactly the quality attribute that is targeted by each test cases.

Also the Web Service platform or the middleware affects the stability of Web Services because the Web Service platform in the provider side may intercept the SOAP request before reaching the Web Service implementation if that request contains some invalid data, the rule-based test cased proposed by this paper makes a distinction between targeting the stability of the middleware and the Web Service implementation.

2 Background

This section will introduce brief definitions of Web Services and fault-based testing techniques.

2.1 Web Service

There is no universally accepted definition of Web Services, as it has been under debate for quite some time. An extensive literature survey on Web Services showed us that none of current definitions (given by different people and organizations) contained all the relevant characteristics of Web Services. In the context of our work, the definition of Web Service includes those relevant characteristics for our work, as it is defined as follows:

Web Services are network (Internet) based modular applications designed to implement SOA, and support interoperable, loosely coupled, integration of heterogeneous application. Web Services are discovered using UDDI and It has an interface that is describe in WSDL, Other systems interact with the Web Services in a manner prescribed by its description using SOAP, these SOAP messages (as well as all other technologies of Web Services) are based on XML and typically conveyed using HTTP.

2.2 Fault-Based Testing Techniques

Fault-based or negative testing is defined as "Testing aimed at showing software does not work" [4].

Testing that a system meets its requirement specifications (validation testing) without applying fault-based testing leave the software system open to vulnerabilities that might not surface until much later in the development cycle or after deployment [5]. In fault-based testing, test cases are written for invalid and unexpected input conditions in order to check how if the system under test will can handle such input gracefully.

Handling the invalid (or manipulated or faulty) input gracefully may include raising an exception with proper error message that describes to the user what happened, while if the system have vulnerabilities to such invalid inputs, then it might reveal so important information that can be used by malicious used to harm the system.

Systems that have an interface which is accessible by public must specially be robust and consequently must have prolific input-validation checks.

The fault-based testing techniques that are important to the research in this thesis are: Interface Propagation Analysis (IPA) which is one of the fault injection techniques, Boundary-value based stability testing , equivalence partitioning with invalid partition class, and syntax testing [4]. All these techniques belong to black-box testing because it is assumed in this paper that the testing is done by the Web Service Requesters who does not have the source code of the Web Service under test. we will describe how test data is derived using these fault based testing techniques

3 Related Work

Most the researches in Web Services testing focus on specification or validation testing in order to make sure that a Web Service meets a Service Requester's requirements [6]; however, there are few researches addressed fault-based testing of Web Services.

Since the stability and other related quality attributes, such as security and fault tolerance, are important to this paper, we will give a summary of the researches that assess stability and other related quality attributes using fault-based testing techniques. After surveying the field of Web Services testing, whether fault or validation testing, the following notices have been concluded:

- Some researches do not specify what quality attribute of Web Services they are assessing.
- Different researchers may be assessing the same quality attribute but they describe or call this quality attribute differently.
- Some researches mention that they want increase trustworthiness of Web Services but without specify which specific requirement of trustworthiness they are targeting.
- Some researches specify that they do negative testing but they do not specify how the negative or faulty test data was generated, in other words which testing techniques have been applied.

Test data generation method in different fault-based testing techniques.

4 Web Services Stability Testing Approach

This section will describe an approach for assessing the stability, input manipulation vulnerability, and fault tolerance to wrong input quality attributes of Web Services. we describes the overall architecture of the Web Services stability testing approach proposed in this paper.

The components of the architecture are described as follows:

- Web Service platform is the platform or middleware that the Web Service Provider is using for his Web Service implementation. Examples of Web Service platforms are Axis [3] and GLUE [4].
- Test case generation rules are the rules that is proposed by this paper for test case generation, these rules depends on the faults that affects the stability quality attribute of Web Services and the fault-based testing techniques. Test case generation rules will be discussed in section 5.
- Web Services test case generator is the component that is responsible for generating test cases based on the WSDL document of the Web Service under test and the test case generation rules.
- Test results component is an XML document that describes the test data together with the actual response of the Web Service under test for each of the test data in each test case.
- Web Service implementation is the source code of the Web Service that is written by the Web Service Provider.
- Automatic Client Generator is the component that is responsible of building a client to the Web service under test and invoking the Web service under test using the test data provided by the Web Service test case generator component.

After defining the different components of the overall architecture, the interaction between those components will be described:

(1). Test case generation rules are designed based on the faults that may affect the stability of Web Services depending on the specification inside WSDL.
(2). Web Service Provider deploys his/her Web Service implementation in a Web Service platform.
(3). The Web Service test case generator component uses the test cases generation rules in step 1 and the WSDL document of the Web Service in step 2 to generate the Web Service test case[4],[3],[7]..
(4). The automatic client generator will generate a client to invoke the Web Service deployed in step 2 using the test case developed in step 3 and then generate the test results document accordingly.
(5). Test Case Generation Rules

Test case generation depends on the input parameters data type XML Schema based specification inside WSDL and the stability related faults that may be resulted based on violating this specification.

A brief description of the attributes or components of the schema in is as follows:

(1) The ID attribute is a unique identifier for different rules
(2) WSDL component test data is based on, since the test cases depending on the information inside WSDL, this attribute specifies the WSDL component that the current test case is based on.
(3) The fault attribute is the fault that is based on a certain element inside WSDL and that the current test case assumes to detect.
(4) Traditional testing technique describes the fault-based testing technique (See section 2.2) that is used to generate test data to assess the fault in step(2).

(5) Traditional test data generation rules describes how the test data is generated depending on the testing technique in step(3).

(6) Valid/Invalid attribute used to specify if the test data are valid or invalid test data.

(7) Web Service data type, this attribute describes the XML Schema-based data type of the input parameter of the Web Service operation under test. XML Schema data types are discussed in [3]. According to [3] XML Schema data types can be categorized to: primitive or derived from primitive simple data types, user-derived data types, and complex data types.

(8) Web Service test data type, this attribute defines the data type of the test data used in this test case. The data type of the test data in not always the same as the Web Service data type because some test cases use for example integer input for an operation that accepts a string as input in order to test if the operation with produce a proper or graceful exception or not.

(9) Web Service test data, this is the actual data that is used to in the current test case.

(10) Expected output, this attribute specifies the robust expected SOAP response or SOAP fault of the Web Service under test based on the current test case.

(11) Quality attribute assessed, this attribute specifies the quality attribute targeted by the current test case. This research mainly concerned with the stability quality attribute, however, other quality attribute, such as security, may also be tested by the same test case.

5 Conclusions and Future Work

Web Services still not widely used because Service Requesters do not trust Web Services that were built by others. To solve this problem all the trustworthiness requirements such as reliability, safety, security, interoperability, etc. must be addressed by researchers and practitioners.

This research proposes an approach to assess the stability quality attribute of Web Services. Stability is a sub-attribute or requirement for the reliability attribute, so improving the stability will improve the reliability and hence the trustworthiness of Web Services.

Test cases are destined in this paper approach based on the XML Schema based input parameter specification inside WSDL and the stability faults that may affect a Web Service based on violating these specifications.

Assessing the stability quality attribute contributes to the assessment of other quality attributes such as security and fault tolerance to wrong input A tool has been implemented that can help the Service Requester to assess the stability of a Web service based only on its WSDL.

The stability of a Web Service may be affected by the Web Service platform or the middleware that this Web Service is deployed in. The test cases designed in this paper distinguish between testing the stability of the platform and testing the stability of the Web Service implementation.

Future work will assess other Web Service trustworthiness requirements especially more research on the security of Web Services.

References

1. Kakas, A., Denecker, M.: Abduction in logic programming. In: Kakas, A., Sadri, F. (eds.) Computational Logic: Logic Programming and Beyond. LNCS (LNAI), vol. 2407, pp. 402–436. Springer, Heidelberg (2002)
2. Möller, R., Haarslev, V., Neumann, B.: Concepts based information finding. In: Proc. IT&KNOWS 1998: International Conference on Information Technology and Knowledge Systems, Vienna, Budapest, August 4-September 31, p. 496 (1998)
3. Möller, R., Neumann, B.: Ontology-based reasoning techniques for multimedia transformation and finding. In: Semantic Multimedia and Ontologies: Theory and Applications (2007) (to appear)
4. Neumann, B., Möller, R.: On Scene Transformation with Description Logics. In: Christensen, H.I., Nagel, H.-H. (eds.) Cognitive Vision Systems. LNCS, vol. 3948, pp. 247–275. Springer, Heidelberg (2006)
5. Peraldi, S.E., Kaya, A., Melzer, S., Möoller, R., Wessel, M.: Multimedia Transformation as Abduction. In: Proc. DL 2007: International Workshop on Description Logics (2007)
6. Shanahan, M.: Perception as Abduction: Turning Sensor Data Into Meaningful Representation. Cognitive Science 29(1), 103–134 (2005)
7. Thagard, R.P.: The best explanation: Criteria for theory choice. The Journal of Philosophy (1978)

Using Concepts in Grid Data Organization

Yan Mao and Li Kai Han

Department of Computer Science, Xi'an University of Arts and Science
710065, Xi-an City
amao0010@sina.com

Abstract. Grid is emerging as a practical standard for information exchange over the Web, while businesses and enterprises generate and exchange large amounts of grid data daily. One of the major challenges is how to searching this data efficiently. Searching can be represented as linked patterns. Some researchers have developed algorithms that reduce the needless results that are generated during searching processing, while others have introduced recording methods that locate the position of elements, enabling the ?earching process to be answered by taking the records without searching the original grid files. In this paper we represent a method that are based on concepts of the data being searched, and introduce content and keyword searches in grid databases.

Keywords: Grid, Searching, Optimization, Algorithms, WSDL.

1 Introduction

In this paper we outline an innovative way to process grid queries that takes into account the concepts of the data, and introduce an efficient algorithm for keyword searches in grid databases. The essence of the approach is that concepts of the data can be used in searching optimization if the concepts of the data are known, otherwise a more traditional approach to searching processing will be adopted. Some of the concepts can be represented in mode languages such as WSDL8 (Web Service Description Language)and grid mode9 but there is other information that can be used in searching processing that cannot be represented in these mode definition languages.

Typically, grid data is simply modeled as a tree structure without the important concepts object class, attribute of object class, relationship type defined among object classes, and attribute of relationship type. We have defined a data model called CRD-FS - Object-Relationship-Attribute Model for Semistructured Data, which includes the concepts in the Entity-Relationship data model together with constructs to capture the hierarchical structure of grid data. With the CRD-FS data model, many concepts of the grid database can be explicitly represented. Concepts that can be represented in the CRD-FS data model but cannot be specified by WSDL and grid mode include:

(1) Attribute vs. object class. Data can be represented in grid files either as attributes or element. So, it is difficult to tell from the grid file whether a child element is in fact an attribute of its parent element or an object. WSDL and grid-mode cannot specify that a child element is an attribute of its parent element.

S. Lin and X. Huang (Eds.): CESM 2011, Part I, CCIS 175, pp. 447–452, 2011.

(2) Multivalued attribute vs. object class. In grid file, multivalued attributes of an object class have to be represented as child elements. WSDL and grid mode cannot specify that a child element is a multivalued attribute of its parent element.

(3) identifier (ID). WSDL and grid mode cannot specify the identifier of an object class which appears as a child element and has a many to many relationship with its parent element. ID and key of WSDL and grid mode respectively, are not powerful enough to represent the identifier of such object classes.

(4) IDREF or Foreign Key. As WSDL and grid mode cannot represent identifiers of some object classes, so foreign key or ID reference of such object classes cannot be specified.

(5) N-ary relationship type. WSDL and grid mode can only specify child elements of a parent element, such a relationship is the parent-child relationship and it is a binary relationship type. Ternary relationship types and N-ary relationship types among object classes cannot be specified by WSDL and grid mode.

(6) Attribute of object class vs. attribute of relationship type. As WSDL and grid mode do not have the concept of object classes and relationship types (they only represent the hierarchical structure of elements and attributes), there is no way to specify whether an attribute of a element is an attribute of the element (object class) or an attribute of some relationship type involving the element (object class) and its ancestors (object classes).

(7) View of grid file. Since WSDL and grid mode cannot specify identifiers and attributes of object classes and relationship types, WSDL and grid mode do not contain concepts to define views of grid file which change the hierarchical order of object classes (elements) in the original grid file.

The above concepts (1 to 6) can be captured in the CRD-FS mode diagram, and because of these concepts, we can define a valid grid view which changes the hierarchical order of object classes using a swap operator.10 With the concepts captured in the CRD-FS mode diagram of an grid database, linked pattern queries on the grid database can be optimized significantly. Using the work we have done with views, we can guarantee that if a searching changes the hierarchical order of nodes, the concepts of the output is consistent with the concepts of the grid file. WSDL and grid mode cannot be used to interpret the output part when the hierarchical ordering of nodes in the output is different than in the searching part. With the concepts captured by the CRD-FS data model, we will be able to interpret grid queries correctly and improve the searching evaluation performance using these concepts.

2 The CRD-FS Data Model

The Object, Relationship, Attribute data model for Semistructured Data (CRD-FS) has four basic concepts: object classes, relationship types, attributes and references, and consists of four diagrams: mode diagram, instance diagram, functional dependency diagram and inheritance diagram. In this paper we are concerned with the CRD-FS mode diagram.

We shows an CRD-FS mode diagram. The rectangles labeled department, course, and student are the object classes. Attributes name, code and stuNo are the identifiers of the object class department, course and student respectively. Each student has a unique stuNo. The attributes title, mark, address and hobby are optional. Attribute hobby is multivalued, while stuName is required. There are two relationship types, called dc and cs. The former is a binary relationship type between object classes department and course, while the latter a binary relationship type between course and student. A department can have one or more (1:n) courses, and a course belongs to one and only one (1:1) department. A course can have zero or more (0:n) students, and a student can take 1 or more courses. The label cs on the edge between student and mark indicates that mark is a single valued attribute of the relationship type cs. That is, the attribute mark is an attribute of a student in a course. From these constraints, we can derive that {course; student}→mark.

3 Using Concepts in Searching Processing

Here we outline how the concepts captured by CRD-FS mode can be used to optimize linked pattern searching evaluation with three linked pattern queries.

Searching 1: Find the stuName values of student elements having stuNo value equals to "c1001". The XPath expression is: //student[@stuNo="c1001"]/stuName.

Using the CRD-FS mode, we know that stuName is a single valued attribute of the student object class and stuNo is the identifier of the student, so stuNo→stuName. To prcess the searching, we only need to find the first student element in the grid file with attribute stuNo equal to"c1001", and then find the value of its subelement stuName. However, if we use a WSDL or grid mode of the grid data, we would not know that stuNo is the identifier of student or that stuName is a single valued attribute of student, so we would need to traverse the whole grid file.

Additionally Wu et al. have proposed an algorithm that concentrates on searching for content or values with concept information as compared to structure-focused searching processing. We will discuss content search in more details in Section 5.

Searching 2: Find the average marks of all the students.

To answer this searching the processor needs to know that stuNo is the identifier of object class student, and mark is a single valued attribute of the relationship type between course and student.

However, a WSDL cannot express the concepts that stuNo is the identifier of student object, and also cannot express that mark is a single valued attribute of the relationship between student and course, that is {course; student}→mark. Without this information, there is no way to know whether the XSearching searching with an aggregation function (or linked pattern searching) is written correctly or not.

Searching 3: For each student, find all courses taken by the student with the marks the student achieved in the course. Consider for example the searching , where a rectangle represents an object class and a circle represents an attribute. On the left hand side the searching is specified, and on the right hand side the output format is given. The lines between the searching part and the output part show the correspondences between the objects in the searching and those in the output. The searching is asking for the marks of students in courses and in the output courses must be nested within student rather than students within courses.

4   Content Search in Grid

Processing a linked pattern searching in grid file includes structural search and content search. Most existing algorithms do not differentiate content search from structural search. They treat content nodes the same as element nodes during searching processing with structure. Due to the high variety of contents, to mix content search and structure search suffers from organization problem of contents and low performance. Another disadvantage is to find the actual values asked by a searching, they have to rely on the original file. Therefore, we propose a novel algorithm Value Extraction with Relational Table (VERT) to overcome these limitations. The main technique of VERT is introducing relational tables to store file contents instead of treating them as nodes and labeling them. Tables in our algorithm are created based on concept information of files. As more concepts captured, we can further optimize tables and queries to significantly enhance effciency.

For example, consider the example grid tree with containment labels. Instead of storing the label streams for each grid tag and value contents, we can store the value contents together with the labels of their parent tags in relational tables. With these relational tables, when a user issues a linked searching , the system can automatically rewrite it to the searching, where the node price, the value node with value greater than 15, and their PC relationship are replaced by a node called price'>15. Then, we can execute SQL in table Rprice to get all labels of price elements with value greater than 15 to form the label stream for price'>15; and perform structure based on label streams of book, ISBN and price'>15. In this way, we save both the stream merge cost of all content values greater than 15 and the structure between the merged label streams for content values and price element.

Moreover, if we know that price is a property of book object class by exploiting the mode information, we can directly put the value contents of price with labels of book object class, instead of the labels of price element. In this way, when processing the linked searching, we can also save the structure between book object and its price property. Note that we can also store the labels of book objects with the contents of other properties, such as title, author, etc., which are not shown due to limited space.

Finally, if we further know that ISBN, title, price, etc. are single valued properties of book object class according to concepts captured by ORASS, we can premerge the content values of these properties into a single relational table with the labels of book objects.With the premerged table, to answer the linked searching, we can simply perform an efficient selection on the pre-merged table without time consuming structure. Note that we should not merge multi-valued properties (e.g.author) into the table to avoid duplicate information.

5   Keyword Search with Concepts in Grid

Keyword proximity search is a user friendly way to searching grid databases. Most previous efforts in this area focus on keyword proximity search in grid based on either a tree data model or a graph (or digraph) data model. Tree data models for grid are generally simple and efficient. However, they do not capture connections such as ID references in grid databases. In contrast, techniques based on a graph (or digraph) model capture connections, but are generally inefficient to compute. Moreover, most of the existing techniques do not exploit mode information which is usually present in grid databases. Without mode information, keyword proximity techniques may have difficulty in presenting results, and more importantly, they return many irrelevant results. For example, the LCA (Lowest Common Ancestor) concepts for keyword proximity search based on tree model may return the overwhelmingly large root of the whole grid database.

With interested object classes, the most intuitive result of keyword proximity search is a list of interested objects containing all keywords. We call these interested objects as ICA (Interested Common Ancestor) in contrast to the well-known LCA (Lowest Common Ancestor) concepts. Also, and more importantly, we propose IRA (Interested Related Ancestors) concepts to capture conceptual connections between interested objects and include more relevant results that do not contain all keywords. An IRA result is a pair of objects that together contain all keywords and are connected by conceptual connections. An object is an IRA object if it belongs to some IRA pair. For example, for searching "grid searching processing", the paper with title"searching processing" and citing or cited by "grid" papers are considered as IRA objects. Further, we propose RelevanceRank to rank IRA objects according to their relevance scores to the searching. RelevanceRank is application dependent. For an intuitive example, in DBLP, for searching "grid searching processing", a "searching process ing" paper that cites or is cited by many "grid" papers is ranked higher than another "searching processing" paper that cites or is cited by only one "grid" papers. Other ranking metrics can also be incorporated with RelevanceRank. For example, for searching"John Smith", we can use proximity rank to rank papers with author "John Smith" higher than papers with co-author "John" and "Smith".

Experimental evaluation shows our approach is superior to most existing academic systems in terms of execution time and result quality. Our approach is also superior or comparable to commercial systems such as Google Scholar and Microsoft Libra in term of result quality.

6 Conclusion

One of the important areas in the organization of semistructured data is providing algorithms that enable efficient searching of the data. Many researchers have investigated matching linked patterns, using clever matching algorithms and included labeling schemes which enable smart ways of determining the relationships between nodes in a tree, without traversing the tree.

In the future we will study how to use other concepts captured in ORASS mode diagrams to further optimize the evaluation of linked pattern queries, provide guidelines of where these optimizations are worthwhile, and show the improvement in processing speed through experimentation. The particular areas we will look at include how specific information in linked queries interact with optimization such as parent child and ancestor-descendant relationships, negation, ordering of nodes, constant values, and output nodes.

References

1. Wu, T., Xue, Y., Cui, Y.: Preserving Traffic Privacy in Wireless Mesh Networks. In: Proceedings of WoWMoM 2006 (2006)
2. Bouam, S., Othman, J.B.: Data security in Grid using multipath routing. In: Proccedings of 14th IEEE International Symposium on Personal Indoor and Mobile Radio Communication (2003)
3. Michell, S., Srinivasan, K.: State based key hop protocol: A lightweight security protocol for wireless networks. In: Proceedings of PE-WASUN 2004 (October 2004)
4. Soliman, H.S., Omari, M.: Application of synchronous dynamic encryption system in mobile wireless domains. In: Proceedings of the 1st ACM International Workshop on Quality of Service and Security in Wireless and Mobile Networks, pp. 24–30 (October 2005)
5. Junaid, M., Mufti, M., Umar Ilyas, M.: Vulnerabilities of IEEE 801.11i Wireless LAN CCMP Protocol. Transactions on Engineering, Computing and Technology V11 (February 2006)
6. Housley, R.: Using Advanced Encryption Standard (AES) Counter Mode With IPsec Encapsulating Security Payload (ESP), RFC 3686 (January 2004)
7. IEEE Std. 801.11i-2004, Wireless Medium Access Control (IAC) and Physical Layer (PHY) Specifications: Medium Access Control (IAC) Security Enhancements,
   http://standards.ieee.org/getieee801/download/
   801.11i-2004.pdf
8. IEEE Std. 801.1X-2004, IEEE Standard for Local and metropolitan area networks - Port-Based Network Access Control (June 2001),
   http://standards.ieee.org/getieee801/download/
   801.1X-2004.pdf
9. Aboba, B., Blunk, L., Vollbrecht, J., Carlson, J., Levkowetz, H. (eds.): Extensible Authorization Protocol (EWP), RFC 3748 (June 2004)
10. Rigney, C., Willens, S., Rubens, A., Simpson, W.: Remote Authorization Dia. In: User Service (RADIUS), RFC 2865 (June 2000)
11. Calhoun, P., Loughney, J., Guttman, E., Zorn, G., Arkko, J.: Diameter Base Protocol, RFC 3588 (September 2003)
12. He, C., Mitchell, J.C.: Analysis of the 801.11i 4-Way Handshake. In: WiSE 2004, Philadelphia, Pennsylvania, USA (October 2004)
13. Mishra, A., Arbaugh, W.A.: An Initial Security Analysis of the IEEE 801.1X Standard, Technical Report CS-TR-4328, Department of Computer Science, University of Marryland (February 2002),
   https://drum.umd.edu/dspace/handle/1903/1179?mode=full

Security Scheme in Wireless Grid

Yue Hong Zhang[1], Li Hao[2], and Zhong Shan Yang[3]

[1] Automatic teaching and research section, Air force second flight Institute
[2,3] Xi'an Communications Institute
710306, Xi-an City
xazyh@163.com

Abstract. In this paper, we considered the two security services of authorization and data security in wireless Grid. The security issues is related to authorization and security, specific to Grid, the characteristics of these services have been outlined. The proposed security solutions for the two services of authorization and security have been categorized into three categories, depending upon the underlying security techniques. The proposed solutions within each classifying are discussed in detail. and then, We will analyze different privacy mechanisms proposed for Grid. For each solution we will address the approach, security issues addressed by the solution, strength of solution, overheads caused and the weaknesses.

Keyword: wireless Grid, classifying, authorization, encryption.

Preface

A security framework have been proposed based on stream cipher for encryption to provide the services of data security, data integrity, and authorization. This framework ensures per packet mutual authorization between the two communicating nodes within the network. The objective of using stream cipher is to allow online processing of the data. Consequently, minimum delay is introduced because of the security provisioning. Two secret security keys, Authorization Key (AK) and Authorization Session Key (ASK), are used for authorization of the supplicant and authenticator. AK is exchanged between the supplicant and the authenticator after initial mutual authorization from the authorization server, whereas the ASK is used for a given communication session between the two nodes. The AK and ASK pair is used by the communicating nodes to generate the permutation vector (PV) which is used for the encryption and decryption of data. In the strongest mode of security, the data is also involved in the PV generation, resulting in the randomness which makes the decryption of the data difficult even if the encryption key of one packet is compromised. The synchronization of the generated permutation vector between the sender and the receiver of the data results in origin authorization of every MPDU. To minimize the security overhead, plain text MPDU is XORed with the PV generated for that MPDU. The authors have proved that the encryption of data using PV provides strong security services of data security, data integrity, and origin authorization.

S. Lin and X. Huang (Eds.): CESM 2011, Part I, CCIS 175, pp. 453–457, 2011.

1   Standardization Efforts and Mutual Authorization

IEEE 801.11i is the defined standard for the IAC layer security of the wireless networks. We dedicate this section to discuss the IEEE 801.11i standard. The section begins with the explaination of the security methods used for the services of authorization and security in the IEEE 801.11i standard. Subsequently, we expose the vulnerabilities in IEEE 801.11i that render the standard prone to security attacks. These weaknesses lead to attacks including: pre-computation and partial matching attacks; session hijacking attacks; man-in-the-middle attacks exploiting vulnerabilities in IEEE 801.1X; and DoS attack exploiting vulnerabilities in four-way handshake. We also briefly discuss the proposed prevention mechanisms for these attacks.

After successful distribution of the encryption key (PMK) and authorization of supplicant using 801.1X, the supplicant (mobile device) and the authenticator (peer mobile device) mutually authenticate each other. This process is based on the four-way handshake. The four-way handshake is initiated when the two nodes intend to exchange data. Although an encyption key PMK is available to both the supplicant and the authenticator, this key is meant to last the entire session and should be exposed as little as possible. The purpose of four-way handshake is to use the PMK and establish two more keys called the Encryption Temporal Key (ETK) and Session Temporal Key (STK).

The first information of the four-way handshake is transmitted by the authenticator to the supplicant which consists of ANonce. The supplicant uses this ANonce and readily available fields: Supplicant nonce (SNonce); Authenticator IAC address; and Supplicant IAC address, to generate the ETK using cryptographic hash function. The second information of the handshake is transmitted by the supplicant to the authenticator consisting of SNonce and Information Integrity Code (IIC), which is encrypted using ETK. The authenticator is then able to generate the ETK and STK. The attached IIC is decrypted using the generated ETK. If the IIC is successfully decrypted, then the authenticator and the supplicant have successfully authenticated each other (Mutual Authorization). This is because the authenticator's generated ETK will only match the ETK transmitted by the supplicant if the two share the same PMK. Third information is transmitted by the authenticator consisting of STK and IIC. The Last information of fourway handshake is the acknowledgement transmitted by the supplicant. The two nodes can exchange the data after successful four-way handshake.

ETK is used to generate Temporal Key (TK), which is used to encrypt unicast informations, while the STK is used to encrypt broadcast and multicast informations. The four-way handshake involves generation and distribution of these keys between supplicant and authenticator and also leads to the mutual authorization of the two.

2   Vulnerabilities in IEEE 801.11i and Security Attacks

A number of security vulnerabilities have been identified in the IEEE 801.11i standard. This section details these vulnerabilities, the attacks launched by exploiting the vulnerabilities and the available prevention mechanisms.

2.1   IEEE 801.1X Vulnerabilities

IEEE 801.1X[6] is used for key distribution and authorization in IEEE 801.11i. The process of authorization involves three entities: Authenticator, Authorization Server and the Supplicant. The protocol assumes that the authenticator is always trusted. Therefore, the supplicant does not verify the informations received from the authenticator and unconditionally responds to these informations. This assumption is the security vulnerability that can be exploited by the adversary. The adversary can act as authenticator and launch the session hijacking attack and the man-in-the-middle attack as exposed in [10]. an adversary can launch session hijacking attack by exploiting the explained vulnerability. The adversary waits until the authenticator and the supplicant complete the authorization process and the authenticator sends the EWP success information to the supplicant. Following this, the adversary sends 801.11 disassociate information to the supplicant with the spoofed IP of the authenticator. The supplicant assumes its session has been terminated by the authenticator as the information is not verified for integrity. There onwards, the adversary gains the access to the network by spoofing the IAC address of supplicant and proceeds with mutual authorization procedure using four-way handshake.

The man-in-the-middle attack launched by the adversary exploiting the same vulnerability. After the initial exchange of EWP request and response informations between the supplicant and the authenticator, the adversary sends EWP success information to the supplicant using its own IAC address. Since the IEEE 801.1X protocol suggests unconditional transition upon receiving the EWP success information by the supplicant, the supplicant assumes it is authenticated by the authenticator and changes the state. When the authenticator sends the EWP success information, the supplicant has already passed the stage where it was waiting for the success information and hence no action is taken for this information. The supplicant assumes the adversary as the legitimate authenticator while the adversary can easily spoof the IAC address of the supplicant to communicate with the actual authenticator. Therefore, the adversary will become the intermediatory between the supplicant and the authenticator. The proposed solutions to prevent these attacks10 recommend the authorization and integrity check for the EWP informations between the authenticator and the supplicant. The solution also proposes that the peer-to-peer based authorization model be adopted where the authenticator and the supplicant should be treated as peers and the supplicant should verify the informations from the authenticator during the process of trust establishment. The peer-to-peer model is suitable for wireless Grid where both the authenticator and the supplicant are wireless peer devices.

2.2 Four-Way Handshake Vulnerabilities

Four-way handshake is the mechanism used for the mutual authorization of the supplicant and the authenticator in IEEE 801.11i. Vulnerabilities in the four-way handshake have been identified and the DoS attack exploiting these vulnerabilities proposed in [9]. The handshake starts after PMK is distributed to the supplicant and the authenticator. The supplicant waits for a specific interval of time for information 1 of the handshake from the authenticator. If the information is not received, the supplicant disassociates itself from the authenticator. Note that this is the only timer used by the supplicant. If information 1 is received by the supplicant, it is then bound to respond to every information from the authenticator and wait for the response until it is received. On the other hand, the authenticator will timeout for every information, if it does not receive the expected response within a specific time interval. Further, the supplicant is de-authenticated if the response is not received after several retries. Also note that both the authenticator and the supplicant drop the information silently, if the IIC of the information cannot be verified.

This mechanism of four-way handshake is vulnerable to the DoS attack by the adversary. the authenticator sends the information 1 to the supplicant. Note that information 1 is not encrypted. Supplicant generates a new SNonce and then generates ETK using the ANonce, SNonce and other relevant fields and responds with the information[2], which is encrypted using ETK. At this point, the adversary sends the malicious information 1 with the spoofed IAC address of the authenticator. The supplicant is bound to respond to the information. It assumes that the information that it sent to the authenticator is lost so the authenticator has retransmitted the information 1. Therefore, it calculates ETK' (different from ETK and over writing ETK) based on the ANonce sent by adversary and sends information again which is encrypted using ETK'. Meanwhile, the authenticator responds to the first information of the supplicant by sending the information that is encrypted using ETK. The integrity check performed by the supplicant, because the supplicant is now using ETK' while the authenticator encrypted the information using ETK. Consequently the fourway handshake process is blocked until the authenticator de-authenticates the supplicant after several retries, denying the supplicant of the service.

3 Open Issues

The strong security offered by asymmetric cryptography makes it an attractive solution for wireless Grid. However, the limited computational and communication capabilities of the devices and the unavailability of centralized certification and authorization servers pose challenges for adopting the asymmetric cryptographic solutions for wireless Grid. A number of light weight security solutions have been proposed as an alternative to asymmetric cryptography, reducing the complexity of security provisioning. However, majority of these protocols do not specify any mechanism for initial credential distribution and verification. Shared secret threshold cryptographic solutions can effectively address the problem of unavailability of centralized certification and authorization server. However, the additional overheads involved in key renewal and partial key accumulation to generate the private key make these solutions less attractive. Consequently, the wireless Grid have yet to meet a complete security solution for authorization and data security that is lightweight, distributed and covers all aspects of the two security services including initial credential distribution and verification.

4 Conclusion

In this chapter, we considered the two security services of authorization and data security in wireless Grid. The security issues relating to authorization and security, specific to Grid, have been identified and the characteristics of these services have been outlined. The proposed security solutions for the two services of authorization and security have been categorized into three categories, depending upon the underlying security techniques. The proposed solutions within each classifying are discussed in detail. Finally, IEEE 801.11i, standard for wireless security is detailed, its vulnerabilities are highlighted and the solutions proposed for the vulnerabilities are discussed. The chapter ends with a note on the open issues relating the two security issues of authorization and security in wireless Grid.

References

1. Baader, F., Calvanese, D., McGuinness, D., Nardi, D., Patel-Schneider, P.F. (eds.): The Description Logic Handbook: Theory, Implementation and Applications. Cambridge University Press, Cambridge (2003)
2. Elsenbroich, C., Kutz, O., Sattler, U.: A Case for Abductive Reasoning over Ontologies. In: Proc. OWL 2006: OWL Experiences and Directions Workshop (2006)
3. Haarslev, V., Mööller, R., Wessel, M.: RacerPro User's Guide and ReferenceManual Version 1.9.1 (May 2007)
4. Hobbs, J.R., Stickel, M., Appelt, D., Martin, P.: Transformation as abduction. Artificial Intelligence Journal 63 (1993)
5. Kakas, A., Denecker, M.: Abduction in logic programming. In: Kakas, A.C., Sadri, F. (eds.) Computational Logic: Logic Programming and Beyond. LNCS (LNAI), vol. 2407, pp. 402–436. Springer, Heidelberg (2002)
6. Mööller, R., Haarslev, V., Neumann, B.: Concepts based information finding. In: Proc. IT&KNOWS 1998: International Conference on Information Technology and Knowledge Systems, Vienna, Budapest, August-4-September 31, p. 496 (1998)
7. Möller, R., Neumann, B.: Ontology-based reasoning techniques for multimedia transformation and finding. In: Semantic Multimedia and Ontologies: Theory and Applications (2007) (to appear)
8. Neumann, B., Möller, R.: On Scene Transformation with Description Logics. In: Christensen, H.I., Nagel, H.-H. (eds.) Cognitive Vision Systems. LNCS, vol. 3948, pp. 247–275. Springer, Heidelberg (2006)
9. Peraldi, S.E., Kaya, A., Melzer, S., Möller, R., Wessel, M.: Multimedia Transformation as Abduction. In: Proc. DL 2007: International Workshop on Description Logics (2007)
10. Shanahan, M.: Perception as Abduction: Turning Sensor Data Into Meaningful Representation. Cognitive Science 29(1), 103–134 (2005)
11. Thagard, R.P.: The best explanation: Criteria for theory choice. The Journal of Philosophy (1978)

Author Index

Agha Mohammadi, Hamid Haji   II-247
AL-Sarem, Mohammed   II-180
An, Peng   II-107
Ao, Zhanyi   I-112, I-117

Bao, Hua   I-14
Bao, WeiGang   I-39
Bellafkih, Mostafa   II-133, II-180
Bing, ZhiGang   I-359, I-392

Cai, Lijun   I-266
Cao, Xiaoxia   II-318
Chang, Guiran   II-409
Che, Xinsheng   II-451
Chen, Deyun   I-98
Chen, Feng   II-323
Chen, Guannan   I-232
Chen, Guixu   I-92
Chen, HaiYan   I-26
Chen, Hao   I-128
Chen, Jia   I-259, I-341
Chen, Jiawei   I-112
Chen, Juhua   I-47
Chen, Qingjiang   II-415
Chen, Shuai-Shuai   II-167
Chen, WenJing   I-123
Chen, Xiang   I-347, I-353, II-396
Chen, Xianlin   II-207
Chen, Ying   I-327
Chen, Yujie   I-163
Chen, Zhaoxue   I-21
Cheng, Ruihua   I-280
Cheng, Wei   II-409
Chu, Chen   I-253
Cui, Lin   I-146

Dai, Bei   I-21
Dai, Dongliang   II-59
Dai, Guoyong   I-47
Deng, Ai   I-32
Deng, Fei   II-86, II-91
Deng, Xiangzheng   I-312, I-317, I-322
Ding, Luwei   II-14
Dong, Fangfang   II-14
Dong, HuiJuan   I-39

Errais, M.   II-133

Fan, Jianbo   II-107
Fan, Ping   II-149
Fan, Xinghua   II-207

Gang, Li   I-186
Gao, Chuan   II-287
Gao, Chunfu   I-298
Gao, Hailin   I-53
Gao, JIan-xin   II-33
Gao, Xiujuan   II-241
Gao, Ying   I-379
Gu, Ming   II-40
Gu, Minjie   I-139
Gu, Zonghai   II-384
Guan, Jing   I-372
Guang, Qin   II-336
Guo, Hanyu   I-226
Guo, Honglin   I-66
Guo, Jifeng   II-329
Guo, LongFei   II-26
Guo, Ning   I-411, II-368
Guo, Ping   II-167
Guo, Rendong   I-170
Guo, Shuxia   I-379
Guo, Yanjun   II-349
Guo, Yuqi   II-200

Han, Li Kai   I-447
Han, SuMin   II-281
Hao, Li   I-453
He, Hong   I-128
He, Xinsheng   I-298
He, YanPing   I-292
Hou, Wei   I-347
Hu, Jianfeng   I-226
Hu, Jilei   I-170
Hu, Liangming   II-323
Hu, Lianjun   I-92
Hu, Lihua   II-144
Hu, Nan   II-33
Hu, Songtao   I-139
Hu, Xiaoming   II-318
Hu, Yongcai   II-415

Huang, Dexiu   II-174
Huang, PingHua   II-281

Jiang, Qunou   I-317
Jiang, Tao   I-379
Jun, Luo   II-273

Kan, Kaihui   II-7
Khashandarag, Asghar Shahrzad   II-247

Leghroudi, D.   II-133
Lei, Lei   I-379
Lei, Qianzhao   II-379
Lei, Wei   II-235
Lei, XiaoYu   II-73
Li, Ang   I-327
Li, Bangyu   II-451
Li, Chuanzhen   I-253
Li, Dongming   I-14
Li, Geng   II-213
Li, GuangMin   I-123
Li, GuoPing   I-123
Li, Haiping   I-411
Li, HongBin   I-8
Li, Hui   I-159
Li, Jin   I-1
Li, JingBing   I-305
Li, Jingjiao   II-101
Li, Jinguo   I-266
Li, Jinhong   I-146
Li, Jun   I-213
Li, Ling   I-273
Li, Meixia   I-219
Li, Qingfu   I-280
Li, QingSong   I-238
Li, Qiong   I-366
Li, QuanLi   I-359
Li, Sheng Qi   I-441
Li, Shuqin   I-14
Li, Tong   II-390
Li, Wei   I-266, II-254, II-261, II-267
Li, Xiaojun   II-59
Li, Xuquan   I-139
Li, Yazhen   I-372
Li, Yizhi   II-323
Li, Yunfei   I-423
Lian, Hao   I-327
Liao, Daixi   I-199
Liao, Dong   II-421
Lin, Ruilin   II-362, II-403

Ling, Daijian   II-7
Liu, Banteng   I-47
Liu, Chun   II-161, II-174
liu, Dejun   I-207
Liu, Feng   I-180, II-384
Liu, Huran   II-219, II-225, II-231, II-299,
      II-305, II-312
Liu, Lijun   I-232
Liu, Min   I-123
Liu, Nian   II-213
Liu, Qin   I-153
Liu, Ruohui   I-53
Liu, Wenfeng   I-428
Liu, Xiaomei   I-213
Liu, Yan   II-384
Liu, Yang   II-33
Liu, Yingjie   I-174
Liu, Zhen   II-14
Lou, Xi'an   I-259
Lu, Guilin   II-116
Luo, Guanlong   I-335
Luo, Hanyang   II-438
Luo, Zhiyong   I-298
Lv, TingJie   II-26

Ma, F.Y.   I-266
Ma, Qiang   II-47
Ma, XingHua   I-392
Mao, Jianlin   I-411, II-368
Mao, Yan   I-447
Mei, Long-Bao   II-287
Meng, Zengshan   II-128
Mirnia, Mir Kamal   II-247

Navin, Ahmad Habibizad   II-247
Nong, Zheng   II-1

Ou, Xiao-qing   I-117

Pan, WenLin   II-193
Pei, Shujun   I-98

Qiao, ZhengHong   II-73
Qin, LiZhi   I-238
Qin, Zili   II-122
Qiu, ChangHua   II-193

Ramdani, Mohammed   II-133, II-180
Ranc, D.   II-133
Raouyane, B.   II-133

Ren, Chunyu   I-79
Ren, Jian   II-451
Ren, Yongsheng   II-293
Ruan, yue   I-47

Shen, Gongqi   I-286
Shen, Jianying   I-134
Shi, Yaqing   I-385, II-73
Si, YaQin   II-96
Søresen, Claus Age   I-207
Song, Dejie   I-428
Song, Hong   I-92
Song, Qiang   II-343
Song, Sanhua   I-73
Sun, Jiaguang   II-40

Tan, Boxue   I-428
Tan, Wenan   II-144
Tan, Zhenhua   II-409
Tang, Bing   II-67
Tang, Jic   I-335
Tang, TieHu   II-193
Tang, YuQiu   I-392
Tang, Zhihao   I-66
Tao, Huanqi   I-85
Teng, Gang   I-248
Teng, Jian-fu   I-128
Ti, Yunqiao   II-254
Tian, Dongfang   I-243
Tian, Xinyu   I-192
Tian, Yang   I-327

Wan, Fang   II-86, II-91
Wan, Li   I-418
Wan, Yuan   II-356
Wan, Zhongping   I-112
Wang, Baosen   I-434
Wang, Bin   I-298
Wang, Dan   II-254
Wang, Di   I-434
Wang, Gang   I-139
Wang, Guoqiang   I-59
Wang, Jian   I-8
Wang, JianDong   I-26
Wang, Jin   II-53
Wang, Jing   II-349
Wang, Jingling   I-253
Wang, Juan   II-349
Wang, Lan   II-356
Wang, Meijuan   I-385, II-73

Wang, Min   I-423
Wang, Minggang   I-341
Wang, Qian   I-399
Wang, Qingdong   II-161, II-174
Wang, Rongjuan   II-200
Wang, Rui   II-343, II-368
Wang, Tianhong   II-434
Wang, Tong   II-144, II-318
Wang, Weishu   II-47
Wang, Xiaochu   I-170
Wang, Yansong   I-286
Wang, Yu   I-273
Wang, Yuling   II-349
Wang, Zheng   II-457
Wang, ZiYun   I-123
Wei, Man   II-261, II-267
Wei, Rui   I-59
Wei, Yaohua   I-139
Wen, Xin   I-312, I-317, I-322
Wu, Haitao   I-192
Wu, Jian   I-39
Wu, Jin   I-32
Wu, Qian   I-248
Wu, Weiwei   I-266
Wu, XiaoLi   II-96
Wu, Xinjue   II-349
Wu, Xuejun   I-47
Wu, Yuchuan   I-85
Wu, Zhenxing   I-253

Xiang, Fenghong   II-368
Xiao, Litian   II-40
Xie, Bo   II-59
Xie, Changsheng   II-161, II-174
Xie, Wu   II-122, II-128, II-390
Xu, Guodong   II-421
Xu, Hui   II-451
Xu, Jin-bao   II-33
Xu, Lei   II-116
Xu, Xian-wei   II-33
Xv, Qi   II-47

Yan, Chengwen   II-374
Yan, Chenyang   II-155
Yan, Hao   I-26
Yan, Hua   I-232
Yan, JingJing   II-26
Yan, Xiujuan   I-226
Yan, Yue   I-253
Yan, Zheqiong   I-341

Yang, Guangming   II-409
Yang, Jinfan   I-73
Yang, Lihui   I-199
Yang, Shen   I-32
Yang, Tong   I-128
Yang, Wei   I-359
Yang, Xue-mei   II-445
Yang, Zhong Shan   I-453
Yao, Jian   II-374, II-434
Yao, Ying   I-192
Yao, Yu   II-107
Ye, Sheng   II-116
Yi, GuiPing   I-359
Yi, Min   II-186
You, Fucheng   I-163, I-174
Yu, JingNuo   I-8
Yu, YongChun   II-96
Yuan, Liuyang   I-112
Yuan, Pin   I-259
Yun, Jianjun   I-335

Zeng, Shuiping   I-146, II-200
Zeng, Xiaohui   I-92
Zhang, Bin   I-411
Zhang, Cheng   II-207
Zhang, Guangsheng   I-207
Zhang, GuangYu   I-39
Zhang, HaiDong   I-292
Zhang, Huacheng   II-122
Zhang, HuaiQiang   I-305
Zhang, HuaPeng   II-20, II-428
Zhang, Huimin   II-122, II-128, II-390

Zhang, Kai   I-105
Zhang, Li   II-67
Zhang, Qianhong   I-199
Zhang, Tingting   I-385, II-96
Zhang, Xiaolin   I-192
Zhang, Xin   II-396
Zhang, Yanzhu   II-101
Zhang, Yong   I-347, I-353
Zhang, Yongping   II-107
Zhang, Yue Hong   I-453
Zhang, Zhen   II-116
Zhang, ZiMu   II-26
Zhang, Zuxin   II-261, II-267
Zhao, Ni   II-20
Zhao, Xiurong   I-207
Zheng, Yuhuang   I-405
Zhijun, Kuang   II-79
Zhou, Jianrong   I-213
Zhou, Qinghua   I-418
Zhou, Sheng   I-273
Zhou, Xinhui   I-372
Zhou, Xue-feng   I-353
Zhou, Yinggang   I-232
Zhu, Guangxi   II-161
Zhu, Hao   II-384
Zhu, Lin   II-167
Zhu, Nanli   II-107
Zhu, Qiang   I-286
Zhu, Shaohua   I-117
Zhu, Youfeng   II-293
Zhu, Zhiliang   II-409
Zou, Meng   II-107